CADOGAN Sadaka

Prague
Budapest

Cadogan Guides
West End House, 11 Hills Place,
London W1R 1AG, UK
cadoganguides@morrispub.co.uk

Distributed in North America by
The Globe Pequot Press
246 Goose Lane, PO Box 480, Guilford
Connecticut 06437–0480

Copyright © Sadakat Kadri and Matthew Gardener 2000

Book and cover design by Animage
Cover photographs: **front** Travel Ink/Stephen Coyne
                     back Travel Ink/John Grant
Maps © Cadogan Guides, drawn by Map Creation Ltd

Editorial Director: Vicki Ingle   Series Editor: Linda McQueen

Editors: Mary-Ann Gallagher, Kate Paice, Claudia Martin
Indexing: Dorothy Frame
Production: Book Production Services

A catalogue record for this book is available from the British Library ISBN 1–86011–958–1

Printed and bound in the UK by Cambridge University Press

Please help us to keep this guide up to date

We have done our best to ensure that the information in this guide is correct at the time of going to press. But places and facilities are constantly changing, and standards and prices in hotels and restaurants fluctuate. We would be delighted to receive any comments concerning existing entries or omissions, as well as suggestions for new features. Authors of the best letters will be offered a copy of the Cadogan Guide of their choice.

Please Note

The author and publishers have made every effort to ensure the accuracy of the information in the book at the time of going to press. However, they cannot accept any responsibility for any loss, injury or inconvenience resulting from the use of information contained in this guide.

About the Authors

Sadakat Kadri: Prague

Sadakat Kadri was born in Fulham of a Pakistani father and a Finnish mother. He studied history and law at Trinity College, Cambridge, and took a Masters degree at Harvard Law School, and currently practises as a barrister in London. As well as writing about Prague, where he has spent several years since 1989, he is an occasional journalist and is now writing a popular history of the Western criminal trial. His hobbies include cooking chicken.

Winner of the Shiva Naipaul travel writing prize, and author of the *Cadogan Guide to Prague.*

Matthew Gardner: Budapest

Matthew Gardner is a writer, traveller and accomplished musician and composer. He has lived all over the world, including Mexico and India, and now lives in a remote valley in western Canada with his wife Alison, a photographer and chef.

Contents: Prague

P9-DCA-987

iii

Contents: Budapest

Prague: Introduction

Prague, wrapped in its legendary magic, is truly one of those cities that has been able to fix and retain the poetic idea that is always more or less drifting aimlessly through space.

André Breton to the Prague Surrealist Group, 1935

The flim-flam of hundreds of tourist brochures makes Breton's homage sound almost clichéd, but there is something mighty surreal about Prague. Floating in the architectural flotsam of a thousand years, its domes, dungeons, rickety rooftops and spires are about as close as life gets to fairyland. Its central bridge is bent, one of its clocks turns backwards, an entire 13th-century town is buried 3m under its alleys, and surveying its domain from the hill above the river is a castle in the air.

The city lies at the crossroads of Europe, and its spirit has been formed and deformed by the cataclysmic pressures of a millennium of continental madness. Dogs of war have dumped on it from every direction, its streets are filled with the petrified dreams of dissembling monks and cuckoo monarchs, the Communists practised their jiggery-pokery behind an iron curtain for four decades—and yet it survived the hullaballoo to emerge as one of the most enchanted cities in Europe. Its spell isn't some two-bit trick with a slipper and a pumpkin, but the almost tangible energy of the images, ideologies and myths with which everyone has grown up. Give it an inch of imagination, and it will unleash a mile.

Years of smears and smokescreens have added to the mystery that now surrounds Prague. It is the capital of Bohemia, which has been a byword for outlandishness for centuries. The kingdom began its ascent into the clouds in the mid-1400s: the pope spread the word that Bohemians made love on the streets, while in France a group of expelled gypsies waved their safe-conducts as they passed through, and the French duly noted that *un bohémien* was a gypsy—as he still is today. By the early 1600s, Shakespeare could get away with describing the landlocked and forested kingdom as 'a desert country near the sea' (*The Winter's Tale*). In 1938 disingenuous ignorance was elevated to foreign policy by Neville Chamberlain. Ten years later, Prague—farther west than Vienna, and considerably closer to Dublin than to Moscow—became lost in 'Eastern Europe'. The city of dreams began a 41-year nightmare; but, in the West, Bohemia did little more than hover somewhere between Bloomsbury and Hampstead. And then in 1989, a few million people pinched themselves, the tin-pot emperors of Communism shivered, and the city returned to where it belongs—the heart of Europe.

Prague is now the capital of the Czech Republic—made up of Bohemia, Moravia and a slice of Silesia—and comprises some 1,190,576 inhabitants (with an inexplicably decreasing proportion of men); 503 spires, towers and sundry aerial protrusions; 495 square kilometres; ten districts; eight islands; seven hills (like most legendary cities); and an agglomeration of what were historically five separate towns. Since 1989 it has barely stopped echoing to the rhythm of of pile-drivers and, under the glare of oxyacetylene torches, the magical metropolis is being transformed into a city fit for the 21st century. It's still scarred by the barbed-wire wounds of the Cold War but, as it busks, dances, works and kisses its way back to the light, the old divisions are being healed on its streets. Prague doesn't *always* feel so dreamy—particularly as you chew through its accursed dumplings or cross swords with a hobgoblin of the bureaucracy—but, if you pack your senses of humour, adventure and romance, a visit is an unforgettable jaunt into a city where history is in the making, and where a thousand years has already been made.

Prague: Travel

The best source of information on holidaying in Prague is still Čedok, the former national tourist agency. Although sloth and inefficiency have characterized it for too long, it can arrange flights, accommodation and a series of entertainments ranging from nights at the opera to dire evenings of 'traditional' beer and sausages in five-star hostelries. For further information, contact them at 53–54 Haymarket, London SW1Y 4RP, ✆ (020) 7839 4414, *www.cedoz.cz*, or your local office. Other agencies that organize holidays to the Czech Republic include Bridgewater Travel at PO Box 2333, Kidderminster, DY14 OYT, ✆ (012991) 271717, *www.bridgewater-travel.co.uk*, which provides a flexible service including charter and scheduled flights and accommodation in hotels and private homes throughout the country. The Czech and Slovak Tourist Centre, 16 Frognal Parade, Finchley Road, London NW3, ✆ (020) 7794 3263 (a private travel agency despite its name), has friendly and enthusiastic staff and can provide a good range of accommodation as well as organize flights, bus and train tickets and arrange tailor-made trips. They also issue tickets for the Prague spring festival, *see* p.20. In North America contact New Frontiers/Nouvelles Frontieres, 12 East 33rd Street, New York NY 10028, ✆ (212) 779 0600, ✆ 1 800 366 6387, *www.newfrontiers.com*. They also have branches throughout the USA and in Quebec City and Montreal. Cultural tour organizers are listed under Specialist Tour Operators (*see* p.4).

For general tourist or travel information contact the Czech Tourist Centres: 95 Great Portland Street, London W1 5RA, ✆ (020) 7291 9925, *cclondon@czech.cz,* or 1109 Madison Avenue, New York, NY 10028, ✆ (212) 288 0830, *nycenter@pop.net*.

By Air

British Airways fly daily from London, and have services from many major North American cities. Go flies twice daily from Stansted (note that it is cheaper to book train tickets to the airport with your flight). Czech Airlines (ČSA) has two services daily from Heathrow and one from Stansted, and daily flights (except Sundays) from Manchester. It also flies directly to Prague from New York, Chicago, Toronto and Montreal. It is possible to buy tickets online at *www.czech-airlines.com*. Delta Airlines (call toll free ✆ 1 800 221 1212) fly daily to Prague from Atlanta and JFK via Paris.

American Airlines: ✆ 1 800 433 7300 (USA), *www.aa.com*.

Air Canada: ✆ 1 800 555 1212 (Canada), ✆ 1 800 776 3000 (USA), *www.aircanada.ca*.

BA: ✆ 0345 222 111 (UK), ✆ 1 800 247 9297 (USA), *www.british-airways.com*.

ČSA: ✆ (020) 7255 1898 (London); ✆ (212) 682 5833 (New York).

Delta: ✆ 0800 414 767 (UK); ✆ 1 800 55 1212 (USA), *www.delta-air.com*.

Go: ✆ 0845 60 54321 (UK), *www.go-fly.com*.

The cheapest deals require 14-day advance booking, weekday departure, and a stay that covers at least one Saturday night and lasts no longer than three months. Under-25s may be eligible for reductions. You could also try Holiday Services, ✆/✉ (01773) 747426, *www. holidayservices.freeserve*, an independent flight specialist that runs cheap scheduled flights to Prague; or Campus Travel, 52 Grosvenor Gardens, London SW1W 0AG, ✆ 08702 401010, which operates regular charter flights to the city. A good place for bargain-hunting in the USA is **Council Travel**, 205 East 42nd St, New York, NY 10001, © (212) 822 2700. There are regular Prague-orientated offers among the classified ads in the UK's Sunday papers and London's *Time Out*; in New York, you could try the *Village Voice*. Visit these websites for more cheap deals: *www.lastminute.com, www.deckchair.com, www.cheapflights.com*.

Prague's small international airport is **Ruzyně**, situated some 20km to the west of the city centre. The taxi journey into town should cost no more than £10 ($15), but trying to guess whether you're being ripped off isn't the calmest way of beginning your hard-earned break, and you might prefer to take one of the many waiting mini-bus shuttles. The drivers are helpful and will usually drop you at or very near your precise destination for approximately £6 ($9) per person. Some car rental companies have offices at the airport, *see* p.8.

Airline Offices in Prague

All are open weekdays only and most close by 4pm. For airport information, call © 334 11 11.

Air Canada (Canada): Revoluční 17, © 24 89 27 30, ✆ 24 89 27 31.

British Airways (UK): Staroměstské nám. 10, © 22 11 44 44, ✆ 22 24 37 20.

ČSA (Czech Republic): Ruzyne 6, © 20 10 41 11, ✆ 24 81 04 26, *www.cas.cz*.

Delta Airlines (United States): Národní 32, © 24 94 67 33, ✆ 24 94 67 31.

Malev (Hungary): Pařížská 5, © 24 81 26 71, ✆ 24 81 47 28.

By Train

There are three time-honoured routes from London to Prague. The quickest is via Paris on the Paris–Praha night express, which you pick up at the Gare de l'Est. Another possibility is to travel through Ostend and Köln, setting off from London Victoria in the morning and early afternoon and arriving in Prague in the morning or late afternoon of the next day. Finally, you could stop off in Berlin, and then catch one of the many Prague-bound trains from Berlin (Lichtenberg), a journey of about seven hours. Fuller details of routes and up-to-date fares can be obtained at British Rail International Inquiries, © 0870 584 8848. All international rail tickets are valid for up to two months and permit an unlimited number of stops. For Eurostar tickets to Paris or Brussels, call © 0990 186 186, or book online at *www.eurostar.com*. To book trains from Berlin, contact German railways on © (020) 7317 0919, *www.bahn.de*.

EU citizens over and under the age of 26 and non-EU citizens who have been resident in Europe for six months are eligible for the **InterRail** pass (currently £269 if you're over 26 or £195 if you're under 26). Passes entitle holders to a month's unlimited travel across Europe, plus 30–50 per cent discounts on trains to cross-Channel ferry terminals. Contact **Rail Europe**, 179 Piccadilly, London W1V 0BA, © 08705 848 848, *www.raileurope.co.uk*. The equivalent North American three-zone **EurRail** pass will only get you as far as Hungary. From there you will have to make your own way to Prague. EurRail passes are valid for 15, 21, 30, 60 or 90 days and, for the under-26s, two weeks' travel will cost $388. Contact **Rail Europe US**, © 1 800 438 7245, *www.raileurope.com*.

Trains to Prague arrive either at **nádraží Praha-Holešovice** or, most likely, **Hlavní nádraží** ('Main Station'). Both are on line C of the metro network. Hlavní Nádraží is by far the grander, four floors' worth of station, three of which somehow emerge on to the street. Train information is provided in an office on the first floor (*open 6am–10pm*) and on the maps and roller timetables on the same floor. The Prague Information Service (PIS) will sell you maps, and dispense more or less wise advice from its booth in the main hall below (*open 8am–7pm*). On the top floor—the core of the original Art Nouveau station—is a shabby dining hall, decorated with stained-glass windows and tiled mosaics (*open 6am–10pm*). En route, be sure to see the magnificent half-dome, some 25m high, that greeted arrivals to Prague until the confused postwar reconstruction of the station. Since 1989, Hlavní nádraží has sunk to the grim level of most European railway stations and you won't want to spend much time there. Staying overnight in the station is a bad idea but, if you are determined to do so, at least avoid nodding off. All you will lose is a few snatched anxiety dreams, and Prague will begin to awaken at 5am.

By Bus

Regular and frequent coach services between London and Prague are run by several companies, including Capital Express and Kingscourt Express. The journey is precisely as cheap as it is hellish (around £50–£80 and two days' recovery time for the round trip), with a ten per cent reduction if you are under 26. Capital has offices at 57 Princedale Rd, London W11 4NP, ✆ (020) 7243 0488, *www.capitalexpress.demon.co.uk*, and U výstaviště 3 in Prague 7, ✆ 870 36 80; Kingscourt is based at 15 Balham High Rd, London SW12 9AJ, ✆ (020) 8673 7500/6883, *www.kce.cz*, and Havelská 8, ✆ 24 23 45 83. For coach schedules and information in Prague, ✆ call 1034 (*daily 6am–9pm*).

To Budapest

By air: Malév and Czech Airlines both have flights daily, taking 1hr 5mins.

By train: Trains go three times a day, taking 9hrs.

By bus: Buses go three times a week taking 8hrs (information ✆ 1034).

Specialist Tour Operators

Several British companies now organize trips to Prague for culture buffs. The following all offer flights, comfortable hotel accommodation and up to 10 days of excursions and like-minded conversation partners, at £500–1,000. Explorations of the musical traditions of the city are run three or four times a year by **Travel for the Arts** at 117 Regent's Park Rd, London NW1 8UR, ✆ (020) 7483 4466, *www.travelforthearts.com*. The trips romp from Mozart to Janáček through all the most melodious halls, stages and churches in the capital. Friends of Covent Garden are eligible for a discount. If you're the solitary type, the company can even arrange an itinerary just for you. **Prospect Tours** at 36 Manchester St, London WIU 7LH, ✆ (020) 7486 5704, organizes another set of musical holidays, and also offers meanders through the city's galleries and churches led by an art historian. Finally **Martin Randall Travel** runs a number of high-quality artistic and architectural tours to Prague, led by very wise lecturers. The company is based at 10 Barley Mow Passage, London W4 4HP, ✆ (020) 8742 3355. For a complete list of reputable specialist tour operators contact the Czech tourist office at ✆ (020) 7291 9923.

Within Prague itself there are a couple of companies that may be of interest: **Wittman Tours**, which specializes in trips exploring the Jewish history of Prague and Bohemia. It organizes regular tours of the Jewish Quarter and the former ghetto at Terezín, often led by Jews who lived through the Nazi occupation, and can arrange individual itineraries on request. The company has an office at Manesova 8 in Prague 2, ✆/✉ 22 25 24 72, *sylvie@wittman-tours*. Another well-reputed Jewish interest tour operator is **Precious Legacy Tours**, Maiselova 16, ✆/✉ 22 32 03 98, *legacy–tours@casanet.cz*. **Praha Magica**, Masna 9, ✆ 24 81 92 18, *info@pragamagica.cx*, *www.pragamagica.cz*, organize cultural tours.

Customs Formalities

A full passport will get you into the Czech Republic, although if it has less than a year to run you could have problems. West Europeans, US and Canadian citizens no longer need visas but, if you plan to stay for longer than three months, the bureaucracy still wants to know. Visit your local embassy in your home country for detailed information. Visitors must be able to prove access to at least 6,000 kčs (£150/$225); a spokesperson for the customs authorities stated that, in practice, the rule was only enforced against people who look homeless and, if you fear you might fit that bill, come armed with a wad of cash or a concertina of credit cards.

On arrival, you're allowed to import unlimited amounts of personal effects and up to 200 cigarettes, two litres of wine, a litre of spirits, and 50ml of perfume. Anything else, including valuable gifts, will attract duty. The standard prohibitions apply to both arrival and departure— no hard porn, no heroin, no Semtex, etc—and there is a 20,000 kč limit on the import and the export of Czech currency. If you have brought anything that even looks like an antique, you'll need the receipt to take it out of the country. The main customs office (Celni uřad Praha) is at Praha 8, Sokolovská 22, ✆ 24 81 62 56.

Getting Around

The curves and cobbles of central Prague have a mobile life of their own. Most of the streets are no more than the patches of ground that no one wanted to build on and, in their medieval madness, they often lead you on a merry dance and occasionally pull off the startling trick of coaxing you back to your starting-point after a 30-minute meander. Things aren't made easier by the name-change mania that gripped the nation after 1989, a problem exacerbated by the cantankerous old Communists and mischievous youths who insist on using the wrong name.

Transport information is dispensed from the enquiry centre, ✆ 24 98 46 42, but you'll be lucky to speak to an Anglophone. Information is available on the web at *www.dp-praha.cz*. Daytime routes of buses and trams are marked on most city maps. You can buy a ticket (*jízdenka*) for the buses, trams and metros from the yellow machines in metro stations and on street corners (make sure that the green light on the top is on). You can also get them in tobacconists, newsagents and several cafés, but you *can't* buy them on trams or buses, so it's worth getting a bunch at a time. Validate them by punching them in the machines that you'll find on board the tram or bus, and in the vestibule of metro stations. Each ticket is valid for one ride, up to 60 minutes long. **Day passes** (*celodenní jízdenka*) covering all three services can be bought from the red machines in most stations; and you can get passes of up to a week from almost any *tabák*. Don't try to validate them. If you are under 10 or over 70, you have a free ride—and if you're not, you should be particularly careful not to cross one of Prague's most distinctive sub-cultures, female pensioners with time on their hands. By law they are entitled to your seat, and may raise hell if you don't offer it spontaneously.

by metro

This is the easiest way to get around town. The chrome-plated Soviet-built network still has the legendary efficiency of totalitarianism, and the three lines and three intersections present few difficulties to even the worst sense of direction (*see* map, p.46). Trains run from around 5am to midnight, every few minutes at peak hours, and stops are scattered all over the centre of town. The junctions are at Muzeum (lines A and C), Můstek (lines A and B) and Florenc (lines B and C).

by tram

These quaint beasts shudder across Prague in droves, rattling and raining down showers of sparks as they go. Tram timetables are so simple that they look mystifying. Each of the city's hundreds of stops has its own, regularly updated, and the times given apply only to that stop. You can usually rely on them almost to the minute. The regular service runs from 4.30am to midnight. Night trams then take over all the major routes; there are nine (routes 51–58), all passing through Lazarská street in the New Town. There is a simple plan of night tram routes at most stops; look out for a white number on a blue background.

by bus

These avoid some parts of the centre, but otherwise most of the same rules apply as for trams. The timetables are less reliable (tram jams are rarer), and, if you're working from a map, take into account that the stops are much farther apart. Night-time service is provided by bus numbers 501 to 512. Night buses are marked on the bus-stop plans, but are only really useful if you are living in one of the hellhole housing estates in the suburbs. The authorities do their best to make sure that things run smoothly: as on the trams, a recorded message announces the name of each stop (which has led to mass confusion on the rare occasions that it's slipped out of synch), and an unseen eye even watches the platforms to snap at you if you look as though you might leap off.

by funicular

The funicular up to Petřín Hill leaves from Újezd and stops at Nebozízek before reaching Petřín. The service runs from 9.15am to 8.45pm.

by taxi

Cabs are the source of much tourist unhappiness. The manners of most drivers have improved hugely since the mid-1990s, when stun guns and revolvers were, on more than a few occasions, used against recalcitrant passengers, but many cabbies will add several hundred per cent to your fare if you let them. As a general rule, you should ask the price before setting off, and have a general sense of the direction in which you want to travel. A fair fare, allowing for a moderate level of extortion, is about £6 ($9) for 3 miles. The least stressful option of all is to dial a cab: two safe, cheap and reliable companies are Profi Taxi, ✆ 61 31 41 51, ✆ 61 04 55 50/5 or ✆ 692 13 32, and AAA Radio Taxi, ✆ 1080 or ✆ 312 21 12. Both firms are used to dealing with foreigners, and the controller will usually speak at least basic English. Tipping is optional but, if you meet a driver who's worth it, the going rate for foreigners is 10 per cent.

by car

Cars drive on the right, usually at very high speed. For the record, the speed limit in built-up areas is 60 kph (just under 40 mph). On open roads that goes up to 90 kph (about 55 mph), and on motorways you can travel at up to 110 kph (70 mph). Seatbelts are compulsory, unless you are less than 1.5m tall, in which case you should sit in the back seat. Driving with *any* alcohol in your bloodstream is punishable by an on-the-spot fine of just under £400 ($600). Finally, don't mess with the trams. They have full right of way, even—nay, especially—if that involves careering across your lane at full speed. At stops without a pedestrian island you should never pass on the right while passengers are being disgorged. Disembarking tramsters comprise a fair proportion of Prague's dead pedestrians each year.

Until the 1970s, motor traffic trundled uninterrupted through the winding alleys and broad boulevards of Prague. However, large tracts of the capital have since been closed or restricted to those with special permits. You can buy a good driving map that shows which roads are navigable (*Praha pro motoristy*), available from all good map shops, but the best rule of thumb is to park on the periphery and continue your journey by public transport. Wenceslas Square and the surrounding streets are off-limits to almost all passenger traffic. If you try to drive along them you'll be waved down by a policeman holding a big red lollipop; he will either fine you or, if no one is looking, let you off with a bribe.

Auto-theft has reached epic proportions. Several car-ringing gangs now operate in the city; immobilizers can only provide limited protection, given that cars are sometimes lifted straight off the road into covered trucks, and you may want to keep your car in an underground car park. You'll find them next to the National Theatre, near the main station, and under the Hotel Intercontinental, Hotel Atrium, nám. Jana Palacha and the Kotva department store. Outdoor guarded car parks are also common, are often safer and are always cheaper; they can be found, for example, in Karlovo nám., Malostranské nám., Národní street, and at both ends of Revoluční street. Otherwise, about 97 per cent of parking in the centre is for residents only. If you park illegally, you're likely to be clamped or towed away within a couple of hours of stopping. The police will provide the address if you call ✆ 158.

Petrol pumps remain few and far between in Prague, and when you get to one you should fill up. Leaded petrol is marked *special*, diesel is *nafta*, and leadfree is *natural* or *bleifrei*. There are 24-hour stations on K Barrandovu, Jeremiašová and Plzeňská streets, all in Prague 5.

If your engine explodes or you otherwise sputter to a halt, call ✆ 154 or ✆ 123 and a car full of so-called Yellow Angels will charge to the rescue. The Angels will tow your hulk to the **24-hour repair service** at Limuzská 12, ✆ 77 34 55, and, if you haven't entirely run out of steam, you can drive there directly. There is a certain etiquette about **road accidents** in the Czech Republic. After the usual exchange of details, apologies, blows, etc., you're expected to report the news to the police on ✆ 42 41 41. If you've moved your car an inch or if you test positive for alcohol, it's curtains for your insurance claim.

The following firms all offer a range of Western cars, and permit drop-offs at offices outside the Czech Republic. All take major credit cards. **Budget**, Hotel Intercontinental, ✆ 24 88 11 11 (*open daily 8–8*); **Europcar**, Pařížská 28, ✆ 24 81 05 15 (*open daily 8–7*); **Hertz**, Karlovo nám. 28, ✆ 29 78 36 (*open daily 8–8*); **Avis**, Ruznyě Airport, ✆ 35 36 24 20 (*open Mon–Fri 7–6, Sat 7–1pm*). A small private firm, **Esocar**, at Spojová 95, ✆ 82 66 37/82 41 24, offers rates that are among the lowest in Prague. On the other hand, if money is no object you might consider cruising Prague in a white stretch limo: chauffeur-driven Lincolns, Buicks and Cadillacs can be hired at Na Marně 4, ✆ 34 27 91, *cinek@appet.cz.*

by motorbike

The maximum speed limit is 60 kph (40 mph) in built-up areas, and 90 kph (55 mph) elsewhere. Driver and passenger have to wear helmets and may not smoke while riding, under any circumstances. Dipped headlights must be used.

Tours and Trips: Inefficient Travel

Messing about on the Vltava is a useless way of getting from A to B, since you have to go back to A eventually, but it's fun. The Prague **Steamboat Company**, Rašínovo nábřeží, ✆ 24 91 76 40, ✆ 24 91 38 62, paddles up- and downstream all summer long. A **horse-and-carriage** is only marginally more functional, and you can mount one at the Old Town Square. You can also catch a **choo-choo train** in the square during the summer, and go on a hooting and jangling trip through town. No Czech rides a **bicycle** across the asthmatic hills of smoky Prague, but odd foreigners can get away with it: hire a mountain bike at 3F Servis on Šumavská 33, ✆ 253 99 82 (*open daily 9–8*). If that sounds too much like hard work, you could float over the city in a **balloon** instead, sipping champagne as you go: call Adyton on ✆ 74 81 36; or tour the city in a chauffeured 1927 Praga Alfa-Tatra vintage car, courtesy of Pavel on ✆ 06071 914915. Finally, the Czech Aeronautical Research and Testing Institute (VZLU) at Beranových 130 in Prague 9, ✆/✆ 850 18 90, offers a number of opportunities to expend truly colossal amounts of energy for no good reason. As well as chartering executive jets and light aircraft, it can put you into an L39 Albatros **turbojet trainer** alongside a watchful man with dual controls. For about $1,000 an hour, you can speed over the Czech Republic in the same plane used to teach an entire generation of Warsaw Pact pilots how to evade NATO and wipe out the West, as and when it might become necessary.

Prague: Practical A–Z

The significance of dates in Prague, like that of street names, has become very obscure as of late. Many anniversaries that were once charged with anti-Communist significance are now all but ignored and the only new public holiday created since 1989—Czechoslovakian Independence Day—was observed only twice before the country that it commemorated disappeared from the map and the holiday was demoted. That, along with the fact that a clutch of Communist feast days were abolished, means that the Czech Republic has a dearth of long weekends. On the other hand, it has an excess of so-called State Holidays (marked with a ★) and Memorial Days (marked with a +) which no one quite knows how to celebrate. Public holidays, during which most of the capital closes down, are listed in bold.

1 Jan	**New Year's Day**
19 Jan	Anniversary of Jan Palach's death. Inexplicably, this lasted as a Memorial Day for only a couple of years after 1989. Scores of people still light a candle at his grave (*see* p.29).
28 Feb	Victorious February. Anniversary of Communist takeover in 1948. Used to involve 'vast popular manifestations' in the Old Town Square.
7 Mar	Tomáš Masaryk's birthday. The first president of Czechoslovakia, stooped, bearded, intellectual and much loved. This short-lived Memorial Day was once celebrated with as much enthusiasm as Victorious February.
April	The year's excitement begins. In the fortnight before Easter, street vendors sell willow switches (*pomlázky*) bedecked with ribbons, and grandmothers to granddaughters across the country suck eggs.
Easter Mon	**Pondělí velikonoční**. A fun-packed day. Until noon, Prague's men thrash their women with the willow sticks to keep them fresh for the coming year. The newly fertilized women then give their menfolk a painted egg, and pour buckets of water over them. The bizarre ritual is universally observed.
30 April	Walpurgis Night. Witches speed unseen through the coal-black night. Bonfires are lit on hills, crossroads and pastures to roast the flying hags and, by tradition, pubescent youths leap through the flames. The festival is still marked with a fire up on Petřín Hill.
May	International Book Fair and Writers' Festival.
1 May	**Labour Day**. Slowly reverting to another day of feasting and fecundity.
5 May+	Anniversary of Prague Uprising (*see* p.28).
8 May★	Day of liberation from Fascism. In 1991, the Czech Republic joined western Europe in celebrating VE Day on the 8th, despite the fact that on that day in 1945 ferocious fighting was still continuing in Prague.
12 May	Anniversary of Smetana's death. Musicians walk from his grave in Vyšehrad to Obecní dům and play his masterpiece, *Má Vlast*. The Prague spring music festival begins.
June	This month sees the annual Golden Golem film festival, which has established itself as a minor fixture on Europe's cinematic scene.
3 June	Anniversary of Kafka's death. Devotees gather to contemplate mortality and genius at his grave (*see* p.124).

18 June	Anniversary of the killing of the assassins of Reinhard Heydrich. Memorial mass is held in the Church of SS Cyril and Methodius (*see* pp.120).
21 June	Summer solstice. Twenty-seven spectres potter about in the Old Town Square (*see* p.50).
July	Karlovy Vary International Film Festival (every even year).
5 July★	SS Cyril and Methodius Day.
6 July★	Anniversary of Jan Hus' death (and birth).
21 Aug	Anniversary of Soviet-led invasion in 1968.
29 Aug+	Anniversary of the 1944 Slovakian National Uprising.
Sept	A festival of spiritual music is held in and out of the city's 630 churches.
Oct	Annual Mozart festival takes place throughout the city. Prague International Jazz Festival, throughout the month; contact ✆ 2481 8277, ✉ 248 18272.
28 Oct★	Independence Day. The anniversary of the establishment of Czechoslovakia in 1918. The day is regularly hijacked by the extreme right, and if you're black you'd do well to avoid large crowds.
31 Oct	All Saints' Eve. Appropriated by accountants and attorneys with pumpkins.
2 Nov	All Saints' Day. The day on which the medieval Church decreed that prayers be said for 'all the dead who have existed from the beginning of the world to the end of time'. Praguers still observe the custom, and turn their graveyards into galaxies of candles.
17 Nov+	Anniversary of the first demonstration of the 1989 Revolution. Candles are lit in Národní street and under the St Wenceslas monument.
5 Dec	St Nicholas' Eve. An event-filled day. Public-spirited folk dress up as devils or angels and, accompanied by a crozier-toting St Nick, stalk the streets of Prague handing out coal to evil-doing tots and sweets to the good ones. The bad ones toss firecrackers.
8 Dec	Anarchists and youths protest John Lennon's death at the John Lennon Wall (*see* p.114).
20 Dec	Tubs containing carp appear on Prague street corners around this time, and the roads foam with rivulets of blood and water. The creatures are the Czech equivalent of the British turkey, and normally placid Praguers spend several minutes each day watching gizzards being removed. Don't stand too close— the *coup de grâce* generally sprays fishy brains across a wide radius.
24 Dec	**Christmas Eve**. Children spend the day trying to fast, in the hope of seeing golden pigs. Carp are taken out of the bath and fried. Baby Jesus or Grandfather Frost bring the presents. St Nicholas makes the occasional surprise appearance.
25 Dec	**Christmas Day**. Nothing happens. More carp is eaten.
26 Dec	**St Stephen's Day**. More carp is eaten.
27–30 Dec	The city continues to eat carp; the bathtubs are replaced by firework stalls. Sporadic explosions occur across the city.
31 Dec	**New Year's Eve**, a.k.a. St Silvester's Day. The city turns into an assault course of gunpowder mortars and jumping-jacks.

If you are looking to abandon your child, you couldn't pick a better city than Prague. Musicians, puppet-shows and jugglers turn the streets into a perpetual playground during the summer, and it's still remarkably safe. Should you succumb to remorse, the city's inexplicable way of engineering unexpected meetings would quickly throw you back into each other's arms.

Maps and (Czech) money are useful ways of drumming up interest before you leave. Good King Wenceslas is another limited way of introducing the country to younger children. There's an easily readable collection of national legends available in English: *Old Czech Legends* by Alois Jirásek, published by Forest Books. Over the years, the country's much renowned animators have also produced an impressive body of children's cartoons (which are sometimes shown at London's National Film Theatre). Nappies and basic medicines are widely available. Stick to bottled water, at least for younger children, since even the government accepts that the mains variety is unsafe for toddlers, although it quibbles about precisely how toddly.

Most bars, cafés and restaurants welcome children, and some foreign-run establishments—such as Kampa Park—have cheap or free deals for kids under 10. (They make up for it with their prices for everyone else.) If you're feeling particularly harried, you might even consider taking your brood to one of the many McDonald's in the city centre (e.g. on Vodičkova or Mostecká streets), where you can stupefy them with carbohydrates and deposit them in a built-in playpen while you plot your next move. Another child-friendly haunt with a children's play area is the Old Town branch of Bohemia Bagel at Masná 2. On a sunny day, an outdoor alternative is the small Childrens' Island (Dětský ostrov) between the Jiráskův and 1 May bridges, which comes with a decent playground and plenty of native playmates.

Sightseeing with children is no problem. The hourly mechanics of the **Astronomical Clock** (*see* p.51) are a thing of endless fascination to most children, and **tower-climbing** is a game that the city caters for well. You can even have fun on the move. **Trams** can be mightily impressive to someone small who's never seen the beasts before; **horse-drawn buggies** and **rowboats** on the river are less useful as means of transport, but just as good if your child has learnt to walk and had enough already (in which context, it should be noted that the municipal transport system is free for children under five and half-price for those under 10).

All ages will appreciate the **National Technical Museum** (*see* p.134), with its clocks and cameras, button-induced noises, and the hundreds of wings and wheels in its transport exhibition. The long tour through the massive coal mine in the basement is a particular adventure. Significantly less anarchistic is the **Police Museum** (*see* p.133), which shows films to teach children how to want to be police officers when they grow up, and has a number of other kiddy-orientated displays. Little Big Brothers will particularly enjoy the bank of closed-circuit TV screens, which enable them to keep tabs on their fellow infants throughout. Best of all is the small electric model car-racing set, intended to help youngsters develop road-safety skills and almost certainly entirely counter-productive. More passive children could contemplate the offerings at the **Toy Museum**, off Jilská street at the bottom end of Prague Castle, replete with display cases full of teddy bears, dolls and model cars. Whether by way of treat or punishment, you could also take your children to the **Waxworks Museum** on 28. rijna 13, or the **Ghost Museum** (Muzeum Strašidel) on Na příkopě 17: the first is probably a little too dull for younger kids, but the assorted goblins, dragons and unicorns at the latter should give them something to think about.

The funfair and dinky seaside-pier architecture of the **Exhibition Park** (Výstaviště) is filled with a mass of pleasure-inducing marvels including a funfair, planetarium, adventure playground and a singing fountain (Křižík) whose water jets dance to both classical and rock music at 6, 7 and 8pm. Up on Letná Park, just outside the National Technical Museum, is a **carousel** (open all year round, weather permitting) and, if there's a **circus** in town, it will almost certainly have pitched up on nearby Letná Plain. You or your offspring would have to be beastly to go to Prague's cruel zoo, but there's another set of attractions on Petřín Hill (*see* p.127). The **funicular** to the top is a thrill in itself, and at the summit is a **planetarium**, *www.planetarium.cz*, an observatory with telescopes for public use, *www.observat. infoserver.cz*, and a **mirror maze**.

Several of the city's theatres cater for children, most reliably the **Divadlo Minor** on Senovážné nám. 28, ✆ 24 21 43 04, and the **National Marionette Theatre** on Žatecká 1, ✆ 24 81 93 22 24. You can find full listings in *Program* (*see* p.20), in the theatre section under the heading *Pro Děti* (for children).

Finally, when push comes to shove and you've finally had enough, dump the kids with one of the following established **babysitting** services: Affordable Luxuries, ✆ 21 66 12 66, 🖂 29 80 24; Agentura Martina, ✆ 86 88 74 18/684 76 30; Babysitting, ✆ 301 17 64/5.

Climate and When to Go

There's nothing extraordinary about Prague's climate. The average temperature hovers around freezing point between December and February (and is often considerably below), climbing into T-shirt weather from May. July and August are the hottest months, reaching the high 20s regularly, and the chill of autumn usually sets in towards the end of September. The driest month is February and the wettest July, when warm showers of Bohemian acid rain drop lazily in the late evening.

average temperatures °C

Jan	Feb	Mar	April	May	June
−1.5	2.5	4	11	13.5	17.5
July	Aug	Sept	Oct	Nov	Dec
18.5	19.5	15.5	9	3.5	0

Millions of tourists visit Prague each year, and about half of them seem to come in August. In that month tourism reaches critical mass, and the city temporarily becomes a combination of Torremolinos and EuroDisney. Praguers take fright and evacuate to their country cottages every weekend, leaving the city almost devoid of Czechs. The August explosion will appeal to high-energy types, but those of a calmer disposition should consider arriving in late June or early July. Even better is early September, when the almost statutory holiday periods of much of Europe are over, but twilight lingers and cobbles remain warm. Prague's buskers are still out in force, its gardens and islands are in late bloom, and the city heaves a sigh of relief at having survived the deluge. As autumn turns to winter, pensive types can watch leaves yellow and die, or head for the city's cafés and restaurants, which develop a jolly intimacy that lasts throughout the big chill. In November, Praguers turn on the central heating and, to the sound of organ recitals and the smell of lignite, they rush towards Christmas. Prague becomes a peasoup of pollution between about November and February, so if you have respiratory problems stay away.

The capital all but closes down on Christmas Eve, but as year's end approaches Prague fills with thousands of people playing with fireworks and looking for a party. On New Year's Day the hangover hits, and hovers over the city for several very quiet weeks. February is the cruellest month, but also the time when you're most likely to see Prague swathed in snow, not the mushy rubbish of Western capitals but the creaking stuff of Good King Wenceslas. Buds pop, sap rises, and public displays of affection reach new heights at the beginning of April. The end of the month is another of the best times to come to the city and, when the Prague spring music festival begins in early May, the tourist season has turned full circle.

Crime and Police

As in the rest of one-time Communist Europe, a massive increase in (usually) petty crime has been an unwelcome aspect of the Czech Republic's transition to democracy. Popular respect for all forms of authority took a battering after the Velvet Revolution, and, while a discredited police force retreated from the streets to lick its wounds, the boom that accompanied economic liberalisation fuelled high-level corruption and kickback scandals which have left many with a deep disrespect for the integrity of their new political and financial institutions. Matters were hardly helped by the reorganization of municipal policing, which is now the uneasily shared responsibility of separate national and local forces. Swaggering bravado and internecine turf wars characterize them both.

All in all, you should probably avoid the lawmen almost as carefully as you do the outlaws. Always carry your passport with you: leaving it at home is a very minor offence, and can lead to hopeful officers spending long minutes angling for a bribe. In a real crisis, look for a patrol car marked *Policie*. Prague's central police station is at Konviktská 14 in the Old Town. The emergency phone numbers are © 156 (municipal police) and © 158 (national police).

Despite everything, the city remains one of the safer capitals in the world. Elementary precautions should keep your property and person intact. However, you would do well to avoid early-morning strolls through Wenceslas Square and the main station: not only are they the most seedy and alcohol-drenched parts of town at night, but during the summer they are also the scene of regular sweeps by squads of Prague police. The most common form of thievery is the gentle art of pick-pocketing. Crooks usually operate in pairs, and are particularly active wherever tourists gather—be especially careful on the Charles Bridge in the summer. Plan for the worst by making notes of your passport details, and traveller's cheque and credit card numbers. Travel insurance policies usually require you to file a report within 24 hours of a theft: go to the main police station at Konviktská 14. You could also contact your embassy for help; the British Embassy is particularly sympathetic and can help you have money transferred out. Optimists could also try the lost property office, Praha 1, Karolíny Svetlé 5, © 24 23 50 85. If you're waylaid—or forgetful—on a train, each station also has its own lost property office.

Lone **women** will probably find Wenceslas Square doubly uncomfortable at night, since it's a well-known promenade for prostitutes and pimps. The same applies to the area around Uhelný trh., which has become Prague's kerb-crawling precinct. The streets are far safer for women than those of London or most large US cities, although keys, knees and umbrellas are useful weapons to keep in reserve. Czech hairspray is a traditional and effective blinding agent, but it has now been superseded by canisters of CS gas, available from all good tobacconists.

Another crime-related issue concerns the explosion of **drug use** that has occurred across Prague during the 1990s. Heroin has flooded into the Czech Republic through its once impermeable eastern borders, and addiction has reached a level that would have been unthinkable in the heady days of Communism. Matters are made worse by the Czech Republic's unworkable drug laws, which do not distinguish between soft and hard drugs and do permit possession (but not supply) of any amount that can reasonably be regarded as for 'personal use'. The rules have brought about the worst of both worlds: creating a lucrative grey market for organized criminal gangs to exploit, while making it enormously difficult to track down the key players. All in all, beware of people with eclipsed pupils, and avoid nocturnal strolls around the nám. Republiky area, which is where many addicts gather to compose their thoughts as the smack runs out.

Finally, anyone black or even marginally off-white should expect to come across a certain degree of **racism**. It's often of a fairly innocent kind, but it can create the occasional uncomfortable situation for foreigners. The concept of a black American is widely understood (although it's best if he or she knows a lot about rapping and so on), but many people are still flummoxed by the idea of a British person who's not white. You'd be very unlucky to come across anything worse than unpleasantness in the city centre; elsewhere, it's unfortunately true that you should remain on yellow alert. However, it's the local non-whites who bear the brunt. One of the most unpleasant of the many genies to slip out of the velvet bottle in 1989 was a contempt for the 30,000-strong Vietnamese population and, most notably of all, the open hatred now expressed towards the country's several hundred thousand Romanies (*cikáni*).

Disabled Travellers

Even the most powerful electric wheelchair is likely to whine to a halt when confronted with some of Prague's hills, and its crowded public transport system can be inaccessible to even the most able-bodied, but at last the city is beginning to address the problems of people with limited mobility. The first post-revolutionary mayor, former dissident Jaroslav Kořán, set the ball rolling by smoothing 3,000 kerbs during his time in office. Olga Havel, the wife of Václav, also worked tirelessly for disabled people until her untimely death in 1996, and the foundation that she created is the capital's most useful source of information for all those with visual, dietary and auditory problems, as well as wheelchair users. It's known as the Výbor dobré vůle (Committee of Good Will), and you'll find it at Senovážné nám. 2, ✆ 24 21 68 83. Extremely helpful English-speaking workers are always around. They can also put you in touch with the Red Cross, which lends wheelchairs out to anyone who needs one.

Three major theatres—the **Estates Theatre**, the **Vinohrady Theatre** and the **Rudolfinum**—are fully accessible to wheelchair users, as are all the city's department stores. Most of the city's museums and galleries can make special arrangements if you call in advance; the **Cubist Museum** (*see* p.132) has been specifically designed to accommodate wheelchairs. Wheelchair-friendly hotels are noted as such in the **Where to Stay** chapter.

The capital is slowly providing for the special needs of blind people. Metro entrances have been bleeping for about a decade; on the trains a voice announces when the doors are about to close and what the next stop will be (the latter also on trams); and traffic lights click or squeak when it's safe to cross.

The Czech Republic's spas are said to alleviate scores of medical conditions, from cerebral palsy to psoriasis. Each watering hole has its particular specialities, and for further information you should contact **Balnea** in Prague at Národní 28, ✆ 24 22 76 44, ✉ 24 21 42 11. Eighteen Czech towns have dialysis centres, and prior arrangments for treatment can be made via your local centre in your home country.

There are numerous UK-based organizations providing specific information and help in planning a trip to the Czech Republic. They include the **British Diabetic Association** at 10 Queen Anne St, London W1M 0BD, ✆ (020) 7323 1531, ✉ (020) 7636 3096/637 3644, and the **Haemophilia Society** at Chesterfield House, 385 Euston Rd, London NW1 3AU, ✆ (020) 7380 0600.

The best source of general information in the UK is **RADAR** at 12 City Forum, 250 City Rd, London EC1V 8AF, ✆ (020) 7250 3222, textphone (Minicom) ✆ (020) 7250 4119, which publishes *European Holidays and Travel Abroad: A Guide for Disabled People*, updated every two years. In the USA, get hold of *Access to the World: A Travel Guide for the Handicapped* by Louise Weiss (H. Holt & Co.).

Electricity

Prague's voltage is usually 220 ac, but you'll need a plug with two round prongs before anything will fire up. Buy adaptors before leaving home. The best is the universal kind, because it can deal with the earthing prong that sticks out of some sockets. The voltage in rooms in private accommodation in an older part of town may be 110 ac. That's fine for US equipment, but UK hairdryers will work at half-speed, while your laptop and fax won't work at all. Pack a transformer, if in doubt.

Embassies and Consulates

Most diplomatic missions are located in Malá Strana, or around the Dejvice area in Prague 6.

Canada	Mickiewiczova 6, 125 33 Praha 6, ✆ 72 10 18 00, ✉ 72 10 18 90
Hungary	Badeniho 1, 160 00 Praha 6, ✆ 33 32 44 54, ✉ 33 2 21 04
Ireland	Tržiště 13, 118 00 Praha 1, ✆ 57 53 00 61 4, ✉ 57 53 13 87
UK	Thunovská 14, 118 00 Praha 1, ✆ 57 53 02 78, ✉ 57 53 02 85
USA	Tržiště 15, 118 01 Praha 1, ✆ 57 53 06 63, ✉ 57 53 05 83

The British Embassy acts on behalf of New Zealanders. Australians should trek on to Warsaw (✆ 48 2 617 60 81).

Emergencies

In an emergency, contact one of the following: Ambulance, ✆ 155; Municipal Police, ✆ 156; National Police, ✆ 158; Fire, ✆ 150. *See* also 'Health and Insurance', below.

Health and Insurance

If you hold a British passport, you're entitled to free medical treatment in the Czech Republic; to qualify, you should complete and have stamped (prior to departure) a form E111, which you can obtain from post offices and travel agents. Prices are still relatively low for everyone else. However, Prague is not a place where you want to undergo major surgery, and you should at least consider taking out health insurance for your stay. Holiday insurance policies differ hugely in their coverage of theft and loss: check, for example, whether stolen cash is reimbursed, and go through the even smaller print detailing exclusions and limitations. The latter may result in your recovering only half a camera, and an even smaller fraction of a lost suitcase. US students with an ISIC card have free (albeit limited) cover from the moment they venture out of the home of the brave.

The best Czech hospital, and the one most accustomed to dealing with foreigners, is the Nemocnice Na Homolce on Roentgenova 2, off V úvalu, Prague 5, ✆ 57 27 21 46. Otherwise, head for one of the clinics below. You can redeem your prescriptions at any pharmacist (*lékárna*). Two of the most central—both of which are open 24 hours daily—are at Palackého 5, ✆ 24 94 69 82, and Belgická 37, ✆ 22 51 97 31.

Foreign Medical Clinics:
Health Centre Prague: Praha 1, Vodičkova 28, ✆ 24 22 00 40.
Canadian Medical Centre: Praha 6, Veleslavínská 30, ✆ 35 36 01 33.
American Medical Center: Praha 7, Janovského 48, ✆ 80 77 56.
General Health Care Corporation: Praha 1, Krakovská 8, ✆ 22 21 01 78.

Dental emergencies: Praha 1, ✆ 24 94 69 81 (*Mon–Fri 7am–7pm, Sat–Sun non-stop*).

Opticians can be found where you see a sign saying *oční optika*. If you can't find one, feel your way to Eiffel Optic, Na příkopé 25, ✆ 24 23 49 66, or Vodičkova 17, ✆ 24 94 68 50 (*open Mon–Sat 9–8, Sun 9.30–6.30*).

Internet

Connect to the Internet at one of the following cybercafés:

Bohemia Bagel, Masna 2. Cheap and fast connections; bagels and bottomless coffee. *Open daily 10–10.*
Café.com, Na poříčí 36. Cold beer, cocktails and computers in a basement bar. *Open Mon–Fri 9am–midnight, Sat–Sun 11am–midnight.*
Cybeteria, Na příkopé 25. Mellow atmosphere, and teas from around the world. *Open daily 10–10.*

The following websites offer some of the most useful Prague-based information and services for foreign visitors to the city. The most comprehensive Czech search engine is at *www.seznam.cz.*

Food and drink: *www.praguepivo.com* (pubs and beer halls), *www.squaremeal.cz* (restaurant reservations), *www.praguefinedining.cz.*

Listings and tourist information: *www.globopolis.com* (the Globe bookshop site), *www.prague-info.cz* (the Prague Information Service site), *www.downtown.cz*, *www.amigo.cz* (gay and lesbian directory).

Music: *www.musica.cz*, *www.czechmusic.cz.*

News and current affairs: *www.praguepost.cz* (the online edition of Prague's weekly English-language newspaper), *www.centraleurope.cz* (regional news).

Travel arrangements: *www.vlak-bus.cz* (train and bus services).

Money

The Czech currency is the crown (*koruna česká*, abbreviated to kč), which is made up of 100 heller (*halér*). The present rate of exchange (late 2000) is 58kč to the pound sterling and 40kč to the American dollar. The exchange rate is likely to adapt itself to price increases, and **almost all prices in the Prague section of this book are given in pounds and dollars.** An exchange rate of £1:$1.50 is assumed. However, it's still only possible to give very rough estimates of how much your stay will cost. Assume prices about 30 per cent lower than those at home and, if hyperinflation hits, you will be in for a pleasant time, even if no one else is. When changing your money, don't bother with the 'black market'. Street transactions invariably end in a confused scuffle, mutterings of 'police!' and the tourist left holding a wad of waste paper or near worthless Polish zloties.

Exchange offices exist in every hotel and accommodation agency, and gleam out of the medieval centre of the town. There are several 24-hour Chequepoints, including one at the foot of Wenceslas Square, on 28. října 13. However, the commission they extract—often 10 per cent—is painful, and you should always change your money at a bank, which usually takes two per cent. Most banks close by 5pm and throughout the weekend. There's a 24-hour banknote-changing machine at the Bank Austria on Havelská 19.

The plastic revolution is well under way, but **cash** is still ubiquitous. Putting aside a high-denomination note, Czech or foreign, can be useful for bribery, but although the practice remains common you should be very careful before attempting it. Slipping someone a sweetener can lead to very embarrassing situations unless you know exactly what you are doing.

Major **credit cards** can now be used in all the swankier restaurants, shops and hotels. Cash advances can be obtained from all banks and exchange offices. Holders of MasterCard, Visa, Cirrus and Plus cards can also use the ATMs scattered around the centre of town. American Express has an office at Václavské nám. 56 (*see below*). Lost Amex cards can be reported on ✆ 22 80 01 11; Visa losses can be reported by calling ✆ 24 12 53 53; for Diners Club losses call ✆ 67 31 44 85; and for MasterCard/Eurocard ✆ 61 35 46 50. In the case of other cards, the Živnostenská banka, ✆ 24 23 24 23, will help you have them cancelled before too much damage is done.

Few shops are yet prepared to accept **traveller's cheques** in payment, but cheques are the only safe way to carry around small fortunes in Prague. If your cheques are pilfered, you can obtain a more or less instant refund at the following addresses: **American Express**: Václavské nám. 56, ✆ 24 21 99 92 during office hours, or at other times call the UK, ✆ (0044) 12 73 57 16 00; **Thomas Cook**: Václavské nám. 47, ✆ 26 31 06, ✆ 26 66 11 (*open Mon–Fri 9–9, Sat 9–5, Sun 10–5*); **Visa and Eurocheque**: Živnostenská banka, Na příkopě 20, ✆ 24 12 11 11 (*open Mon–Fri 8–5*).

Post

Prague's **main post office** is in the New Town at Jindřišská 14, ✆ 24 22 88 56. Fax, telegram, post and telephone services are available at all hours of the day and night. There are several other post offices in the city centre, including one in the Old Town at Kaprova 12, another in Malá Strana at Josefská 4, and one opposite St Vitus' Cathedral in the Third Courtyard of the castle. There is a non-stop post office at Praha 1, Hybernská 15.

Over the last century, Praguers have shown a rather unhealthy attachment to mass-mobilization in the name of sport. Until 1989 the quinquennial highlight of the sporting calendar was a celebration of beauty and youth organized by the Communists and known as the *Spartakiáda*. Every five years, 160,000 identical gymnasts would perform feats of co-ordinated kitsch in the capital's Strahov stadium, watched by 220,000 awe-struck spectators. Very few Praguers will admit it now, but being selected as a cog in the machine was regarded by many as a great honour, and the festival was only the successor to the even more popular *Sokol* movement, founded in 1862 and devoted to celebrating the physical glory of the Czech race. However, the capital seems finally to have lost its fascination with sporting crowds and power. The plug was pulled on the June 1990 *Spartakiáda*, and any lingering traces of beauty and youth evaporated two months later when Mick Jagger and Keith Richards strutted the Strahov stage. Nowadays, the following activities are about as dramatic as leisure gets in Prague.

Football

Prague has four soccer teams—Sparta, Slávia, Bohemians and Dukla—but only the first two are of real interest. The season's Sparta–Slávia match is football as any Englander would recognize it: obscene chants, fireworks lobbed at the goalies, and regular invasions of the stands by riot officers. Sparta fans in particular revel in their reputations as ruffians. Unlike their Western counterparts, who occasionally confound expectations by giving up seats to pensioners and the like, Sparta's most loyal troops are unreconstructed neo-fascist hooligans.

Horse-racing

The city's racecourse is at Velká Chuchle, a 15-minute bus journey from Smíchovské nádraží metro station on line B (Nos.129, 172, 241, 243 or 245).

Mushroom-picking

Czechs have a fascination with fungi—so much so that five people, on average, die each year as a result of eating the wrong ones. If you like to live on the edge, the wooded hills that stretch from Karlštejn to Křivoklát castles harbour scores of edible varieties, and the grasslands around Telč are said to harbour some particularly interesting specimens. Avoid the fate of the five Czechs by taking your mushrooms to the Česká mykologická stanice (Czech Mycological Station) at Karmelitská 14, ✆ 53 26 93 (*open Mon–Fri 8–2*). For a very small fee, the staff will name your fungus and warn you if eating it would, for example, lead to vivid hallucinations.

Snow Sports

It's fashionable to leave Prague with your skis in winter. Slopy pistes can be found at Špindlerův Mlýn, Harrachov and Pec pod Sněžkou, in the Krkonoše mountains near the Polish border.

Swimming and Watersports

Prague's public pools have a long-standing reputation for being over-chlorinated and under-cleaned, but many of the newer hotels have excellent pools, and the 25m pool at the Hotel Axa (*see* p.156) is always open to non-guests. Committed nudists can meet like-minded folk at the Šeberák lake in Prague 4, near K Šeberáku, while the wild expanse of Šárka park (along Evropská on the way to the airport) is a time-honoured spot for Praguers to go skinny-dipping on summer evenings. Finally, you'll find waterskiing and windsurfing facilities at the Slapy Dam, 30km upstream on the Vltava. To get there, catch the signs on the Strakonická highway, which runs south along the river, or take a bus from the terminal outside Anděl metro station.

Telephones

Most **UK mobiles** can be used throughout the Czech Republic, assuming that prior to travel you've contacted your company's customer services department and asked for the roaming facility to be activated. Very few of Prague's **public phones** take cash any more, and if you're going to need to use them you should invest in a card, available from newsagents and tobacconists, post offices, hotels, etc. Prague's telephone system has been in the throes of mass reorganization for the last few years; older numbers may be anything from four to seven numbers long. The word for extension is *linka*.

The **dialling code** to the UK is 0044, to Canada 001, and to the USA it's 001; the code *for* Prague is 00420(2) from the UK and 011420(2) from the USA.

Toilets

There are toilets in every subway station, and in strategic locations across town. If you are desperate, it's acceptable to rush into the nearest café or wine bar and ask for the *záchod*, a.k.a. WC (pronounced *ve tse*). 'Men' is *muži*; 'women' is *ženy*. One of the stranger of the many jobs created to keep Prague's *babičky* off the streets is that of Toilet Paper Custodian, and in several public conveniences you'll find one sitting at a table near the entrance, snarling and mumbling as she folds and neatly lays out small scraps of tissue paper. The procedure varies, but generally you have to pay a couple of crowns for admission and/or a piece of paper. It can all be terribly embarrassing, and it's generally advisable to carry spare supplies. Otherwise, there are few differences between Prague's loos and those of its former Cold War enemies.

Tourist Information

The official **Prague Information Service** (PIS) has two offices: at Betlémské nám. 2, ✆ 54 44 44, *info@pis.cz, www.prague-info.cz* (*open Mon–Fri 8–7*); and Na příkopě 20 (*open Mon–Fri 9–7, Sat–Sun 9–5*). General information in both Czech and English can be obtained on ✆ 54 44 44 or ✆ 187. The PIS also runs sightseeing tours, as does almost everybody else in Prague during the summer. Head for the town hall in the Old Town Square, or telephone ✆ 24 48 25 62/9, ✆ 24 48 23 80. Every newsagent in the centre will sell English-language guides, but the most up-to-date and informed listings are to be found in the *Prague Post.* Another good weekly listings magazine is *Program*, which is predominantly Czech but has English summaries of all its sections, and the *Erotic Guide to Prague* might tickle some fancies. For telephone listings, ring Echoline on ✆ 1051.

When **booking tickets** for a specific event, you're best advised to go directly to the venue concerned. However, if you're pressed for time or want advice in drawing up an itinerary, seats for all the major theatres and operas, as well as for many smaller venues, can be booked for you by Bohemia Tickets International at Malé nám. 13, ✆ 24 22 78 32/24 23 77 27, ✆ 21 61 21 26, *btiinter@login.cz, www.csad.cz\bti* (*open Mon–Fri 9–12 and 1–6, Sat 9–4*); or Ticketpro at Salvátorská 10, ✆ 24 81 60 20, ✆ 24 81 40 21, *orders@ ticketpro.cz, www.ticketpro.cz.* The only place to buy tickets for the Prague spring music festival is at Hellichova 18. It's open for just a month from mid-April onwards, but advance information and tickets can be ordered by post (at a heavy premium) from Bohemia Tickets International, P.O.B. 534, Praha 1–111 21. If you want to buy them in the UK, contact the Czech and Slovak Tourist Centre, p.2.

Prague: History

21

Those who lie on the rails of history must expect to have their legs chopped off.

Rudé právo (Communist Party newspaper), 1979

The 1,000-year history of Prague is one of the most inspiring and tragic of any European city. Glory, betrayal and martyrdom litter its pages, while its magnificent skyline has grown to maturity, bloodied but unbowed, through centuries of invasion and war. Prague's citizens, who conceived nationalism before it even twinkled in the eyes of the rest of Europe, have seen their country both liberated and dismembered in the last few years. What the future holds for the Czech Republic is anyone's guess—but if history is any guide, it's not going to be dull.

The First Přemysl is Found

The story begins with the establishment of Bohemia's first ruling dynasty, the Přemysls, at some time around the end of the 8th century. Myth and history are intertwined but, according to the former, the Čech tribe had established itself at Vyšehrad ('higher castle'), a rocky outcrop on the Vltava River that still bears the same name. Čech himself was a mass-murderer on the run; but it was his son, Krok or Crocus, who went down in legend as the putative founding father. Unable to produce a male heir, he was succeeded by his daughter Libuše.

When the men of the tribe insisted Libuše needed a husband, her response was to go into a trance. Pointing towards the distant hills, she told them to follow her horse, which would take them to a ploughman whose descendants would rule over them for ever. The horse trotted off, and a sturdy farmer named Přemysl was brought back to wed Libuše. A dynasty had begun. The city of Prague (as distinct from the settlement at Vyšehrad) also owes its legendary origins to one of Libuše's prophecies. According to Bohemia's venerable chronicler, Cosmas of Prague (c. 1045–1125), she was overcome by a vision involving two golden olive trees and 'a town, the glory of which will reach the stars'. Again the loyal subjects trooped off to a spot described by Libuše, where they found a man building a door-sill (in Czech, *práh*—hence the name Praha or Prague) for his cottage. Legend has it that this spot was on what is now Hradčany, or the Castle District. Building started in earnest and the rest, as they say, is history.

Archaeological finds and other scanty evidence suggest, in fact, that the first people in the area were a Celtic tribe known as the Boii, who lived here at the turn of the Christian era and stayed long enough to leave behind the name 'Bohemia'. In about the 5th century, the Čechs, a Slavonic tribe from Croatia, are thought to have established a powerful presence in the area, but there's no record of Crocus, and it's only in the later 9th century that the first historically attested Přemysl, Bořivoj, appears on the scene as ruler of Bohemia. The princedom was still an insignificant cog in the Greater Moravian Empire, which included most of the Slavs of Central Europe, and which was engaged in endless bloody tussles with the Holy Roman Empire to the west.

The Great Schism between the Roman and Byzantine Churches had already begun to open up, and German monks were scurrying across the Moravian Empire with their version of the Good Book. Christianity was clearly the coming thing and, in about 863, the empire's ruler, Rostislav, turned to the Eastern Church for help. Emperor Michael sent along Brothers Methodius and Cyril, two Greek Holy Rollers who arrived with a Bible and a liturgy written in a new Greek-based alphabet (Glagolitic, or Cyrillic script) that could deal with the grunts peculiar to the Slavs. Jealous Germans levelled charges of heresy, but the two men remained on fairly good terms with Rome until their death. In Bohemia, Bořivoj was dunked into the new religion by Methodius in about 874. Mass abandonment of storm and fertility gods followed.

Bohemia Takes Off

Although the Slavs had little sympathy for the Holy Roman Empire, its power couldn't be ignored. As the Přemysls struggled to control Bohemia, they began to turn away from the East, and the influence of Germans in Bohemian affairs, which was to become a tragic motif over the next millennium, began to grow. In 885, Pope Stephen V declared the Slavonic liturgy to be heretical. The Přemysls took his word for it and began the switch away from Cyrillic, for which Western tourists can be eternally grateful. Bohemia remained subservient to the Moravian Empire until the beginning of the 10th century, when that empire suddenly disappeared from the map, seized by rampant Magyars who chose to spare little Bohemia.

In about 921, Prince Wenceslas (Václav) became Bohemia's sovereign. A gentle Christian, he may have been a suitable subject for imaginative 19th-century carols but he just wasn't up to the rough-and-tumble of Dark Age intrigue. In 935, he was murdered on the way to Mass by his brother, Boleslav the Cruel. What Boleslav lacked in kindness, he made up for with political skill: he exterminated his remaining rivals, extended his dominions, married his daughter into the Polish ruling family, and successfully resisted political pressures from Rome.

In 973, under the rule of his less cruel son, Boleslav the Pious, Bohemia's strength was acknowledged by the pope, who finally consented to the founding of a bishopric in Prague. Two more Boleslavs followed—Boleslav the Third, who reverted to type and murdered several unruly nobles at a banquet, and his brother, Boleslav the Brave.

Over the next two centuries, Bohemia was pulled ever deeper into the tangled web of the Holy Roman Empire. In the early 13th century, both pope and emperor allowed Bohemia's princes to call themselves kings and wear a crown—which was as unimpressive as it sounds and laid the ground for future emperors to claim the right to appoint Bohemia's king. An explosive brew was also building up at lower levels of society. Under the reign of King Wenceslas I (1230–53) German merchants were invited to Prague and other parts of Bohemia, where they were allowed to govern themselves according to their own laws.

Wenceslas' successor, Přemysl Otakar II, gave further ground to the colonists, quite literally, by founding Malá Strana on the left bank of the Vltava for their benefit in 1257. During his reign (1253–78), the city developed into three autonomous units—the Old Town, the Castle District itself on Hradčany, and Malá Strana. A Jewish community in the area around Malá Strana was expelled to make way for the Germans—if Jews wanted to stay in town, they joined another Jewish community to the north of the Old Town which had been walled into a ghetto some years before. Romanies ('gypsies') are thought to have first come to Bohemia at about this time in the wake of the short but savage incursions of the Tartars. Trade and finds of silver deposits around nearby Kutná Hora helped to fund Prague's first building boom, and its Romanesque basilicas and houses gave way to Gothic grandeur. However, the city's expansion was soon stopped in its tracks—a victim of Přemysl Otakar's own success. By the early 1270s, he had created a Bohemian kingdom that stretched from the Baltic to the Adriatic and was more than enough to shake Germany's princes out of their internecine struggles. Otakar made a last-minute lunge for the emperor's throne in 1273. He missed, and Rudolf, Count of Habsburg, stepped into the imperial driving seat.

Anarchy and Chivalry

In 1306, the Přemysl dynasty sputtered to a halt with the murder by persons unknown of the 17-year-old Wenceslas III. Finding a successor was no easy matter. Anarchic Bohemia badly needed a monarch, and by 1310 everyone was longing for a strong hand. They finally settled on 14-year-old John of Luxembourg, the son of the new German emperor, Henry VII. The young king confounded everyone's expectations and spent most of his reign on a warring spree across Europe. He cared little what Prague got up to as long as it kept the royal coffers full, so burghers and nobles made the most of the new opportunities: the Old Town got a town hall, a legal code and formal supremacy over every other town in the kingdom.

The Golden Age

John's son could hardly have been less like his father. The German princes elected him Emperor Charles IV and offered him the Bohemian crown. In 1356, he regularized the imperial electoral system, putting power squarely in the hands of the princes, thereby undercutting those who had voted against him, and dealing a body-blow to the temporal ambitions of the papacy, which had had an effective veto for centuries. He took advantage of the battering that France was receiving at the hands of the English (the Hundred Years War had only just begun) to reduce it almost to vassal status. He spoke fluent Czech (along with several other languages) and encouraged the development of the country's language and traditions, and he wrapped his reign in a series of legends, going back to Libuše and St Wenceslas. With the help of his friend and former tutor, Pope Clement VI, Prague had already been elevated to an archbishopric in 1344, and Charles got permission to invite monastic orders from the farthest-flung reaches of the Eastern Church. While the Black Death devastated the rest of Europe during 1348, Bohemia lay protected by a screen of mountains and began to emerge as the most vital centre of Gothic art and architecture on the Continent. As befitted a medieval town with pretensions of grandeur, it got a new bridge, cathedral and the first university in Central Europe. For decades this was an academic vortex, sucking in scholars from as far away as Oxford. In the same year Charles founded the New Town, incorporating the straggling settlements outside the city walls into a system of broad streets and marketplaces that must count as the most successful and lasting piece of urban planning in Europe since the efforts of the Romans.

Nationalism and Hussitism

The peace and prosperity enjoyed by Bohemia during Charles' reign were not to last. For two centuries tensions had been building between the country's German and Czech populations. The native nobility, although far from homogenous, resented the political influence wielded by the Germans, and workers were jealous of their economic influence. Popular anger soon found potent expression in a movement for religious reform, one which began a century before the birth of Luther, and was one of the first signs of the conflict that was to tear Europe apart. Charles' policy of inviting scores of religious orders to Prague also aroused hostility as Praguers realized not only that medieval monks and nuns were as prone to screw around as anyone else, but that here they were being subsidized to do it. The Church was brought further into disrepute by one of Charles' personal obsessions, a mania for collecting religious relics. In reaction to a corrupt Church, anticlericals, reformists and chiliastic lunatics of all sorts began to flood into Prague, and the next decades saw the fissures in Western Christianity grow ever wider.

Charles IV's eldest son, Wenceslas IV, took over as emperor and King of Bohemia. He spent most of his reign in an alcoholic stupor, and was soon replaced as emperor by his wily half-brother Sigismund.

In 1402 a young priest, Jan Hus (John Huss), much influenced by the teachings of the Oxfordshire parish priest John Wycliffe, was appointed rector of the Charles University. Although Hus would never have regarded himself as anything but a Catholic, his fiery sermons moved further and further from the party line. His assertion that clerical and even papal decrees had to be tested against Scripture amounted to a direct political attack on the power of the Church. The Hussites preached in the vernacular, and in about 1414 began the practice that was to characterize the movement, allowing the congregation not only the bread but also the wine of the Eucharist, and became known as the Utraquists (from the Latin for 'in both kinds'). Hus was excommunicated in 1411 and was finally burned at the stake on 6 July 1415, to the outrage of his supporters. Wenceslas made clear his sympathies for the nationalists, but he was under constant pressure from his brother to keep the heretics under control. In 1419 things went from bad to worse when councillors at the New Town Hall were defenestrated and killed by a Hussite mob, a novel form of political violence that was to become a regular feature in Bohemia's history. Wenceslas finally succumbed to one of his repeated apoplectic fits.

In 1420, sneaky Sigismund tried to succeed his brother as King of Bohemia. It soon became clear, however, that he intended to restore Church privileges and suppress the Utraquists, and the last straw came in 1420 when Pope Martin V declared a crusade against Bohemia. During the next decade he would announce four more, while the Turks merrily hammered into Christendom. Bohemia found itself at war with most of Europe; even Joan of Arc took an interest in 1429. As early as 1421, a more important division developed among the Utraquists, between moderates who sought a compromise with Rome and a more radical group which was beginning to think in terms of a total break with the Church. The conflict came to a head in 1434 when Pope Eugenius IV granted the right to administer and receive communion in both kinds (an agreement known as the Compacts of Basle). The Táborites rejected the proposals as insufficient, so the moderate aristocrats wiped them out at the Battle of Lipany in 1434.

Sigismund, finally recognized as sovereign of Bohemia, died a few months later. His successor, Albert of Habsburg, followed suit in 1439, remaining alive just long enough to impregnate his wife, who produced Ladislav the Posthumous. He reigned briefly from 1453 to 1457, but the real ruler of Bohemia from 1440 to 1471 was an Utraquist nobleman, George of Poděbrady (Jiří z Poděbrad), who ruled as king from 1458. Although he had high hopes of establishing a native dynasty, he found himself forced to conclude a treaty with the pro-Catholic Vladislav II of Jagellon of Poland, in order to fight off the equally pro-Catholic Matthias Corvinus of Hungary.

Vladislav was elected king in 1471, and it was under his reign that the last flickers of popular Hussitism went out. Anti-Catholic feelings still ran high among the population—a riot against Vladislav's officials in 1483 produced Prague's second defenestration, this time from the Old Town Hall, but the nobility began increasingly to look after their own interests. Taking advantage of the king's long absences (he preferred Buda Castle), nobles introduced serfdom in 1487, and began to brew beer (a long-standing privilege of the towns) on their feudal estates. Many nobles kept to the Utraquist faith, but in their hands it came to signify little more than a tipple at communion. But, even if the first flowering of Czech nationalism was over, Prague and Bohemia had nevertheless established themselves as a centre of anti-Catholicism—and were to pay heavily over the next centuries.

The Habsburgs Arrive

Another would-be dynasty bit the dust when Vladislav's heir drowned; princelings from across Europe headed for Prague to vie for the vacant throne. The fateful choice of the divided electors was Ferdinand I of Habsburg. He seemed tolerant enough for a Catholic and, after years of fratricide, many hoped that a strong monarch might repel the voracious Turks.

In the 1520s, many of Bohemia's Germans fell under the Lutheran spell, while the Bohemian Brethren found affinities with Calvinism. Ferdinand was religious and Catholic, but his opposition to Protestantism was strengthened by more mundane concerns: Catholicism was a usefully universal ideology under which to establish centralized rule; and in Bohemia, Protestantism still had a dangerously nationalistic tinge. In 1547, Ferdinand sweet-talked Prague's Protestants into financing an anti-Turkish army, which then marched westward to attack Protestants in Saxony. Representatives from across the country met in Prague and decided that enough was enough, but Ferdinand's troops massacred the Saxons in weeks, and were back in Prague before the Estates had got their army off the drawing board. The ringleaders were decapitated and Prague's privileges were drastically curtailed. Ferdinand ensured his eldest son, Maximilian, was crowned king while he was still alive and introduced the fiercely proselytizing Jesuit order into Prague in 1556 to counteract the spread of Lutheranism. In 1563, Pope Pius IV launched the militant programme of the Counter-Reformation at the Council of Trent.

Ferdinand died in 1564, to be succeeded as emperor by Maximilian (already King of Bohemia). In return for continued funding for his anti-Turkish forays, Maximilian granted Bohemia's Lutherans the right to organize independently of the old Utraquist church. The concessions enabled him to have his son elected King of Bohemia with little difficulty in 1576 and, when Maximilian died later that year, the same son succeeded him as Emperor Rudolf II.

Rudolfine Prague

The Turks were now within 100 miles of Vienna, the traditional seat of the Habsburgs. The Czech Estates offered to pay off a chunk of the empire's debts, and rebuild the castle, if Rudolf moved to Prague. By 1583, despite lobbying by Viennese nobles, the emperor had decamped to his new capital. Prague became the centre of an empire for the first time in two centuries.

Rudolf was the most singular monarch that Prague had seen since Charles IV. The papacy had high hopes for the young emperor but Rudolf turned out to be a very strange fish indeed, imbued with an almost mystical spirituality that was far from the new orthodoxy the Church was trying to promote. Fanaticism was almost entirely alien to him, but his education left him torn between the ideal of a universal truth and the reality of a Christianity that was being reduced into two armed camps. The sensitive emperor was never able to resolve the dilemma, and teetered between profound pessimism and mild insanity for most of his reign. Legend and history came to remember Rudolfine Prague as a fantastic city of alchemy and astrology, suspended in time, but its surreal atmosphere was very much the product of the moment. The Counter-Reformation was gathering force in neighbouring Austria and Styria; a part-time lunatic and full-time melancholic was on the throne; and mystics and zealots were massing in the city. Prague had become the embodiment of Europe's schizophrenia. It would have taken a genius to steer the empire through its crisis, and Rudolf's temperament was ill-suited to the job. His younger brother Matthias had been intriguing against him since his first major bout of insanity in 1600. By 1606, Matthias had launched an open mutiny, and two years later he forced his brother to hand over all his realms save Bohemia, which was to be Rudolf's posthumous gift.

From Defenestration to Massacre

In 1617, Emperor Matthias proposed his fiercely anti-Protestant cousin Ferdinand as his successor to the crown of Bohemia. The policies of both Matthias and the new monarch turned more militant, and the Bohemians finally took their stand against Catholic rule on 23 May 1618 when they hurled two of Ferdinand's most hated councillors, along with a secretary, through a window. All three survived the 50ft drop: the Catholic Church attributed it to a miracle; others claimed that their fall had been broken by a dungheap. Prague's third defenestration threw Europe into the religious fratricide of the Thirty Years War. Prague's nobles swiftly set about looking for a royal champion to oppose Ferdinand: the only taker was Frederick of the Palatinate, but it's hard to see how the Bohemians could have made a worse choice. The allies he was expected to carry with him flaked away as he spent the winter in Prague, and it soon became apparent that the 'Winter King' had never fought before in his life. The two armies finally met at the White Mountain (*bílá hora*), just outside Prague, on 8 November 1620. The Czech and Hungarian allied armies scattered into headlong and ignominious retreat, a sorry end to two centuries of anti-Catholicism.

The Bohemian Counter-Reformation

The Thirty Years War ravaged Europe until 1648. It had begun as a struggle to assert Habsburg power, but by the 1630s almost the entire Continent was sorting out its political differences by fire and sword. In Prague, Bohemian Protestantism and nationalism were inseparable, and Ferdinand, who had become emperor after Matthias' death, soon hitched the imperial cause firmly to that of the Church. Even before the war's end, he and his monkish allies extinguished the city's ancient powers: Protestantism was made a capital offence, and the independence of the Czech Estates was destroyed. When the dust settled, Bohemia was left with its population reduced by over a third, and the country plunged into a decline that lasted two centuries.

Nothing Happens

Frederick the Great invaded Prague twice in the mid-18th century, but otherwise the city became a backwater where you went when the bright lights of Vienna became too much. The Jesuits led the consolidation of the new faith with a Baroque building programme that transformed the face of the city, but were placed under a worldwide ban by a jealous pope in 1773. In 1781, the despotically enlightened Emperor Joseph II abolished most of the empire's other monasteries and convents. The corollary was the restoration of individual religious freedom for all save the weirdest sects, and Prague's Jewish population was finally allowed out of its ghetto.

The Nationalist Revival

During the early 19th century, Bohemia began to breathe again. Europe's tide of nationalisms swept across the country and, after centuries of German meddling and oppression, Czechs began to hanker for a purely Slavic alternative. The Czech language, which had all but died out, was resuscitated by a handful of writers and researchers—František Palacký and Josef Jungmann being among the most notable. In 1848 the citizens of Prague were up in arms again, this time joined by the rest of the empire in a revolt against Metternich's iron rule from Vienna. The Habsburg empire was slowly dying; composed of a score of different peoples, it was to prove incapable of accommodating the new power of nationalist sentiment. As the empire sickened, the Czech nation quickened.

From Independence to Dependency

As the pattern of European alliances emerged in the years before 1914, many Czechs and Slovaks felt with apprehension that, in any future war, their interests lay firmly in the enemy camp. Lingering pan-Slavism encouraged sympathy even for the corrupt Russia of Nicholas II, while democratic ideals and anti-German sentiment made others look towards France and Britain. When war broke out, two men—Tomáš Garrigue Masaryk and Edvard Beneš—set out on a four-year tour to persuade the world that Czechoslovakia was an idea whose time had come. In 1918, Masaryk signed a deal with Slovak émigrés in Pittsburgh, which was enough to persuade President Woodrow Wilson to give 'Czecho-Slovakia' the green light.

Independence was declared on 28 October 1918 and, within two weeks, Masaryk had been elected president of the new Czechoslovakian Republic. With Beneš, now Foreign Minister, he staked out the borders of the new state. These encompassed the largely German-populated Sudetenland to the west, as well as areas claimed by the Hungarians and the Poles, but at the peace conferences the victors ratified the *fait accompli* with little discussion and no plebiscite.

Although the country's political structures rode the Depression with a stability astonishing in a country so young, the ancient problem of the German minority was soon to explode with unparalleled ferocity. An ongoing separatist movement in the Sudetenland found a champion in Hitler, and Czechoslovakia became the eye of the building European storm. Under the notorious 1938 Munich Agreement, Britain, France and Italy gave Hitler *carte blanche* to seize the Sudetenland. Within six months, the German army had invaded Czechoslovakia as Britain and France remained silent. Only after the invasion of Poland six months later did they declare war on Germany. The war left Prague's buildings almost unscathed. Its population was less fortunate. Tens of thousands of intellectuals, politicians and Romanies were imprisoned or killed. Of the 90,000 Jews who remained in the Protectorate in 1939, only 10,000 survived the war.

When war broke out, Beneš, who had taken over as president in 1935, went to London to establish a government-in-exile. Within the Protectorate itself armed underground movements began to operate, directed largely by the London government. On 5 May 1945, the capital's Resistance groups broadcast a call to arms and thousands rose up against the occupying Nazi forces in the city. The **Prague Uprising** lasted only four days, but street fighting and last-minute executions left up to 5,000 Czechs dead. Plaques and graves throughout the city mark where they fell. On 9 May 1945 the Soviet Red Army entered Prague to a rapturous reception. A provisional national assembly, with Beneš as president, was set up in October, and set about solving Czechoslovakia's German problem once and for all. Mobs lynched collaborators, and the country's three million Sudeten Germans were expelled, resulting in the deaths of thousands.

Communist Consolidation

The Czechoslovakian Communist Party led by Klement Gottwald swept the board in the 1946 elections, with 38 per cent of the votes. Beneš appointed Gottwald prime minister of a coalition government, but Uncle Joe Stalin had no intention of letting his protégé go to bed with a bourgeois. Gottwald's rabble-rousing skills and Beneš' weakness led to the former's assumption of the presidency in February 1948. Within a month the popular foreign minister, Jan Masaryk—son of Tomáš—who was less accommodating to the Communists, had died in a mysterious fall from his office window late one night. A fourth defenestration began 40 years of Communist rule, and the Party was pleased to report 89 per cent support in new elections in May. Within a year the Terror had begun.

From Socialism with a Human Face to Normalization

During the mid-1960s, reformers at the lower levels of the Party began to work on revitalizing its links with the rest of society. In January 1968, Alexander Dubček was elected to the post of First Secretary. Dubček was no closet liberal: his politics were formed in the crucible of the 1930s Soviet Union but, in the heady days of 1968, he finally began to listen, and learn. During the so-called Prague Spring, he proposed ever-more radical reform of the country's political and economic institutions, partly out of his changing convictions but largely at the urging of more committed forces and individuals both within and outside the Party.

The Soviet Union, which had actually backed pliant Dubček for the leadership the year before, began to stir. General Secretary Brezhnev was soon considering how to help the Czechoslovak proletariat stave off 'a return to the bourgeois-capitalist system'. He took soundings of all the other leaders of the Warsaw Pact and, on 21 August, Czechoslovakia was invaded by five armies: the Prague Spring suddenly turned very cold. The cultural and political renaissance of the mid-1960s had been strangled in its cradle. The times were desperate. Fourteen philosophy students at the Charles University drew lots, and agreed to burn themselves alive one by one until press freedom was restored. 'Torch No.1' was Jan Palach. On 16 January 1969, the 20-year-old emptied a can of petrol over himself in Wenceslas Square, and flicked a lighter. Over the next month, so too did many others. In April 1969, Dubček was replaced by Gustáv Husák—Resistance hero, victim of the Terror and supporter of the Prague Spring. Brezhnev is said to have murmured, 'If we can't use the puppets, we'll tie the strings to the leaders'; and within a year, Husák began to dance. Some 500,000 people were deprived of their Communist Party membership, in a process that was called 'normalization' (*normalisace*). When it was finished, the government declared that Czechoslovakia had achieved a state of *reálný socialismus*, an eerie phrase that's usually translated as 'real existing socialism', and a new generation grew up without even the memory of hope.

The Velvet Revolution

Even as late as mid-1989, with Hungary and Poland well on the path to reform, few observers saw Czechoslovakia as likely to follow in the near future. But as the East German regime tottered, refugees from the country began to flood into the West German embassy in Prague. The revolutions of 1989 had begun. On 10 November the West woke to the news that bulldozers were demolishing the Berlin Wall, and on 17 November Prague's students confronted a baton-wielding police force. The filmed scenes of police brutality against students armed with candles and flowers aroused the population from two decades of torpor. For the next six weeks, Prague was enfolded by a 'Velvet Revolution', an anarchic hubbub of strikes, pickets and celebrations which culminated in the election of playwright and recently released political prisoner Václav Havel to the presidency on 29 December 1989.

Truth Will Out

The most dramatic of the messy truths to emerge since 1989 was the realization that Czechoslovakia itself was based on a fiction. The rhetoric of internationalism spouted by Communist leaders had both fuelled and concealed domestic rivalries and, within three years of the Velvet Revolution, Slovakian nationalism grew into a fully blown independence movement. On New Year's Eve in 1992, each more or less amicably waved goodbye to the other, and the Czech and Slovak Republics were born.

The new nation's social conflicts don't have a solution as simple as the 'Velvet Divorce'. The country's Romanies have suffered from official neglect and public ignorance for decades, and the replacement of totalitarianism by majority rule has in many cases done nothing but add a veneer of legitimacy to their stigmatisation. The psychological legacy of Communism also fractures the country. As late as May 1988, the Party had over 1.7 million members—that is, over one in 10 of Czechoslovakia's total population—and humdrum compromises with the regime were struck by millions more. As a result, measures taken since 1989 to break the institutionalized power of the Party have often had an irrational quality, scapegoating individuals for a system in which almost every adult was implicated to some extent. So far the Czech Republic has steered a precarious course between the demands for revenge and the temptation of forgetfulness, but it is only when today's twenty-somethings reach middle age that it will finally be possible to say whether normality has replaced the 'normalization' which plagued Czechoslovakia for 30 years.

But whatever else may happen, it is unlikely that the country will stumble back into Communist dictatorship. Under the leadership of its first prime minister, Václav Klaus, it steadily anchored itself into the mainstream of Europe, joining NATO and placing itself on the fast track to membership of the European Union (currently scheduled for 2003). After elections in 1998, with his government tainted by a series of kickback scandals and a worsening economy, he handed over power to social democrat Miloš Zeman. For all their ostensible political differences, there has been a fair degree of continuity between the policies of both men; but although that consensus might bode well for the stability of the country's political institutions, it has also meant that some of the hard questions for the future remain unanswered. Hidden subsidies and sclerotic industries continue to skew the Czech economy and, as the country gears up for full-scale integration into the European economy, radical reforms will become inevitable. How much that will hurt is rather harder to predict but, unless the burden is evenly spread, the Czech egalitarian tradition—which dates back to Hussitism, and was a cause rather than an effect of the Communist rise to power—might yet again prove that history did not end in 1989.

But no matter how much remains to be transformed in the Czech Republic, Prague itself has not looked back since the mid-1990s, when it suddenly became the bolthole of choice for thwarted writers, desperados and hedonists from across the English-speaking world. That party has since moved on, but the capital has matured into one of the most cosmopolitan and sophisticated cities of the former Communist bloc. Few who can remember Prague in the early 1980s would take seriously the suggestion that capitalism had robbed the city of something worth keeping—and it would need chutzpah indeed to compare the existential dilemmas of globalization with the despair of those years.

There is still no better way to end a history of Prague than with the dour words of the country's first president, Václav Havel, pronounced while the rest of the city was going wild during the euphoric New Year of 1990: 'The happiness is gone. The second act is called crisis. The crisis will be chronic and then the catastrophe will happen. Finally the catharsis will come, and after that everything will start to go well.' By the beginning of the 21st century, the chronology was questionable and the outlook didn't seem quite as cataclysmic. And even if it is, Prague has been through it all before.

The golden ages of Prague have been short and few, and yet the city has one of the richest architectural legacies in Europe. Purists may object that it's a visual cacophony, but anyone with an ounce of romance will be dumbstruck by Prague's Gothic art, the riot of modernism and the unforgettable Baroque skyline. The city now offers one of Europe's most complete if haphazard selections of a millennium of cultural endeavour.

Prague: Art and Architecture

Romanesque

In 965, when most urban centres northern Europe comprised a few wooden hovels, Prague was a thriving town of stone and mortar. The earliest architecture was Romanesque, and the first churches follow a standard basilican ground plan. No one yet understood how the Romans had supported the weight of their roofs, so buildings were either covered with wood or supported with pillars; naves had simple tunnel vaults; tiny rotundas, their tops supported by a circular wall, were built. Prague's best surviving Romanesque church is St George's Basilica; three of the mushroom-like rotundas survive, one on Konviktská street.

Gothic

The architecture that spread from French cathedral design of the later 12th century was named 'Gothic' by Renaissance Italians who felt that it could only have been produced by vandals. The first glimmers arrived in the mid-13th century with St Agnes's Convent, and Gothic features also crept into the Old-New Synagogue: pointed arches and steeples drove heavenwards; walls became a field for rich sculptural decoration; and sheets of glass, framed by decorative tracery, flooded the interiors with light. In the late 1200s, the Vltava submerged the town once too often; the burghers retaliated by burying their town under several metres of earth, and a new one was built in Gothic style, using decoration and glass to a greater extent than ever before.

Under Emperor Charles IV (1346–78) Prague entered the European stage. He imported **Matthew of Arras** from France to begin his new cathedral; but by the mid-14th century, Germany led the field in church design, and in 1353 Matthew's timely death brought 23-year-old **Peter Parléř** to Prague, where he was responsible for St Vitus's Cathedral, one of the grandest late Gothic churches of Continental Europe. It would take five centuries to finish; but Parléř, an accomplished sculptor, and his team left an indelible imprint on the capital.

Bohemian artists also began to produce the first work unique to the country. The oldest surviving paintings date from the early 13th century, and show how artists were breaking free of Byzantium's rigid rules. The individualist trend in Bohemia manifested itself in ever-heavier modelling, which reached a peak in the work of **Master Theodoric,** whose outstanding portraits of saints rank as some of the most distinctive work in 14th-century Europe. Painting and sculpture moved towards a sophisticated and idealized style at the court of Wenceslas IV. In 1420, the outbreak of the Hussite Wars called an abrupt halt to cultural development. When the dust settled, Prague's Gothic architecture enjoyed a series of splendid explosions, epitomized by the magnificent Vladislav Hall.

The Renaissance

Bohemia's first Habsburg monarch, Ferdinand I, crowned in 1526, encouraged the flow of Italian ideas to Prague. He built his sublime Royal Summer Palace (1538–63) and, after a huge fire on the left bank in 1541, a series of imposing Renaissance palaces were built by nobles.

Mannerism

Under Emperor Rudolf II (1576–1611), Prague became one of the leading centres of Mannerist culture in Europe. Mannerism, originally a term of abuse, was a retreat from the notion that art could capture the essence of the world by trying to reproduce it in its most noble form. In a troubled century of religious uncertainty, the attempt to penetrate beyond the appearance of things was part of a widespread search to find a more solid basis for a universal truth. Rudolf II summoned artists to Prague from across Europe, most notably the Milanese painter **Giuseppe Arcimboldo** (1527–93), best known for his allegorical portraits and surreal compositions. Many of the emperor's other favoured painters came from the Low Countries. Among them was **Bartholomeus Spranger** (1546–1611); his style, shimmering with colour and movement, and sophisticated in form and composition, used classical and religious themes and also motifs from alchemy and astrology to glorify the imperial mission. The apotheosis of Rudolf—Christian hero and patron of the arts against dark ignorance—was a theme to which most of his artists turned at some point. **Hans von Aachen** (1552–1615), from Köln, created elegant portraits and religious scenes; but, like Spranger, he also painted nudes, tinged with an unusual eroticism. Rudolf II's curiosity stretched to the natural world, and among his still-life artists was the Flemish **Roelandt Savery**, who arrived in 1604 and produced Europe's first paintings of exotic animals. The emperor's successor, Matthias, spirited parts of Rudolf II's collection over to Vienna a year later; and almost all the rest was stolen in 1648 by Swedish troops. Prague's visual arts were going through another crisis in an atmosphere of quasi-Calvinism, and the Estates sold off an unknown amount of Rudolf II's collection in 1619.

The Baroque

The Baroque style arrived in Prague from Rome in the late 16th century, as the Council of Trent laid down its demand that art was to glorify the Church, and within a century it had utterly transformed the face of the city. The mysterious abstraction of Gothic vaults was replaced by illusionistic paintings and frescoes and the Marian cult and miracle-working icons found their way into almost all the churches. The trick worked; Praguers headed like moths towards the Catholic flames and, by the 18th century, the majority of the city had reverted.

The Baroque used movement, disproportion and unnatural light with a consistency that overwhelmed rather than intrigued. The new architecture elbowed its way into the vast **Waldstein Palace,** which represents a transitional period. When the Thirty Years War ended in 1648, building began in earnest. The majority of Baroque architects in Prague came through Vienna; the most prolific were **Francesco Caratti** (?–1677/9) and **Giovanni Alliprandi**

(1665–1720). Ovoid halls and domes replaced the serene circles of yesteryear; and the palatial façades loudly announced that Prague had lost the war, and the victors had come to stay.

By the beginning of the 18th century, northern Europe had snatched the baton of Baroque, and Prague and Vienna were setting a scorching pace. Two of the city's greatest architects were the Bavarian **Kristof Dienzenhofer** (1655–1722), and his son **Kilian Ignaz Dienzenhofer** (1689–1751); their joint masterpiece, the Jesuit Church of St Nicholas in Malá Strana, is one of 18th-century Europe's finest. The new architecture wasn't entirely alien to the city's traditions. Even in St Nicholas's, the flowing vault harks back to the Gothic style; and the work of Prague-born **Giovanni Santini** (1667–1723), is even more explicitly Gothicizing.

The Baroque reintegrated architecture and sculpture, after the Renaissance insistence that they were independent elements. A tradition was thus established that influenced design into the 20th century. Baroque sculpture began with the relative restraint of **Jan Bendl** (1620–80) and **Matthias Jäckel** (1655–1738) but culminated in the epic works of **Matthias Braun** (1684–1738) and **Ferdinand Maximilian Brokof** (1688–1731).

Baroque painting in Bohemia isn't up to the sculpture. **Karel Škréta** (1610–74) followed Italian art of the previous century, and **Michael Willmann** (1630–1706), painted religious anguish and passion; but the most accomplished works of Prague Baroque were the experiments with light and colour of **Petr Brandl** (1668–1735), and, later, the glorious frescoes of **Franz Anton Maulpertsch** at the Strahov Monastery.

From Neoclassicism to Neo-Gothic

Under the reign of Emperor Joseph II, the city's culture suffered a series of rapid blows. Fripperies had no place in the monarch's coolly rational world. What remained of Rudolf II's collection was auctioned off, and most men of the cloth were turfed out of their monasteries, which were then turned into barracks. The disappearance of religious orders and their huge contribution had serious consequences. There was little originality in the few buildings that appeared in Prague in the years between 1780 and 1850. Architecture was typified by a dry classicism inspired by France; the change was particularly noticeable in heavily Baroque Prague, but neither classicism nor the Empire style which followed had much impact.

Nation-building and Opening the Doors to Europe

In the middle of the 19th century, Prague's architecture was engulfed in the national revival movement (*see* pp.27), and a vogue for rehashing older architectural styles. The favoured choice was the Renaissance. Huge pediments were triumphant, and stacks of disordered columns were considered noble. The result appears most clearly in the National Museum. The later 19th century also saw a wave of restoration of Bohemia's Gothic architecture. However, the zealous bunch concerned, led by **Josef Mocker**, often destroyed more than they created. One exception was St Vitus's Cathedral, to which they began to add a western half some 550 years after construction had commenced. Artists also played a heroic role in the national revival, adorning the new buildings with mythological and allegorical works to express the aspirations of the patriotic movement. By the turn of the century, Habsburg rule had begun to crumble, and political concerns gave way to introspection over what the future held in store.

Art Nouveau and Symbolism

Prague's architecture at the turn of the century was dominated by Art Nouveau and the Europe-wide attempt to escape the tyranny of historicism. This book uses the term 'Art Nouveau', but the Bohemian *secese* was actually a confluence of two currents. The first came from France, and aimed to create a unified new style from natural forms, using extensive sculptural decoration in building, as with the Hotel Evropa and Municipal House. The second form of Art Nouveau originated in Glasgow and used rectilinear structures, abstract, self-contained and stripped of ornamentation. Its leading light was **Jan Kotěra** (1871–1923).

Art Nouveau found decorative expression in the work of sculptors such as **Ladislav Šaloun** (1870–1946) and **Stanislav Sucharda** (1866–1916), and most notably, **Alfons Mucha** (1860–1939) (*see* p.132). Two of the most original artists to emerge during the 1890s were mystical types less concerned with the new forms. The first was the sculptor **František Bílek** (1872–1941), who linked ideas spanning music, literature and religion to produce a fascinating body of work (*see* p.133). **František Kupka** (1871–1957) settled in Paris after 1896; his earliest paintings concentrated on ideas of rebirth and renewal, but, after several years as a medium, he moved on to produce some of Europe's first intentional abstract art.

Cubism

In 1902, a belated exhibition of the French Impressionists and a Rodin retrospective caused a storm among the city's artistic community. Three years later, however, all eyes were on the anguished work of the Norwegian Edvard Munch. It was a crash course in the clash of philosophies that had been building in Europe over the previous decade; whether art should show what the world *looked* like, or express the emotions of the artist and the subject.

Prague's first modernist painting came out of *Osma* (The Eight), a group of artists founded in 1907. Its initial inspiration was the raw force of Munch but, as early as 1910, Czech artists such as **Emil Filla** (1882–1953), **Bohumil Kubišta** (1884–1918) and **Antonín Procházka** (1882–1945) had picked up on Parisian Cubism. For the next decade, Prague was perhaps the most important centre of the new art outside its birthplace. **Josef Čapek** (1897–1945) and **Jan Zrzavý** (1890–1977) also dabbled with Cubism, but were more concerned with the primitivism that had inspired it. Each produced a set of simple and beautiful paintings.

Prague's painters largely followed the lead set by Picasso and Braque, but the sculptors and architects in the Cubist *Skupina* group produced maverick works that are unparalleled. The leading sculptor was **Otto Gutfreund** (1889–1927), whose early work reflects the ideas of Cubo-Expressionism. The most extraordinary experiments of Czech Cubism were made in architecture. Three members of the Skupina, **Pavel Janák** (1882–1956), **Joseph Gočár** (1880–1945) and **Josef Chochol** (1880–1956) tried to restore depth and flexibility to their buildings by using three-dimensional geometrical forms on the façades. The idea was to translate one of Prague's oldest architectural traditions into the idiom of Cubism; you can see examples, at Celetná 34 and Neklanova 2 and 34, of the only systematically theorized and practised Cubist architecture in the world.

Devětsil and Surrealism

The interwar years were among the most exciting in the history of Prague's cultural life. The old world didn't look good after the carnage of war; Czechoslovakian independence had been won; and in the east, a rosy Bolshevik dawn was rising. In 1920, a group of young artists led by **Karel Teige** (1900–51) founded *Devětsil* ('Nine Forces'). The political philosophy of the group was Soviet-style Marxism but, after a brief tinker with 'proletarian art', Devětsil spent the 1920s weaving through a maze of artistic experimentation. In 1924 Teige hurled the group into the mêlée of the European Avant Garde with the *First Manifesto of Poetism*. Like the Soviet Constructivists, he embraced the abstract beauty of the machine age, but he also laid down his theory of 'Poetism', 'the art of pleasure', which was to condition the art produced. The balancing act was precarious—technology had just slaughtered millions—and Devětsil never really united the two elements. The general feeling was that art should be accessible to everyone, not just an élite, yet Devětsil came up with work incomprehensible to anyone who hadn't read every manifesto published.

Though Teige spent most of the early 1920s calling for 'the liquidation of art' (and the Artist), early Poetism joyfully celebrated the imagination. The lyrical poets **Jaroslav Seifert** (1901–86) and **Vítězslav Nezval** (1900–58) worked on 'film poems'; the sculptor **Zdeněk Pešánek** (1896–1965) created visual pianos and perhaps the world's first neon fountain; one of the group's most common forms of art was the collage, or 'pictorial poem'. The group took the view that photography would replace the bourgeois art of painting, though its only full-time photographer was **Jaroslav Rössler** (b. 1902). Two other photographers emerged during the 1920s, **Jaromír Funke** (1896–1945) and **Josef Sudek** (1896–1976); although they were never confined by ideological posturings their prewar interests included beautiful machines and suggestive patterns of objects. The group approved of cinema's popular appeal and its non-élitism; ideas and images could be linked on film in Poetist fashion; and the big screen was an ideal moving blackboard with which to instruct the masses. Devětsil also set up the Liberated Theatre in 1926; it was taken over three years later by the comedy and cabaret duo of Jiří Voskovec (1905–81) and Jan Werich (1905–80) (**V & W**), whose work remains popular.

Devětsil had many interests in common with French Surrealism, and the darker questions raised by Surrealism began to make inroads into the happy-go-lucky early Poetism of painters like **Toyen** (Marie Čermínová) (1902–80) and **Jindřich Štyrský** (1899–1942). Another Devětsil member, **Josef Šíma** (1891–1971), settled in Paris in 1921, and became an important contact between the two movements. In 1932, one of the first international exhibitions of Surrealist art was held in Prague, and in 1934 the Prague Surrealist Group was established.

There was no Surrealist architecture but Prague saw huge activity in the field of design. In the immediate post-war years, Cubist architects developed a short-lived 'Rondocubism' which it was hoped could become a distinctively national style. The theory was impressively realized in the bizarre Banka legií on Na poříčí, designed by Josef Gočár. The façade was emphasized but, in a manner harking back to the Baroque, its elements were amassed and pushed outwards in repetitive curves. The friezes on the Banka legií, by **Jan Štursa** (1880–1925) and Otto Gutfreund, are far removed in their simplicity from Gutfreund's earlier Cubist-inspired work.

Between the wars, internationalism and ideology led most of Prague's architects towards Constructivism and Functionalism. Their basic difference was that the first claimed that mass production and modern materials were beautiful; the second theoretically didn't care, so long as a building served its purpose. By the 1930s the aesthetic differences, although still loudly argued over, were little more than nuances. Already primed by the Art Nouveau of Jan Kotěra, Prague hurled itself into the brave new world of glass and concrete. In 1924, Teige organized Czech participation in the first international Bauhaus exhibition and Adolf Loos built his Müller Villa on the outskirts of the capital, on Nad hradním vodojemem in Střešovice. The most significant modernist construction in Prague was the Baba Housing Estate around Na Babě in Prague 6. Standing outside any movement was radical Slovenian architect, **Jože Plečnik** (1872–1957), who modernized the Castle and designed the Church of the Sacred Heart, one of the most extraordinary religious buildings of the 20th century.

From Nazism to Normalization

The Nazis rolled into town in March 1939 and Prague's cultural life was crushed. Functionalist architecture wasn't glorious; most contemporary art was degenerate. Exile and extermination decimated the intelligentsia. Then, three years after liberation, another tyranny moved in.

With the accession of the Communists in 1948, creativity was sacrificed on the altar of Socialist Realism. A monolithic, officially controlled programme extolling the class struggle and the march to socialism, it produced monumental buildings and Stakhanovite murals and sculptures: the best architectural example is the Hotel International, Prague's homage to the University of Moscow. The pre-war avant-garde was an abomination; Karel Teige lived to see his dreams turn to dust. He's said to have committed suicide in 1951, with a warrant out for his arrest.

After the death of Stalin, the cultural constraints were slowly eased. The Surrealist movement whooped into life again in the late 1950s. Important artists of the period were **Mikuláš Medek** (1926–74) and **Václav Tikal**, and, perhaps most impressive of all, **Jiří Kolář**, who experimented with collage assemblages of image and word. In 1965, Prague's students elected Beat poet Allen Ginsberg as their king and carried him shoulder-high up Wenceslas Square; and by 1968, the mildly insane **Milan Knížák** was slaughtering chickens to loud rock music.

The party ended on the night of 21 August 1968 as 200,000 Warsaw Pact troops turned the Prague Spring into winter. The government launched a programme of 'normalization'. Potential centres of ideological resistance such as theatre companies and the Writers' Union were dissolved and artists who had supported the Prague Spring were anathematized. Intellectuals and artists found work as stokers and taxi-drivers. Scores found fame abroad. The most courageous signed the **Charter 77** manifesto.

Resurrection

Since 1989, some of the artists who left after 1968 have returned. The cultural return is helping to bring new (and old) ideas to the capital for the first time, and the bridge between west and east is helping to untie the ideological knots that could stymie Czech culture. Few Praguers can stomach it when westerners compare capitalist alienation to Communist despair, but the exiles can at least warn that materialism exacts a price. Artists based overseas have held up a mirror to their former compatriots, typified by the stark photographic record that **Josef Koudelka** has made of the neglect and poverty of the country's gipsies.

The attempt to piece together the nation's shattered cultural life draws inspiration from many sources. Young artists have rediscovered the interwar avant-garde, and Surrealism has returned once more. Foreign influences are pouring in, and the city is engulfed by aesthetic debates that began in the west years ago, such as the difference between erotica and pornography. Czech art often has an unselfconscious lasciviousness that can be unpleasant to western eyes. The work of photographer **Jan Saudek**, known in the west for his portraiture, ranges from tender kissing scenes to spanking scenarios with uniformed girls. Note also **David Černý**, whose art has included painting a tank pink, spraying a Trabant gold, and putting up anonymous posters in London to advertise a day of random killing (a joke).

As for the architecture of Prague, it endures. The redevelopers are moving in and the city of *Amadeus* has begun to echo to a faster beat, but the ancient stone jigsaw of the centre will survive. Even the Communists didn't dare tamper with that.

Prague: Seers and Stargazers

Seers and Stargazers

The ear of Rudolfine Prague was attuned to speculations on all the highest planes, and sooth-sayers, croakers, necromancers and prophets of every description found the emperor's court a congenial staging-post. In Rome, the shadow of the stake was a powerful disincentive to weirdness; in Prague, the character of an emperor whose horoscope had been cast by Nostradamus demanded it. His vast curiosity cabinet included mandrake root fetishes (thought to scream when pricked); he apparently carried moss from the bones of a hanged man in his back pocket; and his courtiers were at the sharp end of contemporary scientific thought. Wherever there was a mystery to be pondered, Prague thinkers could be guaranteed to deepen it. The emperor's private secretary published an acclaimed thesis on squaring the circle; others wrote influential works on a Silesian boy reported to have been born with a gold tooth in 1593; and when a bone was unearthed in the capital, the city was consumed by a debate on whether it was an elephant's tusk or the shin of an antediluvian giant.

Two of the earliest visitors to the capital were the extraordinary Jekyll and Hyde duo of John Dee (1527–1608) and Edward Kelley (1555–95?), who pulled into the capital on a coach from Kraków in 1584. Dee, a Fellow of Trinity College, Cambridge, and astrologer to Queen Elizabeth I, was a scholar in search of a question; but quite what drove Kelley, whose experiments in England had included the disinterment and quizzing of a corpse, has never been satisfactorily established. It does a disservice to his warped genius to call him a mere fraud, but Rudolf would still have done well to ask him why he had no ears (they had been shorn for counterfeiting). Instead, the emperor put both men on the imperial payroll. The partnership revolved around crystal balls. With Kelley gazing, and the doctor asking the questions, they had already clocked up hundreds of hours of crystalline conversations with maverick quasi-Christian angels, all conducted and recorded in Enochian, an entirely new 117,649-character language. Rudolf seems, remarkably enough, to have been uninterested in Dee's outline of the hallucinations, and soon dispensed with their services. However, there were plenty of other takers, and the duo were to spend five eventful years in and around Prague.

Rudolf II's court was the Los Alamos of the alchemical age. Europe's wild golden-goose chase peaked in the late 1500s, and to questing types everywhere the emperor was the latest incarnation of Hermes Trismegistus, the mysterious quasi-divinity who had been the first to crack the transmutation secret. Unfortunately, Hermes' gnomic utterances—notably, 'that which is above is like to that which is below; but that which is below is like to that which is above'—kept a tight lid on the Hermetic wisdom. The concept of the philosopher's stone ('the stone which is not a stone, a precious thing which has no value, a thing of many shapes, this unknown which is most known of all') did little to advance matters, but its discovery was one of Rudolf II's obsessions. Anyone who could show proven alchemical ability was given board and lodging, and all the technology that money could buy. As they slaved over their stills, alembics, crucibles and hot-ash baths, Rudolf II's alchemists produced interesting results—hair-restoring potions, hair-removing potions, laxatives, philtres and new recipes for mulling wine—but the nature of the experiments (among other factors) ensured that the stone remained elusive. Congelation, calcination, cibation and mortification were among the standard processes; when those failed, they could be combined with ceration, the addition of wax, or inhumation, which generally involved burying the substance concerned in dung.

The stakes were high in the alchemical quest: possibly eternal life, certainly ultimate wisdom and, depending on the Hermetic tract that you read, anything from a million-fold increase in gold to a thousand billion. The scope for quackery was immense. On one celebrated occasion, a mysterious Arab drew into the capital and invited hundreds to a banquet at which he swore to multiply contributions by a thousand; to general consternation, he and the money exploded into a puff of smoke instead. The dangers were no less dramatic. Dungeons and mercury inhalation were occupational hazards, and in Prague unmasked charlatans faced the added possibility of being paraded in tinsel and hanged from a yellow rope on a gilded scaffold. Alchemical theory had accommodated the risks, by suggesting that the philosopher's stone could take up to 12 years to ripen. By that time a nimble failure could be long gone, leaving behind only a steaming heap of wax and dung; but for those who talked big and failed to deliver, time could run out far sooner.

Kelley was one of those who learnt the hard way. The Englishman had stumbled upon the stone while pottering around the ley lines of Glastonbury during happier times with John Dee. Although his claims were relatively modest (an increase in gold by a factor of 72,330), he was taken on by Rudolf in 1589. He began impressively, transmuting a pound of lead into gold with a drop of blood-red oil (leaving a ruby at the bottom of the pot), and he was promptly knighted by the emperor. By 1591, however, he was under pressure. England's Lord Treasurer had written to ask for 'a token, say enough to defray the expenses of the Navy for the summer', and Rudolf was finding that the gold he was receiving was significantly less than the amount he was paying his knight. Kelley was incarcerated on suspicion of heresy and sorcery. He enjoyed an Indian summer in 1593, when he was reported to be at liberty and making gold 'as fast as a hen will cracke nuttes', but his incredible career was drawing to a close. Suitably enough, no one knows where or when (or, say some, if) he died. Legend claims that he lost a leg or two jumping from a tower and then poisoned himself; a neat variation on the tale is that the fatal draught was an elixir of life that he had prepared for the emperor.

Kelley notwithstanding, alchemists would soon become chemists, and the stargazers of Rudolfine Prague also stood at a turning-point in the history of science. In the space of a few decades, the universe had been shaken to its core. For some 1,500 years, the moon, planets, sun and stars had orbited the Earth attached to Ptolemy's harmonious crystal spheres, but in 1543 the Pole Nicolaus Copernicus had revived the ancient heresy of heliocentricity. No one knew how to look at the universe any more. When a Paduan arrived with a set of concave mirrors, they were snapped up by the thinkers of the court; Giordano Bruno stopped by in 1588 with his theories of infinite worlds; and as comets, a supernova and fateful conjunctions hurtled through the firmament during the last decades of the century, the capital battened down the hatches and prepared for darkness at noon and the end of empires.

Successive imperial mathematicians at Rudolf II's court personified the critical juncture to which the heavens had come. The work of the first, the little-remembered Nicholas Ursus, was inextricably linked to that of the second, the Danish Tycho Brahe, who served between 1599 and 1601. While still in Denmark, Brahe accused Ursus of plagiarism, setting off an arcane intra-Continental row that became vitriolic even for an age when scientists didn't mince their words. Ursus published a defence from Prague in 1597. It interspersed an erudite survey of astronomy's history with constant references to one of Brahe's supporters as 'Snotface', taunts about Brahe's own disfigured nose, and the observation that the Dane's daughter was 'not yet nubile and so not of much use to me for the usual purpose'. Brahe never quite matched his opponent's invective, but he was no more stable, and subjected poor Rudolf to endless astrological prophecies of doom. The emperor was told variously that he would die before 50, that he would be killed by a monk, and that he would follow his pet raven to Hell.

Brahe's successor as imperial mathematician (1601–12), Johannes Kepler, went further than any of his contemporaries in developing a rational philosophy of science, but the wisdom of the ancients continued to permeate his work. His laid down the laws of planetary motion, but linked them to the idea that each of the five planets corresponded to one of the musical ranges from bass to treble. His suspicion of superstition (reinforced when his mother was tried for witchcraft) meant that, when it came to astrology, he was cautious. He suggested that the aspects affected the world only in the limited sense that a peasant could affect the shape of a pumpkin, and he sensibly warned that 'one must keep astrology entirely from the emperor's mind' (although he actually cast several horoscopes for Rudolf). His contributions to scientific debate were incomparably more elegant than those of his predecessors, often written in Latin verse or Ciceronian orations. However, neither the mode of expression nor the caution demanded by the dangerous times fully account for their elliptical sound to the modern ear. His comments on those who now questioned Copernicus' views are a suitably oblique memorial to an absurd Prague that has never quite disappeared.

> *They castrated the poet*
> *Lest he copulate;*
> *He lived without testicles.*

Rabbi Loew

Every community mythologizes its history but, with the legendary Rabbi Loew, Prague's Jews personified it. Loew (as in 'I just *lurve* sushi') was a celebrated scholar in the relatively tolerant Prague of the late 1500s, but the stories that came to envelop his life encapsulated the centuries-old experience of the ghetto—where pogroms and the evil eye were omnipresent dangers, and only the rabbi could really explain why life was so abysmal.

The legends begin on a touching note. When young Loew arrived in the capital, he was smitten by Pearl, daughter of one Reb Schmelke. Schmelke then went bankrupt, but Loew was so in love that he agreed to wait until the dowry could be raised. Impetuous it may have been, but it was only 10 years before Reb Schmelke was back on his feet, thanks to a bag of gold that a contemptuous cavalier tossed at Pearl as he stole a loaf of bread. Loew, by now steeped in the Talmud, declared that that had been no ordinary horseman, but Elijah. The stage was set for an exceptional life.

Certain themes run through all the tales. The ghetto is under constant threat from Christians, the wickedest of whom is Brother Thaddeus, whose very mention brings a hiss to the throat. There is also the occasional good *goy*, most notably the weak but fundamentally sympathetic Emperor Rudolf. Pulling the strings together is mild-mannered Rabbi Loew, who checks Brother Thaddeus at every turn, dares to reveal to the emperor that his real mother was Jewish, and exchanges tips with other super-rabbis across Europe in his dreams. When 300 clerics ask Loew to answer questions such as 'Are the Jews guilty of killing Christ?', his eloquence wins them over to a man. On the innumerable occasions that Rudolf begs him for help, the rabbi rescues him from jail, dethrones an impostor and overturns expulsion edicts. When a jealous flunky persuades the vacillating emperor to order Loew to hold a banquet, the scholar transports a shimmering palace from a distant land into his humble ghetto abode; and to the now jovial Rudolf II's uproarious laughter, the luckless lackey pockets a goblet and is rooted to his seat. The picture of Rudolf that emerges is about as far from reality as it's possible to get. The emperor summoned the rabbi to his castle once, to discuss a matter that was never revealed, which was clearly more than enough material for generations of Jewish myth-makers.

The legend now inextricably linked to Loew is that of the *golem*, or artificial man. The word, meaning 'unformed substance' (or 'unmarried woman') in Hebrew, is first found in Psalms 139:16; and the idea that humanity could create life comes from the mystical cabalistic tradition that each mortal contains a spark of the divine. Jewish history is littered with pre-Loewian *golems*, and they have stalked Europe's ghettos for centuries. Jakob Grimm found one in Poland in 1808, but Rabbi Loew's has become the most famous, turned into a German silent film (1920), a French talkie (1937) and a tale to alarm good Jewish boys and girls everywhere. It all began while Loew was communing with the cosmos one night. He was warned that a great danger loomed, and told to make a *golem*, pronto. With his two youthful rabbi sidekicks, he hurried to the banks of the Vltava. Working by torchlight, the trio built a man out of mud, walked round it several times, and Loew then placed the unknown name of God (the *shem*) in its mouth. 'Joseph Golem' was born. His adventures are laced with slapstick ghetto humour— such as the moment when he follows orders too literally and floods long-suffering Pearl's kitchen—but most are of a grimly heroic nature. Joseph once rescues a girl from being forcibly baptized; and when the community is on trial for ritual murder, he arrives with the exonerating evidence as the verdict is to be announced. The allegation that Jews kneaded Christian blood into their Passover *matzoth* (unleavened bread) echoes throughout and, as well as thwarting the remorseless Brother Thaddeus, Joseph constantly intercepts shadowy Christians wheeling dead babies into the ghetto in order to lay the ground for a pogrom.

Joseph was eventually laid to rest in the roof of Prague's Old-New Synagogue. The annihilation of the capital's Jews gave rise to the last *golem* legend. It had been said that he would return if needed but, as the Nazi cattle trains filled and emptied, those Jews who remained declared that he had died for ever. It sounds likely, but Praguers still claim that, on stormy nights, Joseph's footsteps can be heard on those streets of the ancient ghetto that survive.

Communist Kitsch

When the Czechoslovak Communist Party moved into the driving seat in 1948, official culture embarked on a headlong descent that was to last four decades. The fetish of the Five Year Plan, gigantomania, and the celebration of vulcanization processes were to leave no one entirely untouched.

The Party's first plunge into truly execrable taste was the transformation of President Klement Gottwald into a mummified icon after his death in 1953. The procedure was in its infancy in the Communist world, and Gottwald proved too rotten for formaldehyde—in part because alcoholism had already pickled him. An alarmed government turned to the prop and make-up wizards of the Barrandov film studios, who effectively rebuilt Gottwald in plastic, limb by putrefying limb. Only in 1962, by which time the original president had been reduced to a head, did the Central Committee call it a day. The lecherous drunkard then became 'Czechoslovakia's First Working-Class President', immortalized until 1989 in a metro station, a town, countless roads, museums, a bridge and a banknote.

Stalin himself was the subject of Prague's most mind-boggling piece of cultural junk, when in 1953 the government constructed a 30m-high statue in his honour, glowering from a hillside over Prague's Old Town. Six hundred workers spent 500 days building the colossus, which showed Stalin leading a Soviet worker, heroine, soldier and botanist into the future. The designer, Otakar Švec, did the decent thing and shot himself before its completion, but the Czechoslovak Communist Party apparently had every reason to be satisfied with its magnificent display of unctuousness. But within a year, things had gone badly wrong. Stalin's successor, Nikita Krushchev, let slip that Uncle Joe had, objectively speaking, deformed socialism—and what's more, that a personality cult had grown up around him. The Party took a quick look at its 14,000-ton masterpiece, and shrouded it in scaffolding. In January 1962, a commission was set up. A panicky Mr Štursa, who had seen the project through, wrote to suggest that Stalin could be severed from the soldier, botanist et al., and replaced by 'an allegory—perhaps a woman holding a bouquet?'. The commission never replied, and in October 1962 the dynamite boys went in and destroyed the heroes in a series of night-time detonations.

It's hard to tell whether long-term damage has been done to the Prague psyche by the cultural atrocities perpetrated by their side of the Cold War. During the 1950s, many actually believed in the slush and the cant, but it was in the 1970s and 80s that kitsch very nearly triumphed, by implicating thousands in a world of schmaltz. The aspirations were noble, but they were enshrined in hyperbole which threatened to destroy critical functions entirely. The dangers have become clear since 1989: one example is that years of seeing banners celebrating racial harmony have led many to conclude that anti-racism is somehow equatable with Communism.

Visible vestiges of the Communist interregnum are hard to find these days. The crimson placards that lined Wenceslas Square until early 1990 (saying things like 'We shall overfulfil the plan by 143%!') have been replaced by advertisements for photocopiers and computers; statues have been toppled and history is being re-rewritten. But ghosts survive. Hundreds of megaphones, which once blared martial tunes on festival days, sit silently on lampposts across the capital. Epic friezes and mosaics cling on (notably at the Anděl metro station), spared destruction by their size and yet mutely pleading for it by their ugliness. And most formidable of all is the Hotel International, a masterpiece of Socialist Realism. Since 1989, its pride has turned into insouciance, but it remains as arrogant now as it must have been on that hazy day back in 1954 when the Defence Minister stepped out to unveil his granite erection to a jubilant crowd.

There has been endless talk since the revolution of the need to exorcise the spirit of Communism, and an essential stage will be the opening of a gallery of revolutionary culture. The perfect site exists: the former Communist Party Mausoleum, a marble temple to totalitarian necrophilia (see p.122). The vast sepulchre would take some filling, but there is no shortage of exhibits. The hundreds of statues that now lie in storage across the capital could line the long approach road in welcome—nymphs caressing olive branches would mingle with scrums of bearded thinkers, while droves of bald men with goatees could point visitors onward, ever onward. Several items from the now defunct Museum of the National Security Corps and Army of the Interior Ministry could also find a new home there. They celebrated the valour and vigilance of the border patrol; among the threats to the nation that the brave boys had seen off were packs of strange cigarettes (accompanied by photographs of their bewildered hippy owners) and the home-made helicopter and pretend tank of very hopeful would-be escapees. Most stirring of all was Brek, an almost legendary guard dog who pounced on 60 fleeing miscreants, sustained two shotgun wounds, and was eventually stuffed for his pains.

Prague: Essential Sights

It is hard to draw up a Prague top ten, but if you're only in town for a couple of days—or if you prefer roaming free to following walks—you may want to do so. The following list represents a few of the most impressive sights and experiences that the capital has to offer.

Art Nouveau	Municipal House; Evropa Café.
Baroque churches	Church of St Nicholas; Church of St James.
Bridges	The Charles Bridge. No others.
Cemeteries	Malá Strana Cemetery; Old Jewish Cemetery.
Evening drinking	Evropa Café in winter; Michalská Street in summer; cup of *burčák* on the Charles Bridge in September.
Galleries	St George's Convent (Baroque art); St Agnes' Convent (Gothic art); Tradefair/Veletržní Palace (Modern art).
Gothic architecture	Cathedral of St Vitus; Vladislav Hall; Old-New Synagogue; St Agnes' Convent; Stone Bell House.
Islands	Kampa; Žofín (Slovanský ostrov); Střelecký ostrov.
Modernist architecture	Church of the Sacred Heart; Tradefair/Veletržní Palace; Žižkov Tower.
Museums	Museum of Decorative Arts; National Technical Museum; Military Museum in the Lobkowicz Palace; Anti-Nazi Resistance Memorial.
Preposterous Baroque shrines	Loretto; *Bambino di Praga*; St John Nepomuk's tomb.
Quirky miscellanies	National Memorial (Communist mausoleum); John Lennon Wall.
Rides	Funicular up Petřín Hill; tram 22; rowing on the Vltava.
Romantic strolls	Winding path down Petřín into Malá Strana; Kampa Island; New Town (Nový Svět); streets around St Agnes' Convent.
Views	From a table at Nebozízek restaurant; the orange tiles of Malá Strana from the top of Nerudova street; from a room in the Hotel Praha.
Walled gardens	Waldstein Gardens; courtyard in Clementinum; Vojan Park.

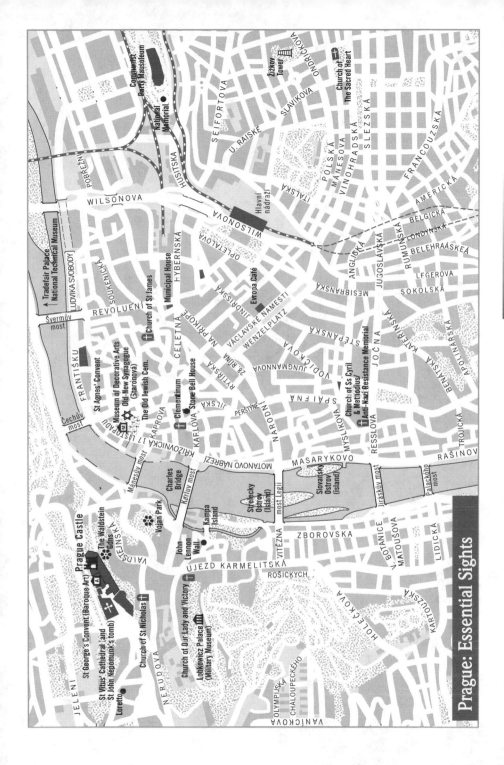

Prague: Essential Sights

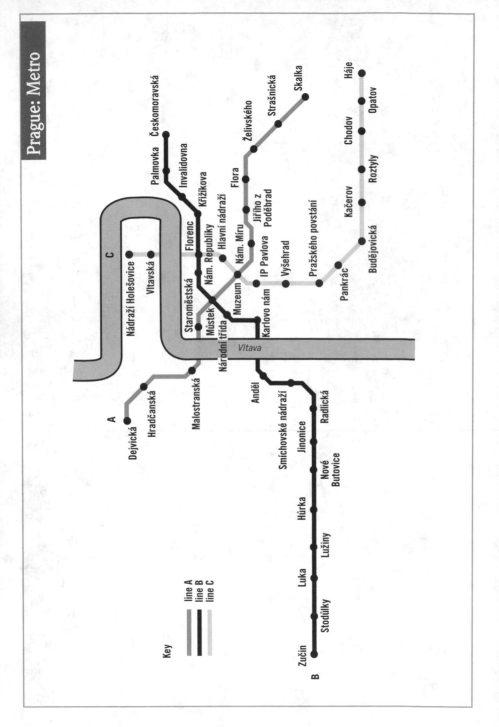

Prague: Metro

Old Town (Staré Město)

Founded and fortified in the 13th century, the Old Town is the Central European fantasy in microcosm. A stroll along the alleys between the town square and the stone bridge will wind you through centuries of legend and history: over subterranean bars which were once ground-level town houses, under the clockwork marionettes that have relentlessly counted out Prague's time for five centuries, and past the ghosts of its countless dead martyrs, miscreants and ideologies. The modernized façades of the Old Town's buildings now pay lip service to the 21st century, but its streets remain a labyrinth of Baroque colour and Gothic gloom. Negotiating the maze will at the very least be enjoyable and, if you allow yourself to get lost, it can sometimes take you back to the pied pipers and magical playgrounds of a half-forgotten childhood dream.

Lunch and Cafés

As well as the following stops, there are innumerable eating posts around the Old Town Square. During summer, overlapping terraces and parasoled tables turn the square itself into one huge (and audaciously overpriced) outdoor café.

Bohemia Bagel, Masná 2. *Open daily 9am–midnight.* Self-service restaurant and café with a children's play area and cheap Internet connections. No cards.

Café Milena, Staroměstské nám. 22, first floor. *Open daily 10–10.* One of the more civilized cafés on the Old Town Square, it was named after the one-time lover of Franz Kafka, whose bust presides over the room.

Café Nuovo, Staroměstské nám. 5. *Open daily 8.30am–midnight.* A smart, airy and popular café which serves excellent coffee, cakes and sandwiches. Daily local and international papers available to customers. No cards.

Clementinum Café-Restaurant, Platnéřská 9. *Open daily 11am–midnight.* Newly and elegantly renovated; try the salmon with shrimp and saffron sauce or the rich chocolate cake.

La Provence, Štupartská 9. *Open daily noon–midnight.* Expensive but tasty French and Italian-style food and long drinks.

Obecní dům Kavárna (in the Obecní dům next to the Powder Tower). One of the most glamorous Art Nouveau cafés in town, recently refurbished.

Red, Hot and Blues, Jakubská 12. *Open daily 9am–11pm.* Good breakfasts and Cajun meals.

Safir Grill, Havelská 12. *Open Mon–Sat 10–8.* Falafel and all the trimmings in the middle of Havelska street market. Takeaway or sit-down meals. No cards.

U budovce, Týnská 7. *Open daily 10am–11pm.* Quirky café-bar with eccentric decoration in a basement off the Tynska street antique shops' alleyway. No cards.

U kata (The Executioner), next to U zelené žáby. *Open Mon–Fri 10am–midnight, Sat–Sun noon–midnight.* A pleasantly down-at-heel pub that trades on the fame of its gory next-door neighbour. Gambrinus and Purkmistr on draught. No cards.

U supa (The Vulture), Celetná 22. *Open daily 11.30–11.* Arched and expansive restaurant, serving light and dark beers and a gamut of juicy, meaty Czech dishes.

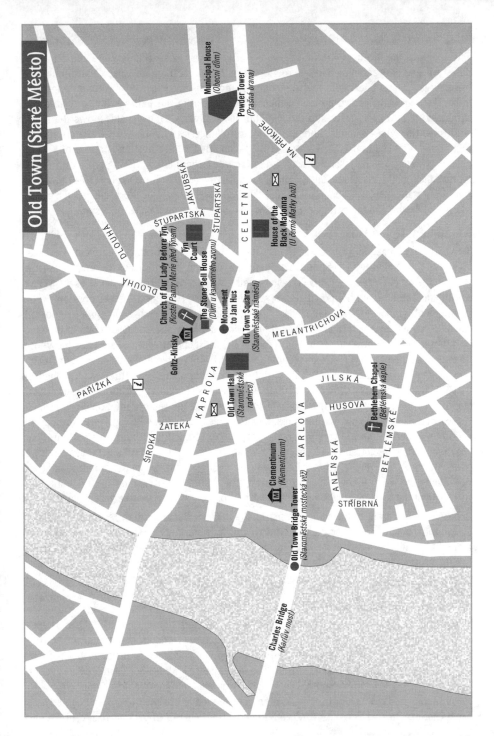

Old Town (Staré Město)

Municipal House
(Obecní dům)

Powder Tower
(Prašná brána)

NA PŘÍKOPĚ

JAKUBSKÁ

ŠTUPARTSKÁ

ŠTUPARTSKÁ

CELETNÁ

DLOUHÁ

House of the
Black Madonna
(U černé Matky boží)

Church of Our Lady Before Týn
(Kostel Panny Marie před Týnem)

Týn
Court

DLOUHÁ

The Stone Bell House
(Dům u kamenného zvonu)

Monument
to Jan Hus

Old Town Square
(Staroměstské náměstí)

Goltz-Kinsky

MELANTRICHOVA

PARÍŽKÁ

KAPROVA

Old Town Hall
(Staroměstské
radnice)

JILSKÁ

Bethlehem Chapel
(Betlémská kaple)

HUSOVA

ŽATEKÁ

KARLOVA

ŠIROKÁ

KARLOVA

ANENSKÁ

BETLÉMSKÉ

Clementinum
(Klementinum)

STŘÍBRNÁ

Old Town Bridge Tower
(Staroměstská mostecká věž)

Charles Bridge
(Karlův most)

The square is the Brothers Grimm in stone. Gothic towers, a sparkling white church and a pastel wave of pink and blue Baroque rooftops provide the location; and, like Central Europe's unexpurgated fairy tales, with their Jew-baiting and sadism, its history is sunk in blood and guts. The merchants of Týn unpacked their wares here from the 12th century onwards and the hawking tradition survives to this day, but it has always been the sideshows that have confirmed the square's status. Romping stomping Wenceslas IV threw parties here until the Old Townies locked him up in 1394; in 1600, scholarly Dr Jessenius (an ancestor of Kafka's epistolary lover, Milena Jesenská) astonished crowds as he fiddled with a corpse during the world's first public dissection; and the plaza's capacity meant that it played host to all the most significant state killings of Bohemian history. Nowadays, the square is the strolling intersection of the Old Town, and the perfect spot to soak up rays, history and a beer on a summer's day.

Monument to Jan Hus

The best place to get an overview of the square is from the steps of this monument. Heretical Hus was burnt alive in 1415, and his death marked the beginning of decades of war in Bohemia. Two centuries later, his Protestant heirs were eradicated at the Battle of the White Mountain; but although the population reverted in droves, Hus never lost his position as the pre-eminent symbol of Czech nationalism. In 1900, as the Austro-Hungarian empire doddered towards extinction, Prague's authorities commissioned a monument to their man, in preparation for the 500th anniversary of his martyrdom. The artist chosen was Ladislav Šaloun, whose lifelong attachment to Art Nouveau techniques (until 1946) placed him outside both the mainstream and the avant-garde of Czech sculpture; and when this sculpture was unveiled in 1915, it was predictably showered with abuse. It shows Hus flowing from the bronze base, standing tall between two groups representing the crushed and the defiant. Some complained that Šaloun had created a sprawling mess, by letting his fascination with light effects run away with him; others found the very idea of allegory too disrespectful, although it's doubtful that they would have preferred Hus to be portrayed as the bald midget that he is thought to have been. However, the very fact that Šaloun was commissioned shows that the municipal arbiters of Prague taste were slowly coming to terms with the 20th century. Compare the work with the pomp of the St Wenceslas Monument (*see* p.116), unveiled only three years before.

A bronze line in front of the sculpture marks Prague's former **meridian**. A Marian column, erected in 1649 to celebrate the Bohemian Counter-Reformation, sent its midday shadow along here until it was toppled by a patriotic mob in 1918. With independence, Prague gave up the increasingly inconvenient tradition of calculating its own time.

Old Town Hall (Staroměstská Radnice)

Open Tues–Sun 9am–6pm, Mon 11am–6pm (until 5pm in winter); adm.

The privileges attached to town life in medieval Europe were immense. Peaceful coexistence and fortifications had always been a way for decent folk to protect themselves against raping and pillage; but a town charter also gave them a degree of political power that was potentially more or less independent of the monarch. The dilemma for a king was that to declare war on uppity subjects could strain resources (although it was still often judged worthwhile), so, when a community had reached critical mass, monarchs tended to cut their losses and hand over a town charter. The Old Town got fortifications and a royal charter in the mid-13th century, and

Wenceslas II grudgingly let Praguers have a clerk in 1296; but Wenceslas put his foot down when they asked for a town hall to put the clerk in. The townspeople had to wait until 1338, when they were able to take advantage of blind King John of Luxembourg. He waved the plans through—but commanded that the town hall be funded from a new tax on wine. That threw the thrifty burghers, but they were able to make a humble start when they bought a house and turned it into the tower in front of you. As the receipts poured in, they were slowly able to add all the buildings on your left. It was a piecemeal process, but the maroon and white 18th-century façades, encrusted with Gothic and Renaissance survivals from earlier days, now house a single interior, stretching from the tower to the end of the block.

On the tower is the town hall's pride and joy, its **Astronomical Clock**, or horologe (*orloj*). Prague woke up late to the idea of clocks—by the time this one was installed in 1410, every other major city in Europe had one—but they were still exotic devices, and the city's burghers were concerned that things should stay that way. Legend has it that, when it was remodelled by a certain Master Hanuš in 1490, the municipal council blinded him to protect its copyright. A peeved Master Hanuš scaled the building, tossed a medieval spanner in the works, and promptly died. Prague's timepiece was out of joint for almost a century, but since 1572 it has ticked away without interruption, the occasional fire and artillery blitz notwithstanding. The arcane clock is a reminder of an age when such machines were regarded as very powerful creatures indeed. Only in the 19th century did the industrial world really begin to operate on the assumption that clocks simply recorded the hours—as far as medieval thought was concerned, it was just as plausible that they created them and, even into the 17th century, the connected notions of clocks, clockwork and perpetual motion were imbued with a mystery that is hard to imagine today. This one purports to tell the time, but that's only the beginning. Its astronomical symbols, pointers and interlocking circles also register the phases of the moon, the length of the day, the equinoxes, Babylonian time, and the dates of innumerable mobile feasts; and all the cogs and wheels whirr with added complication, according to the orbit of the heavens around the Earth. Mechanical magic also treats awestruck spectators to a morality play, all but unchanged for 500 years. Every hour two cuckoo-clock windows open and statues of the 12 Apostles mince past while Death tinkles his bell. The great leveller is pooh-poohed by preening Vanity, and those bugbears of 15th-century Europe, the Turk and the Jew. The latter now lacks his beard and horns, and is politely referred to as Greed, having been sanitized following the town hall's bombardment in 1945. The post-Holocaust decision was understandable; but the paradoxical effect was to whitewash the bloody feature of Central Europe's history that had just reached its culmination. A cock, and delighted children, screech when the ceremony is all over.

The temporal theme is taken up by the painted calendar below the clock showing the monthly labours of rural folk. It's by Josef Mánes, a prolific artist of the 19th-century Czech national revival movement. Bucolic subjects were favoured by Romantics everywhere, and especially so in Bohemia where Germans were popularly seen as an unhealthy brood of urban lounge lizards. Again, the stereotype had connotations that stretched back to darker times: by the early 20th century, some 85 per cent of the German-speakers in Prague were of Jewish origin.

Walk to the modern **entrance of the town hall** (*open March–Oct Tues–Sun 9–6, Nov–Feb Tues–Sun 9–5; adm*) under the Renaissance window (1520). The Latin phrase means 'Prague, head of the kingdom', and was a motto extracted by the burghers from devil-may-care John of Luxembourg. The small Gothic **chapel** on the first floor dates from 1381. A Nazi tank shelled it to smithereens at the height of the Prague Uprising, but it has been restored well, using as much of the original rubble as could be identified. The chapel's main attraction is up on your right as you face the oriel: through a glass door, the **figures of the 12 Apostles** wait on the spokes of two wheels for their moment of glory; if your timing is right, you can be here to see the windows open and the figures twirl into life when the hour strikes.

From the chapel, begin the trek to the top of the **tower**. After gasping—and gasping—at the view, descend again for the **guided tour of the town hall's rooms**. The tour leads past a **memorial cross** made from two charred wooden beams. At least 14 men died in the building during the Nazi assault—it was the headquarters of the committee that led the Prague Uprising. The resistance fighters holed themselves up in the network of late 12th-century **town hall cellars**, until recently host to an instantly forgettable multimedia show. The cellars comprise a number of halls, a well, and a dungeon for those women who were thought to talk too much.

The rest of the tour takes you under painted Renaissance joists on the first floor; on the second, faded Gothic murals and a turn-of-the-20th-century drawing of Prague from Petřín Hill, minus the housing estates on today's horizon. The next two rooms contain four works by Václav Brožík (1851–1901), whose speciality was portraying turning-points of Bohemian history with a turgid solemnity. Until 1526, the country's king was chosen in the town hall, and *The Election of King George of Poděbrady* shows Hussite George being given the nod by the country's nobles in 1458. The equally monumental *Jan Hus' Trial at Constance* is one of several versions churned out by Brožík for the nationalist movement. Among those watching Hus' doomed attempts to present a defence—to charges that included the allegation that he believed himself to be a fourth member of the Holy Trinity—are the great men of 19th-century Bohemia, including Smetana, Dvořák and none other than Václav Brožík himself. The two canvases in the next room are *Charles IV Founding Prague University* and *Comenius in Exile in Amsterdam*.

The **Old Council Chamber**, dating from about 1470, does most to conjure up the years when municipal powers were at their height. Councillors would hammer out policy at the broad table, supervised by the solemn Gothic sculptures. The haunting figure of Christ (*c.* 1410) implores them in Latin to 'Judge Justly, Sons of Man'—a fair plea, since it is here that Master Hanuš' fate would have been decided; summary execution was the norm in politically sensitive cases, when last rites would be swiftly administered in the neighbouring chapel. The councillors found themselves at the receiving end of some rough justice in 1483, when a Hussite mob threw the Catholic mayor and several cronies out of the window in the second of Prague's four defenestrations. The reformers then continued the good work with a pogrom in the Jewish Quarter—eradicating Judaism was widely thought to be a precondition of the Messiah's expected return in 1500. The scene of the first crime is no longer known; the Renaissance window through which light now trickles was installed 40 years later.

Goltz-Kinský Palace

Open Tues–Sun 10–6, closed Mon; free.

This dainty building in the northeast corner of the square dates from 1755–65, by which time Prague's Baroque frenzy had begun to exhaust itself. This is one of the best examples of Rococo architecture in the city, with its frilly stucco garlands and pink and white façade demanding no more than an approving coo from passers-by. Kafka studied here from 1893 to 1901, and the family connection was resumed some years later when his father, no-nonsense Hermann, moved his haberdashery store into the ground floor. But its moment came in

February 1948. A vast crowd gathered in the square to hear Czechoslovakia's first Communist president, Klement Gottwald, roar from the balcony that the dictatorship of the proletariat had arrived. The masses cheered back and paid the price—every year workers were herded back here to celebrate their emancipation, until Victorious February was thrown into the dustbin of history in 1989. The gracious palace has now shrugged off its claim to ill fame, and spends its days hosting the National Gallery's exhibitions of graphic art, and broadcasting light arias and chamber music across the square from the music shop on its ground floor.

Stone Bell House (Dům u Kamenného Zvonu)

The oldest intact Gothic house in Prague, with its creamy façade and stone bell set into the corner, sits to the right of the palace. It was built in the mid-13th century, and Emperor Charles IV is thought to have lived here as a youth—but you won't find it on any photographs older than a decade or two. Thorough remodellings after the late 1600s meant that only in the 1960s did restorers realize what lay within the then unremarkable neo-Baroque house. The onion-skins were peeled away, and the house was opened to the public in 1986. It's now used for concerts and some of the city's most consistently excellent exhibitions of modern art. It will be closed if there's nothing on; check notices outside for details of the next event. The Gothic tower, fronting what is now a Renaissance courtyard, is the richest part of the building, but you'll find fragments of murals, pointed doorways and ribbed vaults throughout. The most complete decoration is in the chapel to your right as you walk towards the courtyard, once entirely covered with murals of the Passion (c. 1310).

Church of Our Lady Before Týn (Kostel Panny Marie před Týnem)

Open daily 10–6; free.

Just to the left of the Stone Bell House is the **Týn School**, its 16th-century façade falling and rising in bulbous imitation of the church that it fronts, usually abbreviated to the Týn Church. The multi-steepled towers of Týn bristle like Gothic missile batteries and dominate the square, but they emerge from behind the school, a fact that has given rise to dark tales of Catholic conspiracies. The church was the hub of Hussitism right up to the 1620 rout and, although the Hussites were by then a minority among Bohemia's Protestants, it is said that the Jesuits decided to humiliate Prague by hiding its former parish church behind a house. In fact, the school and its even more obtrusive neighbour were originally Gothic buildings, and appeared around the same time that the church was founded (1385). Their later reconstructions were just par for the course in Prague. In fact, Týn created its own problems; it was founded on a self-effacing earlier church and just grew, adding the spires over a century later. The legend may have arisen because of the alterations that the Jesuits really did make. As well as the almost sensible decision to melt down a Hussite statue and transform it into the Madonna that now stands between the towers, the monks melted down the bells because they had been given Hussite nicknames, and then recast them into identical copies. (It is worth remembering that this was a time when bells couldn't be touched by women or any non-cleric over the age of puberty.) The lead spires with their countless golden prongs are an aerial signpost over the Old Town, but few ever notice that the tower on the right is significantly broader than its neighbour: medieval rules said that a fat male tower had to protect a slim female tower from the midday sun.

After a fire in 1679 the central vault was rebuilt in Baroque style. The altars and decorations are also largely Baroque but, even more than in St James', they are swamped by the cavernous

Gothic structure of the triple-naved church. At the end of the northern nave, past the 1493 stone baldachin (which now canopies a 19th-century altar) and the tombstone of the dwarf to your left, is a powerful Gothic Calvary of around 1410. From here, cross the central nave. Walk across the high altar and, on the pillar to your left, you'll find the **tomb of Tycho Brahe** (1546–1601), Emperor Rudolf II's imperial mathematician for two eventful years. The red marble relief is relatively flattering. It hardly hints at the gold and silver nosepiece worn by the moustachioed Dane ever since he lost most of the original organ in a duel. Brahe was one of the most colourful men in a court that was hardly dull. Apocryphal legend has it that his own day-to-day activities were conducted according to the Delphic utterances of Jeppe, a homuncular lunatic whom he placed under the table at mealtimes. Nothing became his life so much as his manner of leaving it, the result of over-drinking at a feast when a combination of self-control and a polite reluctance to leave the table caused his bladder to explode.

Near Brahe's tombstone, at the end of the southern nave, is the oldest font in Prague, a tin pot dating from 1414. The Gothic pulpit on the next pillar to the west dates from the 15th century, although the painting and canopy are 19th-century additions. It was from here that rabble-rousing preachers incited generations of congregations to sprees of destruction. Near the pulpit is the rich foliage and drapery of the early 16th-century **carving of Christ's baptism** by Master I. P., a Dürer-influenced artist whose work is also exhibited at St Agnes' Convent (*see* p.71).

Church of St James (Sv. Jakub)

Open Mon–Fri 9–1 and 2.30–4, Sat 9.30–12.30 and 2–4, Sun 2–4.

St James', founded in 1374, escaped the overkill that turned some of Prague's churches into grotesqueries during the Counter-Reformation. Its interior is now one of the most elegant in the city, but it hasn't escaped the Old Town's stormy history. It was the target of iconoclasts in both 1420 and 1611, and was saved only by the courage and cleavers of the Butchers' Guild, whose history is intertwined with that of their church; in 1689 it was ravaged by a huge fire, which destroyed about 800 houses in the surrounding area. By 1739, the interior and the façade had assumed their present appearance. The church vibrates better than any other in Prague and its organ concerts are superb; the schedule is pinned up outside. Above the entrance, rich stucco reliefs depicting the event-filled lives of SS Francis of Assisi, James and Antony of Padua crowd out of the wall. The nave is the second longest in Prague after St Vitus' Cathedral. The illusionists in charge of the Baroque reconstruction wanted it even longer, and tapered the galleries in the narrower bays of the chancel.

Although the Gothic proportions of the hall-church keep the 21 Baroque altars firmly under control, the splendid tableau of the **tomb of Count Jan Václav Vratislav of Mitrovice** (1714–16) tries its hardest to break free, at the far end of the northern aisle. Mitrovice was imperial chancellor of Bohemia at a time of strict control from Vienna, when the most important qualifications for the job were dull ambition and kneejerk reflexes. He may have slipped out of the history books but, when the daunting late Baroque duo of Vienna's J. B. Fischer von Erlach and Prague's F. M. Brokof set to work on this monument, his posthumous fate was clearly seen in more elevated terms. None of the other decorations of the church can quite match the tomb. After a brief look at the ceiling frescoes (*Life of the Virgin* and *Glorification of the Trinity*) and the *Martyrdom of St James* on the high altar, go to the left of the main doors, where you'll find a less carefully crafted monument to human folly: a scraggly **human forearm** hanging from a chain. The rag and bone is what's left of a bloodthirsty miracle that took place in 1400, when a thief tried to pilfer the jewels of the Madonna on the high altar. The Virgin would have none of it and grabbed his arm, refusing to let go despite the prayers and pleas of church officials. The limb eventually had to be lopped off, and has hung ever since as awesome testimony to Divine Justice.

Týn Court

The name 'Týn' comes from the same Germanic root as the English 'town'; this courtyard, dating from the 11th century, was the enclave of the Eastern traders and formed one of the first settlements on the right bank of the Vltava. It had everything—church, inn, and even a hospice in which moribund merchants could expire in comfort. The fun lasted until the late 1500s, when the traders upped and went to the Vladislav Hall and the more abstruse pleasures of Rudolf II's castle, at which point Týn became the peaceful retreat that it remains today. The dignified **Granovský House**, on the far right, built by the customs officer of Týn in 1560, is one of the grandest survivals of the Renaissance in Prague.

The Rest of Old Town Square

The buildings lining the southern side of the square, like those of Celetná, are constructed over older subterranean houses. The plaque marked 'DUKLA' contains a pot of earth from a 1944 battle between the Nazis and Soviet-Slovakian forces; and to the right is a memorial to an earlier watershed in the country's history, the executions of 21 June 1621, which took place on the site of the 27 crosses painted on the ground. After the Battle of the White Mountain, Emperor Ferdinand II wasted no time. The big fish of Bohemian nationalism were put on trial; Viennese judges pondered the evidence and sentenced them to death. A scaffold was set up on this spot, and a grandstand constructed for those nobles lucky enough to find themselves on the right side. The appointed day began portentously—crossed rainbows were seen in the sky—but the executions went like a dream. Dr Jessenius was among those who got their comeuppance and, in a terrible echo of his most celebrated moment, he was virtually dissected himself: tongue extracted, decapitated, then quartered. Mydlář the Axeman was such a virtuoso that Praguers (who have celebrated their national humiliation with gusto ever since) took him to their hearts almost immediately. The hooded hero is still an integral character in the packed universe of Prague childhood. Mydlář plucked and amputated with legendary precision, and 10 of the unluckiest heads were piked and suspended over the Old Town Bridge Tower. All 27 martyrs apparently still come here on the night of the anniversary, on a rather futile hunt for their many other missing appendages.

Next to the town hall is the burnt-out shell of a pink neo-Gothic stump, which used to stretch across to the southern façade of **St Nicholas' Church** (Sv. Mikuláš) in the northwest corner. It was a part of the town hall obliterated by Nazi tanks on 8 May 1945, a week after the suicide of Hitler, and on the same day that Western Europe was celebrating VE Day. The last fighting on the Continent took place in Prague. On 5 May 1945, the city rose up against the Nazis; four days and up to 5,000 dead Czechs later, the Red Army arrived. There seems to have been none of the chicanery that surrounded the Soviet betrayal of the Warsaw Uprising; but US forces—who were within easy reach of the capital—stood idle so as not to breach the terms of the Yalta agreement. Eight competitions were held after 1945 to find a way of filling the hole. Endless Stalinist temples and monumental schemes were proposed, but even the competition organizers seem to have been unnerved by them, and no one ever won. Only in 1998 was the city's unofficial sunbathing green turned into the rank of wooden benches that now stand on the site.

Municipal House (Obecní Dům)

Open daily 10am–11pm.

From nám. Republiky look for the ornate Art Nouveau façade of the **Municipal House**, built between 1906 and 1911 as an unusually successful contribution to the Czech national revival movement. The building stands on the site of the Gothic Royal Court, occupied by Bohemia's monarchs for an unhappy century, deserted for several more, and finally destroyed in the early 1900s. Its replacement, with exhibition halls and auditorium, had the standard patriots' aims of edifying the masses; but, unlike all the other dire architectural monuments of the revival movement, it came late enough to express itself in the language of Art Nouveau. Scores of Prague artists and architects made contributions, and the Municipal House is a cacophonous charivari rather than a tight symphony in the new style: a forest of crystal and mirrors, whiplash curves, organic excrescences and unusually sensual homages to Czechdom and civic virtue. Highlights of the interior include the elegant **café** (*kavarna*) on the ground floor; the Turkish delights of the **Oriental Hall** upstairs; and the **Němcová Hall**, which contains an Art Nouveau aquarium encrusted with brass snails. Next door is the glittering **Sweetshop** (*cukrárna*). No less absurd is the massive **cloakroom** (*šatna*), which you will find with little difficulty. In the circular **Mayoral Hall** (Primátorský sál) are violet windows, and paintings by Alfons Mucha: examples of the sombre late work of the man who produced some of the most distinctive posters of Parisian Art Nouveau during the 1890s. Rising through two floors at the core of the building is the **Smetana Hall**. Every year on 12 May, the Czech Symphony Orchestra arrives here hotfoot from a pilgrimage to the composer's grave in Vyšehrad; and the Prague spring music festival bursts into life with a performance of his symphonic poem cycle *Má Vlast* (My Country). In order to see the above it is best to book a guided tour at the main entrance.

Tethered by a small bridge to the neighbouring Municipal House, the **Powder Gate** (Prašná brána; *open daily 10–6; adm*) is a stately but forlorn reminder of a glory that never was. As long ago as the 11th century, traders with turbans, pelts, spices and slaves would roll into Prague from the East through a gateway here. Although this tower was begun in 1475 amid general festivities and merriment, it was rapidly abandoned by the mercurial Hussites. Later given a temporary roof, a use (gunpowder storage) and an unimaginative name, it was bombarded by Frederick the Great, and emerged in an even sorrier state than before. It was finally put out of its misery by the zealous neo-Gothic touch of the Czech Josef Mocker, and the ornate decoration of the façade, and much of the interior, is his work (1875–86).

House of the Black Madonna (U Černé Matky Boží)

Open Tues–Sun 10–6, closed Mon; adm.

At the corner of Celetná and Ovocný trh is a 20th-century Cubist curiosity, the House of the Black Madonna, which houses temporary exhibitions and a permanent collection of Czech Cubist art on its upper two floors. Designed by Josef Gočár, and built in 1911–12, it is recognizable by the caged Virgin suspended above the portals, a 16th-century remnant of an earlier house on the site. Black Madonnas have long been a popular sideline of the Marian cult in Catholic Europe. When this was built, Cubism was sweeping through Prague's artistic community, and Gočár was one of several Czech architects who hoped to use the principles of Braque and Picasso to restore volume and life to the façades of Prague's buildings without breaking the city's architectural traditions. The experiment sounds shocking, but tradition came out very much the winner: despite the recessed, angular window frames and two-tiered roof, the house slots almost perfectly between its Baroque neighbours. The small exhibition it contains is one of the least exciting in Prague, comprising a few jagged pieces of furniture, minor works of Czech Cubist art, and the architectural plans of several unbuilt buildings, but it is worth trying to sneak past the ticket office just for a quick view of its recently restored keyhole staircase.

Western Old Town

Bethlehem Chapel (Betlémská Kaple)

Open April–Oct daily 9–6, Nov–March daily 9–5; adm.

In 1391, reformers chose to build a church here in which services could be held in the vernacular. The idea was never popular in the medieval Church, which only approved a chapel and began to monitor events closely. Bohemians rose to the challenge and built the largest chapel in the land. With panache, they centred it on the pulpit rather than the altar and, with the Protestant preference for scripture to saints, they thumbed through the Bible for a name. Jan Hus began to preach in the Bethlehem Chapel in 1402, the same year that he became rector of the Carolinum. His sermons filled the 3,000-capacity chapel, which set alarm bells ringing in the Church. Prague's archbishop warned him to pipe down; Hus was excommunicated; and an exasperated pope finally had to have him roasted in 1415. The present building is a modern copy of the original, which was all but demolished in 1786, and there's little to see inside other than daubed sermons preserved on three walls.

Clementinum (Klementinum)

Library open April–Oct daily 9–6, Nov–March daily 9–5; Church of Holy Saviour open for services on Sun and Tues at 8pm.

This was the first Jesuit College in Bohemia and the nerve-centre of the country's Counter-Reformation. The Society of Jesus was founded in 1540 by St Ignatius of Loyola. Waved off by Pope Paul III, members scattered across Europe to confront the Antichrist of reform. Organized on military lines and headed by a general elected for life, the Order made up the advance platoons of the Counter-Reformation. Setting up Baroque base camps and barracks as they moved, the missionaries penetrated deep into Protestant Europe; and during the uneasy peace that preceded the Thirty Years War (1618–48), the Clementinum relit the Catholic flame in a city that had become 90 per cent Protestant.

One of the most successful weapons in the Order's armoury was education. Prague's Jesuit college took shape after 1556, when a 40-strong squad was invited into Bohemia by Emperor Ferdinand I. The Clementinum's success was such that, by the 17th century, non-Catholic families were queuing up to enroll their little ones; and after a short-lived expulsion on the eve of war, the Society returned in force in 1620 to supervise a century of militant reconversion. The Clementinum swallowed up its arch-rival, the Protestant Carolinum, two years later, and only in 1773 did it lose its religious nature. It's now the Czech State Library.

The Jesuits took their architecture seriously. They moved into this site in 1556, but the present complex was built in protracted stages between 1653 and 1723, on the site of 30 odd houses, three churches, 10 courtyards and several gardens. The once graceful ground plan isn't easy to appreciate any more, paved in asphalt and disrupted by the chunk of modern concrete on the left, but its rooms and walkways are filled with surprises.

Down a lonely 100m-long barrel-vaulted passage is a series of 34 stucco cartouches containing scenes from the hectic life of St Francis Xavier, proto-Jesuit and the Order's second saint, who spent the last 10 years of his life in Asia on a one-man baptism drive. His achievements were considerable. On his first stop, he curbed the activities of Goa's syphilis-spreading Portuguese settlers; and in 1549, he gave the Mikado a clock and a music-box and swiftly immersed Japan's first 2,000 Christians, which proved to be something of a mixed blessing when later and less liberal Mikados gave the country its first several hundred martyrs. The scenes here were painted by an unknown Jesuit and are of no artistic merit, but—in this case at least—the Order clearly believed that subject matter alone would be enough to inspire and prepare the hopeful novices. Ignatius' life story is in the corridor immediately below. Unfortunately, it's been sliced down the middle by prefabricated offices: they're called temporary, but they look increasingly permanent.

There's one more stop to complete your Jesuit experience: the small reading room of the Music Library (Hudební oddělení). It contains the Jesuits' fascinating tribute to astronomy: models of the universe, diagrams of eclipses and, on the vault, a Baroque parade of approved thinkers. Although not officially open to the public, it occasionally hosts temporary exhibitions of some of the library's treasures (*open 9am–9pm*). The Jesuits did their best to keep abreast of new learning, but, as the Enlightenment advanced, astronomy became very tricky territory. Prague's Jesuits built their observatory in 1721, and the fresco was painted at some point between then and the tower's remodelling in 1749, as shown by the fact that the original building is part of the background. On the left are seven pretty Mathematical Disciplines, including Gnomonics, the once popular spirit of sundial construction; and under the Latin inscription 'God Gave the World to be Comprehended by Discussion', astronomy's heroes are gathered. Aristotle, doodling in the sand, is in front of Appolonius of Perga, Hipparchus and Ptolemy; on the far right Tycho Brahe, wearing his false nose (*see* p.58) is holding full and frank discussions with Giambaptista Riccioli (1598–1671), the Jesuits' black-robed representative. Riccioli's last-ditch attempt to keep the Earth at the centre of the universe is on the right of the wall in front of you. A century after Galileo and Johannes Kepler had suggested alternative proposals, the Clementinum's scientists still regarded it as the pinnacle of astronomical achievement.

Old Town Bridge Tower (Staroměstská Mostecká Věž)

Open April–Oct daily 10–6; adm.

The Bridge Tower was designed by Peter Parler (*see* 'Charles Bridge'), and completed in the 1390s during the reign of Wenceslas IV. As part of the fortification walls, this titan has had both symbolic and practical functions. After the execution of Bohemian nationalists in 1620, 10 heads putrefied from its first floor; and in 1648 the final hours of the Thirty Years War raged around the tower, when Sweden's army went on a looting spree and the Old Town was saved by a motley alliance of students and Prague Jews. A Europe-wide peace had already been negotiated, but another truce was clearly necessary. It was signed on the middle of the bridge, in a wooden cabin specially partitioned to keep the opposing factions from each other's throat.

The battle destroyed most of the decoration on the western façade of the tower. The east still has its original 14th-century decoration, with sculptures of SS Adalbert and Procopius at the top, Charles IV and Wenceslas IV enthroned below, and St Vitus in the centre. More intriguing are the minor details, which show the whimsical and irreverent spirit that was abroad in the late Gothic art of Wenceslas' court. On the corner to your left is a figure running his hand up a nun's habit, and one of Wenceslas' dalliances is directly commemorated by the birds and scantily clad female figures which appear all over the sides and golden-ribbed vault of the tower. According to legend, they are all in honour of one Zuzana. In 1394, the feckless king was temporarily locked up by disgruntled nobles in the Old Town, and she rowed him to the safety of Malá Strana after he persuaded his captors to let him have a bath. She was only a bathkeeper's daughter, but the king's gratitude knew no bounds—not only did he bed her, but he also raised her hitherto shady profession to the status of a guild.

The view along the bridge from the first floor is impressive—so much so that Communist buggers used to sit here and point eavesdropping equipment and lenses at particularly suspicious conversationalists down below. The listening post was dismantled only in 1990. Just before the viewing gallery at the top is a stone hunchback who guards the tower from evil spirits. Unfortunately, the medieval inscriptions that once used to help him have mysteriously disappeared. Demons were known to read everything they came across in case it contained a curse, and the tower used to contain two Latin phrases—*Signatesignatemeremetangisetangis* and *Romatibisubitomotibusibitamor*—which it was hoped would delay them more than usual. They seem to mean, respectively, 'Take note, take note, you are touching and torturing me' and 'Rome, to you I submit with the force of love', but more importantly, they are both palindromes. With luck, puzzled fiends would never be able to tear themselves away.

Charles Bridge (Karlův Most)

Through the vault of the tower lies the **Charles Bridge** (Karlův most), a curving, swerving ley line through Prague. For centuries the city's energy has squeezed through this narrow channel and, although the coronation processions and fairs of yesteryear have given way to endless troupes of guided tourists, it remains Prague's jugular vein.

There was a wooden way over the river more than 1,000 years ago, if Cosmas the chronicler is to be believed: an incidental detail of his account of the murder of St Wenceslas is that the bridge was damaged in 932, requiring a spot of Divine Intervention to fly the pallbearers across. Nothing is left of that structure, but remnants of the Judith Bridge, built in 1158, survive in the piers of the present work. The Judith Bridge was destroyed by floods in 1342, but the civic pride of Charles IV, who ascended the throne four years later, ensured that Prague didn't remain bridgeless for long. Astrologers were asked to find a suitably auspicious celestial configuration, and in 1357 Charles' architect, 27-year-old Peter Parléř, got to work. For over 400 years, the bridge was Prague's only river crossing. This feat of medieval engineering has survived centuries of deluges and, until 1950, the trundle of motor traffic.

The stark structure of the bridge is perfectly complemented by the 30 sculptures that now line it. The 14th century saw a simple wooden crucifix placed on the bridge; the Counter-Reformation knew a propaganda opportunity when it saw one and, during the late 1600s and early 1700s, an entire avenue of Baroque saints was added to the bridge, inspired by Bernini's 1688 work on the Ponte Sant'Angelo in Rome. The hapless commuters of Prague were a captive audience to what would then have been an awesome array of swooning and gesticulating saints. Many of the works have now been replaced by copies, and there is some lifeless neo-Gothic statuary from the 19th century, but the overall effect of the sculpture is still superb.

The oldest work is the bronze **Crucifixion** (1657), third on your right, flanked by 19th-century work. The Hebrew inscription on the statue was the compulsory contribution of an outspoken Jew, who apparently wandered past in 1695 muttering blasphemies. The fifth statue to your left shows **Francis Xavier** being borne aloft by grateful coolies. It's a copy of a 1711 work by F. M. Brokof which was swept away by a flood in 1890. The river was finally dammed in 1954. Ignatius used to stand on the opposite side of the bridge; after sinking in 1890, he was replaced by the youngest statue here, Karel Dvořák's 1938 sculpture of **SS Cyril and Methodius**.

About halfway across on the right is a small bronze Lorraine Cross embedded in the wall. According to rumour, the Dalai Lama recognized this point as the centre of the universe during his visit to Prague in 1990; and it also marks the spot where **St John Nepomuk** was hurled into the river. Put your hand on it, make a wish and then go to his statue, the eighth on the right. John was a vicar-general of Prague who was put in a sack and dropped into the Vltava in 1383 by Wenceslas IV. Two explanations for the king's act exist: the boring truth is that John appointed an abbot against the king's wishes; far better is the jolly tale put about three centuries later by the Jesuits when they were casting around for a wholesome Catholic rival to Jan Hus. The story is that Wenceslas asked John what the queen had told him during confession. Honest John supposedly replied from the rack that he'd forgotten, and wouldn't tell even if he could remember. Five stars appeared above the bobbing corpse (hence the unusual headgear that you'll see on all the saint's monuments in Prague). The rubbing of a million fingers has meant that tumbling John is still a glittering dot on the oxidized reliefs at the base of the figure. He will get you across any bridge safely, and he's the saint to turn to if someone suspects you of doing something that you just didn't do. He also gets women pregnant.

SS Vincent Ferrer and Procopius on the left deserve a mention; among the feats noted on their statue are the salvation of 100,000 souls, the conversion of 2,500 Jews, 70 exorcisms and 40 resurrections. A downcast devil, Turk and Jew support the saints. If you look over the bridge here, you'll see the statue of **Bruncvík**, a chivalrous character linked to the legend of Roland. The latter was a sanguinary epic of crusading Christianity, but Bruncvík has become enmeshed in a pot-pourri of mythological motifs and Prague legend. Various versions exist, but the most complex is that his invincible sword, buried in the Charles Bridge, will be unearthed in Bohemia's moment of greatest need by a stumbling white horse belonging to St Wenceslas; the saint will be at the head of the lost Hussite heroes who fell asleep in Blaník Mountain in 1434.

Of the petrified melodramas that remain, take a look at Matthias Braun's **St Luitgard**, fourth from the end on your left. Generally agreed to be the best-crafted sculpture on the bridge, it shows Christ letting the blind saint nuzzle His wounds, a vision she enjoyed late one night. Two statues along is F. M. Brokof's pantomime-like tribute to the **Trinitarian Order**, established for the purpose of ransoming Christian hostages from infidel clutches. The founders of the Order stand above a grotto full of captives, guarded by a pot-bellied pasha and a mad dog.

The Baroque hubbub subsides as you near the end of the bridge. An arm of the Vltava separates the island of Kampa (*see* p.114) from the mainland, and on your right are all 13 houses of Prague's so-called 'Little Venice'. The end of the bridge is punctuated by the **Malá Strana Bridge Tower** on the right, which was built in the early 1400s (*open daily 10–6, till 5 in winter*) and the stumpy **Judith Tower**—which, despite the Renaissance decoration, belonged to the 12th-century predecessor of the Charles Bridge. The inseparable duo, wearing tiled top hats and forming the parapet and arch into Malá Strana (*see* pp.102–14) frame St Nicholas' Church and one of the most tempting photo opportunities in Prague.

Jewish Quarter (Josefov)

With its central location and august feel, post-Communist Josefov has at last developed into the bourgeois district of boulevards and avenues that its Paris-inspired designers always wanted it to be. But as you walk through the quiet streets, under the sculptured façades of fantastic neo-Gothic strongholds and Art Nouveau citadels, you can't help but hear whispers from the past. The district used to be Prague's Jewish ghetto and, alongside those parts of it that still stand, there are hundreds of passageways and rooms, silent oubliettes and medieval refuges. However, now they form the cellars of the airline offices, French perfumers and antique stores that have taken over the area. Elsewhere in Prague, history reeks from every stone, but in the Jewish Quarter, it's the transformation that speaks.

Jewish Ghetto

Combined tickets which include entrance to the Maisel Synagogue, Spanish Synagogue, Pinkas Synagogue, Old Jewish Cemetery, Klausen Synagogue, Ceremonial Hall and Old-New Synagogue are available from the ticket office on Jachymova 3. These sights are open Nov–March Sun–Fri 9–4.30, April–Oct Sun–Fri 9–6 , closed Sat; last tickets are sold 30mins before closing time.

No one knows when the first Jews came to Prague. Even ghetto legend, which generally had an answer for everything, was unclear about precisely which lost tribe had made their way here. It often set the date at some point between the Exodus (*c.* 1300 BC) and AD 33—a period that gave the community a watertight alibi to charges of Christ-killing—but folklorists sometimes settled for about AD 135, when the Jews had been expelled from Palestine. Even the last date precedes the arrival of the Czechs by about four centuries. Historical sources suggest that the 10th century is closer to the truth, and it's thought that Jews first lived in two separate communities on either side of the river. By the mid-13th century an unhappy set of events had combined to create a single community here. Přemysl Otakar II wanted the left bank for his new town of Malá Strana (*see* pp.101–14); the Old Town was fortified; and most importantly, the Church in 1179 had announced that Christians should avoid touching Jews, ideally by building a moat or a wall around them. Another set of walls was accordingly built within the Old Town and, three centuries before the word was coined in Venice, Prague Jews began life in the ghetto.

Lunch and Cafés

Kavarna Rudolfinum, Alšovo nábr. 12. *Open Tues–Sat 10–6.* Quiet, refined retreat from the crowds in the grand neoclassical splendour of the Rudolfinum (*see* p.69).

Le Café Colonial, Široká 6. *Open daily 11.30–10.30.* Airy and elegant café, on the edge of the Jewish Quarter, with a range of spicy dishes.

Molly Malone's, U obecního 4. *Open Sun–Thurs noon–1am, Fri–Sat noon–2am.* The best of Prague's Irish pubs; drink Guinness among old sewing machines and sing Gaelic laments with every redhead in town. Big brunches.

Pizzeria Rugantino, Dušní 4. *Open Mon–Sat 11–11, Sun 4–11.* Tasty pizzas.

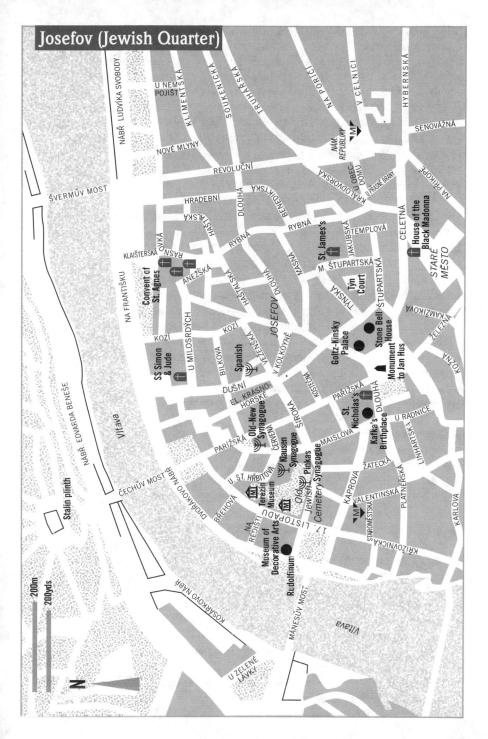

Josefov (Jewish Quarter)

U NEMŠKÁ
POJIŠT

NÁBŘ LUDVÍKA SVOBODY

KLIMENTSKÁ

SOUKENICKÁ

TRUHLÁŘSKÁ

NA PORÍČÍ

V CELNICI

HYBERNSKÁ

SENOVÁŽNÁ

NOVÉ MLYNY

REVOLUČNÍ

NÁM.
REPUBLIKY

KRÁL. DVORSKÁ

OBEC.
DOMU

U PRAŠNÉ BRÁNY

NA PŘÍKOPĚ

ŠVERMŮV MOST

HRADEBNÍ

DLOUHÁ

BENEDIKTSKÁ

RYBNÁ

CELETNÁ

House of the
Black Madonna

STARÉ
MĚSTO

HAŠTALSKÁ

RYBNÁ

RYBNÁ

MASNÁ

St. James's

JAKUBSKÁ

TEMPLOVÁ

KLAIŠTERSKÁ

RÁSNOVKA

ANEŽSKÁ

M. ŠTUPARTSKÁ

NA FRANTIŠKU

Convent of
St. Agnes

HAŠTALSKÁ

JOSEFOV

DLOUHÁ

TÝNSKÁ

Týn
Court

ŠTUPARTSKÁ

KAMZÍKOVA

NÁBŘ. EDVARDA BENEŠE

KOZÍ

U MILOSRDNÝCH

KOZÍ

BÍLKOVA

VĚZENSKÁ

V KOLKOVNĚ

Goltz-Kinsky
Palace

Stone Bell

Monument
House

ŽELEZNÁ

KOŽNÁ

KNĚŽNÁ

Vltava

SS Simon
& Jude

Spanish

DUŠNÍ

EL. KRÁSNO-
HORSKÉ

Old-New
Synagogue

KOSTEČNÁ

PAŘÍŽSKÁ

Monument
to Jan Hus

U RADNICE

DVOŘÁKOVO NÁBŘ

Stalin plinth

ČECHŮV MOST

BŘEHOVÁ

PAŘÍŽSKÁ

ČERVENÁ

ŠIROKÁ

Klausen
Synagogue

Pinkas
Synagogue

Jewish
Cemetery

MAISLOVA

St.
Nicholas's

Kafka's
Birthplace

DLOUHÁ

LINHARTSKÁ

PLATNÉŘSKÁ

U ST. HŘBITOVA

Terezín
Museum

Old

17. LISTOPADU

VALENTINSKÁ

KAPROVA

ŽATECKÁ

STAROMĚSTSKÁ

KARLOVA

KŘIŽOVNICKÁ

KOŠÁRKOVO NÁBŘ

NA
REDIŠTI

Museum of
Decorative Arts

Rudolfinum

MÁNESŮV MOST

U ZELENÉ
LÁVKY

Vltava

200m

200yds

N

The daily routine was much the same as that of Jews elsewhere in central Europe—pogroms, ritual murder allegations, and occasional banishments from the land (on many occasions in the early 16th century, and in 1744–8). By day movement was free, but as the sun set the portcullis would be lowered. The gates would be locked throughout the Easter-Passover flashpoint. Jews didn't mind, as it kept out the crowds eager to avenge Jesus on Good Friday; but the authorities' concerns were no different from those of the mob. Medieval Christendom generally assumed that the Passover lamb was a cunning codeword for Christ and that, unless the gates were locked, Christian babies and virgins would end up on a Passover plate.

During the 16th century, the ghetto became a vortex of Jewish mysticism, as interest in the cabala grew among both Jews and Christians throughout Europe. The mysterious cabalistic tradition—handed down orally from Adam—was reflected in the intellectual search of Rudolf II's court, and the exchange of cryptic data between rabbis and castle scholars became legendary. The period was to inspire a powerful image of the ghetto as a dank universe of miracles and poverty, its 7,000 inhabitants living cheek-by-jowl in a shadowy labyrinth of cramped lanes and subterranean passages. There's more than a little truth to the picture but, although the ghetto was sealed, it wasn't all poor. The richest man in Rudolfine Prague was Jewish.

In 1784, under Emperor Joseph II, the gates were thrown open. Joseph, enlightened despot that he was, was being liberal only in an academic sense. The idea was to wipe the Jews out as an independent community: the use of Hebrew or Yiddish in business was prohibited, and separate schools were banned. That didn't stop him being honoured after 1848, when Jews were finally granted civil rights (Charles IV had made 'imperial serfs' of them in the late 14th century). The ghetto was formally incorporated into Prague in 1850 and renamed Josefov, as it is still known. Integration proceeded apace—rich Jews moved out; poor Christians moved in. By the end of the 19th century, the district had become a stinking slum. The authorities could have repaired the buildings, but they chose to destroy them, along with an irreplaceable part of Europe's history. Broad streets, crowded with turn-of-the-20th-century mansions, now stand over winding medieval alleys. Of the old ghetto, only six synagogues, the town hall and the cemetery were spared, and still survive thanks to Hitler's macabre decision that they would house a postwar 'Exotic Museum of an Extinct Race'. Of the Jews themselves, some 80,000 of the 90,000 who remained in Bohemia and Moravia in March 1939 were killed.

After the war, the government took over the Nazi museum collection. It is hard to see what else could have been done, but the Communists proved unworthy custodians. A monument to a destroyed community was loaded with propaganda exalting the wartime role of the Communists, and incredibly inappropriate attacks on Zionism. Those Jews who remained in Prague continued to run the town hall and two neighbouring synagogues; but even the supposedly autonomous community organization had been compromised, as became clear after 1989—when the chief rabbi was found to have been a police informer. Friction between the State Jewish Museum and the community administration continued until late 1994, exacerbated by a more general conflict over the government's extraordinary refusal to return Jewish property that had fallen into State hands before the Communist accession in 1948. (That policy, which effectively legitimized all expropriations born out of the Nazi exterminations, was overturned in May 1994—so long as seizure was for 'racial' reasons and not 'national or political' ones.) But in October of that year, the State finally relinquished control, and the new Jewish Museum—now run by the Federation of Jewish Communities of the Czech Republic—was opened by President Havel.

The Old Jewish Cemetery

*Starý židovský hřbitov, known in Hebrew as **Beth-Chajim**, or the House of Life.*

The Jewish graveyard, the second oldest in Europe after that in Worms, is an astonishing sight—a flash of a lost world that imprints itself on your memory. For over three centuries until 1787, it was the only burial ground permitted the Jews, its elder trees the only patch of green behind the ghetto walls. As space ran out, it was covered with earth, older gravestones were razed, and a new layer of burials was begun. Subsidence has turned the graveyard into a forest of some 12,000 madly teetering tombstones. Many are half-interred themselves; many have migrated far from the person they commemorate. There are thought to be some 20,000 people under your feet, buried in up to 12 subterranean storeys.

The tombs are marked with the name of the deceased and the deceased's father (for women, also that of the husband), usually with verses pointing out some especially good things about the proprietor. The many hieroglyphs include the benedictory hands of the Cohens, the anointing jugs of the Levites, and other respectable symbols born out of the rigid division of Israeli labour; but the gravestones are also peppered with figures, and even the occasional portrait. As far as the Talmud was concerned, that was the first step towards the Golden Calf. The freethinking Enlightenment is a partial explanation of the idolatrous experiments, but no one really knows what came over the ghetto Jews. Descendants leave scribbled prayers and pebbles on the graves. No one knows where the Jewish custom of placing stones on tombs arose. Legend provides the only suggestion: it claims that the tradition dates back to the Exodus from Egypt, when only rocks were available to mark desert graves. The cracked vaults themselves probably contain more desperate prayers: when the Nazis ripped up Jewish cemeteries elsewhere in Europe, their gruesome harvest often included treasures hidden in broken tombs by Jews whose transportation papers had arrived.

The melancholy of the graveyard has made it a favourite spot for quiet contemplation over the years, but the days when Einstein or Egon Erwin Kisch could come here to ruminate in seclusion are long gone. Despite the tens of thousands of people who now visit annually, wandering between the stones was still permitted as recently as 1992. However, for many reasons—including religious sensibilities and the fact that the cemetery was being padded down by a millimetre each year—walking routes have now been marked out.

The oldest known plot is that of poet **Avigdor Kara**, dating from 1439. In 1389, Kara lived through and lamented the most vicious pogrom in Prague's history, in which 3,000 were massacred—over half of the ghetto's inhabitants. His original gravestone, now in the Maisel Synagogue, has been replaced by a copy which you'll find on the path running along the eastern wall of the cemetery.

Just before the western border wall from the Pinkas Synagogue (*see* p.66) turns to the left is the grave of **Rabbi David Oppenheim** (1664–1736), whose 5,000-volume library eventually went on a tour across Europe, and made it to Oxford's Bodleian in 1829, where it now forms the Oppenheimer Collection. Walking routes permitting, turn right at the path and then right again. There you'll find the grand tomb of **Mordechai Maisel** (1528–1601), the mayor of the ghetto during the reign of Rudolf II. Maisel had to wear a yellow wheel and high hat like any Jew in Rudolfine Prague (badge and hat were an intermittent requirement throughout the ghetto's history) but he died one of the wealthiest men in Europe. His will made dispositions amounting to 17 million gulden, at a time when five would buy a fattened ox. Jewish lore claims that young Maisel was an honest urchin who found a gold coin in a ghetto alley, and tracked down the wealthy rabbinical owner. The proud rabbi wasn't pleased, as he had put it there after a trio of goblins had told him that it would be retrieved by his future son-in-law. But prophecies were prophecies, and the ragamuffin moved in; the goblins eventually returned with several treasure chests, and rabbi, daughter and Maisel lived and died happily ever after. Others claim that Maisel made his fortune thanks to the trading monopoly granted him by Rudolf II.

The best-known of all the cemetery's occupants, the subject of tales that are still told to awestruck New York children, is **Rabbi Loew ben Bezalel** (1512–1609). His tomb, completely covered in pebbles, is along the western wall, roughly opposite the entrance gate. Loew, born in either Poznań or Worms, was one of the leading scholars of 16th-century Jewry. Most of his life was spent in Prague, and in 1597 he took over as chief rabbi of the ghetto; by the time of his death, he was already a legend. The stories surrounding his life—the most famous of which is his golem, a cabalistic precursor of Frankenstein's monster—are detailed on pp.40–1; but his powers apparently extended even beyond the grave. He's surrounded by 30 faithful disciples, among whom is his grandson Samuel. Solemn Samuel set his heart on being buried next to his grandfather; Loew vowed that he wouldn't be disappointed. Bungling ghetto authorities filled the precious plot with another lucky corpse—but dead though he was, Loew had not forgotten. When Samuel expired, the rabbi and his sepulchre budged a couple of feet. Samuel's grave is the thin one on the left.

Pinkas Synagogue (Pinkasova Synagoga)

Set on the south side of the cemetery, the synagogue stands over the 11th-century foundations of what may have been the first synagogue in Prague. Rabbi Pinkas began the present building on this site in 1479, apparently after a dead monkey stuffed with gold coins had been hurled through his window. A man nicknamed Munka (coincidentally) enlarged the synagogue and constructed the late Gothic vault in 1535; and in about 1625, it was given its present Renaissance façade. The first Jews of Prague may have worshipped on this spot and, after the war, the synagogue was chosen to house the Czech monument to the victims of the Holocaust: under the gilded ribs of the red-brick vault were listed the names of each of the 77,297 Czech Jews who died at Nazi hands. The synagogue was reopened in 1991, after being closed for over 20 years of so-called restoration, during which time the Communist authorities allowed the memorial to crumble into indecipherability. They excused themselves by blaming rising damp. As you gaze at the thousands of names, now repainted, only their tragedy can dwarf the scale of that insult.

The Old-New Synagogue (Staronová Synagoga)

This is one of the oldest synagogues to survive in Europe, and is still used by Prague's Orthodox community. There are two explanations for the synagogue's name. One very prosaic offering is that it was coined when the building was newly constructed on an older synagogue; but Jewish legend springs to the rescue with the claim that *Alt-Neu* ('Old-New' in German) is actually a corruption of *Al-Tenai*, or 'with reservation' in Hebrew. Angels and/or outriders of the Diaspora are said to have constructed the synagogue from the rubble of the last temple in

Jerusalem, which they carried over in about AD 135. The name stands as a reminder that, when the Messiah arrives, Prague's Jews have to take it back. Unless the legend is true, the synagogue appeared around 1270. The date was about a decade before the level of the Old Town began to be raised; and as you enter, you sink several feet to the level of (not quite) antediluvian Prague. The first chamber is the vestibule, and through the door on your left is the section where women are segregated during services; the slits through which they watch the goings-on are set into the northern and western walls of the interior. Men are asked to cover their heads before entering the main hall, and you can buy a *yarmulka* with your ticket. The gorgeous Gothic tympanum over the portal, a stylized vine, is divided into sections that represent the 12 tribes of Israel and the three continents of the world then known to Europe.

The splayed chinks of light and the pillar supports show how much the synagogue owed to Romanesque building techniques; but the vaulted naves, and the slenderness of the octagonal pillars themselves, represent the beginnings of Gothic architecture in Prague. The simplicity of the new features shows the influence of the Cistercians, who were tireless monastic messengers of an austere early Gothic style throughout the Continent. The Order had a masonic lodge in Prague, and architectural experts claim that the monks toiled with the Jews to build this synagogue. It sounds unlikely, particularly since the fifth rib of the vault, a feature unique in Bohemia, is thought to have been installed specifically to avoid the defiling symbol of the cross.

In the centre is the *almemar* (pulpit), surrounded by a 15th-century wrought-iron grille. Rabbi Loew apparently fought his final and most heroic battle here, when, alerted by a dream, he hurried to the darkened synagogue and found an apparition waving swords, dripping with gore, and ticking off a list of all Prague's Jews. Ninety-six-year-old Loew realized that this was Pogrom personified, and lunged for the beast. He ripped the scroll from Death's bloody grip, saved the ghetto from extinction, and missed only a scrap containing his name. The banner above the *almemar* was a present from Emperor Ferdinand III, after Prague's Jews, preferring the devil they knew, fought off Protestant Swedes in 1648; they had been honoured with flag rights by Charles IV over 200 years earlier. On the eastern wall is a screen covering the Torah (the scrolls containing the Pentateuch, i.e. the first five books of the Old Testament), in front of which are four messy cushions, where the rabbi used to circumcize wailing infants. The Hebrew psalms on the walls date from 1618 and were recovered in the 1960s, after the neo-Gothic restorer Josef Mocker (whose aesthetic sensitivities often recall those of the Communists) had obliterated them during restoration in 1883. Among the other features that ham-fisted Mocker restored to oblivion were the bloodstains of those who barricaded themselves in the synagogue during the 1389 pogrom. For 500 years the unwashed walls had been a memorial to those elegized by Avigdor Kara, 'destroyed in the House of God by the bloody sword of the enemy'.

The 14th-century bricks of the Old-New Synagogue's roof hide a mystery. Rabbi Loew's golem (whose full name was Joseph Golem according to Jewish legend) eventually ran amok, as man-made creatures do, and went on a rampage through the synagogue. Loew was holding a service in the synagogue when he heard the news and, after consulting the scriptures to work out whether golems could be deactivated on the Sabbath, he went stalking Joseph and eventually turned him back to clay. Suitably chastened by his dabblings with the laws of creation, he announced that he would never make another golem; lifeless Joseph was taken up to the steep brick roof, and has apparently been there ever since.

Interwoven mysteries still shroud the loft. Several curious rabbis are said to have sneaked up during the 19th century, all, needless to say, returning white as sheets and dumbstruck. However, the journalist Egon Erwin Kisch audaciously claimed to have been up and found nothing during the 1920s. The synagogue's small adjoining green contains *Moses Dreaming of Adam* (1905) by the Czech sculptor František Bílek, one of the few Baroque-influenced works by the artist.

Ceremonial House (Muzeum Terezína)

The neo-Romanesque Ceremonial House (1908) has two rooms containing an exhibition of artwork and poetry recovered from the Terezín ghetto in 1945. Terezín is better known to the oustside world as Theresienstadt, a 200-year-old fortress town that was transformed by the Nazis into a concentration camp for deported Jews from across Europe. The Nazis intended it to be the acceptable face of ghettoization, so representatives of the International Committee of the Red Cross were shown around here, as and when the organization took an interest in what was happening to Europe's Jews. The relatively lax regime meant that the camp became a bizarre centre of wartime Jewish culture, with clandestine newspapers, plays and concerts, and even a jazz band ('The Ghetto Swingers'), despite a Nazi decree outlawing such Judeo-Negroid deviancy. However, the laxness was very relative indeed: 85 per cent of the 140,000 people who passed through Terezín did not live to see the end of the war.

Klausen Synagogue (Klausova Synagoga)

The late 17th-century (remodelled in 1884) **Klausen Synagogue** (Klausova synagoga), on the other side of the entrance to the graveyard, was built on the site of a mess of schools and prayer halls, supposedly where Emperor Maximilian I began a ghetto walkabout in 1571. Rabbi Loew taught in an older building. As well as initiating Samuel and others into the secrets of the cabala, he practised his new-fangled pedagogical theories on the ghetto children. Loew believed that the familiar was a better starting-point than the unfamiliar, and that the general would be more easily understood than the particular, which in the 16th century would probably have thrown his classes into utter confusion. The synagogue now houses a small museum devoted to Jewish customs and traditions, including a tearful cycle of early 19th-century paintings devoted to the dolorous deathbed-to-grave duties of the Jewish Burial Societies (*Hevrah kadisha*).

Jewish Town Hall (Židovská Radnice)

The Jewish Town Hall (Židovská radnice; entrance on Maislova) was donated to the ghetto by rich Mayor Maisel in 1586. Originally Renaissance in style, it was given a Rococo revamp in 1765, when the tower and the clock below it were also added. The lower clock has Hebrew figures and, just as the Jewish alphabet is read from right to left, its hands turn backwards.

The town hall is still the administrative centre of Prague's Jewish community. For years it was a symbol of the moribund state of Jewish culture in the capital, but like so much else in the city it has fizzed back into unexpected life since 1989. There are still only about 1,500 registered Jews, but the number is growing and their average age (which used to be about 65) has begun to sink, in the nick of time. Since the revolution, parents have felt freer to discuss all sorts of topics that were once taboo, and many adolescents have recently found out for the first time that they have a Jewish heritage.

Maisel Synagogue (Maiselova Synagoga)

The **Maisel Synagogue** was another of the mayor's gifts to the ghetto, but it was dully re-modelled in neo-Gothic style at the end of the 19th century. The hall contains an exhibition devoted to the history of Jews in Bohemia from the 10th to the 18th century.

Beyond the Ghetto

Rudolfinum

The building's walnut-panelled and cut-glass rooms, ranging around a vast glass-roofed atrium, host temporary exhibitions; but the Rudolfinum is best known as the home of the Czech Philharmonic Orchestra. Its history is not purely cultural: the musicians perform under the globe-clustered chandeliers of the glorious Dvořák Hall (Dvořákův sál), which used to host the legislative sessions of the Czechoslovak parliament until that was prorogued by the Nazis in 1938. The building was also the scene of one of the more surreal episodes of the war. If you look up to the roof, you'll see sculptures lining the balustrades on each side. Each is of a famous musician and, according to the Czech (and Jewish) author Jiří Weil, *Reichsprotektor* Reinhard Heydrich erupted with fury when he noticed that the non-Aryan Felix Mendelssohn was among them. The order was barked that he be toppled, *schnell*, but the hapless workers to whom the task fell found that the statues were nameless. The solution seemed obvious—the Jew would be the one with the biggest nose—but disaster looms and Weil's novel takes off as they accordingly put a noose round the neck of Richard Wagner, the musical demiurge of fascism. No one's quite sure who is who nowadays. Mendelssohn is probably the character second from the riverside, as you face the main steps. According to Weil, Wagner is wearing a beret. However, careful inspection from the rooftop—unfortunately not yet opened to guided tours—reveals that the bewigged character on the street-side balustrade has the largest organ, by a long chalk.

Museum of Decorative Arts (Uměleckoprůmyslové Muzeum)

Open Tues–Sun 10–6, closed Mon; adm. Library open Mon–Fri 10–6, closed Sat–Sun; adm. Temporararily closed for renovation at the time of writing.

The museum was founded in 1885, inspired by the English Arts and Crafts Movement's dream of elevating public taste in the industrial age. Many of its holdings remain in storage, but the small collection on display is a sumptuous one: four rooms of household and palace furnishings from the Renaissance through to the mid-19th century. The work includes escritoires and cabinets inlaid with gemstones, a technique imported from Milan by the Miseroni family, invited to Prague by mineral-mystic Emperor Rudolf II; and timepieces by Erasmus Habermel, who had promised Rudolf the secret of perpetual motion. The rooms also contain Baroque bureaus and chests, pumped into fat curves by the same men who were designing Prague's 18th-century churches, such as Kilian Dienzenhofer and Giovanni Santini. The porcelain—a material that fascinated the 17th-century alchemists of Prague and Europe, according to Bruce Chatwin's *Utz*—includes works from Meissen, the first European factory to unlock the 1,000-year-old Chinese mystery; and from Munich and Vienna, produced after treacherous Dresden workers swiftly spilled the beans. Pewter pots, cobalt jugs and fussy teacups are scattered throughout, and the tapestries include Gobelins. The collection ends with the stark furniture of 18th-century neoclassicism, rediscovered by the Functionalists of the 1920s, and neo-Rococo work of the mid-1800s. The museum has neither the money nor the space to exhibit the rest of its huge holdings, but temporary displays are very occasionally held. They include thousands of posters and photographs, and one of the largest glass collections in the world. The latter begins with 14th-century Bohemian glass (which got off to a flying start under the patronage of Charles IV, another gem-fanatic) and runs through Venetian Renaissance glasswork to Art Nouveau and contemporary pieces.

St Agnes' Convent (Klášter sv. Anežky)/National Gallery of Medieval Art

Open Tues–Sun 10–6, closed Mon; adm.

The oldest remaining Gothic building in Prague, the former convent was founded by King Wenceslas I in 1233, on the urging of his sister Agnes (Anežka) who had just signed up with the Order of the Poor Clares. In 1235, she became the first abbess of the new convent. The Poor Clares were a sister community to the Franciscans and, like bees to a honeypot, the friars arrived next door in about 1240. The nuns happily cohabited with the monks for some 500 years, until stern Joseph II demanded that Prague's religious orders show what purpose they served. Poor Clares and Franciscans were mendicants, and as a result entirely useless. They left in 1782 and, over the next century, hundreds of stray families moved in along with a fair proportion of Prague's tortured-artist community, until the 1890s, when slum clearance loomed. Patriots declared that it was a matter of national pride that the convent be restored, and set up a fund for the purpose. The occupants were swiftly ejected; restoration was completed in 1980. Agnes was canonized as recently as 12 November 1989. The 750-year delay was because her body was never found, despite years of hopeful pottering—a serious impediment to sainthood in a Church that has sanctified mythical characters a few too many times. The long wait meant that, by the time she got the papal thumbs-up, the inevitable legend had arisen that her canonization would be accompanied by great marvels—a prophecy duly fulfilled when the Velvet Revolution began five days later. The first vaulted arcade as you walk clockwise around what was the convent's cloister (about 1360) is the best preserved, but throughout the convent the modern restorers have struck a happy balance between non-intervention and confident reconstruction where necessary.

On the fourth side of the court, a narrow passage leads into the oblong nave of the convent's **Church of the Holy Saviour** (Kostel sv. Salvátora), dating from 1240. King Wenceslas I's wife is buried under a slab in the centre, and on the right is a fake tomb for St Agnes, installed to keep up appearances after her canonization. Ahead is the presbytery (1270–80). On the capitals of the arched entrance are miniature heads of Bohemia's Přemysl kings (left) and queens (right). The building was the first in Bohemia to take up the lessons of French Gothic cathedral architecture—on a tiny but sublime scale. Light floods in through tall arched windows with simple tracery, under a high and graceful ribbed vault.

Through the arch on your left is the presbytery of the **Church of St Francis**; it was built some 70 years after the Holy Saviour, but the nuns had no time for the grandeur of late Gothic and stuck with the simple formula of their pocket presbytery. King Wenceslas I (not the Good one) is buried here. A door leads to a heavily restored hall, now used for concerts despite being covered by a wooden canopy that muffles all the best notes.

In late 2000, the convent re-opened as the **National Gallery of Medieval Art in Bohemia and Central Europe**. The earliest Gothic art in Bohemia dates from the beginning of the 14th century. The slender and elegant Madonnas, their faces half turned away, show how Bohemian art was beginning to escape the rigid formality of its Byzantine progenitors, with ever more robust representations of the human form. The break with Orthodox art had begun to occur across Western Europe; but the second feature marked the birth of Bohemia's independent artistic traditions and, during the few decades of Charles IV's rule, made its painting unique in Europe. Among the works displayed here is a gallant *St George*, plunging a standard into the mouth of a downed dragon (the flag has gone missing, but you can see it in the copy of the work that now stands in the Third Courtyard). The bronze statue, which dates from 1373, was designed as a free-standing work, one of the first in Europe to break out of the Gothic inability to conceive of sculpture (any more than painting or architecture) as an independent art form. That said, it's not easy to see what Europe's proto-sculptor had in mind: puny George is dwarfed by a remarkably life-like horse, recast with the rather different techniques and mentality of two centuries later. Also here is the *Vyšší Brod (Hohenfurth) Altarpiece*. The most notable feature of the nine paintings is their use of contrasting colours to create the illusion of depth, a century before the laws of perspective twinkled in the eyes of the clever Florentines. It's most remarkable in *The Descent of the Holy Ghost*: huddled Apostles swirl in a sea of reds and greens and indigoes, yet the space around them appears almost three-dimensional.

There are several works by **Master Theodoric**, the first of Bohemia's painters to emerge from misty anonymity—and as you gaze at them here, you'll understand why. Bohemian artists' experiments with colour values and facial modelling reach their culmination in these panels, which have a vitality that survives six centuries. Huge saints spread on to the edges of their medallion-studded frames; their powerful human ugliness crowds forward into the small room, and, with just the crow's feet of an eye or the downturn of a lip, Theodoric gives them an expressiveness deeper than anything that came before. The panels are from the Chapel of the Holy Cross at Charles IV's castle at Karlštejn, where there are over 100 more. Theodoric was the emperor's court painter—a radical choice for a man brought up amidst the delicacy of French art, and a choice that almost makes his other quirks seem rather unimportant.

With Charles' death and the coronation of his wastrel son Wenceslas IV in 1378, Bohemian art became increasingly refined. Sophistication replaced spiritual mystery, and the paintings of women take on a doll-like charm. Look, for example, at the languid rosy-cheeked depictions of SS Catherine, Mary Magdalene and Margaret in the *Třebon (Wittingau) Altarpiece* of *c.* 1380. Portrayals of the Madonna become heavily romanticized images of motherhood. The *St Vitus' Madonna* shows the phenomenon in all its treacle; it's also especially apparent in the sculptures. The trend towards humanization takes a different form in most of the depictions of men of late Gothic art: there are rows of hirsute or bald saints, while Christ suffers and is tortured with a greater intensity than ever before.

The central scene of the enormous **Tympanum of the Northern Portal of the Týn Church** (*c.* 1380–90) is the work of either Peter Parler or one of his team then working on St Vitus' Cathedral. Compare its sense of balance and perspective with the clumping neanderthals on either side, flagellating and crowning Christ, which were the work of lesser artists. The tympanum was originally gilded and painted, but the colour has disappeared, along with much of the top scene, where diabolical amphibians struggle with a rather unconcerned angel, ripping a poor soul apart in the process.

By the time you get to the *Lamentation* of *c.* 1510–20, the regular cast of characters mourning the dead Christ have a restraint that's still utterly Gothic, but they have begun to sprout the extra inches and shrunken pinheads that are characteristic of Mannerist art; and a strange sense of movement pervades the sculpture, from the rolling curtain of drapery to the Medusa-like locks of Christ. The floor ends with the carvings of Monogrammist I. P., a shadowy character who lived in Prague between 1520 and 1550, and who left behind a series of masterful woodcuts, showing all the devotion to north European foliage characteristic of the Danube School.

Franz Kafka's Birthplace (Rodiště Franze Kafky)

Open Mon–Fri 10–6, Sat 10–5, closed Sun; adm.

Only the Baroque portal survives from the house that heard baby Franz's first scream in 1883. The author spent almost all his life within the square mile around the house. He once stood near here, tracing with his finger while telling a friend, 'This narrow circle…encompasses my entire life'; and he wrote his final story as he lay dying in a flat over the Old Town Square, 'the most beautiful setting that has ever been seen on this earth'.

Except during the cultural thaw of the 1960s, no serious attempt was ever made to accommodate Kafka's bleak and incomprehensible world into the progressive literary canon of the Communists (which requires a happy ending). Only after 1989 did his books become freely available again. Few people bother to read them now that they're no longer banned, but Kafka as commodity has become hugely popular. The author's remarkable gaze, simultaneously as piercing as approaching headlamps and as doomed as a transfixed rabbit, stare out from T-shirts, mugs and postcards across the capital, while foreign film crews regularly troop into town to re-create his life and loves. The museum (in the ground floor of this building) contains a few photos, accompanying quotations, and a large selection of souvenir booklets and video cassettes.

Prague Castle and Hradčany

From its beginnings as a pagan mound to the day when Václav Havel was sworn in as president, Hradčany Castle has been the backdrop for Prague's history. Its neoclassical veneer now stretches half a lazy mile over the capital, but it's the onion domes and demented prongs of the cathedral, rising from its core, that hint at the true nature of what lies within. This area reveals the city's medieval heart and arcane mind: it includes St Vitus' Cathedral, the monument to a monomaniacal emperor and one of the grandest churches of the 14th century; and the Vladislav Hall, a late Gothic masterpiece with early Renaissance windows through which three men and the Thirty Years War were launched. Exploring the area allows you to sense the forces, large and small, that have made Prague tick so strangely for so many centuries. Every building has its secrets, from the laboratory of Emperor Rudolf II's alchemists, to the minuscule pastel cottages of the 400-year-old Golden Lane.

The shadow of the castle has always fallen between Hradčany and the city below. The district was founded in 1320 as a set of hovels in which the royal serfs could sleep and breed—and although it slipped out of the castellan's personal control in 1598, it never grew into a normal town. Locked into a slowly turning backwater, monks and nobles indulged their peccadilloes here for centuries; today, its cobbles and courtyards are a silent suburb of the castle which many visitors never see. Yet it contains the magnificent libraries and gallery of the Strahov Monastery, Prague's collection of pre-modern European art, the Baroque miracles of Prague's Loreto shrine, and the royal gardens, where the Habsburgs grew their tulips and built the most splendid Renaissance palace north of the Alps.

Lunch and Cafés

Malé Buddah (The Little Buddah), Úvoz 44. *Open 11–10, closed Mon.* A quasi-Buddhist enclave serving vegetarian snacks and lots of tea. Popular among mystical types.

Pálffy Palác, Valdštejnská 14. *Open Mon–Fri 11–11, Sat–Sun noon–midnight.* French food in a Baroque palace.

Sate, Pohořelec 3. *Open daily 11–10.* Spicy Indonesian food and fast service. Vegetarians and non-pork eaters can have the small menu customized to their taste. No cards.

U černého vola (The Black Ox), Loretánské nám. 1. *Open daily 10–10.* Tasty Velkopopovické beer and all the flesh and dumplings you could hope for, in a pub cooperative that donates its profits to a local school for the blind. No cards.

U ševce Matouše (Matthew the Cobbler), Loretánské nám. 4. *Open daily noon–4 and 6–11.* Recognizable by the copper boot that hangs in the vaulted arcade outside. Countless varieties of thick steak; excruciatingly slow service.

U zavěšené kávy (The Hanging Coffee), Radnické schody 7. *Open daily 11am–midnight.* An intimate and smoky café on the curve of the cobbled stairway leading up from Nerudova street. If you want to know what a hanging coffee is, it's all to do with generosity and community: ask someone to translate the little fable painted on the ceiling. No cards.

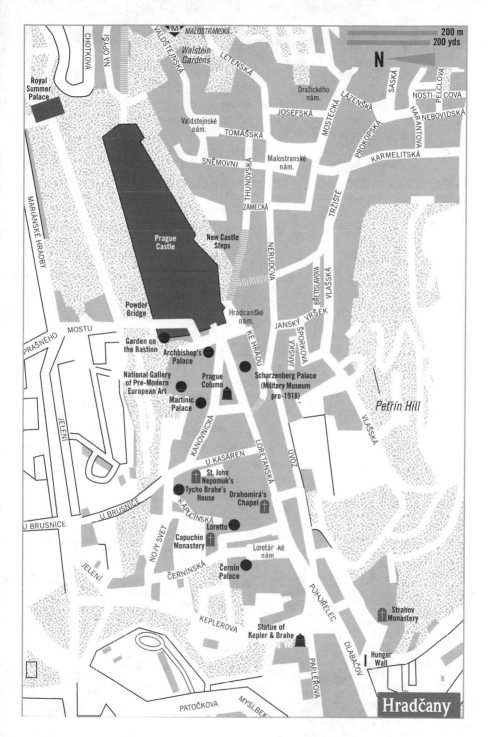

200 m
200 yds

N

CHOTKOVA

NA OPYŠI

VALDŠTEJNSKÁ

M MALOSTRANSKÁ

Walstein Gardens

LETENSKÁ

Royal Summer Palace

MARIÁNSKÉ HRADBY

Valdstejnské nám.

TOMÁŠSKÁ

JOSEFSKÁ

Dražického nám.

MOSTECKÁ

LÁZEŇSKÁ

SASKÁ

NOSTI-COVA

PELCLOVA

HARANTOVA

NEBOVIDSKÁ

PROKOPSKÁ

KARMELITSKÁ

SNĚMOVNI

THUNOVSKÁ

Malostranské nám.

ZÁMECKÁ

Prague Castle

New Castle Steps

NERUDOVA

VLAŠSKÁ

BŘETISLAVOVA

Powder Bridge

Hradcanské nám.

JANSKÝ VRŠEK

JANSKÁ

ŠPORKOVA

PRAŠNÉHO MOSTU

Garden on the Bastion

Archbishop's Palace

KE HRADU

National Gallery of Pre-Modern European Art

Prague Column

Scharzenberg Palace (Military Museum pre-1918)

VLAŠSKÁ

Petřín Hill

Martinic Palace

JELENÍ

KANOVNICKÁ

U KASÁREN

LORETÁNSKÁ

ÚVOZ

St. John Nepomuk's

Tycho Brahe's House

Drahomirá's Chapel

U BRUSNICE

U BRUSNICE

KAPUCÍNSKÁ

Loretto

NOVÝ SVĚT

Capuchin Monastery

Loretár ·ké nám.

JELENÍ

ČERNÍNSKÁ

Černín Palace

POHOŘELEC

Strahov Monastery

KEPLEROVA

Statue of Kepler & Brahe

DLABAČOV

Hunger Wall

PARLÉŘOVA

PATOČKOVA

MYSLBEK

Hradčany

75

Hills were much in demand in the dangerous Dark Ages. Prague's venerable chronicler Cosmas was particularly complimentary about the Hradčany hill, comparing its shape to 'the back of a dolphin or a sea-pig'; and he was writing in the 12th century, when the topography would have been clearer than today. Despite the legend that Prague's history began with the soothsaying of Libuše at Vyšehrad (*see* p.22), the castle is almost certainly the oldest continuously inhabited part of the city. The Přemysls, Bohemia's first dynasty, fortified the area towards the end of the 9th century. They coexisted happily with their neighbours, a community of cockerel-venerating pagans, until Prince Bořivoj got Christianity and founded a church. Relations became strained, the cock-worshippers revolted, and Bořivoj left town for a while. By the beginning of the 10th century, however, the family was firmly in control. Until the end of Bohemian independence in the 17th century, the castle was home to most of the oddballs to rule the country; behind the monotonous grandeur of its façade, it's a vast monument to centuries of regal madness. The castle's **façade** dates from 1753–75, when, after centuries of sieges, fires and royal building projects, it had become a crazed accretion that sorely displeased pernickety Queen Maria Theresa. Although the Habsburgs had moved to Vienna over a century before, she still regarded the palace (and Bohemia) as a pleasant little possession, and hired her Viennese court architect, Nicolo Pacassi, to clean it up. He filled in moats and added neoclassical façades with dull abandon although, behind it all, huge chunks of the medieval castle survive. At least Maria Theresa tried in her tasteless way to make the castle pretty; her son, Joseph II, attempted to turn it into a barracks, and succeeded in part. In the 19th century, the castle was all but deserted by the distant Habsburgs. The last emperor to spend any time here was Ferdinand the Gracious after his forced abdication in 1848. A. J. P. Taylor once claimed that Ferdinand's most significant statement was 'I am the Emperor and I want dumplings'. He brought little glory to the castle but ended his days here. In 1918 it became the seat of the president—a tradition maintained by the Communists, and one that continues today.

The **castle guards**, now resplendent in their bright blue uniforms, wore dull khaki until 1989, but then Václav Havel moved in as president and got a friend, Theodor Pištěk, to design something more jolly. Pištěk's last major job had been as costume designer for *Amadeus*, and

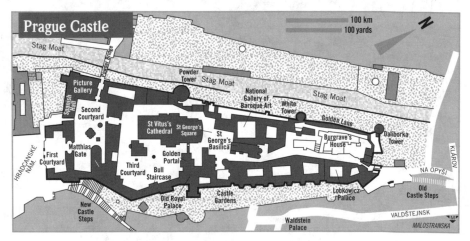

the gulping guards look dimly aware that they are the victims of a presidential prank. Another of Havel's wheezes during the humorous honeymoon that followed the Velvet Revolution was to dress the brass band in red and have them play a tune every Sunday morning. If you're here at midday, keep your eyes left, and on the first floor you'll see them emerge on to the window ledges to blast out a lilting classical piece composed by Michal Kocáb, rock musician and erstwhile MP for central Prague.

First Courtyard (První Nádvoří)

Between the pine flagpoles is the **Matthias Gate** (1614), thought to have been designed by Vincenzo Scamozzi. The Vicenza-born architect worked in the service of Emperor Matthias and visited Prague from 1599 to 1600. He was a close follower of Andrea Palladio, but the elegant serenity of the master's influence gave way in Scamozzi's later work to some of the earliest hints of the Baroque—and this grand gateway is one of the first signs of the new architecture to have appeared in the capital. The Roman triumphal arch is now unhappily immured in a building dividing the first two courtyards, but it originally stood proud and alone between two bridges crossing the outer moats of the castle.

A glass doorway on the right leads to the **Presidential Rooms** and on the left is the **Hall of Columns** (Sloupová síň), built between 1924 and 1926. Three rows of Ionic columns line the walls around the stone staircase, which marches up to doubled iron doors under a copper-panelled roof. The hall is the work of Jože Plečnik (*see* pp.35), who did more to transform the appearance of the castle than anyone since Pacassi. He was appointed Castle Architect in 1920, with an unenviable brief: to modernize the castle in a way unimposing enough to suit the democratic ideals of the new Czechoslovakian state, dignified enough to honour that democracy's president, and tactful enough to complement the existing architectural scheme of the castle. In the context of the monumentalism that surrounded him, it's a balancing act that he carried off with aplomb. The staircase leads up to the **Spanish Hall** (Španělský sál). The hall is used for concerts but otherwise accessible to the public only occasionally. When it is opened, the queues of Praguers that snake through are immense, all curious to see the stucco-encrusted room that used to host the regular meetings of the Communist Party Central Committee. (Before 1989, a tank stationed outside would warn them to keep away.) Interest has been piqued further by the news that in 1995 Václav Havel showed the garish neo-Baroque interior of mirrors and chandeliers to the Rolling Stones, who promptly got their lighting manager to install a computer console and dimmer switches.

Second Courtyard (Druhé Nádvoří)

In the second courtyard is the **Chapel of the Holy Cross**, designed by Nicolo Pacassi, a Baroque fountain (1686) and the disused well. Through the gateway the **Powder Bridge** crosses the Stag Moat, the northern flank of the castle (*see* p.90). The **Castle Stables**, once the home of 300 thoroughbred horses, now thoroughly sanitized, house temporary exhibitions and the **Picture Gallery**.

Picture Gallery (Obrazárna)

Open Tues–Sun 10–6, closed Mon; adm.

The gallery's holdings, including some works of art kept in the castle since the reign of Emperor Rudolf II, are worth a brief visit to get a feel of the emperor's eclectic tastes, and the decline of his Habsburg successors. Rudolf summoned artists from across the Continent to Prague, and the court that he assembled became one of the centres of European Mannerism. His collectomania became legendary, even in an age when curiosity-cabinets-cum-art-galleries were a dime a dozen among Europe's nobles. No inventory survives but, as well as rhinoceros horns, nails from the Ark and the like, Rudolf is thought to have installed some 3,000 pictures and 2,500 sculptures. The gallery was pillaged by occupying Protestant forces during the Thirty Years War: a moderate pruning by the Saxons in 1631–2 was followed by a systematic ransack by Swedes in 1648. (Their naughty Queen Christina later sold most of the loot, reverted to Catholicism and lived off the proceeds in Rome.) The crowning insult came in 1782, when Joseph II publicly auctioned off most of the remaining works.

Perhaps unsurprisingly, most of the works that survived the barbarians and bargain-hunters were of limited appeal. The Swedes and Saxons were discerning hordes, judging from what they left behind. Many lay around in the castle for several centuries before being reattributed in the late 1960s by X-ray-wielding scientists; but they always included a few gems.

The portrait skills of one of Rudolf's court artists, Hans von Aachen, were displayed in two rather atypical works, showing none of the stylized proportions or mild eroticism for which he's best known. It probably had something to do with the subject-matter: his *Head of a Girl* is touched with the affection that a father might be expected to show his daughter, while his full-length *Portrait of Emperor Matthias* flatters the peacock-grandeur of the hated brother who usurped Rudolf's throne. (Aachen waited for Rudolf to die, and then jumped on to Matthias' payroll.) The gallery contained a bust of Rudolf himself by his sculptor, Adriaen de Vries; and the strange work of Joris Hoefnagel, who painted innumerable studies of creatures of the deep and crawlers of the earth, showing a fascination with the order (and decay) of things that was typical of Rudolfine Mannerism (*see* pp.32).

There's an intriguing *Amnon and Tamar* by Lucio Massari. The saga of incest and rape is mysteriously treated as a story of unrequited love: topless Tamar gazes wistfully at her hunk of a half-brother, while the men at the door look as though they're about to break up a tryst rather than leave the scene of the imminent crime. An Oedipal sphinx sitting cryptic under the bed is about the clearest reminder of the incestuous theme. Other highlights are Guido Reni's *Centaur Nessus Abducting Deianeira*, Gentileschi's *Triumphant Amor*, a *Flagellation of Christ* by Tintoretto, Titian's *Toilet of a Young Lady*, and four paintings by Veronese: the *Portrait of a Jeweller, Jacob König* shows his shrewd friend who landed the job of Venetian buyer for Rudolf II. Most impressive of all is the vast *Gathering on Mount Olympus* by Rubens—an exuberant feast of divine nudity in which the gaze of ashen-faced Cassandra, peeking out from the wall of flesh, seems to have been the only concession to a moral message that fun-loving Rubens was able to make. Look out too for the dignified portraits by Jan Kupecký, and an excellent *Still Life with Cards and Letter* by Samuel van Hoogstraten (1627–78). Hoogstraten spent his life exploring the effects of perspective, and this work, an almost abstract composition, is imbued with a sense of experimentation immediately apparent to the 21st-century mind.

The gallery also owns some astonishingly bad portraits of assorted Austrians and Spaniards. Rudolf II may not have been the healthiest of Habsburgs, but if you find the portraits of Marie Eleonoro and Marie Leopoldina you will realize it was with these two that the inbreeding finally took hold.

Third Courtyard (Třetí Nádvoří)

The Third Courtyard contains a large granite obelisk (a memorial to the dead of the 1914–18 war), and, at the far southern end, the offices of the president. On the southern façade of the church is the central **tower**, which dominated the front of the cathedral until its modern completion. It's almost 100m high, although a fair chunk of that (38m) is made up of the multi-storey Baroque dome added by Pacassi in 1770. Four bells hang in the tower, of which the largest is **Sigismund**, an 18-ton monster on the first floor. Bells caused no end of trouble in the 16th century. They couldn't be touched by anyone impure (a category that included all women), and pubescent boys dressed in white had to be engaged to transport them from foundry to belfry. Sigismund, dating from 1549, was the successor to two earlier bells. The first was dragged on sledges from the Old Town by hundreds of pretty urchins in 1534; after several days, they got it to the gate of the castle, only for it to roll out of control and break into pieces. No chances were taken with the next one, which was cast in the castle grounds and hung in 1538—three years before smashing to the ground during the great fire of 1541. Sigismund finally made it in 1549. Like the carillon of Loreto, it survived the great Austro-Hungarian bell massacre of 1918 (*see* p.97) and can be heard booming across Hradčany on Sunday mornings. The ornate golden grille in the arched window dates from Rudolf II's reign (hence the 'R' just above)—so do the two clocks, the higher of which shows the hour, the lower the minute.

To the right of the tower is the **Golden Portal**, once the main entrance to the cathedral. The emphasis on the southern façade is unusual in church design—Charles effectively turned the cathedral round, so that Wenceslas could have the prominence that he deserved (his chapel is just to the right of the doorway). Under the bullet-shaped arches, in another of Peter Parler's touches, ribs spray into the air from the door, again inspired by England and again unique for its time on the Continent. Above the gate is a **mosaic of the Last Judgment** (1370–71) made from thousands of shimmering semi-precious stones and coloured glass. It's thought to have been pieced together by Venetians after a cartoon drawn up by artists in Charles' court, and is the largest on any Gothic building other than Orvieto Cathedral. Kneeling below Christ the Judge are patron saints; to the left, on Christ's right hand, the luckier resurrected corpses emerge from their coffins; to the right, wretched sinners wail and gnash their teeth as they're herded into Hell. The not-so-humble suppliants on either side of the central arch, crowned and ermined, are Charles and his fourth wife, Elizabeth of Pomerania.

Directly opposite the mosaic is the **Bull Staircase**, another ingenious Plečnik construction, which runs down to the Garden on the Ramparts. The garden contains benches, pavilions and two obelisks that commemorate the miracle which followed Prague's third defenestration in 1618 (*see* p.27), when the Virgin Mary supposedly interceded to save the victims from a sticky end.

St Vitus' Cathedral (Chrám Svatého Víta)

> *Open April–Oct daily 9–5, Nov–March daily 9–4; an admission fee is charged for entrance to the western end of the church.*

Prince Wenceslas (a.k.a. Good King) founded the first church, a rotunda, on the site in 929 after receiving St Vitus' arm as a token of friendship from the Saxon King Henry I. He dedicated the church to the saint in honour of the limb, but also because he hoped to convert the local pagans, who worshipped a four-headed war and fertility god called Svantovít (St Vitus in Czech is *svatý Vít*). The trick was made even easier by the fact that Svantovít liked cocks, a symbol shared by Vitus. Between 1060 and 1096 the church was enlarged into a basilica, but it was under Charles IV that the present construction, one of the finest 14th-century churches in Europe, began to take shape. Building commenced in 1344, months after the future emperor had persuaded his ex-tutor, Pope Clement VI, to promote Bohemia to an archbishopric. Charles hoped to make Prague into a great imperial metropolis, and the cathedral was to be its centre-piece. He turned first to a French architect, summoning Matthew of Arras from the papal court at Avignon. Matthew built the east end of the chancel on standard French lines but, luckily for Prague's Gothic architecture, he died in 1352. His replacement, called to the court from Swabia, was **Peter Parléř**, the scion of a distinguished family of German masons. His new plan for the nave inaugurated a half-century during which Prague became the most significant centre of Gothic architecture in Europe. Although the church was unfinished at his death in 1399, most of its notable features are his work. The Hussite wars brought construction to a halt, and the building was closed with a temporary wall which stayed for centuries.

The entire western part of the church, including the grand façade, was only completed between 1871 and 1929. Prague's neo-Gothic mania at the end of the 19th century did its fair share of damage to the town, but the architects' efforts here can hardly be faulted. Their work completed a symbol of Bohemian history, and gave Prague's skyline a focus it had lacked for 500 years. Although there's an almost too perfect industrial precision to some of the pinnacles and sculptures on the façade, you would be hard-pressed to find the joins in most of the building. As you launch your gaze through the mammoth pillars lining the noble arch of the nave, you're in the monument to the greatest king ever to rule Bohemia. Charles, on his way to becoming one of the most powerful men in Europe, almost certainly hoped to be canonized after his death *à la* Louis IX. But he was taking no chances. The Black Death was marching across Europe, and Prague's clerics were warning that the Apocalypse would take place some-time between 1365 and 1375. To add insult to prospective injury, one of the city's leading preachers had recently accused Charles of being the Antichrist. As well as putting his capital firmly on the medieval map, Charles' magnificent offering to God was private insurance that, when weighed in the balance, he would not be found wanting.

The first three chapels on each side date from the early 20th century. Although topped up with older decoration, they are filled with neo-Gothic sculpture that's as lifeless as St Ludmilla, throttled and serene in the first chapel to your right. The stained glass is another modern addi-tion dating from the 1930s. The original Gothic church is thought to have had only one coloured window, and its bold use of clear light was one way in which architect Parléř broke from the church's French origins. The windows have a certain garish splendour, but here at least it's hard not to wonder how different a completed 14th-century church might have been. The window in the third chapel was paid for by an insurance company, and celebrates prudent risk-assessment with the psalm *Those Who Sow in Tears Shall Reap in Joy*.

The original part of the building contains the tower of the old cathedral from which you can get the highest view in Prague, as breathtaking as you would expect from a climb of 287 steps (*open April–Sept; adm*). On the left of the building is the **choir** (1557–61), designed by Ferdinand I's court architect, Bonifaz Wohlmut, and surmounted by a tremendous organ dating from the later 18th century. Originally, it closed the western end of the church, but the whole shebang was moved in the 1920s.

Just to the right is the shining goldmine of the **Chapel of St Wenceslas**, built between 1362 and 1367 by Peter Parléř. Gentle Wenceslas died at the hands of his brother Boleslav in 935, and has wielded more influence from his grave than he ever did during his life. After killing him, Boleslav cheekily decided that to be the brother of a martyr was no bad thing, and he had the remains transferred to the original rotunda in 939. Charles exploited his ancestor in a far more systematic fashion. From the example of St Louis, he had learnt how useful national cults were in cementing together a kingdom, and even before his arrival in Prague he began to turn his ancestor's grave into a shrine. He had the old tomb decorated with silver statues of the Apostles (which his father, John of Luxembourg, immediately pawned to finance his latest foreign adventure); and when the cathedral was begun, he had Parléř change his plans for the nave to build this chapel on the site of the original grave.

There are two doorways. The northern portal in the nave contains the ring to which the saint allegedly clung as he was hacked to death, although the church where the deed occurred, outside Prague, has always indignantly claimed to have the knocker concerned. The arch is flanked by sculptural warnings—on the left, a crumbling figure of Peter denying Christ, and on the right a vicious demon yanking Judas' tongue from his mouth—but the interior is an inviting mosaic of gilt plaster and semi-precious stones, unevenly framing and crowding over the painted Passion scenes below. The chapel is a Gothic painting in three glittering dimensions, suffused with the shot of mysticism that ran through the otherwise eminent worldliness of Charles. The number of stones (about 1,370) corresponds to the date of its construction (and, if Prague's clerics were to be believed, the rough date of the Second Coming); and if you can lay your hands on a Bible, take a look at ch. 21 of the 'Book of Revelations'. The chapel is a model of the Heavenly Jerusalem, whose arrival would herald the end of history.

The full ramifications of the original decoration, which Charles illuminated with 144 perpetually burning candles, would have been hard for the modern mind to appreciate; but impressive as the chapel is, there have been some changes over the years. The emperor and his wife are still kneeling near the crucified Christ over the chapel altar, but the (heavily restored) paintings on the upper part of the wall date from 1509. They show scenes from the *Legend of St Wenceslas*, as well as portraits of Vladislav II of Jagellon and his rather unappealing wife Anne, who flank the arched window. The **tomb** in the centre was once as gold-plated and jewel-encrusted as the rest of the chapel (and contained small reliquaries for 18 more saintly scraps) but Charles' sons proved as impious as their grandfather, John of Luxembourg, had been. Wenceslas IV melted down bits and pieces to make gold coins, while Sigismund turfed the saint out and carted away the whole coffin during his occupation of the castle in 1420. Wenceslas' semi-precious home dates from the early 20th century, and represents one of the rare occasions when Prague's pedantic neo-Gothic restorers didn't even try to match the original work.

The chapel also contains a Gothic **statue** of the saint by Peter Parléř's nephew, Henry; some more odd stained glass (a translucent vision from the late 1960s); and in the south-east corner is a sanctuarium, built here by Charles so that Wenceslas could guard the cathedral's wine and wafers. The emperor also gave the chapel tremendous secular significance by establishing a new coronation ceremony linked closely to the cult of the saint. Much of it took place here, and the forged door in the south-west corner leads to a small room containing the old **crown jewels** of Bohemia. You'll have a job getting to see them, though: the door is closed with seven different locks and to track down the scattered keys you'd have to sweet-talk some fairly imposing figures, ranging from the President of the Republic to the Archbishop of Prague. In any case, any pleb who puts them on signs his own death warrant. The legend was last fulfilled (or just possibly created) in 1942, when *Reichsprotektor* Reinhard Heydrich is said to have sneered with Teutonic arrogance when the grizzled guardian of the jewels warned him of the curse; shortly after trying on the crown, he was cut down by assassins. An extension of the story, which begins to damage its own case, is that Heydrich's two sons also had a go. One died a fairly predictable death on the eastern front, and Nemesis apparently caught up with the other at the end of a mad stallion's hoof.

Good King Wenceslas was one of the first buried here but, like any cathedral worth its salt, St Vitus' in its heyday served as a necropolis for the corpses of the high and mighty. In the central aisle is the white marble **Habsburg Mausoleum** (1566–89), containing the remains of the first two generations to rule Bohemia. Ferdinand I died in Vienna, but the family decided to honour St Vitus' with his posthumous presence to shore up their shaky claim to be the hereditary rulers of Bohemia. His wife joined him, and in 1577 Maximilian II arrived here at the head of a funeral procession that chroniclers noted was the grandest that Prague had ever seen. All three characters were sculpted sleeping on top of the tomb, next to each other and in full regalia. Maximilian's peculiar son, Rudolf II, made his own arrangements (*see* p.83), as well as those of his mother when she died in 1603. The funeral procession that he organized for her was a suitably lavish affair, marred only by the fact that Rudolf himself failed to turn up, despite plans to attend in disguise.

Yet the Habsburg contingent only topped up a church that was already brimming with human tissue, thanks to Charles IV's mania for collecting relics. Cultured and cosmopolitan he may have been, but he was truly medieval when it came to saintly souvenirs. On his jaunts abroad, he begged, borrowed and, according to legend, stole (once, from the pope) about 200 sacred objects. When his nephew, Charles V of France, asked the emperor in 1356 for help in recovering his father (John the Bountiful, who had been confiscated by the Black Prince at the Battle of Poitiers), Charles agreed to mediate with the victorious English only after being given two thorns from Christ's crown and splinters of the True Cross. In 1354 he proudly wrote to Bohemia's first archbishop, 'I do not think that you will find another place in the whole of Europe, except Rome, where pilgrims can seek out so many holy relics as in the cathedral of St Vitus.' Prague did not yield second place to Rome for want of trying.

You can contemplate this in **St Andrew's Chapel**, next to that of Wenceslas. The chapel used to contain a picture known as the *vera icon* (true image). The Vatican also has one—a messy state of affairs, given that the *vera icon* is the miraculously imprinted hanky used by the (anagrammatical) St Veronica to wipe the sweat off Jesus on the road to Calvary. The story goes that Charles set his heart on the thing and asked if he could have it; no way, said the pope, so the cunning emperor asked if he could copy it instead. The weak point of the story is that the pope trusted Charles enough to agree—otherwise, it's not hard to believe the punch line, that the emperor returned the copy and kept the original. The official castle catalogue always used to cast some doubt on its miraculous provenance by listing the work as a 'Gothic panel painting from about the year 1400'; it's a shame that the authorities have now robbed you of the chance to decide for yourself.

In the next chapel is the entrance to the **crypt of the cathedral**. The tour is a confusing journey through the convoluted architectural history of the cathedral. Columns and

82   *Prague: Prague Castle and Hradčany*

tombstones unearthed over the years litter your path as you wend through the 11th-century crypt of the basilica, the cathedral's foundations and those of its original choir, 20th-century masonry, and the northern apse of Wenceslas' rotunda. A plan of the two older churches in the penultimate room may help you piece together the puzzle, although it's hardly less complicated. The wooden steps take you back into the nave, but first take a look at the **royal crypt** in the room to the right, next to more foundations.

The spotlit sepulchre is the bizarre resting place of Bohemia's greatest kings, silently awaiting Gabriel's trumpet in an avant-garde collection of stainless steel and granite sarcophagi—all were given a postmortem and reinterred here during the final stages of the church's completion in 1928–35. You'll find Charles IV here, next to his four wives, who have all been tossed into the same stone box. Rudolf is in his original pewter coffin, but he's a lost and lonely character even in death. He is separated from his forebears (in the mausoleum upstairs), his internal organs (in the Saxon chapel) and his successors (who deserted Prague altogether after the Battle of the White Mountain and now lie in the Capuchines in Vienna).

From the crypt, you emerge back into the centre of the nave, a good point from which to compare the medieval part of the cathedral with its 20th-century extension. From here you can see one of Parléř's most significant contributions to the design of the church, the net-vault of the choir, which breaks free of the purely practical concern of cross-ribbed vaulting (the need to stop the roof from falling down) and shows the move towards abstraction that came to characterize late Gothic architecture across Europe. Parléř is thought to have borrowed his ideas from England, possibly after Charles IV's daughter married King Richard II. The work is actually a model of restraint compared to the exuberance of English vault design over the previous century; nevertheless, it was the first time that the ideas had been used in a major Continental church. Up in the triforium are a series of busts by Parléř and his workshop. They're among the earliest portraits in Gothic art, but you'll need binoculars to see them properly. As well as Charles and family, Parléř and Matthew of Arras are represented—an unusual honour for the time and an indication of the respect that Charles had for his architects.

The line of chapels on the right continues with the **Royal Oratory**, designed for Vladislav II by his court architect, Benedict Ried, and built in 1493. The vault and the entrance are decorated with fantastic branch-like ribs, gnarled stone bows bent across the vault. Ried, like Parléř, had radical ideas when it came to vaulting, as he showed to magnificent effect in his design for the Vladislav Hall (*see* p.85). Opposite the **Waldstein Chapel**, containing the Gothic tombstones of the cathedral's two architects, is a relief showing what looks to be a very orderly iconoclastic rampage through the cathedral, which occurred in 1619.

You're now entering the oldest part of the church, but to go any further you have to get round the incandescent Baroque **tomb of St John Nepomuk**, fashioned from 3,700 pounds of solid silver after a design by Fischer von Erlach the Younger. What John would have made of it all can only be guessed. Larger-than-life angels support the coffin; the swooning saint clutches a crucifix above the lid; and four heavenly bodies float over it all, dangling from wall-brackets. The cleric had been venerated in an unassuming way from the moment he was lobbed off the Charles Bridge in 1383 (*see* p.60), but three centuries later he suddenly found himself at the heart of the Jesuit drive to re-Catholicize Bohemia. The monks needed a native saint, and John fitted the bill—he was untainted (to both sides) by any involvement in Europe's religious schism, he was Czech, and he was dead. In 1715, a canonization committee gathered in

Prague to investigate the old legend that John had been martyred for refusing to tell King Wenceslas IV what the queen had said in the confession box. When his rotting coffin was exhumed from his chapel (opposite the tomb), the confessor's skull was found to contain a lump of organic matter. The committee's three doctors examined it, solemnly swore that it was John's incorrupt tongue—a useful organ, given the basis of his proposed canonization—and the 100 or so commissioners hurried to Rome with the news. The pope promptly beatified John—and sensing that they had backed a winner, the Jesuits pulled out all the stops. Six years later their doctors declared that not only was his tongue still throbbing with life but growing steadily. That clinched it, and in 1729 John was canonized. To make his cult even more palatable to Praguers, the Jesuits filled the castle fountains with beer and wine on his annual feast day. They couldn't quite get the cathedral renamed but, after John was reburied in this awe-inspiring piece of kitsch in 1736, it effectively became the high altar. Curious scientists examined the tongue in the early 1980s and declared that it was actually a desiccated brain. Sadly, it's no longer available for public worship, having been removed to an inaccessible part of St Vitus' treasury. It apparently resembled the condom-like object that is being pointed out by the priggish cherub on top of the coffin.

The next chapel along contains yet more bodily remains: the two Přemysl Otakars in tombs sculpted by Parléř and, under the slab marked with the Habsburg double-headed eagle, a vault containing Rudolf II's exiled viscera. There are also fragments of a mural painting (*The Adoration of the Magi*) which may have been painted by Master Theodoric, court artist to Charles IV (*see* p.32). As you pass the centre of the cathedral, pay your respects to the **altar to St Vitus** on your left, especially if you're afflicted with an annoying twitch or you've been bitten by a mad dog. Vitus hasn't done well over the years, outshone first by Wenceslas and then by John Nepomuk, and his tomb is an insignificant 19th-century affair. At least Charles IV did him the courtesy of cobbling together a full body.

On the left as you pass the next two chapels are two more **oak reliefs**, dating from 1631, which show the flight from Prague of Frederick of the Palatinate (motto: I Know Not How to Turn) after the defeat of his Protestant armies at the Battle of the White Mountain. Malicious they may be—they were commissioned by the victorious Ferdinand II—but both are lovely snapshots of 17th-century Prague, all the king's horses and men galloping in hasty retreat from the medieval castle across the bridge and through the Old Town Square.

On the right just past the choir is an amazing **wooden altar** (1896–9) by the Czech sculptor František Bílek. Its simplicity, and the pain that it exudes, owes much to the humanistic traditions of late Gothic art in Bohemia, but Bílek's Symbolism developed a spiritual language independent of any single religion or country. His *Crucifixion* is a masterpiece: Christ rising slowly from the ropes and nails of his cross, locked into meditation while a heedless humanity despairs at his feet; and on the altar, the return of hope, portrayed by a single arm stretching up with its offering. Bílek's sculpture is a modern addition that works; the Art Nouveau stained glass by Alfons Mucha (a 1931 comic-strip celebrating SS Cyril and Methodius) is one that doesn't. You're back in the 20th-century half of the cathedral. The chapel now contains the grave of Cardinal Tomášek, Archbishop of Prague until his death in 1992, and an ever-more vocal focus of opposition in the years before the 1989 revolution. In 1987, the Communists mocked him as a 'general without an army'; by the time of his death, they had lost the war and the mourners who attended the funeral here included two underground fighters who had become presidents, Václav Havel and Lech Walesa.

Old Royal Palace (Starý Královský Palác) and Vladislav Hall (Vladislavský Sál)

Open April–Oct daily 9–4.45, Nov–March daily 9–3.45; adm.

Since the castle was first fortified, this has been the site of the royal residence, and inside are three layers of palace, spanning the Romanesque and the Renaissance. The older halls are now below ground level—a feature you come to expect in Prague—as a result of the original unevenness of the Third Courtyard, which sloped steeply towards the east until paved during Rudolf II's reign. The topmost palace, and the one you'll see first, is the **Vladislav Hall**.

The hall was built between 1486 and 1502 by Benedict Ried, court architect to Vladislav II of Jagellon. Over the previous century the palace here had been deserted: in 1383 rollicking Wenceslas IV had taken the toadies and flunkies of his court to the high jinks to be found in the Old Town, where he built a new Royal Court, and the castle fell into ruin. For decades the only visitors were passing Hussite mobs or the invading army of Wenceslas' brother, Sigismund. But in 1483 life returned suddenly. Vladislav was now king, and city pressures had become too much—his Catholic officials had just been defenestrated by Hussites from the Old Town Hall, and the final straw came when he opened the windows of the Royal Court one morning to be greeted by an arrow carrying a scrawled message which roughly translates as 'Get out of town, Polack'. He left in a hurry, crossing the Vltava by boat at night, and wasted no time in fortifying and expanding the desolate castle.

Vladislav built a new hall above the old palace partly because of his belief—all too often disproved in the castle's history—that 'high' meant 'safe'; but it was also the expression of the worldly grandeur that now permeated the court. The structure represents the culmination of the Bohemian late Gothic style named after the Polish king (*see* p.85). In its magnificent vault, ribs shoot up like monstrous tendrils from its wall shafts, intertwining across five gently articulated bays and somehow meandering into star-like flower petals in the centre. Ried used anything that seemed to fit the opulence required: the broad rectangular windows are pure Renaissance, sneaking into Bohemia years before the Italian influence began to be felt in Western Europe; spiralling pillars and classical entablatures frame the doors of the hall.

Surrounded by the almost tangible space of the hall (62 x 16 x 13m) you understand the awe of the chronicler who breathlessly recorded, 'There was no other building like it in all of Europe, none that was longer, broader and higher and yet had no pillars.' Horses fitted in here comfortably; mounted stewards and cupbearers lined the sides during banquets; and tournaments were a regular feature. Under the reign of Rudolf II, it became a bazaar; a contemporary engraving shows it full of high-hatted and haggling merchants, and even a small scrum of bargain-hunting Persians. Since 1918, the President of the Republic has been sworn in here, and this was where Václav Havel took the oath of office that ended 40 years of Communist rule in December 1989.

To the right of the entrance is a door leading to the **Ludvík Wing**, built in similar style by Ried in 1502–9, and named after Vladislav's successor, Ludvík of Jagellon (ruled 1516–26). Inside, on the same floor as the hall, are the two rooms of the **Czech Chancellery**. Through the portal of the first room (marked with Ludvík's initials) is the chamber which the chancellor and the governors used to deliberate under the Habsburgs. It was here that Prague's most significant **defenestration** took place on 23 May 1618. Count Thurn and other Bohemian Protestant noblemen confronted the two hated Catholic governors appointed by Ferdinand I, and after explaining their grievances tossed both out of the window to your left. According to a contemporary account of events, 'They loudly screamed "Ach, ach oweh!" and attempted to hold on to the narrow window ledge, but Thurn beat their knuckles until they were both obliged to let go.' Their secretary, Fabricius, protested and followed them down. All three plunged some 50ft, but landed more or less comfortably in a dungheap. After interviewing a number of witnesses, most of whom swore that they had seen the Virgin Mary parachute the men to safety, the Church declared it a miracle. Following the defeat of Bohemian Protestantism at the Battle of the White Mountain, two obelisks were set up in what's now the Garden on the Ramparts to commemorate the glorious event. They mark where the governors came to rest. No similar honour was accorded the humble Fabricius.

Through the first door on the opposite side of the hall, a staircase spirals up to the offices of the **New Land Rolls**, a land registry institution similar to the Norman *Domesday Book*. The walls and ceilings are decorated with scores of colourful crests, the emblems of the clerks between 1561 and 1774. In the next room is a mid-16th-century cabinet containing the rolls themselves, highly unofficial-looking hand-painted tomes decorated with rainbows, planets and various flora and fauna.

Back in the hall, the second door to the left leads into the **Diet**. Originally part of the palace below, it was rebuilt by Ried in about 1500 only to be completely destroyed by the fire of 1541. Ferdinand I's architect, Bonifaz Wohlmut, designed the present room between 1559 and 1563, copying Ried's vaulting and making his own contribution to the hall's Renaissance motifs with two mutant Doric pilasters, twisted like liquorice sticks into three dimensions around the door. The Diet was the supreme court in medieval times, and the place where the Estates met until 1848; if the emperor wanted to meet his Czech subjects (which was not often after the Battle of the White Mountain), they all assembled here. Nobles and clergy sat on either side of the central throne. In case the town representatives were in any doubt about their insignificance in Habsburg Bohemia, they were given one collective vote and left to watch the proceedings from the gallery on your left.

To the left of the Diet is the entrance to the **All Saints' Chapel**. It was built by Peter Parléř as part of Charles IV's palace, but after the 1541 fire its vault was rebuilt, and Baroque additions have left it an unimpressive appendage to the rest of the hall. Opposite is an **observation terrace**, a popular spot from which to look for any lingering remains of the defenestratees' dungheap (unfortunately its rough location is hidden by a covered passage). On the right is the **Riders' Staircase**, built by Ried in around 1500. Knights summoned to amuse the diners with a spot of horseplay would storm up these shallow steps on their steeds. The pointed cutaway section on the portal was to make sure that nothing embarrassing happened to their decorative plumes.

At the foot of the staircase, steps lead down to the predecessors of the Vladislav Hall. At the very lowest level is the Romanesque gloom of the 12th-century **Soběslav Palace**. Impressive though it must have been back in the 12th century, to the modern mind its gloomy arches are reminiscent of nothing so much as a short stretch of railway tunnel. Its most interesting structural feature is a Romanesque fireplace.

On the intermediate level are a number of chambers from various palatial extentions built between the mid-13th and the late 14th century. The largest room is the **Charles Hall**, built by Emperor Charles IV in the mid-1300s. Charles had little use for the sombre cavern that he found awaiting him when he moved to Prague. He used it to store the wines that he brought back from his travels, and built a new palace on top. Although only this hall survives, its high-ribbed grandeur can still hint at a building that was designed to outshine the Paris Louvre, in keeping with the emperor's peaceful megalomania.

St George's Convent (Klášter Svatého Jiří)/National Gallery of Baroque Art

Open Tues–Sun 10–6, closed Mon; adm.

The gallery is housed in the Benedictine St George's Convent, the first in Bohemia, founded by Mlada, the sister of Boleslav II, in 973. She went to Rome to ask the pope to make Bohemia a bishopric, and he not only agreed but also gave her an abbess's staff to take home. The nuns are long gone though, having thrown off their habits when the fanatically enlightened despot Joseph II abolished all the empire's religious institutions in 1782. He turned the convent into a penitentiary for bewildered priests to consider the error of their ways. Despite its venerable age, successive reconstructions have left it a dull building.

One of the most striking works in the collection is the *Epitaph of the Goldsmith Müller*, by Bartholomeus Spranger, which will ambush you with its rather incredible eroticism. Sex permeated the art of the emperor's court—generally in its kinkier forms—and here Spranger has turned Christ into a coquettish pin-up, sly, pouting and wrapped in the strangest loincloth that you'll have ever seen. It was Spranger's memorial to his father-in-law, and bereaved relatives (rare portraits by the artist) line the bottom of the scene. Spranger himself thought it one of his greatest successes, and its almost reflective iridescence is one of the best examples of the feature that typified his work—but quite what the stern mourners thought about being extras in a Mannerist skin-flick can only be suspected. The collection also contains a rippling *Hercules with the Apples of the Hesperides* by Rudolf II's sculptor, Adriaen de Vries, the only full-length work by the artist to have escaped the attentions of the Swedish art collectors of 1648 (*see* p.32). Finally, the landscapes by the Flemish Roelandt Savery show some of the talents of a man whom the emperor sent to the Alps when he wanted to know what they looked like.

Baroque painting begins with the restrained touch of Karel Škréta and, dubiously, its culmination is presented as *St Jerome* by Michael Willmann. Removed from the sensory wonderland of Prague's Baroque churches, Willmann's work, and much of that which follows, has all the unpleasant drama of a fish twitching out of water. The heroic proportions and animation of the country's Baroque sculpture are made no less peculiar in the harsh light of the gallery—but it is far more fun. Their quivering becomes an earthshaking crescendo among the statues of Matthias Braun and Maximilian Brokof, the two greatest sculptors of Baroque Prague. Braun's *St Jude* is the most spectacular example. The sculptor studied in Venice and probably Rome, and with this statue he seems to have made an attempt to capture the ecstasy of Bernini's *St Theresa* in the frame of an octogenarian. The result is heartstopping in every sense, a whirl-wind of frenzied rags and varicose veins. Brokof's armed and arrogant Moors are models of restraint by comparison.

Past the paintings by the Czech Petr Brandl, you'll find the remarkable work of Jan Kupecký (1667–1740), a melancholy Czech exile who spent most of his life shuttling between Vienna and Nuremberg. Kupecký lived off commissions from rich buyers and trod a thin line between flattery and honesty. With his superb *Portrait of the Miniaturist, Karl Brun*, he just about lets the diabolically charming subject, swathed in silk dressing-gown and furry shadow, get away with the concealment of a faraway stare, but he's less sparing of himself. He looks downright shocked by what he found when painting his *Self-portrait with the Artist's Wife*. It might just be what he met in the mirror, but it's worth bearing in mind that his wife was busily being unfaithful at the time. That's her again, clutching a Bible in the next painting, *Penitent Spouse*, and only you can judge what Kupecký thought of the oath of fidelity he had just made her swear.

The Powder Tower

Open April–Sept Tues–Sun 9–5, Oct–March Tues–Sun 9–4, closed Mon; adm.

In Vikářská, the narrow lane to the side of the cathedral, the present buildings date from the early 18th century, but Rudolf II's **alchemists** used to live in earlier houses here. Sunk in the shadows of the cathedral's flying buttresses and vomiting gargoyles, their laboratory was in the **Powder Tower** (Prašná brána), also known as Mihulka. The tower was built as an armoury in the 15th century; a foundry had been set up by the 16th century; and under the reign of Rudolf II, scientists and quacks from across Europe hopefully distilled their aqua vitae and toiled with base metals here. Despite rigid admission tests administered by Rudolf II's quality controller Tadeáš Hájek of Hájek, during which applicants had (among other things) to transmute a pound of lead into gold, a motley crew of adventurers and charlatans were taken on as imperial alchemists. Among them was the incredible English duo of **Edward Kelley and John Dee**. Kelley, who lost his ears in England and his legs in Prague, was a rather magnificent fraud, but Dee was a true Renaissance scholar. He has gone down in legend as the trickster who wormed his way into Rudolf II's confidence by translating bird-warbles; in fact, by the time he arrived in Prague with Kelley in 1584, his Europe-wide reputation was established, thanks in no small part to a giant mechanical dung beetle with which he had amazed the Fellows of Trinity College, Cambridge, some 40 years before. While in the capital, he had his son baptized in the nearby cathedral, but that wasn't enough to placate an alarmed papal nuncio who eventually persuaded the emperor to expel the English sorcerers from the capital. Kelley was to return, and prompt another string of Prague legends (*see* p.38).

Any alchemy that survived Rudolf II's abdication in 1611 ended with the outbreak of the Thirty Years War. The tower was used as an ammunition dump by occupying Swedish forces in 1648, until it blew up. It has since been rebuilt, and now houses a museum devoted to its strange history. The **basement** (through the gate and down a curving set of stone steps) sinks to sub-zero temperatures for much of the year, and is often closed in winter. It contains a selection of objects from the foundry of Tomáš Jaroš, bell-maker *extraordinaire*. Sigismund the Bell was one of his babies, and there are two of his more minor creations here (you're still not supposed to touch). Another object that you can examine at close quarters is the copy of Rudolf II's pewter coffin, each side lined with a set of camp and repellent cherubs.

The next floor contains a paltry selection of weapons—muskets, cannon and a handful of balls—and no mention of the far more interesting lamprey (*mihule*), which gave the tower its nickname. Folklore remembered that the vile creatures were bred here for the castle kitchens but, although the suckered and feelered pseudo-fish were indeed a staple feature of the castle diet, the lamprey tank was actually in another tower which disappeared in the late 1500s. The second level contains retorts, crucibles and stoves used by the alchemists. This was once their laboratory (and the top floor of the tower), as proved by the soot on the roof and the chimney, which survived the centuries thanks to an unthorough replastering.

The last floor contains an elegant collection of late 16th-century **furniture and art**, including a typically icy work by Agnolo Bronzino, *Nobleman in Red Coat*. There's also a portrait of the young Rudolf—a rare chance to see his magnificent Habsburg chin before he was able to muster the hairs for a beard.

Golden Lane (Zlatá Ulička)

The huddled cottages here date from the later 16th century, and look like a Matisse painting come alive—tiny blocks of colour stretching higgledy-piggledy down the street. There's barely enough room inside to fit a cat, let alone swing one. The cottages are built into the castle fortifications, and originally housed 24 of Rudolf II's marksmen. The minuscule passage used to be even tinier: woodsheds and outhouses lined the other side until the 18th century. By then, the neighbourhood was on the decline: scores of grimy artisans had moved in, starved out of the city below by the restrictive practices of the trade guilds, and had taken to tending pigs, goats and chickens. The grunting and gobbling disturbed the nuns of St George's, so the abbess closed down the local pub and wiped out the woodsheds. However, people continued to live here until 1951, when the Communists evicted the last inhabitants and turned the lane into the collection of more or less uninteresting souvenir shops that you see today.

Take a look at the powder-blue hovel at No.22, a tourist-trap Tardis swallowing up a coach-load of Germans at a time. Between December 1916 and March 1917, Franz Kafka lived here and wrote most of the short stories published during his lifetime. His sister Ottla, who actually rented the house, deserves to be remembered in her own right. Married to a German 'Aryan', she was exempted from the first anti-Jewish measures passed by the Nazis but, after seeing her two sisters and their husbands taken away to the Łódz ghetto, she divorced him. In August 1942, she was sent to Terezín (Theresienstadt), and died in Auschwitz after volunteering to escort a children's transport there the following year.

The origins of the street's name have long caused controversy. Nineteenth-century myth-makers transmuted Rudolf's guards into alchemists, cheating Vikářská street of its rightful claim to fame, and creating one of the most pernicious of Prague legends. In fact the lane seems to have been named after goldsmiths who lived here in the later 17th century, but in 1990 a Czech historian hurled a thought-provoking cat among the etymological pigeons. It's well known that the 24 sharpshooters shared one toilet, and even that little closet was several nerve-racking minutes away on the Powder Bridge. Supported by lateral thinking (over 100 people lived here in the lane's glory days), he suggested that the 'gold' referred to was urine, dribbling down the passageway for generations.

The White Tower (Bílá Věž)

The tower, at the westernmost end of Golden Lane, was built in the 15th century as part of Vladislav II's fortifications of the castle, but for about 200 years after 1584 it also served as Prague's central prison. On the first floor are preserved scores of observations scratched into the walls by debtors and delinquents of old. Some of them must have doodled out of boredom, but others would have had more pressing thoughts in mind. Among those held here were the 27 Protestant leaders executed after the Battle of the White Mountain. During the reign of Rudolf II, the few villains in his court unlucky enough to be rumbled were also kept here. One was the already mentioned Edward Kelley, who eventually fell foul of the emperor, and was imprisoned in towers across Bohemia. The nature of the dispute is unclear, but legend has it that Rudolf became convinced that Kelley was withholding the philosopher's stone from him. If he had it, it didn't do him much good—he's said to have been crippled leaping from the windows in an escape attempt, and then to have poisoned himself in the tower. The first floor also contains, next to a lone wooden privy, the tower's torture chamber (*mučírna*). It contains a rack, stocks, branding irons and so on; and should any of them take your fancy, you can buy similar instruments, along with chastity belts and heavy-duty weaponry, in a shop upstairs.

At the topmost level, a corridor, filled with suits of armour, lances, maces and muskets, runs the length of Golden Lane. Archers would once have trained their weapons through the revolving wooden cylinders which still fill the windows. Below you is **Stag Moat**, used until 1743 to breed game for assorted Habsburg hunters. The deer had a rough time: not only were they periodically blown up when artillery pounded this side of the castle, but Rudolf II often insisted on including lions and tigers in his hunting packs, and the animals were regularly decimated by epidemics as they nosed curiously through the slop hurled over them from Golden Lane.

Royal Gardens (Královské Zahrady)

Open April–Oct daily 5am–midnight, Nov–March daily 6am–11pm.

The gardens were founded by Ferdinand I in the mid-16th century and, until the Habsburgs left for Vienna after the Thirty Years War, it was their Prague playground as well as a laboratory for their explorations of the natural world. Shrubs and plants were grown in greenhouses (tulips stopped off for several years on their way from Turkey to Amsterdam, obtained thanks to the untiring efforts of Ferdinand I's ambassador to Constantinople) and, on the slope down to the Stag Moat, Rudolf II grew figs and oranges. The park was laid out as an English garden in the 19th century, after having been devastated during the 17th and 18th centuries: the Swedes and Saxons bombarded the figs, and the rest of the blooms were blown up by the Prussians in 1757. Only the French showed some refinement. They occupied the garden in 1743, but agreed not to obliterate it after the head gardener offered them 30 pineapples.

The gardens were strictly off-limits to the general public until 1989, due to the fact that the adapted 18th-century summer house on your right was the **President's Residence** until that year. Most rulers develop odd phobias eventually, but the Czech Communists elevated paranoia to an impressive level. By the mid-1970s Gustáv Husák had installed a reinforced concrete slab above his Baroque study here, to thwart the rocket attacks and air strikes that he had begun to fear. The garden's spooky associations meant that Václav Havel's late wife, Olga, refused to move in when he was elected president, and it has remained unoccupied ever since.

Beyond the house but on the same side of the gardens is the *sgraffito*-covered **Ball Game Hall** (Míčovna), dating from 1567–9. It resounded with the rackets of the Habsburgs and favoured guests for some 50 years, until the family deserted troublesome Prague for good. The sculpture in front is an *Allegory of Night* by Antonín Braun. Examine the monochrome façade closely. When restoring it after the war, the authorities, in a fit of Communist whimsy, added a few new details to the Renaissance decoration—such as the hammer and sickle discreetly tucked away next to the figure of Justice.

The one-time **Orangerie** stretches along the slope below the garden, which is closed by the graceful splendour of the **Royal Summer Palace** (Královský letohrádek), also known as the

Belvedere. The palace was built between 1538 and 1564 for Ferdinand I. More particularly it was built as a token of love for his wife, although he unfortunately loved her too much: she died while giving birth to their 15th child before the palace was completed. It's the purest example of Italian Renaissance architecture in Prague. Slender Ionic columns swing up and down in happy harmony along the arcade running around the palace, and there are none of the alien Mannerist growths that infected the city's later explorations of the Renaissance (although its roof, an upside-down ship's hull of sea-green copper sheets, defies categorization). The **Singing Fountain** in front of the palace dates from 1568 and tinkles slightly when the water's on. Ferdinand and his entourage would trot through his tunnel to the palace when life at the castle became just too dreary, perhaps to have a ball in the room upstairs. His grandson Rudolf II was less given to revelry: according to Prague's papal nuncio he smiled once during his 26 year reign, when confronted by a diplomatic delegation from Persia scurrying towards him on all fours to kiss his feet. In 1600, he installed an observatory for Tycho Brahe inside the palace. Johannes Kepler also worked here, but his short-lived collaboration with Tycho was fraught with difficulties. Kepler had accepted the Dane's offer of a menial assistant's post only after he and his fellow Lutherans in Styria had been given 45 days' notice to quit by Catholic Archduke Ferdinand; and despite his respect for Tycho's mathematical wizardry, he had already begun to doubt the latter's necessarily ever-more complex model of the universe, in which five planets circled the sun in a flotilla that hurtled round the Earth at different speeds. From the moment that Kepler arrived, he tried to double-check Brahe's evidence. In a series of unhappy letters he reported that the tetchy astronomer would only mention the occasional apogee or planetary orbit over dinner, that he had had to promise to keep all the morsels to himself, and more generally that 'Tycho philosophizes rather queerly'. Brahe's unfortunate death was a stroke of luck for the German astronomer. Although Brahe's heirs guarded his work with equal jealousy (the notation of observable facts was widely regarded as an artistic creation), Kepler managed to weasel them out through disingenuous flattery, and was appointed Brahe's successor as imperial mathematician. As the title suggests, Kepler was subject to Rudolf's occasional quirk, but he got on well with the tolerant emperor, who was correspondingly fascinated by his astronomer's outlandish vision of a heliocentric universe. It all bore fruit in 1609, when he published his first two Laws of Planetary Motion based on the work he did here, with an effusive dedication to the emperor.

Hradčany

Hradčany Square (Hradčanské Nám.)

When a part of Prague can be described as tranquil, it often means that its history is steeped in gore or grinding poverty, but this square has less to hide than most. Many of the grand buildings that line it predate the Battle of the White Mountain and, although it had the standard pillory and gallows, the most impressive judicial murders took place in the Old Town Square where a larger audience could be guaranteed. It never even really had the hurly-burly of a marketplace: a few groceries and trinkets were sold here over the centuries, but the kings and nobles preferred to do their shopping downtown.

On the corner of the square is the façade of the **Martinic Palace**, plastered with cream-on-brown scratchings. The palace was built by the count of the same name in 1620, two years after his defenestrated descent into a dungheap had plunged him into the footnotes of history as one of the minor causes of the Thirty Years War (*see* p.27). The *sgraffito* decoration was redis-covered during restoration in 1971. It's a merry Renaissance retelling of Old Testament stories. On the front is Joseph (of Technicolor Dreamcoat fame). The wife of his master Potiphar is eagerly trying to lie with him, but he doesn't want to know her. The artist seems to have partic-ularly empathized with men wronged by the treachery of the fairer sex: in the courtyard, there are fragments from the story of Samson, wrestling with his lion and tossing a Philistine pillar.

On the opposite side of the square is the eye-catching façade of **Schwarzenberg Palace**, end-less *sgraffito* triangles crawling in diagonal formations across its Renaissance splendour. It was built by a member of the Lobkowicz family, who took advantage of the property slump after the 1541 fire to buy the site. It houses a **Military Museum** (Vojenské muzeum; *open May–Oct Tues–Sun 10–6, closed Mon; ✆ 20 20 20 23*), devoted to the pure joy of olde worlde warfare, from flails to cannon. The **Plague Column** in the woody centre of the square was sculpted by F. M. Brokof in 1726, and was an *ex post facto* offering to appease the fickle saints, who had just done nothing as the plague had stormed through for the second time in 50 years.

Sternberg Palace (National Gallery's Collection of European Old Masters)

Open Tues–Sun 10–6, closed Mon; adm.

The gallery, which used to be the finest in Prague, has recently been decimated by a double-whammy: its superb modern collection has been hived off to the Tradefair Palace (*see* p.134), while many of its older works have been returned to the monasteries and nobles from whom they were confiscated by the Communists. However, it still contains a few excellent pieces.

On the first floor is 14th- and 15th-century Italian art, ancient and classical art and icons, and 15th- and 16th-century art of the Netherlands. The triptychs and diptychs that make up the bulk of the work on this floor are no great shakes, but there are a few paintings worth noticing in the Netherlandish section. One that you can't avoid is *St Luke Drawing the Virgin* (1513–16) by Mabuse (Jan Gossaert), which once adorned the altar of St Vitus' Cathedral. Ever since the 16th century, there has been strong support for the view that Mabuse was too clever for his own good, and this famous painting shows why. A stint in High Renaissance Rome had rather overwhelmed him: not only did he set the legendary painting session in a classical temple (rather than the more conventional studio or cloudy vision) but he cluttered the building with most of the mental baggage that he had picked up during his stay. It's unclear whether you are inside or outside—pillars, balustrades and arches are joined in a way that only perspectival trickery knows how—and the unassuming figures of Mary and Luke are watched over by a hotchpotch of ancient heroes and mythological symbols. To confuse matters further, Mabuse has painted another Virgin and Apostle outside a mutant late Gothic construction in the distance. This floor also contains Pieter Bruegel the Elder's *Haymaking* (1565), a happy landscape of rural harmony which originally formed part of a cycle; only four other Months survive, in Vienna and New York. Finally, have a quick gaze at the exquisite *Bouquet* (1607–8), by Jan Brueghel, flower-painter *extraordinaire*.

On the second floor, the first rooms contain work by German artists of the 14th–16th centuries, including a much reduced selection of works by Lucas Cranach the Elder. The high-light is Albrecht Dürer's *Feast of the Rose Garlands* (1506), regarded as one of the most important paintings of the northern Renaissance. It represents Dürer's deliberate attempt to marry his country's late Gothic art with the technical tricks and new visions of the south, and this work—with its shimmering colour, noble proportions, beauty and use of perspective—was an attempt to beat the Venetians at their own game (Dürer painted it on a visit to the city). It shows Virgin, Child and St Dominic handing out rosy honours to kneeling worthies, and is also one of the first group portraits in northern art. Those attending the outdoor ceremony (any excuse to stick in a landscape) include Pope Julian II and Maximilian I, plenty of bourgeois bigwigs and, hopeful and hairy on the far right, the notoriously arrogant Dürer himself, clutching a small C.V. Rudolf II was obsessed by the artist's work, and had a special yearning for this painting—his father is the character being crowned by the Virgin. When the emperor eventually procured this, 'four stout men' were hired to carry it by hand over the Alps. In 1782, no-nonsense Joseph II put it under the hammer: it was sold for a gulden, but Strahov's monks bought it for a hundred the following year. Although it's been restored and re-restored far too often, it's still the National Gallery's pride and joy.

France and Spain are represented by a handful of minor works, the least unremarkable of which is Goya's *Portrait of Don Miguel de Lardizábal* (1815). The next wing continues with Prague's collection of Italian Renaissance art. The biggest names disappeared when the Swedes pilfered Rudolf II's massive collection in 1648, and several of the best modern acquisitions suffered a similar—though legally sanctioned—fate as a result of the *restitute* law. Of those that remain, look out for the two works by Agnolo Bronzino, *Cosimo de Medici* (1560) and *Eleanor of Toledo* (1540–43), examples of the many portraits produced by the artist for his Florentine patron. Bronzino's relentless accuracy was often a cruel comment on the weaknesses of his subjects but, at least here, Eleanor is more than a match for his piercing eye. The painting commemorates the birth of one of four little Medicis that she produced during the three-year period, and she exudes a cool but almost sensual triumph. Bronzino was to have richer pickings in later portraits, capturing her pain as she spent 12 years dying of tuberculosis.

Prague's Mannerist collection was unmatched in northern Europe until the Swedish heist of 1648, but it's thought to have contained few if any works by El Greco. However, the gallery has one work by him, a *Head of Christ* (1595–7), in which the artist's fervour is reflected in the damp eyes of the Messiah, gazing at a light that only the lucky few are likely ever to see. As usual, El Greco plays havoc with the artistic conventions of an age. Christ the Man, somehow combining humility with an almost superhuman nobility, is framed by a flaming rhomboid, taken from the figure of Christ the Judge in the rigid iconography of Byzantine art. The painting is one of the most unforgettable in the gallery.

Baroque light effects fill the next few rooms. The works include Guido Reni's idealized *Salome with the Head of John the Baptist* and Domenico Fetti's masterful *Christ on the Mount of Olives* (1615), convulsed by rippling movement and illumination. Take a look also at the tempestuous and faintly macabre *Penance of Mary Magdalene in the Wilderness* (1710) by Il Lissandrino (Alessandro Magnasco), the flickering light and nervous brush strokes of whose work make it instantly recognizable. The gallery's Italian collection ends with Canaletto's *View of London from the Thames* (1746), painted from the balcony of Lambeth Palace at the beginning of his 10-year stint in England. The artist had painted too many of his gay Venetian waterscapes to change his ways by then, and this work transforms the Thames into a festive lagoon, with barques and rowing boats messing about on the river while the launch of the Lord Mayor-cum-Doge cruises past. The unfinished Westminster Bridge stretches across in all its pristine glory. The painting is placed next to a painted snapshot by Francesco Guardi, *Palace Courtyard*. It's a rather minute example of Guardi's work, but his almost Impressionistic views of Venice are often contrasted with the detailed deliberation of Canaletto.

The next wing of the gallery contains its collection of Flemish and Dutch art from the 17th and 18th centuries. The first room has two works by the Flemish Roelandt Savery: *Paradise* (1618) and *Landscape with Birds* (1622). Each is an excellent showcase for Savery's claim to art history fame as Europe's first painter of exotic animals. He developed his skills during the decade he spent at Emperor Rudolf II's court and, more particularly, during the time he spent in the imperial menagerie. Although these works were painted after he had left the capital, the subjects are almost certainly accurate likenesses of early 16th-century Prague beasts. A further Prague connection may exist in the case of *Paradise*. The tranquil composition—in which camels, cows and cats, beagles, bucks, boars and birds laze around in prelapsarian innocence— can be viewed as an idealised allegory of the religious stalemate Savery had seen in Bohemia. As you contemplate the blissful scene, it's interesting to reflect that, in the same year as it was painted, Prague's defenestration threw the continent into 30 years of throat-slashing carnage. The room also contains several works by Rubens, including the superb *Expulsion from Paradise* (1620), a preliminary sketch for one of 39 depictions commissioned by the Jesuits for their church in Antwerp. None was used, but even in its stillborn form the study shows the swirling brushwork and the ability to conjure up an instant of dramatic movement that set Rubens apart from every other European artist of his day.

In the next room are landscapes by Salomon van Ruysdael, still lifes by Jan Jansz den Uyl, and a number of notable minor works. They include an oddly spooky *Council of Beasts* (1629) by Cornelis Saftleven, who spent his life perfecting such satires in the days before they became the stuff of wrapping-paper. Look out also for the *Raising of Lazarus* (1640) by Leonaert Bramer, a powerful work sunk in darkness by an artist who is thought to have been the teacher of Vermeer.

The oval heart of the palace that you enter next contains the grandest Dutch and Flemish painting in the gallery. Rubens holds centre stage with his *Martyrdom of St Thomas* (1637–8), showing the dramatic skills of the artist at their larger-than-life best. The Madras saint-killers are caught in mid-hatchet job, while the speared apostle heroically stretches for a palm of martyrdom being proffered by a squadron of exhilarated cherubs hovering overhead. Frans Hals is represented by a masterful *Portrait of Jasper Schade van Westrum* (1645). Like Rubens, the Dutchman didn't waste a brush stroke, and he's captured the brashness of his 22-year-old subject with a typical economy of expression that made him a perennial favourite among artists (and rich American buyers) in the hurried 20th century. The very different portraiture of Rembrandt, kneaded from the palate and laboriously formed on the canvas, is reflected in his *Scholar in his Study* (1634)—an unknown character painted early in the artist's career, but showing the quizzical mystery of facial expression that was to obsess him in later life.

The art of the Low Countries ends with some minor gems in the next room, including the eerie monochrome of *Ships in the Estuary* (1646) by Jan van Goyen, whose lifelong fascina-tion with moody clouds placed him (along with Salomon van Ruysdael) at the forefront of Dutch landscape painting of the 17th century. There are three notable still lifes: *Still Life with Lemon* by Willem Kalf, which depicts sparkling glasses and glistening fruit set off against a dark rug, showing both the contrast and sumptuous display that typifies his work; Jan van de

Velde's *Still Life with Smokers' Requisites* (1647), a strikingly simple example of Dutch still life, lighter glowing and beer unfinished to bring to mind the absent presence of the puffer concerned; and Jan Davidsz de Heem's *Still Life with Fruit* (1652), which exemplifies the more opulent Flemish still-life tradition, dripping with moisture and very active life forms.

Nový Svět

Nový Svět, the name of both a street and the whole hamlet, means 'New World'; Dvořák's symphony has a certain appropriateness, although it is Hovis commercials rather than the Land of the Free that come to mind. The quarter grew up during the 1500s as a set of ramshackle hovels for workers to trudge back to after a hard day's work at the castle. The Capuchins cleaned them up after moving in, and they're 17th-century cottages at heart, despite modifications made over the following 200 years.

The last house on the right was the home of **Tycho Brahe** during his stay in Prague as imperial mathematician to Rudolf II (1599–1601). Brahe was never really at ease in the house, and had incessant problems with his Capuchin neighbours. He complained that the monks had begun to ring their bells in a manner calculated to unnerve him—which sounds like the kind of thing that the Spaniards would do, but Brahe was little better. The Dane had the ear of the emperor throughout 1600, a year in which the rest of Rudolf was plumbing new depths of mental instability, and it's thought that it was Brahe who convinced the monarch to expel the Capuchins a few months after he had invited them in. As the monks packed their bags, Rudolf had another turn and commanded them to remain; and the seesaw of intrigue continued for another year until Brahe set off from this house on the fateful journey to the banquet at which his bladder would explode (*see* p.54).

Along **Černínská**, the little mess of cottages sinking into a dell of grassy cobbles is ridiculously dreamy. In any other town it would have been turned into a warren of wine bars and poster shops long ago. It's not a good idea to say anything vaguely favourable about the Communists in Prague these days, but at least here you can whisper silent thanks for the rigor mortis of their iron grip.

The Loreto

Lorentánské nám. Open Tues–Sun 9–12.15 and 1–4.30, closed Mon; adm.

The original Loreto in Italy was a medieval Lourdes, one of the most visited shrines in Europe. It was the house where the Archangel Gabriel told Mary the good news, rescued from pagan hands and flown over from Nazareth by a flock of angels in about 1291. The cult was wildly popular, and hundreds of imitations appeared across the Continent in the following centuries. After the Battle of the White Mountain, 50 were built in Bohemia as part of the miracle-culture that was constructed to re Catholicize the country. The Prague Loreto wasn't the first, but it became the grandest. The shrine was begun in 1626, only six years after the Catholic victory, and three generations of architects spent a century perfecting it.

The façade (1716–23) was the work of both Kristof Dienzenhofer and his son Kilian (*see* p.33) and it's a charmer: bouncy cherubs and dinky towers cheerfully taunting the armed might of the Černín Palace opposite. The atmosphere inside is altogether less sunny. The Loreto was established by Benigna Kateřina of Lobkowicz, one of the minor relatives of the Spanish Habsburgs who found their way to Prague; it was owned and run by an order founded by a

Spanish warrior-saint; and it speaks the unearthly language of Spain's Counter-Reformation, the mixture of fanatical cruelty and sensual mysticism that spawned both an Inquisition and the art of El Greco. Pleasure and pain are part and parcel of any shrine, but in Prague the new cult was being thrust on to a people who had fought against Catholicism for two centuries: it worked, but only by tapping a morbid superstition and voyeurism that permeate it still.

The **cloisters**, built in 1661 to protect the hundreds of homeless pilgrims from heavenly deluges, are lined with rows of painted saints in recently renovated pine cabinets. The Capuchins knew their audience—suffering and penitence were out, and the cloister is a department store of useful intercessors. Under this one roof, suppliants could get rid of toothaches (Apollonia), sore throats (Blaise) and gallstones (Liborius); if they had lost something, Antony of Padua would find it for them; and Sebastian inoculated them against the plague. You'll find plenty of others here, with their specialities helpfully inscribed underneath.

Halfway round the cloister, you're led into the **Santa Casa**, a replica of the Nazarene hovel itself, complete with rich Baroque stucco reliefs. As you walk through the pedimented portal, you may feel that it's all slightly at odds with your understanding of the Gospels, but have faith—the exterior is the work of mid-17th-century Italians, but inside is what it *really* looked like. The brick room is something of an anti-climax: a sombre box, with a cedar Virgin on the altar, surrounded by smiling silver cherubs who look as though they were put together with tin foil. Set into the bricks on the left are two beams from the original Loreto. Take a look at the relief on the back, which shows the story of the angelic transportation. Christians are slaughtered below—but there's room on the house for two. Madonna and Child sit elegantly on the roof, before being whisked to safety over a rolling Tuscan landscape.

The **Church of the Nativity** fits the cruel and surreal spirit of the shrine well. On the far right is a painting of the tortured martyr St Agatha—the patron saint of women with breast complaints—handing her own severed breasts on a dish to a welcoming angel. Even more macabre are the dummies in the glass cases on either side of the altar. The wax masks and dusty costumes shroud the skeletons of SS Felicissimus and Marcia, another Spanish addition to Loreto's box of tricks.

The most preposterous Iberian introduction to the shrine is in the chapel on the corner before the entrance. The figure with the Castro beard, on the cross to your left, isn't Christ (as you'll probably realize from the sky-blue dress with silver brocade) but the unfortunate Portuguese **St Wilgefortis**. She prayed on the eve of her wedding to be saved from her heathen suitor, and God in His mysterious way decided that the best remedy was facial hair, which she sprouted overnight. The prospective groom was suitably awed, and hastily withdrew from the wedding. Her father was less impressed—he crucified her. She's the patron saint of unhappily married women, and it sounds like the kind of story that should have done a roaring trade in Loreto, but apparently it was a flop. According to one of the workers here, 'a woman with a beard was alien to the traditions of Bohemia'.

Up the stairs just before the entrance, past a blood-drenched sculpture of the Crucifixion, is the **Loreto Treasury**, a priceless collection of glittering monstrances and reliquaries. Most of the jewels behind the reinforced-glass cases were gifts from the quislings and newly rich who now made up Bohemia's aristocracy, and they smell less of pious duty than anxiety that the propaganda machine of Loreto should remain solvent. The Vatican understood the shrine's importance: in 1683 Emperor Leopold I received permission to sell off the precious metals of the empire's churches to finance his war with the Turks, but the Prague Loreto was granted a blanket exemption. There's some superb silver filigree work, but the most impressive bauble is at the far end—the **diamond monstrance**, over 6,200 of the stones sprayed out like the quills of a horror-struck hedgehog. It was designed by Fischer von Erlach in 1699, and formed part of the gift of Ludmilla Eva Franziska of Kolovrat, who left her entire estate to the Madonna of the Santa Casa.

Walking around the shrine, you may have heard the appealing but cacophonous chimes of Loreto's **carillon**, 27 mechanical bells that have been urgently trying to learn a recognizable tune every hour for three centuries. They were among the few to survive a Central European bell holocaust in the First World War, when the Austro-Hungarians turned most of the metal they could find into cannons (Prague's 267 bells were all rung for the last time on St Wenceslas' Eve in 1916). They're synchronized, for want of a better term, by grooved cylinders; their current effort is apparently called 'We Greet Thee a Thousand Times'.

Černín Palace

The palace, though closed to the public, is worth looking at as you leave the Loreto. It is the largest in Prague, and it's a beast: in form, its façade is still Renaissance; in its scale and deliberate repetition it belongs to the Baroque; and its awesome pomp is redolent of past power. Humprecht Černín was one of the wealthiest of the *arrivistes* who moved into the jobs and properties left vacant by Protestant exiles after the Catholic victory at the Battle of the White Mountain in 1620. From his sojourn in Venice as imperial ambassador, he returned in 1664 with money to burn and a handful of half-baked architectural ideas—and this behemoth was the monstrous offspring of his appetites. He tried out plans by Rome's Bernini and rejected them; he tirelessly argued with his Prague architects who tried to endow his baby with some human features; and when he died in 1682 the palace remained unfinished. The family frittered away their fortune to complete it, and they had barely moved in the furniture before they decided to sell it in 1779, only to find there were no takers. In the end, the government moved in. It became a barracks in 1851, and in 1932 the bureaucrats of the Ministry of Foreign Affairs set up shop in its desolate corridors. *Reichsprotektor* Heydrich decided that it, rather than the castle, should house his operations, and from 1941 to 1945 swastikas framed its façade; and then in 1948, Prague's fourth (and, so far, last) defenestration occurred here, when the Foreign Minister, Jan Masaryk, fell from his office window. No one knows whether he jumped or was pushed. On the one hand, he was the popular son of Czechoslovakia's first president, and the Communists had good reason to bump him off; on the other, he was a manic depressive—but it's always a useful subject to bring up in Prague if the conversation starts to flag.

Černín's builders excavated a pagan cemetery full of headless skeletons, and hundreds of tons of earth. The fate of the bones is unknown, but the earthworks lay around in the centre of the square for a couple of centuries, and were only properly patted down in the early 1900s to form the embankment that divides the square into two levels.

Strahov Monastery (Strahovský Klášter)

Strahovské nádvoří 1. Open Mon, Wed and Fri 9–4.30, Tues and Thurs 9–5.30, closed Sat–Sun.

The name Strahov comes from *stráž* ('guard'), and dates from the mid-14th century, when the western gateway of Charles IV's new fortifications around the left bank of Prague was built here. It's an unsuitably militaristic name for the monastery. When founded in 1140, it was called Mount Sion; although fires and armed mobs stormed through with monotonous regularity until the later 18th century, in spirit the monastery has always been a world apart from the bloodshed and religious tomfoolery of the city below. The Premonstratensian canons were an austere order—their insistence on celibacy didn't make them popular among the licentious monks of the day—but they were also an honest and hardworking crew. On their hilltop retreat, they assembled a library that, despite sacks at the hands of Hussite swarms in 1420 and oafish Swedes in 1648, became the finest in Bohemia. The books came in useful in 1782, when Joseph II announced the dissolution of almost all the monasteries and convents of the empire. While nuns and monks everywhere else were being clapped in jail or told to find honest work, the wily abbot at Strahov, Václav Mayer, saved the day by turning it into a research institute for scholars. Strahov was one of very few monasteries to survive in Bohemia. The Communists were tough cookies—in 1950 they mounted a night-time raid, sent the canons to concentration camps, and turned their cloisters into the national literary museum—but the Premonstratensians proved even tougher. Eight hardy survivors shuffled back after the 1989 revolution, and Strahov is once again a functioning monastery. The canons have been multiplying steadily but, although you might glimpse the flash of a white robe, they live in segregated quarters and tend to avoid visitors.

Strahov Art Gallery

Open Tues–Sun 9–12 and 12.30–5, closed Mon; adm.

Most of the works in the gallery, acquired over the centuries by the monastery, were confiscated by the Communists after 1950. Although limited in number, they are unified by a humanistic and sometimes downright secular quality that is rare for monastic collections. The most notable early work is the *Strahov Madonna* (1340–50), whose matronly bulk and squirming infant show clearly the departure of Bohemian art from the orthodoxies of Byzantium, while Lucas Cranach the Elder's *Judith* (*c.* 1530) turns the Old Testament head-hunter into a coquettish girl-about-town. There are several works from the Mannerist court of Rudolf II, including a portrait of the avuncular emperor by Hans von Aachen (1604–12) and an *Allegory of the Reign of Rudolf II* (1603) by Dirck de Quade van Ravesteyn. The latter is typical of the many apotheoses that were produced to celebrate a pipe-dream vision of the emperor's crisis-ridden reign: Peace, Justice and Plenty fondle each other's breasts, while an iron-clad imperial bouncer keeps a curious Turk at the door. Most impressive of all the Rudolfine works is Bartholomeus Spranger's shimmering *Resurrection of Christ* (*c.* 1576), in which the superhuman saviour shoots skyward from his tomb and the phrase 'faster than a speeding bullet' comes inexorably to the modern mind. Among the other works, look out in particular for Gerrit Dou's astonishingly vivid portrait of the mother of his master, Rembrandt (1628–31). The gallery closes with a garish copy of Albrecht Dürer's masterpiece, *Feast of the Rose Garlands* (for the original *see* p.92).

Church of St Roch (Kostel sv. Rocha)

The church was built after Rudolf II had promised the plague-resistant saint a church if he protected Prague from the approaching pestilence. Roch accepted the offer—the bacilli screeched to a halt a few kilometres from the city walls—and although Rudolf took no chances and moved to Plzeň for the duration, he was as good as his word. The peculiar church dates from 1603–12. Gothic architecture lingered late in Bohemia, and the Renaissance influence of the blank niches and pedimented door is almost lost among the tenacious buttresses and tall, tracery-topped windows climbing the façade. St Roch didn't share the luck of the rest of the monastery: once the Strahov parish church, it was closed down by Joseph II in 1784, and now hosts sporadic exhibitions.

Philosophical Hall

The library was built frantically between 1780 and 1782, after Abbot Mayer got wind of the new Emperor Joseph's plans. Designed to provide room for a wider range of books and readers, it was intended to persuade the emperor of the quarter-truth that there was no conflict between rationalism and what the canons had been up to for centuries. Mayer also resorted to a prudent cringe: the haughty figure in gold above the stark façade is the scourge of the monasteries himself.

After climbing the staircase, you'll find yourself in the anteroom. It contains a few illuminated manuscripts and monkish doodles, but it's hard to resist being dragged into the opulence of the hall beyond. Walnut bookcases, strung with overripe gilt Rococo decoration, push through two levels. Any sensible library would stop at the gallery, but here the tomes march on, climbing 15m in all to the ceiling. When the cabinets arrived, the plan for the half-built room had to be changed to accommodate them. There are over 40,000 books, comprising works that Strahov had picked up from benefactors and less fortunate monasteries than itself, all lined up to prove to Joseph that it was providing a useful social service. The emperor seems to have been convinced—he bought the shelves for the monastery, after driving down their market value by abolishing the previous owner. The late 18th-century library represents the very end of the dream, as old as antiquity but restored during the Renaissance, of collecting all wisdom in one place. Humanity was on the verge of knowing too much—but at the organ-grinder desks, scholars could do their best to keep up by spinning through four books at once.

The ceiling fresco, rising from the sombre stacks into a celestial blue, was the last work of the Viennese Franz Maulpertsch, and dates from 1794. It's called *The Struggle of Mankind to Know Real Wisdom*, but there's also another struggle going on, between the sacred and the profane, which owes as much to Joseph II's threat as to the rationalist bent of the Strahov clerics. Christianity gets an honourable mention at both ends, but the woman in the cherubic supernova is not the Virgin, but Providence; and along both sides antiquity's truth-seeking heroes hog the stage. Alexander the Great and pensive Aristotle on the left face Plato on the right; Socrates welcomes his hemlock on the far right; and even Diogenes the Cynic has moved in, lock, stock and barrel, on the far left. Five years after the French Revolution, neither emperor nor Strahov had any sympathy for the troublesome Encyclopaedists—Diderot *et al.* are tumbling into an abyss next to the pillar on the right—but the nefarious *Rational Dictionary* still found its way on to the stacks, inexplicably filed under reference AA.1 by the canons.

Strahov's Premonstratensians didn't just bury their heads in books. They also stared at their collection of curiosities, now in the cabinets outside the hall: monstrous creatures of the deep, a sad crocodile, and cases of shining beetles and butterflies. The display case at the end of the corridor contains a replica of the oldest manuscript in the library, a 10th-century New Testament bound in fussy 17th-century encrustations.

On the right is the **Theological Hall**, built in 1671, during the restoration of the monastery after the Thirty Years War. It doesn't have the solemn majesty of the later Philosophical Hall, but its stucco-laden barrel vault is even more sumptuous. It is decorated with ceiling frescoes, extolling the virtues of True Wisdom. They were painted by a member of the Order in 1723–7 and, although Grecian philosophers don't crowd out the scenes, the secular nature of the allegories shows that the Enlightenment hadn't passed Strahov by. Favoured lay-scholars could work here along with the canons—all were prodded along by the frescoes' Latin inscriptions, dully insistent reminders that 'it is better to acquire knowledge than to make money', 'knowledge is difficult but fruitful', *et cetera ad nauseam*.

The clerics were liberal—but to a degree. They observed the prohibitions of the Vatican's Index, but kept choice selections dangling tantalizingly in the cabinet above the far door. If a prurient canon wanted to flick through one of Galileo's potboilers or a diabolical Hussite tract, he'd have to explain his reasons in detail to the abbot—a cumbersome process that was swept away during the glasnost of the 1780s, when the books were removed into the profanity of the Philosophical Hall.

Lesser Quarter (Malá Strana)

Sloping from the castle to the left bank of the Vltava, Malá Strana's swirling canopy of orange tiles and chalky-green domes covers one of the finest Baroque preserves in Europe. The quarter was founded way back in the 13th century, but a fortuitous fire and the Thirty Years War cleared out the rotundas and Gothic clutter just in time for the arrival of the carpetbaggers of the Counter-Reformation. This area demonstrates their schemes and dreams: from the Jesuit Church of St Nicholas to the gardens of General Waldstein, all glorious tributes to the power of money and architecture. Here also you can see Catholicism on the march, in the apparently ceaseless interventions of the Virgin Mary and the *Bambino di Praga*, a miraculous effigy that's now venerated by millions in Latin America. The hills and gardens of the quarter can have an almost spooky beauty, with all the luscious and peculiar flavours that you'd expect of a Baroque chocolate box.

Lunch and Cafés

Bílý orel (White Eagle), Malostranské nám. 4. *Open daily 8.30am–1am.* Comfy café on the central square, serving food all day long. Its breakfast menu can be particularly useful, though portions are sometimes stingy.

Čertovka, U lužického semináře 24. *Open daily 11.30am–midnight.* This riverside restaurant on the edge of the surging Devil's Stream takes the biscuit for its location. Václav Havel took Pink Floyd here for a drink.

Scarlett O'Hara's, in the U Hradeb cinema complex off Mostecká. *Open daily noon–2am.* An Irish pub—no more and no less—with toasted sandwiches, Guinness and a lot of more-or-less happy drinkers. No cards.

U kocoura, Nerudova 2. *Open daily 11.30am–midnight.* For years, this tavern was a favourite among the ranters, writers and guitarists of the underground, but it's lost its hold since 1989. It's still a good place for Pilsner, Purkmistr and the putrid *pivní.*

U malého Glena (Little Glen's), Karmelitská 23. *Open Mon–Thurs 8.30am–midnight, Fri 8.30am–1am, Sat 10.30am–1am, Sun 10.30am–11pm.* This friendly café (and jazz club by night) serves breakfasts, sandwiches and snacks.

U sv. Tomáše (St Thomas'), Letenská 12. *Open daily 11.30am–midnight; music from 7.45.* One of Prague's best-known and oldest beer halls, with all that that entails: crooners, bassoonists, dumplings aplenty, and droves of homesick Germans. The pretty walled garden is open in summer.

U zeleného čaje (Green Tea), Nerudova 19. *Open daily 10.30–7.30.* A sort of Body Shop for tea freaks. Brews you can choose range from camomile to strawberry, and the food includes healthy pizzas and sandwiches. No smoking. No cards.

History

The name Malá Strana translates roughly as 'Lesser Quarter' or 'Little Side', and is a reminder that the district is something of an upstart compared to the rest of town. Until the 13th

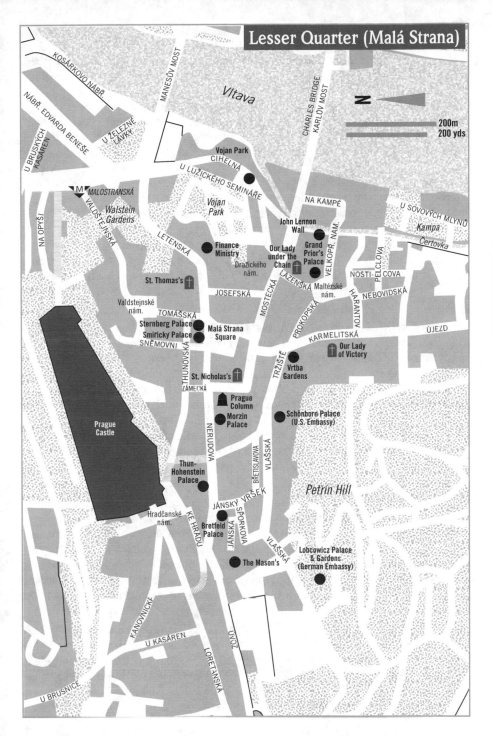

Lesser Quarter (Malá Strana)

Vltava

CHARLES BRIDGE
KARLŮV MOST

N

200m
200 yds

KOŠÁRKOVO NÁBŘ.

MÁNESŮV MOST

NÁBŘ. EDVARDA BENEŠE

U BRUSKÝCH KASÁREN

U ŽELEZNÉ LÁVKY

Vojan Park
CIHELNÁ

U LUŽICKÉHO SEMINÁŘE

NA KAMPĚ

U SOVOVÝCH MLÝNŮ

Kampa

Čertovka

M MALOSTRANSKÁ

Walstein
Gardens

VALDŠTEJNSKÁ

NA OPYŠI

Vojan
Park

LETENSKÁ

John Lennon
Wall

Finance
Ministry

Dražického
nám.

Our Lady
under the
Chain

Grand
Prior's
Palace

VELKOPŘ. NÁM.

NOSTI-COVA

PELCLOVA

St. Thomas's

JOSEFSKÁ

MOSTECKÁ

LÁZEŇSKÁ

PROKOPSKÁ

Maltézské
nám.

NEBOVIDSKÁ

HARANTOV

Valdštejnské
nám.

TOMÁŠSKÁ

Sternberg Palace
Šmiřický Palace

SNĚMOVNÍ

Malá Strana
Square

THUNOVSKÁ

KARMELITSKÁ

ÚJEZD

Our Lady
of Victory

St. Nicholas's
ZÁMECKÁ

TRŽIŠTĚ

Vrtba
Gardens

Prague
Column

Morzin
Palace

NERUDOVA

Schönborn Palace
(U.S. Embassy)

Prague
Castle

Thun-
Hohenstein
Palace

BŘETISLAVOVA

VLAŠSKÁ

Petřín Hill

Hradčanské
nám.

KE HRADU

JÁNSKÝ VRŠEK

JÁNSKÁ

ŠPORKOVA

Bretfeld
Palace

VLAŠSKÁ

KANOVNICKÁ

U KASÁREN

ÚVOZ

The Mason's

Lobcowicz Palace
& Gardens
(German Embassy)

LORETÁNSKÁ

U BRUSNICE

103

century, it was little more than a collection of isolated villages, tucked between the Old Town of Prague and the Romanesque castle. A monkish band of the Knights of St John kept themselves to themselves in the area around Prague's stone bridge; farther south in Újezd, a Jewish settlement worshipped and buried its dead at a cemetery and synagogue that have long disappeared; and a limpet-like community around a market on the lower reaches of the fortification walls eked out an existence from the wealth of the castle on the hill. A few more centuries of urban sprawl might have given birth to a natural town, but ambitious Přemysl Otakar II didn't have the time to wait. In 1257, he issued a general invitation to German merchants to set up shop in Prague, hoping to strengthen the economy and his claim to the crown of the Holy Roman Empire (*see* p.23). With the exception of the monks of St John, the locals were rounded up and expelled, and an entirely new Gothic settlement was built. This 'New Town' became 'Malá Strana' a century later, when Charles IV needed its original name for his new urban development. The German merchants couldn't avoid the religious shenanigans of their Czech neighbours in the Old and New Towns for long. Malá Strana was almost literally wiped out at the very beginning of the Hussite Wars in 1419; and by the time it had recovered in the next century, it had been drawn squarely into the politicking of Central Europe. The Germans got Lutheranism, nobles moved in to be close to the castle, and, in 1541, a huge fire raged through the left bank. Property-hunting vultures of every faith descended on to the smoking plots, and Renaissance palaces and houses rose from the ashes.

A century later, Malá Strana's second mass expulsion took place. The Habsburg victors of the Thirty Years War ejected thousands of heretical losers from their new domain, and handed over vast tracts of confiscated land to the soldiers, monks and flunkies who were to complete the Bohemian Counter-Reformation. Fanatics and time-servers turned the winding and hilly streets into one of the most splendid towns of 17th- and 18th-century Europe. For 300 years, Malá Strana was the provincial playground of the Viennese nobility—and then the toffs lost out as the result of another war. The palaces were snatched in the name of the working class by the Communists in 1948, and many were indeed partitioned into apartment blocks; others were turned into embassies. The last twist in the tale was the restitution law passed in 1990. Exiled merchants, impoverished nobles and long-lost relatives have all tramped back, statute in hand, to reclaim their properties.

There's considerable sympathy for at least the humbler victims of the thieving Communists, but many fear that the *restituce* will be a deathblow to the community. The Communist housing policy, if not egalitarian, was at least random: over the years schizophrenic sculptors, war-widows and orange-jacketed street cleaners have all found themselves allocated crumbling Baroque apartments in Malá Strana. In addition the quarter became a hive of opposition activists and artists, who took over the leaking, gorgeous rooms while more fastidious folk moved away to the warm sterility of suburban high-rise *paneláks*. Amidst the tourists and the diplomats, children played on the cobbles, corpulent men gazed out of 18th-century attics, and each evening the pubs would fill with the gossipy, doleful, laughing and pensive world of non-Communism. It's all changing as the wine bars and antique shops move in. The area has become one of the most desirable residential districts in Prague, and as rents rise and multinationals buy up Baroque blocks the exodus to the suburbs has begun. However, the eclectic community remains one of the tightest knit in town. Even if it's doomed, the nobles et al. will be hard-pressed to transform it by the time you get there.

Malá Strana Square (Malostranské Nám.)

This area has been at the centre of left-bank life for a millennium. Prague's first market is thought to have stretched from here in the direction of Tomášská street to the outer bailey of the castle and, when the Jewish merchant Ibrahim Ibn-Jakub sang the praises of the bargains to be found in Prague in 965, it was the stalls here that he had seen. A rotunda in the middle of the square confirmed its growing importance, and with the foundation of Malá Strana in 1257 the square assumed full municipal functions. A parish church (consecrated to St Nicholas) and a town hall joined the rotunda, and for 300 years the most exciting things to happen in the square were ritual humiliation (the pillory stood on this corner) and strangulation (gallows on the next one up the hill). However, its history hotted up, quite literally, after 1541. The fire that destroyed most of Malá Strana and Hradčany in that year began in the **Sternberg Palace**, the second building over the arcade rising up the hill, and, less than a century later, an even more far-reaching conflagration was sparked off in the **Smiřický Palace**, next along. On 22 May 1618, Albrecht Smiřický invited his noble friends around to discuss what to do with Ferdinand II's hated Catholic governors. They plumped for a defenestration, carried it out the next day, and the Thirty Years War began. Albrecht himself died in the same year and, in a good example of the convolutions of Malá Strana title deeds, the eventual recipient of the traitor's estates was traitor-to-be General Waldstein (*see* p.108), whose grandfather was a Smiřický. The generalissimo is recorded as having said that the worst mistake that the nationalists ever made was to throw the governors out of a window instead of stabbing them. It's a mysterious comment, but it is interesting to note that he had survived one of these fates, and was to perish by the other.

On the corner of Letenská is a Renaissance building over an arcade, known as the **Beseda** (Meeting Place). It's now a rather sorry music club, the haunt of hairy drinkers and lost trendies; but between the late 1400s and 1784 it was Malá Strana's town hall.

Church of St Nicholas (Kostel sv. Mikuláše)

Open daily 10–6; adm.

The Baroque mass of the church and adjoining one-time **Jesuit College** towers over the square. All of Malá Strana now revolves around the odd couple of the tower and dome of the church. The Jesuits would have appreciated the compliment, but their enjoyment of their masterpiece was sullied by endless problems, of which their conflict with the town hall over the **tower** is a case in point.

The Jesuits were given the old Church of St Nicholas in 1623 by fanatical Ferdinand II, who was dishing out newly vacated places of Protestant worship to almost any monkish zealot who was prepared to fight the good fight, and with particular alacrity when it came to Spaniards, who infested his Viennese court. The Order planned to build a new church and college from the outset, but this complex took years to get off the ground. The first problem was that the overstretched Order was impecunious. With the long-term vision of good monomaniacs they clung to their dreams, until in 1653 they were able to present the town hall with firm plans. Serious dispute then arose about who owned precisely which pieces of the architectural jungle in the centre of the square. The crucial stumbling block was an old Gothic tower, standing roughly where the present one is today. The Jesuits hoped to turn it into a belfry, but the councillors angrily claimed that it was Malá Strana's venerable fire post (and a useless one, judging from the blaze that had started a few feet away in 1541). Work stalled for another 20 years, until in 1673 the cunning clerics promised to build the town an even better watchtower if they could start work on their church. The council agreed and the Jesuits swiftly set about destroying the tower, school, vicarage, former town hall, two churches and a street full of cobblers that had occupied their land. Eighty years later, this tower rose almost as an after-thought to the completed church—and the mendacious missionaries connected it to the church and planted saints on it. The sculptures briefly stood on the now empty pedestals on the corners of the tower. An aggrieved citizenry removed them and locked the door, and until 20 years ago the tower—which looks to be part and parcel of the church—was one of the most unusual flats in the capital. The Jesuits' tribulations didn't end there. They put the finishing touches to their church in the 1750s, and had hardly settled in when their Order was placed under a worldwide ban by the pope in 1773. It had served its purpose, and was becoming a little too powerful for the European establishment's liking. The Society found a refuge in Catherine the Great's Russia but, although the Holy See let them start up again in 1814, they did not return to Prague. In a neat little turn, St Nicholas' then became the parish church of Malá Strana. The front door of the tower is at No.29 Malostranská kavárna (556 according to the older system of numbering), and is marked by the crest of the town.

The Jesuits put so much thought into the façade, the pinnacle of Prague's religious Baroque architecture, that it deserves a moment. The Order had a glacial appreciation of human psychology, which you can begin to appreciate by comparing the grim west front of the former Jesuit College (and now maths faculty of the Charles University) on the left, with the seductive face of the church itself. Although there was a 20-year gap between the two façades, and a church might be expected to be grander than a school, the contrast also had a deliberate purpose. The General of the Order, Father Oliva, warned the architects in 1673 that the lay house mustn't have the sumptuousness of the west front of the Clementinum (*see* p.107). With their own building the Jesuits thrust their humility and austerity into the face of the heathens; the richness of the later church façade was all the more inviting as a result. But the Jesuits were no aesthetic puritans. Following the example of their fervent Spanish founder, Ignatius of Loyola, each novice had to go through a month of 'spiritual exercises', during which he progressed from contemplation of sin and damnation to, *inter alia*, a mental munching of 'the loaves and the fishes with which Jesus feeds the multitude'. Ignatius' teaching that God was to be known through all five senses was instrumental in the development of later Baroque archi-tecture, which was given an added punch in Bohemia, where the Jesuits had to seduce a population that had fought Catholicism for 200 years. The façade was the work of Munich-born Kristof Dienzenhofer, and was completed around 1710. It's a development of the undulating rhythm used by Borromini in 1667 for his church of S. Carlo alle Quatro Fontane in Rome.

But it is when you enter the church—which now charges admission fees and calls itself a museum—that the mobility of Prague's late Baroque architecture finally overwhelms you. All of the city's churches built during this period sought to capture hearts and minds for the Church Militant; but none other has the potency of this Jesuit cocktail of illusion, threat and promise. Even hardened cynics are momentarily stopped in their tracks, and it's relevant that this was one of the few churches to be given a full restoration in 1955, at a time when the Communist government's policies of Scientific Atheism were at their height. Inspired by the work of Guarino Guarini, who carried the idea of expressing movement through curves to an extraordinary degree, the decoration and structure create a space that pulls you in every direction. The nave's piers jut out at a diagonal, dragging your attention upwards, while the balconies sway forwards from pier to pier, over vast saints urging you onwards to the high altar. The vault adds to the intoxicating confusion, flowing almost imperceptibly from the pillars into three central bays, while the *trompe l'œil* extravaganza of the 1,500m² **fresco** (1760) makes it almost impossible to say where construction ends and illusion begins. The fresco was the work of Johann Lukas Kracker, an Austrian who is thought to have trained under Franz Maulpertsch (*see* p.33), and wasn't intended to be viewed from any single point, adding even more to the church's fluidity. It opens the vault into the dark drama of the life of St Nicholas. Better known to pagans as Father Christmas, Nicholas was a 4th-century bishop from Asia Minor and the patron saint of perfumers, pawnbrokers and sailors in distress.

The east of the church, from the third vault onwards, is the work of Kristof's son, Kilian Ignaz Dienzenhofer, home-grown and educated by the Jesuits themselves in the Clementinum.

From the nave, the choir and altar seem almost irrelevant, a result not of an unsuccessful union between the work of father and son, but of the overpowering effect of the church as a whole. But by the time you're standing under the diffuse light of the painted dome, it is the nave that has become an appendage. The size of the dome caused terror: no one would enter the church until a commission of experts certified in 1750 that it wouldn't collapse. The painting, by Franz Xavier Palko, is the *Celebration of the Holiest Trinity* (1752–3).

God moves in mysterious ways while you keep your eyes heavenward—but there's little room for doubt when you notice the colossal statues (1755–7) stationed above and around you. The venerable Doctors of the Church standing at each corner of the stunted transepts have physiques more often associated with steroid abuse than religious devotion. Their brutality was no accident. SS Basil, John Chrysostom, Gregory of Nazianzus and Cyril of Alexandria are all associated with the early Christian struggle against heterodoxy in the East, and the Jesuits were drawing a parallel with their own cause in Bohemia. There are equally gargantuan statues of the Order's heroes, SS Ignatius and Francis Xavier, flanking the copper St Nicholas on the high altar. The analogy was clear but the Jesuits hammered the point home: Ignatius and Cyril are each coolly plunging a crozier into the throats of jug-eared heretics.

After the initial shock of the church, as you walk back the trickery reveals itself. As in almost all Prague's churches, the marble is actually scagliola, a painted mixture of plaster and glue; the intimidating saints are plaster casts; and the chapels contain little decoration that stands up to a brief examination. The Jesuits knew that by the time their prey had got as far as the entrance, they were willing victims—and all eyes would soon have been on the equally fake, but splendid, **pulpit** at the end of the nave. It dates from 1765, and is decorated with reliefs of John the Baptist. The shell on which it stands was one of the favourite motifs of the Rococo, but this swirling mass of cream and pink still belongs in spirit to the Baroque.

As you leave, the last chapel on your left is the **Chapel of the Dead**. It was the first to be completed and, with its oval plan, it is the only one to stand outside the scheme of the church. The fresco is *The Last Judgment*, and the chapel contains one of the church's better paintings, a *Crucifixion* by the Czech Karel Škréta (1646).

The Waldstein Gardens (Valdšteinská Zahrada)

Open March–April and Oct daily 10–6, May–Sept daily 9–7, closed Nov–Feb.

This majestic maze of beech hedges, gravel paths and gurgling fountains lazing under the silhouetted spires and halls of Prague Castle is an idyllic summer retreat from the overheating city, as well as a monument to **General Albrecht Waldstein** (1581–1634), the most epic megalomaniac that Prague has ever produced.

Waldstein belongs to the dubious band of men whose influence on Europe is difficult to exaggerate. Friedrich Schiller turned his life into *Wallenstein*, a three-act tragedy, and the general himself was one of the first to recognize his genius. According to his earliest biographer (1643), from the moment when, at the age of 21, he fell off a window ledge in Innsbruck and found the Virgin Mary swooping to the rescue, he 'made it the study of his life to penetrate the future and to discover the high destiny that awaited him'. At its peak, that destiny took him to the command of the combined Catholic armies of the Thirty Years War; and at its end, it left him bedridden with gout, declared a traitor by the empire he had saved twice, and ignobly dispatched by the dagger of an Irish dragoon.

Waldstein made the most of his opportunities. The first came when he landed the widow Lucretia in 1609. She was so hideous that his hagiographer anxiously had to explain that she had slipped the general a love potion. Although that was a gallant attempt to silence the rakish whispers aroused by the general's lifelong lack of *affaires de cœur*, it seems clear that Waldstein was firmly in control when he popped the question. Lucretia was seriously rich— and when she did what wealthy widows should, and caught the plague five years later, the general buried her in style and scooped up a windfall. A second big break came in 1618. While his countrymen were lobbing Emperor Ferdinand's men out of Prague's windows, Waldstein threw in his lot with the imperial cause. The defenestrators were executed; Waldstein snapped up confiscated lands for a song, and was put in charge of the imperial army, which he led through a decade of almost continuous victories over motley Protestant forces. But he was no employee. He provided the army to Ferdinand under a series of lucrative contracts and, with the help of an inflated currency scheme and manic organizational skills, Waldstein soon became the largest creditor of the Habsburg empire. Without the money to pay his general, Ferdinand had to reward him with other assets. Lands and honours poured through his hands, culminating with a princedom in 1627. To his already formidable powers, only the least of which was the right to legitimize bastards, he could now add the privilege of handing the emperor a napkin after he had used his finger bowl, and all but unlimited control over a vast fief in northern Bohemia.

Ferdinand's Jesuit advisers already loathed Waldstein for his pragmatic attitude to a war that they saw as a crusade and, to many, the fact that he could now keep his hat on while chatting to the emperor was the last straw. The intrigues intensified, until in 1630 Waldstein was relieved of his command. It was too late—his superbly run army had become indispensable. When Saxon Protestants retook Prague the following year, Ferdinand hastily recalled his champion, and appointed him generalissimo of the imperial forces. An almost omnipotent Waldstein finally decided to slip the leash. He began to negotiate with the enemies of the empire, and in January 1634 launched open mutiny against Ferdinand. Historians have spent the last three centuries discussing his reasons. Few doubt that he wanted to be king of Bohemia, but the riddle is whether he had been a Bohemian nationalist all along, whether he grew into one, or whether he was a power-mad traitor. The nuances didn't really matter to Ferdinand, and the *dénouement* unfurled. As Waldstein crossed northern Bohemia in a crimson litter, looking for the allies who were suddenly and mysteriously fading away, Vienna's churches were put on alert and ordered to pray, for 'a matter of the first importance'. Four days later, placards appeared across the city blaring that the legendary Waldstein was to be taken dead or alive. The noble renegade's game was up, and he and the commanders who remained loyal to him were finally done to death by Scottish and Irish officers in the town of Cheb. Assassination without trial was still considered rather outrageous, and the crocodile emperor did his best to distance himself from his dastardly deed. As Waldstein's Golden Fleece was returned to him, he murmured, 'They painted him blacker than he was', and the general's name echoed into history with the 3,000 requiems that Vienna's overworked churches were now commanded to say for his errant soul.

Waldstein's character oozes out of both his garden and his palace. When this complex was built between 1623 and 1629, on the site of 23 houses, three gardens and the municipal brick kiln, he supervised every stage of the work. A man who laid down dietary rules for his army's sick chickens wasn't likely to leave his Milanese architects to their own devices. From the entrance, turn left and then right towards his magnificent terrace, or **sala terrena**, through the **avenue of sculpture** by Adriaen de Vries (1545–1626).

These green-streaked deities were among the last works to be produced by Netherlands-born de Vries, who died before completing his master's commission. The sculptor studied in Florence under Giovanni Bologna, the master of Mannerist sculpture, and the figures here show the refinement and elegance typical of both men's work. The themes were inspired by the Italian Renaissance's rediscovery of the classics; but the Mannerist fascination with graceful movement appears throughout. It's most evident in de Vries' version of *Laocoön* on the left, which shows the punishment inflicted on the Trojan family by the Greek contingent on Mount Olympus, after Laocoön Senior had threatened to spoil the gods' fun (he had warned that the big wooden horse outside the gates wasn't to be trusted). The work was inspired by a late-Hellenistic antique that had set Europe's artists a-twittering ever since its rediscovery in a vineyard in 1506. The Italian Renaissance had approved of the ineffable grandeur with which those characters had struggled with their snakes, and the Baroque was to seize on the work's emotion and gore—but this sophisticated composition, twisting and straining with a stylized anguish, stands neatly between the two approaches. Waldstein particularly favoured de Vries' work: not only did it give his palace a distinguished touch, but the man who would be king savoured the fact that de Vries' last, and very proprietorial, Prague patron had been Emperor Rudolf II, until his abdication in 1611.

None of the statues are original. Waldstein's former subordinate and fellow turncoat, Hans von Arnim, left the palace untouched when his Saxon army occupied Prague in 1631–2; but the Swedes were less respectful when they took the city 17 years later. The removal men of rapacious Queen Christina carted the sculptures to Drottningholm Palace, where they remain today, and these works are copies, dating from the beginning of the 20th century.

The avenue of sculpture ends with a fountain of Venus, cast by a Nuremberg sculptor in 1599, beyond which is Waldstein's **terrace**. De Vries' sculptures represent the transition between the harmony of the Renaissance and the dynamism of the Baroque. In a very different way, the terrace (1623–30) also shows the beginnings of the new style. Its Milanese architect, Giovanni

Pieroni, followed the 16th-century rules of proportion to the letter; but the sheer size of these gaping arches and doubled Doric pillars left their spirit far behind. Waldstein clearly appreciated the triumphal possibilities of Baroque architecture, but his greatest tribute to his own genius lies under the stucco vault, in the **frescoes of the Trojan Wars** (1629–30) by Baccio Bianco. Apart from Aeneas, staggering off to found Rome with his father on his back, the assembled heroes and damsels are dressed in the contemporary dress and armour of Waldstein's war. The capricious gods lounge around on the cloudy ceiling, but the general had more faith in himself than in any humdrum deity. He is a dead ringer for ginger-haired Achilles and, on the ceiling of the main hall of the palace, he had Bianco paint him as Mars, riding to war under a dark star.

In a small salon on the left as you face the sala terrena, the general and his second wife (the reputedly less ugly Isabella von Harrach) would dine in the summer, under more heroic frescoes of the Argonauts' quest for the Golden Fleece. The courtyard now contains a café, which serves remarkably good ice cream. It contains a door (closed at the time of writing) leading to what was once Waldstein's observatory. The general's astrological obsessions were another part of his fatal flaw, and an essential component of his elevation to tragic hero by Schiller. The best place to contemplate them is at the **grotesquery** on the southern wall of the garden, near Waldstein's aviary, which used to house 400 songbirds.

The general would stare at this wall and listen to the warbles when the pressures of devastating Europe became too much. Grottoes had become popular across the Continent during the later 1500s, and this pendulous foliage, growing tumour-like into a mass of hidden faces and shapes, reflects Waldstein's mystical pursuits. He had spent some years studying in Padua, a hotbed of the quasi-sciences of the day, and his unorthodox interests were well known even during his lifetime. He had converted from tepid Lutheranism to lukewarm Catholicism, a fairly conventional step for the social climbers of the day, but many of his enemies muttered darkly that he had long since pawned his soul to the devil—a rumour fuelled by reports of a large black hound that he apparently consulted prior to major military manoeuvres. The general took any diabolical secrets he may have had to the grave, but his astrological mania was public knowledge. He had mundane stargazers scattered across his dominions, and seemed to have hit the jackpot in 1628, when Ferdinand asked him to look after the imperial mathematician, Johannes Kepler (*see* p.40). The emperor had little use for the Lutheran son-of-a-witch, to whom he owed 11 years' back pay and who had fled his proto-Counter-Reformation in Styria back in 1600; but Waldstein hoped that the scientist would be a particularly reliable source of inside information as he planned his future. Unfortunately, it wasn't to be. Kepler had long been nagged by doubts as to how powerful planetary aspects really were, and his only comprehensive analysis of the general's fate was something of a deconstruction of astrology. It contained the news that 'the applicant is full of superstition' and warnings that to act on a horoscope was 'arrant nonsense', even though all that the general wanted to know was whether he would die of apoplexy and the star-signs of any enemies that he might have. However, the imperial mathematician was still sufficiently impressed by something that he saw to mention that March 1634 boded ill. The comment turned out to be an over-cautious reference to Waldstein's murder in February of that year.

At the opposite end of the garden is the Riding Hall, which hosts temporary art exhibitions, and a pool around a sculpture of Hercules, another copy of a work by de Vries.

The street is named after Jan Neruda (1834–91), a 19th-century Czech poet and journalist who lived here. His name was later filched by the Chilean writer and 1971 Nobel Laureate, Pablo Neruda, who apparently chose it at random, although he deposited flowers outside Jan's birthplace after finding out who he was. More a chasm than a street, its Baroque and Renaissance façades cling on to the incline. As you grapple with it, spare a thought for the assorted beasts and heralds who once had to lug the paraphernalia of the coronation procession along here, en route to the castle.

The street has more **house signs** than any other in Prague—multi-coloured beasts, birds and apparently random objects which sometimes date back 600 years. They originally followed, in a lowly way, the strict rules of heraldry, but matters slipped out of control as the city grew. House-owners, desperate for an original name, resorted to zoological monstrosities (a house in the Old Town used to be called the 'Stag with Two Heads'); people adopted their property's name and took it with them when they moved; and streets were sometimes consumed by a counter-productive craze for a particular sign. Another grave problem was that people began to forget their significance altogether. Golden geese became white swans, Magi were transformed into musketeers, until in 1770 city fathers called a halt to the collective madness by introducing numbers. At No.6 on the right is the narrow 18th-century façade of the **Red Eagle** (U červeného orla), one of the innumerable variations of the 26 avian species that adorned Prague's houses. The sign, surrounded by an intertwining Rococo cartouche, may have begun life as a vulture, which was the only creature allowed to perch on rocks by the heraldic guilds. The plaster decoration swirls into two less apparent images, sinister faces with dark tadpole eyes gazing out from the stucco above the first-floor windows. There's another sign at the **Three Little Fiddles** (U tří housliček), a small restaurant at No.12. Three generations of violin-makers lived in the house, but legend insists that the sign has more to do with satanic fiddlers who gather here when the moon is full. Other signs to decipher as you walk up the street include a golden goblet (No.16) and a golden key (No.27), both from the 17th century, when castle goldsmiths used to heat and beat their metals along Nerudova; and a golden horseshoe (No.34), recalling the days when steep Nerudova used to be the site of several humbler smithies.

On the left at No.5 is the Baroque **Morzin Palace** (1713–14), now the Romanian Embassy. The palace is an example of the inventiveness of Giovanni Santini, another of the greats of Prague's late Baroque. It was an adaptation of three older houses and, rather than go to the trouble of putting an entrance through the middle building, Santini put a balcony in the centre and had both sides of the façade thrust outwards towards it, making the asymmetry almost unnoticeable at first glance. The tension is thrown into even higher gear by the two atlantes, sombre Moors (the Morzin family emblem) who carry the balcony with ease and make a good job of supporting the rest of the façade. The other sculptures (all by F. M. Brokof) reinforce the illusory balance, both by their position and theme. The balcony is flanked by sunny Day and starry Night, and up on the roof the Four Corners of the World are back to hold the building under their feet.

Atlantes became fashionable during the 18th century, but if you look at the portal of the **Italian Embassy** (Thun-Hohenstein Palace), across the road at No.20, you'll see that they didn't always work. It was built in 1721–6 for the Kolovrats, very soon after the Morzins had moved into No.5. The newcomers liked the idea of having the family emblem supporting the portal. Unfortunately, the Kolovrats' was an eagle, and Matthias Braun duly sculpted these two preposterous creatures. Jupiter and Juno are left to perch above.

Next to the embassy a set of stairs burrow up the hill to the New Castle Steps. Continue the climb up Nerudova, until you reach another set of steps to the left. The house to the left as you face the staircase is said to conceal the walled-up Kuzmack Tunnel, built by an imperial stooge in the 18th century to provide an escape route from the castle in case of siege.

On the opposite side is the Rococo façade of the former **Bretfeld Palace** (1765), now a greying and blue-rinsed set of private apartments, but a centre of merriment in its youth. The first Count Bretfeld threw balls that were renowned across Central Europe, one of which Mozart attended in 1787. He wrote to a friend in Vienna that 'the cream of the beauties of Prague flew about in sheer delight to my *Figaro*', which was played repeatedly in his honour, and, according to legend, he also rubbed shoulders with Giacomo Casanova on the dance-floor. The story sounds a little too neat, given that Wolfgang was in town to conduct the premiere of *Don Giovanni*—but it's not impossible. The ageing lover Casanova had been invited by one of General Waldstein's descendants to pen his kiss-and-tell memoirs in the family castle in 1785, and he lived in Bohemia until his death in 1798.

If you have the energy, a detour to the top of the street will take you past the remnants of two mutant signs (the Red Lion at No.39 and the now very peeled and not-at-all Green Lobster at No.43) to Jan Neruda's birthplace at No.47, itself marked by two very sorrowful suns. Opposite Jan Neruda's house is *Toileta*, a charming sculpture by the Czech Jan Štursa, whose work was marked by a particular affection for the female form until he blew his brains out during a burst of creative angst in 1925. Predictably, generations of snapshooters have been more impressed by the fact that its name is plastered across the base. A final climb up the lane to the castle leads to a postcard view across the roofs of Malá Strana.

Lobkowicz Palace and Gardens

The **Lobkowicz Palace**, now the German Embassy, dates from the early 18th century, and the stately aspect that it presents to the street conceals a beautiful garden and a much more charming façade at the rear of the palace, from which a winding path leads up into the wooded hills of Petřín. The top floors of the side wings were added in the later 18th century, and have disrupted the scale originally intended for the building. The elliptical plan, inspired by the work of Fischer von Erlach, originally bore a close resemblance to a 1665 project by Borromini for the rebuilding of the Louvre in Paris. Louis XIV rejected the design in favour of the grandiose colonnade that survives today and, if you imagine this prior to the alterations, you'll see why Borromini's plans lacked the required pomposity. The English layout of the gardens dates from the late 1700s, but they're still recuperating from the most momentous event in their sheltered history. In September 1989, thousands of East Germans arrived in Prague, dumped their Trabants, and clambered over these railings in the hope of being allowed to go west. They lived on the flower beds for a fortnight until permission was granted—and the rumble of their sealed trains, which President Honecker strangely insisted should pass through East Germany, were the final tremors before Europe's revolutions of 1989. A whimsical tribute to the fleeing Ossies now stands in the garden: called *Quo Vadis*, it's a gold Trabant on four long legs. Sadly, someone has seen fit to sanitize it by knocking off the scrotum with which it was originally endowed.

Church of Our Lady of Victory (Kostel Panny Marie Vítězné)

Karmelitská. Open daily 8.30–4.

This sits on the site of Prague's first Baroque church (1611), which was built by German Lutherans—a paradoxical start to religious Baroque architecture in Prague. After the Battle of the White Mountain in 1620, Ferdinand II gave their church to the Order of Barefooted Carmelites, who had trudged into the city as part of the Catholic squad. The friars, who actually wore sandals, renamed it in honour of the Virgin (their protectress) and, more specifically, in commemoration of her role at the White Mountain, where she had rained down destruction and smites on the enemy. The discalced crew took to their heels again when Saxon troops looted the church in 1631, and the present edifice is a rebuilt version dating from 1640. The Carmelites were finally expelled in 1784 as a result of Joseph II's anticlerical policies; and the church was taken over by the Knights of Malta, whose base was near by and whose cross now adorns the façade. The Knights were themselves expelled in turn by the Communists.

The structure is unimpressive—an ugly development of the façade of the 1568 Gésu in Rome (only the portal on the right remains from the Lutheran church) and an interior that retains much of the Lutherans' rigidity and austerity. The striking late-Baroque gold-on-black decoration is denied the play of light it deserves, since the church's few windows are obstructed by altars. These weren't planned for when rebuilding began, and were only made possible as a result of the miraculous financial assistance of the **Bambino di Praga**, in the illuminated altar on your right. Rome's Barefooted Carmelites put Bernini's *Ecstasy of St Teresa* in their church. The showpiece of the Prague friars was this 1ft-high wax effigy of the Infant Jesus. It's hardly less famous. Italians gave it the name by which it is best known, and the Bambino is venerated throughout the Hispanic world. In Central America, there's said to be a tribe that worships it as a god, and has very confused notions about what *Praga* involves. Intercessory prayers are offered in over 10 languages; during high season coach-loads of more-or-less credulous pilgrims arrive daily. The Bambino's rise to stardom began when Polyxena of Lobkowicz, one of many Spanish brides taken by Czech Catholics during this period, gave the figure to the friars in 1628. It had belonged to Polyxena's Habsburg mother, and had been known to work the occasional wonder in the old country, but its big break came in 1637. The new abbot, picking through the debris of the church (which had remained untouched since the Saxons had swept through) found that the trinket had been tossed behind the high altar, and was missing only its arms. He declared it a miracle. Equally incredible was the discovery, made while the Carmelites were drumming up funds for a new church, that the Bambino would do anything in return for a small sum. After Countess Kolovrat touched it and had her sight and hearing restored, there was no looking back. Cripples and imbeciles poured in, and in 1741 enough money had been made to buy the doll its silver altar; during the early 1700s, it was granted the rights of a Count Palatine. The most mysterious (some say miraculous) tribute came in 1958, when an official delegation from Communist North Vietnam stepped off the plane with a set of silk clothes for the Bambino. To this day, no one knows why. It's been bought and given scores of other costumes. After the Carmelites were expelled, the Order of English Virgins was allowed to continue dressing it, and even through the Communist era a prelate of St Vitus' Cathedral continued changing the Bambino regularly. Look out for outfit No.5, an apple-green number with gold embroidery, which was handed over personally by Queen Maria Theresa in 1754.

Above the altar, there's a dim celebration of the Battle of the White Mountain, but the church's other main attraction is now inaccessible. The power of the Bambino meant that few friars wanted to stray too far during the interval between death and resurrection, and the most fortunate had their corpses put into a catacomb, where they were blow-dried into mummies over the years. Privileged benefactors were also let in. Everyone's still there, but a spot of putrefaction has set in and the smelly chamber is now closed.

Kampa Island

This island (named from the Latin *campus*—field) is one of the gentlest patches of Prague. Separated from the mainland by a mere sliver of a river known as the Čertovka (or Devil's Stream), its grassy enclaves, slowly turning water-wheel and quiet cobbled streets are a step away but a world apart from the hubbub of the nearby Charles Bridge. Like most of the city's idyllic hideaways it has, however, had its ups and downs. A long-standing border dispute with the Vltava River saw its shape change regularly and, despite being strengthened by imported debris from the 1541 fire, the deluges continued until the damming of the river in 1954. The abundant supplies of water meant that Kampa was particularly favoured by Prague's washer-women, who are commemorated both by the stream and by the small early Gothic church of St John at the Laundry, just off the southern tip of the island on Říční.

From the island there are two nearby attractions which are all to often overlooked by visitors to the city. The first is the **John Lennon Wall**, which you'll find across the bridge near the water-wheel in Velkoprevorske nám. The singer was a powerful symbol of nonconformity throughout Communist-ruled Europe after his murder in 1980, and this wall, a colourful tribute to the Beatle-saint, became the site of a surreal struggle between Prague's youth and the police. The former would daub it with pictures and slogans; the VB responded with regular pots of white-wash and, at the height of the subversion, video-surveillance equipment. When a fair proportion of Prague's hippies became government officials after December 1989, it was expected that moody adolescents would be able to doodle at will, but low-key skirmishes with the Knights of St John, whose order owns the wall, resumed for a few tense months in late 1990. The French ambassador rather improbably stepped in to safeguard free expression, and the wall is now encrusted with several years' worth of obscene *non sequiturs* and the scrawled greetings of hooligans from across the Continent. If you're around on the anniversary of Lennon's death on 8 December, come and join the dreamy types who spend much of the night imagining no possessions, greed or hunger. Bring a guitar and brush up on your Lennon lyrics.

A final stop, secluded even by the hushed standards of Kampa, is the **Vojan Park** (Vojanovy Sady) just beyond the north of the island on U lužického semináře (the entrance is set into the blank wall on the west side of the road). The almost hidden park is the oldest in Prague, laid out in 1248 by the Carmelites, taken over by English Virgins and now an integral part of the Finance Ministry. Modern sculptures regularly swing and squat under its willows and fruit trees nowadays, and to the far left from the entrance is a grotto-chapel to the Old Testament prophet Elijah, who, the Carmelites insisted, had founded their Order. Regrettably, it seems that the best statue in the garden, showing an impassioned St John Nepomuk astride a fish, has gone missing.

New Town (Nové Město)

Apart from Wenceslas Square, which no one can avoid, these districts are largely overlooked by most visitors to the city. Given the chocolate-box delights that the rest of the city has to offer, that's easily understandable, but, if you're in town for more than a few days, you could do worse than spend a few hours wandering off the beaten track. The tribulations of the 20th century have been played out and commemorated on its streets, and none of the follies or gems listed below are more than a very short subway journey from the centre. And if you want to see what Praguers get up to while the tourists aren't watching, take a walk. The broad boulevards and Art Nouveau mansions of Vinohrady begin just a few hundred metres north of Wenceslas Square and, as the pavement cafés and property speculators move in, the area is turning into a dowdily Central European version of Paris or Brussels. The gentrifiers of Žižkov, by contrast, are taking Hoxton and Brooklyn as their models and, although the tenements and dusty streets aren't yet quite as cutting edge as Prague trendies would have you believe, scattered squats and dives and Romany pubs can make for a memorable nocturnal mission.

Wenceslas Square (Václavské Náměstí)

Wenceslas Square, actually a half-mile boulevard, is now Prague's commercial heart, but it began its life as a humble horse market in the mid-14th century—at the same time as the rest of the 'New' Town was established by Charles IV. Its expansive lay-out gives a clue as to why the New Town was amenable to modernisation, and goes some way to explain why, thankfully, the winding alleys in the rest of the city have resisted redevelopment so effectively.

National Museum (Národní Muzeum)

Open daily 10–6, except first Tues of the month; adm, free first Mon of the month, www.nm.cz.

The grandiloquent National Museum now seals Prague's central avenue with all the half-pillars, pilasters and pomp that the brown and solemn architecture of the Czech national revival was able to muster. A museum of Bohemian history was a dream of early 19th-century patriots. The grandeur of the neo-Renaissance building (1885–90) built to house it was meant to express the confidence of the Czech national revival movement, but the effect was to shatter the balance of old Wenceslas Square. It encouraged the almost complete renewal of the street's architecture over this century; and paradoxically, the symmetry of the museum, its bulk set off by a golden central dome, now makes it an almost elegant point on the 20th-century exclamation mark that Wenceslas Square has become. Inside, on the first floor under the glassy dome, is a **sculptural pantheon** of some 60 national heroes gazing down from the walls and plinths: an eclectic and eerie collection of work by most of Prague's leading early 20th-century sculptors. Wait for a very, very rainy day before exploring the rest of the building, which houses a stupefying collection of stuffed animals and anthropological knick-knacks. Even the mammoth is fake.

Silhouetted against the National Museum is one of the motifs of Bohemian nationalism, the **equestrian figure of St Wenceslas**. Although a familiar name to English carol singers since

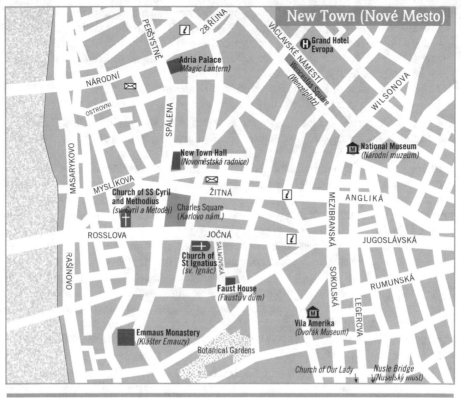

New Town (Nové Mesto)

Lunch and Cafés

Evropa Café, Václavské nám. 25. *Open daily 7am–midnight.* Unappetizing cold snacks at inflated prices with appalling service, but one of the finest Art Nouveau interiors in Prague. The choice is yours.

Le Gourmand, Václavské nám 18. *Open daily 8am–11pm.* Tasty European and Mediterranean self-service food and one of the longest salad bars in town, in conservatory-like kitsch surroundings. No cards.

Institut Français, Štepánská 35. *Open Mon–Fri 9–6, later in summer.* The French Institute's built-in pâtisserie, stylish in a halogen-lit and airy sort of way, and a useful spot for a croissant-and-coffee breakfast. No cards.

McDonald's, Václavské nám. 9. *Open Mon–Sat 8am–1am, Sun 9am–1am.* Cheerful hamburger restaurant, popular among Czechs. No cards.

Novoměstsky pivovar (New Town Brewery), Vodičkova 20. *Open Mon–Sat 11–11, Sun noon–11.* Modern microbrewery, with good pub food.

Palace Hotel, Panská 12. *Open daily 10–10.* Non-smoking salad bar. No cards.

U rozvařilů, Na poříčí 26. *Open Mon–Fri 7.30–7.30, Sat 7.30–7, Sun 10–5.* Staple and unglamorous self-service Czech food with bread, beer and desserts at disconcertingly low prices. No cards.

the 1850s, Good King Wenceslas ruled as a prince rather than a king, until murdered by his notoriously cruel brother, Boleslav the Cruel, in 935. Just to confuse matters, there were eventually four King Wenceslases and the country is now ruled by another (Václav= Wenceslas). The saint's reputation for goodness arose from an obsessive and harmless Christianity, but over the years Wenceslas has metamorphosed from religious to national hero. The legends have followed him, and this figure will apparently gallop into life at Bohemia's moment of greatest need.

The symbolic importance of the statue came to obsess its designer, J. V. Myslbek. The grand old man of 19th-century Czech sculpture, Myslbek began work in 1887 with the idea of Wenceslas as a shaggy Slav; but as the reality of a national state grew closer, he transformed the Dark Age prince into the serene and noble leader you see today. Ardo the stallion had to take weeks off his military duties to pose in the sculptor's studio. When his work was finally unveiled in 1912, Myslbek sighed, 'Now I see it could have been still bigger.' Perhaps—but he needn't have worried. Ever since it was unveiled, it has been a public rallying point: in 1918, Czechoslovakian independence was announced at Wenceslas' feet; after 1948, Communist May Day parades goose-stepped along the square; and after the Soviet-led invasion of August 1968 the monument was the focus for Prague's desperation. In that month, an 11-year-old boy was shot dead as he stood on the steps and pushed a Czech flag down the barrel of a Soviet tank; and on 16 January 1969, next to the fountain of the National Museum, Jan Palach burned himself alive. A week later, 800,000 Czechs followed his coffin past the statue. The happiest moment of the monument's recent history came in November 1989, when Wenceslas and Ardo made it on to television sets across the world, at the head of the demonstrations that finally saw off the shoddy dictatorship.

Directly in front of the statue is a round pedestal where, every year on the anniversary of Palach's death, Prague's bravest dissidents would attempt to lay flowers while its police would attempt to dissuade them. The last arrestee was Václav Havel, jailed for nine months in February 1999 and released just in time for the Velvet Revolution. It's now a permanent memorial to those who suffered or died resisting the Communists.

Around the Square

Just before the central crossroads of the square is the glorious Art Nouveau façade of the **Grand Hotel Evropa** (1903–6). Take a look at its café, on the ground floor. Revolving doors spin you into a shabby and beautiful room of mirrors, mahogany, crystal chandeliers and carriage lamps. It all conforms neatly to a clichéd theme of faded *Mitteleuropäische* elegance, but there's a doubly wistful feel about the place nowadays. For decades, the Evropa played host to some of the most colourful characters of Prague's lowlife: a hierarchy that ran from gum-chewing rent boys and magnificent transvestites up to the mysterious Duchess, whose lifetime of shadowy achievements was said to have included the pleasuring of much of Prague's Nazi High Command on behalf of the Resistance during the war. But she died in 1991 and the pimps and whores have gone for good, helped on their way by the ludicrous decision of the management to charge admission fees to sit in the café. It's still as pretty as it always was, but the sterility of the place nowadays makes it little more than an overpriced tourist-trap.

Across Jindřišská is the Polish Cultural Centre, which once housed the insurance company where **Franz Kafka** began his first job in 1907. Kafka never quite settled in to the Wenceslas

Square location. A week after starting, he was already dreaming of 'someday gazing out of an office window upon sugarcane fields or Muslim cemeteries', and within a year he had moved on. However, he went nowhere more exotic than nearby Na poříčí street and would work in the field of industrial injury for the rest of his life. It was a surprisingly distinguished career: Kafka visited factories across the country, he drafted elegant reports on workplace accidents that he proudly sent to friends, and was even recommended for a national medal in 1918, failing to receive it only because the Habsburg empire collapsed shortly before the papers could be processed.

The rest of Wenceslas Square is a hotch-potch of Prague's early 20th-century architecture. Between the Functionalist Alfa and Tatran buildings on your left is the Hotel Adria, one of the last Baroque façades on the square. The Air India offices at No.13 used to house Aeroflot; some older Praguers still fondly remember the night in 1969 when Czechoslovakia beat the Soviet Union at ice-hockey and they made a bonfire of the furniture.

As you gaze at the façades, you can now safely consider one of the more surreal rumours of the November revolution: that after June 1989, the jittery authorities had a cardboard copy of the entire square constructed somewhere in Slovakia, in which their troops could practise Tienanmen-inspired crowd-control techniques. It has never been found.

On the far side of the street, at No.8, is the **Peterkův dům**, perhaps the most elegant Art Nouveau façade in the capital; it was designed by a 28-year-old Jan Kotěra and shows the precision that would later inspire some of the finest Czech Constructivist architecture (one example is the neighbouring Baťa shoe shop). At the foot of the square is the so-called **Golden Cross**, a junction of shoppers and idle youth which—along with Ardo's tail—is Prague's most widely used meeting point.

On 28. října, you'll see the bizarre crenellations and turrets of the **Adria Palace**. The building is a striking example of the Rondocubist architecture that Pavel Janák, the designer, was trying to develop into a Czechoslovakian national style fit for the 20th century. Modern Prague would have been an architectural curiosity of titanic proportions had he succeeded, but this urban citadel (1923–5) is one of only a few examples that got off the ground.

Charles Square (Karlovo Nám.)

While horses were traded in Wenceslas Square, cattle changed hands here, but until the 19th century this square was always the symbolic centre of the New Town. Charles IV used it for his annual relic displays (*see* p.24), while the **New Town Hall** (Novoměstská radnice) is descended from the 14th-century original. Only the tower (1425–6) has any look of age about it however, since the rest of the building was completely rebuilt during the 19th and early 20th centuries. In 1419 its former windows were the venue for **Prague's first defenestration**. Jan Želivský, a Hussite firebrand of a priest, led a rabble to the building to demand the release of some heretics, and the Catholic councillors apparently lobbed stones at his monstrance. That proved to be a serious misjudgement. The crowd stormed the building, hurled the councillors from the windows, and then bludgeoned to death anyone who survived the fall. The times were violent ones, and Jan himself didn't escape: in 1421 the burghers of the Old Town invited him to their place for full and frank discussions, and beheaded him. The Communists always had a soft spot for radical John, and there's a monument to him here dating from 1960.

Church of St Ignatius (Sv. Ignác)

This church, halfway down the square, once formed the Jesuit encampment in the New Town, along with the neighbouring college (now a hospital). The powerful arches of the chapels and broad nave are laden with half-immured cherubs and angels, and the gold and creamy-pink interior has the usual ostentatiousness of Jesuit architecture. It was built in 1665–70, too early for it to display the fluidity and seductive power of later Jesuit churches such as St Nicholas' in Malá Strana (*see* pp.105).

Church of Saints Cyril and Methodius (Sv. Cyril a Metoděj)

In Resslova, the main street leading off the opposite side of the square, is the Orthodox Church of SS Cyril and Methodius (sv. Cyril a Metoděj). It is recognizable by a pock-marked section of wall that commemorates one of the most dramatic events to occur in Prague during the Second World War. After the killing of Heydrich, whom Hitler had appointed Protektor, seven members of the group responsible holed themselves up here. They were betrayed, and during the early hours of 18 June 1942 over 300 SS and Gestapo soldiers took up positions around the building. Through the night, wave upon wave of machine-gun fire poured into the church, but only as dawn broke did the shooting from within stop. The Nazis entered to find that they had spent the night battling three men—four remained in the crypt. Gunfire resumed, and for another two hours the fighters held out in the catacombs against bullets, tear gas and grenades.

The gouged and battered **crypt** is *open Tues–Sun 10–4, adm.* The entrance is on Na Zderaze street. An 18th-century stone staircase links the crypt to the nave. Catacombs line both sides of the small cellar; until desecrated by the SS they held the bodies of church priests and, in two of the highest, the last men to survive took their lives. They did so only after reaching the end of their ammunition. German troops had pushed a high-pressure hose through a vent and, with water flooding into the pitch-black crypt and the Nazis on the point of blowing open the long-disused staircase, both men blasted themselves with their final bullets. The gashes of the shots still mark the walls. The small exhibition includes photographs of the Nazi assault, taken by a Czech police officer with a camera in his lighter. At the far end of the crypt is a metre-long hollow, smashed away with a pipe while the Nazis pumped gunfire and water through the ventilation hole overhead. Although hundreds of troops had been stationed at sewage outlets along the Vltava to forestall any escape, the crypt is actually next to a Grand Central of Prague sewers. Had they hit the drain, the men would have been home and dry. They were 30cm away from doing so.

Emmaus Monastery (Klášter Emauzy)

This Gothic monastery, to the south of Karlovo nám., had its roof obliterated during an Allied bombing run in February 1945, and the 1960s replacement, flowing into two spires, is one of the most distinctive pieces of postwar architecture in the capital. The monastery was founded by Charles IV in 1347 for Balkan Benedictines, who (thanks to a spot of pressure on the pope) were granted the rare privilege of being allowed to chant their dirges and liturgies in Old Slavonic here. Pope and emperor each hoped that their respective spheres of influence would thereby be extended eastwards, but the Croatians and Dalmatians played their own game. When the Hussites popped round to storm the monastery, the clerics audaciously informed the mob that they fully sympathized with the anti-clerical cause. It was a gamble, but it worked: the confused crowd slunk off and the cowled monks were left to intone in peace. In 1446 they consolidated their position by re-establishing themselves as the only Hussite Order in the world. The Spanish Benedictines recovered Emmaus from their wayward brethren after the Battle of the White Mountain in 1620, and the Order has ebbed and flowed through ever since. It was last evicted by the Communists in the early 1950s, and reinstated in 1990. The monastery's cloisters contain a somewhat battered cycle of Gothic mural paintings, commissioned by Charles himself. Their astrological and alchemical symbolism (as well as a healthy dose of sun-worship) provides a fascinating glimpse into the arcane depths of religious belief in 14th-century Prague. However, long and occasionally futile arguments with the Benedictine bouncer are now necessary before you can get in to see them. Try at the door to your left as you enter the monastery grounds.

South and East of Charles Square

Just farther along the street, where it rolls into Na slupi, are Prague's **botanical gardens** (Botanická zahrada), a sloping retreat of roses, rhododendrons and azaleas (*open Jan–15 March 10–5, 16 March–Oct 10–6, Nov–Dec 10–4*). There are two worthwhile stops farther up the hill on Ke Karlovu street. At No.20 is the **Vila Amerika**, a gorgeous Baroque summer-house designed by Kilian Dienzenhofer and set among sculptures by Antonín Braun. It houses the small **Dvořák Museum**, Ke Karlovu 20 (*open Tues–Sun 10–5, closed Mon*).

The crimson dome of the **Church of Our Lady and Charlemagne** (Kostel Panny Marie a Karla Velikého; *open Sun and hols 2–5.15*) stands at the end of the road. Founded by Charles IV in 1358, the church's unusual octagonal plan was loosely modelled on the Aachen burial church of Charlemagne, one of the many bigwigs adopted by Charles to bolster his political credentials. Like several of Charles' churches, it was deliberately sited to command the horizon of the New Town, and towers over the vast Nusle valley. The most awe-inspiring feature of the church is its remodelled interior, shaped like a single star, 24m in diameter. Legend has it that the architect was a novice who built it with the devil's help; others claim that it was designed in about 1575 by Bonifaz Wohlmut, court architect to Ferdinand I—but either way it's one of the grandest flourishes of (extremely) late Gothic architecture in Prague.

The neighbouring monastery houses the **Police Museum**, which may have a perverse appeal to some, Ke Karlovu 1 (*open Sept–June Tues–Sun 10–5, closed Mon*). From the the 14th-century fortification walls that stretch down from the church, you could also contemplate the gargantuan **Nusle Bridge** (Nuselský most), leaping half a kilometre across the Nusle valley. Some Praguers still suspect that the bridge, which carries six lanes of scooting traffic and two tracks of tunnelling metros, was intended to facilitate any urban military manoeuvres that the Communist government or its fraternal foreign allies might have deemed necessary. It's probably not true, since construction began during the relatively liberal mid-1960s, but it's hard to believe that someone somewhere didn't check that a line of tanks could safely trundle across. The bridge used to be named after Klement Gottwald, Czechoslovakia's first Communist president, and has long been the most popular spot for public suicides in the country. The former regime never got round to releasing the annual figures, but a worker under the bridge made the assertion, fortunately rather unbelievable, that for several years at least one body a month had crashed to a halt outside her shop.

National Memorial (Národní Památník) and Communist Party Mausoleum

Perched high on a ridge from which in 1420 the radical Táborites saw off a papal crusade and set off the action-packed decade of the Hussite Wars, is one of the lesser known marvels of the capital. A 9m-high sculpture of Hussite hero Jan Žižka now sits on the summit, mace in hand and surveying the railway tracks and decrepit housing of the district named after him. The sculpture is the largest equestrian statue in the world, but big though it is the horse slots almost discreetly into the granite edifice which lies just behind it—and it is firmly put into the shade by that building's extraordinary history. Although built in the early 1930s, it was the Communist Party Mausoleum between 1955 and 1989. But the strangest feature is an entire complex of rooms all constructed in the early 1950s for a single purpose—the mummification and display of Klement Gottwald, Czechoslovakia's 'First Working-Class President', an episode which ended rather messily. Under the yellowing tiles of the first room—a refrigerated morgue—the F.W-C.P. was pickled by a team of taxidermists from the Soviet Union, and it was here that the increasingly desperate attempts to keep him together were later made. A hydraulic lift in the nearby annexe used to raise and lower the besuited mummy from casket to slab. Next door is a bank of dials and knobs, regulating humidity and temperature, and manned continuously by ultra-loyal members of the Party. Finally, you come to the engine room. It contains an emergency generator and a maze of tanks, valves and pipes—all installed in pairs, in order that no mechanical failure could ever threaten the immortality of the demigod upstairs. The mausoleum was closed in early 1990, and its future is still undecided. Over the years, a series of bizarre plans have been mooted, the best of them being to install a waxwork of Gottwald's corpse and turn the whole shebang into a memorial to Communist kitsch. Worth investigating.

Žižkov Tower (Žižkovská Věž)

You should have few problems finding this futuristic silver steeple, next to Fibichova street, which at 287m can be seen from virtually everywhere in Prague. At close range the tower is phenomenally impressive, almost ready to begin a sleek and fiery ascent from the broad and quiet square of pastel tenements in which it waits. Since 1992, it has been happily broadcasting TV and radio signals, as well as bouncing wavelengths from passing satellites, but its early working life was plagued with problems. From the moment the Communists began its construction in 1984, suspicious locals began to whisper that it would be used to jam, beam and survey with hitherto unheard-of power. By its completion in 1989, most of Prague had become convinced that the Pražský čůrák (Prague penis) was emitting everything from subliminal propaganda to gamma rays, and under popular pressure the new government invited a team of international inspectors to check. The boffins prodded solenoids, waved Geiger counters, and found nothing. However, urban myth can still tell you about the many mutants born in the neighbourhood, and the strangely incongruous patter that occasionally crackles out of the mouths of passing babičky or their dachshunds. You can mull over the possibilities, and listen out for any odd humming, from a viewing gallery on the 8th floor, or the (fairly basic) café and restaurant on the 5th floor (*open daily 11—11*).

One of the more genuinely spooky things about the tower is that it is built over the ground that served as a **Jewish cemetery** between 1787 and 1891. The Communists destroyed most of it and turned it into a park in the early 1970s, but a small strip still stands to the north of the square. With tottering stones and crumbling inscriptions, it is reminiscent of the Old Jewish Cemetery, but here you're likely to be the only person wandering among the ivy-covered graves and haphazard piles of decommissioned slabs. As you stand under the shadow of the rocket, with the knowledge that the silent graveyard once stretched across the entire square, that can make for a disconcerting experience.

Church of the Sacred Heart (Kostel Srdce Páně)

This 1933 church (next to *Jiřího z Poděbrad* subway station) is a worthy addition to the modern masterpieces of Žižkov. Surrounded by tissue-tinted mansions and with the TV tower in the background, the view from this square is one of the more surreal to be found in Europe. The monochrome church, the eastern façade of which combines the pediments of classicism, the ornamentation of Art Nouveau, two obelisks and a mammoth glass clock, defies categorization. It's the work of Jože Plečnik (1872–1957), a Slovenian who studied in turn-of-the-20th-century Vienna and spent most of his life teaching and designing in Ljubljana. By adapting historical motifs, Plečnik attempted to create a modern architecture that retained the beauty and spirituality of the past; but paradoxically, although that made his work suspect to many of the cube-lovers of the day, it was Prague's hidebound conservatives who eventually had him run out of town. Despite that, it's since the dubious triumph of the concrete block that this church has come back into its own. It now looks not only more human but also more new-fangled than the Constructivist and Functionalist designs of most of Plečnik's contemporaries.

The Olšany and New Jewish Cemeteries

The **Olšany Cemeteries** (Olšanské hřbitovy) began life in 1680 as a repository for plague victims, but since 1784 they have made up Prague's main cemetery, and the 500,000m^2 are still being filled (*open Nov–Feb 9–4, March–April 8–6, May–Sept 8–7, Oct 8–6; accessible from either Flora or Želivského stations on line A of the metro*). The complex comprises 13 different sections, and its tombs range from the stoic neoclassicism of Prague's golden age of tombstone design to the bourgeois wealth of marble obelisks and granite sarcophagi. Rows of white crosses mark the dead of central Europe's endless wars, and there's an entire plot filled with the odd crucifixes of the Russian Orthodox Church. The eastern wall is lined with thousands of urns, arranged in stone display cabinets and counters that look rather like a line of quaint chemist shops. The grounds become a fearsome sight between All Saints' Eve (31 October) and All Souls' Day (2 November), ablaze with candles and filled with silent mourners.

Just to the right of the main entrance on Vinohradská is the **grave of Jan Palach**, the young man who burnt himself alive following the Warsaw Pact invasion in 1968 (*see* p.29). Some 800,000 people followed his coffin here from the Old Town in January 1969, and Alexander Dubček, still clinging to power, ordered that black flags be flown from every public building in the capital. One of the most sordid acts of the profoundly shabby regime that followed was to disinter Palach in 1973 and rebury him outside Prague. He was replaced by an unknown woman, Marie Jedličková, but for 16 years determined mourners decorated her tomb with flowers and candles on the anniversary of his death. In 1990, Palach was returned to his original resting place.

Adjacent to the Olšany cemeteries, on the far side of Jana Želivského street is the **New Jewish Cemetery** (*open Sept–Mar Sun–Thurs 8–4, April–Aug Sun–Thurs 8–5, closed Fri–Sat; men* *are asked to cover their heads*). It has been used by Prague's Jewish community since the end of the 19th century. You'll find the **grave of Franz Kafka** here, at the end of plot 21, about 300m along the path to your right. The writer spent the last months of his life in Berlin and then in a Viennese hospital but, as he once claimed, his home town had claws. Dr Kafka—he had studied law—is buried with his mother, and the father he reviled. All his novels remained unpublished (and incomplete) at his death, and he was mourned only by some close friends. The notice penned two days after his death by his former lover Milena Jesenská is suitably dramatic food for thought as you stand in front of the tomb:

> *He wrote the most significant works of modern German literature, [which] reflect the irony and prophetic vision of a man condemned to see the world with such blinding clarity that he found it unbearable and went to his death.*

The halo of martyrdom settles rather too easily over artists who die young, but uncompromising and screwed-up Kafka, who called writing 'a form of prayer' and completed his last story on his deathbed, probably merits it as much as any cult hero of modern times.

A memorial at the grave commemorates Kafka's three sisters, all of whom died in Nazi concentration camps, and other victims of the Holocaust are recalled throughout the cemetery. As the number of professing Jews in Prague sank even further in the postwar years, the graveyard became one of the loneliest in the capital. No old ladies came to tend the tombs, few came any longer to mourn, and the stones were slowly lost under a riot of dandelions, buttercups and ivy. Restoration has begun, but it remains to be seen if Prague's Jewish community can reverse its decline and take root again. If not, the graves still being dug mark the protracted conclusion to a story that lasted a thousand years.

Prague: Peripheral Attractions

The few square miles covering Hradčany, Malá Strana and the Old Town contain more than enough to keep most visitors busy, but there's a ragbag of attractions farther from the beaten track. Explorers and romantics should all find something to their tastes in the sights listed below, and there are particularly rich pickings for cemetery ghouls. There is also an inordinate number of memorials to Prague's troubled 20th-century history: as well as reminders of genuine tragedy, there are several spots that demand a quiet chuckle in honour of the more ridiculous aspects of totalitarianism. They are all easily accessible by public transport, and are included in the roughly clockwise order in which they circle the Old Town.

Vyšehrad

This ancient crag over the Vltava has spawned a thick web of nationalistic lore and legend. Most Praguers will still be able to reel off the myths, but its romantic heyday was a century ago, when it was infested with poets and painters in search of patriotic inspiration. It's now little more than a pleasant retreat on a lazy afternoon. There's a superb view over the river, but huffers and puffers might appreciate it more on the way down. The area was probably settled way back in the 9th century and, according to the city's oldest legend, soothsaying Princess Libuše was standing here when she came over all funny and prophesied Prague (*see* p.22). In the later 11th century, Vratislav II moved to the rock; the change of royal address lasted almost a century, but the only remaining evidence is the heavily restored Romanesque **Rotunda of St Martin** (Rotunda sv. Martina). Near it are remnants of the fortification walls built by Charles IV around the New Town in the mid-14th century.

The area's landmarks are the twin towers of the **Church of SS Peter and Paul** (Kostel sv. Petra a Pavla), founded in the late 11th century but entirely rebuilt in dull neo-Gothic style a hundred years ago. To the north of the church is the **Vyšehrad Cemetery** (Vyšehradský hřbitov). Established at the end of the 19th century to accommodate the cultural heroes of the Czech national revival, it forms an impressive gallery of modern Czech sculpture. Among the 600-odd corpses of the great and good are those of Smetana and Dvořák. At the far end is a **pantheon** (*slávín*), a mass grave of more than 50 artists and still the final destination of the *crème de la crème*. On the other side of the church are the **Vyšehrad Gardens** (Vyšehradské sady), small but peppered with a selection of strapping sculptures from Czech myth. They are all 19th-century works by J. V. Myslbek (who also sculpted the St Wenceslas monument, *see* p.116). Before leaving the area, be sure to see the **Cubist houses** designed by Josef Chochol (*see* p.34) between 1911 and 1913. There's a little triplet on the embankment below Vyšehrad (Podolské nábř. 6–10), one on Libušina 3, and, most impressively, the prismatic apartment block jutting outwards and upwards from the corner of Přemyslova and Neklanova.

Smíchov

This is one of Prague's most intriguing suburbs, minutes from the centre but a world apart from the golden city. In the 19th century it became the capital's industrial powerhouse and brewery, traditions that continue today. Factories and traffic seem to belch out more greenhouse gases than the rest of the city combined, but the uniqueness of the atmosphere now owes more to the large concentration of Romanies living here. You won't find tinkers' stalls or caravans, but on warm evenings the streets can have the liveliness of an extremely tranquil and Central

European New York City. A convenient place to begin exploring is the **Malá Strana Cemetery** (Malostranský hřbitov), which—despite official opening hours—never seems to get locked. Founded during the 1680 plague epidemic, it has been disused for over a century, and until recently it was one of the more macabre cemeteries to be found in Europe. It still contains an impressive concentration of Baroque and neoclassical sculpture, centred on the monumental cast-iron tomb of Bishop Leopold von Thun-Hohenstein, but it has lost its soul.

Also up here is the lovely **Mozart Museum** (Bertramka), Mozartova 169, Prague 5 (Smíchov), © 54 38 93, *Bertramka@comenius.cz (open daily 9.30–6)*. This charming villa is one of the few houses of the suburban gentry to survive the dark advance of industry into Smíchov during the 19th century. Mozart stayed here on three of his visits to Prague with the musically minded Dušeks, to whom he was close—so close that his relationship with Josefína has caused Praguers to smile knowingly ever since. Legend has it that he once found himself at a loss for what to compose next, and she decided to inspire him by locking them both into one of Bertramka's rooms. Quite how she loosened his creative block isn't made clear, but he apparently emerged clutching either an aria dedicated to her, or the overture to *Don Giovanni*, depending on whom, if anyone, you believe. The story is a gift to the museum owners, who dramatize it in period costume every night during high season, and once weekly during the rest of the year. The building was seriously damaged by fire in 1871, giving the exhibits a certain speculative feel; no one's quite sure whether Wolfgang really slept, studied or was incarcerated in any of the rooms that escaped. If you ask sweetly, the cashier can usually be persuaded to play the English taped guide as you walk through the rooms. The rapid-fire commentary is interspersed with snatches of the composer's greatest hits. Cult followers might appreciate the collection of 13 hairs, a rare relic of the body that notoriously got lost somewhere under Vienna's St Mark's cemetery. Summer evening concerts are held on the outdoor terrace, and at the far end of the garden is a stone table at which the composer is said to have mused.

Petřín Hill

Petřín is the green and wooded hump on the left as you cross the Charles Bridge from the Old Town. The forest that once used to stretch for miles to the south has disappeared, and vineyards no longer clamber up the hill, but its patchwork of gardens still makes for a perfect retreat as temperatures rise in the hazy city below. The best way of getting there is the funicular railway which leaves from a station just above Újezd street, about 100m north of the junction with Vítězná (*see* p.6). Alternatively, the Strahov gardens are linked by paths to Petřín; there's a gate into the Kinský gardens on nám. Kinských; and one of the loveliest walks in Prague is along the path to the north of Nebozízek restaurant, which turns from asphalt to forest as it slowly sinks into Malá Strana's sea of olive domes and orange tiles.

The first stop on the funicular is Nebozízek, marked by a terrace restaurant standing on what used to be a vintner's cottage. In the woods to the south is a monument to the Romantic poet Karel Mácha near which generations of wistful Praguers claim to have necked and spooned for the first time. At the summit is a rose garden and several minor spectacles. On the left is the Baroque **St Lawrence's Church**, and the **Prague Observatory and Planetarium** (*open Tues–Sun, but the hours vary wildly—call* © *24 51 07 09 if you're set on a visit. See also p.13*). Across the lawns to the right is a **model of the Eiffel Tower**, built in 1891 (two years after the original) by the Club of Czech Tourists, and used as a TV transmitting station until 1992. The globetrotting club was apparently very proud of its tower, but at 60m it falls laughably short of the Gallic symbol (*open April–Oct daily 9.30am–10pm; Nov–March Sat–Sun 9.30am–10pm, closed Mon–Fri; adm*). The year of Prague's Jubilee Exhibition was 1891, and the kooky Czech Tourists also contributed the nearby **maze** (*bludiště*), full of wibble-wobble mirrors and a diorama depicting the Swedish attack on the Charles Bridge in 1648. Finally, look out for the remnants of the 14th-century **Hunger Wall** (Hladová zed'), the crenellations and battlements of which crawl unevenly across Petřín as far as Strahov (*open daily 9–5; adm*).

Letná Park

This expanse of greenery was landscaped in the mid-19th century and, though it doesn't have the rolling splendour of Petřín, it offers another enjoyable stroll. One way of entering the park is by climbing the set of stone steps opposite the Svatopluk Čech Bridge (most Svatopluka Čecha), which fork and then rejoin at the graffiti-drenched **plinth of the former Stalin statue**. Uncle Joe was blown up in 1962, but some of his rocky remains are still in the chambers below. With due disrespect, young Praguers used to break in regularly before 1989 to hold parties in the warren of underground passageways. There's a more conventional dancefloor in the nearby **Hanava Pavilion** (Hanavský pavilón) to the west, an Art Nouveau exhibition piece that was moved here in 1898. To the north is the barren expanse of **Letná Plain**, which is entirely devoid of interest, save that it used to host the speech days of the Communists (1 May), and that, on 25 November 1989, it was the site of the demonstration that marked the death of the old régime, when a million people watched Václav Havel shake hands with Alexander Dubček. The nearby **National Technical Museum** on Kostelní is filled with venerable one-time miracles of modern technology and is great fun (*see* p.134).

Holešovice and Troja

These two areas of northern Prague contain the city's largest and wildest park; its most quirky one; the Tradefair Palace, with its impressive collection of 20th-century art; and the Baroque chateau at Troja, next to the tragic city zoo. The two districts are separated by the Vltava, an island and a railway line, but it's possible to make your way on foot from one to the other along a route that runs from Stromovka Park to Troja.

National Gallery's Collection of 19th- and 20th-Century Art/Tradefair Palace (Veletržní Palác)

> *Dukelských hrdinů 47 (Prague 7), Holešovice, ℂ 24 301 024, tram nos. 5, 12, 17, stop 'Veletržní'. Open Tues–Wed and Fri–Sun 10–6, Thurs 10–9, closed Mon.*

The National Gallery of Modern Art, housed in the spectacular Functionalist interior of the Tradefair Palace, pulls off the feat of making 20th-century art and design feel like an artefact already. The Tradefair Palace itself, built between 1925 and 1928, exudes the doomed optimism of those years. Its six balustraded levels, rising under a light-drenched atrium, have the perverse elegance of a Utopian prison wing. In 2000 the collection was completely reorganized by its new director, Milan Knizak, the former Fluxus artist; many of the city's other museums contributed pieces to enable the Tradefair Palace to display the art works within context, and wallpaper, furniture and fittings have been brought in as theatrical backdrops for some pieces in the collection. There is a new bookshop and café, and plans are afoot to devote a wing to a permanent exhibition of contemporary art.

Prague's artists discovered Impressionism, post-Impressionism and Cubism within a few years of each other during the first decade of the 20th century, and the collection shows how profoundly the ferment affected the work of this period. František Kupka's mystical and increasingly abstract art is well represented; look in particular for *The Keyboard, The Lake* (1909), which shows the fascination with painting musicality which he shared with Kandinsky, and *Amorpha, Fugue in Two Colours* (1912), generally regarded as one of the first—possibly *the* first—non-representational paintings of modern European art. Emil Filla's unique work is worth noting, permeated with the moody tension of Expressionism but given form in a fluently developing style. Like Bohumil Kubišta, his most distinctive work was expressed in a style that was Cubist in form but almost Futurist in its dynamic content; but one of his most startling paintings is the early *Reader of Dostoyevsky* (1907), an epiphany probably based on his own experience of being 'completely stunned on the rack of Dostoyevsky's perverse fantasy'.

The combination of psychological drama, *à la* Rodin, and Cubist method is also reflected in several of the gallery's sculptures, but the most distinctively Czech sculpture of this period is the social realist work of the 1920s and 30s. Unlike its monstrously idealized Socialist Realist cousin, this was inspired by a genuine regard for the real lives of little people. Otto Gutfreund was one of the earliest practitioners, but his work went on to influence a whole generation of Czechoslovakian sculptors, including Karel Pokorný, Jan Lauda, Karel Dvořák and Karel Kotrba. Their works are complemented by the gentle naive painting of Jan Zrzavý, and a lengthy collection of Czech Surrealist dreamscapes. Toyen, Štyrský and Šíma are the most eminent painters, but look out as well for the installations of Zdeněk Pešánek, whose pre-war fascination with neon remains unrivalled.

There is a distinctive collection of non-Czech art, including several works by Rodin, including his seminal Age of Bronze. Critics accused him of using a live model to make the original cast in 1875, paradoxically affronted by the fact that the work was so realistic that it lacked the idealism they still required in a nude. Rodin was undaunted and 10 years later those detractors that remained were confronted with the open sensuality of *Martyr* (1885). Rodin's most profound contribution to the 20th century however lay in his attempt to capture the psychological drama of existence in his art; the conviction of *St John the Baptist* (1880) represented his first major attempt down this road, but it climaxed with the dominating work *Balzac* (1898). As Rodin mulled over the meaning of genius, he transformed the novelist into this epic, which he called 'the sum of my whole life'.

The gallery's collection of early Cubist works is the most impressive in Central Europe. The director of the National Gallery during the 1920s, Vincenc Kramář, lived in Paris during the early years of the century and had an unerring appreciation of the emerging style. Works by Pablo Picasso form the core of the collection. The plum is the artist's *Self-portrait* (1907), painted while he was still thinking his way out of the world of appearances. It dates from the same year as his *Desmoiselles d'Avignon* and, like some of those well-known characters, the black-rimmed eyes and stylized features borrow heavily from the primitive sculpture then being studied by the artist. *Cadaqués Harbour* (1910) shows how far Picasso's experimentation had advanced beyond the work being produced by his contemporaries. The style develops through *Mandolin* and *Glass of Pernod* (1911) and *Woman with a Guitar at the Piano* (1911), and explodes into particular obscurity with *Clarinet* (1911) and the murky mystery of *Toreador Playing the Guitar* (1911). By the following year the high-water mark of Picasso's Cubism had passed, and three works here—*A Souvenir of Le Havre* (1912) and the excellent

Boxer (1912) and *Absinthe and Cards* (1912)—show how, with colour and two-dimensional texts, Synthetic Cubism returned to less recondite expressions of space and form. Only a couple of later works by the artist are owned by the gallery: the statuesque *Standing Woman* dates from the period of married tranquillity and his classical phase (1921); the grim *Woman's Head* (*Head in Grey*) is from the war years of bulls and horses (1941).

As well as various pieces of hazy Impressionism, there are a handful of works by the romantic heroes of post-Impressionism. Gauguin's lifetime preoccupation with colour is reflected in his *Bonjour, Monsieur Gauguin* (1889), and his erstwhile friend Van Gogh is represented by the swirling undercurrents of *Green Rye* (1889), created from the lunatic asylum that he entered after his failed knife attack on Gauguin and his more successful assault on his own ear.

There are several notable works from Germanic artists, including Gustav Klimt's luscious *Virgin* (1913). That hangs opposite Egon Schiele's very different vision of feminine fecundity, *Pregnant Woman and Death* (1911), in which the cadaverous couple dolefully contemplate life's bloody terror. Another tortured spirit, Edvard Munch, is represented by three paintings. His *Dancing on the Shore* (*c.* 1900) dates from the height of his creative powers, and was probably intended for his loosely planned *Frieze of Life*, an utterly beautiful contribution to what he called his 'poem of life, love and death'.

Keep your eyes open for two unnerving Expressionist portrayals of the powers-that-be by Wilhelm Thony and Max Oppenheimer. Thony's *Verdict* (pre-1929) is Kafka in monochrome, while Oppenheimer's excellent *Operation* (1912) takes the form of an indictment of the medical profession: a turbulent sea of white coats surrounded by Mephistophelian doctors. Look out, too, for exceptional paintings by Oskar Kokoschka, most painted during his stay in the capital between 1934 and 1938. The Nazis put Kokoschka on their blacklist, and he left shortly before they rolled into town. He spent the war years in London, and his *Red Egg* (1941) is a powerful attack on the common enemy. Elsewhere you will find modern Czech art and sculpture from the last four decades. It includes the Abstract Expressionist work of Mikuláš Medek, and a couple of Day-glo polystyrene turds.

Troja Chateau

U troiského zámku 1, Prague 7, ✆ 689 07 61. Open April–Oct Tues–Sun 10–6, closed Mon; Nov–March Sat–Sun 10–5, closed Mon–Fri.

This Baroque palace to the north of central Prague houses a collection of 19th-century Czech art, but it's the rich, gaudy, illusionistic decoration of Troja itself that makes the journey here worthwhile. It was built in the 1600s by an ambitious Czech nobleman, who was so anxious to please Bohemia's new masters that he submerged his main hall in an apotheosis of the Habsburgs. Painted by the Flemish-born and Roman-trained Abraham Godyn between 1691 and 1697, it is the richest illusionistic painting in the capital. Austrian triumphalism is the order of the day and, as well as innumerable scenes showing the wisdom, prudence and bravery of the kooky clan, the gaudy masterpiece heaps scorn on the Turks, who had just overplayed their hand for the last time. With the relief of Vienna in 1683, the Sublime Porte had begun its relentless decline into Sick Man of Europe, and there are cringing infidels dotted throughout, with one particularly impressive turbanned loser, with *trompe l'œil* shadow, tumbling from the wall. The simple theme returns as allegory in the chateau's small grounds, littered with scenes from a Baroque battle of the gods and giants, and including a series of sculptures cascading down both sides of a stone staircase.

Prague: Museums and Galleries

Prague itself is one big museum and art gallery, and many visitors never set foot inside the collections scattered across the capital. However, there are some curious and beautiful things behind its doors, and this chapter will help you decide what may be worth a visit. Prices are still lower than in many Western countries, and most museums offer a 50 per cent reduction for students, children, pensioners and disabled people. The standard closing day is Monday, with a couple of maverick collections shutting down on Tuesday instead, and you can never count on being allowed into *any* building in Prague if its advertised closing time is less than half an hour away. Otherwise there's really no best or worst time to pay your choice a visit. In some cities you almost have to queue to see each painting or exhibit, but you can usually roam free in Prague's repositories, and in more obscure museums your very arrival may represent the largest crowd of the day. However, there's one minor obstacle to free movement that you'll face in almost every one of the city's museums and galleries: the dreaded and legendary *babička* posted in each room, poised to snap or spring.

Old Town (Staré Město)

Cubist Museum, House of the Black Madonna (U černé Matky boží), Celetná 34, ✆ 24 21 17 32. *Open Tues–Sun 10–6, closed Mon.* A small collection of Cubist art and design, in a building to match with a delightful keyhole staircase. *See* p.56.

Mucha Museum, Kaunitz Palace, Panská 7, ✆ 628 41 62, *museum@mucha.cz, www.mucha. cz. Open daily 10–6.* A small gathering of the Art Nouveau works of Alfons Mucha (1860–1939). For more, visit the Municipal House (*see* below).

Municipal House (Obecní dům), nám. Republiky 5, ✆ 22 00 21 29, *www.obecni-dum.cz. Open daily 10–6.* Permanent and temporary exhibitions of all things Art Nouveau, from poster art to photography. Daily guided tours through the halls and salons. *See* p.56.

Prague House of Photography (Pražský dům fotografie), Husova 23. *Open May–Sept daily 11–7, Oct–April daily 11–6.* Temporary exhibitions of Czech and foreign photographers.

Jewish Quarter (Josefov)

Kafka Museum, U radnice 5, ✆ 232 16 75. *Open Mon–Fri 10–6, Sat 10–5, closed Sun.* Photos and other memorabilia displayed in the writer's birthplace. *See* p.72.

Jewish Museum (Židovské muzeum), Jáchymova 3, ✆ 24 81 00 99, *zmp@ecn.cz, wwwjewish museum.cz.* See p.62 for ticket details. This museum covers most of what remains of the Prague ghetto, and includes several synagogues, the 12-layer Jewish cemetery, an exhibition devoted to Prague's Jewish history, and collections of thousands of Jewish artefacts from across Europe. The artefacts were assembled by the Nazis, who planned to transform the quarter into an 'exotic museum of an extinct race'. One ticket covers the admission fee to the Maisel Synagogue (*see* p.68), the Spanish Synagogue, the Pinkas Synagogue (*see* p.66), the Ceremonial Hall (*see* p.68), and the Old-New Synagogue (*see* p.66).

Museum of Decorative Arts (Uměleckoprůmyslové muzeum), 17 Listopadu 2, ✆ 51 09 31 11, *direct@anet.cz. Temporarily closed for renovation.* A colourful display of the decorative arts from the late 16th century onwards. The massive holdings of the museum also include one of the best glass collections in the world. *See* p.69.

National Gallery's Collection of Medieval Art in Bohemia and Central Europe, St Agnes' Convent (Klášter sv. Anežky), U Milosrdných 17, ✆ 24 81 06 28. *Open Tues–Sun 10–6, closed Mon.* Reopened after renovation and remodelling at the end of 2000 with an excellent collection of Gothic art. *See* p.70.

Prague Castle and Hradčany

Bílek Villa (Bílkova vila), Mickiewicznova 1, Prague 6, ✆ 243 22 02. *Open Tues–Sun 10–6, closed Mon.* A superb collection of the powerful work of František Bílek, one of the most isolated and extraordinary sculptors in modern Czech history. *See* p.34.

Military Museum (Vojenské historické muzeum), Hradčanské nám. 2, ✆ 20 20 20 23. *Open May–Oct Tues–Sun 10–6, closed Mon.* Well-displayed exhibits relating to early military history throughout the world. *See* p.92.

National Gallery's Collection of Baroque Art, St George's Convent (Bazilika svatého Jiří), Prague Castle, ✆ 57 32 05 36. *Open Tues–Sun 10–6, closed Mon.* An underwhelming collection redeemed by a handful of striking works. *See* p.87.

National Gallery's Collection of European Old Masters, Sternberg Palace (Šternberský Palác), Hradčanské nám. 15, ✆ 20 51 46 34–7. *Open Tues–Sun 10–6, closed Mon.* Contains a couple of acknowledged masterpieces (Dürer's *Feast of the Rose Garlands* and Bruegel's *Haymaking*) and a pleasant peppering of outstanding works by Cranach, El Greco, Goya, Rubens, Rembrandt and others. *See* p.92.

National History Museum (Historické muzeum), Lobkovický palác, Jiřská 3, ✆ 53 73 06. *Open Tues–Sun 9–5, closed Mon.* A diminutive museum offering a brief skim through Bohemia's history.

Picture Gallery of Prague Castle (Obrazárna Pražského hradu), Prague Castle, ✆ 24 37 33 68. *Open Tues–Sun 10–6, closed Mon.* Created to hold the collection of Emperor Rudolf II, who gathered artists from across Europe at his court. Less interesting than a hitlist of its treasures (Tintoretto, Titian, Veronese, Rubens) would suggest. *See* p.77.

Strahov Gallery, Strahov Monastery (Strahovský klášter), off Pohořelec, ✆ 20 51 66 71. *Open Tues–Sun 9–5, closed Mon.* A distinguished collection of European art: it's limited in size but, when combined with the opulent 18th-century libraries of the monastery, it makes a visit to Strahov essential. *See* p.98.

New Town

Anti-Nazi Resistance Memorial, in the crypt of the Church of SS Cyril and Methodius, Resslova 9, ✆/✆ 24 92 06 86. *Open Tues–Sun 10–4, closed Mon.* A small and moving exhibition at the site of the pitched gun battle fought between the Nazis and the assassins of Reinhard Heydrich. To reserve a guided tour call Dr. J. Suvarsky on ✆/✆ 24 92 06 86. *See* p.120.

Mánes Gallery, Masarykovo nabr. 250, ✆ 29 18 08, *office@gmanes.cz, www.gmanes.cz. Open Tues–Sun 10–6, closed Mon.* This stylish white Cubist-Functionalist building, hanging over the river and surrounded by ancient trees, is one of the most prominent modern art galleries in town, exhibiting the work of both Czech and international artists.

National Museum (Národní muzeum), Václavské nám. 68, ✆ 24 49 71 11, *www.nm.cz. Open daily 10–6, closed on first Tues of the month.* The splendid neo-Renaissance interior is worth seeing, and the exterior is unavoidable, but otherwise this is a very dull natural history museum. *See* p.116.

Police Museum (Muzeum policie), Ke Karlovu 1, Prague 2, ✆ 29 52 09, *www.mvcr.cz/policie/muzeum.htm. Open Tues–Sun 10–5, closed Mon.* Once devoted to the activities of the National Security Corps, this museum has been cleaned up since the revolution and is now intended to laud the acceptable face of authoritarianism, but is still a rather ominous place. *See* p.121.

Further Afield

Military Museum (Aviation Museum), Exhibition of Aeronautics and Cosmonautics (Expozice letectva a kosmonautiky), just off Mladoboleslavská, Prague 9, ✆ 20 20 75 04. *Open May–Oct Tues–Thurs and Sat–Sun 9.30–6, closed Mon and Fri.* This museum lies miles from the centre of town, but it's well worth a visit. It comprises three hangars filled with a superb collection of propellers, ack-ack guns, jet engines, Spitfires and Tiger Moths, and just about every plane the Warsaw Pact produced until the mid-1960s. As you wander among the sleek silver MiGs and dumpy Suchoi bombers, you can't help but contemplate the aerial death they might have delivered had Europe's Cold

War ever warmed up. Times are changing: the museum's newest acquisition is a cobalt-blue Phantom, handed over by Britain in early 1992. The museum also contains several requisitioned Panzers, lines of Soviet tanks and a couple of tactical rocket launchers. Military parking lots and a still functioning airfield surround the museum. They're off-limits, and an accidental meander through them is the kind of diversion that would probably have got you deported before 1989. Among the planes and personnel carriers, a 1993 visit revealed partially dismantled Warsaw Pact rockets, helicopter gunships and, sitting incongruously pretty in the middle of a hardware graveyard, Prague's notorious Pink Tank, painted by David Černy.

Mozart Museum (Bertramka), Mozartova 169, Prague 5 (Smíchov), ☎ 54 38 93, *bertramka@ comenius.cz. Open daily 9.30–6.* A charming villa where Mozart stayed on three of his visits to Prague. Summer evening concerts are held on the outdoor terrace. *See* p.127.

National Gallery's Collection of 19th- and 20th-Century Art, Tradefair Palace, Dukelských hrdinů 47, Prague 7, Holešovice, ☎ 24 30 10 24, *smsu@ngprague.cz. Open Tues–Wed and Fri–Sun 10–6, Thurs 10–9, closed Mon.* Housed within an exceptionally impressive Functionalist building, this gallery contains the cream of the Czech Republic's modern art collection. Highlights include a priceless collection of Cubist works by Picasso, paintings by Schiele, Kokoschka and Van Gogh, and a comprehensive collection of Czech art, from the early Modernism of František Kupka to the whimsical installation art of the 1990s. *See* p.128.

National Gallery's Collection of 19th- and 20th-Century Czech Sculpture, Zbraslav n. Vltavou, Prague 5. *Open June–Oct Tues–Sun 10–6, closed Mon.* Despite the loss of much of its 20th-century holdings to the Tradefair Palace, this remains one of the capital's finest collections. It's a 30min journey from the city centre, and as a result is only visited by a determined and well-informed minority of visitors. To get there, take buses 29, 241 or 243 from the terminus outside Smíchovské nádraží (metro line B). Get off at Zbraslavské nám., a quiet suburban square just past the second bridge you cross, and the grounds of the low Baroque monastery are to your right. The ground floor is dominated by the work of J. V. Myslbek, the country's most influential 19th-century sculptor. The mainstream of Czech Art Nouveau is represented by Ladislav Šaloun, and a gentle series of small copper and bronze reliefs by Stanislav Sucharda. Upstairs, the belated influence of Rodin, who exhibited in Prague in 1902, is reflected in the earlier works of Josef Mařatka and Bohumil Kafka, both of whom spent a couple of years working in the great man's studio.

National Technical Museum (Národní technické muzeum), Kostelní 42, Prague 7, ☎ 20 39 91 11, *info@ntm.cz, www.ntm.cz. Open Tues–Sun 9–5, closed Mon.* Tremendous fun. The colossal main hall is a Grand Central Station of transport, with infernal steam engines, Bugattis and Mercedes, and long lines of motorbikes dating from 1887. Sailing over everything are 13 aircraft (14 if you include the balloon that's apparently rising through the roof), an impressive assortment of translucent dragonflies and vintage biplanes. Another hall is filled with hundreds of still and movie cameras, including some of the earliest doomed attempts at stereoscopic photography. The history of chronography is recorded in another ground-floor room. Most of the devices are calm enough (look out for the Renaissance pocket sundial), but several of the dropping balls and swinging pendulums tick mercilessly throughout, and erupt into pandemonium at random intervals. No less unnerving is the acoustics exhibition on the first floor, an interactive cacophony of screaming children and every noise from feedback to bird warbles. On the top floor is a small astronomical collection, which includes sextants and astrolabes used by Tycho Brahe and Johannes Kepler in Prague. There are guided tours (at 11am, 1pm and 3pm) down to the belly of the building, a tremendous mock-up coal mine far underground.

Troja Chateau, U Trojského zámku 1, Prague 7, ☎ 689 07 61. *Open April–Oct Tues–Sun 10–6, closed Mon; Nov–Mar Sat–Sun 10–5, closed Mon–Fri.* A beautiful Baroque palace to the north of central Prague with a collection of 19th-century Czech art. *See* p.130.

Prague: Food and Drink

Eating out in Prague is no longer the mediocre chore that it used to be. With new restaurants opening all the time, ingredients improving, and the arrival of immigrant *restaurateurs* from as far afield as Iceland and India, a Prague meal can sometimes even be exciting—the first time that can honestly be said in decades. Although many restaurants still offer little more than a list of steaks, this section should ensure that your culinary experience of Prague doesn't leave a bitter taste in your mouth.

Food

The specialities of the Czech kitchen represent the culmination of centuries of serfdom and peasant experimentation. Favoured vegetables are the turnip, cabbage and potato and, although meat of every description finds its way on to the table, offal is treated with unusual respect. There's a robust suspicion of most herbs other than marjoram and all spices save garlic, and matters are only mitigated by the influence of the hot-blooded Slovaks and their Hungarian neighbours.

The most distinctive delicacy of the Czech kitchen is the *knedlík*, or dumpling. Praguers treat it as the highest expression of the country's cuisine—and if you say that you recently ate an unexciting one, you're almost certain to be told that *you have to know where to go*. Unfortunately, only the most discriminating foreign palate can truly tell the difference in most cases. The main distinction is between the floury *houskový knedlík* and the *bramborový knedlík*, made of mushy potato. Both are usually served with a lump of flesh in a thick gravy, and are staple fare in beer halls. *Špekové knedlíky* are marginally more interesting, mixed with bacon, while *kynuté knedlíky* are downright wild in comparison, centred on lumps of stewed fruit.

You're on tastier ground when it comes to cold meats. Prague ham (*šunka*) is of high quality, but it's generally agreed that the best salamis are the harder Hungarian-tinged varieties, particularly the flat *lovecký salám*, and both *Uherský salám* and *salám alékum*. Sausages are much loved, and you can pick up a *párek* (two long porkers) in stands across the city. The frankfurter-like *Liberecký párek* and the paprika-flavoured *čabajka* are the best varieties. If you avoid pork, you can safely eat *hovězí párky* and *drůbeží párky*, made of beef and chicken respectively.

Decades of acid rain and toxic leaks have left their very dirty mark in the food chain, and you might want to consider the alternatives to red meat. Czech chickens aren't factory-farmed and, with an average lifespan of 42 days, few of them have as much time as they might want to absorb background carcinogens and contaminants. Freshwater fish are another healthy possibility: carp and trout are bred in the lakes of southern Bohemia and, along with the pike and eel that are occasionally found with them, they are widely available in Prague.

Soups (*polévky*) are often delicious, and in cheaper beer halls and cafés they are often the most likely winners on the menu—but among the standard meats and vegetables, there are a few Czech peculiarities of which you should be aware. Broths are often served with a raw egg yolk bobbing along the bottom of the bowl, and the done thing is to puncture it and swish it about before eating. *Dršťková* is one of the most popular soups and comprises floating pieces of a cow's stomach, while *zabijačková polévka* is a pungent concoction made largely of pigs' blood. The name, roughly translated, means 'slaughter soup', although it's also known by the mildly obscene term *prdelačka*.

There are a few other snacks that you'll probably encounter. Waffles (*vafle*) are everywhere, and to find one of the squashy pieces of sponge and cream you generally need do no more than follow your nose. There are also stalls across the city selling *bramborák*, a garlicky potato pancake that is delicious if not greasy. *Ďábelský toust* is a fiercely tasty mixture of meat (usually beef) on toast. *Smažený sýr* is fried cheese, which is more appetizing but no less unhealthy than it sounds. The most common cheeses are tasteless copies of Edam (*eidam*) or Brie (*Hermelín*), but there are a few remarkably malodorous native creations. If you can stand the whiff, they go well with the rich wine. One of the most fetid is *olomoucké syrečky*, and, if you're drinking beer, ask the bartender for some *pivní*. It isn't designed to be eaten by itself— pour some of your drink on to the plate, add chopped onions while kneading gently, and offer the rank concoction around. In the summer, you'll also see hawkers selling bags of Slovakian sheep cheese (*korbáč*), which looks like stringy pieces of fresh pasta. Prague's sweetmeats are fairly unremarkable, although Viennese-style cream cakes are making a comeback to meet the expectations of tourists. Sweet teeth may enjoy *koláče*, tasty titbits topped with curd, and *palačinky*, pancakes that can be atrocious or scrumptious depending on the tosser.

Drink

Czech food may be nothing to write home about, but its beverages can be more compelling— so much so that one in every five Czechs is a registered alcoholic.

Beer

Czech beer needs little introduction: Plzeň is the home of Pilsner Urquell, the first lager and the father of a thousand German imitators, while the brewing town of Budweis (České Budějovice) has become part of the American dream. In fact, the American company Busch actually borrowed little more than the name, and the potent concoction produced in the Czech Republic puts the US slop to shame. (Perhaps realizing that, Busch has kept Czech Budweis off the US market for decades.) Both beers are chock full of alcohol and sugar, all created naturally during the brewing process unlike that in their additive-laden Western rivals. You may already like sweet beers, and if not you should acquire the taste—look out for beer halls and bottles marked *Plzeňský prazdroj* and *Budvar*. Prague produces several beers of its own (such as *Staropramen*, *Braník* and *Smíchov*), which are slightly more bitter. They taste fine to most people, but some of the capital's own beer bores disavow them, and you may hear it claimed that the Vltava is pumped directly through the brewery. Most beer is 12° proof (i.e. about three per cent alcohol), but 10° beer is also sold. In addition to lager, dark beers (*černé pivo*) are popular: *Purkmistr* is the most widely available, while the beer halls at U Fleků (14°) and U sv. Tomáše brew their own treacly varieties. When you have your first draught in a *pivnice* (pub), Praguers claim that you should stick a matchstick into the head to test the quality. The only danger is that, if it doesn't stay erect for at least 10 seconds, you may be accosted by a staggering drunk who'll suggest that you all go elsewhere.

Doomladen predictions that Prague's *pivnices* would all fall prey to a conspiracy of Western brewing companies and hamburger empires have not yet come to pass, and there are still plenty of places to get hammered in traditional style. Trial, error and dubious drinking partners will soon help you assemble a list of favourite watering holes. The freshest-tasting beers are those drawn by hand, and one possible circuit, incorporating six brews, no carbon dioxide canisters, and a stagger across the length of Prague, comprises U černého vola (Loretánské nám. 1;

Velkopopovický kozel), U zlatého tygra (Husova 17; Pilsener), Krušovická pivnice (Široká 20; Krušovice), U staré školy (Bílkova 11; Staropramen), Radegast (Templová 2; Radegast) and U šumavy (Štěpánská 3; Budvar). Any *pivnice* crawl should be undertaken with dedication, since it's only too easy to get mired in the first stop—your glass is replaced and a notch added to your bill before you can say *už nepiju* (roughly 'enough drinking, already'), which soon becomes far too difficult anyway. The procedure reaches almost industrial scale and efficiency at **U Fleků**, where hundreds of people are intoxicated nightly by trained waiters who cruise around with huge tin trays of brimming black beers. The only problem with that inn is that it's long been ceded to Germany by Praguers; if it's Czech company that you want, go down the local *pivnice* or look through those on pp.165–7 for an appropriately authentic oasis. Be warned that, the more traditional a place is, the greater is the likelihood that your arrival will set off grim mutterings among the more florid of the regulars. If you want a real challenge head towards **U zlatého tygra** on Husova 17, a ferociously exclusive hangout for literarily inclined drunks, where the waiters won't serve you if you sit in the wrong place and no one will talk to you if you fail to observe any one of about 137 Czech drinking customs.

Wine

Oenological pontification is a game that is played by waiters in the swankier restaurants in Prague, but it is even less merited than usual in the case of Czech wine. Moravia has the best grapes, but you'd have to have your tongue embedded in your cheek before you could describe any of the wines as cheeky, playful or vintage. With some of the drier whites, you can almost sense scar tissue forming on your oesophagus as you drain your glass, while several reds feel robust enough to chew. However, as French wines lose their monopoly on the world wine market, the lure of the export trade has led some vineyards to revamp their operations and Czech wines may yet become a force to be reckoned with on the Western dinner party circuit. A glass of Czech wine is twice the size of a regular measure in the UK and USA, and if you're a moderate sort you should ask for a *deci*. The quality of the wine makes it particularly suitable for mulling, and during the winter most cafés have a permanently bubbling pot of wine, cloves and cinnamon—ask for *svařené víno*. One other speciality is *burčák*, which is sold and drunk across the capital from late September. It is the first wine of the year, Prague's semi-fermented Beaujolais Nouveau—and it's an impudent little rascal which masquerades as a soft drink until it knocks you senseless. Bohemia also produces sparkling wine (*sekt*), which is good for popping and conspicuously wasting, but it seems to make many people feel very queasy if they drink much of it. Slovakian *sekt* is marginally less sickly, and useful if you want to celebrate on a budget.

Absinthe

In absinthism, the hallucinating delirium is most active, most terrifying, sometimes provoking reaction of an extremely violent and dangerous nature. Another more grave syndrome accompanies this: all of a sudden the absinthist cries out, pales, loses consciousness and falls; the features contract, the jaws clench, the pupils dilate, the eyes roll up, the limbs stiffen, a jet of urine escapes, gas and waste material are brusquely expulsed.

Dr Valentin Magnan

As Dr Magnan's clinical report suggests, absinthe is not a drink to be taken lightly. Indeed, since the Absinthe Murders of 1895 (when Jean Lenfray shot dead his pregnant wife and two children, before messily missing his own forehead), it hasn't often been a drink to be taken at all. For several decades, observers had been luridly documenting the drink's growing popularity among poets, painters and the lower classes in general, and the fact that Lenfray had downed a couple of glasses a few hours before the killings provided the impetus for a full-scale prohibition movement. By the early 20th century, absinthe had been banned by most of the world. But Czechoslovakia never got round to legislating and, in 1991, a restituted distillery owner in southern Bohemia realised that squeezing through the loophole could be very lucrative indeed. He was right—and Mr Hill's green potion has been going from strength to strength in Prague's bars ever since.

The best place to begin an absinthe adventure is the **Akropolis**, a trendy if slightly grungy music bar at Kubelíkova 27 which saw the arrival of the first bottles back in 1991 (*open Mon–Fri 10am–1am, Sat–Sun 4pm–1am*). Several pubs also sell the drink as a chaser; one with a healthy history of absinthe abuse is **U vystřelenýho oka** (The Shot-out Eye) at U božích bojovníků 3 (*open daily 3.30pm–1am*), lodged under a mountainside in Žižkov and filled with friendly young drinkers. There are certain rituals to be observed when drinking absinthe—that's what you might expect of any exotic drink worth its salt but, in the case of absinthe, there are also sound practical reasons. Its active ingredient, wormwood, tastes rather like toxic waste might (the Greek word *apsinthion* means 'undrinkable') so, to render it even half fit for human consumption, sugar has to be added. Historically, this was done by adding water through a sugar cube—a lengthy process, which allowed for leisurely contemplation and hallucination—but in late 19th-century Prague a more dynamic ritual was invented: drinkers are expected to first set alight an absinthe-soaked spoonful of sugar then, once it has caramelized, stir it into the absinthe with water. Although unsanctified by tradition, the procedure has an appealing drama about it, particularly when the molten sugar is added before the flame has quite gone out.

A word of warning may be appropriate. Wormwood is an unpredictable substance —over the centuries, it has been used *inter alia* to treat bad breath, deworm intestines, obtain eternal youth, kill fleas, and prevent flatulence in dogs—and Jean Lenfray's antics are vivid proof of its disinhibiting effects. Although it is extremely unlikely that you would go on a killing spree after a sip (a little-remembered fact about the Absinthe Murders is that Lenfray also downed several measures of crème de menthe, cognac and brandy, and one-and-a-half bottles of wine), those of an unhinged or psychopathic disposition should consume it with care. Tests on small animals have shown that, whereas alcohol kills after a relatively brief spasm of *delirium tremens*, absinthe overdoses are preceded by a whole battery of predicaments—notably hallucinations, automatism, amnesia, *grand mal* epileptic seizures, and the brusque expulsion of waste material mentioned by Dr Magnan. But if you remain undaunted, it awaits you in Prague, and UK citizens can legally bring home one litre. The position in the USA is less clear: to be on the safe side, you could remove the label and pretend that it's mouthwash if stopped at customs.

Miscellaneous Liquors

During your alcoholic meanderings through the city, you should look out for three **native liquors**. *Slivovice* (plum brandy) and *Borovička* (a gin-type drink) are more or less palatable, but the most distinctive is *Becherovka*. Its 20-herb recipe is one of the world's many distilling secrets, supposedly known only to two men, and the mystique surrounding the ingredients, along with the manufacturers' only-too-garrulous bumph about every other stage of the drink's creation, sells several million of the flat green bottles annually. You'll find it sold in every single bar and pub in Prague, although it originates in the spa town of Karlovy Vary. As a result, it is said to calm an upset stomach, as Prague's dipsos are fond of telling foreigners as they drink their way into double figures.

Eating Out

There are several types of eating and drinking establishment in Prague: beer joints (*pivnice*, *hostinec* or *hospoda*), wine bars (*vinárny*), cafés (*kavárny*) and restaurants (*restaurace*). In the days of central planning, each had its prerogatives and permitted menus, but nowadays the only significant difference is between those places devoted to beer, and everywhere else. The former tend to be cheap, smoky, male and unfriendly to outsiders, with the menu restricted to the more humble Czech dishes. The general rule is riddled with exceptions and you should try making a meal out of a pub crawl at least once, but in most cases the best food is to be had in the city's wine bars and restaurants.

The dining culture in Prague is still underdeveloped. The growth of a postwar dinner party circuit was stymied by rabbit-hutch flats, mediocre ingredients and a lack of foreign cookbooks, so only the dedicated few made a habit of eating out. A sociologist might explain the stay-at-home culture in terms of the social atomization engendered by 40 years of repression; another reason was that the menus in most restaurants were quite literally identical. All ingredients, and combinations thereof, required prior approval by hygiene inspectors unless they were enumerated in one of three state cookbooks: *Recipes for Warm Dishes, Recipes for Cold Dishes I* and *Recipes for Cold Dishes II*. The recipes concerned, while extremely hygienic, had about as much zest as the cookbooks' titles, but for over three decades they held sway in the city's kitchens. Although bureaucratic controls remain stringent, things are now improving hugely. Ragrolled and rustic restaurants are replacing the interrogation chambers of yore, while French, Italian and American chefs are finally challenging the spiritual legacy of the state cookbooks. Perhaps most importantly for the long term, a new generation of Czech restaurants is emerging, in which the quality of the dumpling is more significant than its weight.

Reservations

In Prague, more than in many other cities, the more attractive a restaurant sounds, the more advisable it is to make an advance reservation. Tasty food is still at a premium and, during peak holiday periods, you should call at least three days in advance to be absolutely sure of getting a table.

Service

Recent years have seen a general improvement in waiters' table manners, often the result of crash courses in charm instituted by desperate new owners, but it's still too often the case that only the *concept* of politeness has been grasped by Prague's restaurant staff. The theory that the customer is always right runs directly contrary to the convictions of most Czech waiters and, although they usually maintain the pretence, in moments of candour or crisis their superiority complexes will win through. Give as good as you get.

Tricks

Even assuming that you eventually find someone who is prepared to give you a bill, you aren't clear yet. Check your bill carefully and question any strange notches and ambiguous squiggles that you find. At worst, you'll be treated like a moron as the hieroglyphs are deciphered and, at best, your bill will be halved.

Tipping

A tip of 10 per cent is becoming standard, although it is still customary in cheaper Czech establishments to round the bill up to the nearest reasonable zero. Traditionally, your bill is totted up in front of you, and you're expected to say a figure that you want to pay in total, rather than the amount of change you want returned. How much you actually leave depends on your theory of the tip but, given the variable standard of service in Prague, you'll be doing your bit for future generations of visitors by linking the amount to your level of satisfaction.

Breakfast

Spurred on by foreigners' demands, breakfast is finally becoming an established item on Prague menus. It's often still restricted to omelettes, coffee and *hemenex* ('ham and eggs'), but expat-run establishments often have more substantial offerings: try **Red, Hot and Blues** (*see* p.144), **Molly Malone's** (*see* p.144), or the **Globe Bookstore and Coffeehouse** on Pštrosova 6 (*see* p164). The two branches of **Bohemia Bagel** at Masná 2 and Újezd 16 are cheap and cheerful places to snack all day long, while one of the best outdoor spots is **Barock** (see p.142), the attractions of which include freshly squeezed orange juice, only too rare elsewhere in Prague. **Érra** on Konviktská 11 has a breakfast menu which includes muesli and fruit as well as a fry-up; by night it metamorphoses into a gay bar, but during the daytime it's a cosy cafe that's welcoming to all comers. Finally, one time-honoured place in which to start the day is the Art Nouveau **Evropa Café** at Václavské nám. 25. The meal there is deeply uninspired and unjustly expensive, but it has been a Prague institution since the days when you would eat it while perusing one of its many copies of the *Morning Star*. For Sunday brunch, you could join the scores of wasted clubbers who laze around in the back room of the **FX Café** at Bělehradská 120; or listen to jazz in the ineffably elegant surroundings of **Parnas** at Smetanovo nábr. 2.

Late-night Food

If you find yourself with the post-midnight munchies, your options in Prague remain limited. The vegetarian **FX Café** at Bělehradská 120 is an excellent spot to stave off starvation, but after the closure of its kitchen (around 4.30am) filling your stomach requires a descent of several rungs down the sociological ladder. Non-stop food and drink are available at any number of kiosks serving sausages, burgers and other fast foods on the junction between Wenceslas Square and Na příkopé. For true sleaze however, there is still no rival to **Rebecca**, a 24-hour restaurant with a long granite bar at Olšanské nám. 8 in Žižkov. Any taxi driver worth his licence knows where it is, as does every other Praguer who regularly finds him- or herself at a loose end just before sunrise. Its clientele and omnipresent video screens can induce a deep sense of spiritual *ennui* but, if your concerns are for bread alone, its flesh-and-veg meals should help you make it through to dawn.

Vegetarians

Central Europe's meat fetish still exerts a tremendous power in Prague. You'll be confronted with slabs of flesh and bloody carcasses everywhere you go, and even when you order an apparently meatless meal you run the constant risk of being slipped a sausage. However, a number of places now serve a good range of vegetarian dishes, and among the best are the **Lotos** restaurant, the **FX Café** and (for food on the move especially) **Country Life**. To ask whether a place has meatless dishes, say *máte bezmasé jídlo?* Vegans will have as grim a life in Prague as they have everywhere else. However, Country Life and the **Vacek Bio-Market** on Mostecká 3 carry a large selection of lentils, and bread is, of course, widely available.

Restaurants

The following places offer some of the tastiest, best-value and most interesting meals currently available in the capital. The selections are divided into three categories: expensive, moderate and inexpensive. Estimates can only be very rough, but you should expect to pay the following for a **three-course dinner, including wine or beer:**

∞∞∞	*expensive*	£15–30 ($23–45)
∞∞	*moderate*	£8–15 ($12–23)
∞	*inexpensive*	up to £8 ($12)

Several of the places below don't serve full three-course meals, but they have been put into whichever category they would be in if they did. Most foreign visitors will still find eating out to be good value in all but the most exclusive restaurants, but remember that many Czechs would regard even a meal in the moderate category as something of a luxury. If you've asked a friend to join you, you might avoid a lot of embarrassment by asking him or her to choose a place or saying beforehand that you want to pay. All those place listed take credit cards unless otherwise stated. *See* p.179–80 for a basic menu decoder. *Dobrou chut'!*

Old Town (Staré Město)

∞∞∞   **Aqua Bar and Grill**, U plovárny 8 (across the bridge from Pařížská street), ✆ 57 31 25 78, ✉ 57 31 25 74. *Open noon—1am.* Superb food on the banks of the Vltava, in the renovated premises of what used to be central Prague's outdoor swimming pool. In the summer, book a seat on the outdoor terrace.

∞∞∞   **Barock**, Pařížská 24 (opposite the Old-New Synagogue), ✆ 232 92 21, ✉ 232 19 33. *Open Mon–Fri 8.30am–1am, Sat–Sun 10am–1am (kitchen closes at 11pm).* A complete sushi and sashimi menu, along with a range of strictly Western desserts. Its trendiness is a little too self-conscious to be either convincing or attractive, but the staff are friendly and efficient. Also does a very good cooked breakfast.

∞∞∞   **Bellevue**, Smetanovo nábř. 18, ✆ 22 22 14 38, ✉ 22 22 04 53, *bellevue@ prague-finedining.cz. Open Mon–Sat noon–11, Sun champagne and live jazz brunch 11–3.30, dinner 7–11.* Elegant furnishings and attentive service complement the excellent food in this riverside restaurant. If only it wasn't quite so bright.

∞∞∞   **La Provence**, Štupartská 9, ✆ 90 05 45 10, ✉ 90 00 43 14, *provence@czn.cz, www.laprovence.cz. Open 11am–1am.* Oily, marinated and delicious Italian and French dishes, in a lively and central hangout popular with Czechs, expats and Eurotrash alike. Lycra-clad go-go dancers can be found in the **Banana Café** upstairs, while transvestites take the stage on Wednesday nights. A good place to come if you want to feel as if you've just finished a hard week in the fast lane.

Le Café Colonial, Široká 6, ☎ 24 81 83 22. *Open 1.30–10.30.* Airy and elegant restaurant on the edge of the Jewish Quarter, with a range of spicy dishes, tasty fondue and the finest *crème brulée* in town.

Le Saint Jacques, Jakubská 4, ☎/🖶 232 26 85, *www.infor.cz/lesaint-jacques.* *Open Mon–Fri noon–midnight, Sat 6–midnight.* Good French food, accompanied by crooning and violins on most nights. Romantic, in a formal kind of way.

Lotos, Platnéřská 13, ☎ 232 23 90. *Open 11–10.* The vegetarian restaurant of the moment, run by an ex-government spokesperson who retired to devote herself to the vegetable cause.

Opera Grill, Karolíny Světlé 35, ☎ 22 22 05 18. *Open 7pm–2am.* Eating here is an almost camp experience: dainty portions of Continental cuisine are brought to the handful of tables; as diners murmur, a pianist tinkles and everyone marvels at the exquisite sensuality of this tiny hideaway. Formal wear is *de rigueur*, although ideally everyone would lounge in silk kimonos, and puff opium pipes between courses.

Parnas, Smetanovo nábř. 2, ☎ 24 21 19 01. *Open noon–3 and 5.30–11.* Stylish and modern interior, an expansive view over the river to the castle, and a creamy, saucy, sumptuous menu.

Pravda, Pařížská 17, ☎ 232 62 03, 🖶 231 20 42. *Open Sun–Wed 11am–midnight, Thurs–Sat 11am–2am.* Stylish modern restaurant, next to the Old-New Synagogue, serving a pricy but delicious range of dishes from across the world. Indoor and outdoor seating.

Sarah Bernhardt Restaurant (Paříž Hotel), U Obecního domu 1, ☎ 24 22 21 51, *www.hotel-pariz.cz. Open noon–4 and 6–midnight.* Named after the French actress immortalized by the poster of (the Czech) Alfons Mucha, this is one of Prague's better hotel restaurants.

U červeného kola (The Red Wheel), Anežská 2, ☎ 24 81 11 18. *Open 11–11.*

An intimate steak restaurant, tucked away in a sublime corner of the Old Town near St Agnes' Convent.

U Sixtů, Celetná 2, ☎ 24 22 57 24. *Open noon–1am.* Superb Czech and French cuisine in a centuries-old cellar on the edge of the Old Town Square. The red meat and poultry dishes are rich and well flavoured, and the restaurant's Icelandic fish menu is a lodestar in Prague's culinary firmament.

V zátiší (In Seclusion), Liliová 1, ☎ 22 22 11 55, 🖶 22 22 06 29, *vzatisiprague finedining.cz. Open noon–3 and 5.30–11.* Some of the most satisfying food in Prague, in simple and elegant surroundings. Dishes are fresh, light and international in inspiration, ranging from poached salmon in dill sauce to steamed chicken on fresh spring vegetables. There are several (home-made) pasta dishes, and a number of vegetarian choices.

Kogo, Havelská 27, ☎ 24 21 45 43. *Open 11–11.* Easy-going and lively atmosphere, stone oven-baked pizzas, pleasing pastas and delicious fish.

Kozička, Kozi 1, ☎ 24 81 83 08, *kozicka@mbox.vol.cz. Open Mon–Fri noon–4am, Sat–Sun 4–4.* Cellar restaurant and bar, adorned with, among other things, a tin goat. Those who should know claim the food is excellent.

Obecni dům (French Restaurant and Café), nám. Republiky 5, ☎ 22 00 27 70, *www.obecnidum.cz. Open noon–4 and 6–12.* To the left of the main entrance. A bright, busy and elegant Art Nouveau interior, recently restored to a sparkling standard. The beer hall in the basement, ☎ 22 00 27 80 (*open 11.30–11*), serves good Pilsner and Czech food to the accompaniment of oom-pah-pah music.

Red Hot and Blues, Jakubská 12, ☎ 231 46 39, 🖶 232 33 64. *Open 9am–midnight.* This is an attractive US-run Tex-Mex, Creole and Cajun restaurant in the rooms and courtyard of the ancient royal stables. Large breakfasts, piquant Creole dishes and weekend music make this place particularly popular among Prague's wealthier and more homesick expats.

∞ **Reykjavík**, Karlova 20, ℰ 22 22 12 18, ✉ 22 22 14 19, *reykjavik@ mbox.vol.cz*, *www.reykjavik.cz. Open 11–11.* The pre-fabricated steakhouse décor of this place conceals one of Prague's better fish restaurants, serving a daily range of scaly creatures freshly flown in from Iceland. Try the fish soup, which has become a legend in its own lunchtime.

∞ **U 7 andělů** (The Seven Angels), Jilská 20, ℰ/✉ 24 23 43 81, ℰ 24 22 69 55. *Open noon–3 and 6–midnight.* A cosy Czech restaurant serving duck, pork, goulash and dumplings to the accompaniment of jolly accordion music.

∞ **U supa** (The Vulture), Celetná 22, ℰ 24 21 20 04. *Open 11.30–11.* A spacious beer hall, serving as its speciality a rich dark brew called Purkmistr 12°, with a broad range of steak, duck and tasty game dishes. The most impressive item on the menu is the roast suckling pig, basted in beer and lard, which the proud chef will wheel out and slice in front of the drooling diners concerned. For a third of the price, he'll do the same with a goose.

∞ **U zlateho tygra** (The Golden Tiger), Husova 17, ℰ 22 22 11 11. *Open 3–11.* Dank but lively beer hall, patronized by writer Bohumil Hrabal for most of his life and accordingly sanctified by Prague's tourist guides (and Václav Havel, who brought ex-President Clinton here for a beer). Fortunately, the regulars couldn't give a damn, and this is a perfectly pleasant spot for beer and basic food.

◌ **Bohemia Bagel**, Masná 2, ℰ 24 81 25 60 (a second branch at Újezd 16). *Open 7am–10pm.* Easy-going, friendly café with salads and bagels to suit all tastes.

◌ **Klub Architektů**, Betlémské nám. 5a, ℰ 24 40 12 14. A range of cheap, basic and very satisfying meals, in a subterranean chamber or (in the summer) on an outdoor terrace.

◌ **U kata** (The Executioner), U Radnice 6, ℰ 24 23 63 63. *Open Mon–Fri 10am–midnight, Sat–Sun noon–midnight.* Basic Czech pub, next door to the building where the Old Town's 16th-century executioner used to retreat after a hard day's chopping. The menu includes venison and delicacies such as smoked pigs' knuckles.

◌ **U krkavců** (The Raven), Dlouhá tr. 25, ℰ 24 81 72 64, ✉ 232 91 21. *Open noon–3 and 6–midnight.* Cosy wine bar, with resident violinist, in a 13th-century vaulted Roman cellar (the restaurant is hidden under a courtyard some distance from the street). Predominantly a place to come and court over a bottle of *Frankovka*, although the small range of aromatic pasta dishes is delicious. The polite staff are also more than happy to toss together a tasty vegetarian dish.

◌ **U Vejvodů**, Jilská 4. *Open 10am–11pm.* A 14th-century beer hall that has been a little over-sanitized by recent renovation. Popular nevertheless, and its menu of stodgy Czech delicacies can be washed down with refreshing Pilsner lager.

Prague Castle and Hradčany

∞∞ **Peklo** (Hell), Strahovské nádvoří 1, ℰ 20 51 66 52, ✉ 471 83 65. *Open noon–midnight, Mon 6pm–midnight.* An extraordinary dining experience, in the 12th-century beer cellars of the Strahov monastery. The dishes are sparse, expensive and delicious, but the décor isn't necessarily what one might expect: fairy lights line the steps that sweep down from the entrance, and one whole chamber has been made into a disco, complete with glassed-in chamber for the DJ.

∞∞ **U zlaté hrušky** (The Golden Pear), Nový Svět 3, ℰ 20 51 47 78. *Open 11.30–3 and 5.30–midnight.* Wonderful Czech and French food in a cottage on the most romantic alleyway in Prague.

∞ **U ševce Matouše**, Loretanske nám. 4, ℰ 20 51 45 36. *Open noon–4 and 6–11.* Tasty steaks in a cosy location.

U černého vola (The Black Ox), Loretánské nám. 1, ✆ 20 51 34 81. *Open 10–10.* A pub so popular with the locals that the (now defunct) Beer Party had to buy it to thwart the tourist-trap designs of rapacious brewery investors. Great atmosphere, and excellent location for post-prandial strolling.

Lesser Quarter (Malá Strana)

Bazaar, Nerudova 40, ✆ 900 54 51 05 12, ✉ 900 545 15, *bazaar@restaurant. cz, www.restaurantbazaar.cz. Open 12.30– midnight.* A hotch-potch of a menu, ranging from Mediterranean to Thai, in a glittering restaurant which assaults your senses from the moment you enter its candle-lined vestibule and are met by one of the mobile-and-micro-skirt-wielding waitresses. The food is no worse than hit-and-miss and, when the bar gets lively (which is just as random) it's a good place to meet Prague's beautiful people

Circle Line, Malostranské nám. 12, ✆ 57 53 00 21, ✉ 57 53 00 23, *circle line@praguefinedining.cz. Open noon– 11.* Genuinely French cuisine and sea-food in comfortable surroundings.

David, Tržiště 21, ✆ 57 53 31 09. *Open noon–3 and 6–11.* Terribly exclusive restaurant set in a former living room, favoured by diplomatic types and all those with expense accounts.

Kampa Park, Na Kampě 8b, ✆ 57 53 26 85. *Open 11.30–10.45.* A Swedish-run restaurant with a truly excellent reputation among Prague's menu-watchers. Entrées are light on the stomach and heavy on herbal themes, and the riverside location is superb on a summer evening. Kids under 10 eat for free, assuming parental presence.

Pálffy Palác, Valdštejnská 14, ✆ 57 32 05 70. *Open Mon–Fri 11–11, Sat–Sun noon–midnight.* Before 1989, the very notion of this restaurant—set in a panelled chamber of a Baroque palace, with softly spoken waiters guiding you

through a French-inspired menu—would have been enough to make you choke on your dumpling. But it's all true. In summer, eat on the candle-lit terrace.

U malířů (The Painter's), Maltézské nám. 11, ✆ 57 53 00 00. *Open 7pm– 2am.* French cuisine, with some of the highest prices in Prague. But if you can afford it, you won't be disappointed. The pretty interior is another attraction; this has been a restaurant ever since the original 'painter' moved here in 1541

U mecenáše (Maecenas'), Malostranské nám. 10, ✆ 53 38 81. *Open 5–11.30.* A 400-year-old inn off a Gothic arcade, filled with pieces of gallows and firearms amassed over the centuries. The Old Town's 16th-century executioner, Mydlář, used to pop across the river regularly, and his scrawled signature is preserved behind a piece of glass in the front room (although it's the homely back room that you should reserve). Reasonable meals, and a comfortable place to pursue or consolidate a romance.

U modré kachničky (The Blue Duckling), Nebovidská 6, ✆ 57 32 03 08, ✉ 57 31 74 27. *Open noon–3.30 and 6.30–11.30.* The first post-revolutionary restaurant to take Czech food seriously and be taken seriously by the wider world. Extremely popular and rightly so. Game is a speciality. A pleasantly quiet walk away from the Charles Bridge, it's intimate, well-mannered and cluttered with comfortable kitsch.

U tří pštrosů (The Three Ostriches), Dražického nám. 12, ✆ 57 32 05 65. *Open noon–3 and 6–11.* An elegant and cosy restaurant in a Renaissance hotel on the edge of the Charles Bridge.

Nebozízek, Petřínské sady, ✆ 57 31 53 29, *www.nebozizek.com. Open 11–11.* A meal here is pure romance from the moment you step into the funicular railway up Petřín Hill (get off at the first stop). Unexceptional Czech food, but this gleaming white villa, halfway up the hillside, offers a mesmerizing view over

Prague. Take the path towards Malá Strana after your meal: the winding and wooded descent into the district's tiles and spires is unforgettable.

∞ **U Maltézských rytířů** (The Knights of Malta), Prokopská 10, ✆ 57 53 13 24, 📠 53 66 50. *Open 11–11.* Extremely cosy restaurant, serving a small but very tasty selection of Czech dishes. A pianist tinkles away most evenings.

∞ **U svatého Václava**, Karmelitská 24, ✆ 57 53 29 42. *Open 11–11, closed Sun.* Basic but friendly place for lunch: steaks, pasta and Italian ice cream.

◌ **Malý Buddah** (The Little Buddah), Úvoz 44, ✆ 265 99 16. *Open 11–10, closed Mon.* One of the curious teahouses that have recently sprung up in Prague which combine a dedication to more-or-less Oriental mysticism with a devotion to tea. This place also serves (extremely cheap) Chinese food, and, should you feel the urge to worship, there is a small shrine for customer use.

◌ **U hrocha** (The Hippo), Thunovská 10, ✆ 57 31 68 90. *Open 10am–11pm.* Pub grub and Pilsner in the heart of Malá Strana. One of the liveliest and most eclectic melting pots in town, neither alienating to the locals nor patronizing to outsiders. No cards.

◌ **U malého Glena**, Karmelitská 23, ✆ 57 53 17 17, 📠 90 00 39 67. *Open Mon–Thurs 8.30am–midnight, Fri 8.30am–1am, Sat 10.30am–1am, Sun 10.30am–11pm.* A culinary mishmash of Tex-Mex, Czech food and eccentric kebabs in a cosy, friendly and laid-back café. Deservedly popular among both Czechs and foreign visitors.

New Town (Nové Město)

∞∞∞ **Bistrot de Marlene**, Plavecká 4, Prague 2, ✆ 24 92 18 53, 📠 24 92 07 43. *Open noon–5 and 7–10.30.* Chic and intimate French-run bistro, with a decent line in pseudo-home-cooked food.

∞∞∞ **Ostroff**, Střelecký Ostrov 336, ✆ 24 91 92 35, 📠 24 92 02 27, *ostroff@ seznam.cz, www.ostroff.cz. Open 7pm– 1am, closed Sun.* A modern beech and steel restaurant on the lushest and most romantic of Prague's islands. Extremely good Italian food, 160 cocktails, and a superb view of the National Theatre on the far bank of the river.

∞∞∞ **La Perle de Prague**, Dancing House (Tančící dům), Rašínovo nabřeží 80, Prague 2, ✆ 21 98 41 60, 📠 21 98 41 79. *Open noon–2 and 7–10.30.* French gourmet restaurant at the top of the so-called 'Fred and Ginger' building, a curving glass and steel cage that—insists the architect, Frank Gehry—is reminiscent of a ballroom couple. The interiors don't quite live up to the external promise, but the 7th-floor view is fairly spectacular and the food is delicious. Booking recommended.

∞∞∞ **Žofín**, Slovanský Ostrov (Slovansky Island), Zofin 226, ✆ 90 00 06 62, 📠 24 91 91 39, *gastrozofin@eol.cz, www.eol .cz/gastrozofin. Open 11–midnight.* Set on an island next to the National Theatre, this neoclassical palace, where waiters drift silently between tables under crystal chandeliers, tries hard to offer an aristocratic dining experience. Unfortunately, it's a little too bright, a little too stiff and rather too quiet on most evenings. That said, the Czech food is above average, and, if you're sufficiently gregarious (or taciturn) to handle the atmosphere, this is a good place to dine before a night at the opera. Vegetarian and children's meals are also available.

∞ **Cerberus**, Soukenická 19, ✆ 24 81 41 18, 📠 231 09 85. *Open Mon–Fri 11–11, Sat–Sun 3–11.* Modern, stylish Czech-run restaurant serving excellent food.

∞ **De Lux**, Václavské nám. 4, ✆ 96 24 94 44, *delux@delux.cz, www.delux.cz.* Elegant underground restaurant, accessible from a shopping mall at the foot of Weneceslas Square. At the time of writing it serves excellent Thai food, while simultaneously offering salsa classes, lounge music and occasional raves. As that might suggest, this place is still finding its feet, but it is certainly worth investigating.

∞ **Dynamo**, Pštrosova 29, ℗ 29 42 24. *Open 10am–11.30pm.* Minimalist décor, friendly staff and tasty Mediterranean menu. One of several new eateries in this area, which real-estate agents now insist is turning into Prague's restaurant district and should be called SONA (South of Narodni).

∞ **Klášterní vinárna** (Cloisters Wine Bar), Národní 8, ℗ 29 05 96, *www.eol.cz/ klasternivinarna. Open 11.30–4 and 5– midnight.* An elegant restaurant in the low-lit refectory of a former monastery. The food is an unremarkable mix of Czech and Continental dishes, but the surroundings and the nightly pianist make this a suitably stylish stop for dinner before or after a trip to the Magic Lantern or National Theatre.

∞ **Mánes**, Masarykovo nábř. 250, ℗ 24 91 48 99, 🖷 29 73 75. *Open 11–11.* This restaurant is adjacent to the Mánes Gallery (*see* p.133), and shares its elegant Functionalist premises. Comfortable and stylish, with wide leather benches, square tables, an occasional pianist and lovely river views.

∞ **Modrá terasa**, Na Můstku 9, ℗ 24 22 62 88. Above-average Czech food, in a glass penthouse next to the huge clock which overlooks Wenceslas Square. Even if you don't eat here, come for a cocktail and take in the extraordinary view, stretching from the National Museum to the faraway castle on the hill. The restaurant is accessible from the covered area above the main entrance to Mustek metro station: take the tiny lift tucked away in the wall.

∞ **Na rybárně**, Gorazdova 17, Prague 2, ℗ 24 91 88 85. *Open noon–midnight, Sun 5pm–midnight.* A quiet fish restaurant, serving all the piscine edibles to be found in Bohemia's waters as well as several that wouldn't be found dead in them. Although the food is fine, this restaurant's now-fading claim to fame lies in the fact that Václav Havel used to live nearby and popped in regularly with his mates: on the walls of the back room are shaky scribbles by Mick Jagger, Keith Richards, Paul Simon and numerous no-hopers.

∞ **U šuterů**, Palackého 4, ℗ 26 10 17. *Open 11.30–3 and 6.30–11, closed Sun.* A glorified steakhouse run by Belgians, the distinguishing feature of which is that patrons cook their own food on lumps of superheated lava on each table. The management claims, with a straight face, to have thus introduced Prague to the latest concept in dining; the next concept will presumably be to leave a cow, an axe and a bill in the restaurant and go home. That said, the informality and conversational possibilities inherent in handling and frying a piece of meat make this a perfect spot to bring a nervous first date or truculent business contact.

◊ **Adonis**, Jungmannova 21, ℗ 24 94 84 52. *Open Mon–Thurs 10.30–8, Fri 10.30–7, Sat–Sun 11–5.50.* Cheap Lebanese buffet, with all the staples from stuffed vine leaves to salads; fine as fast food, though seats are at a premium.

◊ **Kavárna velryba** (Whale Café), Opatovická 24, ℗ 24 91 24 84. *Open 11am–2am, kitchen until 11pm.* Popular among Czech studenty types and foreign time-wasters. Several tasty snacks, like scrambled eggs with mushrooms and a cheesy 'Pasta chez Velryba'. No cards.

◊ **Novoměstský pivovar** (New Town Brewery), Vodičkova 20, ℗ 22 23 24 48. *Open 11.30 11.30, Sun noon–10.* A modern micro-brewery, set in an underground warren of chambers and serving solid Czech food and a deliciously light unfiltered beer. Good for a quick lunch, but you won't want to linger.

◊ **Pizzeria Kmotra**, V jirchářích 12, ℗ 24 91 58 09. *Open 11am–1am.* The expat search for the Great American Pizza has seen many contenders fall by the wayside over the last few years, but the Kmotra (inconveniently, run by Yugoslavs) apparently gets uncannily close. They're big, fresh and tasty.

U Fleků, Křemencova 9–11, ✆ 24 91 51 18, ✆ 24 92 06 92. *Open 8.30am–11pm*. Prague's best-known beer hall, which has brewed the same 14° beer on the premises since 1459. Five hundred seats and simple Czech food. The shady garden is a pleasant spot for raucous summer drinking, but a fee is now charged to sit there.

U Govindy (Govinda's), Soukenická 27, ✆ 24 81 60 16. *Open 11–5*. A Hare Krishna hangout, offering incense, souvenirs and vegetarian food. The menu is a little tastier than its insipid appearance might suggest, but only a little. No cards.

U kalicha (The Chalice), Na Bojišti 12, ✆/✆ 24 91 25 57. *Open 11am–10.30pm*. Only mentioned because you might hear of this beer hall and think that it sounds interesting. It was mentioned in *The Good Soldier Švejk*, and it's milked the fact dry. No cards.

U Rozvařilů, Na poříčí 26. *Open Mon–Fri 7.30–7.30, Sat 7.30–7, Sun 10–5*. A cheap Czech zinc diner, deservedly popular and patronised by everyone from *babičky* to businessmen.

Jáma (The Hollow), V jámě 7. *Open 11am–1am*. US-style burger and Tex-Mex restaurant.

Further Afield

Hanavský Pavilion, Letenské sady 173, Prague 7, ✆ 33 32 36 41. *Open daily (in theory) 11.30–3.30 and 6–1am. Terrace open till 10.30pm*. An Art Nouveau folly, tucked away on the hill opposite the Old Town. Highly romantic, save for the fact that, unless you telephone first, you can never be entirely sure that it will be open.

FX Café, Bělehradská 120, ✆/✆ 24 25 47 76. *Open 11.30am–5am*. Excellent vegetarian snacks above a throbbing nightclub. Tofu, spinach and avocados make regular appearances on the menu, on top of (slightly crunchy) pizzas and in useful toasted sandwiches. Sofas to lounge in, attractive staff to ogle, and cocktails to binge on. Also worth noting are the late hours here. No cards.

Myslivna (The Gamekeeper's Lodge), Jagellonská 21, Prague 3, ✆ 627 02 09. *Open 11.30–3.30 and 4–11*. The décor is brown and uninspiring, but this long-established restaurant offers the gamiest game in Prague. Come and bag a pheasant, deer or boar, and taste Czech food at its best.

Pizzeria Grosseto, Jugoslávských partyzánů 8, Holešovice, ✆ 312 26 94. *Open 11.30–10*. Italian food, eagerly cooked and served in a home-made brick kiln by keen young Czech staff. The pizzas are vast, the pastas are fresh, and the restaurant is deservedly popular among locals.

Quido, Kubelíkova 22, Žižkov, ✆ 22 72 20 07. *Open 11.30–11*. One of the best-value Czech restaurants in town, with a wide choice of tasty seafood, pasta and poultry dishes. The restaurant is next to Prague's incredible TV tower (*see* p.122), and a post-prandial walk around it can verge on the hallucinogenic.

U cedru (The Cedar), Na Hutích 13, *Open 11–11*. Prague 6, ✆ 312 29 74. Small but delicious selection of Lebanese dishes. The owner left the civil war behind in the late 1970s, but Beirut's shops still provide regular supplies. Picnickers and locals could also note that the restaurant offers a takeaway and delivery service.

Prague: Where to Stay

For a city boasting one of the most extraordinary architectural preserves in Europe, the accommodation that Prague offers its visitors can still be very disappointing. The private market died during 40 years of Communist rule, while, apart from a few five-star palaces built to service the Party faithful and their foreign friends, its hotels degenerated into fleapits the colour of nicotine and rust. But recent years have seen dramatic improvements, with mass modernization of older hotels and the emergence of a new generation of quirky cubbyholes and genteel pensions. Plan ahead and you might at last find a place that does justice to the rest of your holiday.

The hotels in this section are divided into three categories. Those listed as 'luxury' have all the facilities that you would expect, from satellite televisions and mini-bars to 24-hour room service, often along with several (such as trouser presses and faxes in each room) that you might not. 'Moderate' hotels usually offer a less extensive but similar collection of services, for a lower rate. The defining feature of those in the 'cheap' category is price; however, all are clean and well run, with a range of services that will meet the requirements of most short-term visitors. And finally, before booking a hotel room at all, it's worth noting that a private apartment will be cheaper, and may well be more appealing and atmospheric; accommodation agencies are listed towards the end of this chapter.

Whatever arrangements you choose to make, the secret of success is to book well in advance. Several of the agencies mentioned towards the end of the chapter can make hotel reservations for you, although it's worth then confirming your booking at the hotel itself. The approximate price you should expect to pay, for a **double room with bath in high season**, is as follows:

◌◌◌	*luxury*	£110–240 ($165–360)
◌◌	*moderate*	£70–110 ($105–165)
◌	*cheap*	£30–70 ($45–105)

Rates are generally between 20 and 50 per cent lower in off-season (roughly November to March, excluding Christmas/New Year). Almost all the hotels in the first two categories include breakfast in the price. Unless otherwise stated, they all take major credit cards.

Old Town (Staré Město)

This area is perhaps the most convenient location of them all.

◌◌◌
(18) **Grand Hotel Bohemia**, Královdorská 4, ✆ 248 041 11, ✉ 232 95 45, grand-hotel-bohemia@austria-hotels.icom.cz, www.austria-hotels.co.at/grandhotel-bohemia. Luxurious, and hopefully pitched at the business market. The neo-Baroque ballroom seems a good place to hold a conference with a difference, while the rooms come with faxes and trouser presses. It's Austrian-owned and the rates are as high as you'd expect.

◌◌◌
(19) **Paříž**, U Obecního domu 1, Prague 1, ✆ 22 19 51 95/22 19 56 66, ✉ 24 22 54 75, booking@hotel-pariz.cz, www.hotel-

pariz.cz. The extraordinary Art Nouveau façade, turned into a fortress by neo-Gothic turrets and arches, lets you down with narrow dark rooms, and lackadaisical staff. Otherwise a comfortable, attractive and central place to stay. 98 rooms.

◌◌◌
(20) **Ungelt**, Štupartská 1, ✆ 24 82 86 86, ✉ 24 82 81 81. A modernized Gothic house on the edge of the Old Town Square, with tiled floors and airy corridors that make it feel more like a chalet camp than a Prague hotel. Contains 10 spacious and pretty apartments for up to four people, each with cooking facilities.

◌◌◌
(21) **Casa Marcello**, Řásnovka 783, ✆ 231 12 30/231 90 53, ✉ 231 33 23,

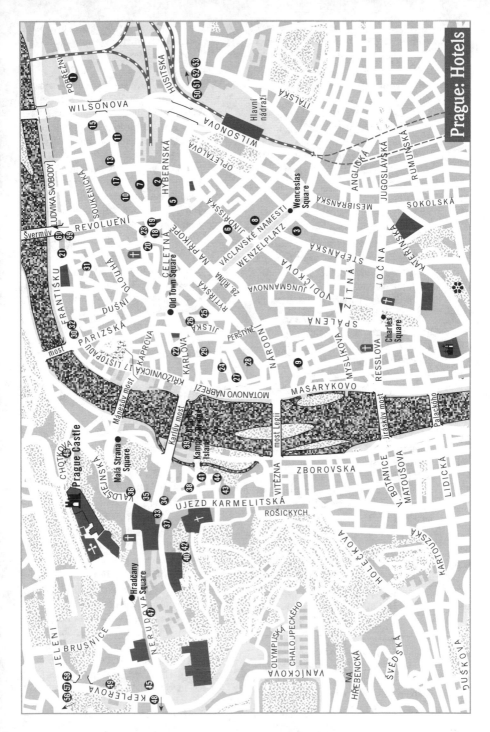

Prague: Hotels

POŘÍČNÍ
WILSONOVA
HUSITSKÁ
Hlavní nádraží
WILSONOVA
ITALSKÁ
LUDVÍKA SVOBODY
SOUKENICKÁ
HYBERNSKÁ
OPLETALOVA
JUGOSLÁVSKÁ
RUMUNSKÁ
SOKOLSKÁ
MĚSÍBRSKÁ
ANGLICKÁ
Wenceslas Square
ŠTĚPÁNSKÁ
KATEŘINSKÁ
REVOLUČNÍ
Švermův
CELETNÁ
NA PŘÍKOPĚ
VÁCLAVSKÉ NÁMĚSTÍ
JINDŘIŠSKÁ
WENZELPLATZ
VODIČKOVA
JEČNÁ
FRANTIŠKU
DLOUHÁ
DUŠNÍ
28. ŘÍJNA
RYTÍŘSKÁ
JUNGMANNOVA
ŽITNÁ
PARÍŽSKÁ
17. LISTOPADU
KAPROVA
KARLOVA
JILSKÁ
PERŠTÝNE
NÁRODNÍ
SPÁLENÁ
MYSLÍKOVA
RESSLOVA
Charles Square
most Legii
KŘIŽOVNICKÁ
MOTÁNOVO NÁBŘEŽÍ
MASARYKOVO
Mánesův most
Karlův most
Kampa Island
most Legii
Jiráskův most
Palackého
CHOTKOVA
Prague Castle
VALDŠTEJNSKÁ
Malá Strana Square
 ÚJEZD   KARMELITSKÁ
ROŠICKÝCH
ZBOROVSKÁ
VÍTĚZNÁ
V. BOTANICE
MATOUŠOVA
LIDICKÁ
KARTOUZSKÁ
JELENÍ
BRUSNICE
Hradčany
NERUDOVA Square
HOLEČKOVA
OLYMPIJSKÁ
CHALOUPECKÉHO
VANÍČKOVA
NA HŘEBENCÁ
ŠVÉDSKÁ
DUŠKOVA
KEPLEROVA

booking@casa-marcello.cz, www.casa-marcello.cz. Plush and intimate, set in a former nun's dormitory on a quiet cobbled street next to the St Agnes Monastery.

U Červené Boty (at the Red Shoe), Karlova 5, ✆ 22 22 10 51, 📠 22 22 10 52. Ring a doorbell through the passageway, go up the stairs, and a grizzled attendant will show you to a choice of four self-catering suites furnished with antiques, all set in a 17th-century building. All mod cons.

Hotel Esprit, Jakubská 5, ✆ 22 87 01 07, 22 87 01 11, 📠 22 87 01 06, *pragueesprit@hotelesprit.cz, www.prague esprit.cz*. Twenty-nine wannabe Art Deco rooms close to a range of nightspots and the Kotva department store. Children up to 15 years old can share free of charge. Disabled access, business facilities, terrace café and a hotel limousine service.

Betlem Club, Betlemské nám. 9, ✆ 22 22 15 74/22 22 15 75, 📠 22 22 05 80, *betlem.club@login.cz*. Family-run pension in a quiet square. The Baroque façade conceals tacky furnishings, but the place is easy-going and central. No cards.

U klenotnika (The Jewellers), Rytířská 3, ✆ 24 21 16 99, 📠 24 22 10 25. Comfortable pension-style hotel, conveniently positioned five minutes from both the Old Town Square and Wenceslas Square—that unfortunately places it squarely in the middle of Prague's red-light district, although the quarter is so low-key that you'll barely notice.

U staré pani (The Old Lady), Michalská 9, ✆ 26 72 67, 📠 26 79 841, *ustarepani@mbox.vol.cz, www.ustarepani .cz*. Simple, clean and modern hotel, a very short walk from just about anything on the right bank of the river. A staid jazz club is annexed to the hotel.

Cloister Inn, Konviktská 14, ✆ 24 21 10 20, 📠 24 21 08 00, *cloister@cloister-inn.cz, www.cloister-inn.cz*. The upmarket cousin of the the infamous Penzion Unitas

(*see* below), which sits below it, while the nuns who own it live next door. Very good value, though be sure you book in advance.

Penzion Unitas, Bartolomějská 9, ✆ 232 77 00, 📠 232 77 09. A cheap and central boarding house in a former monastery, opposite a police station that used to be the central interrogation centre of Prague's secret police. Their interviewees were often held here; Václav Havel spent several unhappy nights in room P6. A gentler group of killjoys now run the show: the hostel is owned by the Sisters of Mercy, and smoking, drinking and staying out beyond 1am are not allowed.

U krále Jiřího (King George's House), Liliová 10, ✆ 24 24 87 97, ✆/📠 22 22 17 07, *kral.jiri@telecom.cz, www.hotel.cz/ ukralejiriho*. Cosy, stylish, Baroque pension in the middle of the Old Town and a stroll away from the Charles Bridge. Extremely good value; book at least two months ahead. Eight rooms.

Jewish Quarter (Josefov)

Intercontinental, nám. Curieových 5, ✆ 24 88 11 11, 📠 24 81 12 16, *prague@interconti.com, www.interconti .com*. Reservations can be made on ✆ (020) 8847 2277 (UK) and ✆ 1 800 327 0200 (USA). Five-star facilities and comfy rooms. Excellent location at the centre of Josefov, newly refurbished, terrace restaurant with great views, swimming pool and fitness club. If only it didn't look like an ugly piece of concrete Lego.

Maximilian Hotel, Haštalská 14, Prague 1, ✆ 21 80 61 11, 📠 21 80 61 10. Classy but humanly scaled hotel on the edge of the Jewish Quarter. Services range from babysitting to business translations, while each room has a fax, and each bathroom has piped music. Underground car park. For overseas reservations, ✆ (020) 8770 0333 (UK), ✆ (1 800) 344 1212 (USA).

Albatros, nábř. Ludvíka Svobody, ✆ 24 81 05 47, 🖷 24 81 12 14. One of Prague's 'boatels', stably moored on the Vltava. Closer to the Old Town Square than Wenceslas Square, but the view is just too far from the Charles Bridge to be dreamy. Two long corridors of clean cabins, all with showers.

Lesser Quarter (Malá Strana)

This picturesque quarter, filled with orange pantiled roofs and smoking chimneys, is the image of Prague you send home on a postcard. If you're happy to pay an arm and a leg, this is the place to stay. Anyone offered lodgings here by one of the accommodation agencies should count himself or herself very lucky indeed.

Hotel pod věži (Hotel Under the Tower), Mostecká 2, ✆ 57 53 20 41/57 53 20 60, 🖷 57 53 20 69, hotel@ podvezi.com. Neat and comfortable hotel, located in a recently renovated Baroque house that is literally steps away from the prettier end of the Charles Bridge. Guarded car-park.

U páva (The Peacock), U Lužického semináře 32, ✆ 57 53 35 73/57 53 33 60, 🖷 57 53 09 19, hotelupava@tnet.cz, www.romantichotels.cz. An absolutely charming hotel, perfectly located and with courteous staff and tastefully furnished rooms. Prices vary according to the view; if possible, pay the premium to get one of the third-floor rooms looking up to the castle over the Vojan Gardens. It's a scene you won't forget. No lift. Eleven rooms.

U tří pštrosů (The Three Ostriches), Dražického nám. 12, ✆ 57 53 24 10/57 32 06 11, info@utripstrosu.cz, www.utri pstrosu.cz. Perhaps the most picturesque hotel in Prague, set in a 16th-century townhouse that is all but built into the Charles Bridge.

U modrého klíce (The Blue Key), Letenská 14, ✆ 57 32 72 50, 🖷 57 32 90 62, bluekey@mbox.vol.cz, www.bluekey .cz. A recently renovated 14th-century Gothic palace, converted into a luxurious hotel. Although next to a tram line, it's quiet and the friendly staff should ensure a suitably luxurious stay. Other attractions include a courtyard, sauna, Jacuzzis and business services. Twenty-eight rooms, some with private kitchenettes.

The Charles, Josefská 1, ✆ 57 53 29 13 14, 🖷 57 53 29 10, thecharles@ bon.cz. An extremely friendly and well-appointed hotel in a converted Baroque townhouse that's a hop, skip and jump away from the Charles Bridge. Velvet curtains, engraved furniture, wood and terracotta floors, Persian rugs, under 400-year-old ceilings with painted beams.

Residence Nosticova, Nosticova 1, ✆ 57 31 25 13/57 31 25 16, 🖷 57 31 25 17, nostic@bohem.net.cz. Full-on luxury in a miniature stone palace, offering accommodation with self-catering facilities, as well as a porter, bar and restaurant if catering for yourself doesn't take your fancy. The spanking-new antiques and medieval props aren't entirely convincing, but fantasy-prone types should enjoy the four posters, and terracotta-tiled bathrooms and cobbled location add to the appeal.

Na Kampe Inn, Na Kampé 15, ✆ 57 53 14 30/57 53 14 32, 🖷 57 53 31 68, nakampe15@nakampe15.cz, www.nakampe 15.cz. Excellent location on Kampa Island with views over the Vlatva. The rooms are bright, airy, simple and classy: wooden floors, beamed ceilings, rugs and so on.

Dům u velké boty (The Big Shoe), Vlasska 30, ✆ 57 53 32 34/57 53 42 09, 🖷 57 53 20 88, rippl@mbox.vol.cz. Extremely friendly family-run pension in a beautifully converted 17th-century townhouse, surrounded by palaces and cobbled alleyways. Only 12 rooms, so advance booking is advisable. In-house laundry facilities, and some fitness equipment. Breakfast not included.

Penzion Dientzenhofer, Nosticova 2,
℃ 53 16 72/53 88 96, 🖅 57 32 08 88,
dientzenhofer@volny.cz. Charming little
pension, in the 16th-century birthplace of
Prague's greatest Baroque architect.
Tucked away on a silent street and
backing on to the Čertovka stream, this
place is so popular that it should be
booked months ahead. Wheelchair access
and basic business facilities.

Sax, Jánský Vršek 3, ℃ 57 53 12 68,
🖅 57 53 41 01, *hotelsax@bon.cz*, *www
.hotelsax.cz*. Sleek, airy and modern, built
under an arrowhead-shaped atrium, and
hidden behind an unassuming Baroque
façade in one of the quietest parts of
central Malá Strana. Good value.

U kříže (The Cross), Újezd 20, ℃ 53 33
26, 🖅 53 34 43, *htl.ukrize@iol.cz*, *www
.volny.cz/hotel.ukrize*. A modernized and
unpretentious hotel in a recently renovated Baroque building.

Penzion U Kiliána, Všehrdova 13,
℃ 561 81 40, 🖅 73 41 10. A tiny guest-
house, comprising two cluttered but
homely rooms behind a café.

Prague Castle and Hradčany

Savoy, Keplerova 6, ℃ 24 30 24 30, 🖅 24
30 21 28, *info@hotel-savoy.cz*, *www
.hotel-savoy.cz*. One of Prague's most
modern and luxurious hotels, Austrian-
owned and entirely reconstructed behind
an impressive Art Nouveau façade. No
subway—your connection to the centre is
by tram or limousine.

Hotel Hoffmeister, Pod Bruskou 7,
℃ 51 01 71 11, 🖅 51 01 71 20,
hotel@hoffmeister.cz, *www.hoffmeister.cz*.
Well-appointed and luxurious modern
hotel. Perched on the edge of a main road,
but a stone's throw from the metro and a
10-minute walk from anything else in old
Prague. Named after Adolf Hoffmeister,
caricaturist and epicure, whose portraits
adorn the walls.

U Krále Karla (King Charles), Úvoz 4,
℃ 57 53 04 84/57 53 35 94, 🖅 57 53 35
91, *ukrale@tnet.cz*, *www.romantichotels
.tnet.cz*. A Baroque house with modernized interior, cluttered with furnishings
that are a little too *faux* for their own good
but very stylish all the same. Set on the
tranquil, romantic and very steep hill
leading up to the Strahov Monastery.

Pyramida, Bělohorská 24, Prague 6,
℃ 33 35 51 09/33 35 81 60, 🖅 33 35 61
59, *hotel.pyramida@orea.cz*, *www.pha
.orea.cz/pyramida*. A vast glass temple
with clean if unexciting rooms, recently
renovated. All have showers. Fitness
centre below, and a short walk from
Prague Castle, albeit one along a dusty
main road. Three hundred and twenty-
five rooms.

U raka, Černínská 10, ℃ 35 14 53/35 43
35, 🖅 20 51 05 11. A quiet stay in one of
the drowsiest and most beautiful streets of
Prague. The log cabin itself is a fairly offen-
sive extension, but it's probably warmer
and much more comfortable than the mess
of ancient cottages that surrounds it. Only
six double rooms, and no meals, but the
owner of this money-spinner can sort out
your dinner reservations once you arrive.

New Town and Vinohrady

Little of this part of town has survived the
extensive redevelopments of the last 100
years, but its buildings span the range from
neoclassical grandeur to Functionalist chic.
In most cases, you can expect your hotel to
be surrounded by shuddering and dirty
streets, but you'll never be more than 20
minutes from the charms of the Old Town
Square. The district includes Wenceslas
Square, which contains a large number of
established hotels that have been omitted
from this edition of the guide; most are well
appointed enough, but it's hard to find a way
of differentiating between their varying levels
of soullessness and lack of value.

Hilton-Atrium, Pobřežní 1, ℗ 24 81 18 96/24 84 11 11, ✉ 24 81 18 96. A spectacular complex of glass and fibre-optic-type decoration, built around an atrium so expansive that some claim to have occasionally seen very small rain-clouds floating across it. Fountains, a 25m pool, an indoor tennis court, transparent lifts and four restaurants make this the perfect hotel in which to lounge, and it offers all the quality that you might expect of a hotel that has included Presidents Clinton and Mandela among its guests. All of Prague is easily accessible by taxi, but the location, on the edge of a jungle of underpasses and motorways, may not appeal to rambling types. Underground guarded car park. Wheelchair access.

Prague Marriott Hotel, V Celnici 8, Prague 1, ℗ 22 88 88 88, ✉ 22 88 88 89, toll free calls from UK ℗ 0800 221 222, from USA and Canada ℗ 800 228 9290, *prague.marriott@marriott.cz, www.marriott .com*. Built in the 1990s, offering un-adulterated luxury and impeccable service at a corresponding price. Contains a well-equipped gym.

Raddisson SAS–Alkron Hotel, Stepanska 40, ℗ 22 82 04 20, ✉ 22 82 01 00, *sales@prgrh.rdsas.com, www. raddisson sas.com/praguecs*, toll-free calls from UK ℗ 0800 374411, from USA ℗ 1 800 333 3333. Recently renovated, with heated marble floors in bathrooms, and Internet access in every room.

Ametyst, Jana Masayryka 11, Prague 2, ℗ 24 25 01 09, ✉ 24 25 13 15. Large German-run hotel, set about half a kilo metre from Wenceslas Square in a leafy residential district. Disabled access.

Hotel Meteor-Plaza, Hybernská 6, ℗ 24 19 21 11/24 19 21 30, ✉ 24 21 30 05, *altours@hotel-meteor.cz, www.hotel-meteor.cz*. Clean and comfortable rooms, equipped with all mod cons. Owned by the Best Western hotel chain. Also has a built-in underground car park, a restored Gothic restaurant, and a conservatory-cum-summer terrace. Eighty rooms.

Palace, Panska 12, ℗ 24 09 31 11, ✉ 24 22 12 40, *palhoprg@palacehotel.cz, www.palacehotel.cz*. Set in a quiet road, opposite the Mucha Museum, this is the only hotel in central Prague where the porter wears a topper and a turquoise cloak. Conference facilities and casino. Built in 1906 in the Viennese Art Nouveau style, the hotel has been completely remodelled, and apart from a whiplash bar and some crazy-paned glass there's no reminder of its past. Guests enjoy an unctuous level of service and superb facilities. Has special rooms 'designed for lady travellers' which are pink, have more mirrors than usual, and come with a red rose.

Renaissance Prague Hotel, V Celnici 7, ℗ 21 82 21 00, ✉ 21 82 22 00, *renais sance.prague@renaissance.cz, www.re naissancehotels.com*. Large and luxurious travellers' paradise with over 300 smart rooms, an in-house travel agency, a fitness centre, and all the extras money can buy. Located close to the edge of the Old Town. Wheelchair access.

Grand Hotel Evropa, Václavské nám. 25, ℗ 24 22 81 17/24 22 84 87, ✉ 24 22 45 41, *hotelevropa@iol.cz*. Prague's legendary Art Nouveau hotel, and still a bargain for all those who like their atmos-phere louche. The rooms themselves are disappointingly stark (unless you manage to nab one of the handful of suites) but the common areas are sumptuous indeed. They're filled with monstrous vases, dusty *chaise longues*, mirrors, lanterns and the fronds and leaves of a hundred scattered plants—all under a vast skylight and within the ovals, arches and wrought iron of the New Art at its most atmospheric.

Jerome House, V Jirchářích 13, ℗ 24 91 21 28/24 91 10 11, ✉ 24 91 21 27, *boheinco@comp.cz, www.bohemia-in coming.cz*. A newly renovated hotel offering some of the most comfortable accommodation in this price category. The stylish interior is offset by a period facade. Located on a quiet cobbled street, a few minutes' walk away from both Wenceslas Square and the heart of the Old Town. Advance booking highly advisable.

Atlantic, Na poříčí 9, ℰ 24 81 10 84, ✆ 24 81 23 78, *htlatlantic@mbox.vol.cz*, *www.hotel-atlantic.cz*. Attractive, well appointed and very reasonably priced.

Axa, Na poříčí 40, ℰ 24 81 63 32/24 81 25 80, ✆ 24 21 44 89, *axapraha@ mbox.vol.cz, www.vol.cz/axa*. This place was once Prague's premier backpacking hotel and, though partially overhauled in recent years, it still has the feel of a comfy student hostel about it. Contains some cheaper rooms with only a wash basin; in the basement is an excellent 25m swimming pool and sauna/massage facilities. Children under six stay free of charge.

Hotel Anna, Budečská 17, Prague 2, ℰ 22 51 31 11, ✆ 22 51 51 58, *reception@hotelanna.cz, www.hotel. cz/anna*. Friendly management and clean and bright rooms, in a leafy location that's a short metro ride to the centre. The only downsides are a grim breakfast room and minuscule lift, both of which you can probably avoid.

Hotel Harmony, Na poříčí 31, ℰ 232 00 16/231 01 35, ✆ 231 00 09. A Functionalist block on a busy street, but friendly and comfortable enough. Sixty well-equipped rooms, some of which have disabled access and facilities, while others come with fridge and TV.

Hotel City Inn, Hybernská 13, ℰ 24 21 67 76/24 22 23 30, ✆ 24 21 40 87, *rezervace@city-inn.cz*. Virtually glued to a railway station, the external grime conceals a clean and quiet interior, with friendly staff, albeit that not all speak English. Demand a room with natural light or you won't get one.

Hotel Merkur, Těšnov 9, ℰ 24 81 09 33/232 38 78/232 35 72, ✆ 23 23 906. If a hotel can be too 'conveniently located', this is one of them, since it's roughly equidistant from the city's main bus and train stations, while a flyover rumbles past a few hundred metres from its main entrance. But the rooms have double-glazing, they're clean and they're relatively cheap. Don't make this your first choice, but don't despair if you end up here, since the Golden City is only a short walk (and even shorter drive) away.

Pension City, Belgická 10, Prague 2, ℰ/✆ 22 52 16 06, *hotel.city@telecom.cz, www.web.telecom.cz/hotel.city*. Large, bright and clean rooms in a well-run and friendly pension. Get a room with a streetside view over the cobbled avenues. The reception desk is open 8am–11pm; call in advance if you are arriving at another time. Free parking.

Hostel Imperial, Na poříčí 15, ℰ/✆ 231 60 12, *hostelimperial@ razdva .cz, www.hostelimperial.cz*. A 1920s hotel offering faded grandeur on a budget. The impressive staircase leads to some good-value, bright and airy rooms with high ceilings and pretty lampshades.

Accommodation Agencies

Prague's housing shortage is chronic. It is notoriously common for families to live together until the children marry, and the claustrophobia that ensues goes a long way to explain the mismatches, extramarital affairs and early divorces that typify young love in the capital. The tourist explosion of recent years has exacerbated the problems but, rather than despair, Praguers have risen to the lucrative challenge by moving in with each other and sending their parents to make marmalade in the country. As a result, you will have few problems in finding private accommodation, and the following agencies all have a variety of properties on their books. All offer the option of one room in a family flat, or a self-contained apartment. The former is rarely as constricting as it sounds, although your hosts may insist on waking you up with coffee and cakes and asking you polite questions about monarchs, presidents and football teams. The agencies can reserve accommodation in the centre if you give them enough warning: specify that you want an address in Prague 1 (although parts of Prague 2 can be just as convenient). *Prices range from about £25–40 ($38–60) per person per night for a flat, and double rooms cost from £10 ($15) a night.*

If you are travelling from the UK, you can arrange accommodation in advance through the **Czechbook Agency**, Jopes Mill, Trebrownbridge, Cornwall TR14 3PX, ℗/℅ (01503) 240629, *info@czechbook.fsnet.co.uk, www.czechbook.fsnet.co.uk*. Or visit the **Czech and Slovak Tourist Centre**, 16 Frognal Parade, Finchley Road, London NW3 5HG, ℗ (020) 7794 3263/3264, free call ℗ 0800 026 7943, ℅ (020) 7794 3265, *cztc@cztc.demon.co.uk, www.czech-slovak-tourist.co.uk*. With the Czech firms listed below, you should make reservations more than a week and less than a month before leaving home. English is spoken in all of them but, where a fax number is given, a faxed request should precede a confirmatory telephone call. Bookings are generally taken on trust: few places in Prague yet accept credit card payment over the phone.

APT-Rent, Ostrovní 7, ℗ 24 99 09 90, ℅ 24 99 09 99, US toll free ℗/℅ 1 800 707 7819, London ℗/℅ (44 20) 7681 2362, *info@apartment.cz, www.apartment.cz. Open daily 8am–8pm*. A 24-hour service from helpful and multilingual staff. Offers private accommodation and can arrange reservations in a broad range of hotels and pensions as well as guided tours, car rental, hotel pick-ups, etc.

Ave, Wilsonova 8 (in the main station), ℗ 24 22 32 26/24 22 35 21/24 61 75 68, ℅ 24 22 34 63, *avetours@avetours.anet.cz. Open daily 6am–11pm*. The largest of the agencies, with several thousand beds on its books, in hotels, pensions, youth hostels and private flats. They have some of the cheapest deals available and provide a range of sightseeing services. They also run a reservations department for accommodation outside Prague: ℗ 24 61 71 32, ℅ 24 61 71 13.

Daněk Apartments, Haštalské náměstí 13, ℗ 231 16 02, ℅ 24 81 06 03. *Open daily 9–noon and 1–6*. A very friendly and obliging company offering a number of attractively furnished apartments in the city centre and further afield, as well as sightseeing trips, car rental, hotel pick-ups and tickets.

International Prague Accommodation Service, Panska 8, ℗ 24 23 23 73/24 22 21 86, ℅ 24 21 50 70, *ipas@sererpha.czcom.cz, www.ipas.cz*. Hotels, pensions and self-catering flats; transport, theatre and concert ticket bookings.

Praga Magica, Masna 9, ℗ 231 22 57/24 81 55 51, ℅ 232 06 05/24 81 55 51, *info@pragamagica.cz, www.pragamagica.cz. Open Mon–Sat 9–6*. One of the friendliest agencies in town, operating a set of its own (modern) apartments in the Old Town and able to offer flexible accommodation from a full range of period buildings, as well as organize hotel or pension bookings. Efficient, centrally located and email literate.

Hostels

Hostels in Prague tend to come and go, as building owners tread water pending major redevelopment of their properties. At the time of writing, two of the most central were:

Travellers' Hostel, Dlouhá 33, ℗ 24 82 66 62/24 82 66 63, ℅ 24 82 66 65, *hostel@travellers.cz*. A fee of $8–18 gets you clean sheets and breakfast, five minutes from the Old Town Square and next door to the Roxy danceclub. Also offers laundry facilities and Internet access.

'Island' Střelecký Ostrov, ℗ 24 91 01 88/24 91 48 49. Decent beds, as well as an outdoor pub, tennis court and open-air cinema on one of Prague's prettiest islands.

Alternatively, the Charles University farms out its student accommodation between June and September, and if you contact **AVE** or one of the other agencies you'll be given plenty of addresses. Finally (and least conveniently) there are year-round hostels in the student dorms up on Strahov Hill around Chaloupeckého street, which you can (almost) reach by taking bus 217, 149 or 143 from Dejvická to Strahov Stadion. The **Estec Hostel** on Vaníčkova 5, ✆ 57 21 04 10, 📧 52 73 43, *estec@jrc.cz*, is the largest, and there are also beds available in nearby Blocks 4, 7 and 11.

Prague: Entertainment and Nightlife

A city that was once among the saddest in the world has turned into one of the hedonistic capitals of Europe. While operas and symphonies resound from Prague's stages, a summer stroll will lead you past the whole gamut of tomfoolery, from sword-swallowing to didgeridoo-snuffling, and a night of debauchery could take you from Romanesque dancefloors to canopied cafés under the stars. It's a far cry from the barren years of yore, when the wicked witches of the bureaucracy often used to insist not just on being invited to the ball but on drawing up the programme. Spontaneity was discouraged and occasionally criminalized, while the work of the country's best playwrights, directors and singers was regularly banned. The energy that always used to be somewhere else has poured back into the city, and so long as you avoid the tourist-trap dross—the shoddy Kafka-itsch plays and *Don Giovanni* puppet shows—you need hardly yawn until you get home.

This chapter can only sketch the outlines of what is one of the fastest-moving aspects of a rapidly changing town. For up-to-date information, examine the listings in the *Prague Post*, scour the Internet sites listed on p.17, and eavesdrop on the conversations of your fellow travellers. Advance booking information is on p.20.

Concerts and Opera

Following a bloody orgy of privatization, Prague Opera acrimoniously split into two separate companies in 1992. The **National Opera**, based in the neo-Renaissance National Theatre on Národní 2, is the more splendid and staid of the two. It has taken very unkindly to the pretensions of its rival, which lives in the almost-as-ornate edifice on Wilsonova 8—once the Smetana Theatre and now cheekily renamed the **State Opera** (Státní opera). Prague opera is competent rather than inspired, and has always depended on vendettas and intrigue for its energy, and as a result the rivalry between the directors and staff of the two companies promises to invigorate it over the next few years. The State Opera has thrown down the gauntlet by announcing an all but impossible number of new productions; and a pained National Opera has responded to the gadfly challenge by ponderously starting to overhaul its conservative repertoire and shoddy props. Battle has been joined and, if public relations officers are to be believed, nothing is ruled in and nothing is ruled out. That may be true, but what you can hope for is imaginative innovation from the former company and dependable quality from the latter.

As well as Smetana, Janáček and other native composers, the work of Mozart is a favourite, thanks to Prague's insistence that his connection to Salzburg was no more than an accident of birth. His music still lilts across the city, honoured by the violins and harmonica concertos of a thousand buskers. If you decide to succumb to what has become a Prague cliché and take in a Mozart opera, you may as well go the whole hog and attend it at the neoclassical **Estates Theatre**, Ovocný trh. (Stavovské divadlo). Among those in whose footsteps you'll be following is Wolfgang himself.

The above venues all act as concert halls from time to time, as does the Art Nouveau **Smetanova síň Obecního domu** (Smetana Hall of the Municipal House) on nám.

Republiky, which now houses the Prague Symphony Orchestra. The Czech Philharmonic Orchestra is based at the **Rudolfinum** on nám. Jana Palacha, which regularly puts on some of the best-value concerts in town. An important venue for **ballet** is the **Palác kultury** (Palace of Culture). A haemorrhage of asylum-seeking talent during the 1970s and 1980s has left Czech ballet in an unimpressive state, but if you want to make your own judgement you'll find the aforementioned palace, a block of concrete erected in the late 1970s, next to the Vyšehrad metro station (line C). There are also regular concerts and recitals in many of the palaces and churches in central Prague. The best acoustics are generally agreed to be in St James' (sv. Jakub), but listening to a symphony amidst the all-encompassing splendour of St Vitus' leaves most people feeling very small and rather overjoyed. There are concerts there (and virtually everywhere else in town) during the Prague spring music festival, booking details for which are on p.xx.

Theatre

The largest theatres are the **National Theatre** (Národní divadlo) mentioned above, and the neighbouring **Laterna Magika,** squatting under what looks like a very big piece of plastic bubble wrap. The first shows suitably unadventurous performances of Shakespeare, Molière, George Bernard Shaw, Karel Čapek and the like (programme information ✆ 24 90 14 48, *www.anet.cz/nd*), while the second combines film, theatre and mime. The granddaddy of Prague's tourist traps, it has degenerated from radical beginnings and international plaudits at the Brussels Expo '58 to a candyfloss multi-mediocrity. The first directors to work at the theatre, who included Miloš Forman of *One Flew Over the Cuckoo's Nest* fame, were soon edged out and it has hardly changed since, although it is perfectly inoffensive. In a similar vein is the Black Theatre, housed in the **Divadlo za Branou II** (Theatre behind the Gate II) at Národní 40. On the basis of one idea—that black-clad actors can move things against a dark stage without being seen—it sparked off an entire genre of gimmickry (called 'black light theatre') that you'll find across the capital, such as at La Fantastika on Karlova 8 and Theatre Image on Pařížská 3, *www.imagetheatre.cz*.

It will probably come as little surprise that, with a playwright in the presidential office, Prague's smaller theatres have been experiencing a renaissance since 1989. However, the experimentalism of their broad repertoires has often had a floundering desperation about it, and a sense that the most important motivation is to make up for lost time. That said, two consistently interesting theatres are the **Divadlo na zábradlí** in Anenské nám., ✆ 24 22 19 33, and the **Divadlo Labyrint** at Štefánikova 57, ✆ 54 50 27. The first was where Václav Havel worked his way from stage-hand to literary adviser in the early 1960s, and had his first play premiered; the second saw the very beginning of the Velvet Revolution in 1989, when the actors of what was then the Realistic Theatre apparently suggested the general strike that was to ring the death knell of the old regime. The **Činoherní Klub** at Ve Smečkách 26, ✆ 24 21 68 12, is also highly regarded by many Praguers; however, its reputation rests on its long association with Oscar-winning film director Jiří Menzel, and it has stultified in recent years. The most innovative programmes, however, are nowadays to be found among the three hydraulically controlled stages of the newly modernized **Divadlo Archa** on Na poříčí 26, ✆ 232 88 00, *www.archatheatre.cz*. With a strong bias towards music and dance, it is also the theatre most accessible to non-Czech speakers, and well worth investigating if experimentalism is your bag. It also has a buzzing café, where you should find someone able to guide you deeper into the dramatic world of Prague: *open Mon–Fri 9am–10.30pm, Sat 10–10, Sun 1–10.*

Finally, you just may want to attend a marionette show while in Prague. Puppeteering has a long tradition in Bohemia and, according to its disciples, it is an under-appreciated art form. You can judge for yourself at one of the street puppet theatres that dot the capital during the summer, or at the **National Marionette Theatre** at Žatecká 1, ✆ 232 25 36. It may help to know that Prague's favourite puppets are the father-and-son duo of Spejbl and Hurvínek, whose plodding worry and agile impudence have enthralled generations of Czech children.

Cinema

Although most of Prague's cinemas have yielded to Hollywood's embrace, there are three that regularly screen cult classics and Czech oldies: the **Dlabačov** in the Hotel Pyramida, at Bělohorská 24, ✆ 33 35 51 09, the **Illusion** at Vinohradská 48, ✆ 22 52 03 79, and the **Pražský filmovy klub** at Václavské nám. 17, ✆ 26 20 35. For a proper night out, head for either the glorious pomp of the **Lucerna**, through the passage at Vodičkova 36, ✆ 24 21 69 72, or spend a laid-back evening in one of Prague's *kinokavárny* (cinema-cafés), such as **Mišmaš**, at Veletržní 61, ✆ 37 92 78. Best of all is the newly relocated **Ponrepo** at Bartolomějska 11, which shares a home with the National Film Archive. For talkies, it uses the quaint technique of simultaneous translation, while silent movies are accompanied by a live pianist. Incongruity is the order of the day: *Hard Times* has been screened to the strains of *Amazing Grace*, and on one memorable occasion all the lines of *Last Tango in Paris* were intoned by an unflappable *babička*, who remained cool as a cucumber even as Marlon Brando built up to the Butter Scene.

Jazz

Prague jazz has had a chequered history. As recorded by writer (and amateur musician) Josef Škvorecký, its savage rhythms were suppressed by Nazism and Communism in turn. The modern low point came in 1986, when members of the spiritedly independent Jazz Section of the Musicians Union were jailed on trumped-up corruption charges; but since 1989 the city's players have revelled in their new freedom. The scene is an eclectic one—ranging from smooth syncopators with oil-slicked hair to goggle-eyed corkscrew heads who have digested one Howlin' Wolf LP too many—but, with a long musical heritage and centuries of folk melodies in the national back catalogue, Prague jazz can be surprisingly relaxed and innovative.

There are three notable venues in the centre of the capital. **Reduta** at Národní 20, ✆ 24 91 22 46 (*open Mon–Sat 9.30pm–midnight*), is the longest established. Although pricey and unusually popular among Scandinavians and Germans, it remains something of a Prague institution: when President Clinton hit the city on his '94 European tour, it was in Reduta that he played his sax (an event promptly commemorated by the management with a bronze plaque). The club is oddly parochial—everyone whoops a little louder if a visiting black person appears on the stage—but its intimacy makes it a good place to fraternize with the band between sets. Look out for Martin Kratochvíl, music mogul, multimillionaire and mean jazz pianist, whose bald head and handlebar moustache are often to be found bobbing around on stage here.

The **AghaRTA Jazz Centrum** at Krakovská 5, *Ⓣ* 22 21 12 75 (*open daily 7pm–1am*), is another cosy spot; as well as being a small shop, it operates as a tranquil café during the day and has a small food menu. **Bugsy's** at Pařížská 10 (*open daily 7pm–2am*) is popular among the city's young urban professionals and, if your idea of jazz is inextricably linked to well-cut suits and long drinks, you'll find no more convivial spot in the capital. And in Malá Strana, be sure to check out the small and smoky basement of **U malého Glena**; its Canadian owner spends much of his life with his ear to the ground, and its weekly programme often repays study. A recent arrival is **Ungelt Jazz and Blues Club** at Týn 2 in the Old Town, which hosts live bands daily from 9pm. Finally, there's the newly re-opened **Café Imperial** on Na poříčí 15, where more or less jazzy bands play amidst restored Art Nouveau splendour on most weekend evenings.

Café Society

In one of his many unpublished stories, Franz Kafka pondered the meaning and origins of café society. Lonely Franz explained to a friend that he imagined a man who wanted somehow to 'make it possible for people just to see others, to talk to them, observe them without getting involved in any relationships, without hypocrisy'. Prague's first café was actually opened by an irascible Armenian who was only looking for a captive audience, but by the early 1900s the capital's coffeehouses had developed a vitality that would turn them into sepia-tinted legend in the grim years and decades that followed 1938. Although everyone from anarchists to anti-Semites had their favoured haunts, the culture transcended its localism and achieved Europe-wide fame. The best-known haunt was the **Café Arco**, the favourite of Kafka, Max Brod and the other 'Arconauts'. It was a beacon for Central Europe's writers, thinkers and shoulder-rubbers until the Nazi invasion. The café survives—after a fashion—at Hybernská 12 but, after several decades spent as little more than an annexe of the nearby railway station, its doors were locked and windows whitewashed in late 2000. It remains unclear in what form it will reopen—common sense grimly predicts that it will be turned into a Kafka theme bar, although Prague's spotty record in the field of heritage-exploitation (both before and after 1989) suggests that it is just as likely to re-emerge as a shoe shop. Those with imagination could also ponder the past at Na příkopě 17. Until 1945, the former palace housed the Café Continental, known affectionately as the Conti by the scarred Junkers, monocled Nazis and generally proud Germans who frequented it. *Untermenschen* entered at their peril.

The mosaic of cultures that made up prewar Prague was shattered by the Nazi invasion. Nostalgic myth subsequently asserted that the city's café-crawlers were always predominantly Jewish and German, but Prague's Czechs were never without their *kavárny*. They regularly reconnoitred at the now destroyed Café Union, and generations of Praguers have famously wasted time at the **Café Slavia**, at Národní 2 opposite the National Theatre. Under its green painting of a lonely absinthe drinker, the Nobel Prize-winning poet Jaroslav Seifert dreamed of meeting Apollinaire in his *Slavia Poems*; the 1920s avant-garde adjourned here whenever things became too stormy at the nearby Union; and until 1989, the unofficial opposition came to exchange ideas and typewritten manuscripts. In 1991, it was closed for renovation and, for seven years, Praguers gazed at its darkened windows and wondered whether it would be replaced by, for example, a rapacious producer of carcinogenic hamburgers. It reopened in 1999, a little more expensive and a little tidier, but otherwise unchanged. The glorious Art

Nouveau **Evropa Café** at Václavské nám. 25 has not fared quite as well, and price-hikes have driven away the old regulars, who once ranged from screaming queens and Romany kings to the animated members of a deaf-and-mute discussion group.

Few of the city's new cafés have the faded grandeur that Central European clichés might demand, but for the first time in decades café society in its true freewheeling sense can be said to be returning to Prague. The process was propelled forward by the influx of foreigners during the 1990s; refugees from the Yugoslavian wars and English-speaking ex-pats showed the city how to lounge in style, and their spiritual legacy survives both in the many establishments now owned by resident foreigners and in some of the most laid-back of the new generation of Czech-run cafés. Anxious dissidents and snooping secret agents may no longer congregate in them, but a trawl through the following stops should provide more than enough characters with which to people your novel.

Nove Mesto and Vinohrady

Café Colubris, Italská 25. *Open Mon–Fri 9am–2am, Sat–Sun 10am–2am.* Sunken, spacious and bluesy café, with furniture to curl up in and an undulating pool table to play drunken games on. Occasional cabarets, gigs and poetry.

Café Imperial, Na poříčí 15. *Open daily 11am–midnight.* Although unassuming from the outside, the ceramic pillars, tiled ceilings and stained glass of this Art Nouveau café, and its location just off the beaten tourist track, make this one of the city's better-kept secrets. The service is a little too laid-back and the food downright dull, but the lively atmosphere and nightly jazz sessions make this well worth a visit. No cards.

Café Louvre, Národní 20. *Open daily 8am–10pm.* Airy coffeehouse and billiard hall, deservedly popular among Czechs and virtually overlooked by most visitors to the city.

Café Meduza, Belgická 17, Prague 2, Vinohrady. *Open Mon–Fri 11am–1am, Sat–Sun noon–1am.* A dusty parlour of a café, filled with dowdy prewar furnishings, and drawing a young, hip and predominantly Czech crowd. The menu is minimal, but drinks are plentiful.

Café Slavia, Smetanovo nábř. 2. *Open Mon–Fri 8am–midnight, Sat 9am–midnight, Sun 11.30am–midnight.* A Prague institution re-modelled for the 21st century, out-pricing all but the richest students from the film school next door, but popular among Prague's chattering classes.

Dobrá čajovna (The Good Teahouse), Václavské nám. 14. *Open Mon–Sat noon–9.30.* One of the odder developments in Prague's café culture over the last few years has been a mushrooming of tea houses, of which this is a typical example. They're popular among the city's more introspective youths, who sit around on pouffes, whispering to each other and sipping tea to the sound of pan pipes and Tibetan dirges.

FX Café, Bělehradská 120, Vinohrady. *Open daily 11.30am–5am.* Comfortable and lively late-night vegetarian café above one of Prague's trendiest clubs. The back room doubles as a venue for various cultural events including poetry readings.

The Globe Bookstore and Coffeehouse, Pštrosova 6. *Open daily 10am–midnight.* An easy-going café that doubles as an English-language bookshop and pseudo-literary haunt. Stylishly decorated, free Internet access and a message board requesting or offering everything from yoga weekends to work as an artist's model. No cards.

Kavárna velryba (Whale Café), Opatovická 24. *Open daily 11am–2am.* Post-revolutionary Prague's first self-styled literary café, and still very proud of it too. Regular readings of Czech poetry are held, and the tables are full of the kind of men who gaze up from their copies of *Ulysses* to see who's watching. One sneaky way of watching them watching you watching them is through the large convex mirror at the bar.

Mánes Gallery Café and Restaurant, Masarykovo nábř. 9. *Open daily 11–11.* Attached to an elegant Modernist art gallery on the banks of the Vltava, this is as popular among the polo-necked and portfolio-clutching crowd as you'd expect.

Obecni dům kavárna, nám. Republiky 5. *Open daily 11–11.* An Art Nouveau café in the newly renovated Municipal House. Piano music and (overpriced) Internet terminals.

Josefov

Blatouch, Vězeňská 4. *Open Mon–Fri 11am–midnight, Sat 2–midnight, Sun 2–11.* A cosy double-decker of a café, popular among soft-spoken Czechs, and the type of expat who just can't stand expats. Sausages, salads and sandwiches. A good spot for mulled wine or a civilized shot of absinthe in the bleak midwinter.

Decorative Arts Museum Café, 17 listopadu 2. *Open Mon–Fri 10am–6pm.* Long and lively café, popular among students from the nearby Philosophy Faculty of the Charles University.

Although sandwiches are available, this is more a place to drink and expound your philosophy, before or after visiting the exceptional museum upstairs.

Malá Strana

Café Savoy, Vítězná 5. *Open daily 9am–midnight.* A century-old café, now daintily restored after having been turned into a carpet warehouse and community propaganda centre by the Communists. Its high-ceilinged splendour seems to appeal particularly to wealthier pensioners.

Jo's Bar, Malostranské nám. 7. *Open daily 11am–2am.* An ex-pat dominated bar, legendarily wild during the 1990s but a pale shadow of its former self since its Canadian founder departed to **Železné Dveře** across the bridge (*see* p.167).

Rubín, Malostranské nám. 9. *Open daily 6pm–4am.* A tiny, smoky, cheap and late theatre-bar, in an arched Gothic cellar.

Bars and Clubs

Prague has finally learnt to party hard. Václav Havel set his compatriots an impressive example during his presidency, with a range of clubbing partners who included Mick Jagger, Lou Reed and the late Frank Zappa; in 1991, in the heat of the moment, he even appointed Zappa to be Czechoslovakia's cultural envoy at large, an appointment swiftly reversed by incredulous bureaucrats. Havel still goes club-crawling occasionally, but with the exponential increase in venues your chances of stumbling into him are fewer than ever before. But you never know.

In a city as protean as Prague, clubs can metamorphose overnight and a constant struggle is being waged for the fickle hearts and flickering minds of Prague's *jeunesse dorée*. To discover the flavour of the moment, supplement the information below with the listings in the *Prague Post*, *www.praguepost.cz*, or look at the popular fortnightly online listings on *www.downtown.cz*. Reggae fans should keep their ear to the ground; although there are several clubs in the capital at any given time, none has displayed much staying power and they are not listed below.

As a general rule, you should avoid the discotheques of Wenceslas Square, unless you have a love for the perverse. They're prohibitively expensive for most ordinary Czechs and as a result teem with disorientated coach parties, lonely businessmen and lowlifes. Unlike any of the places mentioned here, they may also operate dress codes, often changeable at will and used only to keep undesirables out.

For information on all Prague's traditional tipples, see **Food and Drink**, p.138.

New Town (Nové Město)

Klub Mánes (Mánes Gallery Building), Masary-kovo nábř. 250. *Open daily 9pm onwards.* Latin music in a white Functionalist building, balanced on the edge of the Vlatva.

Lucerna Music Bar, Vodičkova 36. A grandiose auditorium, dating from the start of the 20th century (and located above a shopping mall from the same period) which hosts live gigs as well as regular dance nights. Check the *Prague Post* for upcoming events.

Radost (Joy), Bělehradská 120, *www.radostfx .cz. Open daily 9pm–6am.* When it opened in 1992 this was the first hi-tech club to hit Prague; its halogen spots and mind-numbing videos have changed little since, but it retains an air of safe and glitzy glamour. The dancefloor is small but active, with a tendency to favour repetitive beats over boppy pop, while the sofas and seats of the large bar area provide comfy vantage points from which to watch the capital's club culture pass before you. Upstairs is a large bar and café, open for pizzas, coffee, alcohol and conversation until around 5am.

Old Town (Staré Město)

Chapeau Rouge, Jakubská 2. *Open daily 4–4.* Wild, loud and drunk. On most nights, the bar area looks like a scene Hieronymus Bosch might have painted on speed: a fiery tableau of screaming youths in the grip of impulsions, intoxi-cants and illusions beyond human ken. A good place to begin the night if you have no idea where you want to end it.

Karlovy lážné (Charles Baths), just off the Old Town side of the Charles Bridge. Four heaving dancefloors in the erstwhile municipal public baths of Prague. Not a place for leisurely contemplation, but if you want to dance in a disused swimming pool this is the club for you.

Lávka, Novotného lávka 1. *Open 9pm–4am.* Enticing location on an island just under the Charles Bridge, with a view of river, bridge and castle that can be hallucinogenic during a hard night of outdoor dancing. It's during the long hot summers that Lávka takes off, with the holiday-romance scene of swooping pick-ups, hokey

cokeys and unforgettable kisses, all to an un-relenting soundtrack of MTV/Europap at its worst.

Marquis de Sade, Templova 8. *Open Mon–Sat noon–2am, Sun 3pm–2am.* The name nods at the fact that this place was once a brothel, but this dowdy charmer of a bar is now about as risqué as a frayed teddy bear. Eccentric decorations, collapsing upholstery and live music, as and when someone gets their act together to play

Roxy, Dlouhá 33, *www.roxy.cz. Open Tues–Sat 5pm–midnight.* A former cinema, stripped down to its concrete essentials, and usually playing hard-core techno to match. It styles itself as an 'experimental space', but largely sticks to raves of the most traditional kind and, due to the absence of adequate air-conditioning, descending on to the dancefloor is usually like slamming into a wall of sweat. Popular among early 1990s nostalgists, and recreational drug abusers.

Thirsty Dog, Elišky krásnohorské 5. *Open daily noon–2am.* A foreign-owned bar which started its rowdy life during the mid-90s in the Obecni dum, when the Art Nouveau institution was somehow commandeered for a year by a bunch of the city's expat slackers. Sentimentalists who can remem-ber Prague in those days might want to pop in for a beer, but it's otherwise an unremarkable back-packers' hangout.

U bilého koníčka (The White Pony), Staro-městské nám. 20. *Open daily 9pm–4am.* A spacious Romanesque cellar, attractively gloomy despite being hung with a mirror ball and sprayed with lasers. Its unfortunate history, however, is that it was once the place where the youth wing of the Party would come to make whoopee, and—to the suspicious eye, at least —some of the regulars have the distinct air of ageing Young Communists about them. Prague swingers now give it the cold shoulder, but you could at least wander down the steps to peek at the interior.

U zlateho stromu, Karlova 6. *Open 24 hours.* A subterranean entertainment complex, comprising assorted bars, nooks and crannies, and a tiny but highly energetic dancefloor playing Europop cour-tesy of assorted Czech DJs. From the street, this establishment advertises itself as a strip joint but, although more-or-less bored female pole-dancers slink about in one of the rooms, the place is no more louche than any Prague bar, and has long been a favourite among young Czechs.

Železné Dveře (The Iron Door), Michalská 19 (through the passageway and down the stairs). *Open daily 8pm–5am.* Loud, raucous and friendly basement bar, frequented by a gregarious crowd of ex-pats and Czechs. Until about midnight the place stays calm, but then the serious fun begins. Come here for cocktails and bartop dancing; do not come here if you have a flight to catch the next morning.

Lesser Quarter (Malá Strana)

Jo's Garáž, Malostranské nám. 7. *Open daily 9pm–5am.* Funk and house in two cavernous chambers opposite St Nicolas' Church. Popular among backpackers.

Rock Club Újezd, Újezd 18. *Open daily 5pm–3am (café from noon).* This club will forever have a place in the hearts of Prague's post-revolutionary

generation, having been the first to open after 1989. It is now a much-sanitized version of its original grungy, smoky, smelly and squatty incarnation, but it still attracts a diverse and largely Czech crowd of drinkers.

Žižkov

Akropolis, Kubelíkova 27. *Open Mon–Sat 4pm–2am, Sun 4pm–midnight.* A long-standing favourite among trendy Czechs and Czechettes, the smoky bar in the basement is a good place to sip beer and absinthe to a soundtrack of ambient house, while live bands (both Czech and foreign) often play on the stage upstairs.

Further Afield

MECCA, U puhonu, Prague 7. *Open daily 11am–3am.* Prague's latest super-club, housed in a factory conversion.

Gay Prague

Suppressed for several decades as an intrusive symptom of late capitalism, Prague's homosexual culture is finally beginning to throb again. The weekly listings magazine *Program* has a regular gay page. The website *www.amigo.cz* has an English-language option with a variety of information about the gay scene in Prague, the Czech Republic and Slovakia.

Prague's gay scene is still in its infancy, but one of the more established clubs—where you can get up-to-the-minute details of the more transient ones—is **Stella** at Lužická 10, Vinohrady (*open daily 8pm–5am*). It's predominantly male and apparently something of a meat-market, but cruising and cruisable lesbians aren't excluded. Even more relentless is **Drakes** at Petřínská 5, open to men only all hours every day, and offering everything from sex-aid shopping to strip-shows. Smaller, camper and jollier generally is the **A-Club** at Miličova 25 in Žižkov, which holds women-only nights on Fridays (*open Mon–Sat 6pm–6am, Sun 3pm–midnight*). Another mixed gay and lesbian 'disco with sauna' in Žižkov is **Connections** at Husitská 7 (*open daily 9pm–4am*).

Two new popular centrally located gay venues are **Friends Bar** on Náprstkova 1, *www.friends-prague.cz* (*open daily 2pm–2am*), and **Babylonia** on Martinska 6 in the Old Town, which has a sauna, steam baths and massage from 2pm to 2am. If you want more spectacular entertainment, ask around for the latest whereabouts of **Lady Pitchfork**'s roving cabaret troupe; or head out for the louche, camp and comfy **Aqua Club 2000** at Husitská 7 in Žižkov, ℗ 627 89 71/627 80 63, where transvestite shows are held every Friday and Saturday, and peripheral entertainments include a small pool (bookable for private parties), roulette and snooker. That's men only, as is **Érra** (a small bar with dancefloor) at Konviktská 11 in the Old Town, ℗ 22 22 05 68 (*open daily 10am–midnight*), and the small sauna and gym at the **David Club** at Sokolovská 77 in Prague 8, ✆ 232 87 89 (*open daily 2pm–2am*). Finally, when it's time for bed, both men and women should be able to find one at the **Gay penzion David** at Holubova 5 in Prague 5, ✆ 90 01 12 93.

Prague: Shopping

The free market has hit Prague and, as the formerly state-owned retail industry is privatized, the capital's malls and high streets are being transformed. Rusting corrugated shutters are being opened for the first time in years, interiors are being remodelled and relit, and shop windows that spent the last 40 years trying to sell the same dusty jar of gherkins now display Apple Macs and Christian Dior. In the city where a crate of olive oil would once attract a 20-strong queue, you can now buy anything, from a mango to a MiG-50 fighter jet. Unsurprisingly, freedom of choice hasn't been an unalloyed blessing. The homogenising effects of modern capitalism that are slowly making Western high streets into interchangeable copies of each other haven't (yet) overwhelmed Prague, in that the number of foreign and domestic chains is still relatively small, but the city's dependence on the tourist economy is having its own corrosive effect. Scores of shops which once sold a variety of shoddy goods now sell a uniformity of useless ones—and no matter how much you may initially covet a supposedly distinctive Prague souvenir, by the end of your visit you may never want to see a Don Giovanni puppet or porcelain figurine again.

But, despite the problems, all but the very poor and the very conservative in Prague would agree that, so far, the changes wrought since the 1989 revolution have been for the better. For the old and the infirm, forced to hunt an ever-shrinking number of bargains, the queues are getting no shorter; and if inflation spirals out of control they are the ones who will be hurt most. But shops that once formed grim units of mammoth chains called things like 'Meat', 'Tobacco' and 'Fruit-Vegetable' now offer a broad variety of goods, including many home-produced items that are widely available for the first time thanks to improvements in the elephantine distribution network. While few visitors will yet be tempted to shop till they drop, Western designer goods are becoming ubiquitous; if you crave a scent or a suit, Pařížská street is the avenue to investigate, and at the Pavilon shopping mall at Vinohradská 20 (*open Mon–Fri 10–7, Sat 10–6, Sun noon–6*) you can pretend you never left home. Perhaps more importantly, the shortages once caused by centralized production are over. Never again should Praguers have to go through crises such as that of November 1989, when, with the Velvet Revolution at its height, the country's three largest toilet-paper factories seized up—leading, according to legend, to the largest-ever sales of the Communist Party daily, *Rudé právo*.

Certain rituals from the past linger on. In self-service stores, you often aren't allowed to enter without a basket (for which there may be a queue). The fear isn't that you will pocket a pot of yoghurt, but that the number of people in the store would otherwise reach critical mass. Another time-honoured tradition, still occasionally observed, is that you order your goods in one place, pay in another and collect your fetishistically wrapped purchase in a third. There are generally queues at all three spots. Finally, although the quality of service has improved hugely in recent years, you should be prepared to occasionally encounter a rather startling level of rudeness. Enquiries may be met by abrupt and vivid gestures of indifference, while supplementary questions might elicit sarcasm, pity, contempt or abuse.

Shopping Hours

Standard shop hours are 9–7 on weekdays and 9–1 on Saturdays, although extended hours and Sunday opening are becoming common in the centre of the city. There are a few late-night food stores: the Vacek Bio-Market at Mostecká 3 is *open Mon–Fri 6–10, Sat 6.30–10 and Sun 10–10*, while the supermarket section of the Bílá labut' department store at the Muzeum end of Wenceslas Square (Václavské nám.) is open every day until 11pm.

Antique and Junk Stores

The years since 1989 have seen a huge increase in the amount of curiosities and antiques available for sale. They are often the knick-knacks and heirlooms of financially hard-pressed families, but there are sometimes even less pleasant forces at work. A wave of low-level looting has been stripping provincial churches and graveyards of their unguarded paintings and statuary, and an identifiable amount finds its way to Prague's antique stores. If you're tempted by a fishy object, you should ask about its provenance, keep your receipt and declare it to customs on departure. The following places are a couple of the more interesting ones, but you'll find plenty of others (marked *bazar* or *starožitnosti*) on your travels.

Icons Gallery, Pohořelec 9. *Open daily 9–6.* Russian icons, along with various Art Deco glass and metal pieces, including ashtrays and lamps.

Vetešnictví, Vítežná 16. *Open Mon–Fri 10–5, Sat 10–2.* Well-stocked, and a cut above most other junk you'll find in the city. Items regularly on offer include walking sticks, decanters and glassware, coal-fired irons, opera glasses, prewar tin cans, picture frames and stuffed fish. No cards.

Books

Reading is a national pastime. Before 1989, the government, and a fair number of proud Praguers, used to recite sales statistics showing that Czechs read twice as much/quickly as the rest of Europe. The value of the claim was always doubtful, since much officially available literature was dross, and recent years have shown that, given a choice, Czechs will happily sink to the lowest common denominator. Science-fiction and westerns are perennial favourites, while translated accounts of out-of-body experiences and the like can set the capital alight. That said, an honourable minority of true bibliophiles remains. They can often be found in the innumerable second-hand bookstores (*antikvariát*) that have sprung up since 1989, which can be useful places to pick up cheap prints, English prewar curiosities and a potboiler for the trip home. The following shops are the most interesting for English speakers. Art books can also be found in the galleries listed later in this chapter.

Anagram, Tyn 4 (behind the Tyn Church). *Open daily 10–8.* Stylish, friendly and extremely well stocked English-language bookshop.

Antikvariát terra incognita, Masná 10. *Open Mon–Fri 9–7, Sat–Sun 10–6.* Old books, prints, charts and maps.

Antikvariát u Karlova mostu, Karlova 2. *Open Mon–Wed and Fri 10–6, Sat 11–4.* One of the best antiquarian bookstores in the capital, selling old Hebrew texts, a broad range of prints, a regular supply of early 20th-century Baedekers and much else besides. You pay through the nose.

Big Ben Bookshop, Malá Štupartská 5, *books@ bigbenbookshop.com. Open Mon–Sat 9–8, Sun 10–6.* Another very useful English-language bookshop, with a reasonable selection.

Důmknihy, Václavské nám. 4. *Open daily 9–8.* Four floors of wall-to-wall books, CDs and a broad range of international magazines. English-language books are on the top floor.

The Globe Bookstore and Coffeehouse, Pštrosova 6, *www.globopolis.com. Open daily 10am–midnight.* A fixture on the expat scene, as cosy as it sounds, with a good collection of English-language novels and non-fiction works, and a laid-back and very comfortable café in which to read them. Internet access, and a message board.

PNS Noviny-Časopisy, Na příkopě 22. *Open Mon–Fri 7.30–6, Sat 8–1.* The best newsagent in town for Czech periodicals. Even if you don't understand a word of Czech, a browse through the scores of titles here gives a glimpse into the obsessions and tastes of Prague's reading public.

Clothes

Art Deco Galerie, Michalská 21. *Open Mon–Fri 1–5.* Retro chic from the 1920s and 1930s: flapper dresses, accessories, and furniture to match.

Bat'a, Václavské nám. 6. *Open Mon–Fri 9–8, Sat 10–6.* The Bat'a shoe is now part of the furniture in India and many other parts of the developing world, but it only returned to its homeland when properties confiscated from the millionaire family were handed back after the revolution. This shop reopened in March 1992. When built in 1928, the use of glass (and little else) on its façade made the building one of the most innovative examples of Constructivist architecture in Europe. Take in the view from the 6th floor; you could even buy a shoe.

Ivana Follová, Týn 1. *Open daily 10–7.* Czech chic for hip chicks. Twenty designers supply this place with everything from belts and hats to shirts and skirts. High-quality, with reasonable prices.

Modes Robes, Benediktská 5. *Open Mon–Fri 10–7, Sat 10–4 (summer), 10–2 (winter).* A small and trendy women's clothes store, with coffee bar and stained-glass window, that slips into the style continuum somewhere between Portobello and SoHo. Sells clothes designed by its two owners, pitched at the younger woman, and bought by some of the most beautiful people in town. No cards.

Mořská Nemoc, Masná 19. *Open Mon–Fri 10–6, Sat 10–4.* Cheap but fairly stylish secondhand clothes, including clubbing gear and streetwear.

Romantik, Karoliny Světlé 23. *Open Mon–Fri 10–6, Sat 10–1.* Attractive formal wear for men and women, up to and including wedding dresses, as well as a small range of saucy underwear. All items (except the undies) can be hired. No cards.

Crystal, Porcelain, Jewellery and Souvenirs

Stores selling crystal, garnets and porcelain are a dime-a-dozen in central Prague but, if you're determined to compare what's available, your best bet is to wander through Na příkopě, Narodni and Karlova streets, all of which are glittering with more-or-less identical shops. One word of warning is appropriate. Although Bohemian crystal is said to be among the finest in the world, Praguers capitalize on its reputation by producing huge amounts of cut glass. If you are in any doubt at all, take the suspect article and drop it. Crystal usually bounces.

Amfora, in the Lucerna shopping mall, running between Štěpánská and Vodičkova streets. *Open Mon–Sat 10–7, Sun 10–4.* Ceramic items.

Boema, Nerudova 49. *Open Mon–Sat 10–6.* Relatively unusual crystal pieces, along with antique reproductions.

Ceská Keramika, Celetná 4. *Open daily 9.30–7.* Two floors of whimsical and/or traditional Czech pottery and porcelain.

Enyky Benyky, Břehová 4. *Open daily 9.30–6.* More or less wacky souvenirs and art, ranging from painted chamber pots to surrealistic paintings.

Moser, Na příkopě 12 (first floor). *Open Mon–Fri 9–7, Sat 9–4.* A glittering treasure trove of crystal, filling several luxuriously panelled rooms. As well as tortuously wrought goblets, coloured scent bottles and other glassy objets, you'll find silverware and porcelain here. Also has a shop on Malé nám. 11.

Department Stores

Prague's department stores and shopping malls were once palaces of command-economy kitsch, but in recent years they have become showcases for imported Western goods. The closest you'll get these days to a taste of pre-1989 consumerism is in the ornate early 20th-century shopping arcades that are hidden around Wenceslas Square; try the Lucerna complex between Vodičkova and Štěpánská, or the pasáž Rokoko at Václavské nám. 38.

Bílá labut' (White Swan), Na poříčí 23. *Open Mon–Fri 8–7, Sat 8–6.* Once the retail flagship of the Czech command economy, and still the store that's most likely to sell functional, ugly, cheap and shoddy souvenirs. Its smarter sister at Václavské nám. 59 is more modern.

Krone, Václavské nám. 21. *Open Mon–Fri 9–8, Sat 9–7, Sun 10–6.* For anyone who believes that German workmanship is the best in the world. The supermarket in the basement is excellent and can be entered from the Můstek subway vestibule.

Kotva, nám. Republiky 1. *Open Mon–Fri 9–8, Sat 9–6, Sun 10–8.* The largest and best-stocked department store in the capital, with underground parking facilities.

Marks & Spencer, Na příkopě 19. *Open Mon–Sat 10–7.* A little more down-market than its English equivalents, but a good place to buy emergency underwear and so on.

Tesco, Národní 26. *Open Mon–Fri 7–10, Sat 8–9, Sun 9–7.* Prague's best mid-range department store and most centrally located food and grocery supermarket (in the basement). Riding the open-plan escalators and the horseys on the ground floor adds to its appeal.

Food and Drink

Country Life, Melantrichova 15/Jungmannova 1. *Open Mon–Thurs 8.30–6, Fri 8.30–2.30, Sun noon–6.* Vegetarian supplies, including lots of lentils and very tasty bread. Run by Seventh Day Adventists, but the only evidence is the odd opening hours, the good news scattered among the cookbooks and the preternatural contentment of the staff. No cards.

Dionýsos, Vinařického 6. *Open Mon–Fri 10–6.* The best vintners in the capital, with a range of Czech and foreign wines, and a helpful, knowledgeable staff. Delivers too (✆/✉ 29 09 55).

Dům lahůdek, Malé nám. 3. *Open Mon–Sat 9.30– 7, Sun noon–7.* One of the best delis in town, with a particularly good selection of caviar and smoked fish.

Fruits de France, Jindřišská 9. *Open Mon–Wed and Fri 9.30–6.30, Thurs 11.30–6.30, Sat 9.30–1.* A superb collection of imported fruit and veg, with some specimens that will flummox all but the best-travelled connoisseur. If you're cooking to seduce, the cheeses, wild mushrooms, condiments and oils here are prerequisites, and there's an excellent wine selection. As well as imported marks, the shop sells bottles from its own vineyards in Moravia.

J. & J. Mašek Zemanová, Karmelitská 30. *Open Mon–Fri 8–6, Sat 8–noon.* Sumptuous delicatessen selling poultry and a magnificent selection of creatures of the deep, including smoked-salmon steaks, caviare, glistening crustaceans and cooked fish ranging from sprats to sharkfins. Also carries a range of salads and wines. Another essential stop for a stylish picnic. No cards.

Galleries

As well as the places listed below, which largely specialize in established or dead artists, Prague contains scores of galleries showcasing up-and-coming Czech artists: four of the most highly regarded are the **Galerie Behémót** at Elišky Krásnohorské 6 (*open daily 10–6*); **Galerie MXM** at Nosticova 6 (*open Tues–Sun noon–7*); **Mánes Gallery** at Masarykovo nabr. 250; and **Gambra surrealisticka galerie** on Cerninska 5 in Hradčany.

Antikvariát Karel Křenek, Celetná 31. *Open Mon–Fri 10–6, Sat 10–2.* The best place in the city to find Czech graphic art of the first half of the 20th century. Work by many major Czech artists of the period passes through, including manifestos and work produced by the Devětsil group (*see* pp.34–5). Also sells paintings from the same period, older maps and prints, and a selection of books on art history and philosophy.

Galerie Genia Loci, Újezd 11. *Open Mon–Fri 10–6.* A showroom of modern design work. As well as Philippe Starck lemon squeezers and so on, the gallery deals in the cutting edge of modern Czech design: glassware, furniture and household goods.

Galerie Novy Svět, Novy Svět 5. *Open daily 10–6*. Specializes in Pop Art and Surrealism—as well as modern Czech graphic art, this gallery often deals in small works by big names (Ernst, Dalí, Warhol, etc).

Galerie Pallas, Na Perštýné 12. *Open Mon–Fri 10.30–7, Sat 10.30–6*. High-quality Czech art from the first three quarters of the 20th century, including oils and unframed drawings and prints.

Galerie Peithner-Lichtenfels, Michalská 12. *Open daily 10–7*. A vast selection of Czech and Austrian art from the last 100 years, both framed and unframed. Unfortunately, service here is as consistently rude as the holdings are impressive.

Galerie ztichlá klika, Betlemská 10. *Open Mon–Fri 10–6*. Czech etchings, sketches and paintings of the early 20th century.

Pražský dům Fotografie (Prague House of Photography), Haštalská 1. *Open daily 11–6*. The best photographic gallery in Prague, showing the work of Czech and foreign photographers.

Markets

Prague's markets come as a disappointment. Forty years of non-consumption have left a dearth of tradeable second-hand goods, and those that exist have been elevated into pseudo-antiques. The city's oldest market is on Havelská street; most of its bargains are unlikely to appeal to short-term visitors but, if you're stuck for presents, it also sells a range of cheap trinkets and baubles. Rather more interesting, albeit less central, is the market (*tržnice*) on Bubenské nábř. (Vltavská metro; *open Mon–Fri 8–7, Sat–Sun 8–4*), where you'll find an odd collection of liquor stands, flower stalls, DIY halls and knots of Ukrainians and Vietnamese selling pots of caviare and other more-or-less smuggled goods.

Music and Musical Instruments

Classical records and compact discs are cheap and usually well recorded.

Capriccio, Újezd 15. *Open Mon–Fri 9–6, Sat 9–2*. Hundreds of musical scores, many in English and spanning the range from spirituals to electronic keyboard arrangements.

Hudební nástroje, Jungmannova nám. 17. *Open Mon–Fri 9–7, Sat 10–1*. Four floors of Czech- and foreign-manufactured musical instruments, from castanets to clarinets, as well as accessories and a repair service.

Karel Schuss CD-LP, Národní 25 (through the passage). *Open Mon–Sat 11–7.30*. A very wide selection of pop CDs, and second-hand records.

Musica Bona, Jakubská 2, *www.musicabona.cz*. *Open Mon–Sat 9–9, Sun 9–7*. A good collection of classical music, Czech and foreign, at prices that are often lower than elsewhere.

Philharmonia, Pařížská 13. *Open daily 10–6*. One of the widest selections of classical, folk and Romany recordings in Prague.

Popron, Jungmannova 30. *Open Mon–Sat 9.30–7, Sun 10–6*. Pop and dance in all forms, in all formats.

Toys

Česká lidová řemesla (Czech Traditional Handicrafts), Karlova 26. *Open Sun–Thurs 10–6.30, Fri–Sat 10–7*. Wooden toys are sold all over Prague, but this shop contains one of the widest selections: horses to rock and ride a cock on, abacuses, telephones, trolleys and snakes, and an aerial collection of dangling birds. No cards.

ETS, Na bělidle 34 (Prague 5). *Open Mon–Fri 9–5, Sat 9–noon*. Quaint tin train sets, '0' gauge. Ten locomotives, 30 types of rolling stock and a small set of gormless figurines. The shop also sells a cheap type of Czech Meccano called Merkur.

Obchod Loutkami, Nerudova 47. *Open daily 10–6*. Hand and finger puppets and a nightmare-inducing range of tufted, grinning and contorted marionettes. Not a place to get locked into after closing time.

It's sometimes difficult to imagine how Czech could be more alien to English-speakers—although if you want to try, remember that St Cyril provided the Czechs with the script named after him when he arrived. The language seems to have given English nothing other than the words 'pistol', 'robot' and 'Semtex'; and, a few Germanic oddities like 'bratr' (brother) notwithstanding, the only English-tinged Czech words are the same 20th-century neologisms that the rest of the world has also borrowed. The language is Slavonic, with Latin influences, and in its modern form it dates from the 19th century. After 200 years of Germanization in Bohemia, it was painstakingly re-established by a few scholars, with the help of mumbling peasants, a few old texts, and Polish, Serbo-Croat, Bulgarian and Russian dictionaries.

If you try to speak a few words of Czech it's appreciated by most people, although Prague's surlier waiters and shop assistants are still more likely to treat you like an imbecile with a speech defect than to break into a kindly smile. Until the 1989 revolution German was the city's second language, but it has now been firmly overtaken by English. That linguistic shift—which seemed far from inevitable even 10 years ago—has reasonable claim to be the most significant cultural change to hit Prague since the Thirty Years War. By the same token, it has been the most profound legacy of the thousands of English-speaking yuppies, bums and jokers who lived in

Czech Language

Prague during the 1990s; were it not for their tireless proselytising of American and British pop culture, your holiday (and just possibly, the political future of Central Europe) would have been considerably more problematic. The net result is that you'll almost certainly be cornered by someone eager to perfect his or her conjugations and learn a few more obscenities. French is limited to a few sophisticates. Two entire generations were forced to learn Russian, but rarely if ever will you hear it used.

Czech is a phonetic language (pronounced consistently according to its spelling), with none of the shenanigans of silent letters and the like. That's simple enough—the problem is learning how to pronounce the letters. If the language of the English southern middle class is used as a benchmark, the main differences are that c is spoken as 'ts', j is a vowel sound like the English 'y', and r is rolled at the front of the mouth. Ch is a consonant in itself—it's pronounced as in the Scottish 'loch', and you'll find it after 'h' in the dictionary.

A *háček* (ˇ) above a consonant softens it: thus *č* is pronounced 'ch' as in 'chill', *š* is 'sh', and *ž* is the 'zh' sound in 'pleasure'. With *ř*, you venture into territory uncharted by the English language, and every other known language in the world. Even Czech children have to be taught how to pronounce the sound properly; the closest you're likely to get to it is by rolling an 'r' behind your teeth and then expelling a rapid 'zh'. You'll amuse a lot of people by trying to say '*strč prst skrz krk*'—it's a Czech tongue-twister that means 'put your fingers down your throat'.

Vowels are less complicated—*a* is the 'u' in 'up', *e* is as in 'met', *i* and *y* are both as in 'sip', *o* as in 'hot', and *u* as in 'pull'. The sounds are lengthened if the vowel is topped with an accent (´ or, in the case of *u*, also the symbol °)—they're pronounced like the vowels in, respectively, 'bar', 'bear', 'feed', 'poor', and 'oooooh'. The letter *ě* is pronounced as though it were 'ye' as in 'yet' and softens the consonant that comes before it. Accents affect only the sound of a vowel; and when pronouncing a word, it's *always* the first syllable that's stressed.

You don't use a subject (I, you, etc) with a verb, since the ending in itself makes clear who's doing the deed. The English pronoun 'you' has two forms, as in many European languages: *vy* is polite and is used in most everyday situations (and always where more than one person is being addressed); *ty* is widespread among young people, and can be used to address anyone whom you could call your friend (you can also use it to be contemptuous to someone you've never met before). Beware also of the bewildering number of endings any ordinary word can have, depending on which of the seven cases, three-and-a-half genders and two categories it belongs to; if you're looking something up in a dictionary, plump for whatever looks closest. Finally, be alert to the fact that Czechs generally say *no* or *ano*, when they're agreeing to something that's in doubt.

Useful Words and Phrases

yes/no	*ano/ne*	When?	*kdy?*
I don't understand	*nerozumím*	Why?	*proč?*
I don't know	*nevím*	How/what kind of?	*jak?*
Do you speak English?	*mluvíte anglicky?*	How much/many?	*kolik?*
I am English	*jsem angličan(ka)*	Do you have … ?	*máte … ?*
please	*prosím*	post office	*pošta*
Please speak slowly	*mluvte prosím pomalu*	pen	*pero*
		stamp	*známka*
Thank you (very much)	*děkuji (moc)*	envelope	*obálka*
You're welcome	*prosím*	express mail	*expres*
Not at all	*není zač*	telegram	*telegram*
I'm sorry	*promiňte*	telephone	*telefon*
Call a doctor	*zavolejte lékaře*	fax	*telefax*
Let me through,	*pusťte mě,*	I'd like to make a call to…	*rád bych zavolal do…*
I'm a doctor	*já jsem lékař*	I'd like to reverse the charges	*na účet volaného*
Who?	*kdo?*		
What?	*co?*	The number is …	*číslo je …*
Where (is)?	*kde (je)?*	I need the number of…	*potřebuji číslo …*
Where (are you going)?	*kam (jdete)?*	telephone directory	*telefonní seznam*
From where?	*odkud?*	soap	*mýdlo*

toothpaste	*zubní pasta*	sore throat	*angína*
sun-protection cream	*krém na opalování*	thermometer	*teploměr*
medicine for/against	*lék na/proti*	plaster	*náplast*
headache	*bolest hlavy*	bandage	*obvaz*
cough	*kašel*		

Conversation

Good morning	*dobré ráno*	How are you?	*jak se máte?*
Good day	*dobrý den*	Do you come here often?	*chodíte sem často?*
Good evening	*dobrý večer*	Do you have a telephone?	*máte telefon?*
Goodbye	*nashledanou*	May I have the number?	*dáte mi číslo?*
Allow me to	*dovolte, abych se*	Would you like to come	*nechceš zajít na*
introduce myself	*představil*	in for a quick coffee	*kávu?*
Let me introduce	*dovolte, abych vám*	What did you say?	*co říkáte?*
you to ...	*představil*	What did you say? (rude)	*co kecáš?*
My name is ...	*jmenuji se ...*	What are you looking at?	*na co se díváte?*
I'm pleased to meet you	*těší mě, že vás*	What are you looking	*co čumíš?*
	poznávám	at? (very rude)	

Hotel and Shopping

Do you have a free	*máte volný pokoj pro*	supermarket	*samoobsluha*
single/double room?	*jednu osobu/pro dva?*	tobacconist	*tabák*
I'd like the room	*potřebuji pokoj*	antique	*starožitnost*
for ... night(s)	*na ... noc(i)*	book	*kniha*
May I pay by credit card?	*mohu platit kreditní*	cigarettes	*cigarety*
	kartou?	crystal	*křišťál*
How much does it cost?	*kolik to stojí?*	food	*jídlo*
greengrocer	*zelinář*	glass	*sklo*
hairdresser	*kadeřnictví*	newspaper	*noviny*
laundry	*prádlo*	porcelain	*porcelán*
pharmacy	*lékárna*		

Sightseeing

I'd like to go to	*chtěl bych navštívit*	church	*chrám/kostel*
a (concert)	*(koncert)*	chapel	*kaple*
Two tickets for... please	*prosím, dva lístky na ...*	monastery/convent	*klášter*
Do you have a map	*máte plán města?*	castle	*hrad*
of the town?		cinema	*kino*
What building is that?	*co je to za budovu?*	theatre	*divadlo*
How old is it?	*jak je to staré?*	gallery	*galerie*
When are you open?	*jak máte otevřeno?*	museum	*muzeum*
May I take photographs?	*mohu zde fotografovat?*		

Numbers

zero	*nula*	four	*čtyři*
one	*jedna*	five	*pět*
two	*dva*	six	*šest*
three	*tři*	seven	*sedm*

eight	osm	forty	čtyřicet
nine	devět	fifty	padesát
ten	deset	sixty	šedesát
eleven	jedenáct	seventy	sedmdesát
twelve	dvanáct	eighty	osmdesát
thirteen	třináct	ninety	devadesát
fourteen	čtrnáct	one hundred	sto
fifteen	patnáct	one hundred and one	sto-jedna
sixteen	šestnáct	two hundred	dvě stě
seventeen	sedmnáct	three hundred	tři sta
eighteen	osmnáct	four hundred	čtyři sta
nineteen	devatenáct	five hundred	pět set
twenty	dvacet	six hundred	šest set
twenty-one	dvacet-jedna	seven hundred	sedm set
twenty-two	dvacet-dva	one thousand	tisíc
thirty	třicet	two thousand	dva tisíce
thirty-one	třicet-jedna	million	milión

Days

Monday	pondělí	Friday	pátek
Tuesday	úterý	Saturday	sobota
Wednesday	středa	Sunday	neděle
Thursday	čtvrtek		

Months

January	leden	July	červenec
February	únor	August	srpen
March	březen	September	září
April	duben	October	říjen
May	květen	November	listopad
June	červen	December	prosinec

Time

What time is it?	kolik je hodin?	next year	příští rok
morning	ráno, dopoledne	century	století
afternoon	odpoledne	tomorrow	zítra
evening	večer	yesterday	včera
night	noc	the day before yesterday	předevčírem
minute	minuta	the day after tomorrow	pozítří
hour	hodina	now	teď'
(to)day	dnes	later	potom
week	týden	before	před
month	měsíc	after	po
year	rok	during	během
this year	letos		

Travel

How can I get to … ?	jak se dostanu na ?	How far is it to … ?	jak je to daleko do … ?
I would like to go to …	rád bych do …	How long does the journey take?	jak dlouho trvá cesta?
Where is … ?	kde je … ?		

How much does it cost?	*kolik to stojí?*	train	*vlak*
May I have a ticket to … ?	*prosím jízdenku do …?*	taxi	*taxi*
Can I buy a ticket on the bus?	*mohu si koupit lístek v autobusu?*	car	*auto*
Do I have to change?	*musím přestupovat?*	small boat	*lodička*
When does the … leave?	*kdy odjíždí … ?*	pleasure steamer	*parník*
Do I need a reservation?	*potřebuju reservaci?*	ticket	*lístek*
May I have a couchette?	*mohu dostat lehátko/lůžko?*	seat reservation	*místenka*
What's the name of this station?	*jak se jmenuje tato stanice?*	on the left	*nalevo*
		on the right	*napravo*
Let me out	*pusťte mě ven*	straight ahead	*rovně*
airport	*letiště*	nearby	*blizko*
bus- or tram-stop	*zastávka*	far away	*daleko*
metro station	*stanice*	north	*sever*
(railway) station	*nádraží*	south	*jih*
taxi-rank	*stanoviště taxi*	east	*východ*
aeroplane	*letadlo*	west	*západ*
bus	*autobus*	crossroads	*křižovatka*
tram	*tramvaj*	street	*ulice*
		square	*náměstí*
		bridge	*most*

Eating Out

Do you have a table for one/two?	*máte volný stůl pro jednoho/dva?*	breakfast	*snídaně*
Is this seat free?	*je toto místo volné?*	lunch	*oběd*
Could I make a reservation for one/two?	*mohu reservovat jedno místo/dvě místa?*	dinner	*večeře*
		tea	*čaj*
May I see the menu?	*mohu vidět jídelní lístek?*	coffee	*káva*
		with lemon	*s citrónem*
What would you recommend?	*co doporučujete?*	with milk	*s mlékem*
		without milk	*bez mléka*
Do you have vegetarian dishes?	*máte bezmasé jídlo?*	milk	*mléko*
		lemonade	*limonáda*
Excuse me, I'm ready to order	*promiňte, mohu si objednat*	cola	*cola*
		juice	*džus*
		mineral water	*minerálka*
That was delicious/ disgusting	*bylo to výborné/hnusné*	beer	*pivo*
		soda water	*sodovka*
Bon appétit!	*Dobrou chuť'!*	wine (white, red)	*víno (bílé, červené)*

Menu Decoder

dušené	braised	*předkrm*	appetizer
na rožni	grilled	*obloha*	bits and pieces of onion
pečené	roast		and cabbage served as a
smažené	fried		side dish
vařené	boiled	*ovčí sýr*	sheep cheese
hranolky	french fries	*salát*	salad
polévka	soup	*sýr*	cheese

Meat, Fish and Poultry

bažant	pheasant	*platýz*	plaice
biftek	steak	*pstruh*	trout
candát	perch	*pštros*	ostrich
divočák	wild pig (also used to describe a sexually potent man)	*roštěná*	stewed beef
		sardelka	anchovy
		sardinka	sardine
drůbež	poultry	*sekaná*	mincemeat loaf
hovězí	beef	*špíz*	kebab
humr	lobster	*srnčí*	venison
husa	goose	*štika*	pike
játra	liver	*šunka*	ham
jelení	stag	*svíčková*	sirloin
kachna	duck	*telecí*	veal
kapr	carp	*těstoviny*	pasta
klobása ou párek	sausage	*tuňák*	tuna
krab	crab	*úhoř*	eel
králík	rabbit	*uzeniny*	smoked meat products
krocan	turkey	*velryba*	whale
kuře	chicken	*vepřové*	pork
ledvinka	kidneys	*žralok*	shark
maso	meat		

Fruit and Vegetables

ananas	pineapple	*meruňka*	apricot
banán	banana	*mrkev*	carrots
brambory	potatoes	*okurka*	cucumber
broskev	peach	*ořechy*	nuts
česnek	garlic	*pomeranč*	orange
chřest	asparagus	*rajčata*	tomato
cibule	onion	*rýže*	rice
houby	wild mushrooms	*třešně*	cherries
hruška	pear	*tuřín*	swede
jablko	apple	*žampion*	mushroom
jahoda	strawberry	*zelí*	cabbage

Dessert

koláč	cake	*šlehačka*	whipped cream
kompot	compote	*smetana*	cream
palačinka	pancake	*zmrzlina*	ice cream
pohár	ice-cream sundae		

With the Danube, Budapest forms one of the most beautiful cityscapes that exist along a river, probably the most beautiful one in Europe.

Jules Romains

Wherever you are in the city, a point comes in the late afternoon when the Danube beckons. There is a quality to the light here rarely equalled in all the world, a result of the river's wide open space and refractive nature. The whole town is transformed by this slanting luminescence, and seems to be alive with colour, even though the buildings' hues are essentially conservative. At this moment one's feet instinctively head towards the river. The other cities that straddle this most celebrated of Europe's waterways (which is never even close to blue) have resisted her charms, consigning her to a far from central location, but here she is queen, and the atmosphere she commands is one of romance. The most important things to see in Budapest are the two panoramas, so perfect on the Buda side that the whole stretch has been assigned World Heritage status by UNESCO.

Budapest is of course two cities, which grew as separate, divided entities until their union less than 130 years ago, and have maintained their own distinct characters. Buda is hilly, green and dominated by the elevated Castle Hill area, which maintains its medieval village atmosphere, with cobbled traffic-free streets and grand old buildings clustered around the vast Baroque Royal Palace, and the picturesque Matthias church. Up until the 19th century, the majority of its inhabitants still spoke German and kept themselves apart from the expanding metropolis on the other side of the water. Pest is the flat expanse on the east bank, a vibrant, thoroughly modern city in all respects but for the complete lack of skyscrapers.

Almost the entire town was built at the end of the 19th century in an unparalleled period of expansion. After centuries of having to defend itself from invaders and neighbouring empires, Hungary became part of the Austro-Hungarian Dual Monarchy, and set about transforming its

Budapest: Introduction

newly united capital into a city that would compete with and even surpass Vienna in its grandeur. By the 1920s, it was attracting the likes of the Prince of Wales and the King of Italy, making the kind of impact expressed by HL Mencken in 1930: 'This town is really astounding. It is by far the most beautiful that I have ever seen. I came expecting to see a somewhat dingy version of Vienna, but it makes Vienna look like a village.'

Another factor in Budapest's rapid development was the 1896 Hungarian Millennium, the 1,000th anniversary of the arrival in the Carpathian Basin of the city's Magyar founding fathers. In the four years leading up to this date, at least 3,700 buildings were completed. At 80 square miles Budapest had become the biggest city on the continent, with the mainland's first metro system, electric street-cars running since 1880, three bridges spanning the Danube and a fourth well under way,

181

and, also nearing completion, two of Pest's most important constructions: its cathedral, St Stephen's Basilica, and its Parliament. The latter is a vast, spectacular extravaganza, inspired by London's Houses of Parliament and for some a more magnificent achievement. No wonder Mark Twain had this reaction in 1899: 'Budapest was a surprise for me, really. Civilised, cosmopolitan, spacious. Young and ambitious. Can this Chicago-paced development go on forever, one wonders.' In some ways, it is fortunate that the progress was halted, first by two World Wars, then by 40 years of Communism.

Budapest is not what the visitor expects, and nor are its people. The predominant characteristic of Hungarian architecture is an almost obsessive love of the eclectic, a mix-and-match combination of Gothic, Baroque, Renaissance, Romanesque, Art Nouveau and more, interspersed with lawns, parks and gardens scattered around the city itself, and giant plane-trees growing along the roads. The city's inhabitants are as varied as its buildings: from its very foundation, the country has been a melting pot of Slavs, Serbs, Croats, Romanies, Germans, Austrians, Italians, Turks and of course Magyars. The visitor expecting a temperament akin to the Russians will be surprised at how Mediterranean the Hungarians seem. People here are passionate and fun-loving and need little excuse to get dressed up.

In fact, on a superficial level, it already feels as if the 40 years of enforced Communism never happened. Anyone expecting an atmosphere of bleak, apathetic fatalism and crippling inefficiency is in for a surprise. Certain signs are there. The service in shops and restaurants is not great. Hungarians can be very helpful in the street, but if it is their job they tend to be frustratingly indifferent and sluggish. City slickers have to slow down here, since they are surrounded by the pedestrian equivalent of 40 km per hour drivers. On subway escalators, the system of standing on one side so that those in a hurry can walk up or down has not caught on either.

Yet from a visitor's point of view the way Communism slowed Budapest down has been a positive too. The modern age of rapidly advancing technology, multinational corporations and information highways has led elsewhere towards homogenization, all cities resembling one another. In Budapest the effect has been dampened. That is, of course, beginning to change. The malls and the big businesses are moving in. Some believe that the city will be ruined, but much depends on the intelligence of those in charge. Do they allow more businesses to destroy the Pest panorama with their ugly neon signs, or do they have the existing ones removed? Do they allow fast-food outlets to buy up the town's most beautiful buildings and give them *carte blanche* to cover their façades in cheap red plastic signs, or do they set standards, renovate some of those crumbling old buildings, and encourage the highly artistic population to do their own thing with them? Already some positive signs are apparent. There are talks of pedestrianizing certain key areas, which will give them new leases of life. Private enterprises have undertaken renovation works that would never have happened under a state-controlled economy, Gresham Palace or Art'otel for instance, and there are plans to restore the enigmatic Gozsdu Udvar of the old Jewish Quarter. Already capitalism is leading to the normal polarisation: the middle classes are better off, but the number of poor has grown rapidly, and we can expect to see the already considerable number of homeless grow bigger.

The next 10 years will be a decisive period in Budapest's history and its appeal as a tourist destination will certainly alter. Whichever way it goes, now is the ideal time for a visit, so that, in a decade's time, whether it has become an exact replica of every other up-and-coming Western city, or the jewel in Europe's crown, you can say: 'I was there when...'

Budapest: Travel

By Air

Budapest's Ferihegy Airport is 15 miles (20km) southeast of Budapest. The two modern terminals are next to each other: **Malév** (the ex-state airline) uses Terminal 2A; all other airlines use 2B. For information in Budapest, ✆ 296 7000 or ✆ 296 8000 for Ferihegy 2A, ✆ 296 5052 or ✆ 296 5882 for Ferihegy 2B. Malév has direct flights from London, New York, Dublin and major European cities. British Midland (with good prices) and BA fly direct from London, and Delta from New York. Other airlines require changes. One option to save money is taking a cheaper flight to Prague (with Go! for instance) or Vienna, then travelling by bus, train, etc.

Offices in Budapest

Malév: V. Dorottya u. 2, ✆ 235 3535. *Open Mon–Fri 8.30–5, Sat 8–1, closed Sun.*
BA: VIII. Rákóczi u. 1–3, ✆ 318 3299. *Open Mon–Fri 8–5.*
Delta: Ferihegy 2B, ✆ 294 4400. *Open daily 7–3 .*
KLM: VII. Rákóczi u. 1–3, ✆ 373 7737. *Open Mon–Fri 8.30–4.30.*
Lufthansa: V. Váci u. 19–21, ✆ 266 4511. *Open Mon–Fri 8.30–4.30.*

To get from the airport to the centre by **taxi**, look for the board indicating fixed prices in the Arrivals area. The fare should be less than 4,000Ft. LRI, the airport administration, run a **minibus** service, bookable from the airport foyer, that will take you anywhere in Budapest (1,500Ft single, 2,500Ft return). To arrange pick-up for the return, call ✆ 296 8555. A cheaper **minibus** (750Ft single) with Centrum-Airport on the side runs from in front of the terminals and drops passengers at Erzsébet tér in central Pest. The 93 **bus** runs from just outside the terminals (buy a ticket from the machine, and validate it on the bus) to its terminus at the M3 **metro** station in Kőbanya-Kispest. The total journey time to the centre is about an hour.

By Train

Trains depart daily for Budapest from **London** Victoria station. The fare does not compare favourably to the best flight deals. The journey from **Paris** on the Orient Express takes 18½ hours. Trains arrive at Keleti (M2), the seediest (although magnificent in itself) of Budapest's stations. Be especially wary of touts and taxi drivers here. There are left-luggage facilities.

For information in Budapest: MÁV Information, V. Andrássy u. 35, ✆ 322 9035. *Open 18 April–Sept Mon–Fri 9–5.* Or call Keleti Station, VIII. Baross tér, ✆ 313 6835. *Open daily 8–6.*

By Bus

Eurolines, ✆ (01582) 404 511, run London Victoria–Budapest via Brussels, departing four days a week. It takes 29 hours and costs around £80/£120 adult single/return. Buses arrive at and depart from the Erszébet tér bus station. Left-luggage facilities are available.

To Prague

By air: Malév and Czech Airlines both have flights daily, taking 1hr 5mins.

By train: From Keleti station three times a day, taking 9hrs.

By bus: From Erzsébet tér station (information ✆ 317 2318, international information ✆ 317 2562) three times a week taking 8hrs.

in the UK

Budapest City Breaks, 10 Hatton Gardens, London EC1N 8AH, ✆ (020) 7831 7626, ✉ (020) 7404 5588.

Chalfont Line Holidays, 4 Medway Parade, Perivale, Middx UB6 8HR, ✆ (020) 8997 3799, ✉ (020) 8991 2892. Good tours for the disabled.

Danube Travel Ltd, 45 Great Cumberland Place, London W1H 7LH, ✆ (020) 7724 7577, ✉ (020) 7224 8959. City breaks, Grand Prix, spas, Budapest-Prague combinations.

Eurocity Breaks, 243 Euston Rd, London NW1 2BU, ✆ (020) 7388 0888, ✉ (020) 7383 3848. Budapest breaks.

Flexibreaks Travel Service, 7 Seymour Place, London W1H 5AG, ✆ (020) 7723 6999, ✉ (020) 7723 6946. Budapest Spring Festival.

Inscape Fine Arts Tours, Austins Farm, High St, Stonesfield, Witney, Oxon OX8 8PU, ✆ (01993) 891 726. Art and architecture in Budapest.

Martin Randall Travel, 10 Barley Mow Passage, Chiswick, London W4 4PH, ✆ (020) 8742 3355, ✉ (020) 8742 1066. Music and art tours.

Peltours, Sovereign House, 11–19 Ballards Lane, Finchley, London N3 1UX, ✆ (020) 8346 9144, ✉ (020) 8343 0579. Jewish heritage tours.

Prospect Music and Art Tours, 36 Manchester St, London W1M 5PE, ✆ (020) 7486 5704, ✉ (020) 7486 5868. Spring Festival, opera weekends.

Regent Holidays, 15 John St, Bristol BS1 2HR, ✆ (0117) 921 1711, ✉ (0117) 925 4860. Architectural and history tours to Budapest, Bratislava and Prague.

in the USA

Abercrombie & Kent, 1520 Kensington Rd, Suite 212, Oakbrook, IL 60521, ✆ 800 323 7308, ✉ (630) 954 2944, *www.abercrombiekent.com*. Cruises on the River Cloud, city breaks, wine and cooking.

All Europe Tours, 411 West Putman Av, Greenwich, CT 06831, ✆ 800 338 7820, ✉ (203) 869 5986, *www.alleuropetours.com*. Hungarian heritage tours, ecclesiastical art, wine and gastronomy.

Arts & Leisure Tours, 6 Direct Court, Suite 103, Woodbridge, ON L4L 325, ✆ 800 387 4116, ✉ (905) 850 8984, *www.artsandleisuretours.com*. Wine, gastronomy, art and architecture tours in Budapest and elsewhere.

General Tours, 43 Summer St, Keene, NH 03441, ✆ 800 221 2216, ✉ (603) 357 5033, *www.generaltours.com*. City breaks, cruises, etc.

IST Cultural Tours, 225 West 34th St, Suite 1020, New York, NY 10122, ✆ 800 833 2111, ✉ (212) 563 1202, *www.istculturaltours.com*. Fortnight-long musical tours led by experts, visiting Prague, Budapest and Vienna.

Maupintours, 1421 Research Park Drive, Suite 300, Lawrence, KS 66049, ✆ 800 255 4266, ✉ (785) 843 1211, *www.maupintour.com*. Fully escorted city tours.

N&S Connections, 11803 Washington Bd, Los Angeles, CA 90066, ✆ 800 999 0226, ✉ (310) 397 3899. Jewish Heritage tours, Danube cruises, tailor-made itineraries.

Getting Around

Orientation

Finding your way around Budapest is easy. Buda is the hilly part to the west of the Danube, Pest the flat busy area to its east. The river runs near enough north–south, so that when you are in Pest west means towards the Danube, east away from it; vice versa for Buda.

Two circular roads service Pest. The inner semi-circle or **Kiskörút** (Little Boulevard) runs from Szabadság (Liberty) Bridge in the south to Széchenyi Lánchíd Bridge at Roosevelt tér, and consists of Vámház krt., Múzeum krt., Károly krt. and József Attila u. It contains the inner city area of **Belváros**. Where the latter two sections meet, Bajcsy-Zsilinszky út continues north, meeting the outer circular road at Nyugati station. The rectangular section thus formed marks the boundaries of **Lipótváros** (Leopold Town, the City). This inner section from Liberty Bridge to Margaret Bridge hemmed in by these major roads is district V, containing most of what you will want to see in Pest. The outer ring-road, known as the **Nagykörút** (Great Boulevard), runs from Petőfi Bridge to Margaret Bridge, consisting of Ferenc krt., József krt., Erzsébet krt., Teréz krt. and Szent István krt., holding most of the cinemas and many of the decent cheap shops. The districts fan out from the inner ring, divided by the major roads like spokes. Of these, the most important is **Andrássy út**, running northeast to Heroes' Square and City Park.

On the Buda side, the Nagykörút continues, almost making a perfect ring. It runs through Moszkvar tér, Buda's main transport hub, although Móricz Zsigmond körtér southwest of Szabadság Bridge, reached from Pest by trams 47 or 49, can also be useful.

Transport

Budapest is a compact city and the transport service is fast, efficient and cheap. The network consists of three metro lines, buses, trams, trolley-buses and local trains (HÉV). All run about 4.30am–11.30pm. A few night buses ply the busier routes. The same **tickets** are used for all modes of transport, one ticket good for one ride on one vehicle: if you change metro lines, you need to have another validated ticket. Tickets can be bought at counters, from vending machines that may eat your money, at any metro station, but not at all tram or bus stops. After searching hopelessly for a change-eating machine, you may be tempted to ride for free; but beware: plain-clothes inspectors sometimes appear, identified by their red armbands, and pleading ignorance will not spare you a 1,300Ft fine. Get a pass (1 or 3 days or longer), or buy a book of 10 or 20 tickets. Tickets must be validated for each journey. In the metro, this is fairly obvious, but on the buses and trams you might have to watch someone else first. Locate the ticket-puncher, put the numbered end of your ticket in, and pull the black handle down and towards you until it clicks. Tickets cost 95Ft, 10 tickets 900Ft, 20 tickets 1,750Ft, day pass 740Ft, 3-day pass 1,500Ft, weekly pass 1,850Ft, 2-week pass 2,400Ft, monthly pass 3,600Ft (these last two require an ID card: bring a photo). Children up to 6 travel free.

by metro

The metro is fast, regular and easy to use. Trains are identified by destination rather than direction or name. There are three lines: yellow (M1), red (M2) and blue (M3), connecting at Deák tér. They run every 2–3mins; clocks on the platform display the time since the last one. The last metro leaves around 11.10pm. Metro transfer tickets, allowing you to travel on two lines consecutively, cost 150Ft. *See* p.232 for metro map.

by tram

At rush hour, though packed, these are a godsend. The most useful routes are 4 and 6, which follow the Nagykörút all round Pest, terminating at Moszkva tér (at the Buda end of Margaret Bridge the line is disrupted, so you have to get off one 4/6 and on another, using the same ticket). Line 2 hugs the Danube on the Pest side affording great views, and line 19 follows the Buda embankment from Batthyány tér to beyond the Gellért hotel.

by bus

Most buses are very modern, with displays showing the next stop. When you want to get off press the button on the rail next to the doors, otherwise the door may not open. Especially out of the centre, the distance between stops can be very large. Buses with a red square around their number are express and make fewer stops. Those with red numbers follow different routes. A useful route is the 86, following the Buda embankment from Óbuda past the Gellért hotel.

The 6É **night bus** follows the 4/6 tram route round the Nagykörút. 14É and 50É follow the M3 line, 78É follows the M2 line. They run regularly and begin as normal transport ends.

by local train

There are four suburban train (HÉV) lines; you are most likely to use the one from Batthyány tér (M2) to Óbuda. A normal ticket is valid as far as here since it is within city limits.

by boat

Ferries run *May–Sept Thurs–Sun* between Boráros tér, at the Pest end of Petőfi Bridge, and Római part, just north of Aquincum and Óbuda Island. The last ferry stops at the Pest end of Margaret Bridge.

by taxi

This is one area where dishonesty is rife. Taxis that hang around outside major hotels, tourist spots, stations and the airport will often rip you off. Always ask how much the journey will cost before getting in, and check the meter is working. They are prohibited from charging more than the following rates anywhere in Budapest, and should issue a receipt on request: 6am–10pm, 200Ft basic fee, 200Ft/km and 50Ft per minute waiting fee; 10pm–6am, 280Ft basic, 280Ft/km and 70Ft/min for waiting. The following have good reputations for honesty, and dispatchers at the first speak English: **City Taxi**, ✆ 211 1111; **Fő Taxi**, ✆ 222 2222.

by car

Driving in Budapest is a bad idea. The roads are crowded and often under repair, one-way streets are common and badly signposted, and Hungarian drivers are lunatics, obsessed with speed and heedless of any rules. Parking is also difficult. The transport system is excellent: use it. If you do drive, be aware that the use of dimmed headlights is obligatory even during daylight out of city limits; the speed limit is 80km/h unless stated. In city limits it is 50km/h.

Car hire: All the major companies have offices at the airport. Plus: **Americana**, XIII. Dózsa György u. 65 (Hotel Ibis Volga), ✆ 350 2542; **Avis**, V. Szervita tér 8, ✆ 318 4240; **Budget**, I. Krisztina tér 41–3, ✆ 214 0420; **Hertz**, ✆ 296 0999 or V. Apáczai Csere János u. 4 (Hotel Marriott), ✆ 266 4361, ✆ 266 4344.

by bicycle

Riding a bike around town is no more recommended than driving. However, it can be a very good idea in the Buda Hills, or on Margaret Island. Try **Nella Bikes** at V. Kálmán Imre u. 23, or **Tura Mobil** at VI. Nagymező u. 43.

The **Cogwheel Railway** runs from Városmajor Park to Széchenyi Hill (bus 5, 22, 56,156 from Moszkva tér, or a short walk). *Daily 5am–11.30pm every 15mins; 95Ft. See* p.290.

The **Children's Railway** runs from Széchenyi Hill to Hűvösvölgy (bus or tram 56). *Daily 8–5, Sat, Sun and hols every 30–45mins, otherwise mostly hourly; Sept–May closed Mon; adult 130Ft/230Ft, child 50Ft/90Ft.* An old-fashioned '**nostalgia**' **train** runs on weekends and holidays at 9.45, 12 and 2.30, costing 100Ft extra each way (50Ft for kids). *See* also p.290.

The **Chairlift** runs from Zugliget to János Hill (bus 158 from Moszkva tér). *Daily April–Sept 9–6, Oct–Mar 9.30–5; closed alternate Mon; adult 250Ft/450Ft, child 150Ft/300Ft.*

The **Sikló** is a100m funicular from Clark Ádám tér to Castle Hill. The journey takes about 1min. *Daily 7.30am–10pm, closed alternate Mon; adult 300Ft, child 150Ft.*

Tours

by boat

Mahart, ✆ 342 2335, run sightseeing tours from the dock at Vigadó tér. Adult 250Ft/450Ft, child 150Ft/300Ft. The *Duna Bella* combines a 1hr tour with an hour on Margaret Island. The *Danube Legend* does 1hr night cruises with sound and vision shows. They also run a 2hr folklore tour with a three-course dinner and gypsy music and dancing, and a similar trip with operetta. Tickets and information from the dock.

by bus

Budatours, ✆ 374 7070, reservations ✆ 353 0558, run a recommended 2hr tour with tape-recorded guiding, departing from the corner of Andrássy út and Bajcsy-Zsilinszky.

Cityrama offer a whole host of different tours. Pick up their booklet from Vista, ticket offices or V. Báthory utca 22 for details, or call ✆ 302 4382.

IBUSZ, ✆ 485 2700, organize 'live' English tours from Erzsébet tér at 10.30 year-round and 3pm May–Sept, as well as lots of other tours.

Queenybus, ✆ 247 7159, run 3hr tours from the Basilica, some in an open-top bus.

on foot

Budapest Walk run tours from Hősök tere (M1) stop. Informative commentaries.

Budapest Walks, ✆ 340 4232, the original walks company, host tours in English daily 15 April–30 Sept. The Pest tour leaves from Gerbeaud in Vörösmarty tér and lasts 2¼hrs. The Buda Castle tours leave from the Matthias Church.

I.A. Tours offer 3½hr tours including all the major sights, leaving from the steps of the Palace of Arts in Heroes' Square daily.

Jewish Heritage walking tours start at the Great Synagogue every day but Sat. At the end of the tour there is a chance to taste traditional non-kosher Central European Jewish food (except on Sundays).

by air

Indicator, ✆ 249 9824, organize 20min pleasure flights on request: Mar–Nov only.

Sup-Air Balloon Club, ✆ 322 0015, can arrange balloon flights for at least two people (depending on the weather).

Budapest: Practical A–Z

Baths

Budapest is Europe's largest spa town and going to the baths is an integral part of any visit. The waters contain minerals known for millennia to possess curative properties. The Romans built bath-houses at the settlement of Aquincum, which means 'abundant water'. Religious orders promoted the waters for healing in the Middle Ages; by the mid-12th century the custom was widely spread among the Magyars. When the Turks came, bathing became a part of everyday life: Pasha Sokoli Mustapha had the Király baths built within the walls of Víziváros so that even under siege his people could still enjoy a good soak. Along with the Rudas and Rác baths, these are the only significant remains left from the Ottoman period, and all are still functioning today. In the 1920s and 30s, the town's spas helped attract Europe's wealthy and powerful. Today it is a way of life: everyone goes to the baths. The town's gangsters and bouncers are great regulars, but in the baths they rub shoulders with kids, housewives, tourists and the old, who flock here for the relief it offers from aches and pains, arthritis and respiratory complaints.

For first-timers it can seem complicated. Ignore the long menus offering countless types of tub and massage, ultrasound, mud treatment, traction, etc (these are centres of healing as much as recreation). Ask for a ticket for the pool (or baths), give it to the white-clad attendant, and allow yourself to be shepherded through the procedure. You will normally be shown a cubicle, where you change and leave your stuff. In single-sex baths you will be given a minimal cotton garment to cover yourself. You may or may not get a key; usually all you have to remember is the number. The baths generally have a couple of main pools, smaller ones ranging from freezing to very hot, a steam-room and a sauna. Start with the lesser heat, build it up in stages, then go for one of the hot rooms, followed by the freezing cold, then back to moderately hot and so on. Beware of staying too long and standing up too quickly, and watch out for the walls: they get scalding hot. Sweating helps to release toxins, and cleans the skin in a way soap and water never can. Many people in the sauna use loofahs to rub away the top layers of dead skin, encouraging circulation and helping the body to sweat more efficiently. The whole experience is extremely therapeutic, especially for those with joint-related complaints. Massage afterwards is highly recommended. Drink lots of water before, during and after.

Men-only baths are often gay cruising spots. If you aren't interested, just move away politely. You are less likely to be approached in the more touristy baths such as Gellért or Széchenyi. People with **heart complaints** should consult a doctor before going to the baths.

Budapest Card

The tourist card costs 2,800Ft (2 days) or 3,400Ft (3 days). It covers public transport and entry to most sights, and discounts in shops, baths, etc. If you want to see everything quickly it might save money. It's available at main metro stations, tourist offices, travel agencies and hotels.

Calendar of Events and Festivals

Hungarians are a gregarious bunch and need no excuse for a party, yet the normal big events such as Christmas and Easter pass by here fairly quietly. The biggest events centre on the arts: the most important are the Budapest Spring and Autumn Festivals. Of greatest national significance are St Stephen's Day on 20 August and Remembrance Day on 23 October. But there's always something going on, even in July and August when many venues close down.

6 Jan–Ash Wednesday	**Farsang.** Celebrates the end of winter and fattening up before the fasting of Lent. Open-air music, carnivals and balls, culminating in a fancy-dress parade.
Early Feb	**Hungarian Film Festival.** Weekend event highlighting the best Hungarian films. Main venue is the Corvin cinema. Some films are subtitled in English.
15 Mar	**Revolution Day.** Commemorates Petőfi's recital of his *National Song* outside the National Museum. Events there and around his statue in Március 15 tér.
Late Mar/ early April	**Budapest Spring Festival.** The major annual arts event. Classical music, opera, jazz and folk; dance, including folk dance; painting and sculpture; theatre and cinema, often subtitled in English.
	Easter. Mainly passes off quietly with church processions and egg painting. Arts and crafts fairs, e.g. in the Ethnography Museum; free performances of Bach's *St John Passion* in the Lutheran Church. Easter Monday is a rowdy drunken occasion, when men douse women in cheap perfume in exchange for shots of pálinka. It can start as early as 6am, gets ugly by about 10am, and by the afternoon it is better to be off the streets.
1 May	**Labour Day.** No longer involving compulsory homage to Communist bigwigs, this is still a big event organized by trade unions in the parks, especially City Park. Entertainments, contests, talks, games, rides, and lots of food and drink.
End May/ early June	**Book Fair.** Vörösmarty tér's sedate expanse is uglified by a host of stalls, with book-signings, promotions and fringe activities like singing and dancing.
Nearest w/e to 21 June	**World Music Day.** Most venues participate in this French innovation, and stages are set up in open places. All kinds of music are represented.
30 June	**Budapesti Bucsú.** A celebration of the withdrawal of Soviet troops in 1991. *Bucsú* means farewell (and not *au revoir*). Music, theatre and dance events in the city's squares and parks.
Early– mid-July	**World Music Festival** (WOMUFE). A 2–3-day event as good as the performers in Central Europe at the time, becoming more established every year. In the Budai Parkszínpad by XI. Kosztolányi Dezső tér.
14 July	**Bastille Day.** Free food and drink, open-air ball and fireworks. Outside the French Institute at 17 Fő tér, or Felvonulási tér south of Heroes' Square.
Second w/e in Aug	**Hungarian Grand Prix** (at Hungaroring). A major event; all the hotels are full and jack up their prices, restaurants are often fully booked and every bar and café sets up its TV or screen to broadcast the action.
Mid-Aug	**Sziget Festival.** Possibly Europe's biggest rock and pop festival, transforming Óbuda Island into a giant open-air party with big name international acts, beer tents, rave-marquees and every type of music, plus dance, theatre, films etc.
	Budafest. Opera and ballet festival in the State Opera House.
20 Aug	**St Stephen's Day.** Rites at the Basilica, craft fair and folk dancing in Castle Hill, and the procession through the streets with the Holy Right Hand leads up to a climactic firework display from the Citadella, with the Danube lined with over a million people and every cruise ship and river-view restaurant booked weeks ahead. The firework display may move in front of Parliament.

Early Sept	**Budapest Wine Festival**. Chamber concerts in Castle Hill to impress international buyers, but most of the action takes place in Vörösmarty tér, where the stalls let you taste before you buy. There's usually folk dancing.
Mid–late Sept	**Budapest International Music Competition**. Since 1993, this has provided yet another excuse for a lot of first-class classical music.
Late Sept	**European Heritage Days**. Public buildings open up for a weekend, offering the rare chance to see inside some of the city's finest buildings.
Late Sept– mid-Oct	**Budapest Autumn Festival**. Like the Spring Festival but more geared towards contemporary arts. Exhibitions, music, opera, theatre, dance, film.
Late Sept–Oct	**Budapest Music Weeks**.The classical music season kicks off as close to the anniversary of Bartók's death as possible (25 Sept). City-wide events follow, focusing on the Vigadó and the Academy of Music on Liszt Ferenc tér.
Around 1 Oct	**Budapest Marathon and Running Festival**. Along both banks of the Danube. Shorter distances are also raced. Concerts add to the festival spirit.
Early Oct	**Music of our Time**. Two weeks of contemporary classical music.
23 Oct	**Remembrance Day**. Commemorates the 1956 Uprising. Wreath-laying at Imre Nagy's statue, at his grave in the New Cemetery, and in Kossuth tér.
1 Nov	**All Souls' Day**. Make an evening trip to the cemeteries, which stay open late for people to light candles to the memory of their dearly departed.
6 Dec	**Mikulás**. The night before, children put cleaned shoes out on the windowsill, expecting the national Santa Claus to fill them with sweets, fruit and small gifts. If they've been bad, Krampusz the bogeyman might turn up instead.
24–5 Dec	**Christmas** (Karácsony). This is a family affair: almost everything in the city shuts from lunchtime on the 24th until after the New Year.
31 Dec	**New Year's Eve** (Szilveszter). The grandest event is the Opera House ball. The streets are one big carnival, especially the Nagykörút and Blaha Lujza tér.

Children

Budapest is fairly child-friendly. **City Park** has a whole bunch of attractions (*see* p.281). Its Petőfi Csarnok hall often organizes children's activities. Round the back are football fields, basketball and tennis courts, and plenty of room for ball games. The Széchenyi baths have a heated outdoor children's pool, while the lake is great for ice-skating in winter and rowing in summer. There's a good playground between the zoo and the lake, with trampolines and ping-pong tables. The zoo has a good adventure playground and a petting corner. Next door is the circus, and beyond that the Amusement Park, with a smaller version for toddlers next door.

Margaret Island (*see* p.290) is farther away from the traffic. At both ends of the park you can rent bicycles, pedalos, etc. An open train on wheels makes round trips every half-hour. There are wide open spaces and lots of playgrounds. The Palatinus Strand pool is family-friendly with a wave machine and small kids' pools. The farmyard zoo on the east side is a bit sad.

In the **Buda Hills** (*see* p.290) the big attraction is the Children's Railway, a narrow-gauge affair staffed by children in uniforms. The Cogwheel Railway is a fun way to get to its starting point, and at the other end is a giant meadow, Hűvösvölgy.

The **caves** at Pálvölgyi and particularly Szemlő-hegy would appeal to children (*see* p.293), as would the **labyrinth** beneath Castle Hill (*see* p.244).

The **Palace of Wonders Interactive Scientific Playhouse** has weird and wonderful exhibits, with lots of hands-on stuff. The **Transport Museum** and **Telephone Museum** have a fair amount for kids to do, as does the **Natural History Museum**, with a 'discovery room' encouraging experimentation. For older kids, there's the **Planetarium**, at the southwest corner of the Népliget, beyond the edge of District VIII. (*See* pp.296–8 for details of all.)

Cultural activities aimed at kids offer the country's flavour at a level children can appreciate. The **Budapest Puppet Theatre** has anything from Hungarian folk stories to *Grease*: it's the sort of thing you can follow without understanding the dialogue (*see* p.277). The same applies to the fairy tales presented by the **Kolibri Theatre** (VI. Jókai tér 10, ✆ 353 4633, Oktogon, M1. *Shows daily 10am, also Fri–Sun 3pm; box office open daily 2–6; closed summer; adm*). If your kids are brave enough or natural born dancers, take them to a folk-music dance-house (*see* p.324), where they will be taught the steps before the dance begins. The **Budapest Festival Orchestra** give special performances for kids (*Sept–April*), known as Kakaó Koncert because children get hot chocolate at the end (V. Vörösmarty tér 1, or ✆ 266 2312). For **children's activity centres** try: **Almássy tér Recreation Centre** (Szabadidő Központ), VII. Almássy tér 6, ✆ 352 1572, Blaha Lujza (M2). *Open Sept–June Sun mornings*, has special events on other days. **Marczibányi tér Culture House** (Művelődési Ház), II. Marczibányi tér 5a, ✆ 212 4885, Moszkva tér (M2), has classes, clubs and events.

Playgrounds are scattered all over the city centre. The best are in the Károlyi Gardens near Astoria, Erzsébet tér, and Klauzál tér in the heart of District VII. All are new, safe, dog-free, and offer sand-pits and rides. Other handy ones are in Szabadság tér and just north of Kossuth Lájos tér. Look out for the **trampolines** at the Buda end of Margaret Bridge.

Climate and When to Go

In summer Budapest can be uncomfortably hot. Many establishments close in July and August. Winter can be bitterly cold, the average temperature around the freezing mark, troughing in January. So the best time to visit is late March–May or September and October.

average temperatures °C

Jan	Feb	Mar	April	May	June
−1.2	0.8	5.6	11.4	16.3	19.8
July	Aug	Sept	Oct	Nov	Dec
21.7	20.9	16.8	11.1	5.2	0.8

Crime and Police

Most of the crime in Budapest is organized crime. It is generally safe to walk at night, although use common sense in outlying districts, especially District VIII. Beware pickpockets in the tourist areas, especially around crowds and on public transport. There are racist elements around, some within the police force. It is technically compulsory to carry some form of ID at all times, so spot checks can be a convenient excuse for harassment.

Beware tricksters. Never change money on the streets. A common ploy is for a girl to pick up a foreign male and take him to buy her drinks. The bill is extortionate, and the man pressurized to pay. The same tactic is used in red-light venues. (Over-keen females, especially at night and around Districts VII and VIII, might well be prostitutes.) If anyone claiming to be the police asks to see money or a credit card, it is a scam. Demand to be taken to a police station and see how they react. A Tourist Hotline has been set up to deal with complaints or problems: ☎ 438 8080. Or call the police on ☎ 107 or ☎ 112, or contact the Complaints Office, Budapest Municipal Police HQ BRFK: XIII, Teve u. 6. From 1 July to 1 Sept, Tourist Police supposedly patrol the streets accompanied by translators, though none were around at the time of writing.

Customs, Etiquette and Traditions

Hungarians tend to be very polite. Expect to have a lot of doors opened for you. Hand-shaking is very common, and the informal mode of greeting friends is with two kisses on each cheek, but little hugging. Birthdays tend to be quiet affairs here; the big celebrations are name days.

Note that Hungarians do not clink their beer glasses. This is because, after their victory of 1849, during the show-trials, executions and meting out of punishment that ensued, the gloating Austrians continuously clinked their beer glasses in delight. A national vow was taken not to engage in this practice for 150 years. Though this time has actually elapsed, the taboo remains.

Disabled Travellers

Budapest is not really geared up for disabled travellers. Wheelchair access is limited. Most sights and museums are housed in 19th-century buildings with wide steps, although modern renovations are improving wheelchair access. Apart from the M1 metro line and the Airport Minibus, transport is also not adapted for wheelchairs. For more information contact the **Hungarian Disabled Association**, San Marco utca 76, ☎/◉ 388 2388.

Electricity

The Hungarian electricity supply is 220 volts and the plugs are of the standard Continental type with two round pins. Bring the necessary adaptor.

Embassies and Consulates

Australia	XII. Királyhágó tér 8–9, ☎ 201 8899
Canada	XII. Budakeszi út 32, ☎ 275 1200
Ireland	V. Szabadság tér 7/9, ☎ 302 9600
New Zealand	I. Attila út 125, ☎ 331 4908
UK	V. Harmincad utca 6, ☎ 266 2888
USA	V. Szabadság tér 12, ☎ 267 4400

Emergencies

In an emergency, contact one of the following: Ambulance, ☎ 104; Police, ☎ 107; Fire Brigade, ☎ 105. (*See* also 'Health and Insurance', opposite.)

Gay Budapest

Melegek, literally meaning 'the warm ones', is the popular Hungarian expression for gay. Attitudes are traditionally not as tolerant as in many cities, but the situation is improving. *See* p.322 for a list of gay bars, clubs and restaurants.

Gay Switchboard Budapest, ✆ 932 3334, *budapest@gayguide.net, gayguide.net/europe/hungary/budapest*. **Labrisz** (lesbian magazine), ✆ 350 9650, *www.c3hu/~hatter/labrisz*. **Mások** (the only gay magazine), ✆ 266 9959, *www.masok.hu*. **Para Radio**, *para@c3.hu, www.c3.hu.para*. **#Gay.hu** (online magazine), *webmaster@fules.c3.hu, fules.c3.hu/gay.hu*. **Háttér** (support society), ✆ 350 9650, *hatter@c3.hu, www.c3.hu/~hatter*.

Baths known as cruising spots are: Gellért from 4pm, Király in late afternoon on men-only days, Rác on Saturday from 3pm, the sun terrace of Palatinus pool, the mud bath at Lukács baths.

Health and Insurance

No vaccinations are required to enter Hungary. Medicines can be obtained with prescriptions written abroad, and most common over-the-counter drugs are available. Foreign citizens are entitled to first-aid and emergency ambulance treatment free of charge if injured. European nationals will not be entitled to free treatment until Hungary is accepted into the EU.

24-hour emergency departments at V. Hold u. 19, ✆ 311 6816, and II. Ganz u. 13–15, ✆ 202 1370. Országos Baleseti Intézet at VIII. Fiumei u. 17, ✆ 333 7599, specialize in broken limbs and accidents.

24-hour medical care is offered by Falck SOS Hungary, II. Kapy u. 49b, ✆ 200 0100, which has an ambulance service. IMS at XIII. Váci u. 202, ✆ 329 8423, has English-speaking staff.

24-hour dental services: Profident, VII. Károly krt. 1, ✆ 267 9602; SOS Dental Service, VI. Király u. 14, ✆ 267 9602.

Pharmacies with a night service: II. Frankel Leó u. 22; IV. Pozsonyi u. 19; VIII. Rákóczi u. 39; IX. Boráros tér; XII. Alkotás u. 1b; XIV. Bosnyák u. 1a.

Internet

Cybercafés: Vista, VI. Paulay Ede u. 7, ✆ 267 8603, ✉ 268 1059, *www.vista.hu, open Mon–Fri 8–8, weekends 10–6*. **Matávnet**, V. Petőfi S. u. 17–19, *open Mon–Fri 8–8, Sat 9–3*. **BudapestNET**, V. Kecskeméti u. 5, *open 10–10*. **Mathias Rex**, V. Baross u. 4, *open 10–10*. **EasyNet**, V. Váci u. 19–21, *open 9–10*. **AMI**, V. Váci u. 40, *open 10–10*.

Www.budapest.com, Budapest's official homepage; *www.live budapest.com*, articles and listings; *www.timeout.com/budapest*, background and listings; *www.budapestweek.hu*, listings.

Media

Budapest Sun is an English-language weekly, with limited listings. The local listings bible is the weekly *Pesti Est* (in Hungarian but sometimes lists English-language films in English). It is often possible to understand what's happening where and when if you know these few key words: *Bontás* (currently showing), *Színház* (theatre), *Komoly* (serious stuff), *Minden Más* (miscellaneous), *Kiállítás* (exhibitions), *Étal-Ital* (food and drink), *Éttermek* (restaurants).

Scene is a weekly entertainment guide in English. *Budapest in Your Pocket* is quarterly. *Where Budapest*, free in the big hotels, has articles and listings. The *Hungarian Quarterly* is an academic journal in English with reviews, current affairs, and essays on Hungarian literature, politics, etc. News vendors with a good range of foreign press are: House of the World Press, V. Városház u. 3–5; Sajtó és Térképbolt, V. Kálvin tér 3; Hirlapüzlet, V. Váci u. 10.

Hungarian Radio broadcasts news in English at 9pm and 11pm (SW 39.75 KHz and 60.25 KHz).

Money

Hungarian currency is the forint (Ft in this book, sometimes HUF elsewhere). Coins come in 1, 2, 5, 10, 20, 50 and 100Ft; notes in 200, 500, 1,000, 2,000, 5,000 and 10,000Ft. The rate of exchange at the time of writing was £1 = 425Ft, $1 = 295Ft.

Exchange rates vary wildly. The worst rates are in hotels and tourist spots. A common ploy is to advertise a rate that only applies to large sums: always check. The Magyar Külkereskedelmi Bank at V. Szent István tér 11 transfers money from abroad. V. Apáczai Csere János u. 1 has a 24-hour exchange service. ATMs everywhere accept major cards. Credit cards are widely accepted. Leftover forints can be exchanged up to 20,000Ft, more with an exchange receipt.

Opening Hours

Banks: usually *Mon–Thurs 10–4 or 10–6, Fri 10–3*. **Office hours**: *Mon–Fri 8–5*. Most **food stores** are open *Mon–Fri 7–7, Sat 7–2*. Mall shops usually don't open until 10. Other stores open *Mon–Fri 10–6, Sat 9–1*. Almost everything is *shut on Sunday*.

Packing

Budapesters love to dress up, so if you're planning on going out pack your **smart clothes**. A pair of **binoculars** is an excellent idea, so you can see some of the details on the roof of the Post Office Savings Bank from the top of the Basilica. Don't forget **swimming gear** for the baths.

Post

The main post office is at Petőfi Sándor u. 13, *open Mon–Fri 8–8*. The Poste Restante address is Magyar Posta, 1364, Budapest; the office is at the back of the building on Városház u., *open Mon–Fri 8–8, Sat 8–2*. Post offices at Keleti and Nyugati stations *open Mon–Sat 7–7*.

Public Holidays

1 Jan	New Year	**1 May**	Labour Day
15 March	National Day	**20 August**	St Stephen's Day
Easter Monday		**23 October**	Republic Day
Whitsun Monday		**25–6 December**	Christmas

Smoking

It is illegal to smoke in public places (public transport, cinemas and theatres). Many restaurants have a no-smoking policy, and many hotels reserve whole floors as no-smoking zones.

Sport

Big screens go up in bars all over town for sporting events of interest, meaning major soccer tournaments and anything with a Hungarian participating.

Sporting Activities

Swimming is the easiest sport to organize, the best places being the Gellért, Széchenyi or Lukács baths, or the Palatinus Strand on Margaret Island with its 100m-long pool. There are plenty of **tennis clubs**, charging around 1,000Ft per hour. Try Vasas SC, Pasaréti u. 11–13, ✆ 320 9457 (bus 5 from Moszkva tér, M2), *open daily 7am–10pm*; Római Teniszakadémia, III. Királyok u. 105, ✆ 240 9123 (bus 34 from Óbuda), *open daily 6am–11pm*. The SAS Club or the Normafa hotels in the Buda Hills have their own courts. **Bicycles** can be hired at Charles Rent-a-Bike, I. Hegyalja u. 23, ✆ 202 3414.

Spectator Sports

The **Grand Prix** is usually in early August, at the Hungaroring track at Mogyoród, 20km northeast of Budapest. Special buses run from Árpád híd bus station. Tickets from the Ostermann Formula 1 Office at V. Apáczai Csere János u. 11, ✆ 266 2040, or agencies.

Hungarians love **soccer**, but have little to show for it. Going to see a game is likely to be a let-down, as attendance is as low as the quality of play. The top **local clubs** are Ferencvárosi (FTC or Fradi), IX. Üllői u. 129 (Népliget, M3); MTK, VIII. Salgótarjáni u. 12–14 (tram 37 from Blaha Lujza tér, M2); Újpest, I. Megyeri u. 13 (Újpest központ, M3, then three stops on bus 30); Honvéd-Kispest, XIX. Új temető u. 1–3 (tram 42 from Határ u., M3, to the end). For details see *Programme* magazine or the *Nemzeti Sport*. **National games** are better, in the newly built **Népstadion** at XIV. Istvánmezei u. 1–3, ✆ 251 1222 (Népstadion, M2).

The **Budapest Sportcsarnok**, XIV. Stéfania u. 2, ✆ 251 9759 (Népstadion, M2), is where most major indoor events take place, such as **boxing**: capacity crowds of 10,000 watch national hero István 'Koko' Kovács, who became world featherweight champion in 1997.

Tax

VAT (known here as ÁFA) is set at 20% for most classes of purchase, and is reclaimable for those of more than 50,000Ft (not including art and antiques). The cash will be returned to you in forints as you leave the country. The following companies will process the papers for you: Global Refund, II. Bég u. 3–5, ✆ 212 4906; Intel Trade Rt., I. Csalogány u. 6–10, ✆ 356 9800. Food tax is 25%. Drink tax is 12%. A tourist tax of 3% is usually included in hotel bills.

Telephones

The international **code** for Hungary is ✆ 0036; the code for Budapest is ✆ 01. Long-distance calls within Hungary, ✆ 06. International calls from Hungary: dial ✆ 00, wait for the dialling tone, then dial the country code, area code and number (for international codes, *see* p.20). Operator, ✆ 191; domestic directory enquiries, ✆ 198; international enquiries, ✆ 199; sending a telegram in Hungary, ✆ 192.

There are **public telephones** everywhere. Some take coins: 20, 50 or 100Ft. Others take cards, available from post offices, hotels, supermarkets and newsagents, costing 800Ft or 1,800Ft. International calls are very expensive, but you can save up to 40% with an Amtel calling card (available from tourist offices, Vista Internet Café or Keleti station). Send faxes from the Belvárosi Telephone Centre, V. Petőfi Sándor u. 17.

Time

Summer time, from early March to late October, is GMT +2hrs, Eastern Standard Time +7hrs, Pacific Standard Time +10hrs. The clocks go back an hour in winter. Note that Hungarians represent times in a way which can be confusing to Westerners: ½8 means 7.30.

Tipping

Service in restaurants is usually 10%. Tell the waiter how much change you expect. If you say 'thank you' (*köszönöm*) when handing over the bill, it means you expect them to keep all the change. Give a small tip to cloak-room attendants, taxi drivers or changing-room attendants at the baths. Most people leave 10% where appropriate or 50Ft.

Toilets

Like most cities, Budapest doesn't have enough public toilets, though you can usually find one in stations. They always charge (usually 40Ft), even in museums and other public buildings.

Tourist Information

TOURINFORM is the main state-run tourist office. They speak a range of languages and are incredibly helpful, whatever your enquiry. They will help with bookings and are *open Mon–Fri 9–7, Sat, Sun and hols 9–4 unless otherwise stated.*

V. Sütő u. 2 (Deák tér), ☎ 317 9800, ✉ 317 9656, *hungary@tourinform.hu. Open 8–8.*
I. Tárnok u. 9–11 (Castle Hill), ☎ 488 0454, ✉ 488 0474. *Open 8–8.*
V. Steindl I. u. 12, ☎ 253 2956, ✉ 428 0375, *pest-m@tourinform.hu.*
VI. Nyugati Station, ☎/✉ 302 8580, *budapest2@tourinform.hu.*
VII. Király u. 93, ☎ 352 1433, ✉ 352 9804, *budapest3@tourinform.hu, www.tourinform.hu.*
Tourism Office of Budapest: 1364 Budapest POB. 215, ☎ 266 0479, ✉ 266 1482, *info@budapestinfo.hu.* **Hungarian National Tourist Office**: II. Margit körút 85, ☎ 355 1133, ✉ 375 3819, *htbudapest@hungarytourism.hu.* **Infotouch** electronic information terminals are scattered around town at: Astoria passenger underpass; Blaha Lujza tér; upper station of Castle Sikló; Deák tér; Déli, Nyugati, and Keleti railway stations; airport terminal 2; Grand Market Hall; Moszkva tér; Tourinform.

For less official but equally helpful advice, go to **Vista Café and Visitor Centre**, where they cater very intelligently to all a traveller's needs. VI. Paulay Ede u. 7, ☎ 267 8603, ✉ 268 1059, *incoming@vista.hu, www.vista.hu. Open Mon–Fri 8–8, Sat and Sun 10–6.*

Representatives of the Hungarian Tourist Board abroad:

UK: 46 Eaton Place, London SW1X 8AL, ☎ (020) 7823 1032, ✉ (020) 7823 1459, *htlondon@hungarytourism.hu.*

USA: 150 East 58th St, 33rd Floor, New York, NY 10155-3398, ☎ (212) 355 0240, ✉ (212) 207 4103, *htnewyork@hungarytourism.hu, www.gotohungary.com.*

Weights and Measures

The most mystifying measurement you will encounter regularly is the **deci**. In bars and some restaurants, wine, juices and soft drinks are often sold by the deci, which is a tenth of a litre (100ml). If you ask for a glass of wine, it may cost three times more than the number on the menu, which is the cost per deci. When you get used to it, it is easy to tell. Similarly, a **deka** is 10g. In the market, if you wanted 200g of apples, you would ask for 20 dekas.

Budapest: History *by Marietta Pritchard*

The River

The setting is spectacular, theatrical, full of contrasts. On the right bank sits Buda: hilly, verdant, royal, residential. On the other side is Pest: flat, bustling, businesslike, modern. Buda inhabits the eastern edge of small mountains; Pest is the beginning of the Great Hungarian Plain, which stretches, hot, flat and richly agricultural, all the way to the Romanian border. And between the contrasting personalities of two formerly separate cities flows the Danube.

It is here in Budapest that the Danube, Duna in Hungarian, seems most itself, most grandly central to urban life. Only here does the river, which flows from the Black Forest to the Black Sea, become an integral part of a major city. It is not the beautiful blue Danube of Viennese myth (barely visible in Vienna), but the wide, muddy, brown river used and abused by real Hungarians. The river, half a mile wide at Budapest, defines, divides and integrates the city, bringing it commerce, easy transportation and recreation, carrying invaders and unwanted pollution from upstream. The Romans, who designated the Danube as the eastern limit of their empire, also built the first substantial bridge at what is now the northern end of Budapest, connecting their settlement of Aquincum with the dangerous world beyond.

The first permanent modern bridge was the Chain Bridge (Lánchid), completed in 1849. Eventually Budapest was linked together with seven more or less beautiful bridges. When the Germans blew up all the Danube bridges in 1945, separating Buda from Pest once again, the city felt a blow that went to its very soul, not to mention its daily existence. Where else would you find memorials to a bridge? The 'temporary' Kossuth Bridge that spanned the river from after the war until 1956 has its own commemorative markers on both sides of the river.

In addition to their practical uses, the river and its bridges created a sense of identity, even of romance, in the city's inhabitants. Here are some impressions from an unpublished memoir by George Perl, who was born in Budapest in 1895.

> *We lived in a large, comfortable apartment in Pest on the Arany János utca, with Father's law office adjoining, the rooms overlooking the Danube. From our window you could see the Chain Bridge, the first bridge of permanent construction across the river, with two lions guarding either end... Across the river was the castle hill [Várhegy]. On top of the hill, the king's castle and the 'Gothic' Church of Matthias [Mátyás Templom]. The hill, on the Buda side, is about 200 feet above the Danube. From where we lived, you could see a small funicular that ascended the steep hill, mainly used by people with official business. The funicular had a regular schedule, and in the evening a red light glowed on the cabin. From our window on the other side of the river, when darkness arrived, you could see the red signal moving up and down the hill. Gaslight had only recently come to the city, so there was not much other light. In the darkness of the river, the ascending light of the balanced machine gave a little boy a sensation he never forgot.*

For a younger writer, Iván Boldizsár, the river simply and complexly represents life—who you are as a Hungarian. In his story *Meeting the General*, the central character has been hauled in on bogus accusations during the martial law of the Miklós Horthy regime in 1935. As he relives his arrest, the narrator remembers 'the aching emptiness in my stomach in the black automobile as we crossed the Margaret Bridge in the early morning. The despair at the thought that I might not see the Danube again, perhaps for years. They might even shoot me...' (*Present Continuous: Contemporary Hungarian Writing*, 1985, ed. István Bárt, Corvina.) Missing the Danube is the real blow, a fate perhaps worse than death.

Building, Rebuilding

Of course, many other cities are built on riverbanks—Prague, London, Paris, to mention only a few. But Budapest seems to have learned from them all as it has been flattened and rebuilt, flattened and rebuilt again and again. It has its bridges and promenades for pedestrians, Paris-like; a castle and a cathedral on the hill, Prague-like; and a London-inspired Parliament building adorning one bank.

A Hungarian, so the joke goes, is someone who walks into the revolving door behind you and comes out in front of you. The suggestion is of quick, self-preserving reflexes, a little of the charlatan and a kind of witty sleight of hand. Hungarians have had to perfect all of these traits over the centuries, as one wave of invaders, occupiers and destroyers succeeded another. In rebuilding the stage setting of their capital city so often, they have made a virtue of necessity, becoming masters at recycling the past. The result is that things are seldom exactly what they seem. The dramatically located Matthias Church is a 19th-century pseudo-Gothic pile sitting atop a real 13th-century one. The blandly modern Hilton Hotel houses one of the city's oldest structures, a medieval Dominican church and monastery. Even the monuments of the late unlamented Communist era have been transformed into an in-your-face Statue Park on the outskirts of the city, complete with amplified hymns to the People's Socialist Republic of Hungary. In other countries of the former Soviet bloc, such monuments were melted down or broken up. In Budapest it seemed important to hang on to these bits of an unloved past, to confront them in their gigantic absurdity. Knowing what the country endured under Communist rule, this ironic array of totalitarian art brings to mind another saying: *Sírva vigad a magyar* (Hungarians enjoy themselves while weeping). It speaks to the bittersweet pleasures of Hungarian music, art, literature and national character.

Back to the Beginning: A Brief History

Migration, Migration

The history of Budapest cannot, technically, be spoken of until the year 1873, when the two municipalities of Buda on the right bank and Pest on the left bank were united. (The more ancient section of Óbuda was also joined with these two.) But the human history of the region is older even than St Stephen and his sometimes problematic crown.

The earliest settlements in the area we now know as Budapest can be traced to the 2nd millennium BC. Copper and bronze ornamented items and Bronze Age cemeteries with hundreds of graves have been located nearby. Subsequent waves of migrations left their mark, with the **Scythians** arriving from modern-day Russia in the 6th century BC and the **Celts** from what is now France around the 4th century BC. In the 2nd century AD, the **Romans** built a city called Aquincum on the western bank of the Danube, designating it the capital of their easternmost province of Lower Pannonia. Aquincum's population had grown to more than 40,000 by the 3rd century but, as the empire declined, the Romans could not hold off attacks from successive waves of eastern nomadic peoples. When the **Huns**, led by their king Attila, attacked in the 5th century, the Romans abandoned the site. The excavated ruins, now a low-key tourist attraction with its small museum in Óbuda, make a pleasant outing, easily reached by public transport. The fortifications the Romans built on the eastern side of the river to protect them from the barbarians became the beginnings of the town of Pest.

After Attila's death in 453, the **Avars** took over and ruled for several centuries. Finally the conquering **Magyars** or Hungarians got to Hungary in 896, led by their chieftain Árpád. The nomadic Magyars were similar in habits to other central Asian tribes, except for their everlastingly unassimilable language, which was of Finno-Ugric origin. The Europeans confused them with the dreaded Huns, which may account for the eventual name of Hungarians. In their last attempt at European conquest, the Magyars were defeated at Augsburg in 955, after which they retreated to the Carpathian Basin to consolidate and establish a kingdom. A descendant of Árpád, King Géza, was the first to be baptized by missionaries from Charlemagne; they also baptized his son Vajk. This son was to be renamed István or **Stephen**.

Stephen was a strong king, who helped organize a feudal state out of the formerly tribal territories. After his death in 1038, the country continued to develop, despite squabbling among former chieftains and 'pagan' revolts, and despite pressure from the Byzantine and Holy Roman Empires. Then in 1241 the **Mongols** arrived, sacking the city and burning Pest to the ground. But the Mongols quickly retreated with the death of their leader, and the Hungarian king **Béla IV** ordered castles—including one at Buda—built to fortify the country.

Matthias and the Hungarian Renaissance

When the House of Árpád died out with the death of King Andrew III in 1301, the throne was taken over by the Neapolitan Angevin kings, who established the royal seat at Buda, encouraged trade and built a university. In 1456, under the leadership of **János Hunyadi**, the Turks —the next set of invaders—were temporarily staved off at Belgrade. This breathing space before the eventual arrival of the Turks (the newly established Habsburgs, too, were eyeing Hungary) was to provide the country with a fertile era during which Buda became one of the most cultivated courts in Europe. Mátyás, Hunyadi's son, reigned from 1458 to 1490, romanizing his name to **Matthias Corvinus** (his emblem was the crow). He was by all accounts a gifted ruler and a cultural visionary, bringing Italian artists and literary figures to the court and amassing a huge and valuable library, the Bibliotheca Corviniana. Matthias' collection of more than 3,000 volumes was exceeded only by the Vatican's collection. Just as Prague had done 100 years earlier under Charles IV, Buda became a centre of art and learning. Matthias' reign became known as the Hungarian Renaissance. After his marriage to an Italian, Beatrice of Aragon, Matthias' table evidently became as sophisticated as his library, with the importation of such Mediterranean delicacies as onions, garlic, dill, capers and figs.

It was the build-up to this time, the bright shining light of Italian art, the brilliant cultivation of the arts of peace, that the 1896 millennium celebration acknowledged, when the Habsburg Emperor Franz Joseph and his wife the Empress Elisabeth travelled from their seat in Vienna to the Hungarian capital to celebrate the arrival in Hungary of the Magyar tribes led by Prince Árpád in the year 896. Matthias' father's memory was recognized in the construction in the new Budapest park (Városliget) of the Vajdahunyad Castle.

First Turks, then Habsburgs

In 1526 the Hungarians were defeated by the Turks at Mohács, and in 1541 Buda Castle fell. For nearly 150 years Hungary became part of the **Ottoman Empire**, with a slice of the country to the west ruled by the Habsburgs, and Transylvania as a separate principality. Buda and Pest were depopulated, and churches were converted to mosques. Little other building occurred except for defensive fortifications, which were all-important since the Habsburgs were now regularly besieging the city. In 1686 a pan-European Christian army led by the **Habsburgs** and partly financed by the pope mounted a six-week siege to recapture Buda and release the Hungarians from their bondage. At the end, Buda and its castle were in ruins, as was Pest, a result both of the siege and of the post-victory depredations of the 'liberators'.

The Turks left behind little in the way of cultural artefacts except for several fine baths, still functioning, and the Tomb of Gül Baba, a small octagonal chapel with a dome, the only place in Hungary where Muslims come to make pilgrimage. The Turks had made no effort to convert the Hungarians, and, in fact, a strong wave of Protestantism had converted many from the Roman Church to a Calvinist faith. But the Turks' real legacies were twofold: the habit of drinking coffee, a custom that became crucial to the social, literary and political life of Budapest; and the use of that quintessentially Hungarian seasoning, paprika.

The Habsburgs are Coming—and Staying

The Habsburgs, by contrast, left plenty behind. Indeed, there are those who see a nostalgic revival of Habsburgiana in these post-Communist days. The aristocracy is out of the closet and people are renovating buildings in Budapest to Baroquely splendid standards, with the mustard-coloured exterior known as 'Maria Theresa yellow' cropping up all over.

After the defeat of the Turks, Hungary was ruled from Vienna, in a connection that ended only with defeat at the end of the First World War in 1918. The new rulers brought in settlers from Austria and Germany to replace the depleted population, and instituted strong Counter-Reformation measures against the growing power of Hungarian Protestantism. A failed **War of Independence**, led by **Ferenc Rákoczi** between 1703 and 1711, which united nobles and peasantry, is still seen as one of the great moments in Hungarian history. When it was over, the Austrians destroyed fortifications and castles throughout the entire country to make sure no such rebellion would happen again. Reforms that defined the rights of the peasants and initiated public education were introduced under Maria Theresa and Joseph II, but they made small inroads on the essentially imperial-colonial relationship between ruler and ruled.

Although Latin was the official language of government, German and French were the main languages of the privileged; Hungarian was spoken by peasants and now also by an enlightened intelligentsia looking toward revolutionary nationalist ideas. In 1795, seven of these revolutionaries, the 'Hungarian Jacobins', were executed. As in other countries struggling toward nationhood, language became a powerful issue at the end of the 18th century, along with the attempt to define a specifically Hungarian artistic and architectural style. It was important and threatening enough that Ferenc Kazinczy, a leader in the reform of the **language**, was thrown in jail. Anyone who has tried to learn Hungarian as a second language will understand how special this linguistic experience is. Not only must the vocabulary be learned word by word, since there are so few cognates with other languages, but the grammar requires an entirely different kind of thinking. Some might argue that this linguistic uniqueness makes it possible for the best Hungarian minds to think 'outside the box'. A surprising number of Hungarians have won Nobel Prizes in the sciences, including the quantum mechanics physicist Paul Dirac and the father of vitamin C, Albert Szent-Györgyi. Think, too, of Rubik's Cube, an invention almost as baffling as Hungarian grammar. But the pressure to make Hungarian the national language in the 18th and 19th centuries also meant defeating other ethnic/national groups within the country: Germans, Serbs, Slavs, Romanians. Language became a consolidating force even as it isolated its speakers.

Independence Gets on the Agenda

The so-called **Reform Period** of the second quarter of the 19th century is notable for the presence of a star, the liberal politician **Count István Széchenyi** (1791–1860) (*see* p.223). A sophisticated, multi-talented figure, he was an anglophile who admired England's modern inventions, from steam shipping to flush toilets. He founded the Hungarian Academy of Sciences, introduced horse racing, and had the Chain Bridge built. That first permanent crossing was designed by an Englishman, William Tierney Clark, and supervised by the Scots engineer Adam Clark, whose name survives in a square on the Buda side of the bridge.

But liberal reforms within the framework of Habsburg rule were not enough for revolutionaries such as **Lajos Kossuth**, who called for immediate and total separation from Austria. With the help of the nationalist poet **Sándor Petőfi**, Kossuth called for the abolition of the feudal system along with a new constitution that would grant Hungary far greater autonomy. The **Revolution of 1848–9** began, in what was to become a typical Hungarian fashion, by a meeting in a literary and political café, the Café Pilvax in Pest. Here Petőfi recited his *National Song*, a call to arms comparable to the *Marseillaise*. 'Arise, Hungarians, your homeland calls you. This is the moment, now or never.' (*Talpra Magyar, Hí a haza./ Itt az idő/ Most vagy soha.*) Frightened by the show of support for Kossuth, the Austrians acceded to the initial demands, which included making Hungarian the official language, and instituting a ministry headed by, among others, Széchenyi. But Kossuth, now finance minister, upped his demands for even greater separation from Austria. The rebellious Hungarians were easily defeated in 1849 when the new emperor, Franz Joseph, called for help from the tsar of Russia. In the wake of the uprising, the government outlawed public gatherings, theatre performances, displays of the national colours and Kossuth-style beards. Kossuth himself went into exile, energetically promoting the cause of Hungarian liberty in England and America. Széchenyi suffered a nervous breakdown, and eventually committed suicide.

But Hungarian independence was permanently on the agenda, and the idea soon fell on more fertile ground. When the Austrians were defeated in 1866 during the Austro-Prussian War, the weakened empire looked for an agreement with the Hungarians. The **1867 Compromise** created the **Dual Monarchy**, with separate governments and parliaments, but with Hungarians still serving in an army composed of all ethnicities of the empire. Under the new arrangement, the Habsburg emperor was King of Hungary, and the two countries shared finance ministries; but the Hungarian government, with a prime minister, cabinet and parliament, took control of its own domestic affairs. Hungarian finally became the official language of government and universities. The arrangement did not satisfy the most radical reformers, nor did it please members of various ethnic minorities living in Hungary—Slovaks, Romanians and Serbs—whose own national interests were overruled. Still, it marked the beginning of an unprecedented period of peace and prosperity. That period ended with another nationalist eruption and the outbreak of the First World War.

Building a Modern City

One outward sign of the newfound solidity was a population explosion. The combined towns of Pest, Buda and Óbuda had grown from around 62,000 people in 1809 to 285,000 in 1869. By the early 1870s, Budapest was the second largest city in the monarchy. The 1870s also saw the creation of a public works council, based on the London model. Then, when the two main cities were combined into unified Budapest in 1873, an immense architectural plan was implemented, featuring the creation of that still magnificent boulevard, Andrássy út, as well as the rebuilding of Pest's inner city. By 1900, shortly after the millennium celebrations, Budapest had a population of 773,000 and enjoyed modern utilities and transport. The very first underground train in Europe was a series of sedate wooden cars running under Andrássy út. The Parliament building opened in 1902.

Commerce and industry blossomed during this period of relative stability, Hungary's **Golden Age**. With the Danube and the Tisza rivers now regulated, Budapest's milling industry grew to be the largest of any city in the world, based on the country's enormous production of grain. Industrialization and the financial institutions that supported it grew exponentially. Budapest became the centre of a rich intellectual and social life, with poets and literary figures haunting the coffee houses. The journal *Nyugat*, founded in 1908, pushed Hungarian writers toward a less provincial point of view, while helping to define the modern Hungarian 'soul'. The most influential of these writers, poet Endre Ady, claimed to write 'new songs for new times'.

The architecture of today's Budapest reflects the prosperity and style of the turn of the 20th century. The buildings that largely characterize the city's current skyline were built during this period: the faux-Baroque palace, the faux-Gothic Matthias Church, the fantastic Fisherman's Bastion, the Parisian-style Opera House and the London-style Parliament. All of these combine, like the flavours in a good Hungarian *pörkölt*, to create an ambience that may suggest, but never duplicates, any other city.

The First World War and After

In June 1914, Hungary entered the First World War along with the rest of Austria-Hungary as an ally of the Germans. Luckily for the Hungarians, the war was not fought on their soil, but they suffered heavy losses on the Russian and Italian fronts. The war and the defeat that followed underscored the social weaknesses that lay just beneath the heady pre-war prosperity. Ethnic divisions and economic inequality led to political instability. For a brief moment, an independent republic was established under the leadership of Count Mihály Károlyi, and universal suffrage and freedom of the press were proclaimed in 1918. Then in March 1919 a short-lived (four-and-a-half-month) Communist regime was installed under **Béla Kún**, who dealt brutally with all opposition. On 16 November 1919, Admiral (the designation dated from a time when Austria-Hungary still had a navy) **Miklós Horthy** rode into Budapest on a white horse at the head of a Hungarian army, beginning a right-wing regime that lasted until the regent, as he was called, was kidnapped by the Germans in 1944. Under Horthy's '**White Terror**', the Communist Party was banned and a *numerus clausus* restricting the enrolment of Jews in universities was instituted.

Hungary's most devastating wounds from the First World War, politically and psychologically, came from the amputation of its territory by the **Treaty of Trianon**. Romania gained Transylvania and a number of primarily Hungarian towns; and, using the Danube as a convenient border, southern Slovakia got an area packed with Hungarians. Even in post-Communist Hungary, the loss of two-thirds of the country's land in 1920 still feeds nationalist passions.

But during the Horthy regime prosperity, albeit an uneasy one, settled back on Hungary. Despite the backbeat of hunger and social unrest, tourism rose as celebrities and ordinary people from all over Europe and America came to enjoy Budapest's hospitality, its spas, music and good food. The period came to be designated as the **Silver Age**. In 1938, the city was the site of more huge celebrations, the 34th Eucharistic Congress, the 900th anniversary of the death of St Stephen, and the World Scout Jamboree.

A Reluctant Ally

Perhaps the most dangerous result of dismantling Hungary's former territories after the First World War was to send the country into the arms of Nazi Germany at the start of the Second. Hungary was a reluctant and recalcitrant ally of the Germans, although it became a source of natural resources, food and forced labour for the Axis powers. When huge numbers of Hungarians were lost on the Eastern Front in 1943 the government withdrew its troops and began secret negotiations with the Allies. In addition, the Horthy regime, despite its history of homegrown anti-Semitism, refused to go along with the murderous German demands for the ghettoization and deportation of Jews. As the Russians moved in from the east, the British and Americans began bombing the country. Up until now, Budapest had been spared air raids.

In March 1944, the Germans occupied their ally, Hungary, and the round-up of anti-Nazi citizens began. Jews were forced into ghettoes and deported to the death camps under the efficient direction of Adolf Eichmann, who had been sent to Budapest for that purpose. A few thousand of Budapest's Jews survived because of the heroic efforts of Swedish diplomat Raoul Wallenberg, who created fake passports and established safe houses. When the Germans kidnapped Horthy in October, Hungary's murderous **Arrow Cross** fascist party took over. The losses in the last year of the war were huge. Some 500,000 Hungarian Jews were killed, of whom 100,000 were from Budapest. The Nazis occupied Buda Castle, preparing for a siege during the winter. They held out for several months, but the city was finally 'liberated' in February by Soviet forces fighting street by street. The Germans surrendered in April 1945. Seventy-four per cent of the buildings in the city had been damaged and more than a third of them destroyed. Along with Berlin and Warsaw, Budapest was one of the three European capital cities to suffer the greatest damage in the war. More than 50 years later, the scars of war are still visible; the work of reconstruction goes on.

Communism, Real and Goulash

The Hungarians welcomed their Soviet liberators uneasily. The advance guard of Russian troops were known to be a particularly brutal lot, unfamiliar with indoor plumbing, and with a special enthusiasm for raping women and collecting wristwatches. A kind of local government was established, with elections that gave the Communists only 17 per cent of the vote. A new currency, the forint, was created, helping to stave off disastrous inflation, and a land reform act distributed agricultural land to peasant families. But by 1948 a Soviet-style government was put in place, a Stalinist, one-party system, with typically inefficient five-year plans that succeeded in destroying the Hungarian economy, collectivizing farms and emphasizing heavy industry at the expense of agriculture and commerce. A Communist secret police force, the AVO, took over the building on Andrássy út formerly occupied by the fascist Arrow Cross Party. In 1949, the Moscow-appointed hard-liner **Mátyás Rákosi** became prime minister.

In 1951, as part of the effort to extinguish the bourgeoisie, more than 13,000 citizens, 'hostile fascist elements', were stripped of their possessions and deported into the countryside, mostly to the Great Plain, where they were compelled to learn the virtues of hard manual labour in farms and factories. Under Rákosi's cult of personality (the presence of his picture everywhere became a cruel joke), Hungary became a failed Soviet-style economy, driven by a deadly combination of shortage and waste. On the death of Stalin in 1953, Rákosi was replaced by a less extreme Communist, **Imre Nagy**. His more relaxed form of government, the so-called New Course, permitted economic and social reforms. But the struggle between hard-liners and moderates tipped again toward Moscow, and Rákosi was returned to power in 1955.

1956: Revolution Gets the World's Attention

In late October 1956, in the midst of a particularly warm and pleasant autumn, the world watched with horror as Russian tanks rolled into Budapest to crush what Hungarians and others had believed would be a well-supported revolt against Communist rule. The USA and other Western powers, who the revolutionaries had understood were prepared to back their cause with force of arms, were unfortunately distracted by the simultaneous events of the Suez Crisis and did nothing. The mood of dissent had been growing, and several large public gatherings had shown a provocative stance toward the authorities. Students expressing their approval of recent reforms in Poland marched to Bem József Tér, a square honouring a Polish general. Another crowd pulled down the statue of Stalin near Heroes' Square. By evening, Soviet tanks had arrived and, although they were initially pushed back by citizens bearing whatever arms they could lay hands on, they returned in early November to put an end to the uprising. The revolution itself was a failure, costing some 3,000 lives. Exhausted and disillusioned, 200,000 Hungarians left the country to start new lives elsewhere.

But in the long run, the 1956 revolution meant that Hungarians began once more to see themselves as agents, rather than simply as observers or victims of their own history. In other countries, Britain, for one, Communist Party members resigned in protest. Totalitarianism in Hungary was broken, although there were plenty of injustices, executions and imprisonments to come. **János Kádár**, Hungary's new leader, was a relatively moderate figure in the Communist spectrum. His oft-quoted formulation, 'Those who are not against us are with us', suggests an edge of renascent humour, along with the possibilities of a new political and cultural freedom. Economic reforms were eventually initiated, moving toward local enterprises, including small private gardens, allowing for profit and the influence of market forces.

During the 1960s Budapest began once again to rebuild, and the last of the bridges, Elisabeth Bridge, was reconnected in 1963. A reinvigorated, sophisticated culture was on the rise. A new national cinema relatively free from official control gave Hungarians a chance to express themselves to each other, often in an elaborate but well-understood code, while also reaching an international audience. Writers such as István Örkény and György Konrád used the power of irony and humour to reflect on their complex present and past. Örkény's *One Minute Biography* describes his life as a 'continual decline' from the moment of his birth.

Goodbye to Communism

Budapest, which had come to be known as 'the jolliest barracks' in the Eastern bloc, in a country that practised 'goulash Communism', began to live up to its reputation. During the late 1970s, major construction of hotels began, with the Thermal, Forum, Hyatt and others built to accommodate foreigners coming to conferences and sporting events. Mass transit was improved and a new subway system was completed. Meanwhile, more Budapesters were driving their own smoky Communist-bloc cars, Trabants and Ladas, which created brand-new traffic jams, parking problems, and a high level of pollution. Enormous, faceless housing blocks had been built during the 1950s and 60s but, as prosperity grew, so did the attempt to protect the historic face of the city. In 1983, the City Embellishment Association of Budapest was founded to encourage just such preservation and restoration.

In June 1989, Imre Nagy was reburied in an emotional ceremony. That summer and autumn, all over the Eastern bloc, walls and barbed wire came down. The Hungarians allowed thousands of East Germans to go west through its territory. In Budapest, streets and squares shed their Communist designations and recovered their old names. For instance, the unswallowable Népköztársaság út—People's Republic Avenue—returned to its original designation of Andrássy út, recalling once again the 1896 millennial celebration. In 1990, free elections were declared for March. With enormous enthusiasm, Hungarians generated over 100 political parties, of which about six survived. That authentic emblem of capitalism, a tiny stock exchange, reopened, and international investment showed serious interest in the country.

After a series of elections and run-offs, the Hungarian Democratic Forum party (MDF) eventually took power, with a conservative coalition led by Prime Minister József Antall. His government was replaced in the 1994 election by the Socialist Party (MSZP) and their coalition partners, the Free Democrats (SZDSZ), with Gyula Horn as prime minister. They responded to some of the new problems brought in by rapid economic change with austerity and devaluations of the forint, to help contend with a large foreign debt combined with a dropping standard of living for many.

The 1998 elections returned another conservative coalition, with Viktor Orbán as prime minister and Árpád Gönz as president. The concerns of this government include efforts to preserve the environment, reflected in a struggle over a Danube dam on the Hungarian–Slovak border. Hungary is trying to reverse some of the damage wrought by a modern, polluting society, combined here with decades of neglect under the heavy hand of Communism. In addition, despite the rise of an often ungenerous nationalism, Hungarians are making the effort to improve relations with their Slovak and Romanian neighbours.

Endnote

The 1999 István Szabó film *A Taste of Sunshine* delivers a characteristically gloomy message about Hungary's history and the futile attempts of individuals to evade their country's unhappy fate (*balsors*). But the city of Budapest seems to resist this dark vision. It continues to rebuild, to restore, to reinvent itself as a modern post-Communist, post-Habsburg city. It keeps serving up rich, nourishing, tasty meals (along with the occasional Big Mac); playing music that ranges from Romany kitsch to rock to avant garde; publishing and painting and performing in ways that suit its inhabitants as well as the millions of visitors who pass through its streets and over the beautiful bridges that cross and recross the Danube.

Budapest: Art and Architecture *by Edwin Heathcote*

Buda. Pest. Two cities; two architectures. Buda is a typically central European medieval town centre of winding streets, Baroque houses and enchanting courtyards, embellished with a series of picturesque 19th-century additions which blur the boundaries between history and fantasy. Pest is the hard-nosed commercial centre: broad, noisy streets framed by powerful urban blocks, crowded shop windows and quiet courtyards. This clear division of the old and the new should make a guide easy, with the old and interesting stuff in the historic centre all strung along an easy route within a walled city. It is not, however, that easy.

The city is an amalgamation of Buda, Pest and Óbuda, unified in 1877. The city's greatest period of prosperity came after this unification, and the magnificent boulevards of Pest are the manifestation of a dramatic era when Budapest and Chicago were the fastest-growing cities on earth. The building of Pest coincided with Hungary's greatest artistic flowering; its streets are crowded with exquisite architectural decoration and powerful buildings. The wealthy, however, often moved out to the leafy hills of Buda so that the city's finest architecture is widely spread; to see it all is a mammoth undertaking. Whether you have a weekend, a week or a year, the key to the city's architecture is to stroll and look around. Look at the details, the doorways and their wonderful ironwork, wander into the court-yards, sit in the cafés and observe one of Europe's most coherent capitals.

Roman to Ottoman

The history of Hungarian architecture is of dramatic leaps forward and devastating setbacks, a stop-start affair which makes it hard to trace any single line of development. The earliest surviving works were left by the **Romans**: a few morsels, including the military amphitheatre (1st century AD), are in Aquincum, in modern Óbuda. The art and architecture of Hungary's early years (c. 1000–1200) was **Romanesque**; there is little of it in Budapest. The work of art embodying the early Hungarian nation is the **crown** of St Stephen. Its upper section was a gift from Pope Sylvester II (c. 1000), the lower a later Byzantine work; the two pieces were prob-ably joined at the end of the 12th century. Its blend of Byzantine and Romanesque reflects Hungary's position between East and West. Mongol invasions from 1241 destroyed much and once the barbarians retreated the focus of Hungarian building efforts was fortification.

The Buda Castle district and its **Matthias Church** date from this period. The church takes its name from King Matthias Corvinus (1458–90), who brought the Renaissance to Hungary. His rule was the pivotal period between the Gothic and the Renaissance; the buildings from his reign blend Gothic and Classical motifs. A few fragments from this period survive throughout the Castle district, a window here, a door there. The brilliant polychromatic Matthias Church is a true mish-mash, this incarnation dating from the 13th century. It has been remodelled almost every century since. During Turkish occupation the best furnishings were looted—the chandeliers from above the high altar hang in the Hagia Sophia in Istanbul—and it became a mosque. The church went through a Jesuit Baroque phase in the 18th century and was exten-sively rebuilt between 1873 and 1896 by Frigyes Schulek. The Mary Portal on the south side dates from the mid-14th century and indicates the original appearance. The **Royal Palace** also dates from the 14th century but only a few Gothic foundations survive. Some of the finest Hungarian art of the period can be seen inside.

The Turkish invasions of the 16th century swept away Hungary's burgeoning Renaissance and artistically the country stagnated for 150 years. The Turks left few monuments, but they are worth seeing. The **Király Baths** in Buda date from the 1560s and survive in almost unaltered form. The dome in the **tomb of Gül Baba** is original; the rest has been rebuilt several times.

Baroque

Turkish occupation was followed by Habsburg domination from the end of the 17th century. For the next 150 years Baroque, which crept in during the last years of Turkish occupation, defined the city. Baroque was the architectural language of the Counter-Reformation, its curvaceous forms a riposte to the puritanism of Calvinist and Protestant architecture and, although it appeared in secular buildings, its greatest expression was in ecclesiastical architecture. The finest example in the capital is the **Pauline University Church**. Designed by András Mayerhoffer and consecrated in 1748, the church's dark, moody interior is stuffed with frescoes, sculptures and carvings. Completed around the same time was the **Serbian Orthodox Church**, probably also designed by Mayerhoffer, its interior a curious mix of Western and Eastern Christianity. The **Franciscan Church** in Ferenciek tere (1727–43) is also notable.

Although the great Baroque monuments are churches, most 18th-century buildings were affected by the style. The early Baroque was directly influenced by Italian originals; later architects were more influenced by the Austrian style, although artists continued to display skills learned from Italy. The Castle district presents endless examples of Baroque embellishment. Among the finest of these is the **former Buda town hall** in Szentháromság utca, designed in the early 18th century by an Italian, Venerio Ceresola. During this period, a lot of foreign artists, mostly Italian, Austrian and German, were at work in Budapest; there was a snob value in employing them, although many were second-rate. Ironically, with so many foreign artists in Hungary, many Hungarian artists were forced abroad. The problem of retaining talented artists has plagued Hungarian art ever since. **Jakab Bogdány**, a fine genre painter, settled in England in 1688 and was a royal favourite. **Ádám Mányoki** made his name in Germany and Poland.

The Baroque remained a powerful force in Hungarian art and architecture through the 19th century, when it was dominant in the historicist rebuilding of Pest. But gradually, under the influence of changes in Germany, Britain and France, the neoclassical emerged as the style that would most stamp its mark on the city during the first half of the 19th century.

Neoclassicism and Romanticism

The key building of this era was the **National Museum** (1837–44), the last major neoclassical museum in Europe, a magnificent building which wears its influences proudly on its façade: the British Museum, the Altes Museum in Berlin and the monuments of Napoleon's Paris. The rediscovery of ancient Greek culture in the 18th century was an antidote to Baroque excesses. Neoclassicism, the style based on the Greek model, seemed everything Baroque was not: cool, urbane and intellectual. Associated with the French revolution and the American republic, it represented democracy, rationalism and science. With Hungary under the yoke of Habsburg oppression, it was inevitable that Mihály Pollack's museum of national history, culture and aspirations, the distillation of the nation's image of itself, should be executed in a grand neoclassicism. When Sándor Petőfi read his *National Song* on the steps of the museum on

15 March 1848 (*see* p.204), it precipitated the Revolution. Neoclassicism's association with national dignity and expression is shown by the **Museum of Fine Arts** and **Exhibition Hall** (both *c.* 1900) on Hősök tere; although built long after the style's heyday, they were executed in monumental neo-Greek. In art, neoclassicism was represented by sculptor **István Ferenczy**, some of whose exquisitely cool reliefs and statues can be seen in the National Gallery.

Historically and artistically the turning point of Hungarian art and architecture was the failure of the 1848 Revolution. On one hand the defeat led to a self-pity which penetrated the arts to their core. On the other, Hungary's economic success and growth after the Revolution led to the Dual Monarchy and Hungary's nominal elevation to equal partner in the Austro-Hungarian Empire. This blend of inconsolable sadness with national pride and burgeoning wealth led to a peculiarly Hungarian situation. Romanticism's inherent sense of longing and loss struck a deep chord with Hungarian artists. In France, Germany or Britain, Romantic artists celebrated lost worlds of chivalry, the passion of revolution or an emotional desire for ancient pastoral land-scapes; Hungarian artists celebrated death and heroic failure. If you walk through a Hungarian art gallery you will be astounded at the misery, poverty and intense mourning on display. Hungarian art of this period was Europe's most miserable art by far.

That misery gives Hungarian art great power to move. Perhaps its first seminal work was **Viktor Madarász'** *The Mourning of László Hunyadi* (1859), which won a gold medal at the Paris Salon (kept in the National Gallery). It shows the shrouded corpse of the defeated hero; a woman, her face stiffened into a mask by pain and anguish, lays flowers at his feet. Madarász, who fought in the war of independence and lived in Paris, was influenced by his French contemporaries, Delacroix in particular. His dark, brooding paintings, like *Dobozi and his Spouse* (1868), depicting a couple about to commit suicide, are keystones in Hungarian artistic identity. A dark blend of Romanticism and history was the breeding ground for the greatest mid-19th-century painters. Best known is **Mihály Munkácsy**, who lived in Paris but exerted huge influence on Hungarian art. His earlier works dwell on poverty, depression and alcoholism. At his best they are powerful, brooding and unforgettable. **Gyula Benczúr** and **Bertalan Székely** created super-realist historical paintings of defeat and martyrdom. The stronghold of Romanticism and historical genre painting was only challenged at the end of the 19th century, when Hungarian artists brought their Impressionist influences home from Paris.

Eclecticism: Building the Capital

In 1867, the year of the Compromise, the combined population of Buda and Pest was 280,000. In 1900 the population was a million, making Budapest the sixth largest city in Europe. Industrialization, the population boom and the uniting of the city necessitated a huge building programme. Town planning, based around two new concentric ring roads, was based on the Viennese model. The infrastructure and council of public works were based on London. The aesthetic came from the broad, tree-lined boulevards and grand buildings of Paris.

The first step was the building of the earliest permanent bridge between Buda and Pest, the **Chain Bridge** (1839–49). It was followed by the layout of key parts of Pest as aristocratic Buda waned and Pest became the engine of Hungarian recovery. The style of the new city was Eclecticism, a pompous but urbane blend of neo-Renaissance, neo-Baroque and Parisian grandeur. It is defined by powerful rustication (use of a bold, often textured design on masonry blocks which are separated by deep joints), deep cornices and richly modelled façades. The ring roads, Andrássy út and the roads around them are all executed in this style. The sculptures on the façades, mythical figures, caryatids, etc, are astounding in their variety, power and quality. Also on Andrássy is the neo-Renaissance **Opera** (Miklós Ybl, completed 1884), which sets itself between the opera houses of Paris and Vienna and holds its own well. Note also the **Central Antiquarium** at the corner of Bajcsy-Zsilinszky út, showing that the skill of Hungarian architects in handling corners was unsurpassed.

Eclecticism allowed unprecedented freedom of expression with a pick'n'mix range of architectural elements. Imre Steindl's fairy-tale **Parliament** (1884–1902) is an ambitious example of extremist Eclecticism, blending Gothic verticality, a Florentine dome, Baroque planning and Ruskinian dreaming spires with great success. Other examples of Eclectic gigantism are the superbly overblown **bank and exchange buildings** on Szabadság tér (both Ignac Alpár, 1905) and the **New York building** housing the famous coffee house. A blackened façade hints at everything from Florentine palazzo to Solomon's Temple, while the interior is a stupendous Baroque fantasy. Despite the success of Art Nouveau, National Romanticism and Rationalism, Eclecticism still defines the inner city.

National Expression, National Romanticism and Folk Art

After the failed 1848 revolution there was a great desire to rebuild a Hungarian architecture independent of foreign sources, leading to a surge of interest in Hungarian folk art and the origins of the Magyars. Ethnographers traced the nation's roots to Central Asia and India by similarities between Hungarian folk art's motifs and those of other nations. These researches were often spurious but they prompted some remarkable architectural approaches. The first major attempt at a national style was the **Vigadó** (1859–64). Frigyes Feszl blended Byzantine, Islamic and Classical elements to indicate Hungary's position on the border of East and West. It is an odd but distinguished attempt, though it failed to pioneer a new national style. Feszl also assisted Lajos Förster, architect of the **Central Synagogue** (1854–9), where his obsession with Byzantine and Moorish detailing was put to good use. The architect who succeeded (briefly) in reviving the ideal of a truly Hungarian architecture was Ödön Lechner.

Lechner began in the Eclectic œuvre, although his buildings were marked out by verticality and Gothicism rather than the Mannerism and neo-Renaissance of his contemporaries. The **Thonet Building**, 11a Váci utca (1888–9), has elements of the style for which he became known. The functional iron-framed building is clad in rich blue Zsolnay tiles, looking almost Moorish. The flatness of the façade, almost like a tapestry, would have been a shock in an era dominated by deeply modelled Renaissance stucco façades. Lechner's masterpiece, however, is the **Museum of Applied Arts** on Üllői út. Lechner's building was created to house the best international applied arts as a resource for Hungarian designers. The building is a *tour de force* of decorative architecture and the apex of his efforts to create a new architectural direction.

Lechner was greatly influenced by Hungarian folk art's supposed links to India and Central Asia. This fascination with Eastern forms explains the domes and ogee arches, the dragons' heads and Middle Eastern courtyards which so influenced this building. The decorative elements are almost all executed in brightly coloured Zsolnay tiles. **Vilmos Zsolnay** was a ceramicist of world renown who had travelled with Lechner to study design in London. His ceramic factory was pivotal in the spectacular success of Hungarian decorative art. The company's products, in particular its glazed tiles, grace the roofs of a number of buildings that define Budapest's skyline, including the Matthias Church and the **Post Office Savings Bank** (1899–1901), Lechner's other great masterpiece. Lechner was a contemporary of Gaudí, with whom comparisons are instructive: both foreshadowed and influenced Art Nouveau, both wanted to create a regional architecture and both were eccentric geniuses whose work cannot be neatly categorised in broader architectural histories.

Lechner stands alone in the history of Hungarian architecture but he profoundly influenced the next generation. They too wanted a national architecture but, rather than to spurious ethnography, they turned to the folk art and architecture of rural Hungary. Influenced by William Morris and the British Arts and Crafts movement, and Finnish National Romanticism, and inspired by Lechner's attempts, this new generation set about creating a new œuvre. Its rural roots gave this style more success in the country than the city, but Budapest has some examples, the most concentrated area being the **Wekerle Estate** around Kós Károly tér (well off the tourist map), a version of the Arts and Crafts garden suburb. The bastion-like gates around the main square are particularly impressive. Nos.2–3 were designed by Károly Kós, the influential leader of this group. More work by Kós can be seen in the superb buildings of the **Budapest Zoo**. Aladár Árkay's powerful **Reformed Church** (Városligeti fasor 7) of 1912–13 displays influences from Finnish National Romanticism and even American Arts and Crafts as well as from Hungarian folk art (note the abstracted folk motifs in the ironwork and in the decorative tiles).

Károly Kós continues to exert great influence on Hungarian architects, and the modern architects working in an organic vein are inspired by his use of folk art and architecture. Hungary's most internationally renowned architect, Imre Makovecz, who was taught by Kós, owes a deep debt to his mentor's vision of an architecture in touch with its folk roots and archetypes.

Art at the End of the 19th Century

If Hungarian art had been morose in the mid-19th century, it underwent a stunning *volte face* towards the end of the century. **Pál Szinyei Merse**, who spent much of his career in Munich, was a contemporary of the French Impressionists and his work paralleled theirs. Sunny, colourful and *plein air*, Szinyei Merse brought sunshine to the gloom of Hungarian art. He was followed by **József Rippl-Rónai**, who lived in France and represented the post-Impressionist phase of Hungarian art, first going through a black period and then launching into an œuvre saturated with brilliant colour yet with profound emotional content. His works echoed the bold outlines and powerful forms of Toulouse-Lautrec, with graphically simplified figures, but he blended these with the expressive colour of Van Gogh and Gauguin. His painting *Father and Uncle Piacsek next to Red Wine*, with his father's anguished expression and his uncle's contemplative fatalism, is one of the great works of Hungarian art. Rippl-Rónai also designed fine tapestries and ceramics and painted frescoes, and was instrumental in fusing arts and architecture, an ideal of Hungarian Art Nouveau. The artist who stands out from this period as unique and unclassifiable is Tivadar Csontváry Kosztka. Known as **Csontváry**, he was a true eccentric who began painting at 30. His deeply odd paintings blend biblical symbolism, Expressionist emotion and complex symbolism and iconography rooted in Hungarian history. Like Lechner, he was a lone genius attempting to create a distinctive Hungarian genre.

Art Nouveau and Secession

The *fin de siècle* in Budapest was dominated by the **1896 millennium of Magyar settlement**. A huge programme of rebuilding celebrated both this and the phenomenal progress that Hungary had made in the years since 1867. The legacy of the celebrations is staggering. The metro, the first in continental Europe, still runs to Hősök tere, focus of the celebrations, which centres on the Millenary Monument and a grand colonnade beneath which stand György Zala's kings and princes of Hungary. Beyond is the Városliget park, built for the Millennium, within which is Vajdahunyad, an impressive theme-park re-creation of a 15th-century Transylvanian castle. Hősök tere and Andrássy út represent the mainstream of Hungarian art and architecture at the end of the 19th century. Eclecticism and Baroque were virtually unquestioned in their supremacy and only Lechner was attempting to depart from this academicism.

In the first few years of the 20th century, artists and architects reacted against the established appearance of the city in Hungary's Art Nouveau, known as *Szecesszió* after the breakaway from the academic system of Vienna. By Western European standards, Budapest arrived at Art Nouveau late. The highlights occurred in 1905–15, by when this approach was distinctly art vieux in France, Belgium and elsewhere. Nevertheless the Secessionist architecture and decoration in Budapest is fantastically varied, of very high quality and worth examining in detail.

The buildings lining Budapest's main streets were largely completed by the turn of the 20th century but the streets packed with apartment blocks behind the major roads were developed when Hungarian Art Nouveau was at its best. Architects strove towards the building as a realization of the *Gesamtkunstwerk*, a synthesis of all the applied arts, so it is worth looking not only at the overall effect but at the details. Take the exquisitely modelled house by Emil Vidor at **Honvéd utca 3** (1903), which features remarkable organic ironwork doors and intricate majolica flowers in the spandrels of the bay window. Nearby is **Aulich utca 3** by Kálmán Albert Kőrössy (1901): its crumbling façade is in a pitiful state, but raise your eyes to the exquisite Art Nouveau panel which crowns it and the whole façade seems to light up. The same architect designed the best-preserved interior of the era, the **Philanthia florists** (Váci utca 9), where the organicism of the furniture and the exotic arches mirror the flowers and plants in the shop, while Lajos Márk's dark symbolist paintings provide a mysterious background. The streets of Budapest are packed with these delightful and surprising *belle époque* jewels.

Among the larger works of Art Nouveau the **Ferenc Liszt Music Academy** (1904–7) is the supreme *Gesamtkunstwerk*. The mountainous Mannerist elevations give few clues to the sumptuous interior. The ground-floor foyer is adorned with a delicate Secessionist fountain, while the first floor is centred on an exquisite mosaic frieze, *Art is the Source of Life* by Aladár Körösfői-Kriesch. Every surface seems to be clothed in precious material, from golden mosaic to marbles and shimmering ceramics. This is one of the city's finest structures. Another towering work of this era is the **Gresham Palace** designed by Zsigmond Quittner and László and József Vágó in 1905–7, a similarly mountainous structure adorned with jewel-like inlays of gold and swirling Art Nouveau tendrils. The final impressive pudding of Art Nouveau is the **Gellért Baths** (Ármin Hegedűs, 1909–18), with its sumptuously tiled, cavernous interiors.

Perhaps the best place to see the dynamic world of Hungarian Art Nouveau is **Szervita tér**. Number 3 (1906), a strikingly rational building of glass and metal, is crowned by an exquisite mosaic representing figures from Hungarian history and legend by the finest Hungarian decorative artist of his day, **Miksa Róth**. Under the highly decorated gable the lower parts of the building presage the Modern movement. The neighbouring building (1908) goes even further with a stripped, rational façade of marble bolted to the structure behind, elegant bays and attenuated shafts of steel and stone framing an almost wholly glazed façade on the lower floors. Number 5 (1911–12) is by Béla Lajta, a follower of Lechner, who incorporated the advances of the European avant-garde in functional design with subtle, abstracted motifs from

Hungarian folk art to create a modern Hungarian architecture, rational yet rooted in folk consciousness. The façade of this building is a stunning demonstration of his ideas; stripped, expressive and elegant, it is an almost timeless design. These three buildings are a snapshot of this vibrant period, in which architects strove to create work based on function and structural rationalism yet retain Hungarian qualities in the details. Lajta was the most interesting of these architects; some of his finest work is in the Jewish cemetery in Kozma utca: his richly decorated **tombs for the Schmidl and Gries families** are among the pinnacles of European funerary art. He was also responsible for the **Új Színház** (1908–9), Paulay Ede utca. Its stark marble façade and the angular, almost Assyrian, gilded angels of its parapet are stunningly original.

At this time Budapest was the fastest-growing city in Europe. Pest's phenomenal growth was fuelled by rapid economic and industrial expansion: it was the engine of the Austro-Hungarian Empire, a city of factories, banks and pan-European trade. This industry also gave rise to a new field in Hungarian arts: graphic design. The poster became the driving medium in the popularization of Art Nouveau, and graphic design as well as illustration became an important part of the new art. Posters for Tungsram light bulbs, Unicum liquor and Törley Champagne are amongst the most distinctive, each developing a specific brand image and style.

The Secessionist style in art and architecture continued to develop in ever more stripped-down form until the outbreak of the First World War. Its late monuments are among the finest buildings in the city and include harsh but urbane buildings such as Béla Málnai's **Czech-Hungarian Bank**, Nádor utca 6 (1912), and Kálmán Giergl and Flóris Korb's **Luxus Department Store**, Vörösmarty tér 3 (1911), which paved the way for Modernism. But it was to be nearly two decades before architects were once more able to realize such radical schemes.

Modernism

The First World War, the loss of two-thirds of Hungary's territory and its reactionary post-war regime crippled its art and architecture while Modernism was fermenting throughout Europe. György Lukács, the cultural commissioner under Kún in 1919, encouraged radical art and design but the government was not able to put its ideas into practice, and artists who had been associated with it had to flee the country after it failed. Other radical architects left the capital for more promising environments and Hungary lost a generation of brilliant young artists.

The Bauhaus, the German home of radical Modernism, was full of Hungarians. **László Moholy Nagy**, the Constructivist artist and designer, was a key figure in the Bauhaus. **Farkas Molnár**, whose design for a Red Cube House (1922), never realised, was among the first and finest architectural designs to emerge from the school, worked in the office of Walter Gropius, the school founder. **Marcel Breuer**, best known for his invention of tubular furniture, designed the UNESCO building in Paris (1953–8). **Vilmos Huszár** was a key figure of the De Stijl movement in Holland. **Ernő Goldfinger** was pivotal in the development of Modern architecture in England. **André Kertész**, perhaps the finest modern photographer, worked in Paris. **Sándor Bortnyik**, **Andor Weininger** and **Lajos Kassák** all proselytised for European Modernist and Constructivist art in Hungary but were also at the apex of the development of these art forms. Kassák was the most influential: he founded the magazine *Ma* (*Today*) and developed Activism in Hungary. His graphic style has remained a powerful influence on young Hungarian artists.

A few artists scraped a living in Hungary during these lean years. **Lajos Kozma**, an architect and designer who had worked with Béla Lajta, found work designing Ex Libris labels and furniture. By the early 1930s, architects like Kozma were beginning to get work once more as the country slowly liberalised and began to prosper. The **Functionalist model estate** at Napraforgó utca (1931) included works by most of the architects who would later introduce Modernism on a larger scale, and demonstrated the variety and potential of the Functionalist house for social and private housing. A few Modernist villas appeared in the Buda hills as business began to boom and entrepreneurs and industrialists looked for the latest fashions. Farkas Molnár returned from the Bauhaus to design minimal villas and houses, including those at **Lotz Károly utca 4b** (1933), **Cserje utca 12** (1932) and **Lejtő út 2a** (1932). József Fischer's perfect but cold villa at **Szépvölgyi út 88a** was another defining moment of the era. By the mid-1930s, the political climate was more receptive, and Functionalist buildings were beginning to appear in the city centre. Lajos Kozma finally gained substantial commissions: among his finest work is the **Atrium Cinema**, 55 Margit körút (1935–6), a pure and sophisticated piece of urban Functionalism, and **Régiposta utca 13** (1937), a subtler, more understated work.

Towards the end of the decade a more streamlined version of Modernism blended the aerodynamic curves of classic ocean liners and cars with the clean, simple lines of Functionalism. This resulted in a number of wonderful apartment blocks, the best of them the building at **Margit körút 15**, a sleek, travertine-clad apartment block with lifts encased in glass cylinders. Good modern buildings went up in the early years of the Second World War and resumed quickly in the socialist regime of the immediate post-war years. The finest example of architecture from this early, idealistic period of socialism is the **Erzsébet tér bus station** (István Nyíri, 1949). By the early 1950s, however, Stalinism had taken grip and Modernism was out.

Socialist Realism to Post-Modernism

Stalin decreed that modern art was decadent, the preserve of an urban bourgeois elite, and could only have value if it represented the life and work of the people realistically. This art came to be known as Socialist Realism, or Soc-Real. The art of the Stalin era was little different in Hungary to elsewhere: factory workers, young pioneers and strong peasants marching as one. It was a style suited more to murals, posters and graphics than to galleries. The socialist sculptures, some undeniably powerful, that littered the streets of Budapest are now exiled to the sardonic Statue Park (*see* p.293). The images of this era, and of the revolutionary period of socialist art (1919–early 1920s), provided modern artists and illustrators with inspiration and a rich vein of imagery for parody and satire.

The architecture of the period was derivative, a classicism that appeared bolder and stronger than it was, as in the **School of Applied Arts**, Zugligeti út 9–25 (1953–4), with its clumsy classical portico. The national stadium, the **Népstadion** (completed 1953), was Modernist in conception but Stalinist-Classical interiors were tacked on as the political mood changed during its design. Simple and structurally brutal, it remains a well-conceived work. This heroic period of Socialist Realism lasted only a few years, and the late 1950s and early 1960s were dominated by rebuilding the city after the brutal suppression of the 1956 revolution. By the time Hungarian art and architecture recovered from that shock it had fallen into line with Western trends. Architecture from the late 1950s to the 1980s has little to recommend it. The lasting architectural legacy of the Kádár era is the dreadful **concrete tower blocks** which surround the city, although all Socialist capitals were subject to similar abuse.

Art of this era was dominated by a few figures, whose state-sponsored status has inevitably tainted them. **Margit Kovács** was probably the best known. Her naïve, folk influenced ceramics remain popular. **Imre Varga** was one of the regime's most favoured sculptors. His Holocaust memorial beside the Synagogue, a palm tree, each frond engraved with the name of a victim, is a poetic conception and his public sculptures are good. The best-known Hungarian artist of the era was **Victor Vasarely**, who studied under Constructivist Sándor Bortnyik in the 1920s but left Hungary to live in France. The creator of Op Art is well represented in an Óbuda museum devoted to his work.

By the early 1980s Hungary's increasingly liberal politics and tolerant regime allowed artists a degree of expression unthinkable in neighbouring countries. Conceptual and absurdist art were a vehicle for criticism of the regime. Hungarian Pop Art too took on radical overtones, aiming criticism at Soviet political imagery and Western consumer culture. Among the major Hungarian artists in the 1970s and 1980s were the Conceptualist and theorist **Miklós Erdély**; **Lili Ország**, whose works developed from Surrealism to beautiful abstract symbolism; **Imre Bak**, whose work encompasses influences from Kandinsky to Italian postmodernism; and **Sándor Pinczehelyi**, whose paintings, photos and installations use political symbols in critique of both capitalism and Communism. From 1989 the political poster became a powerful and evocative tool, the voice of democracy against the still Communist-controlled mass media. Among the most memorable images were **István Orosz**' poster of the back of the head of a Russian soldier with the caption 'It's All Over, Comrades' (in Cyrillic characters, as Hungarian schoolchildren were forced to learn Russian), and **Peter Pócs** and **László Haris**' blood-soaked crucifixion nails on a numbered gravestone, alluding to the unnamed grave of Imre Nagy.

Nagy was the liberalizing prime minister of Hungary in 1956, murdered by the Communists in the wake of the revolution. One of the most potent uses of political imagery in Hungarian art occurred at his 1989 official rehabilitation and reburial. The setting for the ceremony was designed by **Gábor Bachman**, a film-set designer and artist, and **László Rajk**, an architect and son of a murdered politician. Nagy's coffin was laid out in Hősök tere and the portico of the Exhibition Hall behind it was draped in black fabric. The remains of four other murdered members of the revolutionary government were laid alongside Nagy's body with a sixth, empty, coffin representing the other martyrs of the revolution, and six jet-black, ominously angular catafalques created for the coffins. To one side was a Constructivist gantry from which hung a white pennant, the hole burned out of its centre a memory of the revolutionary flag, the tricolour with the Communist star removed, a poetic representation of a nation's loss.

One of the artists loudest against the inhumanity of Communism was Imre Makovecz. Hungary's best-known architect, Makovecz is renowned for his organic approach to building, his revival of forms drawn from folk art and architecture, and his unparalleled use of sculptural timber forms. At his best, Makovecz realizes expressionistic spaces of incredible vision and power. His finest work in the capital is the **mortuary chapel in the Farkasrét cemetery** (1975), a brooding allegorical building of great power in which the coffin lies at the centre of a ribcage of timber arches, echoing the redemptive story of Jonah and the Whale. Many Makovecz houses can be seen in the hills of Buda; oustanding among these are the pair at **Kondorkert utca 9** (1985–9) and **Törökvész lejtő 25** (1983–6). Makovecz' organicism spawned a school of younger architects attracted by his unorthodox and expressive approach. Ferenc Salamin is one of the finest of this younger generation; his **Kuglics House** (1987–91) can be seen in the hills at Brassó utca 5, while Ervin Nagy's **Swan House** (1996), on the corner of Hattyú utca and Batthyány utca, is a rare example of a large work of urban organicism.

Budapest: Magyar Moods

A horse-drawn carriage winds its way down a steep, narrow road through the jagged mountains of Transylvania. Arriving at an inn, everyone hurries to get inside before darkness falls, but a young Englishman announces to the nervous inn-keeper his plan to go farther. 'There's a carriage meeting me at Borgo Pass at midnight.' 'Borgo Pass?' 'Yes.' 'Whose carriage?' 'Count Dracula's.' (The inn-keeper's wife crosses herself.) 'Castle Dracula?' 'Yes, that's where I'm going.' 'To the castle?' 'Yes.' 'Nooo...' (tremulously). 'You mustn't go there.'

When the count appears, his first two lines are knock-out, delivered with an unmistakable Hungarian accent, for this is the definitive Dracula, Béla Lugosi, one-time Minister for Culture in Budapest. 'I am...Drac-u-la... I bid you welcome.' Wolves can be heard in the distance, causing the count to smile chillingly. 'Listen to them. Children of the night. What mu-u-u-sic they make.' He is an archetype, a manifestation of the dark and uncontrolled, the irrational and ungodly; a product of those mysterious, primordial Transylvanian forests, and the fear and awe they inspire. Yet he wants to go West, and uses this hapless city fool to transport him to England, where he will meet his nemesis in the shape of the Dutch Professor Van Helsing, a symbol of Western Europe, with all its pragmatism and belief in reason, order and progress.

Dracula can be seen as a perceptive study of the East–West divide, and as such says more about the soul of the Hungarians than its author can ever have known. A piece of inspiration on Stoker's part was his setting the opening in Transylvania. For Transylvania, which was a part of Hungary until the Trianon Treaty stole away two-thirds of the nation's land, has always held a very special place in the Magyar heart, and above all represents the past, the East, what some would call the 'real' Hungary. Transylvanians are traditionally regarded as more Hungarian than the Hungarians, their language more beautiful and ancient, their folk songs more archaic. The 1970s repopularization of folk music and dancing had many of the main exponents travelling to Transylvania, the only place where 'the real thing' had survived.

Part of the reason for this could be that the domain 'beyond the woods', along with the eastern counties of the Great Plain, was never occupied by the Turks. It remained a bastion of Magyardom, run as an independent principality, with ruling princes who paid taxes to the Turks, and periodically rose up against them. On the colonnades of Heroes' Square and around the base of the Parliament dome, Transylvanian princes take their place alongside the most celebrated of Hungarian rulers, amongst them Prince Zsigmond Rákóczi, who led an uprising against the Habsburgs in the early 18th century. Giving Transylvania to the Romanians after the First World War was a particularly cruel blow. Thereafter 'Transylvanianism' became ever more pronounced. Budapest gained a garden suburb (the St Imre Colony) designed as a Transylvanian village, complete with Transylvanian names. The cemetery plots where Imre Nagy and the other executed victims of the 1956 Uprising are buried have been transformed to resemble a traditional Transylvanian graveyard.

The most popular historical novels of the 19th-century writer Mór Jókai were those set in 17th-century Transylvania, which he used also as a starting point for a series of Turkish tales, *Midst the Wild Carpathians*, again demonstrating Transylvania's symbolic standing as the gateway between East and West. If later generations of Hungarians chose to romanticize the Turks and the Huns who once ravaged their land, this vague, mysterious sense of affinity must surely be understood as a reaction. Just as a past lover can be recalled with tenderness when a present lover is out of favour, so these invaders from the East came to be seen as not so bad after all compared to the oppressors from the West, the despised, coldly efficient Austrians. And now that the latest wave of occupiers, this time from the East, has been sent packing, the people have turned eagerly, and maybe a little too uncritically, to embrace the West.

Thus swings the pendulum. Hungary is situated in a no-man's land, sandwiched between two modes of existence with deep-rooted ideological incompatibilities. East is East and West is West, and they fight a tug-of-war both in the physical terrain of the Carpathian Basin and in the psychic depths of the Magyar soul. This process can be traced back to ancient roots. When the hunter-gatherer Finno-Ugric tribes moved south from their home in the Northern Ural mountains, they learned stock-breeding and cultivation, started using copper and, later, bronze, and lived in family units within clans. When rising temperatures led to droughts, the Voguls and Ostyaks moved back to the forests of the north and resumed their hunter-gatherer lifestyle. But the proto-Magyars stayed, having learned to adapt to their circumstances. When the domino effect of a wave of migrations from the East forced the Magyars to look for a new homeland towards the end of the 9th century, they appeared to horror-stricken Europeans as just one more ferocious, barbaric Asian horde. Yet whereas previous raiding tribes from the Steppes, such as the fearsome Avars, had been incapable of building upon their triumphs, and had consequently been absorbed by other peoples or disappeared without trace, the Magyars had internal resources of organization and survival skills upon which to build. Though from the East, they possessed certain traits compatible with the West.

The pendulum swung still further at the end of the 10th century. Caught between the Holy Roman Empire and the East, Prince Géza threw in his lot with the Westerners, converting to Christianity. While he continued to worship pagan gods, and remained 'an immensely cruel man, who killed a great many persons in his sudden bursts of anger', he had his son raised in the Christian faith, and by all accounts King (later St) Stephen was a genuinely devoted man, a *Rex christianissimus*. For a state moving towards a settled existence defined by property and security, the Ten Commandments were more than just articles of metaphysical doctrine. They prohibit murder and theft. They protect property, render the question of heredity less ambiguous through the regulation of sexual relationships, and demand humility towards the community and obedience to the king. In short, they encapsulate the Western way.

Stephen is always pictured with an Apostolic cross and a sword: he had to convert his people to the new faith by force. When, eight years after his death, a pagan rebellion broke out which, among other things, resulted in the murder of St Gellért, it revealed discontent not just with the new religion, but with the whole ideology that it entailed. The Magyars were not all happy to be Westernized. It is symbolic that the crown which resides in the Parliament today, supposedly a copy of the one worn by King Stephen, is actually a synthesis of two halves, one sent to Stephen by the pope, the other part of an older Byzantine, Eastern crown.

Ever since, the battle within the Hungarian soul has continued. In the 19th century, the two greatest historical figures represent the two halves: Széchenyi the anglophile reformer versus Petőfi the romantic wanderer. Increasing Westernization of politics, economics and industry led to increasing rejection of modernization, summed up by Mór Jókai: 'I regard with fear your attempts at renewal. You are making the nation lose all that it has, and do not acquire for it what it longs for.' Yet the great poet Endre Ady, for instance, was utterly contemptuous of anything 'Oriental', a word for him synonymous with backwardness. Amidst the explosion of creativity that surrounded him, a new literary journal appeared, symbolically named *Nyugat*: the West. But still Ady described the life of daytime Budapest as 'one huge protracted groan', and returned frequently to his native Transylvanian village to seek spiritual renewal.

Meanwhile a new group of artists was championing once again the call of the East. The virtues of 'the people' had been eulogized thoughout the 19th century, but usually in sentimental, insubstantial ways. Now two major writers, Zsigmond Móricz and Dezső Szabó, began to chart the psychic depths of those Ady considered backward. In the field of music, similar events were unfolding. Bartók and Kodály, dissatisfied with emulating the Austrian model, decided to return to their roots. Avoiding the so-called 'folk' music that had been sentimentalized to the point of cliché, and using the new invention of the phonograph, they scoured the land for genuine, ancient Magyar folk tunes. They found the remnants of a truly archaic music based on unusual scales and complex rhythms, a music with its roots deep in the country's shamanic past. By integrating these elements into their own compositions, they arrived at a synthesis of East and West, which thus constituted a truly Hungarian style.

Certain scholars, desperate to 'prove' that the Hungarians have an Eastern pedigree, had suggested that the Magyars were related to Turks, Huns, Indians, Sumerians, even Tibetans. This encouraged the experiments of architects who had begun to incorporate Eastern motifs into their works. The neo-Moorish style blossomed, resulting in such fabulous buildings as the Great Synagogue. Byzantine elements began appearing, especially in mosaics and stained glass. Neo-Indian came into vogue, most notably in Ödön Lechner's building that now houses the Museum of Applied Arts, whose Moghul-style interior reminiscent of the Taj Mahal was originally painted in gaudy bright colours more suggestive of folk art.

Lechner was the leading exponent in Hungary, and one of the prime movers in Europe, of the movement known as Secession or Art Nouveau, which was to have an extraordinary impact on Budapest. In his 60s, he recalled that since his youth he'd harboured 'a distant ideal of creating a national Hungarian style'. He suggested that some of his peers, such as Miklós Ybl, had similar ideals but had 'come to the conclusion that it was impossible to have a building in the Hungarian style because there had never been any such thing' and had usually settled for the Gothic, which, although a product of the West, retained some of the dark, primitive, irrational power associated with the East. While working in Paris restoring châteaux, Lechner wondered how national styles came into being and came to understand how they evolved through the different influences felt by the nobility in their travels around the countryside. He wondered if 'some similar cross-fertilization' could be used in forging a new Hungarian style. The turning-point came when he met the Transylvanian Jószef Huszka who was urging Hungarian architects to seek inspiration in their native peasant traditions. For him, the native woollen garment known as a *cifraszűr* represented the purest expression of Magyar art, and he compared the woven motifs with those found on buckles from 9th-century Hungarian tribes.

Thus Lechner forged a Hungarian style, known as National Romantic, by combining advanced Western building techniques with patterns, motifs, themes and features that he gathered through extensive research in the countryside. He was not so much an exponent as one of the inventors of the emergent Art Nouveau style, even preceding the great Catalan architect Gaudí whose work, equally inspired by regionalist patriotism, Lechner's so often resembles. Lechner's work, which reached its apotheosis with the delightful Post Office Savings Bank, critically nicknamed 'the Palace of the Gypsy Baron', represents the pinnacle of the era's achievements because, like Bartók and Kodály, he built a bridge between the two halves of the East–West divide. This may be the lesson to be learned from it all: that Hungary has always been at its best when it can unite the warring aspects of its own psychological make-up. The historical personage who best represents this synthesis is the king who more than any other brought a Golden Age to this troubled land. Matthias Corvinus may have become the perfect Renaissance King, but he was born and raised in—where else?—Transylvania. Let us hope that, in their enthusiasm to enter the European community, the Hungarians do not forget the other side of their personality. Time may yet reveal that their greatest asset, as well as their oldest curse, resides in their occupying the land where the twain meet.

The Greatest Hungarian

Some things run in the family. Count Ferenc Széchenyi set a good example of how the aristocracy could work for the benefit of the nation by establishing the National Museum and the National Library through the donation of his own substantial collections. Yet his generosity pales in comparison with the dedication of his son István. What is so impressive about Széchenyi *fils* is the scope of his ambitions, and the clear-headedness with which he set about dragging Hungary out of her feudal past by emulating the systems and technology of the country from which he drew most of his inspiration, England.

A list of István Széchenyi's innovations almost beggars belief. His was the idea to build the first permanent bridge across the Danube, not just for convenience, but with the far-sighted goal of uniting Pest and Buda as a single city. He petitioned and badgered to get support, commissioned the architect and engineer, both British, and had the iron shipped from England. He challenged his country's poverty, condemning in his first major work *On Credit* the antiquated laws which paralysed Hungary's growth by rendering credit impossible. In later works *Light* and *Stages* he showed how the feudal system made the lives of the poor almost unbearable, and was not even beneficial for the landowners who sought to perpetuate it. He drew up a timetable for economic reforms. As well as launching various modern banking and industrial enterprises that sought to rectify the country's financial stagnation, he introduced steam-powered machinery, and experimented with the cultivation of mulberry trees with a view to producing silk. Transport was identified as a key ingredient of England's progress, so he entered into partnership with a British ship-building company, imported British engines, engineers and captains, got involved with the Danube Steamship Navigation Company, and set about regulating the rivers Danube and Tisza. In 1833, he personally sailed Hungary's first steamship down the Tisza to Szeged. He also persuaded the government to build the first steam-powered railways, having been greatly inspired by the Manchester to Liverpool line.

Nothing less than a total overhaul of his nation's mentality was what Széchenyi required, and above all it was the wealthy that he aimed to educate. This was why he became obsessed with horse-breeding and racing. He considered it an intimate part of what made Britain great, and expressed his suspicion that most of his compatriots would be enraged to learn that in fact 'it was them, not their horses, whom he wanted to train'. Leisure-time profitably used was part of his strategy. He established the Hungarian Academy of Sciences and had the first Hungarian National Theatre built in 1837. He introduced ice-skating and rowing, and opened the first 'Club' (the Pesti Kaszinó), based on the English model, meant as a venue for 'the intercourse of minds'. It succeeded in becoming a rallying point for young reformers.

Though not of, he was certainly always for the people. Despite having spent most of his life before 30 abroad, and writing his diaries mainly in German, he was the first person ever to make a speech in the Upper Chamber of the Hungarian Parliament in the Magyar tongue (traditionally, Latin was used). At a time when the Magyars were becoming increasingly chauvinistic towards other ethnic groups within the country, he was the first to raise his voice in opposition to discrimination, and history proved that his concern was not just decent but expedient. He fought over issues of personal hygiene, introduced flush toilets, and made practical suggestions to stem the spread of cholera. Yet for all that, and despite his attacks on certain aspects of Habsburg policies, fate was to cast him in the role of the conservative.

The combination of Lajos Kossuth, a passionate speaker in Parliament and a rabble-rouser who used his newspaper *Pesti Hírlap* to influence public opinion, and Sándor Petőfi, the country's most popular poet, was leading the people down the road to revolution. Széchenyi could not advocate such a path to freedom, partly because he understood that neither modernization nor emancipation of the downtrodden depend on full political sovereignty, and believed the former goals to be of more importance; also because he feared that reaching for the prize of independence too soon would provoke retaliation from the Austrians before Hungary had sufficiently modernized to be able to defend herself. Again, history proved him right. A battle of words began between Kossuth and Széchenyi, and their differing stances—reform or revolution—so polarized public opinion that only a decade or so ago did Budapestian intellectuals stop referring to themselves as Széchenyi or Kossuth supporters as a kind of political shorthand. Yet it was Kossuth, his great opponent, who coined the expression so frequently used to describe Széchenyi, 'the Greatest Hungarian', and referred to him as 'the man whose equal I do not know in my nation's annals'. A surprising source, but a difficult opinion to contest.

Hungary's Answer to Elvis

Jorge Luis Borges once declared that there must have lived a Hungarian poet of Keats' stature, but that, not being able to speak the language, he could neither prove it nor ever know for sure. Did the cryptic wordsmith pick on Hungary simply because the language's reputation for unintelligibility had reached as far as Argentina? Whatever the reason, it is a fair bet that the Magyar Keats is Sándor Petőfi. Not just because he is one of the most widely translated Hungarian writers, his name borne by more streets, squares and buildings than even Széchenyi's, and the first poet seriously studied in Hungary's schools; but also because, if we follow Oscar Wilde's idea of putting his talent into his work but his genius into his life, Petőfi is clearly our man. He led a life that puts the consumptives and mad, bad, dangerous-to-know rascals in their place, and reads like any adolescent romantic's daydream come true. Only his nationality can explain why Hollywood has yet to convert his story into a blockbuster.

He was born in a village in the middle of the Great Hungarian Plain, its vast sweeping expanses open and free, infinite as the sky or ocean. He travelled them extensively with his beaten-up old case, drawing inspiration for his beguilingly simple, direct verse from the countryside and peasants, the themes and rhythms of folk songs. He left school to join a theatre troupe, and wandered across the country acting, with an interlude of two years as a soldier. But his soul was that of a poet, and soon he published his first booklet of verse and got a job as an assistant editor in Pest. He was the first poet to speak of personal feelings, and in the language of the common people, who quickly learned to love him. His *John the Valiant* has been the most popular work of literature in Hungary for the last 150 years. It tells the story of a poor shepherd boy who runs away and joins up with the noble Hussars. After many adventures, such as fighting dragons and giants or taking on the whole Turkish army, he is offered the hand of the King of France's beautiful daughter. Of course, he humbly declines and returns triumphant to his village and the childhood sweetheart he left behind.

At 23 Petőfi met the beautiful 18-year-old daughter of a nobleman who became his own sweetheart. Like the best of true loves, the course of theirs was far from smooth, for her father was opposed to their marrying: the poet, though a national celebrity, had no fixed income and was the son of a butcher. Eventually he gave in, and Petőfi's friend and patron put a mansion at the couple's disposal. During their honeymoon, the happiest time of his life, the poet wrote some lines whose foreboding suggests that for some romantics a happy ending isn't enough:

> The flowers fall... Life runs away so early!
> Oh come, Beloved, will you sit on my knee!

> Today you lean against me so dearly,
> Prostrate upon my grave soon you may be.

Two years later Europe was on fire with revolution. As the spokesman of his generation, Petőfi was at the heart of the action, helping Kossuth to whip up the masses into a frenzy of discontent. Café Pilvax, the favourite haunt of writers and politicians, was the meeting place for a growing group of young, radical, articulate intellectuals and students, later known as the 'Young Men of March', who gathered around our hero and his fellow writer Mór Jókai. News of the riots in Vienna made them decide that now was the time to act. József Irinyi (later to invent the safety match) drafted the 'Twelve Points' of their demands, which went even further than Kossuth's speeches in Parliament. When the crowd reached critical mass, they marched to Kossuth's one-time publisher and, without requesting the permission of the censor, a deliberate flouting of the law, printed copies of the 'Twelve Points' and also a copy of the poem that Petőfi had rushed to finish in time for the event, the *National Song*.

It was a time when the heroism of words and ideas was still a tangible reality, when coffee-shop conversation centred on politics and culture, when men were searching for a way out of the grim realities of an outdated feudalism, ready to follow whoever emerged as leaders. The crowd, numbering in the thousands, headed for the National Museum, and stood below the steps to be addressed by their young leaders, yet still no-one really knew where the day was heading. The turning-point came when our boy launched into his new poem. Beginning 'Rise up, Hungarians!', it employs a brilliant rhetorical use of refrain to emphasize one essential choice: freedom or slavery. Not everyone was impressed. The museum director wrote in his diary: 'Some noisy mob had their hurly-burly outside which disturbed me in my work, so I went home.' But the people were overwhelmed, and what started as demonstration ended as revolution. It has become possibly the most celebrated moment in Hungarian history. Petőfi was 25 at the time. According to legend, his only child was conceived that very day.

A successful revolution turned eventually into a war that was doomed to failure. Our hero naturally took part in the fray. He was seen at one of the very last battles, fleeing towards a cornfield in civilian clothes. Nobody witnessed his death, and his body was never found. And this is where it emerges that after all Petőfi is not the Hungarian Keats, or even its Danton, but its Elvis, because the nation simply refused to believe he had died. He was 'seen' at various places. Rumours circulated that he was still alive, that he'd been taken as a prisoner to Siberia.

Even quite recently a Hungarian millionaire sent a team to Siberia to dig up a grave he believed might have been Petőfi's. (It turned out to belong to a young lady.) It says a lot about Hungary that the man whose popularity reached such dizzyingly irrational heights that the country refused to believe the news of his demise was not a rock 'n' roll singer but a Romantic poet who longed for the open plains and craved nothing so much as to die for freedom.

Madness, Suicide, Genius

Most of us would not respond well to being born into a rich, aristocratic 19th-century family, with all the potential for abuse of power and privilege that entailed. More than likely we would indulge our secret vices outrageously, at best think ourselves admirable and modern for not whipping our servants or claiming *droit de seigneur* over their pretty young wives.

How humbling, then, is the case of Count István Széchenyi (*see* 'The Greatest Hungarian', above), whose superhuman strivings to improve the lot of his countrymen once led him to write in his diary, 'They cut off my wings, I walk on my feet; they cut off my feet, I walk on my hands; they tear out my arms, I crawl on my belly. Anything, as long as I can serve.' Yet his story has a strange ending, often tactfully omitted by Hungarian commentators. When the Revolution failed and Széchenyi found himself pressurized by the Austrian police, he didn't display the stiff upper lip his friends at London's prestigious gentlemen's clubs would have expected, but collapsed, degenerating into a hopeless wreck, eventually committing suicide. There are other strange facts too. He was a restless womanizer, who fell in love with his brother's wife, and pursued this odd relationship to an extent that nobody really knows, but that plagued him with guilt all his life. It has been suggested that his endless philanthropy was the only thing that gave him release from his terrible tensions. Looking again at that diary entry, we may ask who exactly is this 'they' who will cut off his wings and hands? The sad truth, as stated by biographer Boyd C. Shafer, is that 'in his public as well as private life, he went from one crisis to another, often contemplating taking his own life and finally, indeed, doing so'.

In his work *The Man of Genius*, Cesare Lombroso refers to Széchenyi to support his premise that 'genius is a special morbid condition', and that there is 'a resemblance between genius and insanity'. From these bed-mates we can make a *ménage à trois* with the related phenomenon of suicide, and suggest that this trio exert an extraordinary pull upon the Magyar soul. Take the case of Mihály Munkácsy. Based in Paris, he became Hungary's most (perhaps only) internationally famous 19th-century painter. He specialized in scenes of Hungarian peasants or historical canvases, usually very dark, with bitumen-black surfaces. As the often bright, colourful works of the Impressionists changed tastes and Munkácsy's popularity declined, he descended into lunacy. He was institutionalized after a fellow painter found him gibbering to himself, endlessly repeating that the way to be successful in the salons was to paint lighter and lighter. Then there was Baron Ferenc Nopcsa, a palaeontologist who achieved fame through his dinosaur findings, and became director of the Geological Institute. In later life he was overtaken by obsession with Albania. He dressed in Albanian costume, built up the largest library ever assembled about Albania, and was a leading contender for the country's throne. Eventually he flipped entirely, killing one of his Albanian companions and then himself.

The much celebrated artist Csontváry was hardly stable at the best of times. His career began when he heard a voice saying he would be 'the greatest...painter the world has ever seen— greater even than Raphael'. He was teased for his oddity by Ödön Lechner and the rest of the gang at the Café Japán, from which he took refuge through endless wandering. In the end, his schizophrenia, loneliness and lack of understanding reduced him to such a state that he could create nothing but sketches of surrealistic visions. József Attila was a similarly unhappy loner. Though his poetry was loved by the people, he was forever in trouble with the authorities, unsuccessful in love and hopelessly alone. He too succumbed to insanity and threw himself under a moving freight train. Even Liszt, a man described by no lesser a man than Wagner as 'too great, too noble, too beautiful', who 'appeared among the people like a God', suffered from extreme bouts of depression, writing in an 1855 letter: 'I have been so overwhelmed with depression these last eight days that I felt I could no longer go on living.'

To these could be added the hundreds who have used the Liberty Bridge as their jumping-off point for the great beyond, and Prime Minister Pál Teleki, who shot himself in disgust at Hungary's having joined the Nazis in their invasion of Yugoslavia (suggesting that maybe in Hungary, as in Japan, suicide is not looked down upon but seen as a noble way out). Of course, any nation's history books offer multiple cases of madness/suicide, but in Hungary's case these instances are matched by official statistics: despite changes in frontiers and the ethnic composition of the people, and whether you examine Protestants living on isolated farms in the Great Plains, or Catholics crammed into the busy metropolis, the figures for suicide are forever glaringly high. It comes as little surprise that the song that best sums up the atmosphere of hopeless, crushing ennui, the song that for a while the BBC would only play without the words, because otherwise it sparked off an epidemic of suicides, 'Gloomy Sunday', was of course written by Hungarians. And, of course, the man who wrote the music, Rezső Seres, failed to make any money from it, and died penniless aged 60 having spent his whole life as a humble bar pianist. And, of course, he didn't die of natural causes.

Count Dracula, that truly Hungarian creation, despite his apparent lust for life, speaks wistfully of death: 'To die, to be really dead—that must be glorious.' It's no shock to learn that the celebrated author of *Darkness at Noon*, Arthur Koestler, who spent many years establishing the foundation 'Exit' which fought for the right to commit suicide, was also Hungarian. In fact, Koestler was part of a generation that more than any other embodied the last characteristic of the Hungarian trinity: genius. Between 1885 and 1927, seven Nobel prizewinners were born in Budapest. The figure goes up to nine if we include the rest of Hungary, and 13 if those born abroad of Hungarian parents are also included. A tremendous brain-drain occurred throughout the war-torn first half of the 20th century, of which Koestler said: 'I don't think that a comparable exodus of scientists and artists ever existed since the fall of Byzantium.' The modern world owes perhaps more to the inventions of Hungarians than any other race. Hungarians were responsible for the dynamo, the telephone exchange, the transformer, the three-phase locomotive, the carburettor, the theory of jet aeroplanes and concept of rocketry, the electronic computer, the nuclear chain reactor, vitamin C, the theory of stress, the ballpoint pen, the hologram, BASIC programming language, email, Microsoft's Word, Excel and Windows programmes, game theory, Rubik's Cube and so on, and so on. Not to mention philosophers such as György Lukács, writers like Koestler, film giants such as Sir Alexander Korda, William Fox and Adolph Zukor, or billionaire economists like George Soros.

John von Neumann, one of the many to attend Budapest's Lutheran school, is a case in point. As well as a member of the US Atomic Energy Commission, this mathematical genius was a pioneer in the field of computers. His 1945 paper on what is today called the von Neumann computer has been called 'the most important document ever written on computers'. He introduced the binary code and learned electronics in two weeks to build his own computers. In the 1950s he speculated about using light instead of electrons to speed up computers (this came about in the 1990s). Before anyone else, he used electronically controllable computers to explore meteorology, economics and strategy. A pioneer of game theory, itself a forerunner of chaos theory, his 1944 book with Oscar Morgenstern *The Theory of Games and Economic Behaviour* has been described as the greatest paper on mathematical economics ever written. His mini-max strategy of the two-person zero-sum game introduced whole new levels of understanding into the complexities of Cold War relations, and revolutionized American military and political strategy. Hans Bethe wondered 'quite seriously' if a brain like Neumann's does not indicate a species superior to that of man.

Indeed, such speculations attached themselves at that time to Hungarians as a whole. Isaac Asimov has reported: 'A saying circulated among us that two intelligent species lived on Earth: humans and Hungarians.' So much were Hungarians prevalent amongst the atomic pioneers that Fritz Houtermans, the man who first recognised the nuclear origin of stellar power, suggested an explanation: 'The galaxy of scientific minds that worked on the liberation of nuclear power were really visitors from Mars. They found it difficult to speak English without an alien accent...and therefore chose to pretend to be Hungarian, whose inability to speak any language but Hungarian without an accent is well known.' It became a standing joke. Leon Ledermen, director of the Fermilab, has said: 'The production of scientists and mathematicians in the early 20th century was so prolific that many otherwise calm observers believe Budapest was settled by Martians in a plan to infiltrate and take over the planet Earth.'

Why this particular country, this city? One solution is offered by scientist George von Békésy: 'In Hungary we all were involved in an ongoing struggle for almost everything we wanted... People need such challenges, and these have existed throughout the history of Hungary.' As George Marx, author of *The Voice of the Martians* has put it: 'Under a changing climate...old schemes no longer work, such conditions encourage creative individuals. If a very different final truth is offered each month, young people learn critical thinking and become more interested in facts than idioms.' To this might be added the culture of coffee houses, melting-pots of ideas which encouraged open discussion among artists and intellectuals, demanding a certain rigour from those who emerged as its leading lights. Scientist John G. Kemény introduced another factor by suggesting that it is so much easier to learn to read and write in Hungarian than in English or French that Hungarian kids have more time left to study mathematics.

Maybe, without even knowing it, he has brought us to the crux of the matter: language. For what shapes the nature of our thoughts so much as the language in which we express them? And what but thought patterns could connect those three phenomena, madness, suicide and genius, that seem to occupy so prominent a position in the Magyar soul? Such a theory fits with the Hungarians' view of themselves. They love their language, celebrate its utter separation from every other language around them, laugh at jokes nobody else would understand, produce poetry that can never be adequately translated, gabble at uncomprehending tourists as if the very sound of their words were a mantra or magical incantation. In a land of ever-changing boundaries, occupied from the beginning by a heady mixture of ethnic groups, the political definition of what constitutes a Hungarian has increasingly been equated with the language: a Hungarian is a person who speaks the Magyar tongue. For to be sure, nobody but a Hungarian would. Except maybe an undercover Martian.

Budapest: Essential Sights

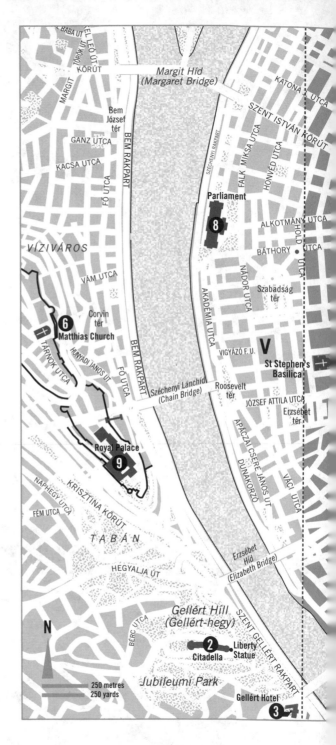

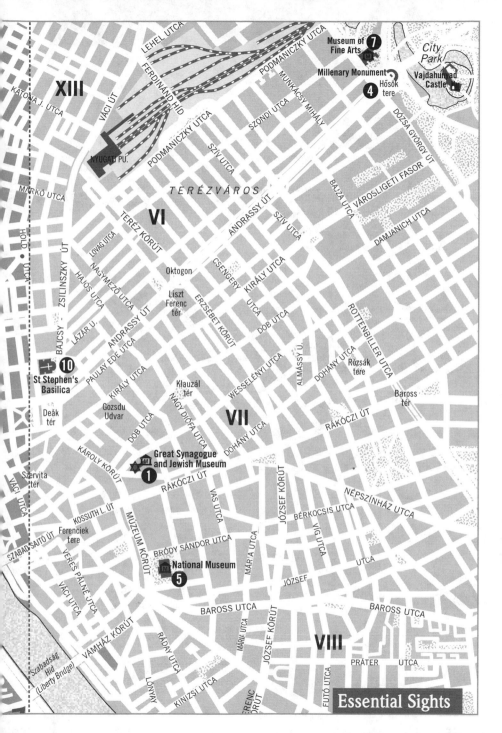

KATONA J. UTCA

LEHEL UTCA

FERDINÁND HÍD

PODMANICZKY UTCA

MUNKÁCSY MIHÁLY

Museum of
Fine Arts **7**

City Park

Millenary Monument

Hősök tere **4**

Vajdahunyad Castle

XIII

VÁCI ÚT

NYUGATI PU.

PODMANICZKY UTCA

SZÍV UTCA

DÓZSA GYÖRGY ÚT

SZONDI UTCA

MARKÓ UTCA

TERÉZVÁROS

VI

TERÉZ KÖRÚT

ANDRÁSSY ÚT

SZÍV UTCA

BAJZA UTCA

VÁROSLIGETI FASOR

DAMJANICH UTCA

HOLD UTCA

BAJCSY - ZSILINSZKY ÚT

LOVAG UTCA

NAGYMEZŐ UTCA

HAJÓS UTCA

LÁZÁR U.

ANDRÁSSY ÚT

PAULAY EDE UTCA

KIRÁLY UTCA

Oktogon

Liszt
Ferenc
tér

CSENGERY UTCA

KIRÁLY UTCA

ERZSÉBET KÖRÚT

DOB UTCA

WESSELÉNYI UTCA

ALMÁSSY U.

DOHÁNY UTCA

ROTTENBILLER UTCA

Rózsák tere

10

St Stephen's
Basilica

Deák
tér

Gozsdu
Udvar

Klauzál
tér

NAGY DIÓFA UTCA

VII

DOB UTCA

DOHÁNY UTCA

RÁKÓCZI ÚT

Baross
tér

Szervita
tér

KÁROLY KÖRÚT

Great Synagogue
and Jewish Museum
1

RÁKÓCZI ÚT

VAS UTCA

JÓZSEF KÖRÚT

BÉRKOCSIS UTCA

NÉPSZÍNHÁZ UTCA

VÁCI UTCA

SZABAD SAJTÓ ÚT

KOSSUTH L. ÚT

Ferenciek
tere

MÚZEUM KÖRÚT

MÁRIA UTCA

VÍG UTCA

UTCA

VERES PÁLNÉ UTCA

BRÓDY SÁNDOR UTCA

National Museum
5

JÓZSEF

Szabadság
Híd
(Liberty Bridge)

VÁMHÁZ KÖRÚT

RÁDAY UTCA

BAROSS UTCA

MÁRIA UTCA

JÓZSEF KÖRÚT

VIII

BAROSS UTCA

PRÁTER UTCA

LÓNYAY

KINIZSI UTCA

FERENC KÖRÚT

FUTÓ UTCA

Essential Sights

231

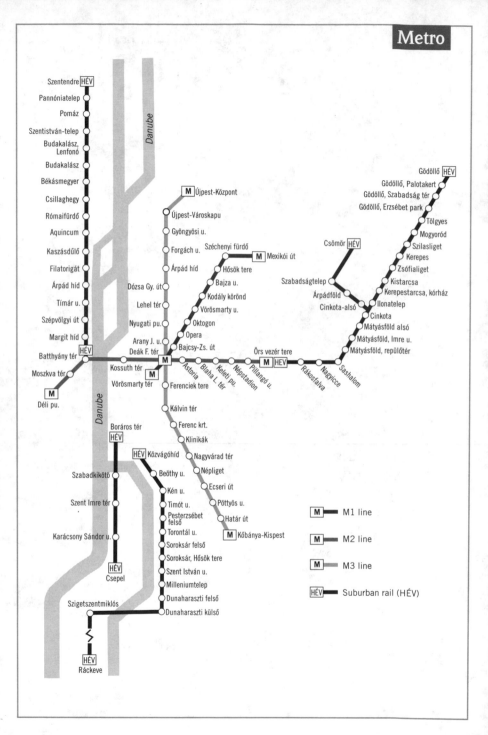

Metro

M1 line

M2 line

M3 line

Suburban rail (HÉV)

232

Castle Hill (Várhegy)

Perhaps the best place to begin is Roosevelt tér on the other side of the Chain Bridge, so that your first view of Castle Hill is in the context of the Buda landscape that it dominates. It's the focal point, bearing the Royal Palace, Matthias Church, the whole centuries-old centre, hanging above the city like a mirage of the past. A mere 60m above the level of the Danube, Castle Hill is not high enough to be aloof. It does not hold itself apart from its surroundings but crowns them.

History

First to see the strategic potential of this location was the Hungarian King Béla IV, who, following the Mongol invasion of 1247, had a fortress built here, recognizing it as a more defensible location than Esztergom. A civilian population grew up around it and, when the 'New Palace' was built during the 1387–1437 reign of Sigismund of Luxembourg, it became the new royal seat in an extended period of peace that culminated in Matthias Corvinus' rule (1458–90), a Golden Age when Buda played a large part in the European Renaissance.

But all that died with the king. A period of decline set in, and this weakness was seized upon in 1541 by the Ottoman Turks, who plundered what they could from the town and left the rest to fall apart around them, a job of destruction finished off in 1686 by the Habsburg-led Christian armies that drove them out. This self-proclaimed royal family built their own palace (though they ruled from Vienna) and restored the town, only to raze it again during the 1848–9 War of Independence. Again the castle was rebuilt and again destroyed, this time in 1945, when German troops, besieged by the conquering Red Army, held out for a month, during which Castle Hill was reduced to rubble. It was the city's 31st siege. Yet once again it resisted the buffeting of history. Phoenix-like, like the Hungarian people itself, it survived.

This persistence is important to remember when roaming those streets, which still follow the same course, dictated by the shape of the castle walls. As the rubble was cleared away after the last destruction, many remains dating back to the Middle Ages were found which would otherwise have been forever hidden. In the rebuilding that followed, these were left visible, and complemented by architectural styles that evoke every period of Buda's eventful history. It would be both easy and unjust to dismiss the whole area as a historical theme park. Instead we should see the preservation of its past as a gesture of pride on the part of a people who have always been a buffer zone between East and West, and have always bounced back.

Lunch and Cafés

Café Pierrot, I. Fortuna u. 14, © 375 6971. *Open daily 11am–1am*. Crêpes, seasonal specials, vegetarian dishes and lunch deals.

Korona Kávéház, I. Dísz tér 16. *Open daily 10–6*. Perhaps the best cakes on Castle Hill.

Litea, I. Hess András tér 4, inside Fortuna Passage, © 375 6987. *Open daily 10–6*. Small bookshop-cum-café, specializing in teas and classical music.

Pest Buda Vendéglő, I. Fortuna u. 3, © 212 5880. *Open daily 12–12*. Intimate and old-fashioned. Gourmet meat-based food. Expensive, but the lunch specials are good value.

Ruszwurm Cukrászda, I. Szentháromság tér 7. *Open daily 10–7*. Budapest's oldest pâtisserie, open since 1827. As much tourist site as coffee shop.

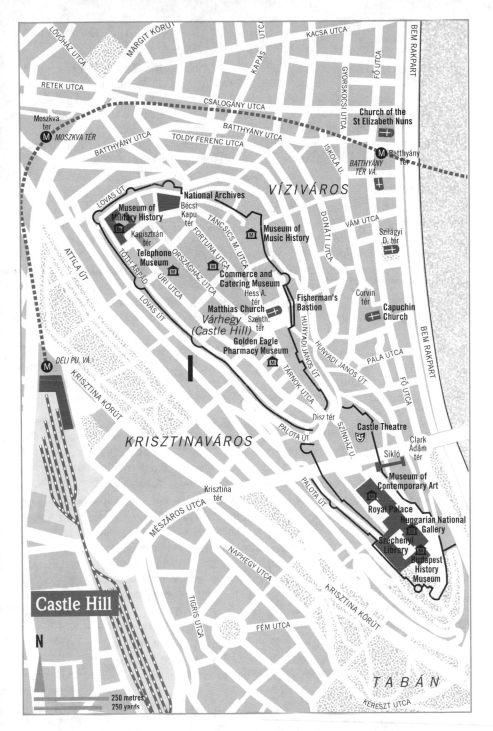

Church of the
St Elizabeth Nuns

Moszkva
tér
Ⓜ MOSZKVA TÉR

RETEK UTCA

LÖVÖHÁZ UTCA

MARGIT KÖRÚT

KAPAS UTCA

KACSA UTCA

GYORSKOCSI UTCA

FŐ UTCA

BEM RAKPART

CSALOGÁNY UTCA

BATTHYÁNY UTCA

BATTHYÁNY UTCA

TOLDY FERENC UTCA

ISKOLA U.

BATTHYÁNY
TÉR VA.
Ⓜ Batthyány
tér

VÍZIVÁROS

LOVAS ÚT

National Archives

Museum of
Military History

Bécsi
Kapu
tér

TÁNCSICS M. UTCA

FORTUNA UTCA

Museum of
Music History

DONÁTI UTCA

VÁM UTCA

Szilágyi
D. tér

Kapisztrán
tér

Telephone
Museum

TÓTH ÁRPÁD

ORSZÁGHÁZ UTCA

ÚRI UTCA

Commerce and
Catering Museum

Hess A.
tér

Fisherman's
Bastion

Corvin
tér

Capuchin
Church

ATTILA ÚT

LOVAS ÚT

Matthias Church

Várhegy
(Castle Hill)

Szenth.
tér

Golden Eagle
Pharmacy Museum

HUNYADI JÁNOS ÚT

HUNYADI JÁNOS ÚT

TÁRNOK UTCA

PALA UTCA

FŐ UTCA

BEM RAKPART

Ⓜ DÉLI PU. VA.

KRISZTINA KÖRÚT

KRISZTINAVÁROS

Disz tér

PALOTA ÚT

SZÍNHÁZ U.

Castle Theatre

Clark
Ádám
tér

Siklo

Krisztina
tér

MÉSZÁROS UTCA

NAPHEGY UTCA

PALOTA ÚT

Museum of
Contemporary Art

Royal Palace

Hungarian National
Ⓜ Gallery

Széchenyi
Library

Budapest
History
Museum

KRISZTINA KÖRÚT

TIGRIS UTCA

FÉM UTCA

Castle Hill

N

TABÁN

250 metres
250 yards

KERESZT UTCA

The Sikló (Funicular) runs daily 7.30am–10pm (closed every other Mon).

However you get up to Castle Hill, it feels like a journey back in time, so it seems most appropriate to take the Sikló. The cars, resembling old-fashioned black and yellow trams, glide up the hill in about a minute. This model, built in 1986, looks like the original from 1870, which functioned up until 1945 when it was taken out by a Soviet shell. To **walk**, follow the slope (negotiable by wheelchair to the top) to the left as you face the Sikló, then take the stairs to your right. Or take the M2 **metro** to Moszkva tér, then pick up the **Várbusz** from beneath the turret of the castle-like building.

The Turul Statue

If you ascend by the steps, this great bronze eagle suddenly looms over you, clutching a sword and squawking defiantly. Wings spread, it is poised for flight, a deft study of suspended movement. This is the **turul-bird**, which occupies a curious place in Hungarian myth. It began its role as national protector by raping Árpád's grandmother; as the hero led the Magyar tribes to conquer the Carpathian Basin, it flew overhead, bearing the sword of Attila the Hun. Descent from an eagle, symbol of the Creator, meant that holy blood coursed through Magyar veins. How ironic, then, that this turul-bird, created in 1905 by Gyula Donáth, was placed here by Habsburg Emperor Franz Joseph to present himself as a second Árpád, founder of a thousand-year Dual Monarchy. Turul-eagles also guard the Szabadság híd and Parliament's main gates.

In the palace gardens is the **statue of Eugene of Savoy**, considered the finest work of József Róna, a self-made man from a poor background. It pays tribute to the man who liberated Hungary by driving out the Turks, though rumour has it that the Austrian Eugene couldn't stand Hungarians. Behind here is the entrance to the National Gallery within the Royal Palace.

The Royal Palace (Budavári Palota)

Whatever your tastes in architecture it is hard not to be impressed by the sheer scale and symmetry of the Royal Palace. Occupying much of the southern portion of Castle Hill and dominating the Buda skyline, its lineage reflects the changing fortunes of the town.

Nothing remains of the castle and fortifications of King Béla IV, and nobody is even sure where it stood. The Angevin Kings, living in less drastic days, built more impressive quarters, bettered by Sigismund of Luxembourg, who commissioned a large Gothic palace, protected by a new set of external walls. But first prize went to the sun-king Matthias Corvinus, who ordered a whole new set of buildings and had the existing ones renovated to suit the latest Renaissance tastes. As the Palace re-invented itself as a melting pot for the latest ideas on art, politics and culture, artists and scholars from all over Europe were commissioned to supply paintings, sculptures, fountains and lavish banqueting halls; and stayed on, no doubt, to enjoy the famous hospitality, state-of-the-art hot and cold running water, wine, women and song.

Alas, the Turks were waiting in the wings to trash the place, using the Royal Palace to stable their horses and store their gunpowder. Defeating them entailed reducing Matthias' pleasure-dome to such tatters that the Habsburgs just had to build a new one. It started small under Charles III (early 18th century), grew to 203 rooms under Maria Theresa, and just kept growing through the 19th century, despite the lack of royalty. The Viennese court left it to be enjoyed by their viceroy, which added to the rancour of the Hungarian public and no doubt fuelled their restless desire for independence. After the great Compromise was made in 1867, large-scale extensions were carried out under Miklós Ybl, then Alajos Hauszmann. This symmetrical neo-Baroque affair was completed in 1905, but never housed an actual monarch. After the First World War put an end to the Dual Monarchy (though not to the Palace, which came off uncharacteristically unscathed), the locals again had to put up with an impostor walking the corridors, this time in the shape of the Allies' viceroy Admiral Horthy. In 1945, of course, the walls came tumbling down again, more completely than ever. The medieval remains uncovered were incorporated into the new structure, which, alas, was based not on the Matthias model but on the vast Habsburg edifice completed by Hauszmann, though with a simpler roof and the addition of a neoclassical dome that is probably its finest feature.

The interiors were not designed with royalty in mind but for the benefit of cultural institutions; and today the palace is occupied by the Museum of Contemporary Art (wing A), the Hungarian National Gallery (wings B,C and D), the Budapest History Museum (E) and the National Széchenyi Library (F).

Hungarian National Gallery (Magyar Nemzeti Galéria)

Open April–Oct Tues–Sun 10–6; Nov–Mar Tues–Fri 10–4, Sat–Sun 10–6; closed Mon; adm.

Unlike many National Galleries, this one really is national. Everything is Hungarian, ranging from the Middle Ages to the present. It is a large collection but not intimidating: a couple of hours should be enough. Paintings are labelled in English, but there is no further elaboration and no guidebooks or tapes. But since these are all artists the layman is unlikely to have heard of, with names that are impossible to get a hold on, who often allude to historical events only a Hungarian would know, it hardly seems to matter. What does matter is that there is much of quality that will help you understand a little better the national soul of the country.

Ground Floor

First port of call is the **Lapidarium**, which displays stone objects reclaimed from the past after the 1945 destruction. Note the black marble statue of King Béla III's head, thought to date from around 1200, and the two red marble bas-reliefs of King Matthias and his wife Beatrice.

Most people agree that one of the highlights of this museum is the collection of 15th- and 16th-century **Gothic altarpieces and panel paintings**, found on both the ground and the first floor. Many seem weird and wonderful to the modern eye, but that is part of the fun. Note the *Madonna* from Bártfy, rare among Gothic art in that it is complete, and the *Death of the Virgin* from Kassa. These, like most of this collection, are from Slovakia, once part of Upper Hungary. Those in the Magyar heartland were mostly destroyed by the Turks.

First Floor

Of the late Gothic altarpieces, look out especially for *The Annunciation* by Master GH and *The Visitation* by Master MS. In the Baroque rooms, most notable is the 1712 *Portrait of Ferenc Rákóczi* by Ádám Mányoki, which might prepare you to go back through the middle section and face the vast canvases of battle scenes that you hurried past. The most unavoidable, right at the top of the stairs, is Peter Krafft's *Zrínyi's Sortie*, which captures that suicidal moment when the army defending Szigetvár took on the Turks outnumbered 50 to one. These skilful, but to many unappealing, works form part of a wave of **nationalism** which shows itself in every aspect of the 19th century, when Hungary was sick of being ruled by the Habsburgs or anyone else. Here the response was a return to the glories, even glorious defeats, of the past. András Török mentions the word *honfibú*, which he translates as 'patriotic sorrow': 'There is the grief of generations behind this word. The grief common to all for their ill-fated country.' Maybe it is the passion of this grief that makes the 19th-century section so exciting. The nationalist fervour is only too evident in Bertalan Székely's historical works such as *The Return of Buda in 1686*, but the grief is there also, maybe more profoundly, in his portraits.

It is easy to see the **influences from the rest of Europe**, particularly France, but for the most part these styles are given a distinctly Hungarian turn, and the artists are at their best when they rise above outside influences and bare their souls, as in László Mednyánszky's dark, brooding, Expressionist oils. A room in wing B is devoted to the works of Mihály Munkácsy and László Paál. The former, who worked largely in Munich and Paris, was one of the few to gain recognition in the rest of Europe. He is well known for paintings with a social conscience such as *The Condemned Cell* and *Tramps at Night*, but also produced landscapes such as the Turneresque *Dusty Road*. Paál mainly painted landscapes of a Realist nature. Also in wing B look out for works by the 'father of Hungarian Impressionism', Pál Szinyei Merse, such as *Picnic in May*. The varied collection of Károly Lotz—whose frescoes adorn the ceilings of almost every major building in town—includes the beautiful, life-size *Woman Bathing*.

Second and Third Floors

These half-empty floors may be a hangover from the days when the favoured forms of art were old, safe and socialist, necessitating some catching up. What is here comprises the 20th-century collection, and temporary exhibitions are also held here. Much of the work on these floors is by **The Eight**, a group from the influential artists' colonies such as Nagybánya, who established Hungary's first avant-garde school. The most notable examples of their work are Róbert Berény's *Woman Playing the Cello*, and Ödön Márffy's *The Old Toll-house at Vác* and *The Oarsmen*. One of the most immediately likeable artists, but probably the worst lit, is Károly Ferenczy. His work seems characterized by a certain serenity, such as in his *Self-portrait: The Painter*, or the informal peasant setting of his *Sermon on the Mount*. Note also the extremely idiosyncratic style of Tihanyi Lajos' portraits.

In the works of the **20th century**, general trends are ever more apparent, though the critics are not always sure what to call them. József Rippl-Rónai has been called Art Nouveau and Impressionist. See his works such as *Woman with a Birdcage* and decide for yourself. Somewhere between Art Nouveau and Symbolism are János Vaszary (*The Golden Age*) and Simon Hollósy (*Dancing Girls at the Outskirts of the Forest*). One artist everyone agrees on, even Picasso, is Tivador Kosztka Csontváry. It seems that this enigmatic, possibly mad, visionary discovered that he could draw when he sketched on the back of a prescription form a dozing oxen tied to a cart outside a chemist's shop. He is considered self-taught, though he studied in Rome, Paris and Munich. When Picasso first saw his work he apparently asked to be left alone with the paintings for an hour with the doors locked, and said, 'And I thought I was the only great painter of our century.' Csontváry is represented by a handful of paintings including *Pilgrimage to the Cedars of Lebanon* and *Ruins of the Greek Theatre at Taormina*. Most of his works, apparently saved after his death just as his family were about to sell them off as tarpaulin, are in Pécs, about 125 miles south of Budapest.

Amongst all this, everyone will surely find much that appeals. In spite of, maybe because of, its difficult history, Hungary has quietly amassed a wealth of artistic achievement of which any country would be proud. And this without even mentioning the **sculpture**. Here you will have to follow the dictates of your own tastes, for if anything this is an even more subjective art form than painting. The pieces here are mostly nudes and extremely well executed, with a life-affirming delight in the beauty of the human form.

At the end, if you still haven't had enough, for a fee you can be taken on a tour of the Palatine crypt below, which was built in 1715. Ask at the reception desk for details.

Museum of Contemporary Art (Ludwig Collection or Kortárs Müvészeti)

Open Tues–Sun 10–6, closed Mon; adm; ludwig@c3.hu.

The excessive use of red marble in the atrium used for temporary exhibitions is a hangover from the socialist days when this wing housed the Museum of the Working Class Movement. With the laughably oversized staircase, this makes it difficult to take many of the artworks seriously. Much of the stuff here is really modern, so much so that no accepted views of what to think of it have yet been laid down. The core of the collection was donated by the German billionaire and art patron Peter Ludwig, who is reputed to have bought at least one painting every day, largely according to his own enthusiasm rather than for investment purposes. Here you will find works of famous 1960s and 70s pop-artists such as Warhol, Rauschenberg, Lichtenstein, Hockney, Jasper Johns and Claes Oldenburg, as well as some lesser-known Europeans and even the odd Hungarian such as Miklós Erdély (*War Secrets*).

Outside the museum is the **Matthias Fountain** on the south wall. It is based on the legend of Szép Ilonka (Helen the Fair), a peasant girl who fell in love with the king when he was out hunting, accompanied by his head huntsman and Italian chronicler. Upon discovering his identity and understanding the hopelessness of her love, she died of a broken heart. To the left is the chronicler, while to the right is poor Ilonka, cossetting the animal her beloved is intent on killing. To the right, two lions guard the gate which leads into the courtyard named after them, within which are entrances to the National Library and the Budapest History Museum.

Budapest History Museum (Budapesti Történeti Múzeum)

Open Wed–Mon 10–4, closed Tues; adm.

This is definitely worth a visit, since it helps to bring Budapest's tumultuous history to life. It is probably best to start on the top floor, where the history lesson begins with artefacts and accounts of those original Magyars descended from the turul-bird. There is little left to show of the intermediate period of the city's past, when the Mongols and Turks seemed bent on all-out destruction, but this deficiency is made good by the splendid, well-designed permanent collection *Budapest in Modern Times*, from the overthrow of the Turks in 1686 to the present.

Downstairs in the basement are exhibited the remains of the **medieval palace** that in its heyday was praised as one of the grandest in all Christendom. Alas, the rooms that it was possible to restore were only of minor importance. The best are the vaulted royal chapel and a Gothic hall which is home to the collection of Gothic statues unearthed in 1974. Ironically, these only survived the Ottoman ravages because in the 15th century no space could be found for them, so they were dumped out in a yard that was later filled in. In summer, a door leads from here to the bastions and courtyards on the palace's southern side.

National Széchenyi Library (Nemzeti Szécsenyi Könyvtár)

Open Aug–June Mon 1–9pm, Tues–Sat 9am–9pm, closed July and Sun; adm.

This library was founded in 1802 thanks to Count Ferenc Széchenyi, father of the famous reformer and national hero (*see* 'The Greatest Hungarian', p.223). He scoured the country for books which he bought out of his own pocket and donated to the nation, a collection of some 17,000 books and manuscripts. Today the library contains five million books, including everything that has ever been published in or about Hungary or was written by a Hungarian. There are also newspapers, journals, small prints, and collections of maps, music and theatre history. Chief among its treasures are the earliest surviving records of the Hungarian language, from around the 13th century, and the *Corviniani*, a collection of ancient books and manuscripts, some beautifully illustrated, which originally belonged to King Matthias. There are usually some items being exhibited.

Matthias Church (Mátyás Templom)

Open daily 7am–8pm. Mass 7am, 8.30am and 6pm, also Sun and hols 10am (Latin mass) and noon.

The square dominated by this church, Szentháromság tér, is the focal point of Castle Hill, thronged by tourists, tricksters, leaflet-distributors and more. All the more reason to arrive early or late. At night the church is more beautiful, and the whole area timelessly romantic. Try to attend a concert in the church: apart from the atmosphere, the acoustics are excellent.

Undoubtedly one of Budapest's finest buildings, the Matthias Church's chequered past began way back in the early 13th century, following the Mongol invasion. It originally resembled the northern French Gothic, before Sigismund of Luxembourg remodelled it into a hall-church in high Gothic style. Matthias, after whom it was named, made his own improvements and was married here twice. Under the Turks, the furnishings were destroyed, the walls whitewashed and the church restyled as a mosque. Back in Christian hands after the siege, it was given to the Franciscans, then the Jesuits, who decorated it in a Baroque style. Poor as its condition was by 1867, it was still considered worthy to host the coronation of Franz Joseph as King of Hungary, for which Liszt's *Coronation Mass* was specially composed.

Much needed reconstruction took place between 1873 and 1896 under architect Frigyes Schulek. Keen to preserve the past, he noted the original features revealed as the walls were pulled down and built them into his new structure, including much of the wall decoration. He also added a lot of his own. Thus, he kept the original tower intact up to the third floor, after which he followed his own vision. Like so much of this district, the building is neither old nor new, but rather a view of many past ages through the distorting lens of the present.

It takes a while to realize why this church makes the impact it does. Partly it is the proliferation of detail, always sure to overawe the senses, and the colourful tiling of the roof. But mainly it is the sheer height of the tower, which raises this church in every way above similar constructions. At 80m it could lose a whole section without appearing squat. Before going inside have a closer look at the front left **Béla Tower**, named after the church's original founder, which has retained many Gothic features; and the stained-glass **rose window** which is unfortunately hidden inside by a pipe organ. Above all, have a good look above the door at the **Mary Portal**, Schulek's reconstruction of one of the greatest pieces of Gothic stone carving in Hungary, depicting the Assumption of the Virgin Mary.

Inside, every inch of wall space has been painted, not like the Sistine Chapel—there are few biblical scenes or figures—but with repetitive patterns of a floral or geometrical nature, sometimes resembling Polynesian, Aboriginal or Native American art, and adding up almost to an Art Nouveau effect. They were designed by Bertalan Székely. The overall effect is one of infinite warmth, in marked contrast to the starkness of so many churches. Here the worshipper—for this is still above all a place of worship—is not overawed and intimidated, but cheered and welcomed. The God who resides in this house feels much more approachable than most. But he still has a penchant for gold. Much of that present is on the altar, whose design was based on Gothic triptychs, and which repeats the Trinity figures from the column outside.

The three arched stained-glass windows on the south wall were designed by Schulek, Székely and Károly Lotz. The participation of these latter two artists helps to explain the overall quality of the art present. Above the Mary Portal are five circular paintings by Lotz showing the *birth and childhood of Christ*. To its right is the original coat of arms of King Matthias. Nearby, inside the Loreto Chapel below the south tower, is a Baroque *Madonna* in Italian style from the 17th century. Legend has it that the original was set into a wall during the Turkish occupation. When the walls were crumbling during the siege of 1686, she reappeared, scaring the Turks out of their wits and assuring them of their imminent defeat.

On the north side in the Trinity Chapel lies the tomb of King Béla III and his wife Anne de Châtillon. Their double sarcophagus lies below a richly carved stone canopy. In the **crypt** is a red marble sarcophagus housing bones from the royal tombs in Székesfehérvár, and a small collection of ecclesiastical treasures and relics. From here a staircase leads to St Stephen's Chapel, containing a bust of the king, and various scenes from his life. More stairs lead to the **Royal Oratory**, exhibiting a replica of the Hungarian crown jewels (the real ones are in the Parliament), and coronation thrones of Emperors Franz Joseph and Karl IV.

The **Holy Trinity Column**, by the church, erected in thanksgiving for the end of the plague in 1713 and in the hopes of fending off another, is surmounted by the eponymous trio: a bearded Father rests his hand on the globe, the Son clutches his cross, and the mystical Spirit is represented by a dove emitting rays of light.

Fishermen's Bastion (Halászbástya)

In the Middle Ages there was a fish market near to this spot and the Guild of Fishermen were responsible for defending this part of the wall. Nowadays, this rampart fulfils a strictly aesthetic function. It was designed by Schulek to complement the Matthias Church. In both, the mood is one of romantic chivalry, playfulness and an almost child-like sense of wonder. With its zigzagging white ramparts, curving stairways and ice-cream-cone turrets (seven, symbolising the Magyar tribes who founded the nation), it looks like it leapt from the pages of a fairy-tale book. It also offers some of the best views of Pest available (for a cheeky 200Ft).

Around Szentháromság Tér

The large bronze equestrian **statue** in the cobbled area between church and bastion represents King Stephen, justly, as a grim and powerful figure. At the end of the 10th century he unified the Magyar tribes into one nation, of which he was the first king. Born Vajk, he became Stephen (or István) when he converted to Christianity and forced his nation to do the same, a move that facilitated their integration into Europe. He is depicted here wearing the famous crown sent for his coronation by Pope Sylvester II. The relief at the back shows Shulek (who designed the neo-Romanesque plinth) kneeling modestly before the king, offering him a model of the Matthias Church.

From this angle the **Budapest Hilton** looks badly out of place and, despite the funky reflections of the church, statue and bastion thrown off by its copper-glass façade, you may wonder why it was allowed to be built. But follow the bastion round to its end, go through the gate (normally open) that leads behind the hotel and you will find yourself in the remains of a medieval church from 1254. This Dominican courtyard, uncovered during excavations in 1902, was incorporated by architect Bela Pinter into the design of the hotel, and now provides the stage for concerts and operettas during the summer season. The hotel's Faust Wine Cellar is a reconstruction from remains of the original monastery wine cellar. At the hotel's front on Hess András tér the façade has been built to integrate remains of a late Baroque Jesuit college. To the left of the entrance is St Nicholas' Tower, containing a copy of the 1486 *Matthias Relief* from Germany, generally considered to be the only genuine likeness of the great man. The overall achievement is admirable, and from the Pest embankment the hotel's bulk looming behind the church is discreet enough to take very little away from the scene.

Hess András tér was named after the man who established the nation's first printing-press. His workshop is believed to have occupied the site of the Fortuna Restaurant. At No.6 is the **House of Hungarian Wines** (Magyar Borok Háza; *open June–Sept Mon–Fri 1–9, Sat–Sun 11–9; Oct–May daily 11–7*), whose extensive cellar holds some 550 different wines from Hungary's 20-odd growing regions, making it one of the biggest wine collections in Europe. For a mere $7–$8 you can help yourself to a selection of 60 or 70 of these, taking as much time as you like, and learn everything about Hungarian wine. There are explanations in English.

Walking the Streets

Don't approach travel as if it were work, racing from one compulsory site to another. In Castle Hill the main attraction is atmosphere, and the past presents itself through the accumulation of details. Wander these ancient streets and observe how each house distinguishes itself through countless tiny variables, hinting at its own secret story. Look at the huge doors; the windows with their bars and boxes; the roofs dotted with spikes, vents, chimneys or tiny windows; the wrought-iron grilles, torch-carriers, sign-holders; the pastel shades, murals, niches, sculptures, plaques. Take in the street-lamps, the cobbled streets, the tiny alleyways and the listed-building (*műemlék*) signs giving details you won't understand.

As you walk away from the Royal Palace past the Sikló, another giant of a building looms, looking like it must contain something terribly important. This is the **Sándor Palace**, presently unused. Its only claim to fame occurred on 2 April 1941 when the prime minister, Count Pál Teleki, shot himself as a gesture of disgust when Hungary joined Germany in its invasion of Yugoslavia only months after signing with them a treaty of eternal friendship. Next door is another grand but under-used building, the **Castle Theatre** (*Várszínház*). Originally built for the Carmelite order in 1736, it housed the first ever play in Hungarian, performed by the first professional acting troupe in 1790. These days it is only used as a studio theatre.

On the other side of Dísz tér (Parade Square) the road splits. **Úri utca** (Lord Street), on the left, runs to the northern end of Castle Hill and is probably its finest street. The stand-out house is No.31, its almost entirely Gothic façade thought to look as it did in the late 15th century, though the core dates back to the 14th century. In 1862 it was redesigned in a Romantic style but, after these decorations were destroyed in 1945, great efforts were taken to restore the medieval façade. No.49, the former Poor Clares' cloister, houses the **Telephone Museum** (*open Tues–Sun 10–6, closed Mon; adm*), containing everything from ancient Bakelite contraptions to state-of-the-art technology, presented in a fun, hands-on way.

The other fork, Tárnok utca, leads to the small **Golden Eagle Pharmacy Museum** at No.18 (*open Tues–Sun 10.30–5.30, closed Mon; adm*). This 15th-century house was the second home of Buda's oldest pharmacy, established after the defeat of the Turks and here since the mid-18th century. A reconstruction of an alchemist's laboratory features various dried creatures along with the alembics. Original texts include an early 17th-century Paracelsus, a 13th-century Roger Bacon and a 16th-century Geber. Look out for the 17th-century Italian map showing Buda's fortifications at the time of the Turkish occupation with Pest nothing but a tiny village. There's no labelling in English but the enthusiastic lady will gladly guide and explain.

From here Tárnok utca leads to **Szentháromság tér** (Holy Trinity Square) and the Matthias Church. On the southwest corner is the former **Buda Town Hall**, one corner bearing a statue of Pallas Athene, protector of cities. Turn left for the famous **Ruszwurm Cukrászda**, whose lavish antique interior makes it as much a part of the historical tour as a great place for coffee and cake. Opposite is the statue of András Hadik, better known as the **Hussar Statue**. These infantrymen, first organized by King Matthias in 1480, wore no armour because their weapon was speed. Armed with sabres, pikes and pointed daggers, they specialized in fast, unexpected attacks, with such success that soon every army in Europe had a similar regiment. The image of the Hussar still holds a place in the heart of the Hungarian people. As well as capturing the poise of effortless understanding between horse and rider, this statue has another interesting feature: its gleaming, smooth testicles. Touching them is believed to bring luck in exams.

From here three streets run roughly parallel to and to the right of Úri u. Táncsics u contains the **Music History Museum** at No.7, in the grand Erdödy Palace where Beethoven stayed in 1800 (*open April–Oct Tues–Sun 10–6, Nov–Mar Tues–Sun 10–5, closed Mon; adm*). In this fascinating selection of 17th–19th-century instruments, the classical exhibits include finely ornamented lyres and a unique tongue-shaped violin, while the folk section has a gardon (a primitive cello), bagpipes, zithers and cowhorns. The emphasis is on the instruments as works of art. As well as temporary exhibits, there is a collection of Bartók's scores and scribblings. Down the street at No.26 is the **Medieval Jewish Prayer House** (*open May–Oct Tues–Fri 10–2, Sat–Sun 10–6, closed Mon*). Foundations of a large synagogue dating back to the 15th century were discovered here. The interest of the museum lies not so much in the small exhibition of tombstones and liturgical objects, but in the space itself, used as a house of prayer during the Turkish occupation.

The **Museum of Hungarian Commerce and Catering**, Fortuna u. 4, is much more interesting than you'd expect (*open Wed–Fri 10–5, Sat–Sun 10–6, closed Mon–Tues; adm*). The commerce section includes early 19th-century advertisements, antique shopfronts, a provincial grocery store, Hungary's first electric billboard (advertising beer) and, the *pièce de résistance*, an HMV dog that taps its paws against the window to catch the attention of passers-by. In the catering section we learn about the men behind the names Gundel and Gerbeau. Keeping up the foody theme on the same street is the idiosyncratic **Pierrot Café** (No.14). Farther left, Országház u. (Parliament Street) gained its name from a period in the 1790s when the Parliament (Diet) met in the large building at No.28, originally a convent of Poor Clares.

At the northern end of Castle Hill, all streets converge on two conjoined squares. To the east is Bécsi Kapu tér, named after the **Vienna Gate**, built to celebrate the 250th anniversary of the recapture of Buda. Climb on top of the gate for a better view of the **Lutheran Church**, built at the end of the 19th century, with its unusual spire. Through the gate and to the right is Europa Grove, so named because in 1972 city mayors from all over Europe planted 16 types of tree in honour of the centenary of the unification of Buda, Óbuda and Pest. Lovas u., curving left under the castle walls, has a collection of Budapest street-lamps dating from 1844 to 1944.

Back on the square, the hulking neo-Romanesque National Archives building is saved from total po-facedness by the multicoloured roof. Next door is the **Military History Museum** (*open Tues–Sun 10–4, closed Mon; adm*) in a former barracks. Permanent displays include 'The History of Hand Weapons from the Stone Axe to the Pistol', exhibits on the 1848 Revolution, and an evocative look at the 'Thirteen Days' of street-fighting during the 1956 Uprising (newsreel footage at 11am and 2pm). Outside is a **statue** of Friar John Capistranus, after whom this bigger square, Kapisztrán tér, is named. This zealous Italian Franciscan urged the Crusaders on to victory in the siege of Belgrade in 1456. Here he stands over a dead Turk, exhorting the soldiers to produce more. Over the road is the **Mary Magdalene Tower**, modelled on the original Baroque spire, after the war destroyed the rest of the church. In the Middle Ages, the Hungarians worshipped here, while the Germans got Matthias Church. The remains of the foundations stand between this strangely solitary tower (housing a private art gallery) and the even more eerie sight of a single tall window. Adding to the oddness is the tower's peal of ornamental bells, apparently capable of rattling through a melody compiled by a jazz pianist.

A chestnut-tree-lined street, Tóth Árpád sétány, hugs the western ramparts of the hill, offering views of the Buda Hills, Gellért and Tabán. The entrance to the Military History Museum is on this street, announced by a collection of historical cannons. Round the corner is the **Abdurrahman Memorial**, a tomb with an inscription in Hungarian and Turkish that reads: 'It was near this site that the last governor [pasha] of the 143-year-long Turkish rule in Buda fell in battle at the age of 70. A valiant foe, may he rest in peace.' The monument was paid for by the descendants of Hungarian soldier György Szabó, who fell on the same day as the pasha.

The Caves

Úri utca 9. Open daily 9.30–7.30; adm.

Castle Hill is topped by an 11m-thick layer of limestone, within which thermal springs have hollowed out a series of natural cavities. The first Magyar inhabitants of the hill developed and connected them. Over the centuries of invasions the cave network repeatedly proved its worth, growing in length and sophistication all the while. Sometimes it was the invaders themselves, such as the Turks, who saw their military potential. In peaceful times, the caves were partitioned and used as cellars. In the Second World War they were used as air-raid shelters for up to 10,000 people and contained a hospital. During the Cold War they held a secret military installation. Nowadays they are touted as a tourist attraction by a private concern. You can visit a small section of the 10km labyrinth of passages. Attractions include copies of the most famous European cave paintings such as Lascaux, reconstructions of historical scenes, images of labyrinths from different ages and cultures, and the chance to prove your bravery and sense of directon by walking around alone. After 6pm the tour is by oil lamp. It sounds good but is probably only worth it for those who really want to see the caves.

Gellért Hill, Tabán and Víziváros

These three areas line the Buda embankment from the Liberty Bridge (Szabadság híd) in the south to the Margaret Bridge (Margit híd) in the north. From the Pest side the geography is easily understood. Gellért Hill (Gellért-hegy) is the steep green expanse to the left, Tabán the flatter green area between this and Castle Hill, and Vízíváros the narrow strip running between castle and river. Each contains a few little gems, worth a visit if you're in the area.

Gellért Hill (Gellért-Hegy)

If Castle Hill is the focal point of the Buda panorama, Gellért Hill is the top tier on the cake and the Liberty Statue its cherry. It is the final piece of inspiration that gives the whole work an entirely new level of meaning. As well a context and backdrop to the Buda skyline, this 460ft dolomite cliff offers the best views of Pest and Castle Hill. For centuries the lower slopes of Gellért Hill were used for cultivating grapevines (a specimen still grows in the courtyard of the Museum of Commerce and Catering). The name Gellért derives from an 11th-century Benedictine abbot from Venice, Ghirardus (Gellért in Hungarian, Gerard in English), who King Stephen asked to help convert the Magyars to Christianity, as well as tutoring his son, Imre.

The Gellért Hotel and Baths

Budapest's most famous hotel sits like a country mansion at the end of the elegant Liberty Bridge, which looks as though, like a driveway, it were constructed for this purpose alone. (In fact it was built for the Millennium celebrations in 1896, when it was opened by Franz Joseph, whose name it originally bore.) By the time the hotel was built, the healing properties of the hot springs that bubbled up at this site had been recognized for at least seven centuries. An old legend has it that spring comes to Gellért Hill three weeks earlier than the rest of Budapest thanks to the dynamic power of the thermal waters. In the Middle Ages a hospital stood on the site, and the Turks, who knew about such things, constructed their own baths. So Gellért was designed very much as a spa hotel to help promote Budapest as a spa town. But it was taken over the year after its completion by Béla Kún's Communist régime, then by the Romanian army, and finally by Admiral Horthy following his entry on a white horse and declaration of intent to cleanse the 'sinful city'.

Despite this interlude, the Gellért lived up to the hopes invested in it, becoming in the 1920s a social high spot for Budapest's upper classes and later enjoying an international reputation that attracted the royal, powerful, rich and famous from all over Europe. Yet after the party-pooper of 1939 it was goodbye to all that: only the outer walls survived the war. Although the interior is not original you would not know it, and the hotel's reputation for excellence has never waned. It is a sight that should not be missed.

The exterior is unabashedly Art Nouveau. The cylindrical form of the towers and turrets lends them an Oriental flavour. Note the lyre and bird motifs on the elaborate balustrades of the

Lunch and Cafés

Marcello, XI. Bartók Béla u. 40, © 466 6231. *Open Mon–Sat noon–10*. Popular and intimate Italian: an incredible range of pizzas, a good salad bar and a no-smoking policy. One of the few options in Gellért.

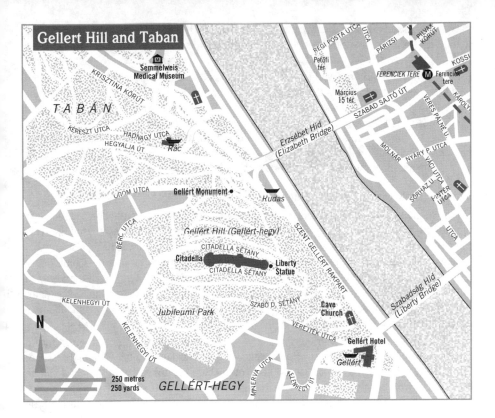

Gellert Hill and Taban

balconies. Step into the busy entrance hall to admire the opulent décor, the mosaics and statues. On the right, at the top of a flight of stairs, is a radiant stained-glass window, which recounts the story of the magic stag, an old Hungarian legend famously rendered in the poetry of János Arany.

Entrance to the **baths** is on the hotel's right flank as you face it (© 466 6166; *open May–Sept daily 6am–7pm; Oct–April Mon–Fri 6am–7pm, Sat–Sun 6am–5pm; adm, reduced rate after 5pm*; trams 47 or 49 from the Kiskörút). They offer sheer opulence, decorated throughout in ornate Art Nouveau style replete with statues, columns, mosaics, glazed tiles, ornate ceilings, lion-headed spouts and myriad other details only the wealthy could once afford. Ignore those around you and imagine that you are royalty. Rarely does life offer the opportunity to partake of so much grandeur for so little money. The baths are mixed-sex, with segregated hot-tubs and steam-rooms. They offer all the variety of pools, plus an outdoor swimming pool and sunbathing terrace. The carbonic gas-rich water is good for those with blood-pressure problems and coronary heart disease.

The Cave Church (Sziklatemplom)

Opposite the entrance to the baths, a path leads a short way uphill (to the right) to the Cave Church (wheelchair accessible). Established in 1926 and based by designer Kálmán Lux on the shrine at Lourdes, the church was intended for the Pauline order of monks. This is the only order indigenous to Hungary, traditionally confessors to the king, founded in 1256 by

Eusebius of Esztergom and dissolved in 1773 by Josef II. It was built and they came—15 of them, back from a 150-year exile in Poland. Unfortunately, in the 1950s the Communists jailed the monks for 'treasonable acts' and sealed the entrance of the church. It was reopened in 1989.

It may be in a cave, but everywhere the coldness of ceiling and walls is enlivened by potted plants, stained glass and art. At the very back a giant bronze Polish eagle contains a copy of the *Black Madonna* of Czestochowa. In the chapel, look for Béli Ferenc's wooden sculptures, and check out some of the whimsical art in the area behind the altar. All of this is rather let down by the gaudy plastic Christ above the altar. But then this is not a tourist attraction: it is a working church, and a busy one at that. A large congregation attends the hour-long masses at 11am, 5pm and 8pm, during which times tourists are asked to remain outside and silent.

The Citadella and Liberty Statue

On the summit of Gellért Hill squats the low, bulky **Citadella**, not an attraction as much as a pinnacle from which to see everything else. The site was chosen by the Habsburgs with this in mind. After quashing the 1848–9 Revolution, they constructed this grim edifice, a stronghold from which to survey and control, and which was impossible to ignore. After the Compromise of 1867, citizens breached its hated walls and called for its destruction. For all that, only in 1897 did the Austrian soldiers leave. Since then it has housed a prison camp, an SS regiment, the homeless, an anti-aircraft battery and, nowadays, a restaurant, café, hotel, nightclub and a small **museum** about the Celtic Eravisci, the first inhabitants of this hill, 2,000 years ago.

Mainly, though, people come for the views, among them that of the adjacent **Liberty Statue**, which is far too tall to take in from below. Designed by Hungarian sculptor Zsigmond Kisfaludi Stróbl, Lady Liberty stands 46ft high (100ft if you include her colossal pedestal), and can be seen clearly from anywhere in Pest. The story goes that this statue was originally commissioned by Regent Miklós Horthy to commemorate his son István, killed in a plane crash on the Russian front. But after the German units were finally prised out of Castle Hill, a Russian marshall supposedly saw this figure in a sculptor's workshop and had the propeller she was intended to hold swapped for a palm leaf, thus creating a monument to the Soviet soldiers who died in the 'liberation'. When the Communists themselves finally got the message and retreated, many wanted the statue destroyed or removed. In the end the statue was recycled. The figure of a Russian soldier (now in the Statue Park) and a plaque listing Russian war casualties were removed. For all that, something about the pedestal, maybe its unnecessary height or functional solidity, mark this out as a Soviet creation.

The Gellért Monument

A quarter of the way up Gellért Hill, facing Elisabeth Bridge, stands this statue of the eponymous saint (bear left on your way down from the Citadella). The pagans he was converting put up with Gellért's evangelizing while King Stephen was alive, but legend tells that in 1046, eight years after the ruler's death, a rebellion erupted against Christianity during which the saint was put into a barrel and pushed off this hill into the Danube. The barrel could have been nail-studded or merely a wheelbarrow, depending which version you choose to believe.

Now that Christianity again has the upper hand, Gellért has been restored to his full dignity. Built in 1904, this near-40ft statue shows him holding his cross aloft in perpetual reproach to the sinners across the water in Pest, while at his feet kneels one of the newly converted Magyar heathen.

An alternative way down the hill involves following the paved road past the viewing spot until you hit a junction, then bearing right and getting lost amidst the maze of lanes and narrow streets. This would appeal to lovers of grand houses and mansions, with which this green area is overflowing. Most of them are embassies. If you keep going down you will, of course, eventually get back to the river and the jumble of roads that carve up the area of Tabán.

Tabán

This area gets its name from the tanning workshops here during the Turkish occupation. The Turks took advantage of the thermal waters, building two magnificent baths, the only part to survive the siege of 1686. When the Turks retreated from Hungary, they still occupied the Balkans, and many Serbs fleeing from them settled here. Around 1700, 95 per cent of the area's inhabitants were Serbian (*Rácok* in Hungarian). As Greeks and Romanies followed suit, a dense, cosmopolitan and essentially impoverished population gave the quarter a run-down, bohemian flavour, famous for its bars, brothels and gambling dens; ancient rambling streets; whitewashed houses with red tile roofs, wine gardens and orchards. Unfortunately, this nostalgic simplicity also entailed open sewers, and in 1908 the City Council declared the whole area a health hazard and razed it. Thankfully the baths survived, as did the splendid **Tabán Parish Church** on Attila út. The arterial roads that now choke it were constructed during the Communist years and mean that the area is only worth visiting for one of its notable sights.

The **Rác Baths** (I. Hadnagy u. 8–10, ✆ 356 1322; *open 6.30am–7pm; women Mon, Wed, Fri; men Tues, Thurs, Sat; adm*), at the foot of Gellért Hill where it meets Tabán, are named after the Hungarian word for Serb. The building contains a Turkish octagonal pool and dome, though its exterior is 19th century. The waters are good for chronic arthritis and muscle and nerve pain, though the baths are now more famous for their gay scene.

The **Rudas Baths** (I. Döbrentei tér 9, ✆ 356 1322; *open Mon–Fri 6am–6pm, Sat–Sun 6am–1pm; adm*), built in the 16th century on a site occupied by baths since the 14th century, are the most atmospheric of the Turkish baths. The original octagonal pool and cupola combined with the dim, rather dank interior, saturated with steam and echoing sounds, make for a potent and timeless experience. Light slants in at different angles through small octagonal windows in the dome. As well as six pools of differing temperatures, including the hottest in town at 46° C, there are three saunas and two steam rooms. A fountain allows you to drink the warm, sulphurous water, supposedly good for gastric complaints. Occasionally, the Rudas pays host to a uniquely Budapestian phenomenon known as *Vizimozi*, basically a rave in the main swimming pool accompanied by silent movies shown on a big screen, or ethno-trance music in the Turkish baths. It also offers bars, a gallery, and a dancefloor in the hallway.

The **Semmelweis Museum of Medical History** (Semmelweis Orvostörténeti Muzeum, I. Apród u. 1–3, ✆ 201 1577; *open Tues–Sun 10.30–5.30, closed Mon; adm*), situated near the Rudas Baths, exhibits items relating to medicine, including a medieval chastity belt and some 18th-century beeswax anatomical models. It's based in the house where Dr Ignác Semmelweis was born: he suggested that childbirth survival rates in hospitals would improve if doctors who had been, say, carrying out post-mortems washed their hands before going on to deliver babies.

The striking white **bridge** which leads from the jumble of roads across to Pest was named after Franz Joseph's wife Elisabeth. Nicknamed Sisi, she was a beautiful and rather tragic figure, unsuited to the straitjacket of royalty. Much loved by the Hungarians, whose language she spoke, she was greatly mourned following her assassination in 1898. This was the only bridge destroyed in the war not rebuilt according to its original form, although it does imitate the old chain bridge's much loved arch. Constructed in 1964, this bridge has almost become a symbol for the city, maybe because it was her first modern yet beautiful construction.

The Chain Bridge (Széchenyi Lánchíd)

Before the 1840s, Buda and Pest were by necessity separate towns because they were divided by the Danube. It was impossible to build a bridge of wood and stone over a river this wide. A pontoon bridge operated between autumn and spring, there were occasional ferries, and in winter the water froze so that sometimes even carts could cross, but still people got stuck on the wrong side for weeks when a sudden thaw set in. Like many examples of 19th-century progress, the first permanent bridge across the Danube was István Széchenyi's initiative. In 1820 he had to wait a week for a ferry across to attend his father's funeral, and decided that it wasn't good enough. He sent to Britain for an English engineer, William Tierney Clark (who designed the similar Hammersmith Bridge), and a Scottish masterbuilder, Adam Clark (no relation), and even had the iron shipped over. In 1849, before it was completed, the Austrians tried to blow it up, but Adam Clark thwarted their plans by flooding the anchorage chambers and destroying the pumps that could have been used to drain them. The colonel who tried to use explosives despite this was blown to pieces. But the Uprising failed, and the bridge was finished off under Austrian command. One bitter irony is that the first person to cross the bridge at its opening was the cruel and much hated General Julius Haynau, at whose behest the equally despised Citadella would be constructed.

A story has it that Adam Clark was so proud of his masterpiece that he swore he would drown himself if the slightest fault was found with it. Eventually it was noted (erroneously) that the splendid lions at either end had no tongues, and Clark duly topped himself. Not true, of course. Actually, he liked the city so much that he married a local girl and stayed to construct the **tunnel** that runs under Castle Hill as a direct continuation of the bridge, whose style it complements. Flanked by two pairs of Doric columns, it was clearly built with an eye to the aesthetic. The joke amongst Budapesters at the time was that it would be a good place to put the new bridge when it rained. Today the Chain Bridge is a symbol of the city, for its beauty as much as its technological prowess. When, 95 years after its construction, the Germans blew up all of the Danube's bridges, this was the first to be reconstructed, and to the same design.

The Sikló running up to Castle Hill starts its journey in Clark Ádám tér. At its foot, a small garden contains a curious concrete doughnut. This is the **Kilometer Zero stone**. Sculptor Miklós Borsos intended it to express not just zero but the beginning of everything, the origins of all life. It signifies that this is the centre of Budapest: all distances in the country are measured from here; and justly so, for this is where the three component towns of Pest, Buda and Óbuda were given their first permanent physical link, paving the way for their official union in 1872.

Víziváros

The thin stretch of land north of the Chain Bridge has been called Víziváros or 'Water Town' since the Middle Ages. While the royal court and its associated gentry enjoyed the views from the hill, people down here were mainly fishermen, craftsmen and traders. The Turks depopulated the area, turned its churches into mosques and left behind the Király baths. The 18th

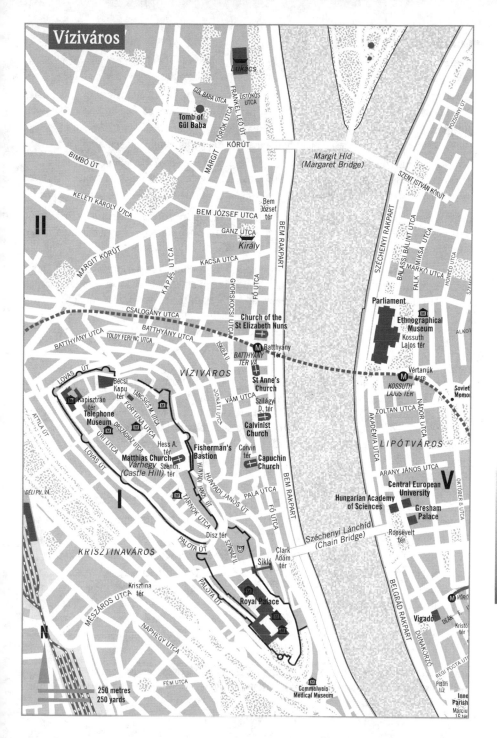

Víziváros

Lukács

GÜL BABA UTCA · FRANKEL LEÓ ÚT · ÜSTÖKÖS UTCA

Tomb of
Gül Baba

MARGIT · TÖRÖK UTCA

KÖRÚT

BIMBÓ ÚT

Margit Híd
(Margaret Bridge)

SZENT ISTVÁN KÖRÚT

POZSONYI ÚT

KELETI KÁROLY UTCA

II

MARGIT KÖRÚT

BEM JÓZSEF UTCA

Bem
József
tér

GANZ UTCA

Király

KAPAS UTCA

KACSA UTCA

GYORSKOCSI UTCA

FŐ UTCA

BEM RAKPART

SZÉCHENYI RAKPART

BALASSI BÁLINT UTCA

FALK MIKSA UTCA

MARKÓ UTCA

HONVÉD UTCA

Parliament

Ethnographical
Museum
Kossuth
Lajos tér

ALKOT

CSALOGÁNY UTCA

Church of the
St Elizabeth Nuns

BATTHYÁNY UTCA

BATTHYÁNY UTCA · TOLDY FERENC UTCA

ISKOLA U.

Batthyány

BATTHYÁNY
TÉR VÁ

VÉRTANÚK
tere

KOSSUTH
LAJOS TÉR

Soviet
Memor

LOVAS ÚT

VÍZIVÁROS

St Anne's
Church

VÁM UTCA

JONATI UTCA

Szilágyi
D. tér

ZOLTÁN UTCA

NÁDOR UTCA

AKADÉMIA UTCA

Bécsi
Kapu
tér

TÁNCSICS M. UTCA

FORTUNA UTCA

ORSZÁGHÁZ UTCA

Kapisztrán
tér

Telephone
Museum

ÚRI UTCA

Calvinist
Church

LIPÓTVÁROS

ATTILA ÚT

LOVAS ÚT

Hess A.
tér

Matthias Church
Várhegy
(Castle Hill)

Szenth.
tér

Fisherman's
Bastion

HUNYADI JÁNOS ÚT

Corvin
tér

Capuchin
Church

ARANY JÁNOS UTCA

Central European
University

V

OKTÓBER 6 UTCA

DÉLI PU. VÁ

I

TÁRNOK UTCA

PALA UTCA

FŐ UTCA

Hungarian Academy
of Sciences

Gresham
Palace

KRISZTINAVÁROS

Disz tér

PALOTA ÚT

SZÍNHÁZ U.

Clark
Ádám
tér

Siklo

Széchenyi Lánchíd
(Chain Bridge)

Roosevelt
tér

BELGRÁD RAKPART

Krisztina
tér

PALOTA ÚT

Royal Palace

Vigadó

DEÁK F. U.

DUNAKORZÓ

Kristóf
tér

MÉSZÁROS UTCA

N

NAPHEGY UTCA

FÉM UTCA

250 metres
250 yards

Semmelweis
Medical Museum

REGI POSTA UT

Petőfi
tér

Inne
Parish

Márciu
15 tér

VÖRÖ

Lunch and Cafés

Angelika, I. Batthyány tér 7. *Open daily 10–11.* A bastion of old-fashioned style. Coffees, cakes, juices, teas, ice creams, 18 bottled beers and even breakfast.

Gusto's, II. Frankel Leo u. 12. *Open Mon–Sat 10–10.* Intimate, classy but informal café. Good range of beer, coffee and spirits, but only cold food and desserts. The tiramisu is famous.

Belgian Brasserie (Belga Söröző), I. Bem Rakpart 12. *Open daily 12–12.* Popular Belgian-style bar/restaurant, with tasty, plentiful food and a staggering range of beers.

San Remo, II. Török u. 6–8. *Open daily 11am–midnight, closed Mon.* Simple, clean Italian-style cellar. Lots of pizzas and seafood, good range for vegetarians, and a good drinks selection.

---

century witnessed a boom time when some of Buda's more socially elevated citizens built many of the grand houses that can be seen here today, but extensive construction a century later put an end to the small-town atmosphere and the advent of the motor-car killed it off.

Today Víziváros has the feel of a neighbourhood that has known better times and will know them again. In contrast to Castle Hill, many grand old buildings have been let go; the churches are closed, the principal square feels seedy, and the main road heaves with traffic. Yet on a Sunday morning when the churches are open and the roads less busy, it is still possible to catch a whiff of the history that permeates these buildings. It is not dead, only sleeping.

Fő Utca

Literally meaning 'Main Street', this thoroughfare leading northwards from Clark Ádám tér dates back to the times of the Romans. Looking up at the façades, it is clear that this has the potential to be a beautiful and refined district when future waves of yuppies restore the wonderful, faded buildings. Check out the three-sided Romantic building at No.2, or the 1811 remodelling of a medieval house at No.20, with its unusual turreted cylindrical window and reliefs. The process of renovation is already beginning: there are plans to pedestrianize the street; and past the ugly Postmodernist pile of the French Institute with its Constructivist sign, already looking dated in a way these older buildings never will, past the **Capuchin Church**, whose fine statue of St Elizabeth has unfortunately been painted brown, **Corvin tér** presents more evidence. What is at the time of writing a mess of construction should by the time you read this be a grassy square with flowers and a fountain.

Over the road are four houses so striking that old local women stop, mouths agape, to admire them. Recently renovated and painted in pastel shades, they are actually the western face of the brand-new **Art'otel** and demonstrate what could be done with the whole street, thus giving our imaginations a much needed boost. A statue of St John of Nepomuk stands in the niche on No.3's Baroque façade, whilst the neoclassical No.5 carries four **reliefs**, the three above the windows depicting King Matthias as farmer, scholar and commander, the one above the door showing the interior of an alchemist's shop.

Fő utca continues in its unrenovated form practically to Margaret Bridge and contains at least two churches that shouldn't be missed. If the traffic gets too much, try the quieter Iskola utca which runs parallel on the left.

The Calvinist Church (Református Templom)

On Szilágyi tér off Fő u., this neo-Gothic church (finished in 1896) was planned by Sámuel Pecz according to a design traditionally used for medieval Catholic churches. It is one of the most distinctive points of the Buda landscape and an extremely complex, impressive construction. Castle-like and angular, squat and solid rather than elegant, and buttressed on all sides, it still manages to achieve a certain sublime beauty: maybe thanks to the three shades of brick used and the glazed, polychromatic roof-tiles, maybe due to its very complexity. Note the unusual shape of the central 10-sided tower, its roof splaying at the last moment to connect with the walls, or the way the spire is set off to one side. Whatever the appeal, viewed from Pest it stands out as one of a trio with the Matthias Church and Fishermen's Bastion, whose romantic yearnings it reflects. The inside is similarly unornamented but aesthetic, its most showy feature the intricate upper half of the pulpit. Unfortunately, it's usually closed.

The **statue** on a fountain in this square is of the church's architect Pecz dressed as a medieval master builder, a guise the sculptor claimed to have seen him wearing at a fancy-dress ball. The square itself is remembered for one of the more grim events of 1945. This stretch of water is one of the areas where Jews and anti-fascists were brought to be shot. Even after the departure of the SS, the Fascist Arrow Cross rounded up and massacred hundreds of Jews here and dumped their bodies in the river. A plaque commemorates the spot.

The Church of St Anne (Szent Anna Templom)

Open only for services, Mon–Fri 6.45–9am and 4–7pm, Sun and hols 9am–1pm.

Located on faded Batthyány tér off Fő u., this twin-towered parish church is one of Budapest's most beautiful Baroque buildings. Commissioned by the Jesuits, work began in 1740 but was interrupted by financial constraints, an earthquake in 1763, and the abolition of the Jesuit order in 1773. It was not consecrated until 1805. It was badly damaged in the Second World War, and almost pulled down during the construction of the metro due to fears that its foundations would be undermined. On the **façade**, note, from bottom to top, the allegorical figures of Faith, Hope and Charity above the entrance, the central niche with a statue of St Anne and the child Mary, the Buda coat of arms in the tympanum, and above it the eye-in-the-triangle symbol representing the Trinity, flanked by two kneeling angels. Farther up loom the distinctive twin towers, crowned by magnificent Baroque spires with funky green square domes.

Much of the interior dates from the 18th century. The spectacular **high altar**, representing in typically Baroque fashion the child Mary being presented by her mother Anne at the Temple of Jerusalem, was completed in 1773, the finest work of Károly Bebó, who also created the gilded Baroque pulpit swarming with cherubs. The painted **ceiling** in the cupola of the chancel is a 1771 depiction of the Holy Trinity by Gergely Vogl, while the side altars by Antal Eberhardt date from 1768. Note also the delicately carved baptismal font and the figurative scenes carved into the Fő wooden panels of the choir pews. Yet for all the gold and excess of decoration, the green wallpaper, carved wooden Stations of the Cross, vases of flowers and oval portraits create a homely, small-town atmosphere, such that, as in the Matthias Church, the God who resides within these walls comes across as welcoming rather than intimidating.

Outside, **Batthyány tér** epitomizes the current nature of Víziváros, surrounded as it is by grand edifices gone shabby. Note, for instance, the old market building that resembles the best kind of railway station but now houses a Spar supermarket, covered in posters and graffiti.

Worth seeing, though, are the bas-reliefs on the façade of the 18th-century **Hikisch house** at No.3. Reminiscent of sketches from an alchemical treatise, they are depictions of the four seasons. The rococo-style house next door is the former White Cross Inn where Casanova is reputed to have stayed. This is the best place for views of Parliament.

Carrying on down Fő utca, you will pass the **Church of the St Elizabeth Nuns,** looking like a big cake. Inside, the Baroque decoration is absurdly rich, with gold-draped figures every-where: fixed to the walls, loafing around the edge of the pulpit or flanking the paintings, admiring them or pointing to encourage us. The altarpiece of St Francis receiving the stigmata is worth seeing, as is the fresco of St Florian saving Christians from a fire in 1810. All the more pity that it too is locked outside service times. Farther on are the Turkish **Király baths** (II. Fő u. 84, ✆ 201 4392; *open Mon–Fri 6.30am–6pm, Sat 6.30am–12pm; men Mon, Wed, Fri only; women Tues, Thurs, Sat only; adm*). One of the most striking and atmospheric of the baths features a 16th-century Ottoman pool and several smaller pools beneath the original cupola. It was completed by the third Turkish pasha in 1570 just inside the Víziváros castle gates, so that the garrison could bathe even during a siege. The classical section was added in the early 18th century. All the normal baths are here. The surviving Turkish section faces Ganz utca; the neoclassical wing facing Fő utca dates from 1826.

Bem József tér is named after the Polish general whose statue it contains. He fought in the Polish uprising of 1830–31, the Vienna revolt of 1848 and the War of Independence in 1848–9. In three months, he led the revolutionary army to free almost all of Transylvania. Here his arm is in a sling, recalling the decisive battle at Piski. Demonstrations often begin here, as did the march on Parliament at the beginning of the 1956 Uprising.

The road changes name but continues, leading (maybe farther than you would want to go) to the peaceful neoclassical complex of the **Lukács Baths** (II. Frankel Leó u. 25–9, ✆ 326 1695; *open May–Sept Mon–Sat 6am–7pm, Sun 6am–5pm; Oct–April Sat only 6am–5pm; adm*). These mixed-sex baths are set in attractive grounds containing two outdoor swimming pools and the normal thermal pools. The waters are said to be good for orthopaedic diseases.

A short detour off Frankel Leó u. takes you to the **Tomb of Gül Baba.** The name of this Turkish Dervish, a member of the Sufi Bektaşi order, means 'Father of the Roses'. Legend has it that he introduced the rose to Hungary and gave Rózsadomb, this area, its name: Hill of Roses. Hungarians revere him for this even though he participated in the hated Turkish capture of Buda (after which he died at the thanksgiving service). His life has inspired works by the Danish writer Hans Christian Anderson and the Hungarian composer J. Huszka. The site has been restored by the Turkish government and surrounded by a colonnaded parapet. The octagonal tomb is a 1962 reconstruction of the one built in the 1540s by the third pasha of Buda, but the dome that covers it is original. The interior is decorated with Arabic callig-raphy citing the Koran, pictures and Turkish carpets. *At the time of writing the tomb was again closed due to construction work, but looked to be reopened in spring 2001.*

The City (Lipótváros/Leopold Town)

Covering the northern section of inner Pest, this is the financial, banking and business heart of the capital, containing its Parliament and cathedral. Planned in the early 19th century and named Lipótváros after Leopold Habsburg II, it is buzzing on weekdays with people in suits talking on mobile phones, and a ghost town at weekends and in the evenings. Since what is of most interest here is the buildings (of which there are too many striking examples to take in), these quiet times are probably the best ones for a visit. There is a lot to see here, and the selection below is only the cream. But, as is so often the case, it is a good idea just to stroll around, get slightly lost, and see what you see.

Roosevelt Tér

At the time of writing, Roosevelt tér, at the Pest end of the Chain Bridge, is a mess of construction. The main reason to come here is to see the Gresham Palace. It is a sad shadow of its former self, but there is enough left to see how it was, and viewed from the Buda side it still outshines the surrounding buildings. It is being renovated by Gresco, who will turn it into the Four Seasons Hotel. If properly restored, it will rank with Budapest's finest buildings, as well as being *the* place to stay. The façade is Art Nouveau, dotted with fragments of glistening gold mosaic designed by Miksa Róth, who also provided the stained glass on the staircase. The plan is for guests to enter through the delicate wrought-iron peacock gates. The restored original glass cupola will be above the reception. At the top the relief of a male head in a ruff portrays Sir Thomas Gresham, founder of the London Royal Exchange. The ugly building next door dominating the square has been nicknamed 'the Spinach Palace' for its unfortunate colour.

At the north end of the square is the neo-Renaissance **Hungarian Academy of Sciences**. The six statues on the main façade represent the Academy's original six departments: law, sciences, mathematics, philosophy, linguistics and history. On the same level are statues of six scientists: from the river, Newton, Lomonosov, Galileo, Miklós Révai (a Hungarian linguist), Descartes and Leibnitz. The building was finished by German Friedrich August Stüler in 1865. The **statue** in the middle of the square is Széchenyi, surrounded by Minerva (trade), Neptune (navigation), Vulcan (industry) and Ceres (agriculture). Farther south is a **statue of Ferenc Deák**, a moderate, liberal politician known as 'the nation's sage'. It is appropriate that his statue should be close to that of Széchenyi, whose belief in the gentle path of reform he shared throughout the turbulent 1840s. Ever opposed to war, he was largely responsible for the 1867 Compromise with Austria that led to the Dual Monarchy. Here he is shown with figures representing Justice, Patriotism, Popular Education, National Progress and Compromise. In 1858 he wrote: 'Primarily the task is to keep alive in the nation a sense and enthusiasm for constitutional liberty, because in a more favourable moment the Hungarian constitution can be restored by the stroke of a pen, and within 24 hours we can again be a free constitutional state.'

The large bronze **relief** on the Akadémia u. side of the academy depicts the moment of its formation. On 3 November 1825, Count István Széchenyi (dressed here in a Hussar officer's uniform) announced to the Diet (Parliament) that he would donate a year's income towards the establishment of a learned society for the development of Hungarian arts, science, language and literature. When asked what he would live on, he answered, 'My friends will support me.' It was the first major act of a life of extraordinary philanthropy (*see* pp.223–4).

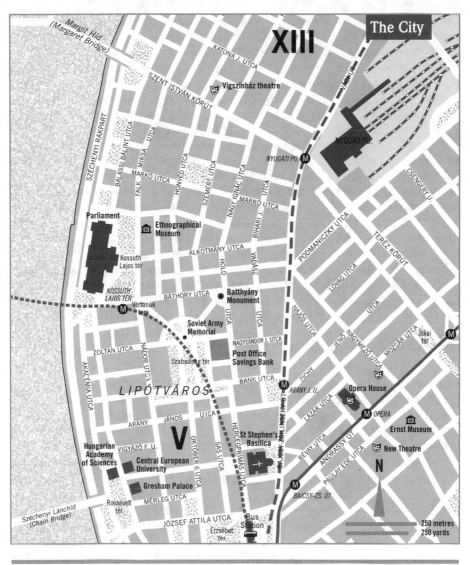

Lunch and Cafés

Café Kör, V. Sas u. 17. *Open Mon–Sat 10–10.* Small, popular bistro.

Café Picard, V. Falk Miksa u. 10. *Open Mon–Fri 7am–10pm, Sat 9am–10pm, Sun 10–10.* Tiny, stylish continental café. Some tasty but light food.

István Cukrászda, V. Október 6 u. 1. *Open Mon–Sat 10–8.* Nice spot for coffee and cake.

Lugas Etterem, V. Bajcsy-Zsilinszky 15. *Open daily 12–12.* Very popular, laid back and friendly; good portions of Hungarian fare.

Szalai Cukrászda, V. Balassi Bálint u. 7. *Open Wed–Mon 9–7.* Great cakes and pastries.

Between Roosevelt tér and Parliament, Akadémia u. is recommended for its buildings, though Nádor u. has the appealing **Central European University**, whose best feature is its interior. Nip inside for a look: just say you're going to the fine academic bookshop if anyone asks.

The Central European University was established by George Soros, a billionaire economist born in Budapest in 1930 at the tail end of a period which saw an unfeasible number of geniuses educated in the city (*see* pp.226–28). His genius expresses itself in an understanding of the complex nature of patterns, and the ways in which certain phenomena are affected by unpredictable human beings. He once made a billion dollars speculating over the fate of the pound (he took a negative view), and was famed as 'the man who broke the Bank of England'. He sums up his beliefs succinctly: 'Countervailing forces usually prevail, but occasionally they fail. That is when we have a change of regime or revolution. I am particularly interested in this occasion. I can do better in the financial markets than dealing with history in general, because financial markets provide a more clearly defined space and the data are quantified and publicly available.' His interest in discontinuities, as well as enabling him to stay ahead of the financial game, showed him a parallel between boom-and-bust economics and the rise and fall of the Soviet Empire. The breakdown of Communism represented for him a turning-point and a great opportunity, of which he urged the nations of the West to make the most by helping the Soviet Union and its satellites through transition. For his own part, he did what he could, setting up Open Society Foundations in 25 countries, beginning with his homeland, and offering access to new ideas through education and the donation of books, photocopiers, funds and so on.

St Stephen's Basilica (Bazilika)

© 332 1790; basilica open Mon–Sat 10–5, Sun 1–5; treasury open daily 10–5, adm.

East of Roosevelt tér, sitting on Szent István tér with its back to the main road, Budapest's cathedral is surrounded by buildings almost as high as itself, so that it tends to creep up on you. This means it's hard to get a good look, except from the front, which is not necessarily a bad thing as this is easily the most attractive part. The back is too overcrowded with competing architectural features, and partially justifies the accusations of ugliness levelled at the building. The sides are nondescript, their lower walls caked with the detritus of pollution.

The Basilica's history has not been blessed. It took over 50 years and three architects to finish it, to the point that it became a standing joke to the denizens of Pest: 'I'll pay up when the Basilica is finished.' It had been talked about for decades by 1851, when work began (having been set back three years by the failed Revolution) under József Hild, whose neoclassical design followed a Greek-cross floor plan. When Hild died in 1868, Miklós Ybl took the helm and was shocked to find cracks in the walls. He had the site fenced off, just in time: eight days later during a storm the dome tumbled down, breaking more than 300 local windows. Ybl began afresh with new plans, including the neo-Renaissance dome that is the church's finest feature today. After he died, the church was finished by József Kauser and consecrated in 1905. During his opening speech, the story goes, Franz Joseph was seen to throw nervous glances at the dome, as you may when the metro goes underneath and the whole edifice trembles. Though it is not shaped like a basilica, it received the title Basilica Minor in 1938, the 900th anniversary of the death of St Stephen, to whom it was dedicated.

The city around the Basilica changed long before it was finished. Originally it had backed on to low buildings and narrow streets but, by the time Ybl took over, the major thoroughfare now called Bajcsy-Zsilinszky had been built, necessitating a second façade. He cleverly provided this by adding the Ionic colonnade surmounted by statues of the 12 apostles. This could explain the overcrowding back there. The dome is 96m high (315ft), the same as the Parliament's dome, this number alluding to the date of the legendary arrival of the Magyar tribes, AD 896. Its four niches carry statues of the four Evangelists. The tympanum between these contains figures of Mary surrounded by Hungarian saints. The main door features carvings of the 12 apostles. Above it is a bust of King (St) Stephen, and higher still a mosaic of the Resurrection.

The interior, which can hold 8,500 people, is spacious, impressive but not oppressive. The marble walls and pillars carry mosaics, paintings and sculptures of a very high standard, mostly produced by Hungary's finest 19th-century artists. The mosaics were designed in Hungary (the dome's by Károly Lotz) and made in Venice. Highlights of the statues are the mournful *Saint Rita*, and the subtle *Joseph*, which has Jesus looking like a normal little boy yet with something intangible extra. Of the paintings, Gyula Stettka's *Golgotha* on the left middle deftly portrays Christ's passion as realistic yet larger than life. Opposite, also excellent, is Gyula Benczur's treatment of a famous scene from Hungarian legend. King Stephen, left heirless after Imre's premature death, is portrayed shrewdly offering his crown, and therefore his country's future, not to the Pope or the Holy Roman Emperor but to the Virgin. Since then she has been considered the Patroness of Hungary. Stephen is featured on the main altar, wearing a halo and a sword, a combination that raised no eyebrows in the past. (Note, for instance the statue of St Ladislaus, the hilt and blade of his sword held up as a cross, a tell-tale crescent symbol protruding from beneath his foot.) The reliefs behind Stephen depict scenes from his life.

Strangely, it was in death that the great king provided the church with its most famous attraction. His mummified **Holy Right Hand** (and forearm), Hungary's most important relic, is daily taken from its chapel and displayed in front of the painting of Stephen offering his crown. It lives in a highly ornate golden model of the Matthias Church, which a 100Ft coin will illuminate. When Stephen was canonized, his tomb was opened, and the corpse's right hand was found to be missing. It was found in the manor of the keeper of the royal tombs. An abbey was designed to contain the hand, but not for long: it made a mini-world tour before it wound up in its new gilded home. The custom has been revived of parading it through the streets every 20 August in a procession celebrating the anniversary of the king's 1083 canonization.

A tiny room contains the few items of the **Treasury**. The best items are monstrances, gifts from abroad. More worthwhile is the panorama from the top (*adm*): this vantage point offers excellent views, including the best view of the roof of the former Post Office Savings Bank. You can get a lift part of the way, but 146 more steps remain. You don't get to see the inside of the church, but the space between the inner and outer domes is a curious spectacle.

Szabadság Tér (Liberty Square)

One thing you will notice about this city centre is the number of trees. This, the capital's largest, most important square, resembles a park. Two roads are flanked by areas of glorious green, inhabited by every type of tree. The southern corners are even devoted to playgrounds. But scattered throughout are objects of great nationalist and political import, and around the edges stand some huge, imposing buildings, most of them banks. The biggest is now the home of Magyar TV, though its original function as a stock exchange suits it better. Built in 1905, incorporating touches of Greek and Assyrian temple architecture, it occupies the whole of the square's western side and would be terribly intimidating were it not for the cheap and nasty MTV Televízió sign above the door. It was on these steps that tens of thousands of people assembled on 15 March 1989, when the air was thick with long-awaited political change, to hear actor György Cserhalmi announce the 15 points of the newly formed opposition parties.

In the park in front is the **Memorial to the Martyrs of the New Building**, a modest monument to a tragic piece of history. The New Building (Újépület) stood here, an enormous Habsburg barracks in which countless Hungarians were imprisoned and executed. Among them were the country's should-be leaders, including, killed on 6 October 1849, its first independent prime minister, Count Lajos Batthyány. Loathed even more than the Citadella, the New Building's destruction in 1897 gave the square its name of Liberty. Across from here is a rather dull **statue** of Harry Hill Bandholtz. He was a US general present when Romanian troops tried to make off with the treasures of the National Museum, which he saved by blocking the doors with censorship seals, official looking enough to give the looters pause.

This northern side of the square reveals it to be not a square at all by arching around in a semi-circle. The façades of the four similar grand buildings on this side curve gently. At the point where the centre would be if the circle were complete stands the **Soviet Army Memorial**, a large white obelisk with a gold star on top. Reliefs at the base depict Red Army soldiers 'liberating' Budapest. Between 1928 and 1945 a flag stood on this spot, permanently at half-mast, over a mound of soil from the territories lost in the 1910 Trianon Treaty, which gave away two-thirds of Hungary's lands and a third of its population. It was accompanied by a quotation from British press baron Lord Rothermere, who campaigned against the unfair treaty, gaining such gratitude that he was even offered the Hungarian Crown. The Soviets removed the flag, and four statues called North, East, South and West which also symbolised the lost territories. This invites the question of why this ugly Soviet memorial has been allowed to remain in this prominent and symbolically charged location when all the others have been removed.

Ironically, it stands close to the former HQ of the Fascist Arrow Cross and right in front of the **US Embassy**. This 1901 building, decorated in a Viennese Art Nouveau style, is where Cardinal Mindszenty, Hungary's Catholic Primate, was sheltered for 15 years following the 1956 Uprising. The situation, exacerbated by Mindszenty's uncompromising attitude and the coverage it received around the world, became embarrassing for the USA and the Vatican, which eventually persuaded him to leave for Austria in 1971. Most of this eastern side is taken up by **Hungarian National Bank buildings**, of which the one on the southeast corner is the most impressive. Built in 1905, it shows an eclectic combination of historical styles. Two large bronze statues in front of the tympanum symbolise agriculture and industry, while a series of limestone reliefs at the first-floor level depict mainly crafts and trades—the means by which the majority made money. This potentially corny idea works thanks to the sympathetic treatment of the subjects, each imbued with an air of nobility. Note also the carved faces representing the many nations of the world.

The Post Office Savings Bank

On Hold utca, behind the National Bank and now belonging to it, sits one of Budapest's architectural highlights, the former Post Office Savings Bank. Ödön Lechner combined Art Nouveau with Hungarian folk art to forge a new nationalist architecture. 'Hungarian style has no past,' he said, 'but it does have a future.' The façade is all curves and gentle colours, simple motifs so delicate and playful that it's hard to do them justice. A wealth of small, lovingly conceived details adds up to a whole much greater than the sum of its parts. If you have children with you, this is one building they will also like. Note the ceramic bees climbing up the gable walls towards the hives on the roofs. The accepted interpretation is that these symbolise savers accumulating their wealth, but anyone familiar with the works of Gaudí, with whom Lechner has much in common, may remember the great Spaniard's interest in the architectural prowess of bees, whose constructions and techniques he was keen to study. These hives and the yellow majolica curlicues are the only hints from below of the extraordinary roof that is the building's finest feature. Here, multicoloured hexagonal tiles from the Zsolnay factory are ornamented with flowers, dragon tails, angel wings and Turkish turbans, a world of fairytale folk imagery. When asked who would enjoy such details, Lechner answered, 'The birds.' The best view of the roof is from the top of the Basilica with binoculars. Even the façade is difficult to see due to a lack of vantage points and the many plane trees.

Just over the road is one of Budapest's still-functioning **produce markets** (*Vásárcsarnok*), startlingly clean and orderly inside. On the way to the Parliament, where Hold u. meets Báthory u., an **Eternal Flame** inside a giant lantern commemorates the execution of Count Lajos Batthyány on this spot (then inside the New Building) on 6 October 1849. He was a conservative patriot, not a revolutionary, who had attempted to find a compromise with Austria and later headed a failed peace delegation. From here it's not far to 3 Honvéd u., which has one of the nicest, most original façades you'll see: very Art Nouveau, very playful (another one for the kids). Note the balconies, each utterly distinctive, and the use of glazed ceramics. There are roses, sunflowers, fruit, and more comparisons to be made with Gaudí.

Imre Nagy Monument

In Vértanuk tere (Martyrs' Square) is the monument to Imre Nagy. After Stalin's death in 1953, the strong-arm dictator Rákosi fell from grace with Moscow, partly because of his personality cult, which surpassed locally even that of Stalin. When Imre Nagy replaced him as prime minister, a period known as 'the thaw' began. Investment policies were implemented encouraging a healthier economic structure; forced collectivization was abandoned and peasants allowed to leave their co-operatives; the ideological atmosphere was relaxed, and silenced writers and poets allowed to re-enter the literary scene. The reign of terror had come to an end. When Nagy's protector in Moscow was dismissed, however, he too was removed from power (after just two years), and his changes criticised and reversed. Though a Communist, he had become much loved, so that, during the 1956 Uprising, the people called for him to speak. Eventually persuaded to address the crowds, he simply urged them to go home. Nevertheless, he accepted the position of prime minister for the 11 or so days when the Uprising seemed to have been successful, and attempted to appease both the revolutionaries and the Soviets.

In the end, the broader political picture sealed the country's fate, the Russians deciding they could not allow Hungary independent rule, and the Western powers agreeing not to interfere. So the Russian tanks appeared, and Nagy sought amnesty in the Yugoslavian embassy. After accepting an armistice, he was imprisoned for two years in Romania, then secretly tried in the spring of 1958 and executed on 16 June. During the trial he could have saved his own life by co-operating, but refused to revise his opinions. Though he never stopped being a Communist, Nagy really believed in the people, their freedom and independence, and he was not prepared to compromise those beliefs in the name of Moscow's policies. This spiritual defection is symbolised by his statue's position on a bridge, his back to the Soviet Army Memorial, looking towards Parliament. Nagy himself is not romanticised, but treated as an imperfect, very human individual, who lived a difficult destiny.

Kossuth Lajos Tér

Like Szabadság tér, this square wants to be a park. Either side of the gargantuan Parliament building are grassy tree-filled areas that could be joined were it not for the car park the size of a football pitch, usually occupied by a dozen vehicles. On the square's southwest corner is a **statue** of the popular working-class poet Attila József. Despite left-wing tendencies, he was too interested in life's bigger questions and the tragically fragile beauty of the human condition ever to conform to any ideology, and was not as popular with politicians as with ordinary people. Sculpted with tremendous empathy, the statue captures all this. The face is forlorn and troubled, too sensitive, too intelligent. Just as much is said about his state of mind by the way he's holding his hat, the coat thrown in a heap beside him. He is one of the greats, and he bears his nation's woes to a degree his fellows will never know. In another life he might have been a Woody Guthrie or a blues singer. He committed suicide in 1937, aged 32.

Right in front of Parliament is a far less enjoyable **statue** of Ferenc Rákóczi II, a prince of Transylvania who led the 1703–11 struggle for independence against the Habsburgs. Latin inscriptions on the plinth read 'For Country and Liberty' and 'The wounds of the noble Hungarian nation burst open'. The sentiment is echoed on the other side of the car park by an odd, Modernist block carrying an **eternal flame** in memory of those who died here during the Uprising of 1956, particularly on 25 October, when Soviet snipers started taking pot-shots at the peaceful demonstrators below, who were socialising with Soviet tank crews at the time. The shots came from the roof of the Ministry of Agriculture, the nicely proportioned neoclassical building behind Rákóczi fronted by a massive Corinthian colonnade. Outside stand unmarked statues of noble peasant types. The *Reaper Lad* seems to be eyeing Parliament with numbed bewilderment, while the *Female Agronomist* looks stubbornly away.

The neo-Renaissance palace next door was built to house the Supreme Court and Public Prosecutors Office, hence the **fresco** on the ceiling of the vast and ornately decorated main hall, which depicts Justitia, Goddess of Justice, surrounded by allegorical representations of Justice and Peace on the right, Sin and Revenge on the left. By Károly Lotz, it outshines his fresco in the Parliament. The palace is now the **Ethnographical Museum** (*open May–Oct daily 10–6, Nov–April daily 10–5; adm*), worth visiting as much for the building as for its contents. On the first floor, starting at the left, 13 rooms contain the permanent exhibition 'Folk Culture of the Hungarians', arranged under the topics People, Institutions, Peasant Work, Crafts, Markets and Fairs, Old House, New House, Folk Art, Childhood, Marriage Ceremonies, Old Age and Calendar Customs. By the 18th century the population of ethnic groups equalled that of Hungarians, so there is a wealth of diversity to be covered. Enlarged old black-and-white photos are often more interesting than the exhibits themselves and give a flavour of how life really was. Throughout the year 2001, the whole museum will be dedicated to an exhibition celebrating the millennium. 'Images of Time' will focus on objects, rites, customs and symbols to explore the many ways in which time is perceived, used, measured and transcended by different cultures.

In the park outside the museum is a **statue** of Lajos Kossuth, the most powerful figure from the struggles of the 1840s. A brilliant writer and speaker, he revolutionised the Hungarian media with his newspaper *Pesti Hírlap*, which he used, along with inflammatory speeches in Parliament, to rouse the people to demand separation from Austria. He was a contrast to the likes of Széchenyi and Batthyány, whose moderate stance he opposed. Széchenyi understood that Kossuth's insistence on revolution threatened to enrage the Austrians and destroy all the progress made by the more subtle path of reform, and history proved him right. When the inevitable war with Austria began, Batthyány stepped down, and Kossuth took up the prime minister's reins. He travelled the country rousing the people to arms, which is the subject of this statue, the six figures around him supposedly typical citizens. Unfortunately, the ensemble looks rather silly, like seven ham actors striking poses. Maybe the original statue was better. It depicted the gloom after the war with Austria was lost. The Soviets had it replaced with the present offering presumably because it was too downbeat, or maybe because Kossuth was surrounded by his aristocratic ministers such as Batthyány, Széchenyi and Eszterházy.

Just northwest of here is another little square, which contains a **statue** of Mihály Károlyi, a.k.a. the 'Red Baron'. He wasn't a fighter pilot but a wealthy landowner who became a radical liberal politician and in 1919 Hungary's first president. This was a very difficult time, at the end of the First World War when the Allied powers were preparing to confiscate two-thirds of Hungary's territory, and the people were swinging ever further to the left. Eventually forced to resign in favour of Béla Kún's Communist party, he went through two separate periods of exile. In this statue by Imre Varga he looks old and sad but stubbornly dignified, standing under two halves of an arch that do not meet.

Parliament (Országház)

To take the tour (in English) go to gate X a few minutes before 10am or 2pm. The cost is 1,300Ft, and it only happens on days when Parliament is not in session.

Occupying 880ft of the Danube embankment, there is no ignoring Budapest's most famous building, based on and reminiscent of the House of Commons in London. A magnificently bold feat of originality and virtuosity, it is so extravagant and pompous that the temptation is to belittle it. The 20th-century poet Gyula Illyés called it 'no more than a Turkish bath crossed with a Gothic chapel'. Even this put-down refers to the eclecticism so integral to Hungarian architecture. The ground plan is Baroque, but the façade is a fusion of neo-Gothic and neo-Renaissance. Designer Imre Steindl wanted 'to combine this splendid medieval style with national and personal features'. Tharaud spoke in 1899 of 'those Hungarian architects, with their bizarre passion for medievalism, without reason'. But there was a reason, which can be understood by comparing this structure with the frigid Baroque Royal Palace on the other side of the water: the Gothic harks back to better days, when Hungary was free to choose its own buildings. Whatever your reactions to the result, awe will be among them. As Patrick Leigh Fermor put it in 1934, 'Architectural dash could scarcely go further.' Upon completion, it was the largest parliament building in the world. The plan is one of perfect symmetry centred on the magnificent dome. The two wings are mirror images down to even the smallest details, one originally holding the House of Commons and the other the House of Lords.

It was in 1843 that the Hungarian Diet (Parliament) decided to build a permanent 'House of the Motherland'. For centuries before, they had met wherever they could. A competition was held which Steindl won. The second- and third-place designs were also used, the former now housing the Ethnological Museum, the latter the Ministry of Agriculture. Work began in 1885 and involved an average of a thousand people every day for 17 years, by which time it was six years too late for the millenary celebrations it was meant to crown, and Steindl was a sick, old man giving directions from a chair. He died five weeks before it was completed.

Inside there are 20km of stairways and 691 rooms. Much of the trimming is painted with 22 or 23 carat gold, 60kg of it. On the guided tour you will only see a fraction of what is there. Just inside the main entrance on Kossuth Lajos tér is a model of Parliament made from 30,000 matchsticks. The 96 steps of the ceremonial staircase, with ceiling frescoes by Károly Lotz, lead to the 16-sided hall below the 96m-high **dome**. These numbers allude to AD 896, when the Magyars arrived in the Carpathian Basin. The dome is the building's finest feature both outside and in, where it is decorated with intricate gilding leading the eye to an exquisite chandelier. Round the giant pillars that support the dome are **statues** of some of Hungary's rulers, including Árpád, Stephen, Matthias, four Transylvanian princes and three Habsburgs. All are staring straight ahead except Árpád, who is looking to his right, as if saying, 'What are those Habsburgs doing here?' Below the dome is the latest resting place of Hungary's crown jewels, including the crown made in the early Middle Ages that came to represent the one sent for Stephen's coronation by the pope.

In the old Upper House, the colour scheme is blue, representing the blood of the lords. Outside the Lords' Chamber, used for conferences since their discontinuation, you'll see the brass ashtrays, numbered so that each member could retrieve his own cigar on returning from hearing the speaker who had lured him away from it. The length of cigar turned to ashes was an indication of the speaker's quality. These days, only the offices of the president, prime minister and speaker are here. All other MPs work in the White House, an ugly modern building farther north, which for 32 years was the powerbase of Communist dictator János Kádár. In those days a red star graced the top of the dome and communist emblems sat where today there are coats of arms and King Stephen's double cross. These days the ruling party is the Young Democrats, whose prime minister is a mere 37 years old. The youngest member of the house at 23, however, belongs to the opposition, while one of the Young Democrats is 90.

A Suggested Stroll

This area is a paradise for lovers of big buildings. Many of the modern ones are just as impressive as the old stalwarts which they are clearly designed to complement. For a first-class selection of both, try this suggested circuit, remembering that not all of the best buildings are on the route, though they are visible from it. From Kossuth Lajos tér walk down Alkotmány u., turn left on to Bihari János u., then left on to Markó u. which crosses Nagy Ignac u. This last and Bihari János retain their quality up to Szent István körút: if you feel like going this far, you could also check out the beautiful **Nyugati Station** building. Constructed by the famous Eiffel company in Paris, it was the largest station in Europe until 1880. Known as the Western Railway Station, this was the site of the first such building in Hungary, from where the first train ran in 1846. Behind it on Váci út (not to be confused with the famous Váci utca in Belváros) is the Postmodern West End City Centre shopping mall. Farther west towards Margaret Bridge on Szent István körút is the delightful **Vígszínház** (Comedy Theatre).

Belváros: The Inner City

The Kiskörút (Little Boulevard) runs along the line of medieval Pest's walls, containing the city centre known as Belváros. Not much remains to identify this as the site of historic Pest: the town was razed when the Turks were driven out in 1686. What can be seen today is mainly a result of the massive expansion at the end of the 19th century. There are a few sights but the thing to do here is stroll—along the Dunakorzó, admiring the views of Buda, whose panorama is so stunning that the whole waterfront stretch has been declared a UNESCO World Heritage site, or around the lively hubs of Vörösmarty tér and Váci utca.

Deák Tér

This is the junction of all three metro lines, just south of the main bus station. In the metro is the tiny **Underground Railway Museum** (*open Tues–Sun 10–6, closed Mon; adm a transport ticket*). The line (now M1) underneath Andrássy út, inaugurated in 1896, was mainland Europe's first metro, and the world's second after London's Metropolitan line. The exhibits are two refurbished carriages on an original stretch of track. Deák tér itself is busy and at night rather sleazy. Its landmark is the squat, spireless **Lutheran Church** with its gently curving green roof. The inside is simple, and can only be seen during services or via the **museum** (*open Tues–Sun 10–6, closed Mon; adm*) next door, whose exhibits include a facsimile of Martin Luther's will and a copy of the first book printed in Hungary, a 1541 New Testament. The more attractive **Lutheran School** a couple of buildings west is a candidate for the best school of all time. As well as György Lukács, the Marxist philosopher who survived his country's changing politics relatively unscathed, and Sándor Petőfi, who didn't, three Nobel prizewinners were educated here, plus pioneer scientists John von Neumann and Edward Teller. The best thing on this square is No.3, housing the **Porsche Bank**, its corner topped by a turret. Across the Kiskörút is the giant mustard-yellow Anker Palace. To the north, Deák tér gives way to the bus station and an ugly construction area, proposed site for a new National Theatre. Political wranglings have stopped work indefinitely. **Erzsébet tér** to the west is a vast square of tree-lined paths converging on the **Danubius Fountain**. The male figure on top symbolises the Danube, while the women on the lower basin represent tributaries, the Tisza, Dráva and Száva. The original, whose basin was carved from a single 100-tonne rock, was destroyed in the war.

Lunch and Cafés

Auguszt Cukrászda, V. Kossuth Lajos u. 14–16. *Open Tues–Fri 10–6, Sat 10–2.* Delightful little old-style coffee-shop.

Csendes, V. Múzeum körút 13. *Open Mon–Sat 12–10.* Decent cheap Hungarian food.

Fatál, V. Váci u. 67 (entrance on Pintér u.). *Open daily 11.30–2am.* Very popular, with huge servings of Hungarian food.

Gerbeaud, V. Vörösmarty tér 7. *Open daily 9–9.* Famous though a bit touristy.

Morik Caffé, V. Erzsébet tér 1. *Open Mon–Fri 7am–11pm, Sat–Sun 9am–11pm.* Classy coffee-shop for connoisseurs.

Zsolnay Kávéház, V. Váci u. 20. Ground floor of the Taverna Hotel. Probably the nicest place to have a coffee on this section of the street.

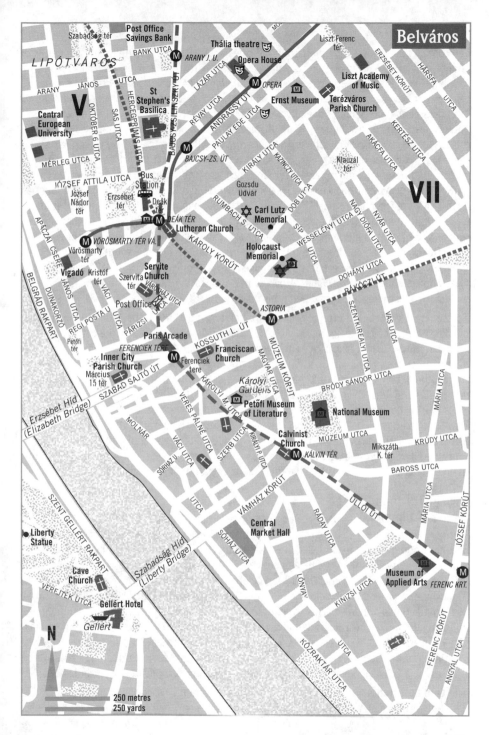

Belváros

Szabadság tér
Post Office
Savings Bank
BANK UTCA
Thália theatre
ARANY J. U.
Opera House
Liszt Ferenc tér

LIPÓTVÁROS

LÁZÁR UTCA
RÉVAY UTCA
OPERA
ANDRÁSSY ÚT
Liszt Academy of Music

ARANY JÁNOS UTCA
St Stephen's Basilica
Ernst Museum
Terézváros Parish Church

Central European University
V
OKTÓBER 6 UTCA
SAS UTCA
HERCEGPRÍMÁS UTCA
BAJCSY-ZSILINSZKY ÚT
PAULAY EDE UTCA

KERTÉSZ UTCA
AKÁCFA UTCA

MÉRLEG UTCA

BAJCSY-ZS. ÚT
KIRÁLY UTCA
KAZINCZY UTCA
Klauzál tér

IÓ7SEF ATTILA UTCA
Bus Station
Gozsdu Udvar

VII

József Nádor tér
Erzsébet tér
Deák tér
DEÁK TÉR
Lutheran Church
RUMBACH S. UTCA
Carl Lutz Memorial
DOB UTCA
SIP UTCA
NAGY DIÓFA UTCA
NYÁR UTCA
WESSELÉNYI UTCA

APÁCZAI CSERE JÁNOS UTCA
VÖRÖSMARTY TÉR VÁ.
Vörösmarty tér
Holocaust Memorial
DOHÁNY UTCA
RÁKÓCZI ÚT

Vigadó
Kristóf tér
Servite Church
Szervita tér
VÁROSHÁZ UTCA
ASTORIA

BELGRÁD RAKPART
DUNAKORZÓ
VÁCI UTCA
REGI POSTA U
Post Office
PÁRÍZSI
ASTORIA

Petőfi tér
Paris Arcade
KOSSUTH L. ÚT
MAGYAR UTCA
MÚZEUM KÖRÚT
SZENTKIRÁLYI UTCA
VAS UTCA

FERENCIEK TERE
Inner City Parish Church
Ferenciek tere
Franciscan Church
BRÓDY SÁNDOR UTCA
MÁRIA UTCA

Március 15 tér
SZABAD SAJTÓ ÚT
KÁROLYI M. UTCA
Károlyi Gardens

Erzsébet Híd (Elizabeth Bridge)
MOLNÁR
VÁCI UTCA
VERES PÁLNÉ UTCA
Petőfi Museum of Literature
National Museum
MÚZEUM UTCA
KRÚDY UTCA

SÖHÁZ U.
SZERB UTCA
KIRÁLYI P. UTCA
Calvinist Church
KÁLVIN TÉR
Mikszáth K. tér
BAROSS UTCA

Liberty Statue
SZENT GELLÉRT RAKPART
Central Market Hall
RADAY UTCA
VÁMHÁZ KÖRÚT
ÜLLŐI ÚT
MÁRIA UTCA
JÓZSEF KÖRÚT

Cave Church
Szabadság Híd (Liberty Bridge)
SÖHÁZ UTCA
LÓNYAY
Museum of Applied Arts
FERENC KRT.

VERÉJTÉK UTCA
Gellért Hotel
KINIZSI UTCA
FERENC KÖRÚT
ANGYAL UTCA

N
Gellért
KÖZRAKTÁR UTCA

250 metres
250 yards

Vörösmarty Tér

Free from traffic and lined by the terraces of cafés and restaurants, dotted with graceful iron lamp-posts and dominated by half a dozen trees, Vörösmarty tér is a focus of social activity—or inactivity, for it is a nice place to just hang out and watch. At the centre is a **statue** of romantic reform writer Mihály Vörösmarty, a giant of 19th-century Hungarian poetry. On the front of the monument are the famous opening words of his *Szózat* (*Appeal*), which became a second national anthem: 'To thy Fatherland be unshakeably true, oh Magyar!' The black spot above this is supposedly the coin donated by a beggar towards the monument's cost. Festivals sometimes take over for a day or a week, and street musicians and artists perform in the summer. Alive and atmospheric, the square never feels busy, tacky or sleazy. This is partly due to the hallowed institution on the north side, the **Pâtisserie Gerbeaud**. This 1861 building has been a café-confectioner's since 1870. Emil Gerbeaud bought it in 1884 and turned it into a landmark, famous as a meeting-spot as well as for its cakes. The three vast rooms that face the square resemble an English palace, exquisitely decorated with turn-of-the-20th-century furniture. The marvellous building with turret-like corners on the square's south side is the **Bank Palace**, housing the Budapest Stock Exchange, which reopened in 1990, 42 years after the Communists closed it down. Ignác Alpár, who designed the Magyar TV and National Bank buildings in Szabadság tér, considered it his major work.

To the north is **József Nádor tér**, flanked by fantastic buildings: the Romantic Postabank building on the south side, its façade alive with detail; Credit Lyonnais on the corner, lovingly restored; the Ministry of Finance on the west side, another Alpác construction, its top ledge boasting a statue of Mercury, god of finance, holding a model of the building on which he stands; the OTP (also Postabank) building on the east with an arcade running through the middle. Overlooking the square from József Attila u. is the ABN Bank building with an Art Nouveau façade. The **statue** in the square's centre is of the archduke whose name it carries. Habsburg Palatine from 1796 to 1847, he was a friend to Hungary. In 1808 he helped establish the Embellishment Commission for the restoration and development of Pest (an ongoing process). The Commission's leading supporter was architect János Hild, whose son József built the neoclassical Gross House, No.1 on this square, next to the Ministry of Finance.

Vigadó Tér to Petőfi Tér

West from Vörösmarty tér is a small square named after the sumptuous Romantic **Vigadó Concert Hall**, whose name approximates to 'making merry'. It was so badly damaged in the Second World War that reconstruction wasn't completed until 1980. It is a beautiful building whose symmetrical façade is richly embellished. The ledge running like a frieze along the top features the heads of Hungarian rulers and celebrities, with the old coat of arms at its centre. The columns carry reliefs of dancers, and statues of musicians line the first-floor ledge in front of the five arched windows. The foyer, *open from 12pm to sell tickets*, grand enough, is a mere prelude to the Great Hall's dazzlingly rich colour scheme. Unfortunately this can only be viewed by audiences, and the awful acoustics make this an undesirable place to see a concert. On the square's railings, look out for a bronze **statue**, the *Little Princess* (1990). Prince Charles has a copy and invited the sculptor, László Marton, to exhibit his work in London.

The **Dunakorzó** has wonderful views of the Buda panorama, especially at night when lights dance on the water and the air is suffused with romance. In the 1900s this area was surrounded by fancy hotels, and the promenade was the place to stroll, to see and be seen. They are trying to recapture that atmosphere, and the tramlines keep the traffic at a distance. Petőfi tér holds a recently made giant Celtic tombstone and the **statue of Petőfi**. More maybe than any other national hero, he stirs patriotism in the Magyar soul, thus his statue—despite its making him look camp and slightly silly—is a popular site for political demonstrations. Behind him is the Baroque Greek Orthodox church (*closed except for services*).

Inner City Parish Church (Belvárosi Plébániatemplom)

Open daily 6.30am–9pm; Mass Mon–Sat 6.30am and 6pm, Sun 9, 10 (Latin), 12 and 6.

Petőfi tér runs into Március 15 tér and Pest's oldest building, the Inner City Parish Church. From the outside it's nothing special. The plaster is crumbling in places and the paint peeling, the niches are empty and the Holy Trinity above the door look sadly decrepit. Even Christ's cross is rusting. Yet this is Budapest's only building east of the Danube to reflect anything like the history encountered on the other side. Sources disagree over how old it is. Some say that a church was founded here as a burial site for the martyred St Gellért in 1046. Others speak of a triple-aisled Romanesque church built at the end of the 12th century. Certainly the first occupant of this site was the 3rd-century Roman fortress Contra Aquincum, whose remains can be seen in the square beside the church. The original was razed during the Mongol invasions, though a single Romanesque arch survives in the southern tower. The 14th-century Gothic replacement provided the basis of what you see today. The Turks converted it into a mosque and then returned it so that for a while it was the only Christian church in Pest. When they were kicked out it was damaged, then in 1723 it burned down. Reconstruction in a Baroque style saw the addition of today's twin towers and façade, resulting in a hybrid curious even by Budapest's eclectic standards: the back is Gothic, the front Baroque. After all that, the church was inevitably war-torn and then almost pulled down when the Elisabeth Bridge was built.

Inside, the historical mish-mash, as well as the grandeur, is much more apparent. The nave features a barrel-vaulted Baroque ceiling and is simple, with little use of gold and few paintings or figures. The chancel is much more ornate, its complex vaulted ceiling-arches edged with geometric shapes. On the right side are five **chapels**. The first three are Baroque; the fourth contains a beautiful Renaissance tabernacle of red marble and white limestone, its pedestal holding the crest of the Pest city council who commissioned it in 1507; the fifth is Gothic. The original high altar was destroyed during the war; this one dates from 1948 and is the work of sculptor Károly Antal and painter Pál C. Molnár. Behind the altar are Gothic sedilias and to the right is a souvenir from the church's time as a mosque, a prayer-niche (mihrab). You can only get a close look at these after Latin Mass on a Sunday. The fine wooden pulpit is neo-Gothic, from 1808. On the chancel's left side is a reconstructed Gothic tabernacle. The chapel before the chancel contains the remains of the church's frescoes. The last chapel holds the extravagant neoclassical tomb of a newspaper editor, constructed in 1835 by István Ferenczy.

Váci Utca

Váci utca runs the length of this district and was once Pest's main road. For the last 150 years it has held Budapest's premier boutiques, where rich ladies would seek the latest fashions, stroll among the gentry and enjoy the sophisticated café terraces. Over 30 years ago the northern half of the street, still considered by natives to be 'the' Váci utca, was pedestrianized, leading to a return of the boom times. It has become increasingly Westernized, so you won't be very surprised by anything you see (unless you look up above the shopfronts). You will end up here anyway. It is gloriously traffic-free and humming with action, a place to watch the natives (who are probably there to watch the tourists). Its lively atmosphere is particularly worth seeking out at night. The southern half of Váci utca was pedestrianized only in 1997. It is calmer and feels a little less like a big tourist trap. Almost every building is a café or restaurant with a terrace, which adds to the convivial atmosphere. Some of them never close.

Szervita Tér

Walking north on Váci utca, just before you get to Vörösmarty tér, a little square overflowing with terrace tables opens up on the right. This is Kristóf tér, and at its centre is a **statue** of a *Fisher-Girl* which originally belonged at a fish-market nearby on the embankment, and apparently caused a stir due to the girl's skimpy attire: strange, given the number of naked classical statues everywhere. Szervita tér is centred on a copy of a 1729 **Immaculata column** with figures of Joseph, Anne and Joaquim at the base. The square was named after its 1732 Baroque **Servite Church**. The most interesting feature of this run-down building is the large **bas-relief** to the right of the entrance, with Christ cradling a dying hero: this 1930 monument is dedicated to the VIIth Wilhelm Hussar Regiment who gave their lives in the First World War. Inside it is excessively lavish, with winged or haloed figures everywhere, lots of gold, and a pastel pink and blue ceiling covered with frescoes: quite a contrast to the Parish Church.

The real reason for visiting this square may elude you until you look up to the west. The building known as the **Turkish Bank House** (which it used to contain) looks at ground level like any other shop (at the moment it is 'Dr Jeans'). Follow it up and it becomes more interesting. The whole façade is covered with vast arched windows. At the top in the playfully curved gable is Miksa Róth's masterpiece, an Art Nouveau mosaic entitled *Glory to Hungary*. Angels, shepherds and heroes such as István Széchenyi, Lajos Kossuth and Ferenc Rákóczi pay homage to a bethroned *Patrona Hungariae* (Our Lady, Patron of Hungary). Two doors to the left, the **Rózsavölgyi Building** is interesting for its distinctions between retail, office and residential levels, a typical trait of the father of Hungarian Modernism, Béla Lajta. The upper storeys' ceramic decoration reveals his earlier links with the Romantic school.

Ferenciek Tere

This is the main route for east–west traffic and very busy, which may blind you to its charms. As ever the key is to look up. Stand where the bridge stretches away before you and you will notice that two near-identical buildings, the **Klotild Palaces**, flank the road like mirror images, creating a gateway for the bridge. This 'gateway' is different but equally impressive coming the other way. Beneath the bridge in the subway is a collection of enlarged black and white photos taken by György Klösz which show details of this area before and after the building of the bridge. Opposite are modern photos of the same region.

On the north-facing wall of the **Franciscan Church** which gives Ferenciek tere its name is a large memorial **relief** recalling the catastrophic flood of 1838 when the whole Inner City was under water and over 400 people died. It depicts Count Miklós Wesselényi, who rescued many in his boat. Over the main road, the corner building smothered with gold-leaf mosaics, ironwork, busts and reliefs is the Párizsi Udvar or **Paris Arcade**. Note the naked figures striking poses either side of the clock (stopped at 12), and the fancy carving around the roof-line and towers. Above the third storey, naked figures appear from the waist up, as if plunging out of the wall. Such details met with disapproval when the building was erected as the Inner City Savings Bank. More in keeping was the theme of bees and the guardian archangel Gabriel on the relief below the gable. Have a closer look at the mosaic inside this porch. Theatrical masks, swirling patterns and gorgon's heads are all the more striking for the colours: gold and an amazing range of blues, greens and reds. Inside it is gloomy and contains nothing worthwhile but a bookshop, but the décor is astounding, full of sculpted wood, wrought iron, Art Nouveau mosaics and stained glass, of which the apotheosis is Miksa Róth's decaying glass dome.

Southern Belváros

In the calm of these narrow backstreets you can catch a whiff of the past and the true spirit of the present. There is little sightseeing to be done. Between Ferenciek tere and Kálvin tér are the **Károlyi Gardens** off Magyar u., a pleasant park with a children's playground, and the **Károlyi Palace** at Károlyi Mihály u. 16, which held the Museum of Hungarian Literature and a Contemporary Literature Centre. It has closed for a major overhaul but may be open by the time you arrive. There are plans for a café, bookshop and state-of-the-art library. Kálvin tér contains the **Calvinist Church**, worth a quick look. Plain but elegant on the outside, the interior possesses its own grandeur. Decoration is almost non-existent, as befits the denomination, but the ceiling is enlivened with brass reliefs of floral motifs, particularly effective on the dome. The combination of the church's many curved planes particularly pleases the eye, drawing it back to the centre, in this case the altar, without so much as a cross.

National Museum (Nemzeti Múzeum)

Open mid-Mar–mid-Oct Tues–Sun 10–6, mid-Oct–mid-Mar Tues–Sun 10–5, closed Mon; adm.

This grand neoclassical edifice is just off Kálvin tér. The huge central portico consists of eight Corinthian columns supporting a large tympanum filled with statues, chief among them Pannonia, the name of the ancient Roman province that occupied western Hungary. Opened in 1848, when it was far from the centre of town, it soon played host to one of Hungarian legend's most important scenes. A huge crowd gathered on 15 March 1848 to listen to the leaders of the young revolutionaries, and heard the popular poet Sándor Petőfi recite his now famous *National Song*, marking in a sense the beginning of the revolution. 'Choose! Now is the time! Shall we be slaves or shall we be free?' he cried, and the people chose.

As with the National Library, the National Museum was the inspiration of the great Count Ferenc Széchenyi, father of István. The count's extensive collection of manuscripts, prints, coins, coats of arms and maps was the basis of the museum's collection. Today the exhibits tell the story of Hungary's history in two halves: from the foundation of the state to its reconquest from the Turks, and from the end of the Turkish wars to the 1990s. Its two great treasures are **St Stephen's Sword** and the **Coronation Mantle**, both on the first floor. In the basement is a **Lapidarium** with a collection of Roman remains, mainly tombstones.

The permanent exhibitions are upstairs. On the ceilings and walls above the grand staircase are a series of **frescoes** completed in 1873 by Than Mór and Károly Lotz. The main images are symbolic representations of abstracts like Imagination, Inspiration and Enthusiasm for

Beauty, while a frieze all round the top of the walls has scenes from Hungarian history, from St Stephen's conversion to Christianity up to the founding of the museum, a helpful prelude to the coming history lesson. A look at the **family tree** in room 1 may help you with the convoluted dynasty of Hungary's early kings. It all begins with the turul-bird. You will probably get more out of the museum if you brush up on your Hungarian history beforehand, although there are explanations in English. The notes on individual exhibits are not given in English, on the other hand. On the positive side, dotted around are touch-screen information panels on History, Economy and Social Struggle, Science and Technological Development, Culture and Arts, and Who's Who in Hungarian History. There is so much here of quality that it seems almost invidious to pick out individual examples of what is on show. It begins with a lot of weapons and religious relics and ends rather poignantly with a collection of Communist-flavoured street-signs, such as Leninváros, with red paint slashes across them.

Museum of Applied Arts (Iparművészeti Múzeum)

Open daily 10–4; adm.

East of Kálvin tér on Üllöi u. is one of Budapest's most interesting museums, worth visiting as much for the building as for the exhibitions. Designed by Ödön Lechner and Gyula Pártos, it is a significant example of Lechner's blending of traditional folk art with more eclectic elements and Art Nouveau to forge a national architecture. It features a wonderfully colourful patterned roof trimmed with yellow majolica, which also enlivens the beautiful dome. Tiles on the façade create flower and foliage patterns, markedly around the rose window above the porch. The steps up to the door are flanked by banisters of yellow ceramic curlicues. Inside, all white, it resembles the Taj Mahal. Originally it was highly decorated with colourful Hungarian folk motifs. The main permanent exhibition, 'Arts and Crafts', is a disappointment. The works are housed in unaesthetic, outdated cases, and nothing is labelled in English, though laminated sheets (available in English) explain the techniques used in each type of craft. However, the main attraction of the museum is its consistently superb temporary exhibitions, of which there are normally three or four. Chief among them, and due to remain for the foreseeable future, is the excellent Art Nouveau exhibition. Exhibits are labelled in English, and a sophisticated booklet gives an introduction to the genre. There are many fine pieces from all over Europe.

West of Kálvin Tér

Farther round the Kiskörút to the west of Kálvin tér is the magnificent **Central Market Hall**, resembling a grand old railway station, an impression maintained inside by the height of the ceiling and the iron staircases and walkways. Outside it is a particularly attractive, striking building with a fancy iron gate, lots of arches and a funky yellow, green and red roof. Inside it is incredibly clean and ordered, to the extent that one could almost think it existed just to impress tourists, yet thousands of Budapestians buy their groceries here every day. It is definitely worth looking inside, if only for the sausage stalls, where lumps of pork fat are sold by the kilo. Upstairs is food (including a good, rustic-style restaurant), souvenirs and lots of linen. Next door is another notable building, the neo-Renaissance **University of Economic Sciences**, originally the Main Customs Office. The façade overlooking the river has 10 allegorical statues. It is worth going through the river-facing main entrance to check out the inner courtyard, once a customs hall, now an atrium, which contains a large bronze **statue of Karl Marx**. A bridge arches over the courtyard, commonly known as the 'Bridge of Sighs'.

Andrássy Út to City Park

Starting at one of Budapest's busiest junctions, where Deák tér, Erzsébet tér, József Attila körút and the Kiskörút collide, Andrássy út runs northwest in a straight line for 2.5km, the central axis of Terézváros (Theresa Town), better known as district VI. It is worth a stroll along this most august of Budapest's boulevards just to admire the grandeur of the buildings, amongst them the State Opera House. But the main reason for coming here is the nightlife: the area around Andrássy út is easily the city's most lively quarter. The boulevard culminates in Heroes' Square (Hősök tere), a site of prime national importance flanked by two imposing edifices, including the excellent Museum of Fine Arts. Beyond lies City Park, a must for anyone with children, containing the fairy-tale Vajdahunyad Castle, the zoo, circus, amusement park and the most family-friendly spa complex in town, the Széchenyi baths.

Andrássy Út

Roads that just evolve rarely run straight, and sure enough Andrássy út was rigidly planned. Following the 1867 Compromise with Austria and birth of the Dual Monarchy, Budapest was reinvented as an imperial capital and for once had the luxury of wealth and peace with which to realize mighty ambitions. Heavily influenced by Haussmann's redevelopment of Paris, Andrássy út was conceived as a grand boulevard in the style of the Champs-Elysées. Inaugurated in 1884, the rather pompous result of these grandiose plans has carried a variety of names. First it was Sugár út (Radial Avenue), then it was named after the 19th-century statesman Count Gyula Andrássy, a name which natives upheld through the Communist designations Sztàlin út (1949–56) and the catchy Népköztársaság (Avenue of the People's Republic), and which officially returned in 1990.

The first part of Andrássy út as far as Oktogon is by far the liveliest, and should definitely be visited, preferably at night. The triangle bounded by Király út (south of Andrássy), Bajcsy-Zsilinsky and Teréz körút is a maze of small streets buzzing with restaurants, bars, cafés and clubs. This section is lined with closely built, eclectic but mainly neo-Renaissance buildings, as well as shops, offices and cafés.

Lunch and Cafés

Café Vian, VI. Liszt Ferenc tér 9, ✆ 342 8991. Excellent selection of beer and wines, coffees, juice and cocktails. Good food.

Ket Szerecsen Kávézo, VI. Nagymező u. 14. *Open Mon–Fri 8am–1am, Sat–Sun 11am–1am.* Food is light and mainly Italian-style; good lunch specials.

Komédiás Kávéház, VI. Nagymező u. 26. *Open Mon–Fri 8am–midnight, Sat–Sun 3.30pm–midnight.* Small, old-style theatrical café.

Művész Cukrászda, VI. Andrássy út 29. *Open daily 9am–midnight.* Old-style café with genuine class; great location.

Pesti 1998, VI. Paulay Ede u. 5. Popular place next to Vista. Hungarian food.

Vista, VI. Paulay Ede u. 2. A nice, busy café-restaurant; vast choice of breakfasts.

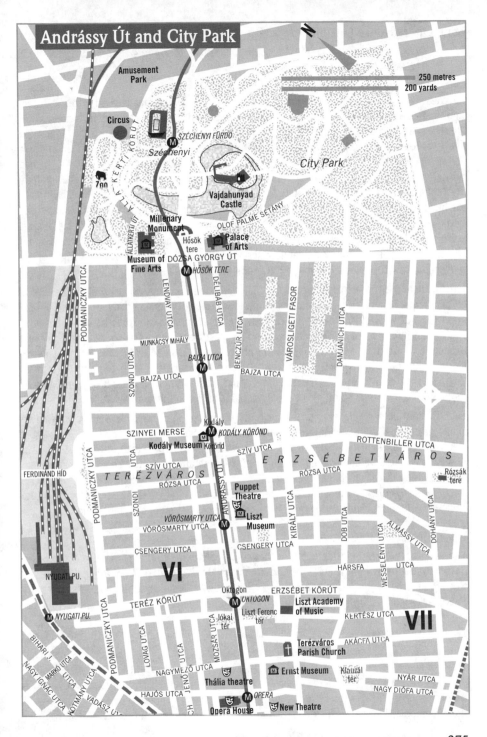

Andrássy Út and City Park

Amusement Park

Circus

SZÉCHENYI FÜRDŐ

Széchenyi

City Park

Zoo

Vajdahunyad Castle

Millenary Monument

OLOF PALME SÉTÁNY

Hősök tere

Palace of Arts

Museum of Fine Arts

DÓZSA GYÖRGY ÚT

HŐSŐK TERE

LENDVAY UTCA

DÉLIBÁB UTCA

BENCZÚR UTCA

VÁROSLIGETI FASOR

DAMJANICH UTCA

MUNKÁCSY MIHÁLY

SZONDI UTCA

BAJZA UTCA

BAJZA UTCA

BAJZA UTCA

Kodály

KODÁLY KÖRÖND

SZINYEI MERSE

Kodály Museum Körönd

SZÍV UTCA

ROTTENBILLER UTCA

ERZSÉBETVÁROS

PODMANICZKY UTCA

FERDINÁND HÍD

TERÉZVÁROS

SZÍV UTCA

RÓZSA UTCA

SZONDI

RÓZSA UTCA

Rózsák tere

Puppet Theatre

ANDRÁSSY ÚT

KIRÁLY UTCA

DOB UTCA

ALMÁSSY UTCA

DOHÁNY UTCA

VÖRÖSMARTY UTCA

VÖRÖSMARTY UTCA

Liszt Museum

CSENGERY UTCA

CSENGERY UTCA

NYUGATI PU.

VI

WESSELÉNYI UTCA

HÁRSFA

UTCA

TERÉZ KÖRÚT

Oktogon

OKTOGON

ERZSÉBET KÖRÚT

Liszt Academy of Music

NYUGATI PU.

Jókai tér

Liszt Ferenc tér

KERTÉSZ UTCA

VII

BIHARI J.

MARKÓ UTCA

NAGY IGNÁC UTCA

VADÁSZ U.

NOTMÁNY UTCA

LOVAG UTCA

JENŐ UTCA

MOZSÁR UTCA

PODMANICZKY UTCA

NAGYMEZŐ UTCA

Terézváros Parish Church

AKÁCFA UTCA

Ernst Museum

Klauzál tér

NYÁR UTCA

Thália theatre

HAJÓS UTCA

OPERA

NAGY DIÓFA UTCA

Opera House

New Theatre

State Opera House (Állami Operaház)

VI. Andrássy út 22, © 331 2550; adm for obligatory guided tour; box office open Tues–Sat 10–7, Sun 10–1.

One of the most sumptuous buildings in Budapest, its interior is even more impressive than its outside, making a night at the opera a grand occasion at a comparatively good price. This neo-Renaissance building was the crowning achievement of Miklós Ybl, who designed the Basilica. He spent nine years overseeing the Opera House's construction and is said to have checked every cartload of bricks. Its first musical director was the acclaimed father of Hungarian opera Ferenc Erkel, who also took up the conductor's baton for the grand opening in 1884. Liszt had written a work for the occasion but it contained elements of the Hungarian rebel melody *Rákóczi March*, and so was not performed. After all, the Compromise had been reached, and the building's funding came mainly from Habsburg Emperor Franz Joseph. Gustav Mahler and Otto Klemperer have been musical directors here, and Puccini directed two of his operas. During the siege of Budapest in the winter of 1944–5, the vast cellars gave shelter to thousands, and the building survived relatively unscathed. In 1981 major renovations began and it reopened on its 100th anniversary on 27 October 1984 as brilliantly sparkling as new.

Either side of the entrance are **statues** of Liszt (right) and Erkel by Alajos Stróbl. Niches at the corners of the first floor contain **statues** of the four muses of opera, Terpsichore, Erato, Thalia and Melpomene (dance, love poetry, comedy and tragedy). On the stone balustrade around the second-floor terrace stand **statues** of the greatest **opera composers** (with the notable exception of Puccini). At the front (left to right): Rossini, Donizetti, Glinka, Wagner, Verdi, Gounod, Bizet. On the left side: Monteverdi, Alessandro, Scarlatti, Gluck, Mozart, Beethoven. On the right side: Mussorgsky, Tchaikovsky, Moniuszko, Smetana. There is also an Egyptian motif, with the 'needles' on the corners of the balustrade and the sphinxes to left and right.

Even without buying a ticket or taking the tour, you can go into the lobby. The gilded vaulted ceiling is covered with wonderful **murals** by Bertalan Székely and Mór Than. The marble columns, mosaic floor and chandeliers are upstaged by the sweeping main staircase. Even this, however, is just a prelude to the bits you won't see, the **auditorium** where a bronze chandelier weighing three tons illuminates the 23-carat gold leaf and the fresco of *The Greek Gods on Mount Olympus* by the genre's master, Károly Lotz. The royal box in the centre of the circle has sculptures representing the four operatic voices: soprano, alto, tenor and bass.

Up Andrássy Út to Oktogon

The neo-Renaissance building opposite that so complements the Opera House is the **State Ballet Institute**. Behind it on Paulay Ede u. is the **New Theatre** (*Új Színház*), whose Art Nouveau façade is unusual even by Budapest's standards. Note the little monkeys above the 1950s-style doors forlornly holding blue ceramic globes, the brass Egyptian-style figures lining the roof and the chintzy blue letters carrying the theatre's name. It was designed by Béla Lajta as a music hall, then redesigned many times before being returned in 1990 to its original form.

Nagymező út has been dubiously dubbed 'the Broadway of Pest'. Optimistic as this may be, it does contain a handful of theatres and clubs, such as the Operetta, Moulin Rouge and the beautiful **Thália Theatre**. On the other side of Andrássy út is the **Ernst Museum** (*closed for renovation, but due to reopen soon*), which usually displays contemporary avant-garde and small temporary international exhibitions. Inside are benches and banisters by Ödön Lechner and a wonderful 1911 post-Impressionist stained-glass window by József Rippl-Rónai. Nearby is **Terézváros Parish Church**, with a graceful tapering tower that draws one's attention to the cross at its pinnacle. The simple, elegant interior has some good paintings and a fine neoclassical high altar but is usually locked. On the corner diagonally opposite is a run-down but still superb Romantic-Gothic building, **Pekáry House**.

A little farther up Andrássy út, scrutinising the traffic that passes it, is a **statue** of popular romantic novelist Mór Jókai on the square that bears his name. On the other side of the road is **Liszt Ferenc tér**, the most happening square in town. Pedestrianized, full of trees, benches, statues and terrace tables, it feels utterly Mediterranean and civilised. One statue is of journalist and poet Endre Ady, but the eye-catching one is of Ferenc (or Franz) Liszt. Even sitting he looks like a crazed, slightly dangerous maniac, which, if you listen to his music, is probably what he was. Erected to commemorate the centenary of his death, it contains a cameo of the sculptor (the bald man on Liszt's lapel). At the far end of the square is the **Ferenc Liszt Music Academy** (*Zeneakadémia*), an extraordinary Art Nouveau building. A wealth of features adorn the façade, including a statue of Liszt, many strange mythological faces and musical motifs, and reliefs of children playing instruments representing the development of music. Inside is even grander. In the centre is a beautiful **mosaic**, while the walls above the entrances to the main auditorium carry a **fresco** by Hungarian Pre-Raphaelite Aladár Körösfői Kriesch entitled *Hungarian Wedding Procession in the 14th Century*.

Where the Nagykörút meets Andrássy út is **Oktogon**. Four enormous, very similar-looking buildings constructed in an eclectic mix of styles in 1873–4 face off against one another, their façades and the roads between them making a perfect octogon. Though it's surrounded by fast-food outlets and all-night restaurants, the effect is still quite impressive. This area never sleeps, largely because buses service the Nagykörút 24 hours a day. Like the boulevard on which it stands, Oktogon maintained its name while being officially subjected to others. It was Mussolini tér under the Horthy regime and November 7 tér, recalling the date of the Bolshevik Revolution so important to Hungarians, under the Communists.

Oktogon to Heroes' Square

The section of Andrássy út running to Kodály körönd is noticably wider, the thoroughfare flanked by secondary local-traffic roads separated off by sidewalks lined with trees, traditional lamp-posts and park benches. Though still close together, the buildings here are not so given over to commercial usage, so their self-important demeanour is more apparent. Amongst them is the **Franz Liszt Museum** at Vörösmarty u. 35 (*open Mon–Fri 10–6, Sat 9–5, closed Sun; adm*). A couple of rooms in Liszt's former house lovingly display the composer's belongings down to nutcrackers and handkerchiefs. There are pianos and organs, portraits and busts of the master, and notes about his life mainly centred on his friendships with Augusz and Zichy, but not even touching upon his rampant womanizing. You'd have to be a real enthusiast to get much out of it. Close by is the Academy of Fine Arts containing the child-friendly **Budapest Puppet Theatre** at No.69 (© 321 5200; *shows winter Mon–Thurs 3pm, Fri–Sat 10.30am and 4pm; closed summer; adm*). Fairly innocuous these days, the building at **No.60** has a notorious past. During the Horthy era, the ultra-right-wing regime made it their secret police headquarters, locking up, beating and torturing Communists here. During the Second World War the Arrow Cross used it for the same purposes, this time the victims mainly Jews. After the war, the Communists kept the tradition alive, their secret police doing a fair amount of 'persuading' here, especially in the brutal 'dark fifties'. They probably used many of the same implements, though the legendary giant meat-grinder for disposing of bodies was never found.

Kodály Körönd, like Oktogon, is defined by four massive buildings, but is much more sedate and elegant, and is generally considered one of Budapest's most beautiful squares. The symmetrical neo-Renaissance edifices are near identical, though No.1 is better preserved and covered in attractive gilt *sgraffiti*. It was once the home of composer, researcher and teacher Zoltán Kodály, who incorporated traditional folk melodies into his work and travelled the country to collect and preserve them. Now it houses his archives and the **Kodály Memorial Museum** (*open Wed 10–4, Thurs–Sat 1–6, Sun 10–2, closed Mon–Tues; adm*). The house is in its original state, with furniture, various manuscripts, and the composer's collection of folk art. At one point the square was named Hitler tér, which prompted Bartók to state that he didn't want his body to be buried in Hungary so long as anywhere was named after Hitler or Mussolini.

The boulevard gets more stately as it heads towards Heroes' Square, the buildings now detached mansions and villas, many containing embassies and the like. Building buffs can veer left down **Bajza u.** for a look at Nos.42 and 44, then cut through to the parallel road **Munkácsy Mihály u.**, where Art Nouveau façades abound, particularly at Nos.19b, 21, 23 and 26. That Andrássy út was designed as a grand driveway leading to the Millenary Monument becomes clearer the closer you get, like a crescendoing drum-roll. However, it is a long walk. The M1 metro runs beneath the road, and the no.4 bus follows the same route.

Heroes' Square (Hősök Tere)

In concept akin to the Arc de Triomphe, in execution more like London's Trafalgar Square, this vast paved arena is distinct in one significant way: being far from the city centre, it is rarely full of people. Even the odd tourist bus makes hardly a dent on the acres of space. In the evening this emptiness, together with the smooth surface, makes it a paradise for skaters of all kinds, performing tricks and weaving past each other, oblivious of the stony faces of ancient ancestors. The square and its contents, like the boulevard that leads to them, represent a conscious act of Magyar nationalism, born of a short-lived era of prosperity. Coming at the end of the 19th century, it happened to coincide roughly with the millennial anniversary of the Magyars' conquest of the Carpathian Basin. Though nobody knew exactly when this occurred, a date for celebrations was fixed at 1895, then changed to 1896 when it became clear not everything would be ready. The date has been official ever since and dictated such details as the height of the Basilica and Parliament domes.

Approaching the square, centre of attention is the **Millenary Monument**, with the Archangel Gabriel atop an imposing 120ft column. Legend has it that Gabriel appeared to King Stephen in a dream, instructing him to convert the pagan Magyars to Christianity and offering him the crown of Hungary, shortly after which a crown arrived from Pope Sylvester II. To augment the symbolism, the archangel is standing on a globe holding the Hungarian crown and an apostolic cross. Despite the setting back of celebrations, the column and statue were still a year late, and were deemed unstable. While a reinforced column was prepared, the statue was sent to the 1900 World Exhibition in Paris where it won the Grand Prix. At the column's base are equestrian statues of Prince Árpád and the chieftains who led the Magyar tribes into the region. They look like a marauding bunch, with wild beards and moustaches and horns attached to their hats or even their horses' heads. In front is a block of stone traditionally used for wreath-laying ceremonies. This **Heroes' Monument** carries the inscription: 'To the memory of the heroes who have sacrificed their lives for the freedom of our people and national independence.'

At a respectful distance behind the column is a two-part semi-circular **colonnade**. On the top, four groups of symbolic figures represent, from left to right, *Work and Wealth, War, Peace* and *Knowledge and Glory.* Between the columns are statues of Hungary's most important rulers, from King Stephen to Kossuth. The Transylvanian princes were only added after the Second World War, when they replaced statues of Habsburg rulers. Below, **reliefs** contain legendary scenes from their lives—Stephen receiving his crown from the Pope, Matthias being presented with a model of the church—though most of them are battle scenes. During the short-lived Council Republic period of 1919, the revolutionary Soviets had the whole square draped in red and the column covered by a huge red obelisk bearing a relief of Marx. Focal point of fervent sentiments that it is, many important gatherings have taken place here, most recently the ceremonial reburial on 16 June 1989 of Imre Nagy, which symbolised the beginning of a new democratic era. His coffin was accompanied by five others, four representing other leaders executed after 1956, the fifth representing unknown victims of the time.

The composition of the square is best taken as a whole, the column and Magyar chieftains flanked by the colonnades and, pulling back the focus, the colossal galleries on either side of the square. To the right is the neoclassical red brick **Palace of Arts**, whose steps were used for Nagy's reburial ceremony. The colourful mosaic that fills the tympanum represents St Stephen as patron of the arts. Behind the portico's six massive Corinthian columns, a three-part **fresco** depicts *The Beginning of Sculpture*, represented by figures of Vulcan and Athene, *The Source of Arts*, with Apollo and the Muses, and *The Origins of Painting*, with images from ancient mythology. Two smaller frescoes in between depict allegorical figures of *Painting* and *Sculpture.* Inside is the **gallery** (*open Tues–Sun 10–6, closed Mon; adm*). Four rather spartan white rooms house exhibitions of chiefly modern art.

Museum of Fine Arts

Open Tues–Sun 10–5.30, closed Mon; adm.

On the north side of the square a neoclassical building with Italian-Renaissance, Romanesque and Baroque-revival influences is an appropriate building for the excellent Museum of Fine Arts, the European equivalent of the National Gallery. Eight gigantic Corinthian columns support a portico whose tympanum bears a relief with a completed copy of a fragment on the Temple of Zeus at Olympia, depicting the *Battle of the Centaurs and Lapiths.* The exhibitions have been made to conform to the gallery rather than vice versa, so the interior is just as grand, particularly the sweeping staircases and the Grand Hall. For some time now the museum has been undergoing renovations and exhibits are constantly being moved around. Consequently the floor plan on the tickets is incorrect; the notes below simply list the contents and no locations. At the time of writing one wing of the first floor is closed with all the paintings squeezed into the other, a truly intense experience. Most exhibits are labelled in English.

The **Egyptian Collection** is interesting enough if you haven't been to a better one. Highlights include some good painted sarcophagi, the head of a statue of a New Kingdom young man, a young lady bearing the standard of Hathor, some Late Period bronze sculptures of Harpocrates, Osiris, a raven and a cat, and an elegant Saite period cat.

The **19th-Century Collection** focuses on French artists of that period. Here are all the big names: Monet, Manet, Renoir, Delacroix. There are some familiar works such as Cézanne's *The Cupboard*, Toulouse-Lautrec's *These Ladies in the Refectory* and Courbet's vast and wonderful *The Wrestlers*. With a few notable exceptions like Monet's *Plum Trees in Blossom*, Pissarro's *Le Pont Neuf* and Gauguin's exotic *Black Pigs*, however, the works of these famous artists are not their best, and the better art on display is the work of lesser names: Dagnan-Bouveret's *Landscape with Trees*, for instance, or Carriere's ethereal *Maternity*. There are some fine **sculptures** also, such as Carpeaux's *Laughing Girl with Roses* and Clésinger's *Lucretia*. Highlight of the collection though, and on their own ample justification for a visit to this museum, are five sculptures by Rodin, including *Eternal Springtime* and *The Kiss*.

The **Old Masters Permanent Gallery** is the real *raison d'être* of the museum. The core of the collection was purchased from Count Miklós Eszterházy in 1871. Comprising 70 works, the **Spanish Collection**, clustered around El Greco and his school, is probably the finest in the world outside Spain. It offers some vivid altar-pieces, seven El Grecos, including *The Agony in the Garden* and *The Penitent Magdalene*, and five Goyas including two of the portrayals of common, humble folk for which he is famous, *The Knife-Grinder* and *The Water-Carrier*. There are also some excellent works such as Cerezo's powerful *Ecce Homo*, Ribera's plaintive *Martyrdom of St Andrew* and Velázquez' *Peasants at Table*,

In the smaller **German Collection** are Hans Baldung Grien's long, sumptuous, wonderfully stylised portraits, *Adam* and *Eve*. The three portraits by Christian Seybold are worthy of scrutiny, one of himself, one of his daughter, and the irrepressible *Laughing Man with Brawn*. Look out also for Dürer's *Portrait of a Young Man*, whose cheer is of a far subtler nature; the elder Jörg Breu's *Elevation of the Cross*; two works by Maulbertsch, *Scene with a Young Man* and *Christ on the Cross*; and Holbein's interesting *Dormition of the Virgin*.

The **Italian Collection** is more impressive and contains many stars, such as Raphael's so-called *Eszterházy Madonna* and Titian's *Portrait of the Doge Loredan*. Other first-class portraits include Giorgione's *Self-portrait* and *Young Girl*, and Bronzino's *Young Lady*. The latter was a favourite of late Canadian author Robertson Davies, who would have seen great depths in his allegorical *Venus, Cupid and Jealousy*. Other key players in the Italian dream-team are Tintoretto's *Supper at Emmaus*, Veronese's *The Crucifixion*, Bassano's *The Road to Calvary*, and Tiepolo's *St James Conquers the Moors*.

The **Dutch Collection** is dominated by Brueghels. The younger Pieter provides the marvellous *Blind Hurdy-Gurdy Player* and *Affray between Peasants and Soldiers*, whereas the elder Pieter's quite different *St John the Baptist's Sermon* has the preacher addressing a group of Flanders peasants. The elder Jan's *Paradise Landscape* is another major work. Look out also for Rubens' *Mucius Scaevola before Porsenna*, and Sebastien Vrancx's *Outdoor Banquet*.

Other exhibits include the **English Collection**, a let-down: a few mediocre portraits by Hogarth, Reynolds and Gainsborough. There is also some mainly very bad modern art, a selection of historical paintings, and some Medieval Italian works. The collection of **Antiquities** consists mostly of Greek ceramics that didn't fit in other collections, although there are some decent 5th-century BC Attic red-figure vases.

There are plans to re-open the **Prints and Drawings Room**, which will rotate works from the museum's holdings by the likes of Leonardo, Raphael, Dürer and Picasso. The museum holds temporary exhibitions of 20th-century art, usually featuring major artists. The shop sells a decent selection of postcards, framed prints, posters, books, ceramics and jewellery. The café behind it is a good place to recover from sensory overload afterwards.

City Park (Városliget)

Heroes' Square is the gateway to the City Park, also created as part of the 1896 millenary celebrations. Over 200 halls and pavilions were erected here, displaying the agricultural, industrial and commercial life of the country. A bridge runs from the square over a lake that in winter is transformed into Europe's finest skating-rink, a marvellous scene when flood-lit at night. Originally, skaters used the lake's frozen surface but an artificial surface was added in 1926 that unfortunately uglifies this whole section of the water. The clubhouse down below operates a café and plays host to various events like live music or sporting competitions.

Across the water, hanging there like a fairy-tale mirage, is the picturesque **Vajdahunyad Castle** (© 343 1345; *open April–mid-Nov Tues–Fri 10–5, Sat–Sun 10–6; mid-Nov–Mar Tues–Fri 10–4, Sat–Sun 10–5; closed Mon; adm*). It is not an authentic castle but was designed by Ignác Alpár especially for the 1896 celebrations, intended to illustrate in one cohesive building all the different architectural styles found throughout Hungary. Erected as a temporary structure, it was so popular with the public that Alpár rebuilt it in more permanent brick. On the road to the castle is a **statue of the architect** dressed as a medieval guild-master. The building is arranged in chronological order, most of the sections using details copied from some of Hungary's most significant historic structures, or inspired more loosely by the work of a particular architect whose style reflects his age.

To the left of the gate are towers copied from former castles in Upper Hungary, now Slovakia. To the right is a copy of the tower of Segesvár in today's Romania. The courtyard on the left contains the Romanesque wing, including a copy of the still-standing 1214 Benedictine Chapel of Ják in western Hungary. The portal, which is its finest feature, is also the part most true to the original, carrying statues of the 12 apostles. To the left is a chapel incorporating elements from the 11th to 13th centuries. Opposite, to the right, the Palace section mixes elements of the Romanesque and Gothic, while to the left the section based on the 15th-century Transylvanian Vajdahunyad Castle is pure Gothic. This is the finest part and most visible from across the lake. Farther left, Renaissance style is represented by a small building with a balcony based on Sárospatak Castle in eastern Hungary. Next door, the large yellow Baroque section is inspired by details from various 18th-century mansions. This part contains the **Agricultural Museum** (*opens same hours as Vajdahunyad Castle; adm*), which traces the history of hunting and farming in Hungary, including the development of tools and some interesting varieties of livestock. Facing the entrance is the very popular **Statue of Anonymous**, the first Hungarian chronicler, from whom much information about the Middle Ages has reached us. The words on the pedestal are those with which he signed his work, and translate as 'The notary of the most glorious King Béla'. Since there were four kings bearing that name in that era, the chronicler's identity remains a matter of speculation, thus the name Anonymous and the hood which shrouds the figure in wonderfully Gothic mystery. Behind him, a small **lake** surrounded by boardwalks and willows is a pleasant place for a picnic or a daydream.

The bulk of the park stretches off to the south and west, encompassing the **Transport Museum** (*open Tues–Fri 10–5, Sat–Sun 10–6, closed Mon; adm*) and the **Petőfi Hall**, both of which might hold some interest, especially for kids. The museum explains how Hungarian transport expanded and flourished around the turn of the 20th century, and features vintage locomotives, scale models of trains, cars and steamboats, and posters and regalia covering a period of 100 years. The Petőfi Hall is a major venue for rock and pop events, as well as an informal youth centre that hosts films, theatre, parties and a roller-skating club for children, a decent weekend flea-market and occasional raves. Behind the building a stairway leads to the **Aviation and Space Flight Exhibition** (*open mid-April–Sept Tues–Fri 10–5, Sat–Sun 10–6; Oct–mid-April Tues–Fri 10–4, Sat–Sun 10–5; closed Mon; adm*), with a nice collection of old aeroplanes.

To the north, on the other side of the busy road that bisects the park, stands a grandiose yellow neo-Baroque building containing not an embassy or summer palace but the **Széchenyi Baths** (XIV. Állatkerti körút 11, ✆ 321 0310; *open April–Sept daily 6am–7pm; Oct–Mar Mon–Sat 6–5, Sun 6–4; adm*). At the entrance a statue depicts geologist Vilmos Zsigmond, who struck upon the hot spring while drilling a well in 1879. Apparently the water comes from deeper within the Earth's crust than any of the other baths, thus reaching the surface at a higher temperature (74–5°C). Inside the grand entrance hall is a series of **mosaics**, centred on the central dome, of a quality to rival anything in Budapest, plus an extraordinary fountain. This is one of the nicest of the baths, and certainly the most accessible. Everything is here: indoor pools of different temperatures, steam room, sauna, a heated outdoor pool where bathers play chess on floating boards, a swimming pool and a children's pool with water jets and waves, plus plenty of room for sunbathing, and a restaurant. The masseurs here are recommended. The inside looks like a run-down Victorian sanatorium, though more atmospheric than ugly.

North of the baths, along Állatkerti körút, you'll find from east to west an amusement park, a circus and a zoo. The **amusement park** (*Vidámpark*; ✆ 343 0996; *open April–Oct daily 10–8, Nov–Mar daily 10–6*) is not likely to impress you or your kids. The rides are old-fashioned and shabby, while the rickety roller-coaster is frightening for the wrong reasons and the ghost train not at all. There are a few newer scarier rides, though, and you may find the lack of sophistication endearing. The gilded merry-go-round, dating from the park's opening before the war, is certainly appealing and a reminder of the fact that this was the setting for Ferenc Molnár's play *Liliom*, on which the musical *Carousel* was based. Next door is a smaller funfair for toddlers. The **Municipal Circus** (*Fővárosi Nagycirkusz*; ✆ 343 8300) next door has been housing shows year-round since it was built in 1971, but there has been a circus on the site since 70 years before that. Acts involving the exploitation of animals are still a major feature.

Budapest's **Zoo** (*Állat-és Növénykert*; ✆ 343 6075) is an altogether more venerable establishment. Dating back to 1866, an initiative of the Academy of Sciences, it contains, as well as all the usual animals, some important examples of Art Nouveau. The very gateway, covered with fakirs and animals, is a good introduction. The same architect, Kornél Neuschloss-Knüsli, is responsible for the Elephant House, which resembles a large Moorish mosque decorated with majolica and ceramic animals. The Bird House designed by Károly Kós in a National Romantic style allows the birds to fly freely. There are also two greenhouses full of exotic plants and a garden of bonsai trees recently donated by the Japanese ambassador. For all that, it still retains the unpleasant flavour of an old-style zoo in which the comfort of the animals was never the highest priority; but renovations are underway to rectify that and to make it a more child-friendly environment, including the opening last year of a new children's playground. All the best animals are found around the big mountain to the right of the entrance.

The Old Jewish Quarter

District VII, or Erzsébetváros, is the slice of Budapest's pie clockwise (or south) from District VI, which is the area around Andrássy út. The old Jewish quarter covers the innermost part of this district, traditionally located between the two circular roads—here called Károly körút and Erzsébet körút—with Király út to the north and Dohány út to the south. From the outset it has been a testament to anti-semitism, its very foundation dating from the 18th century when Jews were still prohibited from living within the city walls. Ironically, as a 3rd-century AD gravestone inscribed with a menora proves, there were Jews living here at least six centuries before the Magyar founding fathers arrived. When the city outgrew its walls, new laws prevented Jews from buying property. The second half of the 19th century brought a relaxing of these property laws, leading to a rapid rise in the Jewish population in this quarter. In 1867 Jews gained formal emancipation, partly as a reward for enthusiastic support of Kossuth during the revolution. Jewish rights and assimilation crested towards the end of the century, some even rising to the ranks of nobility or gaining seats in the Chamber of Deputies. By 1939 there were about 200,000 Jews in Budapest, many of them living here in a thriving community that had its own kosher shops, restaurants, places of worship and clubs, while striving to assimilate itself and achieve acceptance in a city where anti-semitism never really stopped being an issue (Mahler complained about it when he was director of the Opera House).

A community yes, but the area was never a ghetto until 1944. Before that, the Hungarian government had avoided putting all the Jews in one place for fear that this would encourage the Allied forces to bomb the rest of the city. Such considerations were eventually abandoned when the Nazis and Fascist Arrow Cross walled off the whole area and herded the remaining Jews inside as a prelude to deportation. Since the men had already been taken away to do forced labour, which literally worked them to death, the 70,000 crammed into this small area were mainly women, children and pensioners. Due to disease, malnutrition, random killings and the cold, many of them never made it through the winter (though they fared better than those outside the city, 90% of whom perished in the Holocaust).

Today the city's remnant of 80,000 still constitutes the largest Jewish community in Central Europe. Despite Communist attempts to homogenise the area and a tendency of younger, wealthier Jews to move to quieter, more attractive districts, a sense of cultural identity has survived, fuelled by a resurgent interest in roots and religion, as well as increased contacts with the international Jewish community. The best way to get a taste of this spirit is to wander around the shabby, often decaying and bullet-pocked streets, and no introduction could be better than a visit to the magnificent Great Synagogue on Dohány út, which was one of the two entrances to the ghetto of 1944.

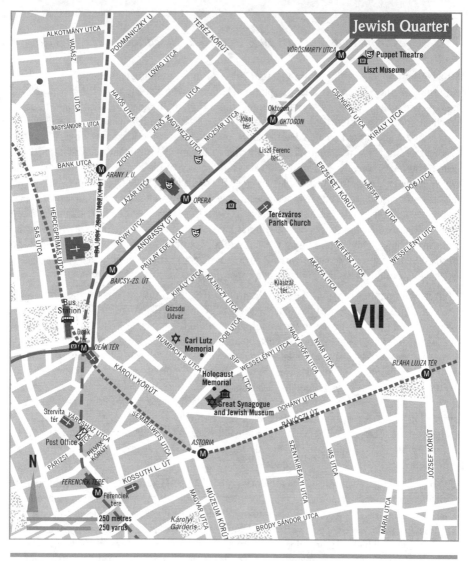

Lunch and Cafés

Fröhlich Cukrászda, VII. Dob u. 22. *Open Tues–Thur 8am–5pm, Fri 8am–2pm.* Hungary's only kosher pâtisserie, with an excellent reputation.

Hanna, VII. Dob u. 35. *Open Mon–Thur and Sun 7am–3.30pm, Fri 7am–10pm, Sat 11–3.30.* Kosher food that those in the know rate highly. Feels like a canteen. For Sabbath meals, order and pay the day before.

Zazie, VII. Klauzál tér 1–2, © 321 3405. *Open daily 12–12.* A bright, arty space. The menu, like the chef, is French. Very reasonable prices.

Great Synagogue

Open Mon–Thurs 10–5, Fri 10–3, Sun 10–2, closed Sat (service 9–12) and at Passover; adm.

Situated on the edge of the Jewish Quarter, this enormous building is tucked discreetly up a side road off the Kiskörút so that, despite its size, you won't see it until the last moment. Before even arriving here, the corner building where Dohány u. meets the Kiskörút (No. 3a) is worth attention. Its flattened corner holds a relief of a classical couple flanking an angel whose hands they hold, backed by a golden mosaic. Opposite this on the Kiskörút side is a fabulous Gothic building with much decoration, right-angled balconies jutting out point first, a central dome, and four impressive gilded Art Nouveau mosaics across the fourth floor. These are mere trifles, however, next to the Great Synagogue, Europe's largest synagogue, and the second largest in the world after Temple Emmanuel in New York; it can hold almost 3,000 people and has to be closed in winter because it's too big to heat. In the last decade, $40 million has been spent on its restoration, footed by the Hungarian State and an assortment of Jewish associations in the USA, chief among them the Emmanuel Foundation, fronted by Tony Curtis (né Bernard Schwartz), whose father was a Hungarian emigrant. It was money well spent, for this is truly one of Budapest's most outstanding constructions.

Built in a Romantic style in 1854–9 by Viennese architect Ludwig Förster, it incorporates many obvious Byzantine and particularly Moorish qualities. The patterns in the brickwork were inspired by ancient ruins in the Middle East, while the colours—yellow, red and blue—are representative of the Budapest coat of arms. This reflects other indications that the 19th-century Jews wished to assimilate with rather than distance themselves from their gentile fellows. The twin towers, for instance, are reminiscent of church steeples, and the presence of an organ (which was played on many occasions by Liszt and Saint-Saëns) is not a very Jewish feature and was opposed by more orthodox adherents. For its congregation was and is not strictly Orthodox, espousing also certain Reformist elements in a uniquely Hungarian synthesis called Neolog. Thus the presence of the Arc of the Torah (*bemah*) is at one end rather than central, which is Reformist, but men and women sit separately (men on the ground floor, women in the gallery), which is Orthodox.

The outside of the synagogue avoids the brick-building trap of excessive squareness through its arched colonnade, doors and windows, the latter richly decorated with grilles and surrounds. Star-shaped motifs and Arabic curlicues abound, along with ceramic friezes at three levels. Two octagonal towers topped with gold-trimmed onion domes loom above a large rose window, below which a Hebrew inscription from the Book of Exodus reads, 'Make me a sanctuary and I will dwell among them' (25,8). The interior, designed by Vigadó architect Frigyes Feszl, is just as grand and clearly Eastern in its influences. The floor is inset with eight-pointed stars, the balconies surmounted by gilded arches, and the ceiling adorned with arabesques and Stars of David. Outside in the courtyard, a collection of humble headstones marks the mass grave of those 2,281 Jews who died here during that bitter winter of 1944. Part of the brick wall that surrounded the ghetto can still be seen, with a plaque commemorating its liberation by the Soviets on 18 January 1945.

The staircase up to the **Jewish Museum** (*open April–Oct Mon–Fri 10–3, Sun 10–2, closed Sat; adm*) bears a relief of Tivadar (Theodore) Herzl, the founder of the Zionist movement, who was born and educated here. It seems particularly appropriate that he should hail from a community continually struggling for emancipation within a country that has always faced the same struggle. The museum's foyer contains that highly significant 3rd-century AD gravestone inscribed with a menora (seven-branched candlestick).the exhibition displays items from Hungary and abroad, mainly from the 18th and 19th centuries but some dating back to the Middle Ages, arranged according to the festival for which they were used. This includes some exquisitely crafted objects and books such as the Chevra book from Nagykanizsa, dating from 1792. The last room documents through photos, clippings and examples of anti-semitic propaganda the nightmare of the Holocaust in Hungary.

Monuments and Memorials

Behind the courtyard is the **Heroes' Temple**, a squat, square building resembling a Moghul tomb, erected in 1931 to pay tribute to the 10,000 Jewish soldiers who died fighting for Hungary during the First World War. Since it is a working synagogue, it is not open to the public. Beyond it, farther down Wesselényi utca, a garden contains Imre Varga's 1991 **Holocaust Memorial**, which channels all that pain and sorrow into the poignant form of a metallic weeping willow in the shape of an inverted menora. Each leaf bears the name of a family lost in the Holocaust. The broken marble slab in front contains the single word 'Remember'. The inscription from the Talmud on the plaque closer to the railings reads 'Whose pain can be greater than mine?'

The garden is named in honour of **Raoul Wallenberg**, a Swedish consul who is believed to have saved as many as 20,000 Jews by placing them in safe houses or even rescuing them from Auschwitz-bound trains. The day before the liberating Red Army arrived, he went forward to meet them and was never seen again. After years of silence, a Soviet official announced in 1957 that Wallenberg had died in a Moscow prison 10 years earlier. They had believed him to be a spy. The Hungarian authorities were wary of the case. In April 1949, a sculpture of the hero depicting a male figure struggling with a snake disappeared on the eve of its unveiling and emerged years later, used for a different function, outside a factory in East Hungary. A copy appeared and remains in front of the Radiology Clinic on Üllői út, but was only acknowledged as Wallenberg in 1989. Even in 1987, a statue by Imre Varga (commissioned by the US Ambassador) was shoved miles away on an arterial road in Buda (at the junction of Szilágyi Erzsébet fasor with Nagyajtai u., four stops on tram 56 from Moszkva tér). So the naming of this garden could be seen as a conscious and political act on the part of the Jewish community, who begin their plaque: 'May this park commemorate as an exclamation mark for the post-Holocaust generations the name of the Swedish diplomat Raoul Wallenberg'.

From here, cross over on to Dob u. and head back towards the Kiskörút, and opposite No.11 you will see the bizarre **memorial to Carl Lutz**, the Swiss diplomat who helped many Jews to survive by issuing them with Swiss or Swedish papers, a ploy later adopted by his colleague Wallenberg. A gold figure attached to the wall seems to be throwing down a sheet to a woman wrapped in bandages lying on the floor below. Locals know it as 'the figure jumping out of a window'. A quote from the Talmud on the easily missed plaque reads: 'He who has saved one life, it's as if he had saved the whole world'.

The 'Ghetto'

Most of what there is to see in this quarter is found on and around Dob u. At Nos.5 and 7, and at No.4 Rumbach Sebestyén, are buildings with unusual Art Nouveau façades. Down

Rumbach Sebestyén to the left is a **synagogue** of the same name, built for worshippers of a more conservative persuasion. One of the only works in Hungary of Viennese architect Otto Wagner, its Moorish façade is similar to that of the Great Synagogue, with many fine features. Owned by the state, it is currently closed and up for sale. The same is true of the amazing **Gozsdu Udvar**, a passageway linking seven courtyards between Dob u. 16 with Király u. 11. Abandoned and crumbling, this series of inelegant but enigmatic concrete squares with a dog-leg in the middle is eerie and atmospheric. Stand in the middle and look back towards the entrance and what you will see is a series of squares alternating light and shade, growing in size with perspective, thus illustrating what the Greeks called 'gnomonic expansion'. These days it is locked at the Király u. end, presumably for safety purposes. Run down as it is, not much effort is required to imagine how it was at the beginning of the 20th century when this was the bustling heart of Jewish Budapest, filled with shops, artisans and immigrants. A private concern wishes to convert it into a cultural centre with bars, art shops, workshops and galleries, the equivalent of London's Covent Garden. As a short building-lover's detour, Síp u. 11 is worth seeing for its Gothic arches, gargoyles and statue of a knight, and the Art Nouveau building on the corner of Síp and Dohány, Metroklub, is wonderfully strange.

These days the community's central focus is on Kazinczy utca, a little farther down Dob u., shortly after Hungary's only kosher pâtisserie, Fröhlich Cukrászda, whose appearance doesn't live up to its reputation. To the left of Dob u., some decaying buildings at the Király end of Kazinczy have a certain nostalgic charm, especially No.51. Király u. 34 also has an interesting façade with Art Nouveau influences. The **Orthodox synagogue** is here, its Art Nouveau façade elegantly following the curve of the street. It is a plain building apart from the very top, whose undulating curves could be of Polynesian origin. Below this, amidst Stars of David and leaf patterns, big Hebrew letters read: 'This place is none other than the house of God and the gate to Heaven.' For gentiles, entrance through the gate is unfortunately not allowed, but it's worth going through the doorway to the right, where a courtyard contains the back of the synagogue and an Orthodox complex including a Jewish school and the kosher Hanna restaurant. The buildings between here and Wesselényi u. are interesting if only for the radically differing architectural approaches they display. Note particularly the Wesselényi side of the corner building, with two giant topless angels spreading their wings. The building opposite is also worth a look, as is Wesselényi 17, which has nice Art Nouveau mosaics. There is also a beautiful Art Nouveau building farther down Dob u. at No.53.

If Kazinczy holds the local focus, the heart of activity is still centred on **Klauzál tér**, a block farther down Dob u. It was the heart of the 1944–5 ghetto as well, when—as Wallenberg bravely complained to the Germans—50,000 people were crammed into living space intended for 15,000. Nowadays, its centre is given over to one big playground, and the scene of so much suffering now echoes with the sound of children's laughter.

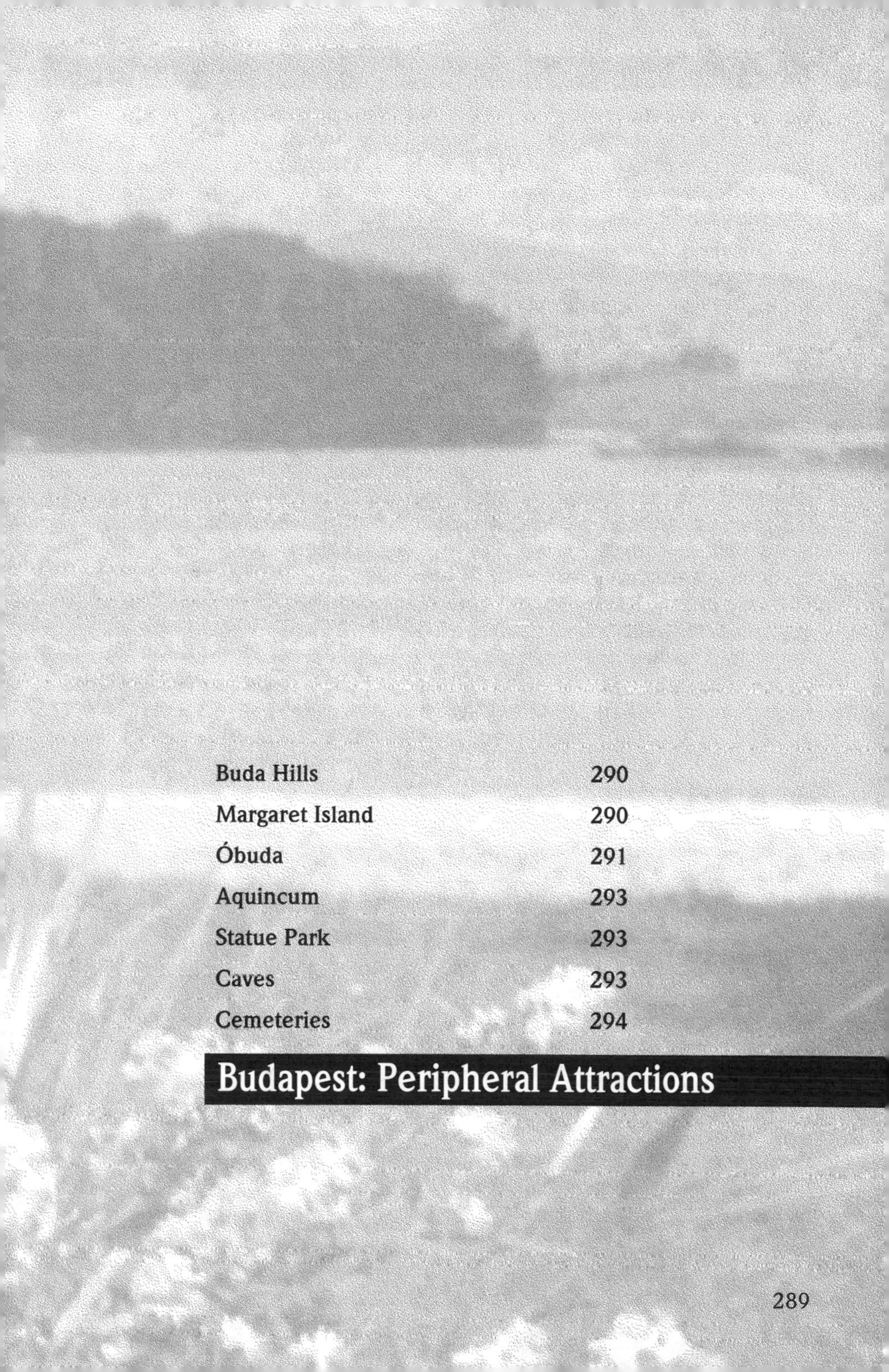

Budapest: Peripheral Attractions

Forested countryside stretches to the west of Buda, perfect for walking and cycling. There are established trails with signs indicating distance, or duration in minutes (p) and hours (ó). Budapesters like to get back to nature too, so the tranquillity factor is reduced at weekends. Particularly popular, especially with children, are the Children's Railway and the Chairlift, which can be combined with the Cogwheel Railway to form a circuit, described below.

The **Cogwheel Railway** starts in the Városmajor park, opposite the cylindrical Budapest Hotel (*a couple of stops west of Moszkva tér by buses 22, 56 and 156, or trams 18 and 56; trains leave every 15mins daily 5am–11.30pm, normal ticket required*). The terminus at Széchenyi-hegy is a short walk from the start of the **Children's Railway**. This narrow-gauge railway (760mm) covers 11.1km in about 45mins, mostly through dense woodlands. Built by youth brigades in 1948, it is run by uniformed 10–14-year-olds (except the engineer), giving the whole experience a slightly magical feel (*trains run Mon–Fri every hour 8am–5pm, Sat and Sun every 30–45mins 8.45am–5pm; closed Mon Sept–May; adm.*)

To visit the **Budakeszi Game Park**, alight at Szépjuhászné from the Children's Railway, catch the 22 bus and ask the driver for the *Vadaspark*. The entrance is a 15min walk past the Hotel Tanne. Apart from the animals in enclosures (wild boar, deer, etc), you're likely to see little but butterflies and flowers. It is a beautiful place to wander, however, and usually empty. A wooden lookout tower offers a nice view of the hills, forest and village. The terminus of the Children's Railway, **Hűvösvölgy**, is a large meadow equally good for tranquil meandering. Buses run from here day and night back to Moszkva tér. It is also worth leaving the Children's Railway at **János-hegy** and following the trail across to the Chairlift. From here it is a short but steep walk up to the four-tiered neo-Romanesque **Erzsébet Lookout Tower**, designed by Frigyes Schulek, who built the Matthias Church and Fishermen's Bastion. On the highest spot in the Buda Hills, it offers superb views. The **Chairlift** descends 235m in its 1km journey, taking about 15mins. Its Hungarian name, *Libegő*, means 'floater', and this is exactly what it does, about 8m above the ground, enough to bother those scared of heights and excite children who relish gentle doses of danger (*runs May–Sept 9.30–6, Oct–April 9.30–5, closed alternate Mon; adm*). Bus 158 runs from Zugliget at the bottom back to Moszkva tér.

Margaret Island (Margit-sziget)

Trams 4 and 6, or bus 26 from Nyugati station.

Margaret Bridge (Margit híd) is the northernmost bridge you are likely to encounter. It is easily recognisable by the 'elbow' in its middle, a 150° angle which allows it to continue the line of the outer ring road (Nagykörút) of which it is a part. At this elbow, a third section leads to Margaret Island. Essentially one big park, Margit-sziget is greatly appreciated by Budapesters, offering as it does a slice of tranquillity minutes from the city centre.

Named the 'Isle of Rabbits' in the Middle Ages, the island was used by the Árpáds as a royal game reserve. From the 12th century onwards various monastic orders replaced the hunters: Premonstratensians, Franciscans and the Order of St John. Béla IV had a convent built for the Dominican nuns, of which his daughter Margaret was the best-known inmate. Tradition has it that during the Mongol invasion of 1242–4, Béla vowed that if Hungary survived he would have her brought up as a nun. In 1252, aged nine, she was confined to the convent, where she died 19 years later after many holy acts, which won her canonization (in 1943) and a place of honour in the Hungarian historical pantheon. In a change of pace, the Turks destroyed most of the island's holy buildings and used it for a harem. Open to the public since 1869, the park's popularity with lovers generated the saying 'Love begins and ends on Margaret Island'.

The island is primarily attractive as a park, especially for children. There are plenty of open areas for games and sports, playgrounds, and much natural beauty. At either end, facilities can be rented including roller-skates, bikes, two-seater pedal-cars and electric cars. Choice and prices are greater at the northern end. Along the road, which runs down the western side, are the **Alfréd Hajós Swimming Pools**, designed by and named for the gold-medal winner of the 100m and 1,200m swimming races at the first modern Olympics in 1896. More fun, and extremely popular in summer, is the **Palatinus Strand** bathing complex, 300m farther on. There are seven open-air thermal pools, a water chute, wave machine, segregated terraces for nude sunbathing (a gay favourite), and a 100m pool, one of the longest in Europe.

East of here is the oval-shaped rose garden; southwest the scant remains of a 13th–14th-century Franciscan **church**. East of the rose garden is a small **game reserve** with goats, donkeys, peacocks and cranes. North is the park's most prominent feature, the 57m **water tower**. A pioneering structure when built in 1911, it now houses exhibitions in the summer, and is next to an open-air theatre that hosts operas, rock operas and plays. To the southeast stand the **ruins** of the Dominican church and convent, a series of low walls (*currently being renovated*). A marble shrine within marks Margaret's original burial place. Farther north stands the 1931 reconstruction of a 12th-century **Premonstratension Chapel** in the Romanesque style. The bell hanging in the tower was made by master craftsman Hans Strous, lost for centuries, then found in the roots of a tree torn out during a storm in 1914.

Two giant **hotels** stand sentinel over the northern end of the island. The Danubius Grand is one of Budapest's classic hotels, built as a sanatorium in 1873 by Miklós Ybl. The **baths** to which it was attached are contained within the ugly Thermal Hotel next door. To the west is a **rock garden** whose warm-water ponds contain tropical fish, bullrushes, sculptures and lilies of varied colour. A network of small canals and bridges links the ponds and paths. What with the artificial waterfall and a small gazebo, this is one of the most attractive areas in the park. Public toilets can be found between here and the hotels, or at the water tower.

Óbuda

HÉV train to Árpád híd from Batthyány tér. Bus 6 from Nyugati station, or 86 from any stop on the Buda promenade.

Situated on the Buda side, level with the northern tip of Margaret Island, Óbuda was the first settlement of any significance in this area. The Romans used the Danube as the boundary of their province Pannonia. A legionary camp and fortifications were established there to defend the border against the barbarians beyond, and by the 2nd century BC a thriving civilian settlement had grown around the camp, centred around Aquincum 3km to the north of Óbuda. The arrival of the Huns marked the end of the Roman era. In the Middle Ages, Árpád and his successors built their royal residence here and the town flourished, but when Béla IV moved the royal seat to the more strategic location of Castle Hill, this original Buda (the ancient Hungarian word Ó means old) lost its importance along with its name. After the Turkish occupation, it enjoyed a renaissance as a market town, producer of wines and gastronomic centre.

Today, Óbuda, plagued by an ugly rash of tower blocks and housing estates, is the sort of area many people go on holiday to get away from. There are Roman ruins scattered around but they are mainly disappointing. **Flórián tér**, Óbuda's main square and an unpleasant junction of major roads and fly-overs, was built over the nucleus of the Roman military camp. Various remains, including some elegant columns, stand in the grassy centre, while the underpass is dotted with display cabinets and relics, and the Roman Baths Museum, a series of badly reconstructed low walls. South from here on Pacsirtamező u. the remains of a large **Amphitheatre** (at the junction with Nagyszombat u., a 30min walk), though limited, are quite impressive. Built in the 2nd century AD with an arena larger than that of the Colosseum in Rome, it could seat up to 15,000 spectators. North of Flórián tér (northwest up Vörösvári u. then right on Vihar u. as far as Meggyfa u.) is the **Hercules Villa** (*open 15 April–end April and Oct Tues–Sun 10–5, May–Sept Tues–Sun 10–6, closed Mon and Nov–14 April; adm*). A series of **mosaics** are preserved where they were found. Under the first canopy an almost complete mosaic portrays Hercules shooting the centaur Nessos. The third canopy contains a mosaic of Alexandrian origin once composed of 60,000 stones and depicting Hercules about to vomit at a wine festival. It would be spectacular if complete, but sadly the three central figures are cut off just above the waist.

Rome enthusiasts apart, most will prefer to concentrate on some of the galleries and museums in the area. With the notable exception of the **Kiscelli Museum**, about 1km southwest of Flórián tér at Kiscelli u. 108, most of these are centred on two very attractive squares which, with their cobbled streets, old buildings, antique lamp-posts and a ban on traffic, recapture some of Óbuda's former glory. Right opposite the HÉV exit on **Szentlélek tér** a splendid old white building resembling a large farmhouse contains the **Vasarely Museum** (*open Tues–Sun 10–5, closed Mon; adm*), with an exhaustive collection of Op Art by one of the fathers of the genre, Victor Vasarely, exhaustively exploring spatial distortions and optical illusions with geometric patterns. It's a bit tedious if you're not a fan. In the square to the left stands a fine newly erected Holy Trinity column. On the right, where the two squares merge, the Baroque Zichy mansion (Zichy Kúria) holds the **Kassák Museum** (*open Mar–Sept Tues–Sun 10–6, Oct–Feb Tues–Sun 10–4, closed Mon; adm*) and a local history exhibition. Lajos Kassák was a radical constructionist and publisher whose left-wing but anti-authoritarian stance led him into conflict with almost everyone. The museum contains works of avant-garde painting, sculpture, literature and typography, and, like the last one, is an acquired taste.

Literally meaning Main Square, **Fő tér** remains to this day the focal point of the town. Surrounded by a fine theatre (*Városháza*) and a clutch of restaurants still making a living from Óbuda's *bon-vivant* reputation, this square magically keeps the fragile ambience of a medieval village. The 18th-century Copf-style house at No.4 contains the **Zsigmond Kun Folk Art Museum** (*open Tues–Fri 2–6, Sat–Sun 10–6, closed Mon; adm*), a collection of mainly 19th-century folk art: pottery, textiles, carvings and furniture, presented in the former home of this connoisseur who gathered them from all over greater (pre-Trianon) Hungary. At the northeast corner of the square is the strange sight of three metallic and miserable-looking women sheltering beneath umbrellas. This is the start of Laktanya u., and the statue composition a prelude to the **Imre Varga Gallery** at No.7 (*open Tues–Sun 10–6, closed Mon; adm*), with a substantial collection by this striking and versatile artist responsible for the Holocaust Monument and the statue of Károlyi Mihály close to Parliament. As well as copies and photos of these and other major works, such as his *St Stephen* and composition of *Our Lady of Hungary* which stand in the Hungarian Chapel of St Peter's in Rome, there are many excellent sculptures.

Aquincum

Grounds open mid-April–end April and Oct Tues–Sun 9–5, May–Sept Tues–Sun 9–6; museum opens at 10 on the same days; both closed Mon and Nov–mid-April; adm. HÉV from Szentlélek tér or buses 34, 42 and 106.

Roughly 3km to the north of Flórián tér, alongside Szentendrei u., stand Budapest's major Roman ruins, the former town of Aquincum. The site is on the right just before the railway bridge. Starting life as a military camp and growing to become provincial capital of Pannonia Inferior, Aquincum was a buzzing civilian town of 40,000 inhabitants. No buildings survive, but the arrangement of the foundation walls and the underground piping give a fair idea of the scale and layout of the town, including the remains of a public baths, houses, a market place, a forum, law courts, an old Christian church, and a shrine to the Persian sun-god Mithras. The neoclassical **Aquincum Museum** contains locally found relics such as statues, pottery, tools, mosaics and jewellery, as well as a reconstructed 3rd-century Roman water organ. Across the road by the side of the HÉV station are the ruins of the civilian town **Amphitheatre**, which could seat 8,000, considerably smaller than the military one in Óbuda. No ticket required, just walk around the surrounding bank peering through the vegetation.

Statue Park (Szoborpark)

XXII. Balatoni u., ℂ 227 7446, www.szoborpark.hu; open Mar–Nov daily 10–6, Dec–Feb Sat–Sun and hols 10–dusk; adm. Take red-numbered bus 7-173 from Ferenciek tere (M3) to its terminus at Etele tér, then a Volán bus to Diósd-Érd from gate 2 or 3 (not included on a Budapest travel card).

After the fall of Communism in 1989, instead of destroying all those Socialist monuments the Hungarians consigned them to a kind of retirement home on the edge of the city, far from impressionable young eyes and tormented older eyes, but close enough so that Hungarians can visit them and jeer, laugh or curse in catharsis. It's also a pretty unique tourist attraction. Here you will find all the old favourites like Marx, Lenin and Engels, plus idealized happy workers, victorious soldiers, and martyrs galore. Many of them are frighteningly massive, like the Red Army soldier that stood at the foot of the Liberty Statue on Gellért Hill. Aesthetically most interesting are Imre Varga's **statue of Béla Kún**, and the giant charging **sailor** based on a 1919 call-to-arms poster. Each of the 43 monuments represents a facet of Hungarian history. You're given most of the information you need with the ticket, but for those with a special interest the 600Ft guidebook is a worthy investment. The half-hearted should be warned, however, that it's a long way to go and many people find the site small and disappointing.

Caves

Since Buda's caves were created by the action of hot thermal waters from below rather than cold rainwater from above, their appearance is unique, consisting of strangely beautiful rock sculptures. The two that are open to visitors are situated in the Buda Hills not far from Óbuda. They are reached from Kolosy tér (itself reached by bus 86 from Batthyány tér, M2 or Flórián tér in Óbuda, or bus 6 from Nyugati station, M3). The larger and more impressive is **Pálvölgyi** (II. Szépvölgyi u. 162, ℂ 388 9537; *bus 65 from Kolosy tér; open Tues–Sun 10–4, closed Mon; adm*). This is the longest labyrinth discovered in the Buda Hills. The 30min tour involves narrow passages, steep climbs and some 600 steps. The stalagmites and stalactites are awesome, and many formations protruding from the rock face resemble animals. About a 10min walk away is the **Szemlő-hegy** cave (II. Pusztaszeri u. 35, ℭ 315 8849; *bus 29 from Kolosy tér; open Mon and Wed–Fri 10–3, Sat–Sun 10–4, closed Tues; adm*). Not as big, impressive or convoluted, this system is maybe more striking. Instead of stalactites the walls are covered with bulbous, cauliflower-like mineral formations called 'cave pearls'. The air is so clean and pure that the lowest level (not on the 25min tour) contains a therapy centre for respiratory illnesses. A small museum displays cave finds from all over Hungary.

Cemeteries

Kerepesi Cemetery, next to Keleti station (M2), was declared a 'decorative' cemetery in 1885, meaning it is where the establishment of each age buried those it chose to honour, be they poets, politicians, artists, architects or war heroes. It thus provides an interesting perspective from which to view Hungary's turbulent recent history. All the big names are here, often easily reached by the wide avenues that criss-cross the vast orderly area. The main mausoleums, placed at key junctions, are those of Kossuth (by Alajos Stróbl), Batthyány and Deák, but look out also for the particularly beautiful tomb of popular singer Lujza Blaha.

Farkasréti Cemetery on Németvölgyi u. (tram 59 from Moszkva tér) in the Buda Hills is mainly visited for the extraordinary **Mortuary Chapel** built by Imre Makovecz, situated just to the right of the main entrance. A prime example of his 'organic architecture', the whole wooden structure resembles a giant oesophagus of some exotic creature. Another delightful spot for a stroll, the cemetery is overcrowded with graves and trees, and contains a rich and varied assortment of tombstones, some of them bearing famous names. Béla Bartók is buried here, with Georg Solti alongside him. Visit the information building to the left of the main gate for a map showing the locations of the cemetery's inmates.

One grave in particular attracts people—almost exclusively Hungarians—to the other major burial ground, **Újköztemető Cemetery**, way out at the edge of District X at Kozma u. 8–10 (*trams 28 or 37*). It is here that Imre Nagy was secretly buried in 1958, along with other key figures from the 1956 Uprising, and a large number of civilians dumped in a mass grave. After the ceremonial funeral of 1989 in Heroes' Square, they were reburied in the same plot (301), which is right in the farthest corner, about 30mins walk from the main gate—not far enough to stop Hungarians from secretly placing flowers on the anonymous grave before 1989, which were duly removed by Soviet policemen. At the beginning of one of the paths leading into plot 300, which contains the mass graves, is a **Transylvanian Gate** inscribed with the words 'Only a Hungarian soul may pass through this gate'. In the middle of the plot stands a wooden campanile, a type of decoration traditionally found in old Hungarian cemeteries, in front of panels listing the names of over 400 victims of the Uprising. Adjacent to Nagy's simple grave is György Jovánovics' **Monument to the Martyrs of the 1956 Revolution**, which could be seen as a 'deconstructed' early Christian basilica or as a symbolic passage through purgatory.

Alongside this cemetery lies Hungary's largest **Jewish burial ground**. There are many grand tombs here, but the most striking, not far from the entrance, to the right of the main path, is that of the **Schmidel family** designed by Ödön Lechner and Béla Lajta. A central mosaic in green and gold tiles, representing the Tree of Life, is surrounded by flamboyant turquoise ceramics and floral motifs.

Budapest: Museums and Galleries

Castle Hill

Budapest History Museum (Budapesti Történeti Múzeum), I. Dísz tér 17, Wing E of the Royal Palace (Várbusz from Moszkva tér, M2). *℗* 375 7533. *Open Wed–Mon 10–4, closed Tues; adm.* The capital's history from the defeat of the Turks to the present. *See* p.239.

Golden Eagle Pharmacy Museum (Arany Sas Patikamúzeum), I. Tárnok u. 18 (Várbusz from Moszkva tér, M2). *℗* 375 9772. *Open Tues–Sun 10.30–5.30, closed Mon; adm.* A reconstructed alchemist's laboratory. *See* p.243.

Hungarian National Gallery (Magyar Nemzeti Galéria), I. Szent György tér 6, Wings B, C & D of the Royal Palace (Várbusz from Moszkva tér, M2). *℗* 375 7533. *Open April–Oct Tues–Sun 10–6; Nov–Mar Tues–Fri 10–4, Sat–Sun 10–6; closed Mon; adm.* Hungarian art from the 13th century to the present. *See* p.237.

Military History Museum (Hadtörténeti Múzeum), I. Kapistán tér 2–4 (Várbusz from Moszkva tér, M2). *℗* 356 9522. *Open Tues–Sun 10–4, closed Mon; adm.* Permanent displays cover the 1848 Revolution, and the 'Thirteen Days' of street-fighting during the 1956 Uprising. *See* p.244.

Museum of Hungarian Commerce and Catering (Kereskedelmi és Vendéglátóipari Múzeum), I. Fortuna u. 4 (Várbusz from Moszkva tér, M2). *℗* 175 6249. *Open Wed–Fri 10–5, Sat–Sun 10–6, closed Mon–Tues; adm.* History of Budapest's shopping and advertising. *See* p.243.

Museum of Contemporary Art (Kortárs Müvészeti), I. Szent György tér 6, Wing A of the Royal Palace (Várbusz from Moszkva tér, M2). *℗* 375 9175, *ludwig@c3.hu. Open Tues–Sun 10–6, closed Mon; adm.* Modern art from the USA, Europe, Russia and Hungary. *See* p.239.

Music History Museum (Zenetörténeti Múzeum), I. Táncsics Mihály u. 7 (Várbusz from Moszkva tér, M2). *Open April–Oct Tues–Sun 10–6, Nov–Mar Tues–Sun 10–5, closed Mon; adm.* Instruments from the 17th–19th centuries. *See* p.243.

National Széchenyi Library (Nemzeti Könyvtár), I. Szent György tér 6, Wing F of the Royal Palace (Várbusz from Moszkva tér, M2). *℗* 224 3848. *Open Mon 1–9pm, Tues–Sat 9am–9pm, closed Sun and July; adm.* Over two million books. Exhibits on the first floor, occasionally of book illustrations. *See* p.240.

Telephone Museum (Telefon Múzeum), I. Úri u. 49 (Várbusz from Moszkva tér, M2). *℗* 201 2243. *Open Tues–Sun 10–6, closed Mon; adm.* The development of the phone, presented in a fun, hands-on way. *See* p.243.

Tabán

Semmelweis Museum of Medical History (Semmelweis Orvostörténeti Muzeum), I. Apród u. 1–3 (Tram 19 from Batthyány tér, M2). *℗* 201 1577. *Open Tues–Sun 10.30–5.30, closed Mon; adm.* Medical items from all over the world. *See* p.249.

The City

Ethnographical Museum (Néprajzi Múzeum), V. Kossuth Lajos tér 12 (Kossuth Lajos tér, M2). *℗* 312 4878, *www.hem.hu. Open May–Oct daily 10–6, Nov–Feb daily 10–5; adm.* Permanent exhibition on 'Folk Culture of the Hungarians'. Throughout 2001 the museum will be showing 'Images of Time'. *See* p.262.

Belváros

Lutheran Museum, V. Deák tér 4. *℗* 317 3413. *Open Tues–Sun 10–6, closed Mon; adm.* Exhibits include a copy of the first book printed in Hungary. *See* p.266.

Museum of Applied Arts (Iparművészeti Múzeum), IX. Üllôi u. 33–7 (Ferenc körút, M3). *℗* 217 5222. *Open daily 10–4; adm.* Permanent exhibition on Arts and Crafts and superb temporary ones, including the long-lasting Art Nouveau exhibition. *See* p.272.

National Museum (Nemzeti Múzeum), VIII. Múzeum körút 14–16 (Kálvin tér, M3). *℗* 338 2122, *hnm@hnm.hu, origo.hnm.hu. Open mid-Mar–mid-Oct Tues–Sun 10–6, rest of year Tues–Sun 10–5, closed Mon; adm.* Hungary's history illustrated by relics ranging from church pews to Communist propaganda. *See* p.271.

Underground Railway Museum (Földalatti Múzeum), V. Deák tér metro station, near Károly körút exit. *Open Tues–Sun 10–6, closed Mon; adm.* Two old carriages on an original stretch of line. A nostalgic slice of history. *See* p.266.

Andrássy Út

Agricultural Museum (Mezőgazdasági Múzeum), Vajdahunyad Castle (Hősök tere, M1). ✆ 343 1398. *Open April–mid-Nov Tues–Fri 10–5, Sat–Sun 10–6; rest of year Tues–Fri 10–4, Sat–Sun 10–5; closed Mon; adm.* The history of hunting and farming in Hungary. *See* p.281.

Aviation and Space Flight Exhibition, Petőfi Csarnok Hall, Városliget (Széchenyi fürdő, M1). ✆ 343 0565. *Open mid-April–Sept Tues–Fri 10–5, Sat–Sun 10–6; rest of year Tues–Fri 10–4, Sat–Sun 10–5; closed Mon; adm.* Two halls full of old planes, gliders and helicopters. *See* p.282.

Ernst Museum, VI. Nagymező u. 8 (Opera M1). ✆ 341 4355. *Currently closed for renovation, but due to re-open soon.* Contemporary avant-garde and small temporary exhibits. *See* p.276.

Ferenc Hopp Museum of Eastern Asiatic Arts (Hopp Ferenc Keletázsiai Művészeti Múzeum), VI. Andrássy u. 103 (Bajza utca, M1). ✆ 322 8476. *Open Tues–Sun 10–6, closed Mon; adm.* Massive collection of a businessman-traveller with many antique pieces from India, China and Tibet.

Franz Liszt Museum (Liszt Ferenc Emlék Múzeum), VI. Vörösmarty u. 35 (Vörösmarty u., M1). ✆ 322 9804. *Open Mon–Fri 10–6, Sat 9–5, closed Sun; adm.* The composer's belongings in his former house. *See* p.277.

Kodály Memorial Museum and Archive (Kodály Emlék Múzeum és Archívum), VI. Andrássy u. 87–9 (Kodály körönd, M1). ✆ 352 7106. *Open Wed 10–4, Thurs–Sat 1–6, Sun 10–2, closed Mon–Tues; adm.* Zoltán Kodály's house, with manuscripts and folk art. *See* p.278.

Museum of Fine Arts (Szépművészeti Múzeum), XIV. Hősök tere (Hősök tere, M1). ✆ 343 9759. *Open Tues–Sun 10–5.30, closed Mon; adm.* Unmissable art collection. *See* p.279.

Palace of Arts (Műcsarnok), XIV. Dózsa György u. 37 (Hősök tere, M1). ✆ 343 7401. *Open Tues–Sun 10–6, closed Mon; adm.* Exhibitions of chiefly modern art, often very good. *See* p.279.

Transport Museum (Közlekedési Múzeum) XIV. Városligeti krt 11 (Széchenyi fürdő, M1). ✆ 343 0565. *Open Tues–Fri 10–5, Sat–Sun 10–6, closed Mon; adm.* Antique vehicles, model boats and railways etc, with captions in English. *See* p.281.

The Jewish Quarter

Jewish Museum (Zsidó Múzeum), VII. Dohány u. 2 (Astoria, M2). ✆ 342 8949. *Open April–Oct Mon–Fri 10–3, Sun 10–2, closed Sat; adm.* In the Great Synagogue. Items from Hungary and abroad, mainly 18th–19th-century. The last room documents the Holocaust in Hungary. *See* p.286.

Further Afield

Aquincum, III. Szentendre u. 139 (HÉV to Aquincum). ✆ 250 1650. *Grounds open mid-April–end April and Oct Tues–Sun 9–5, May–Sept Tues–Sun 9–6; museum opens at 10 on the same days; closed Mon and Nov–mid-April; adm.* The most worthwhile of the scattered remains of Aquincum. *See* p.293.

Béla Bartók Memorial House (Bartók Béla Emlékház), II. Csalán u. 29 (Bus 5 from Moszkva tér). ✆ 394 2100, *bartok-1981@matav.hu. Open Tues–Sun 10–5, closed Mon; adm.* Set in beautiful grounds, this Art Nouveau villa was Bartók's last Hungarian home before he left in disgust at the country's increasing fascism. The concert hall, often used for chamber concerts on Fridays, features the painted wooden panels of a 1740 church, plus many works of art often depicting the man himself. His study, personal objects and folklore collection are all displayed, along with the Edison phonograph he used for collecting old folk tunes.

György Ráth Museum (Ráth György Múzeum), VI. Városligeti fasor 12 (Bajza utca, M1). ✆ 342 3916. *Open Tues–Sun 10–5.45, closed Mon; adm.* Permanent collections of Chinese and Japanese art and curios, plus temporary offerings from other Far Eastern countries. Excellent displays with commentaries in English.

Imre Varga Gallery (Varga Imre Galéria), III. Laktanya u. 7 (Árpád híd HÉV). ✆ 250 0274. *Open Tues–Sun 10–6, closed Mon; adm.* The rich and prolific output of Hungary's most successful 20th-century sculptor. *See* p.292.

Kassák Museum, III. Fő tér 1 (HÉV to Árpád híd or tram 17 to Kiscelli u.). ✆ 368 7021. *Open Mar–Sept Tues–Sun 10–6, Oct–Feb Tues–Sun 10–4, closed Mon; adm.* Avant-garde painting, sculpture, etc. *See* p.292.

Kiscelli Museum (Kiscelli Múzeum), III. Kiscelli u. 108 (Bus 86 from Batthyány tér, M2, then bus 165). ✆ 250 0304. *Open April–Oct Tues–Sun 10–6, Nov–Mar Tues–Sun 10–4, closed Mon; adm.* On a forested hilltop between Óbuda's Flórián tér and the Pál-Völgyi caves, this 1745 Baroque Trinitarian monastery contains a selection of major Hungarian artworks from about 1880 to 1990, including Rippl-Rónai's *My Parents After 40 Years of Marriage* and János Kmetty's Cubist *Városliget*. There are some fine 18th–19th-century engravings of Budapest, with the brand-new Chain Bridge and the Great Synagogue. The bombed-out shell of a Gothic church is now an eerie gallery, providing a striking setting for spectacles such as operas and fashion shows

Margit Kovács Museum (Kovács Margit Múzeum), Vastagh György u. 1 (HÉV or bus to Szentendre). ✆ 06 26 310 790. *Open April–Oct daily 10–6; adm.* A vast collection by the popular ceramicist-sculptor. At times bordering on twee, and far too tame and homely for some art-snobs, Kovács' work is loved by most for its moving and profound rendering of common themes, as well as its undeniable idiosyncracy. Nor was she afraid to experiment with styles and media, always displaying a deft and unique touch.

Museum of Hungarian Literature (Petőfi Irodalmi Múzeum), V. Károlyi Mihály u. 16 (Ferenciek tere, M3). ✆ 317 3611. *Open Tues–Sun 10–6, closed Mon*; *temporarily closed for renovation but due to re-open soon.* Exhibits normally revolve around the country's principal writers.

Natural History Museum (Természettudományi Múzeum), VII. Ludovika tér 6 (Klinikak, M3). ✆ 313 0842. *Open Wed–Mon 10–6, closed Tues; adm.* Good for kids, with an interactive 'discovery room' encouraging experimentation.

Open Air Village Museum (Szabadtéri Néprajzi Múzeum/Skanzen), Szentendre (Szabadságforrás u. HÉV to Szentendre, then Skanzen bus from stand 7, every 40min–1hr, taking a longer route in the afternoon). ✆ 06 26 312 304. *Open April–Oct Tues–Sun 9–5, closed Mon; adm.* On an area of 115 acres, the plan of this museum is to represent farms, villages and agro-towns from 10 regions of Hungary. Though only four have been completed, this is still an impressive exhibition of rural architecture,and could easily fill half a day. Every second Sunday craft workshops are held, offering the visitor hands-on experience of such skills as basket-weaving or pottery, and festivals are celebrated with dancing and other folkloric merrymaking. All very child-friendly.

Palace of Wonders Interactive Scientific Playhouse (Csodák Palotája), XIII. Váci út 19 (Lehel tér, M3). ✆ 350 6131, *info@csodapalota. hu. Open Mon–Fri 9–5, Sat–Sun 10–6; adm.* A new interactive scientific centre for kids, with lots of fun things to do: mazes, lasers and so on.

Planetarium, at the southwest corner of the Népliget (People's Park), about 3 miles southeast of Pest, out beyond the edge of District VIII (Népliget M3). ✆ 265 0725. *Open Mon–Fri 9.30–3.30, Sat–Sun 10–4, laser shows at 7pm; adm.* In the city's largest park, this popular attraction shows the movements of the planets. Evening laser shows are accompanied by music.

Statue Park (Szoborpark), XXII. Balatoni u. (Take red-numbered bus 7-173 from Ferenciek tere, M3, to its terminus at Etele tér, then a Volán bus to Diósd-Érd from Gate 2 or 3). ✆ 227 7446, *www.szoborpark.hu. Open Mar–Nov daily 10–6, Dec–Feb Sat–Sun and hols 10–dusk; adm.* A kind of Communist theme park, where all the old statues were dumped. *See* p.293.

Trafó Galéria, IX. Liliom u. 41 (Ferenc körút, M3). ✆ 215 1600, *www.trafo.hu. Closed July and Aug.* There are all sorts of things going on at this hip and happening venue: exhibitions of art, photography, mixed media and indefinable installations, plus poetry, dance, film, comedy, music, raves and combinations of the above.

Vasarely Museum, III. Szentélek tér 6 (HÉV to Árpád híd or bus 6 or 86). ✆ 250 1540. *Open Tues–Sun 10–5, closed Mon; adm.* Works by the Op Art pioneer. *See* p.292.

Zsigmond Kun Folk Art Museum (Kun Zsigmond Népművészeti Gyűjtemény), III. Fő tér 4 (HÉV Árpád híd). ✆ 368 1138. *Open Tues–Fri 2–6, Sat–Sun 10–6, closed Mon; adm.* Mainly 19th-century folk art. *See* p.292.

Budapest: Food and Drink

Hungarian Food

The image conjured up by the words 'Hungarian food' are of stodgy dumplings, thick stews, lots of meat and lard, and paprika in everything. While this cliché contains some truth—meat is ubiquitous—Hungarian cuisine is rich and varied. Cross-fertilization is one of the keys. The Mongols may have razed the country, but from them the Magyars learnt the secrets of stewing meats in their own juices, the basis of *tokány* stews. The great Renaissance king Matthias is said to have imported the likes of dill, capers, figs, turkey and garlic from Italy. The most famous Hungarian flavour, however, came with the Turks. Paprika is not ubiquitous, but is used subtly, and often sweet and fragrant. Along with onions, fat (traditionally lard, but now just as often sunflower oil or butter) and, often, smoked bacon, it forms the basis of the classic stews called *pörkölt*, which usually include cubed meat. *Paprikás* is the same thing with sour cream. These are the dishes we know as goulash; *gulyás* is actually a thick meat soup cooked slowly with onions, vegetables, paprika and potatoes or small noodles. In their milder, unground form, paprika peppers are the basis, with tomato, of the classic summer dish *lecsó,* a kind of ratatouille often served with meat. In winter an old favourite is stuffed cabbage, *töltött káposzta*, made of sauerkraut, minced pork and smoked sausage dumplings, and other smoked meat.

The Austrians had an inevitable influence on Hungarian cuisine. From them came schnitzel, meats fried in breadcrumbs (*rántott*), and the cooking of vegetables in a roux of lard and flour and/or sour cream (*főzelék*). The biggest influence, however, was from France. In the 19th century the Francophile tastes of aristocrats encouraged chefs to lighten the traditional fare, substituting butter for lard, and introducing such subtleties as herbs and truffles. The chefs' names are often attached to the dishes they inspired. József Dobos, whose name has been immortalised by his invention of the chocolate-layered *Dobos torta*, helped to popularize these innovations through his highly influential Hungarian-French cookbook.

As well as these dishes, a typical menu will offer a range of meats, often including pheasant, wild boar, hare, venison, goose, goose liver and duck, cooked in a variety of ways, usually with sauces containing fruit, wine or cheese. They are generally delicious. Fish from Hungary's many rivers and lakes is also abundant: the delicious pike-perch and trout, abundant carp and rather bony catfish. Particularly worth trying is the hot and sour fish soup called *halászlé*. Vegetarians can expect little or nothing, though: theirs is a credo alien to the Magyars, for whom healthy eating for centuries meant shovelling down enough fat to make it through the next winter. Breaded and fried mushrooms (*gombafejek rántva*) and cheese (*rántott sajt*) feature heavily. Salad (*saláta*) has no fixed meaning and could amount to a pile of pickled cabbage, gherkin or pepper. Among desserts, look out for the strudels (*rétes*), apple, cherry or curd-cheese. Curd-cheese balls (*túrógombóc*) are also recommended, as are the pancakes stuffed with walnuts and topped with chocolate sauce named after the famous chef (*Gundel palacsinta*). It's fun to stretch the culinary experience to a second venue and have coffee and a delicious cake or pastry in a *cukrászda*.

Breakfast-lovers will be horrified to learn that the morning meal doesn't really fit into the Hungarian scheme of things. Few places bother with it at all.

Traditionally, culinary class-barriers have not existed, so menus in the cheapest and most expensive restaurants can be virtually identical. The food in the expensive place will normally be superior, as will the surroundings, but the greatest difference will be in the service. Don't expect to find Hungarian waiters gracious or particularly good at their jobs: they are still recovering from a period when doing a job well was not expected. You can generally expect even the cheapest place to have a menu in English and a waiter who knows enough English to take your order. Just because you have finished your meal, do not expect the bill to materialize until you ask for it. Check to see if service is included: that the menu says it won't be doesn't mean a thing. And check the price of items such as drinks before ordering: some places hike up the price of drinks outrageously (though these have generally not made the list below).

The approximate price for a **three-course meal with wine** is as follows:

∞∞∞∞	**luxury**	6,000Ft +
∞∞∞	**expensive**	4,000–6000Ft
∞∞	**moderate**	2,000–4,000Ft
∞	**inexpensive**	up to 2,000Ft

Wine

Hungary's 20 wine-producing areas have a tradition as long and accomplished as those of France, Italy or Spain, broken by 40 years of Communism, from which the industry is still recovering. Grape varieties include Cabernet Sauvignon, Merlot, and Pinot Noir for reds, Chardonnay, Sauvignon and Riesling for whites, and local Central Eastern European varieties. There are also some rosés and natural sweet whites. The Hungarian wine with the greatest reputation is of the latter kind: Tokaji Aszú, which Louis XIV called 'the wine of Kings, the King of wines'. It is made using grapes desiccated by long hours of sunshine and *botrytis cinerea*, or noble rot. The number of hods of these raisin-like grapes added to each batch of base-wine made from non-botrytised grapes is expressed by a number from three to seven *puttonyos*, the higher the number the greater the quality, the finest known as Tokaji Eszencia. The mixture of grapes is then refermented, without all of the sugar turning to alcohol.

Of the reds, the most famous, not necessarily the best, is known internationally as 'Bull's Blood' and locally as (Egri) Bikavér, Eger being the best-known but not the only region to produce it. Indeed, some of the finest hail from the Szekszárd area, which generally makes some of the best red wine to be found. The other key region for reds is Villány, whose wines are the most full-bodied, with high tannin and alcohol content. Eger reds tend to be more delicate and complex. For whites the North Balaton area is recommended. The small Somló region produces very acidic whites, said to be utterly unmistakable. Otherwise, Chardonnays are generally a good bet, as is the Tokaji Furmint or Hárslevelű. Note that Hungarian sparkling wine can be every bit as good as champagne and considerably cheaper.

Beer

Hungary is not historically a beer-drinking nation and, while the younger generation are moving in this direction, Hungarian brewers are yet to catch up. Dreher, the most common brew, is acceptable ice-cold on a sweltering day. Borsodi is only slightly better. The best bet is to look for Czech beers such as Budweiser Budvar (not to be confused with the inferior American product) or Pilsner Urquell. Even better are the Belgian beers such as Leffe and Belle Vue. Guinness and Murphy's are also popular. Normally two sizes are offered: a *korsó* is almost a pint, a *pohár* almost a half. Some places sell glasses by the decilitre (deci).

Spirits

The most famous national spirit is *pálinka*, a strong fruit brandy or *eau de vie*. The best is apricot (*barack*), but also worth trying are plum (*szilva*), pear (*körte*) and cherry (*cseresznye*). A national institution is Unicum, a dark brown liqueur containing 23 different herbs, with a horribly bitter taste and a kick like a mule.

Restaurants

Buda

Castle Hill

∞∞∞ **Alabárdos**, I. Országház u. 2, ✆ 350 0851. *Open noon–4 and 7–11, closed Sun.* In a 15th-century Gothic building, this feels like a banquet hall, with paintings of knights, swords and shields. Specialities of ancient Hungarian cuisine are put together with an expertise that explains the prices. There's a lot of game choices and even a couple of veggie dishes. The service is impeccable, the selection of drinks vast.

∞∞∞ **Pest Buda Vendéglö**, I. Fortuna u. 3, ✆ 212 5880. *Open daily noon–midnight.* Intimate and old-fashioned with a pianist playing schmoozy favourites. Gourmet meat-based food, excellent wine list, attentive service. Expensive; lunch specials are good value.

∞∞∞ **Rivalda**, I. Színház u. 5–9, ✆/✉ 489 0235, *rivalda@nextra.hu. Open daily 11.30–11.* By the Castle Theatre, decorated with classy but over-the-top theatre regalia. Seating is also planned for the expansive cobbled courtyard. Co-owned by an ex-Gundel chef, with a menu that aims at quality rather than range of choice. Try the goat's cheese and fennel, filet mignon with caramelized garlic and the hot chocolate ganache. A few good veggie options.

∞ **Aranyhordó**, I. Tárnok u. 16, ✆ 316 4239. *Open daily 11–11.* The best reason to eat here is for the cellar dining area, so authentic it's damp. Upstairs is light and clean with a vaulted ceiling, stained glass and bad historical murals. The terrace is okay but for the traffic and fake grass. Basic Hungarian fare, little for veggies.

∞ **Fortuna Spaten**, I. Hess András tér 4, ✆ 375 6175. Agreeable terraced seating in the cobbled courtyard. Food is cheaper than most and with bigger portions than the more expensive places. Gypsy music in the evening. Less attractive inside; cheap self-service area upstairs.

Víziváros

∞∞∞ **Jardin de Paris**, I. Fő u. 20, ✆ 201 1147. *Open daily noon–midnight.* It's overpriced and, apart from frogs' legs and some seafood, offers much the same fare as most. But it has tables in a beautiful courtyard, surrounded by an overgrown garden and a house engulfed by vines. Add the trees, torches and jazz band and you have a very romantic night-time setting.

∞ **Belgian Brasserie** (Belga Söröző), I. Bem Rakpart 12, ✆ 201 5082. *Open daily noon–midnight.* Batthyány tér (M2), then tram 19 or walk. Popular Belgian-style bar-restaurant, stylishly fitted out, with a pleasant Hungarian crowd. A staggering range of beers, including Belle Vue Kriek and Leffe (light and dark) on tap. Starters include brioche, snails and frogs' legs, followed by mussels or meat dishes with a French slant. Tasty, plentiful food, good service.

∞ **Horgásztanya Vendéglő**, II. Fő u. 27, ✆ 212 3780. *Open daily noon–midnight.* Fishing-themed: nets everywhere, an upside-down boat complete with plastic fisherman stuck to the ceiling. Famous for their fish soup but they also rustle up marjoram veal steak with brains, mushroom and bacon, or dishes fried on lava stone. Nice terrace. Nothing for veggies.

∞ **San Remo**, II. Török u. 6–8, ✆ 212 1991. *Open 11am–midnight, closed Mon.* Batthyány tér (M2), tram 4 or 6. Simple, clean Italian-style cellar. Lots of pizzas and seafood, good range for vegetarians, and a good drinks selection.

Elsewhere in Buda

∞∞ **Kéhli**, III. Mókus u. 22, ✆ 368 0613. *Open Mon–Fri 5pm–midnight, Sat and Sun noon–midnight.* HÉV to Árpád híd or bus 86 or 6. Authentic Óbuda restaurant with a plain country feel. Traditional but fancy home-made food, with French leanings and some veggie options. Their classic dish is the hot-pot with marrow-bone. Staff somewhat lax, and prices somewhat high.

∞∞ **Kisbuda Gyöngye**, III. Kenyeres u. 34, ✆ 368 6402. *Open noon–midnight, closed Sun.* HÉV to Árpád híd or bus 86 or 6. Intimate little Óbuda establishment with a plush, old-style interior and an excellent reputation. Expertly prepared Hungarian cuisine, such as medallions of veal with goose liver in a truffle sauce. Attentive service, and a fine selection of wines, malt whiskies and *pálinka.*

∞∞ **Remíz**, I. Budakeszi u. 5, ✆ 275 1396. *Open Mon–Sat 9–1am, Sun noon–midnight.* Bus 22 from Moszkva tér (M2). Situated in the Buda Hills not far from Moszkva tér. Highly recommended for the best traditional Hungarian cuisine; summer barbecues in the wonderful garden are particularly popular.

∞ **Hemingway**, XI. Kosztolányi Dezsö tér 2, ✆/✇ 381 0523. *Open daily noon–midnight.* Almost any bus/tram from Gellért Hotel. A great spot in a nice park. The spacious interior resembles an English colonial club from bygone days, but the music is upbeat, except for the mellow live bands, and the vibe modern. Roasted chicken with potato purée, some pasta options and a few surprises like gazpacho. As much a bar as a restaurant.

∞ **Krúdy Bohém Kávéház**, III. Fő tér (Hídfő u. 16), ✆ 250 3647. *Open daily*

10–1am. HÉV to Árpád híd or bus 86 or 6. Maybe the best option on Óbuda's main square. The interior resembles a Victorian drawing-room, with antique leather divans and lots of small pictures. The courtyard is pleasant and quiet, the beer cellar's barstools are wooden horses with leather saddles. The menu features meats in imaginative sauces. The prices are very reasonable for the location.

∞ **Náncsi Néni**, II. Ördögárok u. 80, ✆ 397 2742. *Open daily noon–11.* Bus 56 from Moszkva tér (M2), or Children's Railway then walk. Most famous place in town for home-cooked Hungarian cuisine. Top marks for quality and quantity, and a thoroughly authentic experience. Try the braised wild boar cutlets, or the sizzling seafood Thunderbolt. Booking is essential.

✇ **Élet-Ház Bio Centrum**, XII. Böszörményi u. 13–15, ✆ 212 5881. *Open noon–5, closed Sat–Sun.* Bus 102 from Déli pu (M2). For those seeking really healthy, organic vegetarian food, this is an oasis. Cheap, tasty and filling, but don't expect too much choice. Part of a health-food shop (*open Mon–Sat 9–9*).

✇ **Gigler**, III. Föld u. 50c, ✆ 368 6078. *Open Tues–Sat noon–10, Sun noon–4, closed Mon.* HÉV to Árpád híd station, bus 86 or 6. Cheap and cheerful option in Óbuda. The interior and courtyard are basic but the food is authentic home-cooked Hungarian fare, tasty, plentiful and cheap.

✇ **Marcello**, XI. Bartók Béla u. 40, ✆ 466 6231. *Open noon–10, closed Sun.* Popular and intimate Italian: an incredible range of pizzas, a good salad bar and a no-smoking policy. One of the few options in Gellért.

✇ **Márkus Vendéglő**, II. Lövöház u. 17, ✆ 212 3153. *Open Mon–Fri 11–1am, Sun noon–midnight, closed Sat.* The pleasant interior and only quite noisy terrace attracts Moszkva tér's more respectable denizens. Along with the standards there is a good range of fish, salads and options for vegetarians, plus a decent wine selection and a few quality bottled beers.

Szent Jupát, II. Retek u. 16, ✆ 212 2923. *Open 24 hours.* It may not look like much (upstairs is better), but this place is an institution, not just for its opening hours but for the legendary size of the portions. It's good food too.

Pest

City (Lipótváros)

∞∞∞ **Lou Lou**, V. Vigyázó Ferenc u. 4, ✆ 312 4505. *Open Mon–Fri noon–3 and 6.30–11, Sat 6.30–11, closed Sun.* Two beautiful little rooms covered with small pictures. Excellent French-Hungarian haute cuisine, well presented, and an impressive wine list. Attracts a well-to-do crowd.

∞ **Biarritz**, V. Kossuth Lajos tér 18, ✆ 302 3943. *Open daily 11am–midnight.* Very popular with locals. Nice terrace and a snazzy light modern interior. Food is variations on the standard themes (sour duck ragoût soup or marinated beef with anchovies), with two dishes for veggies.

∞ **Café Kör**, V. Sas u. 17, ✆ 311 0053. *Open 10–10, closed Sun.* Small and popular bistro near the Basilica, simply but tastefully furnished. The brevity of the menu belies the quality of the food. A good place for a steak. Breakfast until 11.30am.

∞ **Garage Café**, V. Arany János u. 9, ✆ 302 6473. *Open Mon–Fri 11–2am, Sat and Sun 5pm–2am.* Much nicer than the outside suggests. Brick walls covered with odds and ends such as a bicycle and a ladder, with a giant glitterball in the middle. The clientele is well-heeled locals or expats. Service is very professional. International/Hungarian: Cajun black-bean soup, teriyaki chicken, fajitas; in well-cooked large portions. Good choice of beers. Highly recommended.

∞ **La Fontaine**, V. Mérleg u. 10, ✆ 317 3715. *Open daily 10–midnight.* French specialities in well-furnished, spacious surroundings. The food is good rather than excellent, portions adequate rather than big. Good wine selection, friendly service

and reasonable prices, especially if you have the three-course lunch special.

∞ **Via Luna**, V. Nagysándor József u. 1, ✆ 312 8058. *Open daily 11am–11.30pm.* The dining room resembles an Italian country villa. Various pastas and sauces, including some for veggies. Risottos, lots of fish and pizzas, some salads and steaks.

∞ **Csarnok Hal Vendéglő**, V. Hold u. 11, ✆ 269 4906. Opposite the Post Office Savings Bank, with tables on the quiet street and a simple, pleasant interior. Regular Hungarian fare with lots of fish dishes and some nice touches like fried Camembert, or caviar for 600Ft. Good choice of bottled beers. Often open late.

∞ **Danko**, V. Hercegprímás u. 18, ✆ 269 0220. *Open Mon–Fri 7am–11pm, Sat 8am–11pm, Sun 8am–4pm.* Good food with interesting options; very cheap. Cold wine and cream soup, sirloin Lyonnaise for 650Ft, roasted mackerel, and veggie dishes like aubergine (eggplant) gratin. Cheap wine; lots of breakfast options.

∞ **Gandhi**, V. Vigyázó Ferenc u. 4, ✆ 269 1625. *Open noon–10.30, closed Sun.* Healthy, vegetarian food, organic if possible, not all Indian, in the calm and relaxing ambience of a small cellar with a warren of rooms decorated with mandalas, pictures of holy figures and a rock-pool in the corner. Two set menus change daily. Also teas, fresh juices and desserts.

∞ **Gourmand**, V. Október 6 u. 19, ✆ 312 7873. *Open Mon–Fri 9–5, Sat and Sun 9–4.* Bright interior with vaulted ceiling and Mediterranean feel. The menu is ordinary but very cheap, with good, plentiful food.

∞ **Lugas Étterem**, V. Bajcsy-Zsilinszky 15, ✆ 302 5393. *Open daily noon–midnight.* Best views of the back of the Basilica from this terrace across the main road. Very popular, laid back and friendly, offering good portions of well-cooked Hungarian fare. There are a few veggie choices, like grilled courgette (zucchini) with dill and cheese sauce, plus salads. Drinks include juices and a decent selection of wines.

Belváros

∞∞∞ **Corvinus** (Keminski Hotel), V. Erzsébet tér 7–8, ☎ 429 3777. *Open daily 6pm–midnight.* Generally considered one of Budapest's best restaurants. Setting, presentation and service are impeccable. The menu is small, international and cleverly put together.

∞∞∞ **Iréne Légrádi Antique**, V. Bárczy István u. 3–5, ☎ 266 4993. *Open noon–3 and 7–midnight, closed Sun.* Close to Deák tér. Extremely high class. Feels like dining in an antique shop, which is what it is. The best of Hungarian cooking with great service: one of the best restaurants in Hungary. Gypsy music in the evening.

∞∞∞ **Képíró**, V. Képíró u. 3, ☎ 266 0430. *Open daily 10am–2am.* Bright artistic interior of an eclectic nature: Art Nouveau stained glass, Japanese windows, Greek columns, with gentle jazz. Haute cuisine: marinated salmon with asparagus mousse, rosé suprême of duck with balsamic-cherry ragout, spinach soufflé with forest mushrooms. Good selection of wines and whiskies. Great-value lunch specials.

∞∞∞ **Cosmo**, V. Kristóf tér 7–8 (upstairs in Cyrano), ☎ 266 4747. *Open daily noon–3 and 6–11.* The avant-garde décor aiming at elegance is in poor taste, but the garden out back is delightful. Food a little more daring than most places. Scallops in white wine sauce; frog-fish in spicy pesto bacon-rings; *mocca blanco* for dessert.

∞∞∞ **Cyrano**, V. Kristóf tér 7–8, ☎ 266 3096. *Open daily noon–5.30 and 6.30–11.* Just off Váci utca, the terrace is wonderful for crowd-watching and the food good. Inside is dark and cavernous, with strange wrought-iron fixtures, a beautiful ceiling and interesting art. The menu is French-international with a few vegetarian options like spinach sponge roulade.

∞∞∞ **Empire** (in the Astoria Hotel), V. Kossuth Lajos 19–21, ☎ 317 3411. *Open daily 7–10, noon–3 and 6.30–11.* Sumptuous like an old-fashioned drawing room, a taste of a bygone age. Hungarian and international food. Gypsy music in the evenings.

∞∞∞ **Kárpátia**, V. Ferenciek tere 7–8, ☎ 317 3596. *Open daily noon–3 and 6–11.* An extraordinary interior, bold, busy and very medieval, the walls covered in heavy patterns, much like the Matthias Church. There is a pleasant covered area outside. The food is traditional Hungarian cuisine cooked to perfection; the service is good.

∞∞∞ **Légrádi Testvérek**, V. Magyar u. 23, ☎ 318 6804. *Open 6pm–midnight, closed Sun.* Not quite as luxurious as its sister restaurant, and a little more relaxed. Drawing-room atmosphere: enjoy the celebrated cuisine of the famous Légrádi brothers beneath a fine painting of a man finding his wife in bed with her lover.

∞∞∞ **Múzeum Kávéház Étterem**, VIII. Múzeum körút 12, ☎ 267 0375. *Open 10am–1am, closed Sun.* Established in 1885, still with much of the original décor including Károly Lotz frescoes. Good food, sumptuous surroundings, with an excellent reputation. The menu is enormous. Very good wine list. Booking essential.

∞∞ **Fatál**, V. Váci u. 67 (entrance on Pintér u. near Main Market), ☎ 266 2607. *Open daily 11.30–2am.* Very popular; be prepared for a wait. Enormous servings of traditional, well-cooked Hungarian food, with a lot of choice. Set in a tasteful country-style cellar. Service can be slow and inattentive. The name isn't a warning: a *fatál* is a wooden dish.

∞ **Csendes**, V. Múzeum körút 13, ☎ 267 0218. *Open noon–10, closed Sun.* Standard Hungarian food in a dim but pleasant room full of locals, which is a good sign. Not haute cuisine, but cheap and plentiful.

∞ **Govinda**, V. Belgrád Rakpart 18 (just north of Sörhaz u.), ☎ 318 1144. *Open noon–9, closed Mon.* Vegetarian set meal changing daily but basically an Indian thali: dal, two vegetable dishes, puri, rice, chutney. Healthy, filling and tasty, not very spicy. Drinks are good, especially cassis. Upstairs has a view of the Danube.

Around Andrássy Út

Articsóka, VI. Zichy Jenö u. 17, ✆ 302 7757/8. *Open daily noon–midnight.* Light and airy, popular and lively. The menu is sophisticated Italian, with some nice innovations: stuffed squid with risotto *alla milanese.* Veggie dishes include baked artichoke hearts with gorgonzola. Lots of wines and cocktails. Book.

Barokk, VI. Mozsár u. 12, ✆ 331 8942. *Open daily noon–midnight.* This slightly musty cellar with a vaulted ceiling resembles a Baroque drawing-room. The waiters wear period costume and the food lovingly re-creates authentic 17th- and 18th-century fare: consommé, paste of game Casanova-style or poppy-seed parfait.

Bombay Palace, VI. Andrássy u. 44, ✆ 332 8363. *Open daily noon–2.45 and 6–11.15.* Extremely elegant and stylish restaurant serving authentic and varied Indian food cooked by genuine Indian chefs. Good vegetarian options, as one would expect. Service impeccable and helpful.

Velvet, VI. Andrássy út 19, ✆ 322 7896. *Open noon–midnight, closed Sun.* This used to be a private member's club and still has that atmosphere of opulence and attentive service, along with the wood, brass, and leather armchairs in the saloon. Sophisticated Hungarian: salmon grilled with three different peppers and a champagne sauce, goose liver braised in red wine with cinnamon-apple. Pretty good wine list too. Good-value lunch menu.

Cactus Juice, VI. Jókai tér 5, ✆ 302 2116. *Open Mon–Thur noon–2am, Fri and Sat noon–4am, Sun 4pm–2am.* This basement pub has an unfortunate Wild West theme and speakeasy feel but excellent food. Well-prepared Hungarian fare with imaginative twists and portions so big some dishes require two plates. Try the Giant Pork BBQ with home-made pickles. The menu suggests a wine to complement each meal. Some choices for veggies, and a good selection of beers.

Chez Daniel, VI. Szív u. 32, ✆ 302 4039. *Open daily noon–3 and 7–11.* Real French food cooked by French chefs and voted best French restaurant two years running. The small, bright courtyard is a delightful place in which to enjoy first-class, reasonably priced food. Booking essential.

Marquis de Salade, VI. Hajós u. 43, ✆ 302 4086. *Open daily 11–1am.* At the Bajcsy-Zsilinszky end of the road. Owned by an Azerbaijani and featuring chefs from many different countries. The vast menu has salads, meat, seafood and veggie choices. In a small, intimate cellar scattered with Eastern rugs. Book.

Pesti 1998, VI. Paulay Ede u. 5, ✆ 266 3227. Popular light and breezy place next to Vista, serving authentic Hungarian fare.

Sir Lancelot, V. Podmaniczky u. 14, ✆ 302 4456. *Open daily noon–1am.* A theme restaurant with a rowdy party atmosphere. A long murky cellar with wagon-wheel candelabras, suits of armour, shields, etc. Guests sit at wooden benches, eat with their hands and drink beer from tankards. The staff wear medieval garb, minstrels play, and there's sword-fighting after 10pm. Huge portions of traditional meaty fare. There's a champion selection of over 100 Hungarian wines. Booking essential.

Elsewhere in Pest

Fausto's, VII. Dohány u. 5, ✆ 269 6806. *Open noon–3 and 7–midnight, closed Sun.* High-quality, genuine Italian food. The pasta is home-made, the sauces exquisite. A gastronomic delight with service to match and a well-chosen wine list.

Gundel, XIV. Állatkerti u. 2, ✆ 321 3550. *Open daily noon–4 and 6.30–midnight.* Founded in 1894, Gundel is a legend: the most famous restaurant in Hungary, the highest-praised in Central Europe, and among the best in the world. The interior is exquisite, the garden a delight and the menu adds refinement to traditional Hungarian dishes. Of course it is expensive, and a little stiff and formal. The

Sunday lunch buffet is a good compromise at 3,400Ft (served *11.30–3*).

∞ **Carmel Pince**, VII. Kazinczy u. 31, ✆ 342 4585. *Open daily noon–11.* Apart from a few Jewish dishes, the menu is Hungarian-international. Lots of fish dishes, and a few choices for veggies. Try the lemon veal fricassée, or the Carmen Cornucopia for two. Attentive service and a good selection of wines.

∞ **Robinson**, XIV. Városligeti tó, ✆ 343 0955, *Open daily noon–4 and 6–midnight.* An island restaurant (about 12ft from the shore) in City Park, bravely placed opposite Gundel. A friendly, laid-back atmosphere in beautiful surroundings. The French-inspired, cleverly planned menu changes regularly. Excellent, well presented food.

∞ **Bagolyvár** (The Owl's Castle), XIV. Állatkerti u. 2, ✆ 343 0217. *Open daily noon–11.* Gundel's sister restaurant is in a rustic Transylvanian building with wooden beams. Quality traditional home-cooking, prepared and served only by women.

∞ **Fészek Művész Klub Étterem**, VII. Kertész u. 36, ✆ 322 6043. *Open daily noon–midnight.* Tram 4 or 6 from Nyugati tér (M3) or M2 metro to Blaha Lujza tér and walk. In a leafy interior courtyard surrounded by arcades and old street-lamps. The best of Hungarian cuisine (nothing for veggies). Good, plentiful food at a good price. Highly recommended.

∞ **Hanna**, VII. Dob u. 35, ✆ 342 1072. *Open Mon–Thur and Sun 7am–3.30pm, Fri 7am–10pm, Sat 11am–3.30pm.* In a courtyard behind the Orthodox Synagogue. Kosher food that those in the know rate highly. Feels like a canteen. Order and pay at the back, then sit and wait. For Sabbath meals, order and pay the day before.

∞ **Krónikás**, XIII. Tátra u. 2, ✆ 329 2048. *Open daily noon–midnight.* Tram 4 or 6 from Nyugati tér (M3), tram 2 from Kossuth tér (M2) (close to Szent István korut). This cosy cellar's ambience is spoilt by too much light and poor, barely audible music, but the food is excellent and good value. All meat, including wild boar, pheasant, hare, etc, cooked in tasty sauces.

∞ **Művész Bohém Kávéház**, XIII. Vígszínház u. 5, ✆ 339 8008. *Open daily 10–1am.* Beautiful old salon, as much a restaurant as coffee shop, with meats and fish and the likes of chestnut soup with brandy. Live piano every night. Reasonable prices given the atmosphere.

∞ **Zazie**, VII. Klauzál tér 1–2, ✆ 321 2405. *Open daily noon–midnight.* A bright, arty space. Strange Gilliamesque contraptions hang from the ceiling holding colourful conical lampshades. The menu, like the chef, is French: veal and pistachio pâté en croûte, rabbit braised in carrot juice, sun-dried tomato and thyme. Very reasonable prices.

Cafés and Coffeeshops

Coffee was introduced here by the Turks a century before it was heard of in Paris or Vienna. The burgeoning coffee culture reached its apotheosis at the turn of the 20th century, when there were between 400 and 600 cafés in Budapest. At a time when most people lived in cramped, dark surroundings with few amenities, coffeeshops were a convivial place to relax and socialise. As atomic physicist and Nobel prizewinner Eugene Wigner put it, 'In such places you were not only allowed to linger over coffee, you were supposed to linger, making intelligent conversation about science, art and literature.' These were forums for views to be aired and disseminated. The 1848 Revolution even began in the Café Pilvax, Petőfi's regular haunt, where he spent so much of his time that he advised his friend János Arany to address any letters there. Cafés would list on the wall like a menu those publications to which they subscribed, and provided paper and ink for the journalists and writers who spent much of their time gaining inspiration from the free flow of ideas and opinions. Naturally, they were favoured by the whole intellectual and artistic community. Different groups or professions, artists, writers or businessmen, would have their own coffeeshop. Thus the Japán on Andrássy út was the regular den of artists and architects such as Ödön Lechner, József Rippl-Rónai and Csontváry, whereas the New York was dominated by writers, clustered around dramatist Ferenc Molnár, who, so the legend goes, threw its key into the Danube on the opening night so that it might never close. Like many others, it never did. Regulars would stumble in at 3 or 4am to enjoy 'hangover soup'. Food was available round the clock, often better quality than at many restaurants, and the head-waiter, who enjoyed a social position of unparalleled importance, might let hard-up artists eat their 'writers' plate' on credit. It says something for the standing of coffeeshops that the New York, which opened in 1894, was designed by the architect in charge of the Royal Palace, Alajos Hauszmann.

The New York is the only survivor of those glory days. So much were they bastions of free thought that the Communists naturally closed them down. After the Communist years, with the promise of consumerism to come, even the optimists harboured no real hopes of a return to the cöffeehouse days. But somehow, gloriously, it has (to an extent) happened. All over the city, new establishments have opened with a genuine sense of style. Not just sad reproductions of former glory, they often succeed in being 'old-style'—wood, mirrors, polished brass surfaces, tasteful pictures, plush seats and marble tables, with declared intent to function as a place where ideas are fostered, and the newspapers scattered around—in a new, modern way. The Central Kávéház on Ferenciek tere is a perfect example. The coffee (espresso rather than Americano) is probably better than it ever was. Along with this rebirth, the kind of trendy cafés found in Paris, London or Amsterdam, modern alternatives to pubs and bars, are also represented in abundance: Café Miró, for instance, or Café Vian. Generally alcohol is as available here as caffeine. Finally, Budapest is famous for its pâtisseries, known here as *cukrászda*, selling a variety of creamy gateaux, tortes, tarts, pastries and pies, freshly made on the premises. Often the shabbiest places sell the best produce. The locals always know.

Buda

Angelika, I. Batthyány tér 7, ✆ 212 3784. *Open daily 10am–11pm*. On the river side of St Anne's Church, this is a bastion of old-fashioned style, complete with vaulted ceilings, gilt mirrors, lamps, chandeliers and marble tables. Impressive selection of coffees, cakes, juices, teas, wines, spirits, cocktails, ice creams, 18 bottled beers and even breakfast.

Café Miró, I. Úri u. 30, ✆ 375 5458. *Open daily 9am–midnight*. The most successful stylish modern spot in Castle Hill, decked out to resemble a large-scale piece of art by Miró, and with a terrace offering views of Matthias Church. Mixed clientele in the day, buzzing with locals in the evening. Good drinks, but if you're hungry eat elsewhere.

Café Pierrot, I. Fortuna u. 14, ✆ 375 6971. *Open daily 11am–1am*. At the Béksi Kapu tér end of the street, this comfortable little café is bursting with character and eclectic charm. It is halfway to being a restaurant, with crêpes, seasonal specials like asparagus, vegetarian dishes and lunch deals. The bar has a good range of beer and wine as well as speciality coffees and cocktails. Live piano-playing.

Daubner, II. Szépvölgyi u. 50, ✆ 335 2253. *Open daily 9am–7pm*. Buses 6 or 86 to Kolosy tér, then bus 65. One of the strong contenders for the 'best cakes and ice cream in town' prize, which explains the almost perpetual queues. Not very conveniently located, but a must if you're in the area. No sitting area or coffee (they're busy enough already).

Gusto's, II. Frankel Leo u. 12, ✆ 316 3970. *Open 10–10, closed Sun*. Tram 4 or 6 or walk from Batthyány tér (M2). Very popular small café with a terrace on a quiet street. Intimate, classy but informal with a clientele to match. Good range of beer, coffee and spirits, but only cold food and desserts. The tiramisu is famous.

Korona Kávéház, I. Dísz tér 16. *Open daily 10–6.* Not much to look at, but the rumour is that this pâtisserie has the best cakes on Castle Hill.

Litea, I. Hess András tér 4, inside Fortuna Passage, ✆ 375 6987. *Open daily 10–6.* Small bookshop-cum-café with tables scattered around between the shelves, specializing in teas and classical music. Some books in English, mainly about Budapest.

Ruszwurm Cukrászda, I. Szentháromság tér 7. *Open daily 10–7.* Budapest's oldest pâtisserie, open since 1827, its interior including some fine *chaises longues* and an old ceramic stove. As much tourist site as coffeeshop, with the views of the Matthias Church a bonus. Staggeringly busy.

Lipótváros

Café Mirákulum, V. Hercegprímás u. 19, ✆ 269 3207. *Open Mon–Fri 9am–1am, Sat 2pm–1am, Sun 4pm–midnight.* Tasteful, bright café-bar with Art Nouveau prints and a laid-back atmosphere and clientele. Fair selection of beers and wines, coffee, teas, juices and shakes. Some food (cheap).

Café Picard, V. Falk Miksa u. 10, ✆ 311 8273. *Open Mon–Fri 7am–10pm, Sat 9am–10pm, Sun 10–10.* Tiny, stylish continental café near Parliament. Excellent strong coffee, some tasty but light food, plus beer, wines and juices.

Coquans, V. Nádor u. 5, ✆ 266 9936. *Open Mon–Fri 7.30–7.30, Sat 9–6, Sun 11–5.* IX. Ráday u. 15, ✆ 215 2444. *Open Mon–Fri 8–6, Sat 9–5, Sun 11–5.* II. Fény u. market, 3rd Floor, ✆ 345 4275. *Open Mon–Fri 7–5, Sat 7–2, closed Sun.* Chain of small, modern but tasteful cafés serving a range of good coffees and the odd croissant.

István Cukrászda, V. Október 6 u. 1, ✆ 331 3274. *Open 10–8, closed Sun.* Nice little spot for coffee and cake near the Basilica. Pay downstairs; your order arrives upstairs in the dumb-waiter.

Szalai Cukrászda, V. Balassi Bálint u. 7. *Open 9–7, closed Tues.* An old-style institution run by the same family for generations. Housed in rather drab surroundings just north of Parliament. The cakes and pastries have an excellent reputation.

Belváros

Auguszt Cukrászda, V. Kossuth Lajos u. 14–16, ✆ 337 6379. *Open Tues–Fri 10–6, Sat 10–2,* closed Sun–Mon. Astoria (M2). Delightful little old-style coffeeshop hidden away in the corner of a courtyard. Good coffee and cakes, and an oasis of sophistication away from the downtown bustle.

Bon Café, V. Károly körút 10 (in courtyard). *Open Mon–Fri 8–8, Sat 9–2, closed Sun.* Playfully arty, unpretentious coffeeshop near Astoria. Serves a good breakfast (English 725Ft; Continental 480Ft), plus omelettes, baking and desserts. Coffee, teas, juices, a large selection of non-alcoholic drinks, and a good choice of bottled beers, wines and cocktails.

Café Cinema, V. Semmelweis u. 2. *Open daily 9am–midnight.* Big café near Astoria with a low funky ceiling and subdued lighting. Very atmospheric, alive with the chatter of a young, cheerful crowd. Good prices for coffee, cakes, juices and a fair selection of wines, liquors and cocktails.

Central Kávéház, V. Károlyi Mihály u. 9. *Open Sun–Thurs 8am–midnight, Fri and Sat 8am–1am.* Vast old-style coffeehouse on Ferenciek tere with extremely high ceilings and clever decoration. Leather upholstery, marble tables and the gold, green and orange colour scheme add to the feeling of grandeur. Reasonable prices; intimate seating upstairs. The food is surprisingly good.

Europa Kávéház, V. Szent István körút 7–9, ✆ 312 2362. *Open daily 9am–11pm.* Trams 4 or 6, or Nyugati pu (M3). Extremely popular old-style coffeehouse on the Nagykörút, offering canapés, ice cream, cakes, cocktails and a good range of beer. Next to a take-away *cukrászda, open 9–8.*

Gerbeaud, V. Vörösmarty tér 7, ✆ 429 9000. *Open daily 9–9.* The place to sit and enjoy coffee and cake at the social heart of Belváros. Sit out on the terrace to watch the crowds; inside is replete with turn-of-the-20th-century antique furniture and fittings. They also do breakfast, cold food and beer, but at a price. Round the corner is a slightly cheaper stand-up version and an expensive restaurant. The whole affair is quite touristy, and service rushed.

Morik Caffé, V. Erzsébet tér 1, ✆ 266 9882. *Open Mon–Fri 7am–11pm, Sat and Sun 9am–11pm.* Classy old-style little coffeeshop near the Basilica, with constellations on the ceiling. A paradise for connoisseurs, with dozens of choices of beans freshly ground and served in fancy china.

Museum Cukrászda, V. Múzeum körút 10. *Open 24 hours.* Near the museum, cute and old-fashioned inside, small terrace outside. Coffee, cakes and alcohol at any time. The choice of music doesn't always fit the pleasant interior.

River Café, V. Párizsi u. 6. *Open daily 10am–midnight*. Atmosphere like a small French café on a quiet side-street near Váci u. and Ferenciek tere. Some meals also (about 2,500Ft).

1,000 Tea, V. Váci u. 65. *Open Mon–Sat noon–9, Sun 3–8*. Very chilled-out little tea-room in a courtyard off the southern end of the street. The atmosphere is pure zen, with some seating on the floor around low tables or outside at tea-chest tables. Only tea sold, about 30 varieties.

Zsolnay Kávéház, VI. Teréz körút 43, near Nyugati station (M3). Upstairs in the Béke Radisson Hotel, another contender for the best cakes in town.

Zsolnay Kávéház, V. Váci u. 20. Ground floor of the Taverna Hotel. Probably the nicest place to have a coffee on this northern section of the pedestrian street. Outside is a slightly raised terrace, inside is an old-style lounge, all wood and windows with a piano-player and fountain. Good cakes.

Around Andrássy Út

Café Eckermann, VI. Andrássy út 24, ✆ 374 4076. *Open 8–10, Sun 9–10*. Calm, modern place with great art, a nice terrace and a decent selection of coffees, teas, snacks, juices, wine and beer. Free Internet, but you won't get near it.

Café Mediterrán, VI. Liszt Ferenc tér 10, ✆ 344 4615. *Open daily 11am–2am*. All about sitting outside on the terrace, drinking and chatting. The selection of drinks is poor but the atmosphere good and the clientele cheerful. The action goes on till late then moves to 'Undergrass' beneath the café (*open 8pm–5am for dancing, entry 300Ft*).

Café Vian, VI. Liszt Ferenc tér 9, ✆ 342 8991. Next door to the above, more intelligently run and about as popular. The terrace is smaller and more elegant. Inside is big, comfortable and artistically decorated. Excellent selection of bottled beer and wines, plus coffees, juices and cocktails. Food includes omelettes, salads, croissants and desserts. Clientele sophisticated and not necessarily young.

Két Szerecsen Kávézó, VI. Nagymező u. 14, ✆ 343 1984. *Open Mon–Fri 8am–1am, Sat and Sun 11am–1am*. Pastel shades, high vaulted ceiling,

fan and art work all help create a Mediterranean feel to complement the terrace outside. Food is light and mainly Italian-style; good lunch specials. Extremely popular with a smart crowd; often packed at night.

Komédiás Kávéház, VI. Nagymező u. 26, ✆ 302 0901. *Open Mon–Fri 8am–midnight, Sat and Sun 3.30–midnight*. Small, old-style theatrical café, all wood, mirrors, brass and plush seating.

Művész Cukrászda, VI. Andrássy út 29, ✆ 352 1337. *Open daily 9am–midnight*. Old-style café with genuine class, just over the road from the opera. Cakes and coffee are nothing special and a little more expensive, but the location is great.

Vista, VI. Paulay Ede u. 2, ✆ 269 6032. On top of everything else, Vista has a nice, busy café-restaurant with a vast choice of breakfasts. The restaurant offers Hungarian and international food (spinach gnocchi, salmon farfale), for about 2,800Ft. Occasional live jazz in the evening.

Further Out

Fröhlich Cukrászda, VII. Dob u. 22, ✆ 321 6741. *Open Tues–Thur 8am–5pm, Fri 8am–2pm, closed Sat–Mon*. Though not much to look at, Hungary's only kosher pâtisserie, near the Great Synagogue, has an excellent reputation, especially for the *flodni*, an apple, poppy-seed and walnut pastry.

Nándori Cukrászda, IX. Ráday u. 53. *Open 10–6, closed Sun*. Trams 4 or 6. Inconveniently placed near the Petőfi Bridge, but recommended for its quality pastries.

New York Kávéház, VII. Erzsébet körút 9–11, ✆ 322 3849. *Open daily 9am–10pm*. Budapest's last remaining genuine coffeehouse from the pre-war era. Opened in 1894, it is a blend of neo-Renaissance and Art Nouveau. Though the exterior is all but hidden by the wooden props that have held it up since it was barged by a Russian tank in 1956, the interior is still magnificent, containing all the sumptuous details of a palace. The sculpted bronze, mirrors, stained glass, frescoes and the curvy pillars flanking the staircases are only slightly faded, and make it look like a museum piece, which, since only tourists can afford the inflated prices, is what it is. But it's a spectacular museum, worth paying double the going rate for a coffee and tolerating the arrogant waiters to see.

Budapest: Where to Stay

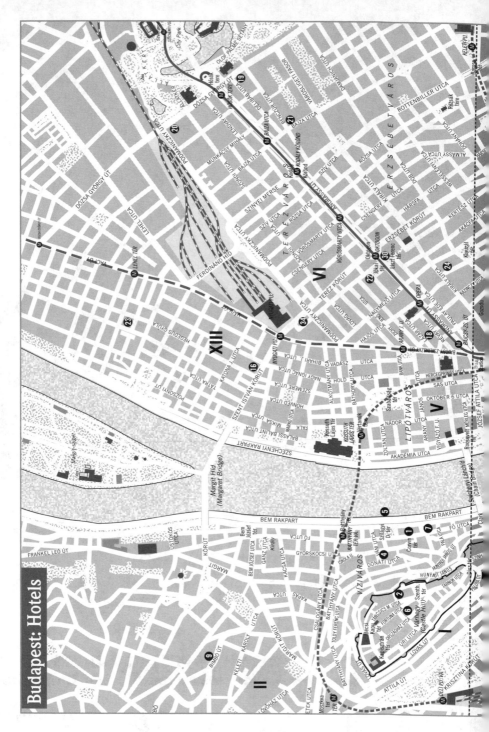

Budapest: Hotels

312

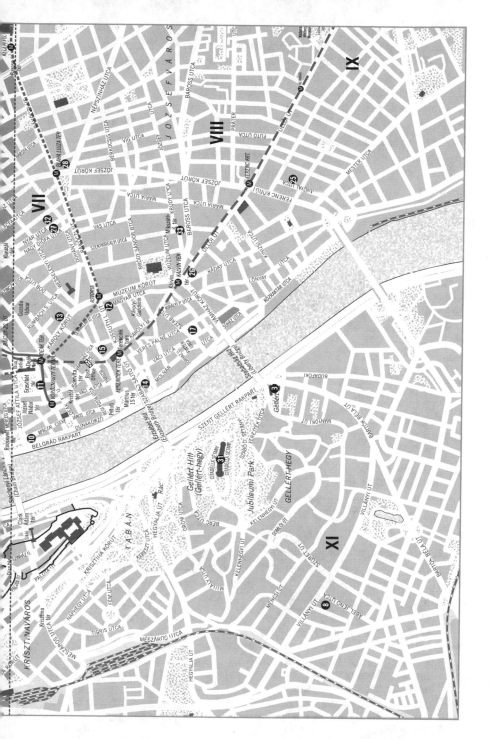

313

There are plenty of luxury hotels in Budapest, usually offering little extra other than service, accountability, and a lot of facilities you are not likely to use, from conference rooms to solariums. There are also a good many cheap hostels. What is lacking, especially around the centre, is mid-range options, and those that exist are usually big, impersonal institutions. There are some exceptions, which you should book as early as possible. You will find plenty of small, homely and attractive lodgings in the Buda Hills, but they are away from the centre, often involve a walk, and are reached by transport that stops running shortly after eleven.

Even the cheapest of Budapest's hotels seem to be kept spotlessly clean. All but the cheapest have TVs, mini-bars and non-smoking rooms or floors. Most rooms are rather small, and double rooms often have two single beds rather than one double. Ask when you book.

Prices for hotels are most frequently quoted in Deutschmarks (DM), even when payment is expected in forints. The approximate price you should expect to pay, for a **double room with bath in high season**, is as follows:

∞∞∞∞	*luxury*	400+ DM
∞∞∞	*expensive*	250–400DM
∞∞	*moderate*	100–250DM
∞	*cheap*	up to 100DM

Another possibility worth considering is short-term rental of an **apartment**, usually cheaper than hotels and allowing for greater freedom. The best place to start looking is at the efficient and helpful **Vista Visitor Centre**, VI. Paulay Ede u. 7, ✆ 267 8603, 📧 268 1059, *incoming @vista.hu, www.vista.hu.* Check out pictures of the flats on the website, arrange everything by e-mail and pick up the keys from the office when you arrive. **Pansio Centrum Info-Centre** acts for many smaller companies with flats in all districts: XII. Szarvas Gábor u. 24, ✆ 200 8874, 📧 200 8869, *pansiocentrum@mail. matav.hu, www.minihotels.net.* Other agencies (*opening hours for all are roughly Mon–Fri 9–5*) include:

Budapest Tourist, in underpass of Nyugati station, ✆ 322 6565, *open Sat 9–12*; or VIII. Baross tér 3, across the square from Keleti station, ✆ 333 6587; or in the mall by the metro entrance at Déli station, ✆ 355 7167; or VII. Erzsébet körút 41, ✆ 342 6521, *open Sat 9–1.*

Cooptourist: Skála Metro department store, opposite Nyugati station, ✆ 312 3621; or V. Kossuth tér 13, ✆ 332 6387; or V. Bajcsy-Zsilinszky u. 17, ✆ 311 7034.

IBUSZ, Ferenciek tere 10, on corner of Petőfi Sandor u., ✆ 318 1120; or in Nyugati Station.

Longer-term rental is more difficult to arrange. These agencies are not geared for it, and landlords are notoriously dishonest, demanding large deposits and not returning them. Try the listings in the daily *Expressz* and ask Tourinform or Vista to make the calls for you.

Buda

∞∞∞∞ **①** **Art'otel**, I. Bem rakpart 16–19, ✆ 487 9487, 📧 487 9488, *budapest@artotel.hu, www.parkhtls.com.* Batthyány tér (M2). This well-located hotel is new and nicely conceived. The interior is designed in a tasteful, artistic manner. US artist D. Sultan's works are displayed throughout the hotel. The rooms are a good size and very stylish, with nice bathrooms. The west wing consists of four renovated Baroque houses on Fő utca, retaining a historic feel with high vaulted ceilings and old doors. West-facing rooms have views of the Matthias Church. Usual facilities, including parking and sauna.

Budapest Hilton, I. Hess András tér 1–3, ✆ 488 6600, 📠 488 6644, *hiltonhu @hungary.net*. Várbusz from Moszkva tér (M2). The building incorporates medieval remains, its wings linked by corridors running through an old church tower. Described by the Hilton president as the most beautiful pearl in the whole string.

Gellért, XI. Gellért tér 1, ✆ 385 2200, 📠 466 6631, *resoff@gellert.hu*, *www. danubiusgroup.com/danubius/gellert. html*. Trams 47 and 49 from Deák tér. This sumptuous and historical building, as much tourist attraction and thermal bath as hotel, has slightly old-fashioned but tasteful rooms of a good size, with decent bathrooms and large windows. First-floor rooms have balconies. Baths free to guests.

Astra Vendégház, I. Vám u. 6, ✆ 214 1906, 📠 214 1907. Batthyány tér (M2). Beautiful 300-year-old building. Spacious rooms with stereos, luxuriously decorated with furniture from Italy or Transylvania, original paintings and big beds. Cellar bar with pool table. The manager goes out of his way to be helpful and there is 24-hour reception. Highly recommended.

Dunapart, I. Szilágyi Dezső tér 33, ✆ 355 9001, 📠 355 3770. Batthyány tér (M2). This boat moored in front of the Calvinist Church has 36 neat, tiny rooms. The lobby tries to look like a luxury hotel, but you're paying for the location and the novelty. Rooms facing the river have excellent views of Parliament but cost no extra, so book early and ask for one.

Kulturinnov, I. Szentháromság tér 6, ✆ 355 0122, 📠 375 1886, *mka@mail. matav.hu*. Várbusz from Moszkva tér (M2). In the neo-Gothic Hungarian Cultural Foundation building. Rooms are big, simple and clean with high ceilings. Those on the road side can be noisy. Friendly, personal, and the price is right.

Victoria, I. Bem Rakpart 11, ✆ 457 8080, 📠 457 8088, *victoria@victoria.hu*, *www.victoria.hu*. Bus 86 from Batthyány tér (M2). Tastefully decorated rooms with big beds but rather small bathrooms. Front rooms have river views. Buffet breakfast in a pleasant room, but no restaurant. Polite and friendly English-speaking staff.

Buda Hills

Ábel Panzió, XI. Ábel Jenő ut. 9, ✆/📠 185 6426, ✆/📠 209 2537/8. Tram 61 from Moszkva tér (M2) or Móricz Zsigmond Körtér. On a quiet street out of the centre. Lounge and some (more expensive) rooms decorated with exquisite taste. Antique furniture and the owner's fabulous paintings. The veranda overlooks a tree-filled garden. This place is highly recommended.

Beatrix Panzió, II. Széher u. 3, ✆/📠 394 3730, *beatrix@pronet.hu*, *www. beatrixhotel.hu*. Bus or tram 56 from Moszkva tér (M2), then a 200m walk. This friendly and well-placed B&B has won lots of awards. Good-sized rooms with decent bathrooms. Lovely front garden with terraces and a pond. Sauna, safes and a helpful owner with good English.

Kapu, XI. Ugron Gábor. u. 9, ✆ 319 2985, 📠 319 2983. Bus 139 from Déli pu (M2) and 500m walk. A very attractive house; well-decorated rooms, with Asian rugs on wooden floors. Very quiet and private, with sauna, bar, parking and a big garden with a terrace at the front.

Normafa, XII. Eötvös u. 52–4, ✆ 395 6505, 📠 395 6504, *hotel2000@matav net.hu*, *hotels.hu/normafa_hotel*. Bus 21 from Moszkva tér (M2). Huge but quite attractive hotel complex on acres of grounds in a very quiet neighbourhood. Upstairs rooms are bigger; some have balconies. Free fitness room and pool; solarium, sauna and tennis court. The restaurant is popular in its own right.

Uhu Panzió, II. Keselyű u. 1a, ✆ 394 3876. Tram 56 from Moszkva tér (M2) and a 1km walk, mostly uphill. Hard work to get to, but a lovely house in exquisite taste. Nine rooms, simple but tasteful. Nice garden with views. 10pm curfew.

Walzer Hotel, XI. Németvölgyi u. 110, ✆ 319 1212, 🖷 319 2964. Tram 56 from Moszkva tér (M2). Beautiful building close to tram stop. Large rooms with plush interiors and mock-antique furniture. Big bathrooms, good restaurant and a big garden with terrace. Credit cards accepted.

Buda Villa Panzió, XII. Kiss Áron u. 6, ✆ 275 0091, 🖷 275 1687, *budapansio @usa.net*. Bus 156 or 28 from Moszkva tér. Beautiful family home with 10 very nice, tastefully furnished rooms. Garden with patio. Parking.

Dominika Apartman Hotel, XI. Lidérc u. 13, ✆ 246 0062, 🖷 246 0092, *dominika.apartman@mail.matav.hu*. Bus 8 from Ferenciek tere (M3) and a 400m walk. Small but stylish, modern rooms in a nice house on a quiet street. Big garden with swimming pool. Bar and parking.

(9) Gárdonyi Panzió, II. Bimbó u. 25b, ✆ 326 7742, 🖷 326 8895. Bus 11 from Batthyány tér. Small family B&B. Homely well-furnished decent-size rooms, some with balconies, and with their own bathrooms, not always en suite. Use of small kitchen. Very good value.

Helios Panzió, XII. Lidérc u. 5a, ✆ 246 4658, *roomheli@matavnet.hu*. Bus 8 from Ferenciek tere (M3). Classily decorated rooms, some with balconies. Excellent views. Big, beautiful garden at back, and a terrace at the front. Parking, and helpful staff. Recommended.

SAS Club Hotel, XII. Törökbálinti u. 51–3, ✆ 246 4643, 🖷 246 4931. Bus 8 from Ferenciek tere (M3). Forty rooms in spacious grounds with restaurant, slide and swings, and two tennis courts. Sauna and solarium included in price. The rooms are big, simply but pleasantly furnished.

Unikum Panzió, XI. Bod Péter u. 13, ✆/🖷 319 3784. Bus 139 from Déli pu (M2). This family-run hotel has nicely decorated, big rooms. Bathrooms with showers, parking, a decent restaurant, and an old lady who speaks English. Quiet, high up and excellent value.

Vadvirág, II. Nagybányai u. 18, ✆/🖷 394 4292. Bus 5 from Moszkva tér or Erzsébet Bridge and 800m walk. Pleasant rooms, some with balcony, some with bathtubs. Very attractive front garden on a quiet street. Sauna and parking.

Central Pest

(10) Hyatt Atrium, V. Roosevelt tér 2, ✆ 266 1234, 🖷 266 9101, *www.hyatt.com*. Ugly and soulless outside, inside it really is an atrium: a glass-roofed courtyard with plants hanging from the balconies. The lobby is full of palm trees, and there's a glider plane suspended in the middle. Even the lift is beautiful.

(11) Kempinski Hotel Corvinus, V. Erzsébet tér 7–8, ✆ 429 3777, 🖷 429 4777, *hotel@kempinski.hu*, *www.kemp inski-budapest.com*. A Postmodern extravaganza: glass, granite and steel put together with taste and imagination. The interior is equally well executed. Rooms are nicer and slightly larger than most, and bathrooms the best in town. Great care has been taken over the details. Parking, pool, sauna, fitness rooms. Its Corvinus restaurant is one of Budapest's finest.

(12) Astoria, V. Kossuth Lajos u. 19–21, ✆ 317 3411, 🖷 318 6798, *astoria@ hungary.net*, *www.danubiusgroup.com/ hungarhotels/astoria.html*. This landmark hotel is a piece of history, exuding a turn-of-the-20th-century atmosphere. The tired rooms offer nostalgia rather than luxury.

(13) Carmen Mini-Hotel, VII. Károly körút 5/b (2nd Floor), ✆ 352 0798, 🖷 252 4976, *carmen@mailmatav.hu*. Small hotel close to Deák tér. The climb up the grim staircases is off-putting, but the rooms are clean, bright and reasonably spacious, if a bit noisy. Staff are pleasant and helpful.

(14)(15)(16) City Panzió Mátyás, V. Március 15 tér 8, ✆ 338 4711, 🖷 317 9086, *matyas@ taverna.hu*. **City Panzió Pilvax**, V. Pilvax köz 1–3, ✆ 266 7660, 🖷 317 6396, *pilvax@taverna.hu*. **City Panzió Ring**, V. Szent István körút 22, ✆ 340

5450, 📠 340 4884, *ring@taverna.hu*. This small chain of hotels offers modern, clean no-nonsense rooms with no real personality. They are well located and moderately priced. Rooms are the same in all three, but Mátyás is preferable for location and the outside of the building.

Peregrinus Elte Hotel, V. Szerb u. 3, ✆ 266 4911, 📠 266 4913. Small hotel in a quiet but central location. Good-sized airy rooms with high ceilings in a renovated old building. Good value.

Around Andrássy Út

K & K Hotel Opera, VI. Révay u. 24, ✆ 269 0222, 📠 269 0230, *kk.hotel. opera@kkhotel.hu*. This large chain-hotel feels smaller and more friendly than most. Rooms are bright and tastefully furnished with big windows. Luxury services including health club and sauna. Buildings are connected by a relaxed bar area.

Délibáb, VI. Délibáb u. 35, ✆ 322 8763, 📠 342 8153, *inn-side@matavnet.hu*. Close to Heroes' Square, set in a grand old building. Rooms are quiet, good-sized with high ceilings and personal, if not wonderfully decorated. A bit slack, though.

Liget, VI. Dózsa György u. 106, ✆ 269 5300, 📠 269 5329, *hotel@liget.hu*. Near Heroes' Square, this building is a mish-mash of shapes, colours and textures. The lobby is bright and shiny, centred on a long, curving bar. Rooms are small but agreeable. Well run with professional staff.

Radio Inn, VI. Benczúr u. 19, ✆ 342 8347, 📠 322 8284. Close to Kodály körönd, the institutional and dated feel of this large hotel is made up for by the huge rooms with big windows, separate toilets and bathrooms, and small kitchens. In the back are two nice gardens surrounded by trees. A good option at this price.

Medosz, VI. Jókai tér 9, ✆ 374 3000, 📠 332 4316. The only advantages here are location and price. The exterior is ugly, the lobby poor and the rooms small and rather tawdry.

Elsewhere in Pest

Danubius Grand, XIII. Margitsziget, ✆ 329 2300, 📠 329 3923, *margotel@ hungary.net, www.danubiusgroup.com*. Bus 26 from Nyugati station. At the north end of Margaret Island. The thermal waters can be enjoyed free in the attractive bathing complex of the Thermal Hotel, reached by an underground tunnel. Rooms are decorated in fine taste. Parkside rooms have balconies; bigger rooms have smaller bathrooms. Ask about discount packages and therapy offers.

Sydney Apartment, XIII. Hegedűs Gyula u. 52–4, ✆ 236 8888, 📠 236 8899, *reservation@sydneyaparthotel.hu, www. sydneyaparthotel.hu*. A 5min walk from Lehel tér (M3). Standard flats have bedroom, lounge, kitchen and bathroom, all spacious, exquisitely and artistically decorated, with all the accessories you could want. Indoor pool, Jacuzzi, sauna, steam room, gym, in-house masseur, laundry facilities, car park, and a terrace giving on to the courtyard.

Ambra Apart Hotel, VII. Kisdiófa u. 13, ✆/📠 321 1533, *ambrahotel@mail. matav.hu, www.ambrahotel.kosep.com*. A 5min walk from Opera (M1), offering fully equipped, decent-sized apartments, decorated in pastel shades. Extras include a sauna and Jacuzzi. A great deal.

Corvin, IX. Angyal u. 31, ✆ 218 6566, 📠 218 6562, *corvin@mail.datanet.hu*. Close to Ferenc körút (M3), in a building with lots of character, this modern little hotel has small but clean and pleasant rooms, a parking lot, a good restaurant and a big, attractive garden at the back.

Ibis Centrum, IX. Ráday u. 6, ✆ 215 8585, 📠 215 8787. This pleasant, professional hotel gives value for money. Rooms are modern, clean, simple and quiet. Windows are a bit small, and bathrooms are small with showers but no tub. Three no-smoking floors. There's an open-air 'garden' on the first floor. Parking and a safe.

King's, VII. Nagydiófa u. 25–7, ☎/📠 352 7675. A kosher establishment. Rooms are okay, but not very aesthetic. Those facing the street are a bit noisy.

Nemzeti, VIII. József körút 4, ☎ 477 2000, 📠 477 2001, *nemzeti@pannonia hotels.hu, www.hungary.com/pannonia /nemzeti*. Blaha Lujza tér (M2). Luxurious turn-of-the-20th-century décor. There's a non-smoking floor, parking and a very nice restaurant. Rooms are bright and pleasantly decorated.

Sissi, IX. Angyal u. 33, ☎ 215 0082, 📠 216 6063, *hsissi@matavnet.hu*. Next door to Corvin in an eclectic building. Smart, modern and a bit more stylish than most, with tastefully decorated rooms. Garden and a conservatory for breakfast.

San Marco Panzió, III. San Marco u. 6, ☎/📠 388 9997, *saiban@elender.hu*. Bus 60 from Batthyany tér (M2). A family-run B&B in Óbuda; the helpful, friendly owner speaks excellent English. Five attic rooms, two of which share a bathroom, the others having showers. Highly recommended.

Hostels

Caterina Hostel, VI. Andrássy u. 47, ☎ 342 0804, 📠 352 6147, *caterina@ mail.inext.hu*. By Liszt Ferenc tér. The kitchen and bathroom are nicer than those in other backpacker hostels. Great TV and use of a stereo, but the Internet is expensive and there are no personal lockers. Very safe. They also rent local apartments.

Citadella, XI. Citadella sétány, ☎ 466 5794, 📠 386 0505. Bus 27 from Móricz Zsigmond körtér. Inside the Citadella, so great views but quite a hike to get there. Rooms are off a white, circular, tunnel-like corridor, surreal to walk round.

Marco Polo Hostel, VII. Nyár u. 6, ☎ 344 5367, 📠 344 5368, *info@hostel marcopolo.com*. Their slogan 'Hotel services for hostel prices' sums it up. The building is beautiful, with a courtyard and cavernous cellar bar-restaurant with TV, pool tables and computers. Rooms are small and pleasant if childishly decorated. They offer a free bus service from Keleti station. Astoria is the nearest metro.

Museum Guest House, VIII. Mikszáth Kálmán tér 4, ☎ 318 9508, *museumgh @freemail.C3.hu*. A warren of small rooms with dormitory beds everywhere, on a lovely and quiet square behind the National Museum. Friendly atmosphere with helpful staff. Use of kitchen and Internet, private lockers, keys (no curfew).

Yellow Submarine Youth Hostel, VI. Teréz körút 56, 3rd Floor, ☎/📠 331 9896, *yellowsubmarine@mailinterware.hu*. Nyugati pu (M3) or tram 73. A friendly and helpful hostel used by a backpacking crowd. Own keys, lockers, Internet access, use of kitchen, breakfast included. But you won't necessarily get a good night's sleep.

Camping

Csillebérci Camping, XII. Konkoly Thege M. u. 21, ☎ 395 6527, 📠 395 7327, *www. datanet.hu/csill*. Bus 21 from Moszkva tér (M2). *Open all year*. Large site with space for 1,000 campers; can get crowded in summer. There are also bungalows. Lots of facilities, including swimming pool, tennis courts and a safe. 500Ft per person, plus 600Ft per tent and 1,000Ft per car.

Római-Fürdő Camping, III. Szentendrei u. 18, ☎ 368 6260, 📠 250 0426. HÉV to Római-Fürdő from Batthyány tér. *Open all year*. Huge site next to the road. All the usual facilities, plus use of the nearby pool. Bungalows, laundry and a safe. 800Ft per person, plus 700Ft per tent and 1,000Ft per car.

Zugligeti Niche Camping, XII. Zugligeti u. 101, ☎ 200 8346. Bus 158 from Moszkva tér (M2). *Open April–Oct*. Situated opposite the Chairlift, this is the most pleasant and smallest site, set in the woods around a terraced ravine. There are bungalows to rent, a safe, and a pleasant little restaurant. 600Ft per person plus 400Ft per tent.

Budapest: Entertainment and Nightlife

Bars and Clubs

It is hard to identify a typically Hungarian bar culture, unless you mean the many dark, rather desperate-looking places where alcohol is more a question of need than recreation, or those filled exclusively with beer-swilling men. The *borozó* is a cheap wine cellar, usually full of unsteady-looking early drinkers; the *söröző* is a beer-cellar, but not like those found in Prague; the *presszó* is a dingy style of café-bar. You won't find many of these listed below. What you will find is theme bars, English or Irish pubs, cellar jazz-clubs, discos, speakeasys, cafés and an otherwise mixed bag. The line between bar, café and restaurant is blurred: check pp.307–10 too. There are few worthwhile bars or clubs on the Buda side.

Buda

Libella Bár, XI. Budafoki u. 7, ✆ 209 4761. *Open daily 8am–2am.* Trams 47, 49 and 19. Close to the Gellért Hotel. Smart but simple locals' drinking den for a quiet beer and a game of cards. Interesting photos of odd details from around Buda.

Oscar Café, II. Ostrom u. 14, ✆ 212 8017. *Open Mon–Fri noon–3 and 5–2am (till 4am Fri), Sat 5pm–4am, Sun 5pm–2am.* Moszkva tér (M2). The atmospheric interior with its cinematic décor attracts a mixed, young, fairly smart crowd.

Polo Pub, I. Batthyány u. 4, ✆ 201 7962. *Open Mon–Fri 12–11, Sat 5–11, closed Sun.* Batthyány tér (M2). Cosy and friendly pub in an English/Irish vein, with a snazzy mezzanine containing booths. Small drinks selection, good beers, some snack food.

Rác Kert, I. Hadnagy u. 8–10, ✆ 214 6793. *Open daily 2pm–4am.* Bus 5, 7 or 8, tram 19, night bus É78. Next door to the Rác Baths, this is easily the most happening bar this side of the Danube. Packed with a young, bohemian, trendy crowd there to party. Live music Wed–Fri and big-screen sports.

Zöld Pardon, XI. Goldmann György tér. *Open daily 5pm–4am.* Tram 4 or 6. Outdoor spacious drinking area near the water next to Petőfi Bridge on the Buda side. Snack food, a few decent beers.

Central Pest

Becketts, V. Bajcsy-Zsilinszky u. 72, ✆ 311 1033. *Open daily noon–1am.* Nyugati pu (M3). On the corner of Alkotmány u. An Irish pub, extremely popular, especially with expats and tourists, who don't mind the inflated prices. Good food and a fine range of beers. Live music on Fri and Sat nights.

Egri Borozó, V. Bajcsy-Zsilinszky 72, ✆ 302 1724. *Open daily noon–midnight.* Nyugati pu (M3). Small wine cellar with an arched ceiling and a warren of small rooms at the back, selling wine from the Egri region at very cheap prices (600Ft for a litre). Packed with a young, pleasant local crowd.

Fat Mo's, V. Nyáry Pál u. 11, ✆ 267 3199. *Open Mon–Wed noon–2am, Thurs–Fri noon–4am, Sat 6pm–4am, Sun 6pm–2am.* Ferenciek tere (M3). A long cellar bar, heaving every evening. Live jazz and blues on Sun, Mon and Tues; Thurs–Sat party nights with DJs. American-style food (3,500Ft).

Fregatt Pub, V. Molnár u. 26, ✆ 318 9997. *Open Mon–Fri noon–1am, Sat and Sun 5pm–1am.* Ferenciek tere (M3). English-style laid-back cellar pub, with live jazz most evenings.

Irish Cat Pub, V. Múzeum krt. 41, ✆ 266 4085. *Open daily 11am–2am.* Kálvin tér (M3). Friendly little Irish boozer with a good range of beers. Can turn into a bit of a meat-market in the evenings.

Jazz Garden, V. Veres Pálné u. 44a, ✆ 266 7364. *Open daily 6pm–1am.* Kálvin tér (M3). With plastic trees and a black ceiling dotted with stars, the sensation of being in a garden is a little eerie. Jazz nightly. The pastel-coloured restaurant offers the regular fare plus some veggie choices (3,200Ft). Reasonably priced drinks. 500Ft entrance.

Old Amsterdam, V. Királyi Pál u. 14, ✆ 266 3649. *Open Mon–Fri noon–2am, Sat and Sun 6pm–2am.* Kálvin tér (M3). A pleasant little pub with a great selection of draft beers and bottles. Some live jazz and blues. A great food selection, especially for vegetarians (2,800Ft).

Talk Talk, V. Magyar u. 12–14, ✆ 267 5758. *Open Sun–Thurs noon–midnight, Fri and Sat noon–2am.* Astoria (M2). A modern minimalist interior with tasteful iron chairs and a cosy mezzanine. The clientele is young and trendy, the waitresses aloof. As much a café-restaurant as bar.

Around Andrássy Út

Benczúr Ház, V. Benczúr u. 27. *Open daily 5–2.* Bajza utca (M1). Friendly venue specializing in trad jazz, folk and world music, attracting a more mature audience. Concerts inside or in the garden.

Café Aloé, VI. Zichy Jenő u. 37. *Open daily 5–2.* Oktogon (M1). Small, unpretentious bar in a comfortable, warren-like cellar, frequented by a laid-back, arty crowd. Leffe and Stella on draught at very low prices, and a surprisingly good wine list.

Club Seven, VI. Akácfa u. 7, ✆ 478 9030. *Open 10am–5am, closed Sun.* Blaha Lujza tér (M2). Upstairs is a small, fairly sophisticated bar. Downstairs resembles a classy supper-club and the small dancefloor is packed. The party goes on late.

Crazy Café, VI. Jókai u. 30, ✆ 302 4003. *Open daily noon–1am.* Nyugati (M3). This long cellar bar has an astounding selection of draught and bottled beers. Live music and karaoke. The restaurant is done out like a jungle, with plastic vegetation and stuffed animals. Imaginative menu (3,500Ft).

Hades Jazztaurant, VI. Vörösmarty u. 31, ✆ 352 1503. *Open Mon–Fri 11.30am–2am, Sat 5–2, Sun 5–11.* Wacky cavern whose style combines classical Greece, Dante, jazz and stucco. Piano music every evening but Fri and Sun; agreeable ambience. Good selection of wine and food at reasonable prices.

Média Club Étterem, VI. Andrássy u. 101, ✆ 322 1639. *Open 10–midnight, Sun 10–4.* Bajza utca (M1). Really a restaurant, but better used as a drinking-hole; the best spot on this section of the boulevard. Fine terrace outside the journalists' club.

Old Man's Music Pub, VII. Akácfa u. 13, ✆ 322 7645. *Open daily 3–3.* Blaha Lujza tér (M2). Probably the most fun, popular and crowded nightspot in town. Mainly disco, with live blues, jazz or funk earlier in the evening. Book a table if you want to see the stage. The menu is surprisingly good.

Piaf, VI. Nagymező u. 25, ✆ 312 3823. *Open daily 4–4.* You usually have to knock to get into this place, and the door-staff are offputting. Inside the atmosphere is wonderfully louche, with heavy red velvet, dim lighting and jazzy music. Seedy but sophisticated. Turn up late, preferably half-cut.

Tütü Tangó, VI. Hajós u. 2, ✆ 322 6456. *Open daily 11.30–midnight.* Situated near Opera on the south side of Andrássy út, trendy and very popular.

Upstairs the décor is bright and sophisticated; lively and friendly clientele. Downstairs there is sometimes live music and a Latin-inspired dancefloor.

Undergrass, VI. Liszt Ferenc tér 10, ✆ 322 0830. *Open 8pm–4am, closed Sun.* Under Café Mediterran. A long, metallic cellar bar with a small dancefloor. Not unbearably crowded: you can hear each other talk in the bar, then nip next door for a boogie.

Further Out

Darshan Café, VIII. Krúdy Gyula u. 8, ✆ 266 7797. *Open 8–midnight, Sun noon–midnight.* Kálvin tér (M3) or bus 9 from the Kiskörút. Small, dark and sleazy, this arty bar attracts a young, studenty crowd. The art is eclectic European, the drinks selection lamentable, the bar service slow.

Darshan Udvar, VIII. Krúdy Gyula u. 7, ✆ 266 5541. *Open Mon–Thurs 11–1am, Fri 11–3am, Sat 6pm–3am, Sun 6pm–1am.* A laid-back, spacious bar-café behind the National Museum. The atmosphere is mellow and trendy, bohemian but respectable. Cheap food (1,800Ft); good draught beers.

Long Time Music Restaurant, VII. Dohány u. 22, ✆ 322 0006. *Open daily 6pm–2am.* Astoria (M2). Cellar club playing live jazz every night. Not that atmospheric unless it's a busy night. Good menu with a few veggie options (about 2,900Ft).

Nincs Pardon, VII. Almássy tér, ✆ 351 4351. *Open Thurs–Sat 9pm–4am.* Trams 4 or 6. Atmospheric, dimly lit, warren-like cellar bar, decorated with tile mosaics. Laid-back and arty clientele, mainly showbiz/media regulars. Tiny dancefloor.

Nothin' but the Blues Pub, VIII. Krúdy Gyula u. 6, ✆ 484 0040. *Open summer 5pm–1am, winter noon–1am, closed Sun.* Kálvin tér (M3) or bus 9 from the Kiskörút. A cellar bar with a lively clientele. Guinness and Kilkenny on tap. No live music.

Paris, Texas, IX. Ráday u. 22, ✆ 218 0570. *Open Mon–Fri 10am–dawn, Sat and Sun 4pm–dawn.* Very nice bar close to Kálvin tér with a French feel. Lively but intimate. Great atmosphere with a mixed crowd. Food by the pizzeria next door, including veggie options and some decent breakfasts (2,000Ft). Particularly buzzing on Thurs and Fri.

Yes Pub, Hegedűs Gyula u. 1, ✆ 329 3105. *Open daily 10am–6am.* Nyugati pu (M3). Atmospheric little late-night boozer, surprisingly friendly and pleasant, with seating upstairs or in the cosy cellar.

Gay Bars, Clubs and Restaurants

Action Bar, V. Magyar u. 42 (Kálvin tér, M3), ✆ 266 9148 (*daily 9am–4am*).

Amstel River Café, V. Párisi u. 6 (Ferenciek tere, M3), ✆ 266 4334 (*Mon–Fri 9am–11pm*).

Angyal Bar, VII. Szövetség u. 33 (Blaha Lujza tér, M2), ✆ 351 6490 (*Thurs–Sun 10–dawn*).

Capella, V. Belgrád Rakpart 23 (Ferenciek tere, M3), ✆ 318 6231 (*Mon and Tues 9pm–2am, Wed–Sun 9pm–5am*).

Club 93 Pizzeria, V. Vas u. 2 (Astoria, M2), ✆ 338 1119 (*daily 11am–midnight*).

Darling, V. Szép u. 1 (Astoria, M2), ✆ 267 3315 (*daily 7pm–3am*).

Kis Sün Restaurant, VI. Podmaniczky u. 29 (Nyugati pu, M3), ✆ 269 4072 (*daily 11–11*).

Mystery Bar-Klub, V. Nagysándor József u. 3 (Arany János u., M3), ✆ 312 1436 (*Mon–Sat 9pm–4am*).

No Limit, V. Semmelweis u. 10 (Astoria, M2) (*daily 10am–5am*).

Theatre

Walking around Budapest, you may come across a large crowd of well-dressed people chatting, flirting and behaving as if they were at a cocktail party in the middle of the street. You're in front of a theatre. A night at the theatre is a social occasion which begins outside. Minutes before the performance starts, everyone glides to their seats and continues to flirt, wave and look around to see who else has shown up. The one drawback for foreigners is when the show begins and you don't understand a word. Still, a few places offer occasional performances in English; or pick a play you know well—there's usually Shakespeare somewhere—and try to follow the action. *Pesti Est* is the best bet for listings, along with their free monthly dedicated to theatre and music, *Pesti Súgó*. Or look in one of the ticket agencies on Váci u. Note that nearly all the theatres **close for the summer** (*June–Sept*).

International Buda Stage, II. Tárogató u. 2–4, ✆ 391 2525. Tram 56 from Moszkva tér (M2). *Box office open daily 8–7.* English and Hungarian theatre, music, dance and concerts. Simultaneous translation into English during Hungarian shows.

Katona József, V. Petőfi Sándor u. 6, ✆ 318 6599. Ferenciek tere (M3). *Box office open daily 2–7.* The best-reputed mainstream theatre company.

Kolibri, VI. Jókai tér 10, ✆ 311 0870. Oktogon (M1). *Box office open Mon–Fri 9–6, Sat and Sun 9–1.* Small theatre showing some productions in English, usually by amateur companies.

Merlin International Theatre, V. Gerlóczy u. 4, ✆ 266 4632. Deák tér metro. *Box office open daily 2–7.* The most professional venue offering English-language performances.

Radnóti, VI. Nagymező u. 11, ✆ 321 0600. Oktogon (M1). *Box office open daily 1–7.* A well-respected company offering sophisticated classics.

Szkéné, XI. Müegyetem rakpart 3, ✆ 463 2451. Trams 18, 19, 47, 49. *Box office open Mon–Thurs*

9–4, Fri 9–2.30, Sat and Sun 1hr before shows. A long-established venue for alternative theatre, in the Technical University building, near Gellért hotel.

Thália, VI. Nagymező u. 22–4, ✆ 312 4230. Oktogon (M1). *Box office open Mon–Fri 10–6, Sat and Sun 2–6.* Very attractive theatre hosting theatre, dance, musicals and foreign troupes.

Trafó, IX. Liliom u. 41, ✆ 456 2044. Ferenc krt. (M3). *Box office open daily 5–10pm. Closed July–Aug.* Very lively venue, with all sorts of events, often crossing over between art forms: art, poetry, music, theatre, exhibitions, dance, comedy, etc.

Új Színház, VI. Paulay Ede u. 35, ✆ 351 1406. Opera (M1). *Box office open Mon–Fri 2–7, Sat and Sun 4–7. Closed June–Aug.* Bizarre Art Nouveau building appropriately housing off-beat productions.

Vígszínház (Comedy Theatre), XIII. Szent István krt. 14, ✆ 329 2340. Nyugati pu. (M3). *Box office open Mon–Fri 1–7, Sat and Sun 1hr before curtain.* Wonderful Baroque theatre focusing on comedy; some big musicals.

Classical Music and Opera

The classical scene in Budapest is booming, and audiences are well known for their enthusiasm. Yehudi Menuhin called this 'the town of Bartók, Kodály, Doráti and the very responsive concert public'. It is thanks to these first two, who scoured the country for folk melodies which they incorporated into their own works, that Hungary found its own true classical voice. Ever since, the genre has thrived, subsidized during the years of Communism, and fed by a rich vein of young talent, the legacy of Kodály's groundbreaking musical education principles. The best **orchestras** are the Budapesti Fesztivál Zenekar, the Nemzeti Filharmonakusok, the MRT Szimfonikus Zenekara, and the Liszt Ferenc Chamber Orchestra. **Choirs** are generally even better, the Nemzeti Énekkar, MRT Énekkar and MRT Gyermek Kórusa (a children's choir), all rated very highly. The Bartók String Quartet (Bartók Vonósnégyes) are also always worth seeing. The **Hungarian State Opera** company puts on a wonderful show, and a night spent at the magnificent Opera House is one of the most truly memorable experiences Budapest has to offer, a piece of sumptuous luxury much more affordable than in most countries. To find out what's on try *Where Budapest* or *Budapest Program* in English, *Pesti Est* or *Pesti Súgó* in Hungarian (all free), or pop into one of the ticket agencies or Vista. The State Opera publishes its own **monthly schedule**, available at the Opera House or at ticket agencies.

As well as the venues listed below, look out for events at St Stephen's Basilica, the Lutheran Church, the Great Synagogue, Kiscelli Museum and the Old Music Academy in the Liszt Museum. Note that most venues close for the summer months, when **open-air venues** are set up for music of all kinds, the main ones being Budai Park Stage, XI. Kosztolányi Dezső tér, ✆ 466 9849 (tram 49 from Deák tér/Kiskörút); Vajdahunyad Castle in City Park, ✆ 342 3198 (Hősök tere, M1); Városmajor, ✆ 356 1565, just east of Moszkva tér (M2).

Bartók Memorial House, II. Csalán u. 29, ✆ 394 2100. Bus 5 from Moszkva tér (M2). Quality chamber concerts, usually on Fri evenings.

Erkel Színház, VIII. Köztársaság tér 30, ✆ 333 0540. Blaha Lujza tér (M2). *Box office Tues–Sat 10–7, Sun 10–1 and 4–7 (show days only).* Number two opera house, with a totally different feel. A vast, socialist building, usually hosting less high-profile productions, ballets and musicals.

MATÁV Zeneház, IX. Páva u. 10–12. Tram 4 or 6 to Boráros tér. *Box office Mon–Fri 9–6, in June 9–2. Closed July and Aug.* Home of the MATÁV orchestra, recently renovated, with great acoustics and an intimate capacity of 200.

Mátyás Templom, I. Szentháromság tér 2, ✆ 355 5657. Várbusz from Moszkva tér (M2). Tickets from the door of the church. A striking venue, usually used for organ recitals. The audience cannot see the player. The poor acoustics are unsuitable for the choir and orchestra works also performed here.

Óbuda Társaskör (Óbuda Society Circle), III. Kiskorona u. 7, ✆ 250 0288. HÉV to Árpád hid, or tram 1 from Árpád hid (M3). *Box office daily 10–6.* Small venue surrounded by high-rise blocks, but hosting very good chamber concerts, recitals and an eclectic range including some jazz.

Opera House (Magyar Állami Operaház), VI. Andrássy u. 22, ✆ 353 0170. Opera (M1). *Box office Tues–Sat 10–7, Sun 10–1 and 4–7 (show days only).* Everything you could want from an opera house. Productions are lavish and dramatic, with extravagant sets and costumes.

Vigadó, V. Vigadó u. 5, ✆ 338 4721. Vörösmarty tér (M1). *Box office Mon–Fri 10–6, Sat 10–2, Sun 5–7. Closed July and Aug.* A beautiful building and location, but terrible acoustics.

Zeneakadémia (Franz Liszt Music Academy), VI. Liszt Ferenc tér 8, ✆ 342 0179. Oktogon (M1). *Box office Mon–Fri 10–8, Sat and Sun 2–8. Closed late July–Aug.* The Nagyterem (Large Concert Hall) is the best venue in town, with excellent acoustics.

Folk Music and Dance

Dance houses (*táncház*) were formed during the Transylvania-inspired folk-tradition revival in the 1970s. A few places around town have weekly gatherings, at which outsiders are welcome, usually with the chance to learn the steps beforehand. More polished, less authentic folk dancing or gypsy concert shows aimed at tourists take place more or less nightly at the **Budai Vigadó** (I. Corvin tér 8), the **Duna Palota** (V. Zrínyi u. 5) or the **Bábszinház** (VI. Andrássy u. 69). Phone ✆ 317 2754 or pick up one of their ubiquitous leaflets for details.

Belváros Cultural Centre (Belvárosi Művelődési Ház), V. Molnár u. 9, ✆ 317 5928. Ferenciek tere (M3). Very popular for dance Sat night. *Children learn from 5pm, adults from 7pm.*

City Cultural Centre (Fővárosi Művelődési Ház), XI. Fehérvári u. 47, ✆ 203 3868. Tram 18 from Moszkva tér or 47 from Deák tér. *Dance house Tues/Fri 5.30–6.30 for kids; Fri 6.30–12 for adults.*

Csángó Dance House, XII. Marczibányi tér 5a, ✆ 212 5789. Moszkva tér (M2). Loud energetic, Csángó music and dancing (*Wed from 8pm*). On

Thurs the popular group Muzsikás play from 8pm in a relaxed atmosphere with little dancing.

Fonó Budai Zeneház, XI. Sztregova u. 3, ✆ 206 5300. Tram 18 from Moszkva tér (M2) or 47 from Deák tér. Alight at Fehérvári u. 108. In a former aluminium factory, one of the best music venues. Acoustic music: folk, jazz, etc. Transylvanian groups every Wed. Outdoor stage in summer.

Gyökér Club, VI. Eötvös u. 46. Nyugati pu (M3). Transylvanian dance house (*Thurs from 8pm*), and straight Hungarian (*Fri from 9pm*).

Cinema

There are plenty of English-language cinemas. *Pesti Est* often has an English-language film listing. Many old movie houses survive, a few showing art-house films. The best multiplex, in a graceful old building, is **Corvin**, VIII. Corvin köz 1, Ferenc krt. (M3). Arthouse venues: **Blue Box**, IX. Kinizsi u. 28, Ferenc krt. (M3); **Cirko-gejzír**, VIII. Balassi Bálint u. 15–17, tram 2; **Hunnia**, VII. Erzsébet krt. 26, Blaha Lujza tér (M2); **Metro**, VI. Teréz krt. 62, Nyugati pu (M3); **Művész**, VI. Teréz krt 30, Oktogon (M1); **Örökmozgó Filmmúzeum**, VII. Erzsébet krt., tram 4/6 to Wesselényi u.; **Tabán**, I. Krisztina krt. 87–9, tram 18 from Moszkva tér; **Toldi Stúdió**, V. Bajcsy-Zsilinszky u. 36–8, Arany János (M3).

Dance

There are a host of modern Hungarian dance groups, most of whom are represented by the **Contemporary Dance Theatre Society**, XI. Kőrösy József u. 17, ✆ 366 4776 (trams 4/6 on the Nagykörút, 47/49 on the Kiskörút; *open Oct–May Tues–Thurs 4–7*). The **Hungarian National Ballet Company** (Magyar Nemzeti Balett) performs at the State Opera House and the Erkel Theatre. See the Opera House's publication for details (*see* p.323). The organisers of the dance shows at seasonal festivals provide information on these and most of the main dance companies: **Táncfórum**, I. Corvin tér 8, ✆ 201 8779 (Batthyány tér, M2; *open Mon–Fri 9–3*). Check what's going on at Trafó (*see* p.322). This is where the highly acclaimed company **Moving House** (Mozgó ház) usually perform when they're not touring.

Jazz and Rock

Big rock bands play at the **Petőfi Csarnok** in City Park. There are a few smaller venues where you can check out a local band. Funk, soul or Latin tends to be lumped under jazz, and many bars, pubs and clubs offer live bands on a fairly regular basis. *See* pp.320–21 for details.

Budapest: Shopping

Like most formerly Communist cities, Budapest has gone consumer-mad, opening its doors to all the major brand names from the West, and embarking on a passionate love affair with shopping malls, the bigger the better. High-street fashions are still a few steps behind but a number of talented young native designers are producing original, quality garments. Getting clothes made is an affordable option, and trawling the second-hand shops and flea markets for a quirky retro bargain can be fun. The specialist local products most suitable as gifts include folk art (although much of it is naff and mass-produced for tourists), handmade porcelain and ceramics from the world-famous factories of Herend and Zsolnay, and local wines.

Budapest excels in the range and quality of art and artefacts. A staggering quantity of galleries carry works from Hungary's past, as well as showcasing the talents of today's artistic community. The many antique shops around V. Falk Miksa utca and the southern end of Váci utca will let you know what you are legally entitled to take from the country. For real bargains, junk and kitsch head to a flea market and haggle. The best window-shopping is on Váci utca and its many sidestreets and courtyards, the north end overflowing with souvenirs, folk art and Western clothes shops, the south lined with antiques, jewellers, boutiques and cafés.

Antiques

BÁV, V. Bécsi u. 1–3. Paintings, jewellery and gifts. VI. Andrássy u. 2. Objets d'art.

Judaica Gallery, VII. Wesselényi u. 13. Where to head for Jewish relics.

Pintér Antik Diszkont, Falk Miksa u. 10. A vast maze stuffed with goodies.

Relikvia, Fortuna u. 14. Probably the best bet in Castle Hill, but expect no bargains.

Art

Art Kortárs Galéria, V. Galamb u. 4. Features two artists, one the owner of the Ábel Panzió Hotel.

Bolt Galéria, Leonardo Da Vinci u. 40. Modern.

Dovin Galéria, V. Galamb u. 6. Showcases renowned young contemporary artists.

Godot Studio, Madách Imre u. 8. Established names from the modern art scene.

Mai Manó, the House of Hungarian Photography, VI. Nagymező u. 20. Old and new photographs.

Miró, VI. Teréz krt 11–13. Contemporary photos.

Pandora Galéria, VIII. Nepszínház u. 42. Classic.

Qualitás Galéria, V. Haris köz 1. Classics by well-known Hungarians.

Várfok Galéria, Várfok u. 14. Younger artists.

Books

Bestsellers, V. Oktober 6 u. 11. Best for novels and has a fair selection of books about Budapest.

Bibliotéka Antikvárium, Andrássy u. 2. Antique and second-hand books.

Ferenczy Galéria, V. Ferenczy István u. 28. Art books and some posters and prints.

Írók Boltja (Writers' Bookshop), VI. Andrássy u. 45. Good selection of Hungarian literature in trans-

lation at the back, and places to sit at the front.

Központi Antikvárium, Múzeum krt 13–15. Antique and second-hand.

Litea, Fortuna Passage off I. Hess András tér 4. A small selection, mainly on Budapest, and a café. The Váci u. 22 branch carries Hungary and travel.

Rhythm'n'Books, V. Szerb u. 21–3. Good range, new and used, and will trade.

Ceramics

Haas and Czjek, VI. Bajcsy-Zsilinszky u. 23. Has a large selection of porcelain and glassware.

Herend Porcelain, V. József Nádor tér 11 and V. Kigyó u. 5. Famous for its fine porcelain since 1826.

Herend Village Pottery, II. Bem rakpart 37. Has a good selection of hand-painted crockery.

Zsolnay Porcelain, V. Kigyó u. 4. Younger than Herend; given to greater artistic experimentation.

Clothes

for women

Emilia Anda, V. Váci u. 16b, Taverna Passage. Said by many to make the best clothing in town.

Manier, V. Váci u. 48. Unique and trend-setting clothes, eccentric handbags and jewellery, shoes.

Manu-Art ,V. Múzeum krt 10. Simple, natural-fibre clothes handmade by local designers.

Monarchia, V. Szabadsajtó u. 6. *Haute couture* from local designers; classic with daring edges.

Ria Divat, I. Bem József u. 22. Budapest's first private boutique, with a wide, well-chosen range.

Tango Classic, V. Apáczai Csere János u. 3. Exclusive clothing handmade by local designers.

V-50 Design Art Studio, V. Váci u. 50. Minimalist women's clothing and slightly eccentric hats. Bigger selection at V. Belgrád rakpart 16.

for men

Fleischer Shirts, VI. Paulay Ede u. 53. Hand-made shirts at good prices.

Grisby, VI. Paulay Ede u. 67. Grisby clothing from Barcelona at reasonable prices.

Merino-Szivárvány, V. Petőfi Sándor u. 18. Old-fashioned store with an in-house tailor.

Sixville Fashion Store, V. Kecskeméti u. 8. Elegant but simple suits extremely well tailored by a local designer, using Italian and homespun fabrics.

vintage

Ciánkáli, VII. Dohány u. 94 and IX. Vámház krt 9. The best collection of vintage clothes around, plus shoes and jewellery.

Iguana, VIII. Krúdy Gyula u. 9. Gloriously tacky throw-backs to the 1960s and 70s.

Department Stores and Malls

Corvin Áruház, Blaha Lujza 1–2. One of the old department stores selling a bit of everything.

Duna Plaza, VIII. Váci u. 178. Mall with a multiplex and bowling alley.

Fontana, Vací u. 16. An old department store.

Mammut, Széna tér. Mall popular with the middle classes.

West End City Center, VI. Váci u. 1–3. A giant Postmodern mall next to Nyugati Station.

Flea Markets

These can be great fun, though you'll have to turn up early to get the bargains among the junk: things that haven't yet come back into fashion in Budapest or kitsch memorabilia. Even the inflated tourist prices can be extremely low, though haggling is essential. Decide on your maximum, start haggling at a third or half of what you're willing to pay, and don't ask the price unless you're willing to buy. It is worth going along just for the people-watching.

Ecseri Piac, XIX. Nagykőrösi u. 156 (bus 54 from Boráros tér), *Mon–Sat 7–3*. In a vast lot in an industrial area: follow the crowds, or get off at the used-car yard and walk through it the way you came.

Józsefvárosi piac, VII. Kőbányai u. 21–3 (tram 28 or 37). There are no used goods or antiques here, just regular goods, such as clothes, of dubious provenance and at knockdown prices. It's known

locally as the Chinese market: most of the phoney brand-name goods were probably made there. There are bargains to be found, but be careful, of pick-pockets and of being cheated.

Városligeti Bolhapiac, in the Petőfi Csarnok in City Park (Széchenyi fürdő, M1), *Sat and Sun 7–2*. A Hungarian garage sale full of old books, records, toys, badges and Communist relics.

Folklore

Anna Antikvitás, V. Falk Miksa u. 18–20. Good selection of beautiful embroidered linens.

Folkart Centrum, V. Váci u. 14. The first stop for all kinds of authentic Hungarian souvenirs.

The Great Market Hall, near Kálvin tér. The best for authentic costumes and linens: first floor.

Tangó Romantic, V. Váci u. 8. Clothes made from Hungarian linens; the shop opposite sells the fabrics.

Food and Drink

markets

Central Market, Vámház krt. The biggest and grandest covered market, and still serves about 30,000 shoppers a day.

Also V. Hunyadi u., V. Hold u., VII. Klauzál tér, VIII. Rákóczi tér, Fény út near Moszkva tér, XIII. Lehel tér (M3).

vegetarian and health foods

Bio-ABC, Múzeum krt 19. Soy and organic products, teas, oils, herbs, etc.

Egészségbolt, XII. Csaba u. 3, close to Moszkva tér. All the health-food basics.

Életház Biocentrum, XII. Böszörményi u. 13–5, near Déli station. A good selection plus restaurant.

Reformkuckó, VI. Teréz krt (in courtyard). Juices squeezed on the spot (bring a container).

wine

Budapest Wine Society, I. Batthyány u. 59.

La Boutique des Vins, V. József Attila u. 12.

other products

A Vörös Oroszlánhoz, VI. Jókai tér 8. Wide range of teas.

Coquan's, V. Nador u. 5, IX. Ráday u. 15, II. Fény u. Market, 3rd Floor. Excellent coffee.

Lekvárium, VII. Dohány u. 39. Good range of pickles and preserves.

Rothschild, VII. Dob u. 12. Kosher products.

T. Nagy Tamás, V. Gerlóczy u. 3. The best cheese shop, with over 150 cheeses to choose from.

Jewellery

Bartha Ékszer, V. Semmelweis u. 19 (in passage). Art Nouveau silver and gold jewellery.

Ómama Bizsuja, V. Szent István krt 1. **Ómama Antique**, II. Frankel Léo u. 7. Both have second-hand and antique costume jewellery.

Toys

Fajáték Bolt, IX. Vámház krt 1–3. Handmade wooden toys.

Fakopáncs, VIII. Baross u. 50 and Jószef krt 50. Wooden toys and puzzles.

Gondolkodó Logikai Játékok, VII. Király u. 25. The name means 'Thinking Logical Games', and that just about sums up the stock. All kinds of puzzles and mind-expanding games.

Játék Ajándék, upstairs in the Central Market Hall. Traditional handmade wooden toys.

Játékszerek Anno, VI. Teréz krt 54. Stocks 19th-century toys, lovingly reproduced. Perfect gift material.

Maci Kuckó, V. Párizsi u. 6b. Teddies and all that goes with them.

Puppet Store, V. Párizsi u. 3. Handmade hand puppets.

Art and Architecture

Andrási, G., et al, *The History of Hungarian Art in the 20th Century* (Corvina). A thorough overview, with plenty of small pictures and extensive commentaries.

Éri, Györgyi, et al, *A Golden Age: Art and Society in Hungary 1896–1914* (Corvina). This beautifully illustrated book captures the Art Nouveau age that has so extensively left its mark on Budapest.

Gerle, János, et al, *Budapest: An Architectural Guide* (6BT, Budapest). A small guide to the city's 20th-century architecture. Nearly 300 buildings are briefly described in English and Hungarian.

History and Politics

Bodor, Ferenc, *Coffee Houses* (City Hall). Brilliant and entertaining snap shots from the age of Budapest's glorious coffee culture. Most of the cafés are now, alas, closed.

Gerő, András (ed.), *Modern Hungarian Society in the Making* (CEU Press). Interesting collection of essays on the last 150 years of Hungarian political, social and cultural history.

Kontler, László, *Millennium in Central Europe: A History of Hungary* (Atlantisz). A heavy academic tome, the most recent overview of Hungary's history, written by a Hungarian.

Lukács, John, *Budapest 1900* (Weidenfeld/Grove Press). A key turning-point in Budapest's history, accurately and evocatively captured in this erudite yet readable account.

Sugar, Peter (ed.), *A History of Hungary* (I B Tauris). A thorough, readable account of Hungary from before the conquest to the end of Communism, with a brief epilogue on the transition to democracy.

Zsachár, Zsófia (ed.), *Encounters: A Hungarian Quarterly Reader* (HQ Society/Balassi Kiadó). Articles from the journal dealing mostly with the turbulent history of Hungary in the 20th century.

Biography, Memoir and Travel

Magris, Claudio, *Danube* (Collins Harvill). Translated from the Italian, this is as much philosophy or auto-biography as travelogue, but it captures the spirit of the river beautifully.

Móra, Imre, *Budapest Then and Now* (New World Publishing). A personal, eye-witness account of the many changes that besieged Budapest in the 20th century, divided into short, digestible chunks.

Pressburger, Giorgio and Nicola, *Hommage to the Eighth District* (Readers International). Evocative, eye-witness recollections of Budapest's Jewish community before and during the Second World War.

Szép, Ernő, *The Smell of Humans* (CEU Press, Budapest/Arrow, UK). One of many works on the Holocaust in Hungary. Superbly written and thoroughly harrowing.

Török, András, *Budapest, A Critical Guide* (Pallas Athene). Not thorough enough to be used as your only guide, but insightful and funny, and therefore great preparatory reading.

Literature

Ady, Endre, *Poems of Endre Ady* (University Press of America). Widely considered Hungary's finest and most influential poet, his style, full of resonances and allusions, is notoriously difficult to translate.

Cushing, George F., *The Passionate Outsider: Studies on Hungarian Literature* (Corvina). A good overview.

Czigány, Loránt (ed.), *The Oxford History of Hungarian Literature from the Earliest Times to the Present* (Oxford University Press). A comprehensive collection, presented chronologically, with good commentaries on the political and social background.

Esterházy, Peter, *Helping Verbs of the Heart*; *A Little Hungarian Pornography*; *She Loves Me*. Novels by Hungary's most successful and influential modern writer.

Budapest: Reading and Viewing

Fischer, Tibor, *Under the Frog, A Black Comedy* (Penguin/New Press). A witty and easy-to-read fictional account of the 1956 Revolution.

Határ, Victor, *The Right to Sanity* (Corvina). Határ is one of the most versatile and difficult writers of the 20th century. This reader offers a good introduction to his work.

The Kiss: Twentieth Century Short Stories (Corvina). Thirty-one examples of Hungarian literature.

Kosztolányi, Dezső, *Skylark* (CEU Press); *Anna Édes* (Corvina); *Darker Muses* (Corvina). Novels by the man widely considered to be the best Hungarian prose writer of the 20th century.

Krúdy, Gyula, *Adventures of Sinbad* (CEU Press/Random House). His most famous work, exploring the fading delights of turn-of-the-20th-century Budapest. *Sunflower* (Corvina). A late, beautiful novella.

The Lost Rider: The Corvina Book of Hungarian Verse (A Bilingual Anthology). A good collection of Magyar poetry through the ages, particularly suitable for those with a smattering of the tongue.

Madách, Imre, *The Tragedy of Man* (Corvina). A work of genius, compared with Dante, Byron and Milton, which seemed to come out of nowhere. A drama in verse, it explores the human condition.

Molnár, Ferenc, *The Paul Street Boys* (Corvina). A classic story for children, but its humour, psychological depth and moving poignancy make it equally suitable for adults.

Móricz, Zsigmond, *Be Faithful Unto Death* (Penguin). The first line of Vörösmarty's famous patriotic 'address' provides the title of this late 19th-century work that offers insights into the Magyar soul.

Örkény, István, *One Minute Stories* (Corvina). These grotesque miniatures offer hilarious and insightful glimpses into the complex Hungarian psyche.

Food

Gundel, Károly, *Gundel's Hungarian Cookbook* (Corvina). The great master of Hungarian cuisine first shared his secrets in 1934. It has been through 30 editions, which suggests what the Hungarians think of it.

Lang, George, *The Cuisine of Hungary* (Penguin/Random House). A complete overview of Hungarian cooking, including its history and how to do it yourself. Well written and beautifully illustrated.

Films

The Witness (1969), Péter Bacsó. A satirical comedy about the Socialist authorities in the 1950s.

Szindbád (1971), Zoltán Huszáric. Striking techniques and imagery, plus the collaboration of many talented artists, led to the great success enjoyed by this screen adaptation of Gyula Krúdy's most famous hero. The last days of an aging hedonist are atmospherically and sensuously documented.

Little Valentino (1979), András Jeles. A dark film revealing much about the seedier side of the city and the values of the late 1970s. For all its malice and darkness, it is still a delight to watch.

Psyché (1980), Gábor Bódy. This two-part esoteric *tour de force* traces the adventures of a fictitious poet from the 1770s up to the present.

Mephisto (1981), István Szabó. An Oscar-winning classic based on the novel by Klaus Mann, depicting the struggles of a German actor in the first half of the 20th century.

Kiss, Mummy (1986), János Rózsa. Worth seeing for its insider's view of modern, day-to-day Hungarian life in an upper-middle-class family.

Meeting Venus (1991), István Szabó. The story of a conductor and the diva he loves.

Woyzeck (1992), János Szász. A world-famous, exhilarating piece of idiosyncratic film-making, brilliantly shot to maintain a brooding atmosphere of apocalyptic tension.

Out of Order (1998), Andrew Vajna. A distinctly Hungarian but uncharacteristically high-budget work by this Hungarian-born Hollywood director.

Sunshine (1999), István Szabó. Explains a lot about the last 100 years of Hungarian history, particularly from the perspective of Budapest's Jews. Starring Ralph Fiennes, it explores the rise and fall of successive oppressive dictatorships, the strangely cyclical nature of events, and some of the darker aspects of the human (and specifically Hungarian) condition.

No other language that uses Latin script is as baffling as Hungarian. Normally in a European country you would expect to be able to understand a few written words, the basics, the essentials. Come to Hungary with such expectations and they are soon dashed against the harsh rocks of impossible letter combinations, absurdly long words, and endless accents. Try to learn a little of the lingo and despondency quickly descends. The easy explanation for this is that Hungarian is one of the few languages in Europe that is not of Indo-European origin. During the course of trying to work out where the Magyars originally came from, linguistics were called upon, and found that the core vocabulary of Hungarian, the basic words that have descended through millennia, is related to languages in the Finno-Ugric family, though far too distantly for Finns and Hungarians to understand one another. This places their origins in Western Siberia and the northern part of the Ural mountains.

The problem is compounded by the fact that the Hungarians, who have managed to avoid the usual fate of small countries surrounded by large predatory empires—that of having their language carefully eradicated—love their language and are reluctant to learn anybody else's. In tourist situations like hotels and restaurants, there is usually someone who speaks some English, but in ordinary shops, museums or at the baths, for instance, even rudimentary communication has to be conducted in sign language. If they do have a few words of something, it is likely to be German. Latin languages will gain no glimmers of recognition. In desperate circumstances, seek out a young person. There's no point trying to learn to speak the language, whose grammar is as absurdly difficult as its vocabulary. What follows is a glossary of words and expressions that might make life easier for you and the Hungarians you encounter. If you do make the effort, they may find it hard to hide their amusement at your pronunciation, but they will love you for it.

Pronunciation: Hungarian pronunciation is fairly straightforward and consistent. Letters and combinations of letters are always pronounced in the same way; there is no nonsense with silent letters and the like. The stress pattern is regular, with the first syllable slightly emphasized and each following syllable clearly and evenly pronounced. Accents denote a longer vowel (except for é and á). Double consonants are pronounced longer.

In dictionaries and listings, words beginning with ö and ő count as separate letters, with their own listings after o. Sz also counts as a separate consonant.

a: like o in hot	ö: the sound that starts earth	cs: like ch in touch
á: like a in far	ő: like the u in fur	sz: like s in sit
e: like e in send	u: like u in put	zs: like s in pleasure
é: like a in day	ú: like u in rule	j: like y in yes
i: like i in hit	ü: like u in the French tu	ly: like y in yes
í: like ee in feet	ű: the same but longer	gy: like d at the start of dune
o: like o in open	c: like ts in hats	ny: like n in new
ó: is the same but longer	s: like sh in cash	ty: like t in tulip

Hungarian Language

The Basics

yes/no/maybe	*igen/nem/talán*	Do you speak English /German?	*Beszél angolul /németül?*
please	*kérem*	I am English /American	*Angol/amerikai vagyok*
thank you/thanks	*köszönöm/kösz*	I don't speak Hungarian	*Nem beszélek Magyarul*
OK/very good	*jó/nagyon jó*	I (don't) understand	*(Nem) értem*
good/nice	*szép*	What is your name?	*Mi a neve?*
bad/ugly	*csúnya*	My name is...	*A nevem...*
hello (to one person)	*szervusz*	Nice to meet you	*Örvendek*
hello (more than one)	*szervusztok*	police	*rendőrség*
hello (familiar)	*szia*	doctor	*orvos*
goodbye/'bye	*viszontlátásra/viszlát*	ambulance	*mentőautó*
excuse me (to get past)	*szabad?*	I feel ill	*Rosszul vagyok*
excuse me (for attention)	*bocsánat, uram*		
I beg your pardon?	*Tessék?*		
Can you help me?	*Kérhetem a segítségét?*		

Shopping

I would like...	*Kérek...*	men's/women's	*férfi/női*
How much is this?	*Ez mennyibe kerül?*	antique dealer	*antiqvárius*
expensive/cheap	*drága/olcsó*	bank	*bank*
big/small	*nagy/kicsi*	bookshop	*könyvesbolt*
free/no charge	*ingyen*	chemist	*patika/gyógyszertár*
open/closed	*nyitva/zárva*	department store	*aruház*
entrance/exit	*bejárat/kijárat*	market	*piac*
sale	*akció*	post office	*postahivatal*
this one/that one	*ez/az*	shoe shop	*cipőbolt*
push/pull	*tolni/húzni*	souvenir shop	*ajándékbolt*

Sights

arts centre	*művelődési ház/központ*	hill	*hegy* or *domb*
art gallery	*képcsarnok*	island	*sziget*
bridge	*híd*	lake	*tó*
castle	*vár*	library	*könyvtár*
chapel	*kápolna*	monument	*műemlék*
church	*templom*	museum	*múzeum*
cinema	*mozi*	palace	*palota*
courtyard	*udvar*	ruin	*rom*
exhibition	*kiállítás*	tower	*torony*
garden	*kert*	town	*város*
gate	*kapu*	valley	*völgy*
		wood or park	*liget*

Directions

left/right/straight on	*bal/jobb/egyenesen*	emelet	*floor*
where	*hol*	utca/út	*street/avenue*
Where is the...?	*Hol van a...?*	tér/tere	*square*
How far is...?	*Milyen messze van...?*	körút	*boulevard*
address	*cím*	sétány	*walk or promenade*

Time

minute	*perc*	now	*most*
hour/half an hour	*óra/félóra*	Monday	*Hétfő*
day/week	*nap/hét*	Tuesday	*Kedd*
month/year	*hónap/év*	Wednesday	*Szerda*
morning/afternoon	*reggel/délután*	Thursday	*Csütörtök*
evening	*este*	Friday	*Péntek*
today/tomorrow	*ma/holnap*	Saturday	*Szombat*
yesterday	*tegnap*	Sunday	*Vasárnap*

Numbers

one	*egy*	twenty-one	*huszonegy*
two	*kettő/két*	thirty	*harminc*
three	*három*	forty	*negyven*
four	*négy*	fifty	*ötven*
five	*öt*	sixty	*hatvan*
six	*hat*	seventy	*hetven*
seven	*hét*	eighty	*nyolcvan*
eight	*nyolc*	ninety	*kilencven*
nine	*kilenc*	one hundred	*száz*
ten	*tíz*	one hundred and ten	*száztíz*
eleven	*tizenegy*	two hundred	*kétszáz*
twelve	*tizenkettő*	one thousand	*ezer*
twenty	*húsz*	one million	*millió*

Transport

bus	*autóbusz*	platform	*vágány*
tram	*villamos*	boat	*hajó*
trolleybus	*troli(busz)*	aeroplane	*repülőgép*
train	*vonat*	airport	*repülőtér*
underground	*metró*	departure	*indulás*
bus stop	*buszmegálló*	arrival	*érkezés*
railway station	*pályaudvar*	ticket	*jegy*
station	*állomás*	seat (place)	*hely*

Eating Out

I'd like...	*Szeretnék egy...*	red wine	*vörösbor*
I am a vegetarian	*Vegetáriánus vagyok*	white wine	*fehérbor*
The bill please	*Számla, kérem*	beer	*sör*
menu	*étlap*	coffee	*kávé*
wine list	*itallap*	tea	*tea*
tip	*borravaló*	sugar	*cukor*
breakfast	*reggeli*	milk	*tej*
lunch	*ebéd*	fruit juice	*gyümölcslé*
dinner	*vacsora*	mineral water	*ásvány-víz*
restaurant	*étterem/vendéglő*	glass	*pohár*
salt	*só*	bottle	*üveg*
pepper	*bors*	cheers	*egészségedre*

Menu Decoder

előételek	*starters*	libamáj zsirjában	*roast goose liver*
főételek	*main courses*	hortobágyi palacsinta	*pancakes stuffed with minced pork, covered with sauce made from pork stew, mushrooms and sour cream*
zöldség	*vegetables*		
édességek	*desserts*		
leves	*soup*		
csirke	*chicken*		
bárány	*lamb*	Bakonyi sertéshús	*pork in mushroom and sour cream sauce*
marha	*beef*		
máj	*liver*	kacsasült	*roast duck*
sertéshús	*pork*	töltött paprika	*stuffed peppers*
kolbász	*sausage*	pörkölt	*stew, usually meat*
hal	*fish*	paprikás	*pörkölt with sour cream*
süllő	*pike-perch*		
pisztráng	*trout*	paprikás csirke	*paprika chicken*
ponty	*carp*	halászlé	*hot and sour fish soup*
sajt	*cheese*	gombafejek rántva	*breaded and fried mushrooms*
tojás	*egg*		
rántott	*fried in batter*	saláta	*salad (often pickled cabbage, gherkin or pepper)*
főttburgonya	*boiled potatoes*		
hasábbburgonya	*chips/fries*		
rizs	*rice*	rétes (almás/cseresznyés/túrós)	*strudels (apple/cherry/curd cheese)*
zsemlegombóc	*dumplings*	túrógombóc	*curd cheese balls*
jókai bableves	*bean soup with vegetables, smoked pork and small dumplings*	Gundel palacsinta	*pancakes stuffed with walnuts and topped with chocolate sauce*

Italic numbers refer to maps; **bold** numbers indicate main references

Index

335

BUDAPEST

Birds of Budapest know what beauty means.

Royal Palaco in Buda Castle

Buda or Pest, Malcv Hungarian Airlines will fly you there in comfort and safety. Budapest for Art, Architecture, Music, Good Food and traditional Hungarian warmth and hospitality.
Call Malev Hungarian Airlines reservations 020 7439 0577
22-25A Sackville Street, London, W1X1DE

MALEV Hungarian Airlines

Giving Wings to Your Dreams

Cadogan Guides are available from good bookshops, or via **Grantham Book Services**, Isaac Newton Way, Alma Park Industrial Estate, Grantham NG31 9SD, ✆ (01476) 541 080, 🖷 (01476) 541 061; and **The Globe Pequot Press**, 246 Goose Lane, PO Box 480, Guilford, Connecticut 06437–0480, ✆ (800) 458 4500, ✆ (203) 458 4500, 🖷 (203) 458 4603.